MASTERPIECES OF CHRISTIAN LITERATURE
IN SUMMARY FORM

———

c. 96 to 1695

MASTERPIECES

of

CHRISTIAN LITERATURE

in Summary Form

Edited by
FRANK N. MAGILL

Associate Editor
IAN P. McGREAL

VOLUME ONE—C. 96 TO 1695

SALEM PRESS
INCORPORATED
NEW YORK

ACKNOWLEDGMENTS

The articles describing the following works were prepared in whole or in part by reference to the editions indicated. The editors and staff gratefully acknowledge the use of these editions.

The First Epistle of Clement to the Corinthians; The Epistle of Barnabas; The Seven Epistles of Ignatius, The Shepherd by Hermas, and *The Epistle to Diognetus.* From *The Apostolic Fathers.* Translated by Kirsopp Lake. Published by William Heinemann, Ltd. and Harvard University Press, and by The Macmillan Company.

The First Apology and *The Second Apology* by Saint Justin Martyr. From *The Writings of Saint Justin Martyr* in *Fathers of the Church* (Volume 6). Translated by Thomas B. Falls. Published by Christian Heritage.

The Apology of Athenagoras. From *Ancient Christian Writers.* Translated by J. H. Crehan, S.J. Published by The Newman Press.

The Apostolic Tradition by Hippolytus. Translated by B. S. Easton. Published by The Macmillan Company.

Against Celsus by Origen. Translated by Henry Chadwick. Published by The Cambridge University Press.

The Incarnation of the Word of God by Athanasius. Translated by a Religious of the C.S.M.V.S. S.Th. Published by The Macmillan Company.

Ecclesiastical History by Eusebius of Caesarea. Translated by Kirsopp Lake. Published by Loeb Classical Library, Harvard University Press.

The Life of Antony by Athanasius in *Ancient Christian Writers* (Volume 10). Translated by R. T. Meyer. Published by The Newman Press.

The Longer Rules and *The Shorter Rules* by Saint Basil of Caesarea. From *The Ascetic Works of Saint Basil.* Translated by W. K. L. Clarke. Published by The Society for Promoting Christian Knowledge.

The City of God by Saint Augustine. Translated by Gerald G. Walsh and others. Published by Fathers of the Church, Inc.

Seven Books of History Against the Pagans by Paulus Orosius. Translated by Irving Woodworth Raymond. Published by Columbia University Press.

The Enchiridion on Faith, Hope, and Love by Saint Augustine. From *The Basic Writings of Saint Augustine.* Published by Random House, Inc.

Tome by Saint Leo I. Translated by E. H. Blakeney. Published by The Society for Promoting Christian Knowledge and by The Macmillan Company.

The Bazaar of Heraclides by Nestorius. Translated by G. R. Driver and Leonard Hodgson. Published by The Oxford University Press.

The Divine Names by Dionysius, the Pseudo-Areopagite. Translated by C. E. Rolt. Published by The Society for Promoting Christian Knowledge.

On the Holy Trinity by Boethius. From *The Theological Tractates.* Translated by H. F. Stewart and E. K. Rand. Published by William Heinemann, Ltd. and G. P. Putnam's Sons.

Pastoral Care by Saint Gregory I. From *Ancient Christian Writers.* Translated by Henry Davis. Published by The Newman Press.

The Ladder of Divine Ascent by Saint John Climacus. Translated by A. L. Moore. Published by Harper & Brothers.

Ecclesiastical History of the English Nation by Saint Bede. From *Baedae Opera Historica*. Translated by J. E. King. Published by Harvard University Press.

The Fountain of Wisdom by Saint John of Damascus. From *The Writings of Saint John of Damascus*. Translated by Frederic H. Chase. Published by Fathers of the Church, Inc.

The Steps of Humility by Saint Bernard. Translated by G. B. Burch. Published by Harvard University Press.

Soliloquy on the Earnest Money of the Soul by Hugh of St. Victor. Translated by K. Herbert. Published by The Marquette University Press.

Know Thyself by Peter Abelard. From *Abailard's Ethics*. Translated by J. Ramsay McCallum. Published by Basil Blackwell.

Policratus by John of Salisbury. From *The Statesman's Book of John of Salisbury*. Translated by J. Dickinson. Published by Alfred A. Knopf, Inc.

Benjamin Minor by Richard of St. Victor. From *Richard of Saint-Victor: Selected Writings on Contemplation*. Translated by Clare Kirchberger. Published by Faber and Faber, Ltd.

Retracing the Arts to Theology by Saint Bonaventura. From *Saint Bonaventure's De Reductione Artium Ad Theologiam*. Translated by Sister E. R. Healy. Published by The Franciscan Institute.

The Journey of the Mind to God by Saint Bonaventura. Translated by George Boas. Published by The Liberal Arts Press.

Ordinatio: Oxford Commentary on the Sentences of Peter Lombard by Johannes Duns Scotus. From *Duns Scotus: Philosophical Writings*. Translated by Allan Wolter. Published by Thomas Nelson and Sons, Ltd.

The Divine Comedy by Dante Alighieri. Translated by H. R. Huse. Published by Rinehart and Company.

The Little Flowers of St. Francis. Translated by Leo Sherley-Price. Published by Penguin Books.

De Corpore Christi by William of Ockham. From *The De Sacramento Altaris of William of Ockham*. Published by The Lutheran Literary Board.

The Adornment of the Spiritual Marriage by John of Ruysbroeck. Translated by C. A. Wynschenk, Dom. Published by J. M. Dent and Sons, Ltd.

The Revelations of Divine Love by Lady Julian of Norwich. Translated by James Walsh, S.J. Published by Harper and Brothers.

The Cloud of Unknowing. Edited by Justin McCann. Published by The Newman Press.

The Following of Christ by Gerhard Groote. Translated by Joseph Malaise. Published by The American Press.

Treatise on the Church by John Huss. Translated by David S. Schaff. Published by Charles Scribner's Sons.

The Imitation of Christ by Thomas a Kempis. Translated by Leo Sherley-Price. Published by Penguin Books.

Of Learned Ignorance by Nicholas of Cusa. Translated by G. Haron. Published by Rutledge and Kegan Paul.

The Scale of Perfection by Walter Hilton. Translated by Evelyn Underhill. Published by John M. Watkins.

An Open Letter to the Christian Nobility of the German Nation; The Babylonian Captivity of the Church; and *A Treatise on Christian Liberty* by Martin Luther. From *Works of Martin Luther*. Published by The Muhlenberg Press.

The Bondage of the Will by Martin Luther. Translated by Henry Cole and Edward Thomas Vaughan. Published by Sovereign Grace Union.

On the Errors of the Trinity by Michael Servetus. Translated by Earl Morse Wilbur. Published by Harvard University Press.

A Short and Clear Exposition of the Christian Faith by Ulrich Zwingli. From *Zwingli and Bullinger* in *The Library of Christian Classics* (Volume XXIV). Translated by G. W. Bromiley. Published by SCM Press and The Westminster Press.

Foundation of Christian Doctrine by Menno Simons. Translated by Leonard Verduin. Published by The Herald Press.

The Life of St. Teresa of Ávila by Saint Teresa of Ávila. Translated by David Lewis. Published by The Newman Press.

A Treatise of Reformation Without Tarrying for Any by Robert Browne. Published by George Allen and Unwin, Ltd.

The Dark Night of the Soul by Saint John of the Cross. Translated by K. F. Reinhardt. Published by Frederick Ungar Publishing Company.

The Declaration of Sentiments by Jacobus Arminius. Translated by James Nichols and W. R. Bagnall. Published by Baker Beck House.

Introduction to the Devout Life by Saint Francis of Sales. Translated by Allan Ross. Published by Burns, Oates and Washbourne, Ltd.

De Religione Laici by Edward Herbert, First Lord of Cherbury. Translated by Harold Randolph Hutcheson. Published by The Yale University Press.

Didactica Magna by Johannes Amos Comenius. Translated by M. W. Keatinge. Published by A & C Black, Ltd.

Pensées by Blaise Pascal. Translated by W. F. Trotter. Published by P. F. Collier and Son.

The Practice of the Presence of God by Brother Lawrence (Nicholas Herman). Translated by Sister Mary David, S.S.N.D. Published by The Newman Book Shop.

The Creed of a Savoyard Priest by Jean Jacques Rousseau. Translated by Barbara Foxley. Published by J. M. Dent and Sons, Ltd., and by E. P. Dutton and Company.

The Journals of Henry Melchior Mühlenberg. Translated by Theodore G. Tappert and John W. Doberstein. Published by The Muhlenberg Press.

Religion Within the Limits of Reason Alone by Immanuel Kant. Translated by Theodore M. Greene and Hoyt H. Hudson. Published by Open Court Publishing Company.

Early Theological Writings by Georg Wilhelm Friedrich Hegel. Translated by T. M. Knox. Published by The University of Chicago Press.

On Religion: Speeches to its Cultured Despisers by Friedrich Schleiermacher. Translated by John Oman. Published by Harper and Brothers.

The Phenomenology of Spirit by George Wilhelm Friedrich Hegel. Translated by J. B. Baillie. Published by Allen and Unwin, Ltd.

The Christian Faith by Friedrich Schleiermacher. Translated by H. R. Mackintosh and J. S. Stewart. Published by T. & T. Clark.

The Essence of Christianity by Ludwig Feuerbach. Translated by George Eliot. Published by Harper and Brothers.

Concluding Unscientific Postscript by Søren Kierkegaard. Translated by David F. Swenson and Walter Lowrie. Published by The Princeton University Press.

Christian Discourses by Søren Kierkegaard. Translated by Walter Lowrie. Published by The Oxford University Press.

Training in Christianity by Søren Kierkegaard. Translated by Walter Lowrie. Published by The Princeton University Press.

The Attack on Christendom by Søren Kierkegaard. Translated by Walter Lowrie. Published by The Princeton University Press.

The Christian Doctrine of Justification and Reconciliation by Albrecht Ritschl. Translated by H. R. Mackintosh and A. B. Macauley. Published by T. & T. Clark.

Lectures on Godmanhood by Vladimir Solovyev. Translated by Peter Zouboff. Published by Dennis Dobson, Ltd.

The Grand Inquisitor by Fyodor Dostoevski. From *The Brothers Karamazov*. Translated by Constance Garnett. Published by Random House, Inc.

Systematic Theology by Augustus Hopkins Strong. Published by The American Baptist Publication Society.

Practical Christianity by Rufus M. Jones. Published by The John C. Winston Company.

What is Christianity? by Adolf Harnack. Translated by Thomas Bailey Saunders. Published by Harper and Brothers.

The Philosophy of Religion by Harald Höffding. Translated by B. E. Meyer. Published by Macmillan and Company, Ltd.

The Quest of the Historical Jesus by Albert Schweitzer. Translated by W. Montgomery. Published by A. & C. Black, Ltd.

Personalism by Borden Parker Bowne. Published by Houghton, Mifflin and Company.

The Person and Place of Christ by Peter Taylor Forsyth. Published by The Independent Press.

The Meaning of God in Human Experience by William Ernest Hocking. Published by The Yale University Press.

The Social Teaching of the Christian Churches by Ernst Troeltsch. Translated by Olive Wyon. Published by The Macmillan Company.

The Problem of Christianity by Josiah Royce. Published by The Macmillan Company.

The Idea of the Holy by Rudolf Otto. Translated by John W. Harvey. Published by The Oxford University Press.

A Theology for the Social Gospel by Walter Rauschenbusch. Published by The Abingdon Press and The Macmillan Company.

The Plan of Salvation by Benjamin B. Warfield. Published by The William B. Eerdmans Publishing Company.

The Epistle to the Romans by Karl Barth. Translated by Sir Edwyn C. Hoskyns. Published by The Oxford University Press.

Theology as an Empirical Science by Douglas Clyde Macintosh. Published by The Macmillan Company.

On the Eternal in Man by Max Scheler. Translated by Bernard Noble. Published by Harper and Brothers.

Christianity and Liberalism by J. Gresham Machen. Published by The William B. Eerdmans Publishing Company.

The Faith of the Christian Church by Gustaf Aulén. Translated by Eric H. Wahlstrom. Published by The Muhlenberg Press.

I and Thou by Martin Buber. Translated by Ronald Gregor Smith. Published by T. & T. Clark.

Love, the Law of Life by Toyohiko Kagawa. Translated by J. F. Gressitt. Published by The John C. Winston Company.

Religion in the Making by Alfred North Whitehead. Published by The Macmillan Company.

Freedom and the Spirit by Nikolai Berdyaev. Translated by Oliver Fielding Clarke. Published by Geoffrey Bles: The Centenary Press.

Philosophical Theology by Frederick Robert Tennant. Published by The Cambridge University Press.

Selected Letters by Baron Friedrich von Hügel. Published by J. M. Dent and Sons, Ltd.

Christ and Society by Charles Gore. Published by Charles Scribner's Sons.

Agape and Eros by Anders Nygren. Translated by Philip S. Watson. Published by The Society for Promoting Christian Knowledge.

Christus Victor by Gustaf Aulén. Translated by A. G. Herbert. Published by The Society for Promoting Christian Knowledge, and The Macmillan Company.

The Faith of a Moralist by Alfred Edward Taylor. Published by Macmillan and Company, Ltd.

The Destiny of Man by Nikolai Berdyaev. Translated by Natalie Duddington. Published by Geoffrey Bles.

The Growth of the Idea of God by Shailer Mathews. Published by The Macmillan Company.

Lectures on Calvinism by Abraham Kuyper. Published by The William B. Eerdmans Publishing Company.

The Natural and the Supernatural by John Oman. Published by the Syndics of The Cambridge University Press.

The Vision of God: The Christian Doctrine of the Summum Bonum by Kenneth E. Kirk. Published by Longmans, Green, and Company.

Church Dogmatics by Karl Barth. Translated by G. T. Thomson. Published by T. & T. Clark.

The Divine Imperative by Emil Brunner. Translated by Olive Wyon. Published by The Lutterworth Press.

The Two Sources of Morality and Religion by Henri Bergson. Translated by R. Ashley Audra and Cloudesley Brereton. Published by Henry Holt and Company.

The Living God by Nathan Söderblom. Published by The Oxford University Press.

Nature, Man and God by William Temple. Published by Macmillan and Company, Ltd.

Being and Having by Gabriel Marcel. Translated by Katharine Farrer. Published by The Beacon Press.

Jesus the Lord by Karl Heim. Translated by D. H. van Daalen. Published by The Muhlenberg Press.

The Parables of the Kingdom by Charles Harold Dodd. Published by Nisbet and Company.

A New Critique of Theoretical Thought by Herman Dooyeweerd. Translated by David H. Freeman and William Young. Published by H. J. Paris and The Presbyterian and Reformed Publishing Company.

True Humanism by Jacques Maritain. Translated by Margot Adamson. Published by Charles Scribner's Sons.

Worship by Evelyn Underhill. Published by Harper and Brothers.

The Cost of Discipleship by Dietrich Bonhoeffer. Translated by R. H. Fuller. Published by The Macmillan Company.

The Philosophical Bases of Theism by G. Dawes Hicks. Published by The Macmillan Company.

The Wisdom of God by Sergius Bulgakov. Published by The Paisley Press, Inc. and Williams and Norgate, Ltd.

The Christian Message in a Non-Christian World by Hendrik Kraemer. Published by Kregel Publications.

The Idea of a Christian Society by Thomas Stearns Eliot. Published by Faber and Faber, Ltd.

A Philosophy of Religion by Edgar Sheffield Brightman. Published by Prentice-Hall, Inc.

Christian Doctrine by J. S. Whale. Published by The Macmillan Company.

The Meaning of Revelation by H. Richard Niebuhr. Published by The Macmillan Company.

The Nature and Destiny of Man by Reinhold Niebuhr. Published by Charles Scribner's Sons.

Prayer by George Arthur Buttrick. Published by Whitmore and Stone.

The Screwtape Letters by Clive Staples Lewis. Published by The Macmillan Company.

Christ and Time by Oscar Cullmann. Translated by Floyd V. Filson. Published by The Westminster Press.

Dogmatics by Emil Brunner. Translated by Olive Wyon. Published by The Lutterworth Press.

The Idea of Christ in the Gospels by George Santayana. Published by Charles Scribner's Sons.

The Source of Human Good by Henry Nelson Wieman. Published by The University of Chicago Press.

The Divine Relativity by Charles Hartshorne. Published by The Yale University Press.

God Was in Christ by Donald M. Baillie. Published by Charles Scribner's Sons.

Theology of the New Testament by Rudolf Bultmann. Translated by Kendrick Grobel. Published by Charles Scribner's Sons.

Ethics by Dietrich Bonhoeffer. Translated by Eberhard Bethge. Published by The Macmillan Company.

Faith and History by Reinhold Niebuhr. Published by Charles Scribner's Sons.

God's Grace and Man's Hope by Daniel Day Williams. Published by Harper and Brothers.

The Living Word by Gustaf Wingren. Translated by Victor C. Pogue. Published by The Muhlenberg Press.

Basic Christian Ethics by Paul Ramsey. Published by Charles Scribner's Sons.

Christ and Culture by H. Richard Niebuhr. Published by Harper and Brothers.

The Christian Understanding of God by Nels F. S. Ferré. Published by Harper and Brothers.

Introduction to the Philosophy of Religion by Peter Anthony Bertocci. Published by Prentice-Hall, Inc.

Systematic Theology by Paul Tillich. Published by The University of Chicago Press.

Time and Eternity by Walter T. Stace. Published by The Princeton University Press.

Natural Religion and Christian Theology by Charles E. Raven. Published by the Syndics of The Cambridge University Press.

Christian Theology: An Ecumenical Approach by Walter Marshall Horton. Published by Harper and Brothers.

The Divine Milieu by Pierre Teilhard de Chardin. Published by Harper and Brothers.

Faith and Knowledge by John Hick. Published by The Cornell University Press.

The Form of the Personal by John Macmurray. Volume I, *The Self as Agent,* published by Faber and Faber, Ltd. Volume II, *Persons in Relation,* published by Harper and Brothers.

The Reality of Faith by Friedrich Gogarten. Translated by Carl Michalson, and others. Published by The Westminster Press.

Christianity and Paradox by Ronald W. Hepburn. Published by C. A. Watts and Company, Ltd.

Christians and the State by John Bennett. Published by Charles Scribner's Sons.

Commentary on Galatians by Ragnar Bring. Translated by Eric Wahlstrom. Published by The Muhlenberg Press.

The Nature of Faith by Gerhard Ebeling. Translated by Ronald Gregor Smith. Published by The Muhlenberg Press.

Our Experience of God by H. D. Lewis. Published by George Allen and Unwin, Ltd. and The Macmillan Company.

ALPHABETICAL LIST OF TITLES

PREFACE

Man's most disturbing intellectual problem is his relationship to the infinite and the eternal. For as long as he has had a rational intellect, he has pondered over the mystery of birth and death, the whence and whither of his existence. Alone and in ignorance yet sensing a kinship with nature and the rhythm of the seasons, he has in the past chosen as the object of his reverence such diverse images as the sun, the sea, mountain peaks, even gods and goddesses he himself had to invent.

About two thousand years ago Jesus Christ appeared on the earth, representing man's first visual, physical contact with the Deity his senses told him surely existed. This book is a survey of the historical, philosophical, and devotional literature that has grown out of Christ's divine revelation, an event that has already affected the lives of billions of people and will unquestionably influence billions to come.

Masterpieces of Christian Literature in Summary Form, which examines this body of literature from the Protestant viewpoint, is one of two works dealing with the subject. The Roman Catholic interpretation is entitled Masterpieces of Catholic Literature in Summary Form. Obviously, the books selected for review are somewhat the same for both works up to the time of the Reformation, but with different interpretations, the emphasis oriented toward the separate doctrines established by these two divergent groups. Such differences do not affect the basic structure of Christianity, however, founded as it is on the towering faith of the early Church Fathers, the passionate dedication of the early martyrs, and the great conviction of Church leaders in the Middle Ages.

Included in Masterpieces of Christian Literature are two-thousand-word essay-reviews of three hundred books dealing with the Christian movement, beginning with The First Epistle of Clement to the Corinthians, written near the end of the first century. Approximately thirty percent of the titles included appeared prior to the Reformation, an indication of the honor and reverence in which these early works are held by Christians everywhere.

Because of the vast number of books under consideration for inclusion in Masterpieces of Christian Literature, the co-operation of scores of professors of Christian literature at many leading universities and divinity schools was sought in connection with the final selection of the three hundred titles to be reviewed. These scholars were asked to name the three hundred books in the entire range of Protestant literature which, in their opinions, had been most influential in the development of Protestantism. I wish to acknowledge with thanks the generous response of these individuals, whose suggestions have helped to broaden the scope of our work.

Assisting the editors in interpreting the three hundred books under consideration was a writing staff of forty scholars and specialists, whose names and academic affiliations appear elsewhere in this volume. In addition to the writing staff, we have had the invaluable assistance of eight special consultants in various fields of Protestant scholarship, and the untiring aid of Dr. Jean Faurot, Professor of Philosophy at Sacramento State College, whose many helpful suggestions reflected his years in the pulpit as well as on the university campus. To all these scholars I wish to express my appreciation for the dedicated way in which they turned to the task of making this book as useful a Protestant reference as possible for the historian, the student, the minister, and the serious layman.

All the articles in MASTERPIECES OF CHRISTIAN LITERATURE were written expressly for this book. While every effort has been made to interpret the original book in the light of the best current scholarship, each article is animated by the insight of the individual scholar who undertook to interpret the particular book under discussion. The main points to be elaborated upon are listed in italics at the beginning of the article under the heading PRINCIPAL IDEAS ADVANCED.

Arrangement of the articles is chronological rather than alphabetical by book title, so that the orderly development of Christian thought will be clearly evident. However, two indexes enable the user to locate any article promptly without regard to chronology: a title index at the front of the book, an author index at the end. For those who wish to consider certain types or groupings from the literature available, such as Church History or Existential Theology, for example, a Category Index is included that lists seventy-five classifications under which the various articles fall.

I am sure that Associate Editor Ian P. McGreal and all staff members share my hope that MASTERPIECES OF CHRISTIAN LITERATURE will serve a useful purpose for those who wish to examine, or review, the great expressions of Christian thought that have sprung from the hearts and minds of Protestantism's most revered leaders.

FRANK N. MAGILL

SPECIAL CONSULTANTS IN PROTESTANT SCHOLARSHIP

GLANVILLE DOWNEY
Professor of Byzantine
Literature, Dumbarton Oaks
Research Library and Collection
of Harvard University
Eastern Orthodox Church
Apostolic Fathers and Early
Christian Church
New Testament

HELMUT H. KOESTER
Associate Professor of New
Testament Studies, Harvard
Divinity School
Early Christian Church
New Testament

SAMUEL LAEUCHLI
Professor of Church History,
Garrett Theological School
Church History

DONALD A. LOWRIE
Formerly of the University
of Paris
Eastern Orthodox Church
Russian Spiritual Classics

JOHN MACQUARRIE
Professor of Systemic Theology,
Union Theological Seminary
Modern Christian Thought
Contemporary Theology

JOHN T. McNEILL
Professor Emeritus, Union
Theological Seminary
Reformation Writings

HEIKO A. OBERMAN
Associate Professor of Church
History, Harvard Divinity School
Church History
Medieval Christian Thought

PAUL RAMSEY
Professor of Christian Ethics,
Princeton University
Christian Ethics
American Church History

PROJECT STAFF MEMBERS

	GRADUATE SCHOOL	PRESENT AFFILIATION
Gregory T. Armstrong, Th.D.	Heidelberg University	Vanderbilt University
Walter F. Bense, B.D.	Western Conservative Baptist Theological Seminary	Harvard University Divinity School
Peter Bertocci, Ph.D.	Boston University	Boston University
Ernest Cassara, Ph.D.	Boston University	Crane Theological School, Tufts University
Kenneth Cauthen, Ph.D.	Vanderbilt University	Crozer Theological Seminary
John W. Chandler, Ph.D.	Duke University	Williams College
Gerald R. Cragg, Ph.D., Litt.D.	McGill University; University of Cambridge	Andover Newton Theological School
Frank B. Dilley, Ph.D.	Columbia University	Smith College
Bernhard Erling, Ph.D., Th.D.	Yale University; University of Lund	Gustavus Adolphus College
Jean Faurot, Ph.D.	University of Toronto	Sacramento State College
Robert L. Ferm, Ph.D.	Yale University	Pomona College
Frederick Ferré, Ph.D.	University of St. Andrews	Dickinson College
A. Durwood Foster, Th.D.	Union Theological Seminary	Pacific School of Religion
David H. Freeman, Ph.D.	University of Pennsylvania	University of Rhode Island
John D. Godsey, Th.D.	University of Basel	Theological School, Drew University
Robert B. Hannen, Ph.D.	University of Glasgow	Berkeley Baptist Divinity School
Howard Hunter, Ph.D.	Boston University	Boston University School of Theology

John A. Hutchison, Ph.D.	Columbia University	Claremont Graduate School
William A. Johnson, Ph.D.	Columbia University	Trinity College
W. Paul Jones, Ph.D.	Yale University	Princeton University
John H. Lavely, Ph.D.	Boston University	Boston University
Clarence L. Lee, B.Th.	Lutheran Theological Seminary	Lutheran Theological Seminary at Philadelphia
Robert Lee, Ph.D.	Columbia University	San Francisco Theological Seminary
Edward L. Long, Jr., Ph.D.	Columbia University	Oberlin College
Ian P. McGreal, Ph.D.	Brown University	Sacramento State College
Clyde Manschreck, Ph.D.	Yale University	Methodist Theological School
Louis Martyn, Ph.D.	Yale University	Union Theological Seminary
Carol Morris, B.D.	Crane Theological School, Tufts University	State College at Framingham
John Pemberton, B.D.	Duke University	Amherst College
Catherine Rau, Ph.D.	University of California	Moorhead State College
Theodore Runyon, Th.D.	University of Goettingen	Candler School of Theology, Emory University
Calvin O. Schrag, Ph.D.	Harvard University	Purdue University
Frederick Sontag, Ph.D.	Yale University	Pomona College
Robert B. Tapp, Ph.D.	University of Southern California	Scripps College
Theodore G. Tappert, D.D.	University of Western Ontario	Lutheran Theological Seminary at Philadelphia
Kenneth Thompson, Jr., B.D.	Union Theological Seminary	Southern Methodist University
Hugh Vernon White, Ph.D.	Stanford University	(Emeritus) Pacific School of Religion
E. David Willis, B.D.	Princeton Theological Seminary	Harvard University
William Young, Th.D.	Union Theological Seminary	University of Rhode Island

THE FIRST EPISTLE OF CLEMENT TO THE CORINTHIANS

Author: Saint Clement of Rome (fl. c.96)
Type of work: Epistle on Church practice
First transcribed: c.96

PRINCIPAL IDEAS ADVANCED

Disorder and strife in the Church are caused by jealousy.

The way to peace and concord is through obedience to established authorities, the elders (presbyteroi).

Christ rules the churches through the Apostles, the bishops appointed by them, and the approved successors of the bishops.

The epistle entitled "First Clement" is traditionally attributed to Clement, the third or fourth bishop of Rome. It is formally a communication from the Church in Rome to the Church in Corinth which had sought its help and counsel. Controversy had arisen in the Church of Corinth, and some of its members had rebelled against the authority of its leaders, called sometimes elders (*presbyteroi*) and sometimes bishops (*episcopoi*). The letter begins with a testimony to the godliness and peace that had formerly prevailed in the Church, and special mention is made of "obedience to your rulers, and fitting honor paid to the older among you (*presbyterois*)." Humility and wisdom had protected the Church from "sedition and schism." But now all this is changed. "Thus 'the worthless' rose up 'against those who were in honor,' those of no reputation against the renowned, the foolish against the prudent, the 'young against the old.'" Faith and virtue have suffered accordingly.

The root causes of such disruption are set forth step by step, and the Corinthian Church is called to repentance and a return to humility, order, and peace. This summons is developed in terms of God's dealing with the nation Israel and with individuals. It concludes with a declaration of the divine ordering of the Church and the establishment of authorities for its government. The virtues involved and illustrated are obedience, concord, and humility. It is pointed out that the source of enmity between brethren is jealousy. This is illustrated by the stories of Cain and Abel, of Jacob and Esau, of David and Saul, and others. Both Peter and Paul were persecuted and opposed through jealousy, but they triumphed over it by their endurance and won spiritual victory. This lesson is driven home and then the greatness of repentance is praised, and examples of it are found in Noah and Jonah. Both men preached repentance, and those who repented were accepted by God even though they were aliens.

God's call to repentance in the Psalms and through the prophets is put before the Church in Corinth.

The letter then dwells on the need for obedience. Enoch and Noah are examples of obedience, as is also Abraham, whose obedience reaches its high point in his offering up of Isaac. Lot also was obedient, but his wife shows the doom of the double-minded. Even the harlot Rahab was approved of God for her faithfulness in the face of danger. So the brethren in Corinth are summoned to a life of obedience, and urged to hold fast to those who truly seek peace and to shun the hypocrisy of those who only profess to do so. There follows a call to be humble and to follow Christ, who Himself fulfilled the ideal of Isaiah 53. The prophets are praised for their humility, as are also Job, Abraham, and Moses. Finally, the fifty-first Psalm is quoted at length to show David the king humbling himself before God, and the Corinthians are urged to follow such great figures in this necessary virtue.

The writer then shows how God calls His flock to concord through the orderliness of creation, and in the succession of day and night and of the seasons. We should be faithful to Him even though we offend proud and foolish men. The Holy Spirit calls us to righteousness and peace. God blesses the sincere and obedient, and judges the evil. The demand for reverence and obedience toward God is supported and sanctioned by the evidence of His power, seen in the Resurrection, which appears both in the raising of Christ and in nature. The story of "the bird called the Phoenix" is narrated by Clement and is applied as an aid to the understanding and acceptance of the Resurrection. God knows all things;

we are His portion and we should seek His blessing, as did men of ancient times. Let us do good, for we are made in His image. He will accept and reward all who do His will. God's gifts are righteousness, truth, holiness, faith, and immortal life. But doom awaits the sinner. All these gifts come through Christ.

After this weighty background of religious and moral exposition, the exposure of the causes of conflict among brethren, and the requirement of humility, repentance, and obedience to God, the letter turns to the issue of authority in the Church. An analogy is found in the chain of authority in an army with its lower and higher officers, and with generals themselves subject to the Emperor. The head and the body also represent the fact of rule and subordination. In all this order of higher and lower each serves the other. The rich really serve the poor, the wise the simple. Each serves in his place. God's wrath will destroy those who are foolish and conceited and who do not respect the order of authority. There is such an order in Israel's service of God. The High Priests and the Levites have their duties; "the layman is bound by ordinances for the laity. . . . Let each one of us, brethren, be well pleasing to God in his own rank, and have a good conscience, not transgressing the appointed rules of his ministration, with all reverence."

The government of the Church is now declared in terms of its origin: "The Apostles received the Gospel for us from the Lord Jesus Christ; Jesus the Christ was sent from God. The Christ therefore is from God and the Apostles from Christ . . . in accordance with the appointed order of God's will." The Apostles preached "and they appointed their first converts, testing them by the Spirit, to be bishops, and deacons of the future believers." They anticipated strife over succession to the office of bishop and "added the codicil that if they should fall asleep, other approved men should succeed to their ministry." It is therefore not right to remove any thus appointed "with the consent of the whole Church," and who have served faithfully and well. This is the offense which had been committed in the Church of Corinth: "For we see that in spite of their good service you have removed some from the ministry which they fulfilled blamelessly."

This judgment on the wrong done in the Church of Corinth is followed by an exhortation to return to the former state of concord. The appeal of Paul against partisanship is invoked. The brethren in Corinth are in fact disloyal to the presbyters "on account of one or two persons." They should put an end to all this and obey the commands of Christ, especially His command to love. All should pray for forgiveness, especially the leaders of sedition, as Moses prayed for those who made the golden calf. The offenders should offer to depart and leave the flock in peace. Many noted and innocent persons have left their cities to put an end to strife. So pray that the present transgressors may be given a spirit of meekness and humility. Deliverance is promised for them in Scripture if they repent. To the troublemakers themselves is addressed a direct injunction to "submit to the presbyters, and receive the correction of repentance, bending the knees of your hearts." And a final appeal is made to all to be obedient to Christ: "Receive our counsel, and there shall be nothing for you to regret."

THE EPISTLE OF BARNABAS

Author: Unknown, but attributed to the Apostle Barnabas
Type of work: Christian exegesis of the Old Testament
First transcribed: Unknown, but probably between 70 and 100

PRINCIPAL IDEAS ADVANCED

Christians must be warned against a Judaic conception of the Old Testament.
Any literal interpretation of the commands of the Law should be avoided and a symbolic exegesis is rather to be followed.
An evil angel used the device of the literal interpretation of the ceremonial law to deceive the Jews, and Christians must give the Old Testament an entirely different interpretation, one in keeping with their belief in Jesus Christ as the true revealer of God.

The *Epistle of Barnabas,* although anonymous, is ascribed by tradition to the Apostle Barnabas, who was a companion of St. Paul, and it was obviously intended for a community in which Alexandrian ideas prevailed.

Early authors, such as Clement of Alexandria (c.150-c.215), actually quote it as Scripture, but it was never accepted into the canon. Origen (c.185-c.254) refers to it as a Catholic epistle, and it was included in the Codex Sinaiticus, the manuscript of the Greek Bible. Despite the fact that the *Epistle* is not accepted as part of the Scriptures, its influence is beyond question.

It begins, as do many of the epistles which are included in the New Testament, with a greeting to the community addressed. The reason given for the sending of the letter is that the author—who does not identify himself by name—has an interest in strengthening Christian conviction through correct teaching. Immediately the author sets forth the three doctrines of the Lord: the hope of life makes Him the beginning and the end of faith; His righteousness is the beginning and the end of judgment, and love and joy are the testimony of the works of righteousness.

The writer of the letter views his own days as evil, and for this reason, he writes, these ordinances of the Lord must be sought out diligently. Fear and patience will help faith, while long-suffering and continence are its allies. The author then begins his searching and his exposition of these ordinances, beginning, as is so often the case in the epistles, with a consideration of the Jewish law and of the Christian's release from it. God abolished the law for Christians and set forth a new law in Jesus Christ, one which is without the yoke of necessity. This new law has its obligation from God and is not made by man. The writer fears that the final trial is at hand, which means that it is all the more important for man to seek out those things which are able to save him.

The author admonishes his readers not to live alone but to come together and to seek out a common good. Be spiritual, he writes; be a temple consecrated to God. Christ endured too, offering up even His flesh, and because He did we are sanctified by the remission of sins, by His sprinkled blood. Nor are we left alone to understand the times. The Lord has also given us knowledge of the past, and wisdom for the present, together with understanding for the future. A man deserves to perish if he has knowledge of the way of righteousness and still turns away to darkness. God's Son came in flesh so that we might have a way of beholding Him in order to be saved. He has opened the way for men, through His death, by completing the total of the sins begun by those who persecuted God's prophets.

Turning to the Old Testament, the author begins to expound passages there to indicate that the prophets anticipated the coming of Christ. The Christians, for instance, are actually the ones whom God brings into the good land; they have been made perfect as heirs of the covenant of the Lord.

Christians are fortunate, the author of the letter tells his readers, in that the good Lord has made all things plain beforehand, so that we can know Him to whom we ought to give thanks and praise for everything. All we need to do is to learn to read the signs, to interpret the Scriptures figuratively and not literally.

Since the Old Testament contains passages which are apparently in conflict, one of the important jobs of interpretation is that of reconciling inconsistencies. The Old Testament reports the Christian message in an indirect, not a direct, fashion, and, consequently, a Christian reader must learn to discern hidden meanings in what he reads. Christ is present in the Old Testament, writes the author, just as He is in the New, but since Christ is mentioned only symbolically in the Old Testament, a Christian reader must learn to understand symbolism. When the Old Testament speaks of the sacrificial calf, for example, the Christian reader must realize that the reference is to the sacrifice of Christ.

The author of the *Epistle of Barnabas* then asks why it is that the Jews were not able to understand the Christian symbolism which runs through the Old Testament. The answer is that the Lord's voice was not clear to the Jews. The coming of Christ could have been recognized even in the practice of circumcision, had the Jews been enlightened enough to understand the symbolism of what they believed.

"Barnabas" especially concerns himself with the allegorical and Christological interpretation of the ritual law of the Old Testament and of details from the Old Testament narrative; he does not discuss truly prophetical passages or the ethical law of the Old Testament.

The distinctive character of the author's mode of allegorical interpretation is provided by his analysis of the number 318, found in the following passage (Genesis 14:14): "And when Abram heard that his brother was taken captive, he led forth his trained men, born in his house, three hundred and eighteen. . . ." The number is interpreted to mean "Jesus crucified," since the numerals of this number in Greek, taken in their letter value, are the two first letters of the name "Jesus"

together with the letter "T," which is taken to symbolize the Cross of Christ.

Everywhere in the original message of the prophets the new message of the Cross is to be found, a message which can be discerned symbolically by the enlightened eye of the Christian. Did the prophets understand that they were actually foretelling the Cross and the Crucifixion of Christ? No, God acted through the prophets to conceal in their message a significance which could be discerned only after Christ's coming. Passage after passage is examined, and the author of the *Epistle* concludes that God wished to reveal in the Old Testament everything concerning His Son. The Old Testament could not be understood before Christ, but now every facet of Christ's life can be discerned beneath the literal meaning of the Old Testament stories.

Jesus inherits the covenant, the central Jewish religious concern, and He does what it cannot do; namely, redeem its followers from their sin. But what is one to do with apparently literal facts? The world, the book of Genesis tells us, was created in six days. The author understands this passage to mean that the Lord will make an end to everything in six thousand years, since each day is a thousand years to God. Everything, then, will be completed in six thousand years. The Sabbath must no longer be celebrated as the day upon which God rested after creation; Christians celebrate the eighth day upon which Jesus rose from the dead. Every factor of Jewish observance is thus altered and transformed, and new meanings are read into old.

What about such a central doctrine of Judaism as that of the Temple? Christians may now take passages referring to the Temple as signifying the new man created through the Resurrection of Christ. The doctrine of the Temple could not have had such a meaning to the pre-Christian Jews, but now it can be seen that the meaning of the Temple was symbolical, hidden there by God in order that it might be revealed later. God dwelt in the Temple; God dwells in Christians now created anew.

The Jews had a literal temple; the Christians now have a spiritual Temple; thus, the author indicates the pattern for all reinterpretation of the Old Testament. Since Christianity is a spiritual religion, it has spiritual meaning, and thus all Old Testament statements are to be interpreted spiritually, not literally. Christians must learn to read everything anew, giving to what formerly had only a literal meaning a new spiritual meaning, thus demonstrating that their eyes have been opened through God's revelation. Giving a spiritual rendering to literal passages is itself a proof that one understands the spiritual nature of Christianity and the revealed truth in Christ.

The author, then, having demonstrated how the Old Testament is to be given a spiritual reinterpretation, begins a summary of an idea drawn from the traditional Jewish-Christian catechism, also to be found in the *Didache*. There are two ways of teaching and power, one of Light and one of Darkness. By the Light the Lord rules from eternity to eternity, but the way of Darkness prevails in the present time of iniquity. The way of Light demands that one be zealous in one's works, and that each man demonstrate a love of the Maker and a fear of the Creator. Furthermore, the way of Light involves glorifying Him who re-

deemed men from death; it requires that all men be simple in heart and rich in spirit, that they hate all that is not pleasing to God, that they hate all hypocrisy, and that they hold fast to the commandments of the Lord.

Having made this introduction to the way of Light, the author of the letter provides a long explanation of the characteristics of the Christian life, drawn from the tradition of exhortative writings to be found in late Judaism and early Christianity.

The way of the Black One, he continues, is crooked and full of cursing, a way of death and of eternal punishment. Along this path are the sins which destroy men's souls: idolatry, adultery, murder, pride, and other offenses against God.

The ordinances of the Lord have been given to us for good reason, the author writes, and he who does what God requires will be glorified in the Kingdom of God, whereas he who chooses the other path will perish with his works. Since there are two paths from which men may choose, there is a resurrection and an eventual recompense for choosing properly. Moreover, the day of accounting is near at hand, when all things will perish with the Evil One and only those who have followed the way of Light will be saved from this destruction.

The letter closes, then, on an urgent note. The author pleads with his readers: Be taught by God and seek out what the Lord requires of you, in order that you may be found faithful in the day of Judgment. While yet you occupy a body, do not fail in any of God's commandments, but seek them out and fulfill them. The hour of destruction and of reckoning is at hand and nothing else could possibly be more important. The matter is desperate, but the way has been made clear by God's revelation, even in the Old Testament, once it is read through enlightened eyes.

THE SEVEN EPISTLES OF IGNATIUS

Author: Saint Ignatius, Bishop of Antioch (c.35-c.107)
Type of work: Pastoral letters
First transcribed: c.107

PRINCIPAL IDEAS ADVANCED

The authority of Christ is present in the churches through the Apostles and the leaders appointed by them.

Unity and peace in the Church and the validity of the Church are acquired through faithful adherence to the bishop, and to the presbyters and deacons.

True Christian life and fellowship, together with the hope of immortality and eternal life, are based on the real earthly existence of Jesus Christ, and on His death and bodily resurrection.

These letters were written by Ignatius, Bishop of Antioch, on his way to martyrdom in Rome. While at Smyrna he wrote to the churches at Ephesus, Magnesia, Tralles, and Rome. Later at Troas he wrote to those at Philadelphia and Smyrna, and to Polycarp, bishop of Smyrna. The letters all show the elevation of spirit of one who regarded himself as "theophorus," a God-bearer, and who voluntarily and even eagerly went to his death as a martyr to the faith. They are full of warm expressions of love for the churches and of prayers and exhortations for their faithfulness, unity, and peace. Frequent mention is made of individuals, and of the bishop's gratitude for their prayers for him and for their blameless lives. Ignatius constantly refers to the purpose of his journey, protesting his unworthiness for such a role, praying for strength, and asking for the prayers of the churches. Ignatius shows great concern for his own church in Antioch which he has been compelled to leave, and he asks the other churches to choose worthy representatives and to send them to the Antioch brethren to comfort and encourage them in their trial.

The dominating theme of the letters is the bishop's concern for the unity of the church in each place, its purity of doctrine, and its faithfulness in life and worship. These virtues of unity, purity, and faithfulness are grounded in the leadership and authority of the bishop, the presbyters, and the deacons. A typical and inclusive statement of this position is found in Smyrneans VIII: "I. See that you all follow the bishop, as Jesus Christ follows the Father, and the presbytery as if it were the Apostles. And reverence the deacons as the command of God.

Let no one do any of the things appertaining to the Church without the
bishop. Let that be considered a valid
Eucharist which is celebrated by the
bishop, or by one whom he appoints.
2. Wherever the bishop appears let the
congregation be present; just as
wherever Jesus Christ is, there is the
Catholic Church. It is not lawful
either to baptise or to hold an 'agape'
without the bishop; but whatever he
approve, this is also pleasing to God,
that everything which you may do may
be secure and valid."

The epistles are not systematic treatises. Rather, they are composed of
brief and often disjointed paragraphs
written apparently under pressure both
of time and of emotion. The main
theme is clearly the divinely bestowed
authority of the bishop, presbyters, and
deacons, and the fact that the integrity
and validity of the churches rest upon
this foundation. There is no New Testament canon yet; hence, the Church
depends completely on the successors
and the Apostles.

Frequent warnings against false
doctrine reveal primarily the danger of
Docetism, which denies the real earthly
life, ministry, suffering, and the death
and resurrection of Christ. There is
no charge that this heresy actually exists in any of the churches, but Ignatius is very much conscious of such a
possibility. Over against the false doctrine of "semblance" he lays great emphasis upon the full reality of flesh and
spirit, the visible and the invisible.
This simple dualism runs through the
whole conception of Christ, the
Church, and the Christian life. Not
only did Christ live and suffer and die
in the flesh, but He also arose from the
dead: "After his resurrection he ate
and drank with them as a being of

flesh, although he was united in spirit
with the Father." So Ignatius prays for
the churches "that in them there may
be a union of the flesh and the spirit
of Jesus Christ, who is our everlasting
life, a union of faith and love, to
which is nothing preferable, and
(what is more than all) a union of
Jesus and the Father." This "flesh and
spirit" reality of the Church is based
on the presence of Christ in spirit, but
also upon the visible authority which
He has delegated through the Apostles
to the bishop, presbyters, and deacons.
The "dispensation of the new man
Jesus Christ" is found in this fellowship and obedience and in "breaking
one bread, which is the medicine of
immortality, the antidote that we
should not die, but live for ever in
Jesus Christ."

The life of the Christian also is a
life in the spirit and in the flesh. It is
first obedience to the bishop; "do
nothing without the bishop." But it is
also a pure moral life, a life of honesty
and uprightness, and of faithfulness
in marriage. The Christian life is "in
the flesh," but it is not a carnal life.
"But even what you do according to
the flesh is spiritual," writes Ignatius,
"for you do all things in Jesus Christ."
Moreover, this faithfulness in moral living wins the favor of God just as unrighteousness incurs His condemnation. By faithfulness the Christian "attains to God." He is "full of God,"
and he is thereby assured of resurrection and eternal life. The bishop does
not seem to fear or even to be aware of
a "doctrine of works"; moral purity appears as direct obedience to God and in
full participation in the life of the
Church. Thus is conceived as of one
piece the saving work and power of
Christ, the Church united with the

bishop and the presbyters, the sacramental efficacy of the Eucharist, the moral life of the Christian believer, and the hope of resurrection and eternal life. The theological basis for all this is the Incarnation: "Wait for him who is above seasons, timeless, invisible, who for our sakes became visible, who cannot be touched, who cannot suffer, who for our sakes accepted suffering, who in every way endured for our sakes."

Ignatius shows a lesser but real concern for the Judaizers. He warns that those who listen to them will be led astray. The prince of this world has hidden from the Jews the Virgin Birth of Christ. One should not listen to the Jews; one cannot be a Christian and live as a Jew.

Ignatius writes as a pastor. His care for his own church is frequently expressed. He counsels Polycarp to foster the fellowship of the church by frequent meetings, by personal humility and interest in the members, by care for the widows, and by positive teaching which will make the people less subject to any influence of false doctrine. He lovingly charges Polycarp to "Be sober as God's athlete," for "The prize is immortality and eternal life."

The "care of all the churches" occupies the greater part of all the letters. But the suppressed and often openly expressed theme of martyrdom is climactic. The bishop's vivid conception of resurrection and of the unity of flesh and spirit, his faith in the risen Christ, and his deep assurance of his own resurrection cannot remove the emotional tension and spiritual exhilaration with which he contemplates his own death. He writes especially to the Romans about this, for they are to be his immediate Christian companions before he goes to death: "Suffer me to be eaten by the beasts, through whom I can attain to God. I am God's wheat, and I am ground by the teeth of wild beasts that I may be found pure bread of Christ. Rather entice the wild beasts that they may become my tomb, and leave no trace of my body, that when I fall asleep I be not burdensome to any." As he approaches Rome he lives through this trial in anticipation. The ten soldiers that guard him already test and prepare him by their harsh treatment. He sees in this physical suffering a figure of the attacks upon his spirit of temptations, and his fight for faithfulness to his Lord. Now, he lives no longer for this world but for the higher world of the spirit. Thus he wins the victory in advance and prepares for the time when the flesh as well as the spirit must face the moment of violent death. The letters provide a powerful support for all Christians who are called upon to face a similar trial—and triumph.

THE APOLOGY OF ARISTIDES

Author: Aristides (fl. second century)
Type of work: Christian apologetics
First transcribed: c.124

Principal Ideas Advanced

There is one true living God, the creator of Heaven and earth, who is worshiped by the Christians, whereas the barbarians and the Greeks have given themselves to the folly of worshiping many gods which are merely subjective creations of their own imagination, and which are unfitting examples for human conduct.

The Christians possess the true knowledge of a holy and just God and live exemplary lives modeled after His precepts so that the very continuance of the world is due to their intercession, and they are, therefore, unjustly harassed by their persecutors.

The *Apology of Aristides* is of importance as a witness to the character of early Christianity. The history of Eusebius mentions Aristides as one of the early Christians who defended Christianity before the Roman emperor Hadrian (117-138). Aristides is one of the foremost apologists of the second century. Like Justin Martyr (c.100-c.165), Tatian (fl. c.160), Melito (d. c.190), Athenagoras (second century), Theophilus (later second century), and others, Aristides sought to win recognition for Christianity throughout the Roman Empire by putting an end to the false rumors against the Christians. The Apologists tried to make known the true nature of Christianity and to put an end to the persecutions. They appealed to the cultured members of society by arguing that Christianity is the highest wisdom, the true answer to the questions of the philosophers, and by attacking the error of polytheism and its effects on morality.

The work of Aristides was lost for centuries. The first two chapters were rediscovered in 1878 when the monks of St. Lazarus of Venice published a Latin translation of an Armenian text. The authenticity of the Armenian fragment remained in dispute until 1889,

when a Syriac version of the *Apology* was discovered at the Convent of St. Catherine on Mount Sinai. The publication of the Syriac text led to the discovery that the greater part of the Greek text is contained in the widely-circulated medieval romance, *The Life of Barlaam and Josaphat.*

The original date of Aristides' *Apology*, according to Eusebius, is 124, when the *Apology* was presented to Hadrian. A second superscription in the Syriac version causes some scholars to assign the work to the time of Antonius Pius (138-161), but it is most likely that Eusebius's early date is correct.

Aristides' argument may be divided into three parts. The first seeks to demonstrate the existence of God; the second, the foolishness of polytheism; and the third, the truth that Christians alone possess the purest knowledge of God and live a life in keeping with God's holiness.

Aristides begins by claiming that philosophical contemplation of the beauty and the majesty of the world discloses that God is the power that moves the world and what it contains. As the cause of motion God is greater than the world, and although His nature is not fully comprehensible, it is reasonable that a philosopher should stand in awe of Him.

God is not born, nor made; His nature is unchangeable and without end. He is perfect and without defect; all things are in need of Him, but He is in need of nothing.

Mankind is divided into four classes, Aristides writes; there are the Greeks, the Barbarians, the Christians, and the Jews. The barbarians trace the origin of their religion to many gods, to Kronos and Rhea; they worship things, mere images or idols made in honor of the elements, rather than their creator. The earth, the waters, fire, the winds, the sun, the moon, and the stars are not gods. Only God is imperishable, invisible, and unvarying, holy, blessed, and immortal. The earth and the waters were created for man, and put under his rule. The winds of themselves have no authority; they too serve man by transporting his ships, and scattering seeds. Man is able to keep the winds in check so that they may be of service to him. Nor does man himself have the nature of a God, for man is born and dies; he has defects, and he is destroyed by animals and the elements.

The Greeks have gone even further than the barbarians in their error concerning God, Aristides continues, for the Greeks have introduced numerous fictitious gods, some females, others males; some are adulterers, others murderers. Their gods are wrathful, passionate, and envious; some are thieves, or cripples; some are sorcerers, some insane; they are kidnaped, struck by lightning, and seduced by other gods; they are perverted, incestuous, and vain. By worshiping such false gods the Greeks accepted folly and absurdity, and in emulating the gods they com-

mitted the same foul practices themselves, thereby bringing wars, famines, captivity, and desolation upon themselves.

Aristides writes that the Greeks sacrifice their children to Kronos; they burn them alive in honor of a god who has children, who went mad, and was bound and mutilated by his son Zeus. The latter is made king of the gods, a god who changes himself into men and animals, into a swan, and an eagle.

Such tales cause wickedness in men, Aristides argues, for by imitating their gods, men practice adultery, defile themselves with their sisters and mothers, have sexual relations with other men, and kill their parents. Such gods are worse than demons.

A god such as Hephaistos is lame and needy, Aristides points out; Hermes is a thief, greedy for gain, a maimed magician; Asklepios is a physician that was killed by lightning; Ares is a jealous warrior who covets sheep, commits adultery with Aphrodite; Dionysus arranges nocturnal orgies, teaches drunkenness, abducts women, eats snakes while mad; Herakles kills his own children while insane, casts himself into a fire and dies; and Apollon utters oracles for men so that he can be rewarded.

Such gods lead to corruption, delusion, and the defilement of nations, Aristides maintains. To believe in such gods is unworthy of the philosopher. The true God is not in need of sacrifices. The gods of the Greeks are based on myths, idle tales, and superficial speculations; the very deeds of such gods are at variance with the righteous laws of men.

The Jews approach the truth more than any other nation, Aristides concedes, for they recognize that God is one, the omnipotent Creator; they worship God and not His works; they show compassion to the poor, and they are just; but they, too, err in their worship of angels, their ritualism, and their rejection of the truth which the Christians have found. From its beginning the Christian religion has centered about Jesus the Messiah, the Son of the most high God, who descended from Heaven, born of a Hebrew virgin. The teachings of Christianity can be read by all in the Gospel. This same Jesus, God incarnate, was pierced by the Jews, buried, rose again after three days, and ascended to Heaven. The Christian religion grew because of the preaching by Jesus' twelve disciples.

Aristides continues his zealous arguments by claiming that the Christians trust and know the God who created the heavens and the earth, in whom are all things and from whom are all things come; the true and living God, besides whom there is no other. From this God the Christians have received commandments as to how they should live, and because of their hope in the world to come, their lives are at present exemplary. Christians do not commit fornication, nor adultery; they do not lie, steal, or covet what is not theirs. They honor their parents, are kind to those near to them, are upright and honest in their judgments. They do not worship idols; they do to others what they would have others do to them. They comfort their oppressors and do good to their enemies; their women are pure and modest, and their bondsmen are treated as brethren; they love one another, are charitable to widows and orphans, hospitable to strangers, solicitous of the well-being of prisoners, observing the teachings of their Messiah with care, and living justly and soberly as their Lord has commanded them. Each day and every hour the Christians praise and give thanks to God for their food and drink; they rejoice at the birth of a child, and give thanks when a righteous man passes from the world to be with God, but when one of them dies in his sins, they grieve bitterly.

Aristides contends that the teachings of the Christians are readily available in their writings, the study of which is able to give full assurance of their veracity. The very earth abides through the supplication of the Christians, who are innocent of the monstrous impurity attributed to them by their persecutors. The Christians are just and good; their spirit is long suffering and they have compassion for those who revile them.

Aristides concludes his apology by stating that the Christians pray that those who wrong them in ignorance may come to purity of heart and receive the forgiveness of their own sins, thus becoming members of the most blessed race—the "new . . . third race"—of men upon the face of the earth, and thereby escaping the final judgment that will come upon those who are without the knowledge of God. Aristides' faith that "Verily this is a new people, and there is something divine in it" illuminates his work.

THE SHEPHERD

Author: Hermas (second century)
Type of work: Account of revelations
First transcribed: c.130

PRINCIPAL IDEAS ADVANCED

Revelations are made to Hermas by the Church, which appears in the form of a woman; by a shepherd, the angel of repentance; and by the great angel, who is in charge of all Christians.

Sin and baptism are the main themes of the revelations.

It is possible to live a sinless life after baptism, but for those who sin after baptism, the message given Hermas offers a final opportunity of forgiveness for those who repent and do penance.

The *Shepherd*, the most voluminous writing among the works produced by the Apostolic Fathers, achieved almost canonical standing, together with the New Testament Book of Revelation. The book was written in Rome by a man who had no particular office in the Church. The author writes with the self-consciousness of a prophet (as does the author of the book of Revelation), but the book nevertheless contains a great deal of traditional material. The message of the book is presented in the form of various "Visions," "Mandates," "Similitudes," and "Parables," to which detailed instructions for proper interpretation are appended.

As the work begins, Hermas is described as walking along a road. He becomes sleepy. Led by a spirit, he crosses a stream and kneels to pray. Then the heavens open, and a woman whom Hermas once secretly desired appears and greets him. She accuses him of having sinned by desiring her in his heart, and she tells him that he must repent. When the vision ends, Hermas ponders the question as to how he can be saved, and he reconsiders his overt actions, for even his unuttered desires have been shown to be sinful.

While he is reflecting, a great white chair appears before him and a woman in shining garments comes to occupy it. Hermas tells her the reason for his grief, and they discuss sin and the means for its restitution. The lady reads to him, speaking of the glory and the power of God, and then she is borne away as the first vision closes.

The second vision comes a year later, when he is again walking near the same spot. Again the ancient lady whom he had seen the year before appears. This time she has a little book, which she tells him to take away and copy. He does this, and only later does he begin to understand the things written there. The message is primarily concerned with Hermas's relationship to his family, and with his duties as a Christian toward them. At the close of this vision it is revealed to Hermas that the Lady who appeared to him was the Church. She is old because she was created first of all things, and for the sake of the Church the world was established.

Hermas's third vision comes after a

period of fasting, when the Lady appears to him in response to his desire to know fully the meaning of his previous revelations. This time six young men come with her, and they listen to Hermas as he recites his sins. She explains the glory which is due to one who is a martyr for the faith, and then Hermas has a vision of a great tower being built on water by a company of young men. It is so built of shining square stones that the tower appears to be of one stone. On his demand, the Lady begins to explain the vision to Hermas. The tower is the Church, and it is built upon water because the lives of those who comprise it have been saved through the water of baptism. The best stones which go into it are the Apostles, bishops, and teachers—men who served God in reverence and holiness. The other stones used represent those who have suffered for the Lord, those who are upright and preserve His commandments; but the stones thrown away represent those who did not repent. Stones with cracks represent those with malice in their hearts. Round stones, which must be cut before they can be used, signify those who have faith but also riches. Hermas and the lady then discuss how those who are rejected may repent so as finally to be fitted into the tower.

Seven women, representing faith and the other central Christian virtues, then appear, and Hermas is told to follow them in order of importance, faith being first. Hermas demands to know why the Lady appears different at different times, sometimes young, sometimes old. A long explanation is given which concerns the various types of people who make up the Church through repentance, and which calls attention to the Church's antiquity and to its continual renewal.

In Hermas's fourth vision he sees the type of the persecutions to come. A great beast comes to threaten him, and again he meets the ancient Lady. She explains to him that he escaped destruction from the beast because he was not double-minded; his singularity of faith preserved him from the beast's destruction.

The shepherd, who inspires the title, appears in the fifth revelation; he tells Hermas that he has come to dwell with him the rest of his days, Hermas having been handed over to his care. The shepherd, who is the angel of repentance, commands Hermas to write down the commandments and parables which the shepherd gives him.

The second part of the book contains the twelve mandates which the shepherd gives to Hermas, and their detailed explanation.

The first mandate is to believe that God is one, that He has made all things and contains all things and is Himself alone uncontained. Simplicity is the theme of the second mandate, since the innocence of simplicity keeps one from evil-speaking and encourages one to live according to God. Love truth: this is the injunction of mandate three, since by doing so one receives a spirit free from lies. One who loves truth abstains from the sin of lying and thus shall live with God. Purity is commanded in mandate four. Healing can be given to the one who sins here, although it can come only from the One who has the power over all. He who sins and is given repentance in baptism, Hermas is told, ought not to sin again but ought to live in purity. There is no second repentance given. Remission of sins is available only if the commandments are kept.

Mandate five tells Hermas that he should be long-suffering and prudent, and that if he is, he shall have power over all evil deeds and shall do all righteousness. The Lord dwells in long-suffering, but the Devil dwells in ill-temper. Temper destroys the servants of God and leads them away from righteousness. It cannot, of course, lead astray those who are filled with faith, but it does mislead those who are vain and double-minded. Long-suffering dwells with those who have faith in perfectness, and it turns out to be the chief virtue. Hermas is told that if he is able to master this commandment, he will be strong enough to keep all the other commandments given to him.

Mandate six explains the first mandates. Hermas is further told to believe only the righteous and not to believe the unrighteous. Two angels are with all men, one of righteousness and the other of unrighteousness. The angel of righteousness is delicate, modest, meek, and gentle, whereas the angel of wickedness is ill-tempered, bitter, and foolish.

Fear is the theme of mandate seven, for the fear of the Lord is the means for keeping His commandments. However, do not fear the Devil, Hermas is told, for by fearing the Lord you are given power over the Devil and need have no fear of him. Temperance, the quality of mandate eight, is said to be two-fold: it causes one to refrain from evil, and it also causes one not to refrain from the good but to do it. Hermas is then given a specific list of acts to be avoided and acts to be performed.

Mandate nine enjoins Hermas not to be double-minded. He is directed to purify his heart from all the vanities of this world. Doubt is the worst enemy of faith and causes double-mindedness. Unless he repents, every double-minded man will have trouble being saved. Grief, mandate ten tells Hermas, is the sister of double-mindedness. Grief is more evil than all the other spirits and is more terrible to the servants of God because it corrupts man more than any of the other spirits, wearing out the Holy Spirit. However, grief can also bring salvation. For if a man grieves over an ill-tempered act, grief may lead to repentance and salvation; but if a man fails in his work because of double-mindedness, and if he grieves over this, then the Holy Spirit is grieved also and worn out. Therefore, to combat grief, put on joyfulness, which always is acceptable to God, since the joyful man does good deeds, has good thoughts, and despises grief. But the mournful man is wicked. If grief is mixed with intercession at the altar, it does not permit the intercession to ascend in purity.

Mandate eleven reveals a man sitting on a bench, and Hermas is told that the man is a false prophet, one who corrupts the understanding of the children of God. Hermas naturally asks how one can discern the false from the true prophet, and he is told: Test a man by his life. A true prophet will be meek, gentle, and lowly minded, whereas the false prophet will exhalt himself, be impudent and shameless, and lead a life of great luxury. Most important, if a person accepts rewards for his prophecy, then he is a false prophet. The vision ends as Hermas is told to have faith in the Divine Spirit.

Mandate twelve, the last of the mandates, concerns desire. The same man continues to instruct Hermas.

Hermas is to put away from himself every evil desire and to put on only desires which are good and holy. A wicked desire is cruel and hard to tame, and it destroys men. Carnal desires are the worst; serving only good desires will enable one to overcome wicked desires. To serve good desires, Hermas is told, means to work righteousness and virtue, to fear the Lord, and to have both faith and meekness.

The angel of repentance has been speaking to Hermas, and the angel concludes the last mandate by saying that these commandments are given so that one may continue pure after repentance by following the commandments. Hermas is not sure that a man is able to keep such commandments simply from his own power, but he is told that whoever believes that the commandments can be kept will be able to keep them; and this assurance is important since without keeping the commandments there is no salvation. Man, after all, is the lord of all creatures and should be able also to be the lord of the commandments. If you have only the name of the Lord on your lips, Hermas is told, that will not do; but if you have the Lord in your heart, then you will be able to master these commandments. If you purify your heart from the vain desires of the world, and if your heart is pure towards the Lord, then these commandments can be kept, the angel of repentance assures Hermas.

The third part of the work presents ten parables, or similitudes, some quite brief and direct, some quite long and involved. On the whole they are rather simple and straightforward in their meaning. For each parable or vision, Hermas is given a detailed and allegorical translation of its meaning. They are not mere stories but elaborately constructed illustrations. The first parable points up the fact that since Christians are like strangers in a foreign land, they ought not to secure for themselves more than the bare minimum of what they need for temporary living.

The second parable describes the two types of servants of God, the rich and the poor, who may complement each other and thus aid each other in achieving salvation. The rich man rests upon the poor and gives him what he needs; the poor man is rich in intercession and confession. The third parable explains that in this world righteous men and sinners appear to be the same and cannot easily be distinguished. Parable four continues this theme, explaining that the righteous will be known in the world to come through their fruits. The acceptable and proper mode of fasting is the subject of parable five; true fasting involves serving the Lord with a pure heart and keeping His ordinances.

Parable six begins by considering Hermas's perplexity over the previous parables and his concern to understand them properly. The angel of repentance appears again and attempts to calm Hermas's perplexity, assuring him that he can both understand and keep the commandments. Then Hermas is presented with a vision of different types of shepherds. One represents the shepherd of luxury and deceit, another the shepherd of punishment; it is luxury which provides the main stumbling block to the good life. In parable seven Hermas continues to express his uncertainty concerning the punishment given to those who have not repented, but parable eight turns to a new theme and concerns a great willow tree and the various kinds of branches which Hermas sees being cut from it. These represent various kinds of lives, and some are so fruitful that they are sent directly to become part of a tower, which represents the Kingdom of God. Useless branches are those who have not observed God's law. Some whose lives were not acceptable on first inspection are given a second chance and through repentance are made acceptable for entrance.

Parable nine is the longest parable; it is a vision of twelve mountains, each with a different appearance. Twelve maidens and six men are building a tower with stones taken from these mountains. The tower is built upon a rock which contains a gate. In elaborate detail the different stones are described, and they are pictured as representing various kinds of lives. And, again, some stones are immediately acceptable for inclusion in the tower, the Kingdom of God, and others must first be reshaped through repentance. Others are never fit to be used and are rejected. Again the message is, repent while there is still time.

The tenth and final parable promises every good thing to Hermas if he keeps the commandments given to him. All the lusts of the world will be made subject to him, so that nothing will impede him. Whoever keeps the commandments has life and honor from the Lord; whoever does not is delivering himself to death. To keep the commandments means to minister to others. If anyone sees another person laboring under the yoke of the lusts of the world, he should help him in his distress and thus gain great joy. Whoever does not rescue another from such distress incurs sin and becomes guilty. The building of the tower, which is the Church, has been broken off so that, through such actions as that of obeying the commandments and ministering to others, each man might have the opportunity to prove his worth and to gain inclusion for himself in the tower. With this injunction to Hermas to obey and to transmit the commandments, the visions of Hermas abruptly end.

EPISTLE TO THE PHILIPPIANS

Author: Saint Polycarp of Smyrna (c.69-c.155)
Type of work: Pastoral letter
First transcribed: c.135

Principal Ideas Advanced

The fruit of faith in Christ is a life of love and purity; Christ Himself provides the example which all Christians should imitate.

Christians are citizens of a heavenly Kingdom and will reign with Christ if they are obedient to His commandments.

Christians are to pray for civil authorities even when the authorities persecute and hate the Church.

The letter of Polycarp of Smyrna to the church at Philippi is one of the documents belonging to the corpus of early Christian literature known as the works of the Apostolic Fathers. Of all the writers whose works are included in this group, Polycarp has probably the most impressive credentials for being considered an "Apostolic" writer, since it is quite possible that he had some personal associations with the Apostle John during Polycarp's youth (see, Eusebius's *Ecclesiastical History*).

Polycarp must have been a central figure in the Church of Asia as early as the first decade of the second century. He was a significant Church leader for more than half a century. Ignatius, Bishop of Antioch, while on his way to his martyrdom in Rome, visited Polycarp, and the letters which Ignatius wrote to the church at Smyrna and to Polycarp himself show the affection he felt for Polycarp and the faith he had in Polycarp's importance to the advancement of Christianity. The fact that there is a somewhat larger body of knowledge about Polycarp than about most figures from the second century is itself evidence in support of the claim that Polycarp played an important and creative part in the building of the early Church.

Two incidents from Polycarp's life, recorded in Irenaeus's *Against the Heresis* (182-188), throw valuable light upon Polycarp's character and temperament. One concerns a trip which Polycarp made to Rome about the year 155. During his stay in Rome he became involved in the problem of determining the correct date for the celebration of Easter, and although he and Anicetus, the leader of the Roman Church, were unable to agree on the same practice, they nevertheless remained in friendly communion with each other; Bishop Anicetus, as a sign of friendship and recognition, permitted Polycarp to celebrate the Eucharist in the Church of Rome. The other incident concerns a meeting which took place between Polycarp and the arch-heretic Marcion (d.c.160). In this meeting Polycarp exhibited none of the charity and tolerance which he had shown in his disagreement with Anicetus. Rather, he firmly denounced Marcion as the "first-born of Satan."

These same two attitudes—charity and tolerance in matters of Church practice and discipline, and implacable opposition to every distortion of the essentials of the Christian faith—are strongly reflected in the Epistle to the Philippians.

The occasion for the writing of the letter was a scandal which had developed in the church at Philippi. A presbyter by the name of Valens had evidently used his position in the church for financial profit and thus had violated the strong feelings of the church against the accumulation of wealth. Polycarp wrote in a spirit of fraternal concern for the church and the wayward presbyter, urging the church to be moderate and understanding and Valens to be truly repentant.

The over-all tone of the letter, therefore, is one of gentleness and restraint. Yet flashes of anger do show forth when Polycarp considers those "who bear in hypocrisy the name of the Lord, who deceive empty-headed people." What Polycarp had in mind here were the heretics who denied the reality of Christ's incarnation and consequently rejected the Apostolic accounts of the Crucifixion and the Church's teachings concerning the resurrection of the body. It is possible that he had

Marcion and his followers specifically in mind when he wrote these words, since he used the same expression he had used of Marcion—"first-born of Satan"—to describe these hypocrites and deceivers.

One obvious fact which emerges from a reading of this letter is that the writer can hardly be called an original thinker. For the most part, Polycarp was content to express his thoughts by means of a patchwork of Scriptural quotations. It is not necessary to conclude from this technique, however, that Polycarp was incapable of originality. Rather, it would seem that he deliberately adopted the technique because it was consistent with his own theological point of view. The entire message of Polycarp can be summed up in the words "Stand fast in the faith delivered to you." His purpose in writing to the Philippians was not to advance new and original ideas, but to remind the church at Philippi of the faith which it had been taught. In short, Polycarp's chief concern was for the preservation of the Church's tradition—a tradition which he clearly identified with the message of the Apostles.

Closely related to this emphasis on the preservation of pure doctrine in the Church is the emphasis on pure living. Again, in the area of morals and conduct, Polycarp showed no interest in presenting his readers with novel arguments and sophisticated expositions, but rather encouraged them to pattern their conduct after the life of Christ. By imitating Christ's example—particularly his purity, patient endurance, and forbearance—the church at Philippi could be assured of an exalted position in the Kingdom of God when the saints would reign with Christ and judge the world.

Behind the oft-repeated encouragement, "Be steadfast," must be seen the constant threat of persecution which faced Christians in the early centuries. Polycarp would one day prove his own steadfastness by his heroic martyrdom. Perhaps the clearest indication of the charitable spirit of this man is to be found in his plea that Christians pray for those who persecute and hate them.

THE FIRST APOLOGY and THE SECOND APOLOGY

Author: Saint Justin Martyr (c.100-c.165)
Type of work: Apologetics
First transcribed: c.150; c.160

PRINCIPAL IDEAS ADVANCED

Truth and right are equal for all men, and all men should be treated equally.

Christians should be treated justly and should not be unlawfully condemned by prejudice, malicious gossip, and false accusations, for in killing Christians, the ruler does them no harm but condemns himself to everlasting perdition.

Christians are loyal citizens, for they have been instructed by God to obey the government in secular matters; there is nothing in Christian belief or practice that is detrimental to the welfare of the state.

The First Apology and *The Second Apology* are the works of Justin Martyr, the second century apologist, and the first outstanding defender of Christianity against the attacks of non-Christians. Justin Martyr was born at the beginning of the second century (c.100-110) in Samaria. Before his conversion to Christianity (c.130), he frequented the schools of the Stoics, the Peripatetics, the Pythagoreans, and the Platonists. After his conversion, Justin opened a school of philosophy at Rome, where he openly and fearlessly engaged in apologetic controversy until his martyrdom about 165.

The First Apology was written at Rome about the year 150. The petition is directed to the Emperor Antoninus Pius, to the Emperor's sons, to the Senate, and to the Roman people as a whole. *The Second Apology* is assigned by critics to the latter part of Antoninus Pius's reign (147-161), although in his *Ecclesiastical History,* Eusebius states that it was addressed to Marcus Aurelius (121-180). It is most likely that *The Second Apology* is not an appendix to the first, but an independent petition, written at Rome between 155 and 160.

The First Apology can be divided into three main divisions. The first twenty chapters deal with the proper relationship between the authorities of the State and Christians; Chapters 21 to 60 seek to demonstrate the superiority of Christianity over paganism, and Chapters 61-68 offer explanations of Christian practices. At a time when the Christian religion was grossly misunderstood, such explanations were significant features of the Christian apology.

Justin Martyr first asks the rulers of the state for justice, for fair treatment to Christians, based upon facts, not prejudice. As citizens, Christians can rightly be called upon to give an account of their life and doctrine; they in turn can expect to be judged in accordance with philosophy and piety, not by force and tyranny. To inflict injustice is more detrimental to the tyrant than to his victim. In fact, the Emperor may be able to kill Christians, but he is unable to harm them, unless he can convict them of being sinful persons or criminals.

To punish Christians simply because they call themselves Christians, without showing they have done evil is, says Justin, to act unjustly. To call Christians atheists because they refuse to worship pagan idols is to overlook the fact that Christians do worship the most true God, the God who is alien to all evil and is the Father of all virtue. Christians worship God the Father and the Son who came forth from Him and the Prophetic Spirit, and they pay homage to Him in reason and truth, and teach His doctrine to anyone who wishes to learn it.

If some Christians have been arrested and convicted of crimes, writes Justin, this is no reason for condemning other Christians. Whoever is convicted of a crime ought to be punished as a criminal, not as a Christian.

Christians do not wish to live by lying; they desire to make their abode with God, the Father and Creator of all, and they make haste to confess their faith in the belief that the righteous will be rewarded, and that the wicked will be assigned to eternal torment.

Christians do not worship idols made with human hands, Justin asserts; such practice is both stupid and disrespectful to God, who is of ineffable glory and form. God has no need of the material gifts of men, but is Himself the giver of all things. God approves only of those who imitate his inherent virtues; namely, justice, temperance, and the love of man.

To the accusation against the Christians that they owe allegiance to another kingdom and are thus guilty of treason and are unable to be good citizens, Justin Martyr replies that the Kingdom of which Christians speak is not of this world but is a Kingdom that is with God.

Christians, more than all other men, are good citizens and allies in fostering peace, since they believe that it is impossible for the wicked to hide from God, and that each man receives eternal punishment or salvation according to the merits of his actions.

As citizens Christians have been instructed by their Lord and Savior, Jesus Christ, to pay their taxes to the officials of the state. While the Christian worships God alone, in other things he joyfully obeys the powers that be and acknowledges the rulers of this world, praying that they may have sound judgment, lest by their wickedness they incur in the everlasting fire the penalty of their misdeeds.

Christianity is indeed superior to pagan religion; for what Christians believe, they learned from Christ and the Prophets who spoke the truth. Jesus Christ alone is properly the Son of God, since He alone is the first begotten of the Father, and having become man by His will, He taught Christians their doctrines for the conversion and restoration of mankind.

To hate Christians because of the name of Christ, writes Justin, and to execute them as criminals, although they have committed no crime, while others are left unmolested in spite of their bizarre and divergent beliefs and practices, is to be grossly unfair. Christians are accused of cannibalism, incest, and sexual orgies, whereas in fact such charges are false, while others who allow newly born children to be raised in prostitution or to perish remain unpunished.

To refute the charge that Christ was a worker of magic rather than of miracles, Justin points to the prophecies which predicted that events were to happen before they actually took place. The books of the Prophets foretold that Jesus Christ would come to us born of a virgin, that He would reach manhood, that He would heal the sick and raise the dead to life, that He would be hated and crucified, that He would rise from the dead and ascend into Heaven as the very Son of God. It was further predicted that the Gentiles rather than the Jews would believe in Him.

The fact that prophecies have been fulfilled does not mean that everything happens by fate and that man does not have the power of choice. Without the free faculty to shun evil and to choose good, a man is not responsible for his actions no matter what they may be. Men were created with the ability to choose good of their own accord, and thus they are responsible when they freely choose what is evil.

Christians do not hold that men who lived before the birth of Christ were unaccountable for their actions. As the first-begotten of God the Father, Christ is the Logos of whom all mankind partakes. Anyone who lived by reason (*logos*), such as Socrates and Heraclitus, even though he may have been considered an atheist, is a Christian. All those who have lived *reason-*

ably, in accordance with the Logos, are in fact Christians.

A reasonable man must be persuaded that since so much of what the Prophets have predicted has already come to pass, those things which were likewise foretold, but are yet to happen, shall with certainty happen. Two comings of Christ have been foretold by the Prophets; the first, which has already occurred, was that of a suffering servant; the second, which will take place, is when He shall come gloriously from Heaven with His angelic army. He shall then raise to life the bodies of all men, and He shall separate the righteous from the wicked, condemning the latter to sensible pain for all eternity and to eternal fire together with the evil demons.

The myths that have been fabricated by the pagan poets are taught to the young without any proof of their truth, says Justin. Such myths were first related through the instigation of evil demons and were designed to seduce and to deceive men. For when the demons heard the Prophets predict the coming of Christ, they produced tales, thinking that they would thereby arouse the suspicion that those things foretold of Christ were on a par with the fabulous tales of the poets. The demons were unable to convince men that there will be no Hell fire to punish sinners, nor could they keep Christ unknown after His appearance on earth. They were able, however, to cause Christians to be hated and to be executed by unreasonable men, who indulged their passions in evil ways. Christians do not hate their persecutors, but pity them and desire their conversion. The Christian has no fear of death, for death is but the beginning of eternal life, free from pain and want.

Christian practices have been slandered and distorted, Justin insists. The rulers of Rome should understand that a Christian who is regenerated through Christ consecrates himself to God. Those who believe pledge themselves to live righteously, and they are taught in prayer and fasting to ask God to forgive their past sins. The new convert is baptized with the washing of water, in the name of God, the Father and Lord of all, and of Jesus Christ, and of the Holy Ghost. Christians are baptized to obtain in the water the forgiveness of past sins, and to be regenerated. Christians do not indulge in sexual orgies or cannibalism; their worship is simple and pure. Newly baptized persons gather with other believers for prayer. They partake of bread and wine mixed with water, the Eucharist, of which only he can share who has accepted the truth of Christianity, who has been baptized for the remission of his sins and for his regeneration, and who lives according to the principles of Christ. The bread and wine which Christians eat and drink is regarded as the flesh and blood of Christ, who died for man's salvation.

Christians come together each Sunday to remind one another of the truths of their faith, to partake of the Eucharist, to read the writings of the Apostles and the Prophets, to pray, and to show their gratitude to God by collecting gifts to take care of all those in need, such as the orphans and widows.

The beliefs of the Christians ought to be respected if they are in accordance with reason and truth; they are to be despised if they are deemed erroneous; but in no case ought death to be inflicted on those who have done no wrong. Those who continue to be unjust shall not escape the future judgment of God. In the words of the Emperor Hadrian, justice demands: "If anyone accuses the Christians and proves that they broke the law, you must assign the punishment in accordance with the gravity of the crime. . . . If anyone shall accuse these persons [the Christians] merely to calumniate them, you arrest him for villainy and inflict penalties against his guilt."

The Second Apology consists of fifteen short chapters written in protest against the unjust execution of three Christians by Urbicus, the prefect of Rome, solely because they dared to confess that they were Christians.

Justin reports that Christians are sarcastically asked why they do not kill themselves and go immediately to God, thereby saving the state the trouble. Why do they confess to being Christians? The answer is simply that man is not the master of his own life. God created the world for the sake of mankind; God is pleased with those who follow His perfections and are displeased with evil. If Christians were to commit suicide, no one would be instructed in the divine doctrines, and they would be acting in opposition to the will of God. Christians confess their faith on being interrogated because they have done no wrong and they believe that it is wicked to lie.

The further question as to why God permits Christians to be persecuted when He has the power to help them is answerable in terms of man's free will and in terms of the hatred of demons who are permitted to persuade men to do evil.

Justin concludes by suggesting that a wise ruler will for his own sake judge the case of the Christian with justice, lest he condemn himself in the eyes of God by convicting the innocent.

THE DIDACHE
or
THE TEACHING OF THE TWELVE APOSTLES

Author: Unknown
Type of work: Code of Christian ethics (first part); manual of Church order
(second part)
First transcribed: Probably the middle of the second century

PRINCIPAL IDEAS ADVANCED

The way of life is marked out by two commandments and their implications:
(1) Love God and your neighbor, and refrain from doing to people what you
do not want done to you; and (2) commit neither murder nor adultery.
The way of death is by violation of these two commandments.
There are definite rules by which churches should: (1) celebrate baptism, the
Eucharist, weekly services of worship; (2) test the genuineness of visiting teach-
ers, apostles, and prophets; and (3) elect bishops and deacons.

Every Christian should always stand ready for the Lord's coming "on the clouds of the sky."

It will help preclude misunderstanding to state at the outset, and in brief compass, what we do *not* know about the *Didache*. We know neither the author's name nor where he lived. We cannot be certain whether he borrowed "The Two Ways" from the *Epistle of Barnabas* (written about 100), or whether both depend upon an earlier Jewish-Christian catechism, itself derived from stoical philosophy, possibly the *Cebetis tabula*. Within tolerable limits we can fix the date of composition, as indicated above; but we do not know, at every point, whether the author is quoting an old document representing first century thought and practice, or whether he is speaking about Church morals and Church orders which were actually followed in his own day.

Other factors which are more certain enable us to read the *Didache* intelligently and help us to see in this document one of the most important pieces of early Christian literature. We may be quite sure that the longer title (*The Teaching of the Twelve Apostles*) is not to be taken literally. In their own time the original Apostles were active in forming and transmitting teaching materials. It is quite obvious, however, that in its present form the *Didache* comes from the second century. In the first instance it must, therefore, be read and interpreted against the background of what we know about life in the second century Church. Such an approach does not exclude one's finding first century customs preserved in the *Didache,* as we shall presently see.

With some degree of probability we may assume that the author employed not only a Christian catechism stating "The Two Ways," but also a late first century document stating regulations for ordering Church life. The latter source was very probably written in Syria—it contains quotations from Matthew's Gospel—and it may be that the *Didache* itself found its origin in that country, though a case may also be made for Alexandria.

The image of two ways is a very old device, employed by the ancient Hebrews for imparting moral instruction: "Thus says the Lord: Behold, I set before you the way of life and the way of death." (Jeremiah 21:8). Use of the same device extends well down into the Christian era, examples being found in Rabbinic literature (*Pirge Aboth* 2:1) and in the New Testament (Matthew 7:13-14; II Peter 2:15). Indeed, when the Christian Church was still a sect within Judaism, it was natural enough for it to be known as "The Way" (Acts 9:2, for example). Thus, the form itself of the *Didache* 1:1-6:2 is an index of its *Jewish*-Christian character. It is not completely fanciful to compare it with the Rabbinic tractate *Pirge Aboth* (*Sayings of the Fathers*), with the understanding that in the *Didache* one hears the voice not of many rabbis, but of only one: Jesus.

The author's method is, in part, to give two or three maxims, then to explicate these basic statements in specific exhortations. Love for God and neighbor, and the "golden rule" (in its negative form) mean in practical terms to pray for our enemies, to turn the other cheek, and to give to everyone who begs. It is important to see that the author works out his explication by quotations from Jesus' words in most instances, but without clear reference to the highly eschatological note which permeated Jesus' teaching. Thus the injunction, "If someone deprives you of your property, do not ask for it back . . . ," is followed by the practical comment: "You could not get it back anyway!" And the exhortation to make donations is qualified in a practical way by a saying of unknown origin: "Let your donation sweat in your hands until you know to whom to give it." Thus the author of "The Two Ways" has assembled words of moral exhortation from various sources—chiefly Jesus' sayings, but also Old Testament verses and even unknown sayings which are merely practical and may have been in general use. He obviously believes that these exhortations convey the true meaning inherent in the basic maxims of the Way of Life; they are also eminently practical suggestions.

The Way of Death is explicated in a similar manner, though in much shorter compass. Persons who follow this way are guilty of all kinds of immorality, they hate truth, they "have no pity for the poor, . . . and are thoroughly wicked." The author of the *Didache* shares with the unknown author of "The Two Ways" a keen interest in *practical* instruction. For he summarizes this first part of his writing with the eminently sensible statement: "If you can bear the Lord's full yoke, you will be perfect. But if you cannot, then do what you can."

In the second part of the *Didache* the reader is provided with advice about food, baptism, prayer, the Eucharist, the Apostles and prophets, the Lord's Day, the election of bishops and deacons, and true eschatology.

Baptism is to be preceded by the moral instruction contained in "The Two Ways." The candidate is to be baptized in running water, if such is available. If not, other arrangements may be made, including affusion.

The Christian is to pray the Lord's Prayer (the text given by the Didachist is similar to that of Matthew 6:9-13) three times each day.

In his directions for celebrating the Eucharist, the author allows the cup to precede the loaf. The Eucharistic prayers which he gives for recitation bear marks of an early age and may have originated in Judea. The one for the cup reads: "We thank you, our Father, for the holy vine of David, your child, which you have revealed through Jesus, your child. To you be glory forever." According to the author, the Eucharist is to be celebrated as a real supper.

Perhaps most interesting are the regulations pertaining to prophets. We know from the New Testament not only that there were prophets in the early Church, but also that they were known by the title "prophet" (I Corinthians 12:28). From what we find about prophets in the *Didache*, we may conclude that this itinerant office continued into the second century and that it soon became necessary to distinguish genuine from false prophets: "If he stays three days, he is a false prophet." "If he asks for money, he is a false prophet." ". . . not everybody making ecstatic utterances is a prophet, but only if he behaves like the Lord." ". . . if someone says in the Spirit, 'Give me money,' or something else, you must not heed him."

True prophets are, however, greatly

to be venerated, "for they are your high priests." Whereas others are to follow the set prayers in celebrating the Eucharist, "in the case of prophets, . . . you should let them give thanks in their own way." Genuine prophets and teachers have a right to be supported by the church members. They are to receive the members' first fruits. (This reflects a rural setting).

The ministry of bishops and deacons "is identical with that of the prophets and teachers." This affirmation points toward a period when the monarchical episcopate had not yet been established. Indeed, the author must adjure his readers to value bishop and deacon as highly as prophet and teacher.

The final chapter presents the Didachist's summation of eschatological teaching. New Testament quotations are again employed. "Be ready, for you do not know the hour when our Lord is coming." Thus the primitive Christian belief in the coming of the Lord is still alive, yet it is necessary for the faithful to persevere in the remaining time. At the end, "The Lord will come, and all his saints with him. Then the world will see the Lord coming on the clouds of the sky."

Thus, the *Didache* is an invaluable source for our understanding of Christian ethics and Church order in the late first and early second centuries. A modified kind of Jewish-Christian ethics evidently sufficed for the Didachist's church and others. It is true that in his final chapter the Didachist penned an eloquent plea for the maintenance of the Christian eschatological hope, but he did not feel compelled to relate that hope to the ethical teaching of the two ways which he propounded in the first six chapters. With regard to Church order, the *Didache* shows that it had become necessary formally to regulate celebration of the sacraments and to lay down definite rules governing the authority of Church officials.

ADDRESS OF TATIAN TO THE GREEKS

Author: Tatian (c.110-c.172)
Type of work: Christian apologetics
First transcribed: Second century

PRINCIPAL IDEAS ADVANCED

The wisdom of Christianity is the true philosophy in comparison with which the philosophy of the Greeks is mere idle quibbling, a collection of conflicting human opinions which lack both credibility and profoundity.

The pride of the Greeks in their inherent superiority is unfounded, for by wisdom they know not God, and they have given themselves to the worship of their own conceit; thus, they shall suffer for their ignorance when the Judge of all mankind holds them accountable for their wickedness.

Tatian belongs to the Christian apologists of the second century, although toward the end of his life he apparently accepted the Gnostic heresy and advocated the practice of extreme asceticism. Little of his life is known other than that he was an Assyrian who embraced Christianity in Rome, where he was instructed by Justin Martyr (c.100-c.165). In addition to his attack on the enormities of paganism, in his *Address to the Greeks,* Tatian is credited with an early *Harmony of the Four Gospels,* a very valuable testimony to the early recognition of the Gospels by the primitive churches.

The *Address to the Greeks* is Tatian's only extant work. It is a biting attack on the Greek claim to superiority, as well as a persuasive argument to show that the Gospel of Christ is the highest wisdom.

The Greeks, writes Tatian, are vainly proud in their superior attitude toward barbarians, when in fact they owe their own institutions to foreign invention. For astronomy, they are indebted to the Babylonians; for alphabetic writings, to the Phoenicians; for the writing of history, to the Egyptians. Furthermore, the Greek pursuit of philosophy has produced nothing noble; the Greeks gather in rather solemn assemblies of dogmatic philosophers, each of whom gives vent to the crude fancies of the moment. The Greeks hate the opinion of others, and they vie for fame, wise in their own conceited arrogance.

The Christian, on the other hand, obeys the ruler in civil matters; he honors his fellow men, but he fears only God, and he will obey no man who orders him to deny the living God. The Christian will never adore what God has made; he will never worship the sun or moon, nor speak of the stones as gods. God alone is to be worshiped, and He is a spirit, not pervading matter, but the maker of the forms that are in matter.

God, says Tatian, is the invisible creator of sensible and invisible things. God in the beginning was the necessary ground of all being; no creature was then in existence. The Logos came forth from Him as the first-begotten work of the Father, and the Logos then begat our world, after first creating matter, which, unlike God, had a beginning and was brought into existence by the framer of all things.

After the consummation of all things, there will be a resurrection of bodies, but not because of a cyclical return, as the Stoics affirm. The periods of mortal existence will be completed once for all, and judgment will be passed upon man by the creator God. The Christian is not troubled by the ridicule of the Greeks, for the Christian believes that after death he will live again. Although his body may be destroyed, he will be restored by the Sovereign God.

The heavenly Logos has made man an image of immortality; thus, since incorruption is with God, man too shares in the principle of immortality, with the freedom of choice to do good or evil. Man is not determined by fate, but is responsible for his deeds. Man is superior to fate, and he is free from the need to obey arbitrary deities or wandering demons.

To believe in the Greek deities is absurd, Tatian insists. Who can wisely believe in a God who becomes a tree, a dragon, a swan, or an eagle? Who can reverence gods who eagerly await presents, and who become angry when they do not receive any?

Man was not created to die, but he destroys himself by the wrong exercise of his freedom and thus he becomes the slave of sin. In itself the soul is mortal, but it is possible for it not to die. When the soul does not know the truth, it is dissolved with the body for a time, but it is to be resurrected with the body at the end of the world, and the soul will then receive punishment. If, however, the soul has acquired knowledge of God, it dies not, although it is dissolved for a time. When it enters into a union with the divine spirit, the soul ascends to heavenly regions. The Spirit of God abides with those who live justly, but not with those who follow demons and false appearances.

Man is not merely a rational animal; only croaking philosophers could believe such an absurdity. Man is made in the image and likeness of God. The human soul consists of many parts; it manifests itself through the body, and it never appears by itself without the body. Man ought to seek what he once had: unity of the soul with the Holy Spirit. By repentance and faith man has conquered death, and the Spirit of God dwells within him.

According to Tatian, the demons are inspired with frenzy against men and they pervert the minds of men so that men are unable to ascend the path to Heaven. Demons turn men from the pious acknowledgment of God, and the demons make use of the productions of nature for evil purposes; they deceive instead of heal. At the bottom of demon worship, Tatian insists, lies human depravity.

The world was excellently constructed, Tatian claims, but men have corrupted their world. Men should remember that death is not to be feared and that if anyone is healed of an illness, God alone is to be credited with the cure. Everything that hinders man in his attainment to perfection is to be put aside.

When the Christian announces that God was born in the form of a man, the Christian utters no myth. The Incarnation is in no way comparable to the mythical tales in which Athene assumes the form of Deiphobus in order to please Hector; nor is the Christian belief like those Greek stories in which a goddess becomes an old woman.

The philosophy of the Christians, says Tatian, is older than that of the Greeks. The Egyptians themselves bear witness to the claim that the Jews left Egypt under the leadership of Moses, who is more ancient than the heroes of Greece. Many of the philosophers altered what they learned from Moses, and whatever they could not understand they misrepresented as if it were a fable.

The Christian is interested solely in the truth, not in vain glory; nor does the Christian allow a variety of conflicting beliefs. Popularity and temporal fame, together with everything that rests upon human opinion, are renounced by the Christian. The Christian's sole interest is in obeying the commands of God and following the law of the Father of immortality, for what comes from God surpasses all earthly gifts. The Christian philosophy is not the possession of a few idle rich; it is taught to the poor without fee. Anyone can hear, the old and the young, male and female. Those who laugh at Christians now will weep hereafter, writes Tatian.

Those who would learn the Christian philosophy are readily admitted for instruction, no matter what their appearance or previous faith. All are invited to inspect the sober character of Christian institutions, and to discover the Christian freedom from all forms of lewdness and impropriety.

Tatian concludes his fervent apology by insisting that the Christian knows who God is, and he lives the life that is according to God, always prepared to submit his doctrines to examination, never fearful that they shall be found wanting in wisdom, but ever certain that his philosophy is the wisdom of God and the power of salvation.

THE APOLOGY OF ATHENAGORAS

Author: Athenagoras (fl. second century)
Type of work: Christian apologetics
First transcribed: c.177

PRINCIPAL IDEAS ADVANCED

Christians are not atheists because, although they do not worship gods, they worship the God who created the world.

While pagan thinkers have sometimes come by means of reason to believe in God, Christians have this faith through prophecy.

Christians regard God as Father, Son, and Holy Spirit; God is therefore powerful in unity and rich in diversity.

The world was created good, and the evil that is in it is due to the defection of some of the ministering spirits whom God placed in control over it.

Christians, far from being guilty of the immoral practices charged against them, obey higher ethical principles than do the pagans.

Athenagoras's *Presbeia peri Christianōn,* sometimes referred to by its Latin title, *Legatio pro Christianis,* is commonly known in English by the name *Apology,* in spite of the fact that this term does not appear in the Greek title. It is also known as the *Embassy for Christians,* and as *A Supplication for Christians.* But by whatever name, the work belongs to the same general class as the celebrated apologies of Justin Martyr (c.100-c.165) and Tertullian (c.160-c.220). Addressed to emperor Marcus Aurelius and his son Commodus, the *Apology* is a defense of Christians against the familiar charges of atheism, cannibalism, and incest.

In reply to the charge that Christians are atheists, Athenagoras explains that Christians do not worship gods of wood and stone, because they believe that God is entirely separate from matter, being "unbegotten and invisible, beheld only by mind and thought." Christians also believe that there is but one God, the maker of all things. But they ought not to be charged with atheism for this, because many of the poets and philosophers also believed in one god, and yet they were not atheists.

Athenagoras says that pagan thinkers came to believe by guesswork in one God, for they were inspired to seek the truth by the divine breath that is present in all men. The Christian belief has a surer foundation, resting on teachings of the prophets, who spoke not by their own understanding, but as God moved their lips. Athenagoras supposes that his readers will agree that it is entirely reasonable to put one's faith in prophecy. Nevertheless, he produces a logical demonstration designed to prove that there can be only one God if God is understood to be the maker and ruler of the universe.

In the course of his explanation Athenagoras gives one of the most complete accounts of the Christian doctrine of God to come down to us from these early times. Christians, he says, "hold God to be one, unbegotten, eternal, invisible, suffering nothing, comprehended by none, circumscribed by none, apprehended by mind and reasoning alone, girt about by light and beauty and spirit and power indescribable, creator of all things by His Word, their embellisher and master." He explains that, while Christians say that God has a Son, their teaching is not to be confused with that of pagan myth. Every notion that the Son had a beginning must be put away, for God is "eternal mind," and the Son of God is "the Word of the Father in thought and power." Father and Son are one God, he says, "the Son being in the Father and the Father in the Son by the wonderful union of the Spirit." He describes the Holy Spirit as "an outflow from God, flowing out and returning like a ray of the sun." Is it not astonishing, he asks, to hear Christians called atheists "who call God Father and Son and Holy Spirit, proclaiming their power in unity and in rank their diversity?"

Athenagoras argues that "goodness" is included in the nature of God, and he suggests that the material world, which owes its being to Him, is naturally good also. But he maintains that when God created the world, He also created "a multitude of angels and ministers" whom He set in charge of his handiwork. Angels are pure spirits, endowed with free choice, he argues; and while some angels were faithful to the task appointed to them, others became "heedless and wicked." The latter, says Athenagoras, are responsible for the irrational elements in the world. Furthermore, these evil spirits enslave the minds of men, who worship them under "the fancies of idol-madness."

As to the second and third charges, that Christians devour the flesh of children and engage in illicit unions, Athenagoras says that Christians do not consider themselves besmirched by the unproven calumnies which their enemies circulate. He points to "some kind of divine law and sequence," which seems to determine evil men to fight against the good, and he cites the persecution of Pythagoras, Heraclitus, Democritus, and Socrates. He expresses his conviction that the philosophical persons to whom his *Apology* is addressed will realize that because Christians desire above all things to live blamelessly in the sight of God, they will not fall short when measured by human laws. However, Athenagoras answers the charges against the Christians, and in doing so he preserves to posterity a clear account of Christian ethics in his day. Furthermore, his work provides a thoughtful consideration of the problem of evil.

Sexual morality among second century Christians was governed by the principle that even a lustful thought is evil. Recognizing that the "kiss of salutation" might be abused, the law of the Church warned specifically against "a second kiss for the motive of pleasure," since "if any one of us was even in the least stirred to passion in thought thereby, God would set him outside eternal life." Athenagoras points out that among the Christians virginity was recommended in both sexes, married persons indulged their passions only for the purpose of begetting children, and second marriages were forbidden.

A similar principle governed the Christian attitude toward taking human life. Christians, writes Athenagoras, will not even attend gladiatorial spectacles because they consider it "nigh unto murder itself" even to look at these shows. They do not even defend themselves when others strike them or plunder their goods. As for murdering children, they do not countenance the practice of exposing infants, and they consider abortion to be murder.

Athenagoras explains the Christians' adherence to this severe moral code on the grounds of their conviction that man is a spiritual being who must appear before God in judgment for the deeds done in the body. Christians do not consider it a great calamity when they suffer malice in this world, because they are assured that the divine Judge will repay them more than they have lost "in the shape of a gentle, humane, and equitable way of life on the other side." "We shall then abide with God as heavenly spirits," he says, "not as fleshly creatures, even if we have

bodies, and by His aid shall be changeless and free from suffering in our souls."

The Christian belief in the resurrection of the body, mentioned briefly in the *Apology,* is the subject of a further discourse by Athenagoras, called *The Resurrection of the Dead.* For apologetic purposes, at least, Athenagoras did not find it necessary to appeal to the Resurrection of Christ as evidence for the Christian belief, but he based the belief upon God's purpose in creating man, His justice, and man's composite nature. In contrast to the dualistic tendency of the Greek mystery religions, the Christian religion, Athenagoras insists, contends that man was created "neither for the soul by itself nor for the body in isolation," but to achieve "one harmony and concord of the whole living being." Thus, if man is to endure beyond the grave in his integrity, the body must be resurrected and reunited with the soul. Athenagoras proves that man was made to live eternally, from the fact that man, of all God's creatures, has been endowed with rational judgment for the contemplation of eternal truth. Here, indeed, Athenagoras is more in agreement with Greek modes of thought. "One would not be far wrong," he writes, "in describing the end of a life of understanding and reasoning judgment as a perpetual and inseparable companionship with those realities for which the natural reason is principally and primarily adapted, in the unceasing and exultant contemplation of our Benefactor, and of all that He has decreed."

Almost nothing is known of Athenagoras personally. One source says that he was born in Athens; another, that he was the first head of the catechetical school in Alexandria, and that he had Clement of Alexandria (c.150-c.215) as one of his students. Scholars disagree as to the value of these notices. It is abundantly clear from his writings themselves that Athenagoras was well-schooled in Greek literature and philosophy, and disciplined in the art of dialectic. In the *Apology* he does not content himself with stating the Christian position, but he carries the argument onto pagan ground and shows the absurdity and immorality of those religious practices which Christians were censured for omitting. Athenagoras's repudiation of Greek polytheism does not, however, diminish his appreciation for Greek poetry and philosophy.

One is tempted to say that Athenagoras is more Greek than Christian, because there is no mention in either of his surviving works of such central Christian teachings as the Incarnation and the sacrificial death of Christ, and of man's sin and his need for redemption. It would be a mistake, however, to minimize the Christian content of his work. Some parts of the Christian teaching were more pertinent than other parts to the accusations against which the Christians had to defend themselves, and, at the same time, some Christian ideas were more intelligible than others to the Hellenistic mind. In the interests of his apologetic, Athenagoras advanced only the relevant parts of the Christian faith, and he kept back such ideas as might complicate his task of defending Christianity. "These thoughts," he writes, addressing Marcus Aurelius, "are but a few out of many, and trivial rather than lofty, but we do not wish to trouble you with more. Those who taste honey and whey can tell if the whole be good by tasting even a small portion."

THEOPHILUS TO AUTOLYCUS

Author: Theophilus of Antioch (d. 181 or 188)
Type of work: Apologetics
First transcribed: Latter half of second century

PRINCIPAL IDEAS ADVANCED

The inspired Scriptures provide mankind with the true account of the nature of God, the origin of the world, and mankind, for they have been given by the Holy Spirit of God, and are sufficient to persuade the intelligent pagan that his own gods are but absurd fantasies.

The highest wisdom is not to be found in the follies of the poets and the speculations of the philosophers but in the truth of God possessed by Christians.

Theophilus of Antioch was a second century apologist, a kindred spirit to Justin and Irenaeus, and the successor of Ignatius as bishop of Antioch, a position he occupied from 168 until his death in 181 or in 188. Theophilus was one of the first commentators on the Gospels, if not the first; he was probably the first Christian historian of the Old Testament, and was the founder of the science of Biblical chronology. Little is known of his personal history. From his writings it is apparent that he was born a pagan and was converted by studying the Scriptures.

The three books now entitled *Theophilus to Autolycus* are the only remaining works of Theophilus. They are characterized by a gentleness and a contempt for paganism and cover the same material treated by Justin Martyr and the other early apologists. Their purpose is to convince Autolycus, an intelligent pagan who scorned Christianity, that the Scriptures are superior in every way to pagan philosophy and poetry and ought therefore to be accepted and believed.

Theophilus does not consider it a reproach to be called a Christian, for a Christian is a lover of truth who would be serviceable to the true God, not to idols, which are the works of human hands, and which neither see nor hear.

The true God can be seen by the eyes of the soul and the ears of the heart, after first casting away all manner of sin and evil deeds. God's appearance is indescribable and ineffable; it cannot be seen by the eye of flesh, for His glory is incomprehensible, His power incomparable, and His goodness inimitable. For the true God is without beginning, unchangeable in nature, the ruler and creator of the universe; He is known by His works and can be beheld through them. From observing a ship sailing into a harbor, we infer that a pilot is steering it; likewise, we can perceive that God is the pilot, the governor of the universe. When the mortal is put off, and incorruption, immor-

tality, put on, God will then be seen in all His glory.

Faith in God is necessary, Theophilus writes, if eternal happiness is to be obtained. After the resurrection it will be too late to repent. In all matters faith is the leading principle. The farmer must trust the earth; the traveler, the pilot of his ship; the patient, the physician. It is not difficult to believe that the God who has once brought mankind into existence will again bring man back from the dead.

God has exhibited much evidence that enables man to believe in the resurrection. Analogies can be found in the dying of the seasons, in planting and harvesting, in the cycles of the moon, and in recovery from sickness.

The Scriptures are able to produce trust in their own veracity, for they contain accounts written by holy Prophets who by the Spirit of God foretold events that were to happen before they occurred, predictions that have been and continue to be fulfilled. Those that put their trust in the truth of God will receive everlasting life, peace, joy, rest, good things in abundance, and such happiness as neither eye hath seen, nor ear heard. For unbelievers and despisers, who are obedient to unrighteousness rather than truth, there is in store wrath, anger, anguish, tribulation, and everlasting fire.

Deities of the pagans, such as Saturn, Jupiter, Bacchus, and Venus, are simply representations of human sinners. Their deeds of incest, adultery, lust, drunkenness, and wanton revelry are unworthy of imitation and lead to the absurdity of idolatry.

The pagan practice of worshiping the king is also foolishness, for the king is not a god. The Christian is, however, a loyal citizen who honors his king, not by worshiping him but by praying for him, by giving him the honor that is his due. The king is subservient to the true and living God, and is a man appointed by God, not to be worshiped but to rule justly. To honor and to obey a just king, to pray for him, and to be subject to him is to do the will of God, who has established the governments of the earth.

It is the height of folly and absurdity to worship men as gods, and to worship statuaries and carvings, which when made are of no value, but which on being purchased become objects of worship. When one reads of the birth of the gods, they are reminded of men, and only afterwards of gods. It is certainly strange that the gods who once lived on Mount Olympus can no longer be found anywhere now that the mountain lies deserted.

The philosophers and poets of the pagans are in disagreement with themselves, Theophilus writes. The Epicureans deny the existence of God, and hold that the world is uncreated and nature is eternal, while still others regard matter as being coeval with God, who formed the world out of the material at hand as an artist plies his craft. Others describe the origin of the world and the gods in speculative terms.

The truth is to be found in the writings of the Prophets, men of God, who were moved by the spirit of God and hence were God-taught; since they were made wise by God Himself, whatever they wrote is the wisdom of God. With one accord the Prophets teach that all things were made by the Word of God out of nothing, for nothing was coeval with God. The world was created that man might dwell therein in obedience to God's commandments.

Instead of living happily in paradise, man yielded to temptation by freely disobeying his creator, thereby incurring God's wrath and curse, which can be removed solely by a new obedience to the will and commandments of God.

Secular history gives no account of the matters disclosed in the Scriptures because the poets and historians were born much later and did not possess the Spirit of God. They had no means of knowing the truth, which is possessed by Christians alone, not because the Christians are of any inherent virtue, but because they have been taught by the Holy Spirit, who spoke through holy men of old.

The Christian learns from God Himself that all things are arranged by His providence, that He is a holy lawgiver who would have each man act righteously and be pious, refraining from all wickedness and uncleanliness, doing good to every man, and loving all, even his enemies.

The Christians are innocent of the many false charges brought against them, insists Theophilus. They lead a quiet and peaceful life, submissive to the powers that be in secular matters, rendering honor to whom honor is due. It is unthinkable that they should eat human flesh; they are forbidden even to be spectators at gladiatorial spectacles. It is inconceivable that they participate in sexual orgies, "for with them temperance dwells, self restraint is practiced, monogamy is observed, chastity is guarded, iniquity exterminated, sin extirpated, righteousness exercised, law administered, worship performed, God acknowledged: truth governs, grace guards, peace screens them; the holy word guides, wisdom teaches, life directs, God reigns."

Theophilus concludes by writing

that reason and wisdom demand that Christians who are zealous in the pursuit of truth and who practice a holy life should not be subjected to savage tortures and persecutions by those who in their folly have themselves lost the wisdom of God and have failed to find the truth.

AGAINST HERESIES

Author: Saint Irenaeus (c.130-c.200)
Type of work: Systematic theology
First transcribed: c.182-188

PRINCIPAL IDEAS ADVANCED

The teachings of the Gnostic heretics are refuted by reason, by the Scriptures, and by the teaching of the Church.

God created the world out of nothing, by His Word and Spirit, and made man a free agent.

When, by disobeying his Maker, man lost the gift of divine fellowship, the Son of God became man in order to restore that which was lost.

Men become partakers of immortality through Christ's gift of the Holy Spirit; and, in the last day, their bodies shall be raised up to participate, with nature itself, in incorruptible glory.

Irenaeus's most important work, commonly known by the short title, *Against Heresies,* was called by its author *The Detection and Overthrow of False Gnosis.* Polemic rather than didactic in its design, the work first gives a detailed exposition of the various Gnostic systems, then patiently marshals logic, the Scriptures, and Church doctrine in an assault against particular Gnostic claims. *Against Heresies* is an indispensable historical source for the student of Gnosticism, but to most readers Irenaeus's book is chiefly interesting for its mature and competent statement of Christian doctrine.

That Irenaeus develops his positive theology in opposition to the rival teachings of the Gnostics instead of treating it topically is no great disadvantage. Irenaeus was in possession of a fully articulated system of doctrine; and the reader has no trouble in recovering his doctrines of the Godhead, Creation, Man, the Incarnation, Salvation, and Last Things. In fact, because Irenaeus's theology is confessional rather than speculative, its worth is more apparent in a controversial setting than it would be if stated in a more schematic form.

As the term "Gnostic" indicates, the early heretical groups were chiefly distinguished by their claims to be possessors of superior knowledge. They maintained that in the nature of things there are three kinds of men: carnal men, animal or psychic men, and spiritual men. The Gnostics, of course, claimed to be of the spiritual variety, and they boasted that they had a special knowledge which had been handed down orally from Christ by those who were able to receive it. The public teaching of Christ, together with His death and resurrection, was, they said, for the benefit of animal men, who, lacking the element of spirit, must always be subject to authority. The Gnostics denied that Christ was truly man; the divine Christ, they said, merely simulated manhood in order to lead men godward. The Gnostics used Scripture when it suited their purposes, but their doctrines were mostly fanciful constructions modeled on Greek theogonic myths. They had elaborate explanations concerning the emanation from an unnamable primal Being of a celestial hierarchy consisting of Aeons, Principalities, and Powers; and they traced the origin of the physical world to an indiscretion on the part of one of the Aeons, by the name of Sophia. The whole scheme of redemption was, in their view, an attempt to compensate for this indiscretion, and, by saving a spiritual heritage out of the world, make it possible for Sophia to achieve reunion with the Highest.

In *Against Heresies,* Irenaeus employs three kinds of arguments to overthrow the Gnostic teachings. First, he appeals to reason, and to the *consensus gentium.* A simple exercise in dialectic enables him to show that if there is any reason to believe that there must be a Being above the highest Aeon, the same reason requires us to believe in a still higher Being, and so on *ad infinitum.* The plain fact is, says Irenaeus, all nations of the world, whether by tradition handed down from their first progenitors, or by reasoning from the evidences in nature, are con-

vinced that there is one God, and that He is the Creator of the world.

But Irenaeus rests his arguments mostly on the teachings of Scripture, devoting the greater part of his work to exposition of the key passages from the Old Testament, the Gospels, and the Epistles. In opposition to the arbitrary use which the Gnostics made of the Bible, he laid down the principle that each passage must be interpreted in harmony with all the remainder of Scripture, and he urged at the same time that men bring a "sound mind" to the study of these writings, and that they interpret the obscure parts in the light of those which are clear and unambiguous, rather than follow the contrary practice.

In the third place, Irenaeus put great store by the authority of the Church as the interpreter of Scripture and as the depository of the teachings of Christ. As offering a contrast to the endless diversity that was to be found among the Gnostic doctrines, Irenaeus could point to the uniform confession of the Church. He refutes the Gnostics' claim to possess a secret oral tradition by pointing out that the bishops of the Church in every city are direct successors of the Apostles. He cites his own case as an example: in his youth, he had been a hearer of Polycarp (c.69-c.155), Bishop of Smyrna, who in turn had been taught by the Apostle John and by other of the Lord's disciples. Irenaeus further argues, against those Gnostics who were disposed to pick and choose among the Scriptures, that all the four Gospels were of Apostolic origin; and he reasons that Paul could not have delivered a separate gospel, as some of them claimed, otherwise Luke, who traveled with him, would have dropped some hints of it in The Acts of the Apostles.

It is evident, says Irenaeus, that the Gnostics are late-comers, by comparison with the Church's bishops, and that they can only be understood as deviating from the right way. What that "right way" is, the confession of the Church makes clear. Irenaeus cites, on several occasions, a confessional formulary which, he says, was used by churches in all parts of the world. Obviously, it is an early form of what we know as the Apostles' Creed. "The path," he says, "of those belonging to the Church circumscribes the whole world, as possessing the sure tradition from the apostles, and gives unto us to see that the faith of all is one and the same, since all receive one and the same God the Father, and believe in the same dispensation regarding the incarnation of the Son of God, and are cognizant of the same gift of the Spirit, and are conversant with the same commandments, and preserve the same form of ecclesiastical constitution, and expect the same advent of the Lord, and await the same salvation of the complete man, that is, of the soul and body."

Drawing upon Scriptures for proof, Irenaeus seeks to show that there is but one God, the Father of all, and that, far from there being an interminable succession of divine personages emanating from the One, there was with God before the creation of the world only "the Word and Wisdom, the Son and the Spirit." It is characteristic of Irenaeus not to enter upon any investigation of the internal relations of these three, nor to inquire what was happening before God created the world. God, he says, has revealed to us all that is profitable for us to know;

notably, that He had need of nothing outside of Himself when He brought the world into existence, but that He devised it in his own Mind and created it by his own Power. "For God did not stand in need of these [intervening Aeons], in order to the accomplishing of what He had Himself determined with Himself beforehand should be done, as if He did not possess His own hands. For with him were always present the Word and Wisdom, the Son and the Spirit, by whom, and in whom, freely and spontaneously, He made all things."

In discussing the creation of man, Irenaeus recounts that God the Father consulted with the Son and with the Spirit, saying, "Let us make man in our image and in our likeness." In opposition to the Gnostic contention that some men are naturally carnal, some animal, and some spiritual, Irenaeus maintains that the essential characteristic of all men is that, being made in God's image, they are free to determine what they will make of themselves. Irenaeus introduces the distinction between "image" and "likeness," which has become official Roman doctrine. God's image, according to this view, is the free and rational constitution which is inalienable from man; God's likeness is the gift of incorruptibility which man lost as a result of disobedience.

Irenaeus holds that the plan for man's salvation is clearly taught both in the Old and the New Testament. In discussing the question why man was not made perfect and thereby prevented from falling into sin, he cites, by way of illustration, the story of Jonah. Just as Jonah learned through trial the justice and the goodness of God, so man, having been permitted to follow his own devices to the brink of destruction, is taught by his undeserved deliverance to love God with all his heart and to seek his good in God alone.

Man fell into sin by following Satan. In this way, he lost his "likeness" to God and became liable to judgment. But, says Irenaeus, God sent His Son into the world in order that those who follow Him may recover their lost inheritance and be reunited with God in their resurrected bodies. Irenaeus is careful to oppose the Gnostic view that Christ did not become truly man. While holding firmly to the teaching that Christ is "truly God," present everywhere in His creation, Irenaeus insists that He was "united to and mingled with His own creation, . . . and thus took up man into Himself, the invisible becoming visible, the incomprehensible being made comprehensible, the impassible becoming capable of suffering, and the Word being made man, thus summing up all things in Himself."

Irenaeus accepts the teaching of Scripture and of the Church that Christ was born of a virgin, that He suffered, rose from the dead, and ascended bodily to Heaven. A characteristic feature of his theology is the doctrine that Christ, as the new Adam, "sums up" or "recapitulates" in Himself all that man is and can become. By his victory over temptation, Christ accomplishes the obedience which Adam failed to perform; by His suffering and death, He redeems those who have been led into captivity by Satan; by the gift of His Spirit, He restores to men their likeness to God.

Irenaeus stresses the continuity between the Old and the New Covenants, insisting that believers under the former are just as much members of Christ's body, the Church, as those under the latter. He further teaches that Christ did not repudiate the Ten Commandments, which, he says, merely reaffirm those natural precepts which God, from the first, implanted in mankind. In opposition to Gnostic antinomianism, he maintains that no one can be saved who does not obey the commandments.

Those who accept salvation in Christ, says Irenaeus, all become spiritual men; but they are such not by nature but by Christ's gift of the Spirit to them. By the Spirit dwelling in them, believers are joined to Christ and to each other in the Church. The Spirit also makes them partakers of eternal life, by restoring the bond between man and God which our first parents lost by their disobedience. While emphasizing man's spiritual inheritance, however, Irenaeus is careful not to lose sight of man's physical constitution. The mystery by which bread and wine are, by the Word of God, made the body and blood of Christ is, he says, a pledge that our bodies, nourished by Christ, shall, by God's Word, rise at the appointed time, and receive the gift of immortality. Nor, according to Irenaeus, shall man be alone in his glorification. A diligent student of Daniel and the Apocalypse, Irenaeus argues that, after the overthrow of Antichrist, the earth itself shall be renewed in the likeness of paradise, and believers of all generations shall be raised up, to live forever with Christ. Irenaeus is no universalist. Christ's coming, which will be for the resurrection of believers, also will be for the damnation of those who have not agreed to follow Him. For, says Irenaeus, God has given men free choice in these matters; and knowing that some will despise his dispensation, God has prepared a place for them, although, as far as Irenaeus cares to indicate, their punishment is simply the loss of those goods from which they have voluntarily excluded themselves.

With Irenaeus, Western Christendom found its characteristic theological stance. Distrustful of speculation, he purchased certitude by limiting the scope of man's investigation into divine things. He did not repudiate reason, maintaining that God's plan for man's salvation is completely rational. He insisted, however, that love, rather than knowledge, is necessary to lead men's souls to their perfection. It was, in his view, no little thing that Gnosticism had no martyrs, whereas the Church numbered its martyrs by thousands.

THE APOLOGY OF TERTULLIAN

Author: Tertullian (Quintus Septimius Florens Tertullianus) (c.160-c.220)
Type of work: Apologetics
First transcribed: c.197

PRINCIPAL IDEAS ADVANCED

Roman justice is outraged when Christians are persecuted; if Christians are enemies of the state, it is wrong to encourage them to deny their affiliation; if there is some doubt whether they are enemies of the state, their alleged crimes should be inquired into.

The charge that Christians deny the Roman gods is true; but Romans ought to refute the denial rather than persecute those who make it.

The charges that Christian worship is immoral and that the Christians are disloyal citizens is false; Christians are the best supporters of imperial government, but they are enemies of pagan civilization.

Born in North Africa, the son of a Roman centurion, Tertullian was educated at Rome in rhetoric and philosophy, and he probably practiced law there. After being converted to Christianity in 195 or 196, he was ordained a presbyter, and he served the Church in Carthage. He is considered the father of Latin Christianity, not merely because he is the first theologian to employ the Latin tongue, but also because of his influence on Cyprian, Augustine, and Jerome. The *Apology* is the best known of his numerous writings because it gives the most comprehensive statement of the Christian position, and because it is free from certain extravagances found in his other writings; the work reflects both Tertullian's mastery of his subject and his legal competence.

The *Apology* was written against the background of the imperial persecution of the Church, and it was intended to instruct the Romans concerning the true nature of the Christian faith. With the logic of a trained pleader and with a minimum of passion, Tertullian criticizes imperial edicts and the manner in which they have been implemented by the courts; in effect, he pleads for freedom of religion. He mentions the famous correspondence (c.112) between Pliny the Younger (62-113) and the emperor Trajan (c.53-117), in which the latter replied that, although Christians were not to be sought out, they should be punished if any informed on them. "O miserable deliverance,—under the necessities of the case, a self-contradiction!" Tertullian cries; "It forbids them to be sought after as innocent, and it commands them to be punished as guilty." In the same connection, he points to the use made of torture. Ordinary offenders, he says, are tortured to make them confess their crimes; but Christians are tortured to make them deny their beliefs. The whole judicial procedure thus becomes a farce. Instead of pressing the inquiry, to be certain that only the guilty are punished, judges offer the defendants every opportunity to escape what the law demands—provided they recant. At the same time, the defendant is denied the securities which Roman law guarantees a common criminal; for, if a man is charged with murder or incest, the court insists on evidence that a specific crime has been committed; but if a man is charged with being a Christian, all sorts of rumors and prejudices (for example, that in the Lord's Supper a child is sacrificed and his flesh and blood eaten, and that in the Love Feast incest is committed) are assumed to be true, but never proved.

Tertullian's argument has a positive and a negative side. On the one hand, the author gives a careful, detailed exposition of the beliefs and practices of the Church of his day; on the other

hand, as a former pagan, well-placed for observing Roman society, he gives a telling exposé of the immorality and irreligion of those who put the Christians to death.

Christians are charged with not believing in the gods of the Romans. This is true, says Tertullian, but it is no scandal. There are tribes throughout the Empire which do not believe in the Roman gods, yet they have permission to practice their religion. Moreover, philosophers, such as Socrates, are held in honor, in spite of the fact that they deny the gods. In any case, when matters of this sort are in dispute, arguments ought to be heard; if their beliefs are false, they should be refuted; if simply ridiculous, they should be laughed to scorn. Nothing is accomplished by killing those who hold unconventional beliefs. As a matter of fact, Tertullian reminds his readers, it often happens that persons who scorned the Christian teaching when they were ignorant of it were converted to Christianity once they learned what it is.

According to Tertullian, Christians worship "the One God" who by His word and power has created and sustains the world. Although He is not visible, every man has some notion of Him because He is manifest both in the works of nature and in the native testimony of the soul itself. In evidence of the latter, Tertullian cites such pagan expressions as "God is great and good," "May God give!", and "I commend myself to God." But, says Tertullian, for our better knowledge of Him, God has also given us a written revelation of Himself. Tertullian stresses the antiquity of this revelation, which was given to the Hebrews. It antedates Homer, the tragic poets, and the philosophers, who, in Tertullian's opinion, probably drew upon it. Then, in the reign of Tiberius, God bestowed His grace in ampler measure, when "He appeared among us, whose coming to renovate and illuminate man's nature was pre-announced by God—I mean Christ, that Son of God." The prophecies had said that Christ would come twice, once to suffer, and once to reign. The Jews, among whom he made His appearance, did not adequately distinguish these two comings; therefore, they rejected Him, delivered Him to death, and tried to conceal the truth when He arose from the grave. Tertullian is convinced that these were matters of public knowledge. He alleges that Pilate became a Christian and reported everything to Tiberius, who actually presented the claim of Christ's divinity to the Roman senate, which, however, refused to consider the claim on the grounds that the senate must originate business of this sort.

As to the pagan divinities, Tertullian holds the view, known anciently as euhemerism, that the gods are men who, after their death, were made objects of worship. There are, then, in actuality, no gods other than God. But, according to Tertullian, there are devils, which take advantage of men's idolatrous propensities and appear to them as gods in order to enslave their souls to darkness.

Another charge which had to be met was that Christians gathered secretly for immoral and criminal purposes. Tertullian shows great patience in dealing with this report, which he regards as absurd. He points out the well-known characteristics of rumor, and shows that, if one's knowledge of religious practices is limited to paganism, it is easy for him to imagine all sorts of sordid things about the new religion, because human sacrifice and temple prostitution have played a prominent part in many ancient cults. He also notes that for the Romans of his day feasting was connected with all sorts of unbridled acts; so that when the Romans heard of a Christian "love feast," their imaginations fed upon their own excesses. Still, he maintains, it is difficult to reconstruct these orgies in the manner in which they are supposed to take place. Try to conceive of the Christians, who will not even permit the practice of abortion, plunging the knife into an infant's breast! Or, try to imagine the confusion of the banquet scene in which, after the lights have been extinguished, each one present is under obligation to commit incest. Each one would have to take careful note while the lights were on where his relations were sitting! And pity the person who has no mother or sister, because he cannot be a true follower of Christ!

The simplicity of Christian worship must be difficult for those to grasp who are accustomed to the florid festivals of Gaia or of Bacchus, writes Tertullian. The service of Christ consists in reading the Scriptures, in prayer, in exhortation and censure. Once a month, Christians gather donations for the poor and the unfortunate. They call one another "brethren," not in the hypocritical manner of those who curry favor of one another, but because of their common mother, Nature. Thus, Christians think of pagans as their brothers and sisters; but they feel special kinship toward those who have been led to the common knowledge of God. They have all things in common, says Tertullian, except their wives, which is the opposite of what is the case among their neighbors. Their modest supper, called *agape,* that is, "affection," stands in sharp contrast to the Roman feast. The measure of their eating and drinking is evidenced by the fact that after the meal, each participant is asked to sing a hymn to God, either one from Scripture or one of his own composition. As the ritual commences, so it closes, with prayer. If the noninitiate needs a model to help him imagine it, let him think of a Roman lawcourt instead of a Roman banquet.

More serious, perhaps, was the charge that Christians were disloyal to Caesar, inasmuch as they refused to offer sacrifice to him as to a god. (Here, Tertullian's argument against sacrifice becomes an attack on the ideological basis of the Roman Empire.) Tertullian insists on the distinction made in the Gospels between that which is Caesar's and that which is God's. Christians are even willing to call Caesar "lord," so long as it is understood that this is not a title of divinity. They also pray for Caesar and for the preservation of Roman rule. This they are instructed to do, as part of their duty to God, from whom rulers receive their authority. Moreover, because of the prophecy that when the Empire is overthrown the Antichrist will come, Christians have special interest in strengthening the existing order.

The same kind of reply is brought to the charge that, in causing the sacrifices to be neglected, Christians are responsible for various natural calamities. The charge had better be turned against the heathen themselves, says Tertullian, considering the hypocritical and perfunctory manner in which they perform their religious rites. If the well-being of the Empire depended on the gods, as is maintained, then the pagans should take it that disasters are a warning to themselves. But since, in reality, it depends upon the one God, whom Christians serve, such prosperity as Rome continues to enjoy must be the result of the prayers of Christians. In any case, says Tertullian, there were natural catastrophies before there were Christians.

Writing at a time when it was not even dreamed that Christianity might become the imperial religion, Tertullian saw no possibility of compromise between Christianity and secular culture. The civil disabilities imposed by the government upon Christians were, in his opinion, the manifestation of "a certain system" which is opposed to God and His truth, and he was determined to fight this injustice. The existence of organized opposition to Christianity did not surprise Tertullian or particularly disturb him; but in his apology he challenges the assumption that government must serve this pagan outlook. Tracing the mischief to the Greek and Roman practice of deifying civic values, he argues for the complete secularization of the political order, and for complete religious toleration. He insists that by paying taxes and obeying the laws, as well as by their prayers, Christians do fulfill their obligations as citizens. Tertullian can boast that no Christian is ever hailed before the court for any crime except that of bearing the name "Christian," and he maintains that because the Christians obey a higher law than Caesar's, they contribute more than any other group to the welfare and stability of the empire. There is, therefore, no political argument for requiring Christians to worship Caesar, or for persecuting them to death.

But if there is nothing in his obedience to God that prevents the Christian from fulfilling the duties of a citizen, there is much, according to Tertullian, which prevents him from making peace with the civilization which the Caesars represent. In spite of what Tertullian calls man's "naturally Christian soul," which continues to witness to the existence and perfection of the one God while he offers his sacrifice to idols, mankind has fallen under the power of demons, and it has systematically ordered its existence in enmity against God. Here Tertullian anticipates the theme of Augustine's *City of God*, even outdoing his illustrious successor in the rigor with which he sets the community of God over against the community of this world. What, he asks, has Jerusalem in common with Athens? What concord is there between the Christian and the philosopher? All the world's wisdom is folly in God's sight;

its righteousness, shame; its boasting, vanity. The Christian is falsely accused of undermining the government, but he is rightly understood to have stripped himself of all the ambition and pride of the world, and to have turned his face away from the amusements and delights in which the pagans rejoice. That is why Christians are willing, if necessary, to go to death rather than compromise.

Asked why, then, he complains because they are persecuted, Tertullian replies that the Christian attitude is that of a soldier who, without courting death, is prepared to meet it without flinching, or of the hero who endures torture without betraying his cause. If such sacrifice is glorious when endured for the cause of city or empire, how much more so when it is for the cause of God!

THE STROMATA
or
MISCELLANIES

Author: Saint Clement of Alexandria (Titus Flavius Clemens) (c.150-c.215)
Type of work: Spiritual instruction
First transcribed: c.200

PRINCIPAL IDEAS ADVANCED

Faith in the Gospel is necessary and sufficient for salvation, but knowledge is also necessary for Christian perfection; Christianity is the true Gnosticism.

The Divine Logos is the author of the Jewish Law and of Greek philosophy, both of which were given to prepare men for the teaching of Christ.

Christ is the Logos manifest in the flesh to bring men into union with God; through faith, Christ leads men to knowledge, and to the unitive love in which they find perfection.

The title *Stromata*, given by Clement to his main work, is sometimes translated "Miscellanies." Literally, it means "Carpets," and in late Hellenistic times the term was a characteristic designation for a composition which sacrifices system for wealth and variety of contents. Clement stated that his purpose in writing *The Stromata* was to preserve the doctrinal tradition which he had been privileged to hear from his teachers. There was, in Clement's opinion, something dubious about committing to writing for the many what had hitherto been communicated only orally to selected hearers. An author, because he has no control over the reading of his book, may well be casting pearls before swine. To avoid this result, Clement adopted the stratagem of hiding the spiritual seed in a vast amount of erudition, confident that such a procedure would effectively conceal the secret tradition from unworthy readers while taking away nothing of value from those who were able to receive it.

Clement had traveled widely and studied under several teachers before coming at last to one whose teaching impressed him as being truly divine. This was Pantaenus (died c.190), who was at that time head of the Christian catechetical school in Alexandria. Clement became Pantaenus's associate, and he later succeeded Pantaenus as head of the school.

In this center of Hellenistic culture, the Christian teacher was compelled to take some sort of stand with respect to pagan learning. The average Christian in Alexandria was inclined to hold that no reconciliation was possible between the Gospel and Greek philosophy. But Alexandria was also a hotbed of that synthesis of Christian teaching and Greek speculation known as Gnosticism. As between these two positions, Clement stood firmly on the side of Catholic teaching. He maintained that

faith in the teaching of the Scriptures is both necessary and sufficient for man's salvation. But, in opposition to the popular attitude, he taught that Greek philosophy has its legitimate uses, both as preparing men's minds to receive the Gospel and as edifying their minds after they have believed. Clement's own learning is impressive, prompting one modern historian to speak of him as "the pioneer of Christian scholarship," and the seven books of *The Stromata*, in addition to their importance in Christian thought, are a treasure-trove for antiquarians interested in reconstructing pagan civilization.

Clement justifies his use of pagan learning on the ground that every good thing comes from God, including craftsmanship and knowledge. The Christian has no more reason to turn away from poetry, geometry, rhetoric, and dialectic than from agriculture, or architecture, or medicine. They are all diverse expressions of the same Wisdom, which, in another context, is the object of faith. On the level of sense experience, Wisdom is called "right opinion"; on that of manual dexterity, it is called "art" (*techne*); when concerned with first causes, it is called "reason" (*noesis*); and when based on proof, it is called "knowledge" or "science" (*gnosis*). The same Wisdom, however, "when it is occupied in what pertains to piety, and receives without speculation the primal Word," is called "faith."

In Clement's opinion, there is no basis for setting knowledge in opposition to faith. Faith is a "voluntary preconception," that disposition of the mind to receive and assent to truth, without which knowledge of any sort is impossible. This is the teaching of Isaiah,

"Unless ye believe, neither will ye understand." Heraclitus was merely paraphrasing the Hebrew prophet when he wrote, "If a man hope not, he will not find that which is not hoped for, seeing it is inscrutable and inaccessible." Faith is assent and an act of the will; for, says Clement, "the intellectual powers are ministers of the will."

Clement's discussion of faith and knowledge must be considered in relation to the gnostic controversies of that day. Alexandrian Gnostics claimed that faith is for the simple, and that Christians who advance to higher stages of spirituality possess knowledge "which is as far removed from faith as the spiritual is from the animal." Clement, for his part, not only asserts that there is no knowledge which does not rest on faith; he also goes on to say that those who believe in the revelation of God through Christ are the true Gnostics. On the other hand, Clement gives small comfort to those who, having confessed their faith in the Gospel, think they can neglect their spiritual growth. Viewed in this light, faith is the foundation (spoken of by the Apostle) upon which some build with wood, hay, and stubble, while others build with gold, silver, and precious stones. Or, again, it is that milk which suffices for babies, but is not adequate food for mature men and women. As the true Gnosis, Christianity demands mental as well as moral discipline. Speaking and acting, says Clement, are rational work, and can be done well only by one who is trained in intellectual matters.

Clement accepts the widely popular Platonic and Pythagorean world-view, according to which God the Father, the Unbegotten Being, transcends the possibility of knowledge; but the Son of God, who is Wisdom, Knowledge, and Truth, manifests the Father, and is therefore the proper object for gnosis. The Son, as the author of creation, is the first principle both of action and of thought, of morals and of philosophy: "Whence also He alone is Teacher, who is the only Son of the Most High Father, the Instructor of men." Because of His love for men, the Son clothed himself with human nature in order to communicate His Wisdom to the Apostles and, through them and their successors, to all who have the will to achieve perfection. But He is also the Lord of Providence, who inspired Moses and the Prophets of Israel, and revealed the truth to those Greeks "who have philosophized accurately."

Himself a convert from paganism, Clement made the conversion of the Greeks his special concern. His earliest work, entitled *The Exhortation to the Heathen* (*ho protreptikos*), employed the art of rhetoric in the effort to persuade pagans to forsake their former religion and embrace the benefits conferred through Christ. His second work, *The Instructor* (*paedagogus*), has the practical aim of counseling converts in fundamental Christian morality. Both works were thought of as preparatory, in the sense that they were intended to bring men to the position where they could profit from the Teacher, who would "guide the soul to all requisite knowledge." Some scholars think that Clement intended to write a third book with the title, "The Teacher," forming a trilogy. Others hold that *The Stromata* fills the place indicated in this outline. What is illuminating, in either case, is Clement's underlying conception of Christianity as the authentic regimen by which the Divine Logos labors to bring men to perfection: "Eagerly desiring to perfect us by a gradation conducive to salvation, suited for efficacious discipline, a beautiful arrangement is observed by the all-benignant Word, who first exhorts, then trains, and finally teaches."

Clement insists that God's revelation to Abraham, to Moses, and to the prophets of the Old Testament was an important stage in Christ's endeavor for man's salvation. In opposition to the followers of Marcion (died about 160), who held that the Jehovah of the Jews was an inferior deity and that the Law of Moses is evil because it appeals to fear and not to love, Clement argues that insofar as fear turns men away from evil and sets them on the path of Wisdom, it is good. "Such a fear," says Clement, "leads to repentance and hope." But it is a distortion to hold that the teachings of the Old Testament are servile and degrading. On the contrary, says Clement, they are superior to the vaunted teachings of the Greeks who, Clement holds, borrowed their best sayings from the Hebrews. Moses, according to Clement, was the greatest of moralists, legislators, and philosophers; he could have received his pre-eminent wisdom only through "the first expounder of the divine commands, who unveiled the bosom of the Father, the only-begotten Son."

But just as the religion of the Old Testament was a means used by the Son of God to prepare the Jews for accepting the Gospel, so, according to Clement, philosophy was ordained to bring the Greeks to Christ. Clement is professedly an eclectic where philosophy is concerned, using the term to stand for no particular sect but for "whatever has been well said by each of those sects, which teach righteousness along with a science pervaded by piety." Hellenistic philosophy had many religious overtones, and the wisdom which it professed to love could fairly be described as "rectitude of soul and purity of life." For Clement, this was nothing else but "the knowledge of the Son of God" which the Apostles proclaimed in its fullness; and he could say to them what Paul said to the worshipers of the Unknown God, "Whom ye ignorantly worship, him declare I unto you." Clement does not admit that philosophy is itself sufficient for man's salvation but that, like the Law, it "shut up unbelief to the Advent." Those devotees of philosophy who died before Christ's coming had their chance to believe when Christ preached in Limbo, but those who live in the dispensation of the Gospel must turn from philosophy and believe the teaching of the Apostles.

Clement's teaching concerning the person and work of Christ has never entirely satisfied orthodox theologians. He makes the Logos central to his doctrine of creation and providence, as well as to his doctrine of salvation; and he seems to regard the manifestation of the Logos in the flesh as necessary for man's salvation. But his account of Christ's human nature does not agree with that which the Church has come to affirm. For example, Clement agrees that Christ partook of food, but he explains that He did so not because His body required sustenance, but in order that the disciples might not be misled into supposing that they were seeing a phantasm. Moreover, says Clement, Christ was "inaccessible to any movement of feeling—either pleasure or pain"; and, although He underwent death, yet He "suffered no harm."

Clement's teaching about the Savior is, however, quite consistent with his teaching concerning the plan of salvation. As Clement sees it, God's purpose in making the world was to bring into existence complete or perfect men. But a complete man is one whose soul is at one with God. It is by faith, and then by knowledge, that man rises to this union. Indeed, knowledge, when it is perfect, becomes love—not the love of desire, but the love of fruition and peace. In our earthly life, says Clement, it is impossible for men to get rid of certain appetites which are essential to the maintenance of the body, but these are the only desires which need to remain. For the rest, the advanced Christian, the true Gnostic, the high-souled man, is free from every passion, having "obtained the affinity to the impassible God which arises from love."

Such being the salvation which Christ came to make possible, it is scarcely to be expected that the perfect humanity of the Savior would exhibit those very weaknesses which men must overcome. The problem of saving man from sin, as Clement views it, does not consist in freeing him from the guilt of past sins but, rather, in converting, disciplining, and instructing his soul. By assuming our nature in its perfection, the Son of God brought humanity and God for the first time into effective union. By His life and teaching, Christ instructs others how to achieve this goal.

Clement concedes that the Scriptures open salvation to the many, who experience the "first saving change" when they pass from heathenism to faith, or from law to Gospel. But these are saved only in the first degree. Besides his

public teaching, Christ also taught his Apostles the gnosis which leads to perfection. This knowledge, Clement claims, "has descended by transmission to a few, having been imparted unwritten by the apostles." Great preparation and previous training are necessary to receive it. But those who can obey it achieve here and now a foretaste of eternal bliss, and, in the world to come, will take their places with the Apostles in the highest sphere. "Such an one," writes Clement, "is wholly a son, passionless, gnostic, perfect, formed by the teaching of the Lord; in order that in deed, in word, and in spirit itself, being brought close to the Lord, he may receive the mansion that is due to him who has reached manhood thus."

While holding that perfection involves turning away from the world toward God, Clement does not advocate the kind of asceticism which requires a person to mortify the flesh and to relinquish all his belongings. On the contrary, Clement says that men who have not attained to perfection are likely to be harmed by poverty and suffering, and prevented from carrying out their spiritual endeavors. He therefore enjoins his readers to make the necessary provisions for their bodies "to keep the soul free and unimpeded." In opposition to the teaching of the Marcionites and other Gnostic groups, Clement affirms the goodness of the material world. On this ground, he commends the married state. Not everyone ought to marry, he says, "but there is a time in which it is suitable, and a person for whom it is suitable, and an age up to which it is suitable." Celibacy is good, but marriage is better. It opens the way to higher attainment, providing "more varied preparatory exercise" through the temptations arising from wife and children, domestics, and possessions. Still, the aim of all Christian striving is to get rid of all desire, not simply to get the better of our passions. Thus, the family man (or woman, for Clement says that the way of perfection is open to both) achieves the Christian ideal only if he conducts the affairs of his household "without pleasure or pain" and preserves his soul "inseparable from God's love." Such a man is mild, beneficent, magnanimous. Having put to death the old man, with his passions and lusts, he holds himself above both pleasure and pain. Thus Clement writes, "If the Word, who is Judge, call; he having grown inflexible, and not indulging a whit the passions, walks unswervingly where justice advises him to go; being very well persuaded that all things are managed consummately well, and that progress to what is better goes on in the case of souls that have chosen virtue, till they come to the Good itself, to the Father's vestibule, so to speak, close to the great High Priest. Such is our Gnostic."

THE EPISTLE TO DIOGNETUS

Author: Unknown
Type of work: Christian apologetics
First transcribed: Unknown, probably second or third century

PRINCIPAL IDEAS ADVANCED

Neither the pagan religions, with their worship of idols, nor the Jewish religion, which ignores Christ, can be tolerated.

The beliefs which Christians hold must be understood if they are to be effective; Christian character at its best must be held up as an example, and the benefits which this life offers should be explained to converts.

What the soul is to the body, Christians are to the world.

Both the author and the one addressed are unknown in the *Epistle to Diognetus,* but the letter clearly stands out as one of the early classics in Christian apologetics, the art and practice of explaining Christianity and its practices to nonbelievers. Diognetus, who is addressed in the letter, is taken as one exceedingly zealous to learn the religion of the Christians, as one who has been asking clear and careful questions about them. Who is the God, he wants to know, in whom these Christians believe? How is He worshiped, and what is the love which Christians have for one another? Diognetus has obviously been impressed by the way Christians disregard the world, by the way in which they despise death, and particularly by the fact that they do not accept the Greek gods. These observed facts have made him anxious to know more about these Christians and their beliefs.

The writer, in replying to Diognetus, first asks him to clear himself of all prejudice, for undoubtedly he has heard many false reports about the Christians, their practices, and their beliefs. If he is to learn about Christianity profitably, he must become a new man; he must prepare himself to listen to a new story. Concerning the gods of the day, the writer tells him: look with your eyes; idols are made of ordinary stone and clay like any perishable vessel. These idols are dumb and blind, without souls, lacking feeling, and they can be made by men into other forms if men wish. The idols do not move, and they decay. Are these things to be called gods? How can it possibly be that because Christians cannot acknowledge such material objects as gods, they should be hated? These pagan idols need to be protected from harm themselves; they do not protect men. How can Christians be expected to pay heed to such fragile gods?

The writer, then, takes it as almost obvious that the pagan idols are not worthy of worship. The Jewish God, however, is not such a series of perishable objects. He is a mighty spirit Who protects His people. Why, then, since the Christian religion began among the Jews, are the Christians not worshipers of the Jewish God? Jews worship the one God, master of the universe. The author then refers to the Jewish law, to their food regulations and their custom of sacrifice. In brief compass the author gives the Christian argument against observance of Jewish law, describing it as encouraging silliness, fussiness, and pride. The Christian cannot accept the Jewish belief that the religious life consists in complete observance of the letter of the law, particularly since men take pride in mere obedience to law. Law is a matter of human observance, whereas the mystery of the Christian's religion cannot be learned from men.

The distinction between Christians and other men, actually, is neither in country nor language nor custom. Their teaching has not, they believe, been discovered by the intellect or by the thought of busy men. Christians are not advocates of any human doctrine. They live in Greek and barbarian cities, and they follow local customs, yet still they exhibit their wonderful and admittedly strange character as sojourners in their own fatherland. Christians share all things as citizens and yet suffer all things as strangers. Every foreign country is their fatherland, and every fatherland is nevertheless a foreign country to them. They must conform to the flesh, but their lives are not patterned after the flesh. Their time is spent on earth, but their real citizenship is in Heaven.

The irony of Christians' lives is that their Gospel directs them to love all men and yet they are persecuted by all men. Their belief teaches them that even when they are put to death they gain eternal life. Christians may be dishonored, but they are glorified in their dishonor. When a Christian does a good deed and is treated as an evil-doer, he rejoices in his ill-treatment as does a man who receives life.

Given such a reception, warred upon by Jews and persecuted by Greeks, how does the Christian look upon his role in the world? It can be stated very simply: What the soul does for the body, Christians do for the world. The soul is spread to all parts of the body; Christians are found throughout the cities of the world. The soul dwells in the body but is not of the same substance as the body; Christians are recognized in the world but their religion remains as invisible as the soul. The soul has been shut up in the body but actually sustains the body; Christians are confined in the world as in a prison but actually sustain the world.

Although this position in the world is not a pleasant one, God has appointed Christians to it and they must not decline to serve in this way. It is no earthly discovery which has been given to men. What Christians believe, in truth, is that the almighty, all-creating, and invisible God Himself has founded among men the truth from Heaven. They believe nothing less than that the holy and incomprehensible Word has been established in their hearts. No angel or intermediary has been sent to do this. The very framer and creator of the universe Himself has come to do this. He who ordered the world in the beginning and sustains it now has been sent to men to establish the religion the Christians hold. Did such a world-creator come in sovereignty and fear and terror, as one might suppose? No, what the Christians assert is that even such a mighty one as this came in gentleness and meekness. He was sent as God and yet He was sent as Man to men. He came saving and persuading, not compelling, since Christians do not believe that compulsion is an attribute of God.

Such actions do not seem to be the works of man, the author of the letter continues. Such an unexpected event in such unexpected form is a miracle of God. Christians are punished for their beliefs, but the more they are punished the more they seem to multiply, a proof that God Himself came as a man to men. The Christians are thrown to wild beasts and asked to deny their Lord, but they do not, and

they are not put down but multiply instead. Such a coming of God as the Christians announce was a calling, not a pursuing. The creator of the world was sent in love, not as a judge, and the proof of this lies in the Christian's increase of power in the face of treatment that might otherwise put an end to the religion. In dealing with Christian beliefs, the oppressors of the Christians are dealing with God Himself and not with the inventions of men.

The Christians claim, then, for their revelation nothing less than the true knowledge of God revealed. In Christ, what God is was revealed, and before His coming no man knew or could discern what God is like. Foolish philosophers have thought God to be fire or water, but such views are unacceptable. Now God has manifested Himself, and He is revealed by Himself, not by men. Yet He is revealed through faith, by which alone it is possible to see God. Before the coming of Christ, God seemed to neglect us and to be careless, but then He revealed His true nature through His beloved Child. Now we know that God alone is good, kindly, long-suffering, free from wrath, and true.

All of this was planned from the beginning, the author writes, but it was revealed at a particular time through God's Child. We lived as men before this time—governed by unruly impulses, carried away by pleasures and lusts—and the coming of God's Son was planned in order to prove to us that it is impossible for us by ourselves to enter into the Kingdom of God. We are able to do so only by the power of God, and His revelation demonstrates this to us and enables us now to enter God's Kingdom. God Himself took pity on our sin, gave His Son as ransom for us, the Holy for the wicked, the innocent for the guilty. Nothing else could cover our sins but God's own righteousness. We were convinced of our own inability to attain life, and now we have a Savior who is able to save.

What does the Christian do now, believing as he does in this divine act for his salvation? The author answers Diognetus: By love he should imitate this example of God's goodness. It is possible for man to imitate God's goodness if God wills. Happiness now for the Christian is not domination over his neighbors; it is not in wishing to have more than the weak, nor is it in the possession of wealth or power. Rather, the imitator of God is the man who takes up the burden of his neighbor, who wishes to help others, and who ministers to others.

If a man does this, if he imitates God after the example given by God's sacrifice in Christ, then even while he is occupied on earth such a man will see that God lives in Heaven, and he will begin to speak of the mysteries of God. Anyone who understands this way will begin to admire those who are persecuted; no one can deny such a God, and He will condemn the conceit and error of the world. When one learns the true life of Heaven and despises the apparent death of this world, then he comes to fear the death that is real, the loss of eternal life.

The writer of the epistle concludes by declaring that, as a disciple of the Apostles, he is becoming a teacher of the heathen. If one speaks with pain, commanded by the will of God to do so, then he becomes a sharer through love of all the things revealed by God. Knowledge does not kill, the writer asserts; only disobedience kills. Thus, Christians claim to possess a new knowledge through their revelation, and it gives them life. They die only if they are disobedient to God by not proclaiming and sharing the message given.

OCTAVIUS

Author: Minucius Felix (Second or third century)
Type of work: Christian apologetics
First transcribed: Latter half of second century, or first half of third century

PRINCIPAL IDEAS ADVANCED

To the pagan accusation that Christianity is foolishness, destitute of reason, and filled with obscene and lustful practices, the answer is given that reason itself discloses that the contents and constitution of the world are determined and governed by God; Christ was God in the world.

Pagan religion rather than Christianity is filled with foolish and obscene practices, for the moral practices of the Christians are above reproach; they do not worship monsters, devour infants, or hold incestuous banquets.

Minucius Felix, author of the *Octavius,* was a master of Latin style. He stands at the very fountainhead of Latin Christianity, and he demonstrated by his writing that Christians were not illiterate or devoid of learning. Prior to his conversion, Minucius Felix is said to have been an advocate at Rome. Little is known of his personal history or of his writings other than the *Octavius.* The date of his celebrated apology is a matter of dispute. The question is whether Minucius borrowed from Tertullian or whether Tertullian borrowed from Minucius. If the latter alternative is the case, then the *Octavius* was probably written around 166, and Minucius flourished during the reign of Marcus Aurelius. If, on the other hand, Minucius borrowed from Tertullian, he must have flourished at the beginning of the third century, and the book could not have been written before 205.

The *Octavius* is a Christian apology written in the traditional Roman form of an imaginary dialogue. The disputants are the pagan Caecilius and the Christian Octavius. The author Minucius (who gives evidence of a thorough acquaintance with Cicero and other Latin writers) plays the role of arbitrator between the disputants.

The argument opens with Caecilius's assertion that all things are uncertain and doubtful in human affairs, and that everything is probable rather than true. It is therefore to be deplored that Christians, who are generally illiterate, should dare to be certain concerning the nature of God. The world shows no sign of being governed by divine providence.

Caecilius continues by arguing that every nation, especially the Roman, has paid homage to its own deities in order that it might gain dominion over the earth. When the Roman auguries have been observed, good fortune has resulted; whereas, when they have been neglected, the consequences have been unfortunate. The impiety of the Christians toward the gods exceeds that of all others, for they despise the temples, reject the gods, and, while fearing to die, after death are indifferent to the torments of the present. Furthermore, the religion of the Christians is a foolish superstition, a conspiracy that ought to be rooted out and execrated, a religion of lust and incest. Christians adore the head of an ass, worship the virilia of their priest, worship a crucified man, and initiate young novices by having them eat an infant covered with meal. They strive in every way to conceal their worship, for they have no altars, temples, or images.

Continuing his indictment of the Christians, Caecilius charges that their one God is unknown to every nation; the Christians can neither show Him nor behold Him, and yet they threaten the whole world with conflagration and assert that the conflagration will be followed by the resurrection of the body and by rewards and punishments. Such old women's fables are spread abroad.

Such religion, says Caecilius, is to be repudiated, for what is above us is nothing to us, and things which are as uncertain as is religion ought not to be disturbed, lest superstition be introduced and all religion be overthrown.

On behalf of the Christians Octavius replies that Christians are not to be reproached because they talk about heavenly things, for wisdom is implanted by nature. The poor are not to be despised, for intelligence is not given to the rich alone. When a person utters his thoughts about divine things, what is most important is not the position of the speaker, but the truth of what he says.

It is of course true, says Octavius, that man ought to know himself and to see what he is, whence he is, and why he is. His reason will then show him that the constitution of the world and everything in it is governed and administered by a Deity of most excellent intelligence, who takes care not only of the world as a whole but also of its individual parts.

The Lord and Creator of the universe is far more glorious than the stars and the parts of the world, says Octavius. The Lord orders everything by His word; He can neither be seen nor fully understood, and yet when all His titles are laid aside, His glory is most fully seen.

Poets and philosophers have attained a glimpse of the unity of God, Octavius concedes, but men have been carried away by fables and have believed in monstrous falsehoods; they have worshiped their own kings and the inventors of the arts, and thus they have adopted men as gods. Men of antiquity fell into ridiculous and absurd practices which have been elaborated by the poets, so that even Plato wanted to banish the poets from the state.

Gods cannot be made from dead people, Octavius argues, since a god cannot die, nor can a piece of metal or wood become a god simply because men consecrate it and pray to it. The rites associated with many religions are truly cruel and obscene, comic and pitiable: "Naked people run about in the raw winter. . . . Some sacred places are crowned by a woman having one husband, some by a woman with many; and she who can reckon up most adulteries is sought after with most religious zeal. . . ." During pagan rites, Octavius charges, men castrate themselves, but if God wished for eunuchs, he would have caused men to be born as such.

The Romans did not gain power from observing superstitions, Octavius suggests. On the contrary, the Romans began with crime, and they grew by the terror of their own fierceness, by their irreligious audacity and violence. They grew rich from pillage, from the spoils of the gods and the murder of priests. They became great not because they were religious but because they were irreligious with impunity.

Demons fly from Christians and then introduce hatred and fear of the Christians in the minds of the ignorant, who then unjustly charge them with horrid crimes which no one has ever proved against them. The gentiles do themselves engage in infanticide, incest, and monstrous acts of worship. They expose their newborn children to the elements, and they perform abortions, whereas Christians regard such practices as wicked and sinful.

The Egyptians worship a mere man whom they propitiate and consult in all things, and to whom they slaughter victims, whereas the Christ that was crucified was innocent of all crime; in truth, He was God.

The banquets of the Christians, says Octavius, are modest and temperate; incestuous love is unheard of, and even modest association between the sexes causes some to blush.

The worship of the Christians is not concealed, he continues; Christians build no temples because they realize that God cannot be enclosed in limits made by man, and no likeness can be made of Him; He is present everywhere. To cultivate innocence is to supplicate God; to cultivate justice is to make offerings unto Him; to abstain from fraud is to propitiate Him. God is beheld in all His works; He is near to us and infused within us, so that we live in Him, and our most secret thoughts are known to Him.

God does not forsake those who follow Him, Octavius declares; it is man who first foresakes God. Nor is it to be wondered at if this world is to come to an end, since what has a beginning also has an end. Yet the God who made man from nothing can raise him up unto life eternal. The pious and the righteous shall then be rewarded with everlasting happiness, while the unrighteous shall receive the eternal punishment which is their due and just reward.

Christians now suffer as a discipline, not as a penalty. The tortures they endure for the sake of Christ are spectacles worthy of the name they bear, and their suffering in the name of God is a fitting testimony to the truth they profess.

The dialogue ends with Caecilius's being convinced of the truth of the Christian faith. His objections are answered, and the pagan world is shown that Latin prose can be utilized in the service of the Christian faith.

The *Octavius* is important as one of the most charming and elegantly styled apologies of the early Christian period. As a work directed at cultivated pagans, the *Octavius* exhibits a remarkable impartiality in its treatment of pagan beliefs and practices, and its dignity and literary excellence made it widely influential.

THE APOSTOLIC TRADITION

Author: Hippolytus (c.170-c.236)
Type of work: Church manual
First transcribed: c.217

PRINCIPAL IDEAS ADVANCED

Laws for Church organization and for the conduct of worship are taken from the practices in Rome; the Roman practice is truly Apostolic.

The Apostolic tradition concerns ordination by bishops, the routine for new converts, the rules for fasting, and the procedures for instruction and prayer.

Hippolytus's *Apostolic Tradition* is the oldest and most important of the ecclesiastical constitutions, and it is one of the most important sources of information concerning the development of Church practice during the first three centuries. The work played a major part in the development of the liturgy in the East, as well as in the development of Canon Law. In particular, the description of baptismal procedures is important as constituting the first distinctively Roman creed.

For Hippolytus, tradition is the most important source of Church practice. In his work he addresses the churches, urging them to hold fast to the Apostolic tradition. Ignorance of the tradition causes lapses into error, he claims, and he suggests that with careful instruction liturgical errors could be avoided.

The instructions which Hippolytus gives are simple injunctions with no explanations appended; the instructions are directives, handed down as authoritative, and they need no support, the author claims, other than their existence as expressions of the tradition of the Church, as means by which true doctrine and correct observance are conserved.

To ordain a bishop, Hippolytus advises, the people, with the presbytery, must assemble on a Sunday. Such other bishops as are already present are to lay their hands upon him, while the presbytery and the people stand by in silence. Together they are to pray in their hearts for the descent of the Holy Spirit. Hippolytus then gives verbatim a prayer which one of the bishops present is to recite. The prayer calls upon God, the Father of our Lord Jesus Christ, to pour forth His Spirit. Then God's blessing is asked upon the servant being consecrated, so that he may serve his flock well. As he is being made bishop, all offer him the kiss of peace, after which the deacons bring him the offering and he blesses it with a prayer.

When the consecration is concluded, the new bishop recites what amounts to a catechism, a short version of the essential beliefs of Christianity. If oil, cheese, or olives are offered, he gives a prayer of sanctification. However, if it is a presbyter who is being ordained, the procedure is somewhat different. Those who are already presbyters touch him, while the bishop lays on hands,

and offers a shorter prayer. When a deacon is ordained, the bishop alone lays on his hands, since a deacon is ordained not to the priesthood but to serve the bishop and to carry out his commands. Therefore, the deacon does not receive the Spirit that is possessed by the presbytery; he receives only what is confided to him under the bishop's authority.

Although the presbyter does receive the Spirit, in common with the clergy, the presbyter has only the power to receive but not to give the Spirit, Hippolytus declares. For this reason a presbyter does not ordain the clergy. At an ordination, a presbyter merely seals while the bishop ordains. On the other hand, if one has been in bonds for the Lord or has been insulted for defending the name of the Lord, then this in itself gives him special status, and he is dealt with differently.

Although Hippolytus gives the specific words of the prayers to be recited, he says that it is not necessary for everyone to say the exact words prescribed. Each may pray according to his own ability. Widows, readers, and virgins all follow under various special rules. Anyone with the gift of healing may be considered as having already made his gifts manifest.

Part Two begins with a discussion of new converts, who are first to be admitted as hearers of the Word. First they are brought to the teachers in front of the assembled people and examined as to their reasons for embracing the faith. Testimony must be furnished that each convert is competent to hear the Word. Whether the person is a slave, the wife of a believer, an unmarried man, each situation involves slightly different rules for his reception and for his disposition after reception. Next the convert must be asked his trade, since not all trades are acceptable, some not at all, and others only if modified. A heathen priest, for instance, must be rejected, says Hippolytus, but a concubine who has reared her children and been faithful to her master may become a hearer. Each catechumen, after such examination and specification, must spend three years as a hearer of the Word. However, Hippolytus admits, if a man is zealous and perseveres well in the work, his character, and not the time spent as a catechumen, is the decisive factor.

When the teacher finishes his instruction, the catechumens pray by themselves, after which the teacher prays over them, lays his hands upon them, and dismisses them. Baptism, which is a further step, can only come after the life of the person has been investigated. Each person desiring baptism must have a sponsor, who must testify that the candidate lives soberly and is active in well-doing. When those who are to be baptized have been chosen, they are to fast on Friday and then to assemble on Saturday, to kneel before the bishop in prayer. After the bishop has exorcised all evil spirits, the chosen ones are to spend the night in vigil, listening to reading and instruction.

At dawn a prayer shall be made over the water to be used for baptism. Then, as each one presents himself for baptism, a presbyter shall take hold of him and command him to renounce Satan and his works. Then, while standing in the water, the deacon questions the one to be baptized about his beliefs: Does he believe in God, the Father Almighty? Does he believe in Christ Jesus, the Son of God, and the Holy Church, and the resurrection of the flesh? When the one to be baptized answers that he believes, he is baptized three times. He is then brought to the bishop for the laying on of hands and anointing with oil, with an appropriate prayer for each act given by the bishop. Water, milk, and wine are brought and each consumed, with the symbolism explained to the one newly baptized.

Part Three begins with a discussion of the rules for fasting. Others may fast more frequently, but the bishop may fast only when all the people do, since his office of breaking bread requires that he eat of it when it is brought to him to be blessed. The next important ceremony to be discussed and described is that of the Lord's Supper. No catechumen is allowed to sit at the Lord's Supper during his period as a hearer. Others are admonished to eat silently, attending such instruction as the bishop may give during the meal. Each one eats in the name of the Lord.

The balance of Part Three gives a series of similar minor regulations. For example, in the paschal season no one is to eat before the offering is made, with certain exceptions outlined. The deacons are to assemble daily before they go to their duties. The closing injunction is that burial shall be provided at a modest cost. By the end of Part Three Hippolytus has left behind the major doctrines and ceremonies of the Church and has begun on the minor regulations, points which need to be covered, about which controversy can arise, but which do not concern major Church doctrines.

Part Four is actually quite short. In fact, the whole of the reporting of the tradition is very brief and is done in abbreviated style. Some specifications concern the central practices of Christianity, and it is obvious that if such tradition were not preserved, the Church would become quite different. However, mixed with these major specifications are minor regulations, so that it is sometimes difficult to tell where the essential points leave off and the noncrucial ones begin. When regulations are specifically fixed, there is an unfortunate tendency to place all of them on a similar level, to make the most obscure point seem as important as the crucial doctrine.

The first point for Part Four concerns the beginning of the day. Before work, hands should be washed, and prayer should be said to God. If instruction in God's Word is to be given on that day, each one should go willingly to that first. One should be zealous in desiring to go to the church for instruction, since that is the place where the Holy Spirit abounds. However, if there is to be no instruction at the church on any given day, then each one shall take home a Bible and read what he finds profitable. At the third hour of the day, public or private prayer is to be made, since it is that hour at which Jesus was nailed to the cross. In like manner all should pray at the sixth hour during the day, since that is the hour at which there was great darkness during the Crucifixion. At the ninth hour of the day each person, wherever he is, is to offer a prayer of thanksgiving for the Resurrection.

Prayer is to be given again at night, just before going to bed, and the final prayer of the day is to be given at midnight, when the instructions are to rise from bed. Why this midnight prayer? Because, our author tells us, all creation rests for a moment at this hour. Then, at dawn, the next day begins with another prayer.

This accounting of the tradition of the Church, which has been received and is to be transmitted to each new group, closes with the assertion that if these ways are accepted with thanksgiving and right faith, they will give edification in the Church and eternal life to believers. If this Apostolic tradition is kept, Hippolytus writes, then heretics cannot prevail to lead the members of the Church astray. Heresy, he feels sure, is increased when Church leaders do not follow the tradition, do not learn the purposes of the Apostles, but instead follow their own ways. Thus it is no small matter whether these specifications for observances are followed or not. The traditional rules are not incidental rules, to be changed if they are not found convenient. In observing these traditional practices, it is thought, the very heart of the Christian faith is preserved and protected. Tradition is not accidental, and, if it is Apostolic, directly descending from Jesus and His Apostles, and their instruction, then keeping the traditional observances is the very path to religious health and purity of belief.

ON FIRST PRINCIPLES

Author: Origen (c.185-c.254)
Type of work: Systematic theology
First transcribed: c.220-230

Principal Ideas Advanced

The source of all Christian doctrine is in the Scriptures of the Old and New Testaments and in the Apostolic tradition of the Church.

The Church has clear teachings on God, the Creator; Jesus Christ, His incarnate Son; and the Holy Spirit; but some points such as the origin of the Spirit and of the good angels are unclear.

Both God and the Devil are active in the created world, but man is given a rational soul and free will to direct himself in the ascent to God.

The Scriptures are filled with mysteries which are understood by any man who shares the mind of Christ and uses the threefold method of interpretation to discover the literal, moral, and spiritual senses of Scripture.

Origen has the distinction of having written the first textbook of systematic theology in his *On First Principles.* Although incomplete by modern standards or even by those of the fifth century, the work represents a great achievement in the history of Christian thought. Origen himself recognized that there were not clear teachings on every subject, but so far as possible he set forth the fundamentals of Christian doctrine as he knew them. As models or analogies he had the works of pagan Platonists, and he too was informed and influenced by the philosophy of middle Platonism. No doubt his experience as a student of philosophy and as a teacher of catechetical classes revealed to him the need for such a Christian handbook of theology.

This work was written while he was serving as the head of the Christian school in Alexandria before his exile in 230-231 to Palestine. It has survived the later purges of Origen's writings only in a Latin translation by Rufinus (c.345-410), an Italian churchman who tried to correct the controversial or unorthodox passages of Origen. The remaining excerpts and fragments of Origen in other Greek authors indicate that Rufinus translated Origen rather freely. *De principiis* is, nevertheless, a tolerably accurate statement of Origen's thought in his middle years. Especially to be observed are his own frequent warnings and qualifications that many points were still speculative and had not then been clarified by the Church.

On First Principles consists of four books which treat the following themes: God and the spiritual beings, the material world and man, free will and morality, and the Holy Scriptures. The long preface to the first book discusses the derivation of Christian doctrine from the inspired Scriptures and the tradition of the Apostles and the Church. Origen distinguishes here between clear and unclear teachings. In the former category are the basic doctrines of the trinitarian God, the soul, the Resurrection, and the creation of the world. Unclear are such matters as the origin or generation of the Holy Spirit and the origin of the good angels. In acknowledging this uncertainty Origen reflects faithfully the position of the Bible on these points.

The doctrine of God is taken essentially from the Bible. God is an incomprehensible Spirit who reveals

Himself to the pure in heart. He is a simple intellectual nature. The Second Person of the Trinity, Jesus Christ, has two natures and many titles. He is the only-begotten Son, without any beginning, the eternal Word of God. A long discourse on the significance of such titles as Wisdom, Truth, and Light follows. It is from the goodness of God that the Son is born and the Spirit proceeds. The Holy Spirit is also known from the Scriptures where He exercises great authority. The Spirit reveals God to man and works with the other two Persons in the regeneration of man. Although Father and Son work in saints as well as sinners, the Holy Spirit is given only to the worthy; for God gives existence, Christ provides reason, and the Holy Spirit is the source of holiness.

The first book goes on to discuss the defection or fall of men, rational natures, the coming consummation or perfection of all rational creatures, and the origin of incorporeal and corporeal beings. It is here that we note some of the concepts for which Origen could later be accused of heresy. He considers the stars to be living beings with souls implanted from without by God. He also discusses the angels and ranks them according to merit.

The material world is as much under God as the spiritual or heavenly, but it is much more diverse. No creature in the material world is privileged to enjoy an incorporeal life. There is always a body even when the corruptible puts on incorruption. The world, of course, has a beginning, and it has many ages without repeating itself. So for example, there are the Old and New Covenants, but only one God.

We detect in this first book the traditional anti-Gnostic, anti-Marcionite polemic against separating or differentiating between the God of the Old Testament and the God of the New. This line of thought is continued in a chapter on justice and goodness, two qualities of God that must go together.

It is in the second book's treatment of the incarnation of Christ that we find the best-known errors of Origen. He is, naturally, orthodox in his acknowledgment of Christ's majesty and divinity and of the miracle of the Incarnation, but his concept of pre-existent souls, one of which was found worthy to become the soul of Christ by union with the Logos, was quite naturally fated to be rejected by the Church. Even Origen admits that his ideas are speculative. He shows no intention, however, of abandoning the doctrine of pre-existent souls, for he goes on to declare that the souls, when cooling, fall away into sin. On the mysterious doctrine of the Holy Spirit or the Comforter, Origen was hesitant to make pronouncements. It follows from the pre-existence of souls, he argues, that there can be only a fixed number of rational beings to inhabit the earth, but he holds that their number is sufficient. He defends the free will of these beings and sees them rewarded according to merit, because God is just. At another place, however, Origen anticipates a universal salvation. Certainly there will be a general resurrection of the body if simply because it is the body which dies and therefore must be raised. (Such an argument is by no means new with Origen although it fits very well with his teaching on the soul.)

Book III of De principiis turns to the question of free will and its consequences. Origen recognizes the shortcomings of men, particularly their need for self-knowledge and the knowledge of God. He believes, however, that God is perfecting man, that men are vessels who prepare themselves by being purged. The human soul is engaged in an ascent to the highest good or God, who is reached in eternity. There are, on the other hand, opposing powers, such as the Devil and his demons, but these powers are the cause of only part of man's sin. Many transgressions are due to man's free choice. Man is confronted by a variety of human temptations which seem inseparable from his having a body.

From this discussion of free will and sin, Origen turns rather abruptly to the problem of the creation of the world. In conforming to the Genesis account, he maintains that the world had a beginning in time, but he goes on to assert that there is a logical need for several worlds because a new heaven and earth is promised in Scripture. If a new world is coming, it is likely that others have preceded this one, but never more than one world can exist at any given time. Scripture points most clearly, however, to the end of this world. It is then that God's image in man will be perfected. Man will complete his ascent and be glorified in the likeness of God. All vice will be purged, and God will dwell in every man. Man will receive a spiritual body, and death will be destroyed.

The fourth book on the Holy Scriptures is an especially valuable account of Origen's handling of the Bible. It is almost a description of his hermeneutics. Fundamental is, of course, the fact that the Scriptures are inspired books. The traditional evidence for this inspiration is presented, in particular the fulfillment of prophecy. How-

ever, when Origen considered the proper way to read the Bible, he found it necessary to deal with prophecies which had not been visibly fulfilled. At this point, he argues, the need for a spiritual or allegorical interpretation of Scripture is obvious. He points out that many previous misunderstandings of the Bible arose from literal readings, and he would correct this error. He cites the importance of sharing the mind of Christ when reading the Scriptures, a principle that appears repeatedly throughout the history of Christian exegesis.

The doctrine of the threefold interpretation of Scripture is based on Proverbs 22:20ff., as found in the Septuagint text. The three steps or aspects are the flesh, soul, and spirit, corresponding to the nature of man. Not all passages of the Bible contain all three forms of wisdom, but since most do, there is often a three-fold meaning of the Bible. The literal meaning is sometimes offensive or a stumbling-block, but God's intent is to keep us from stopping at the literal meaning and thereby missing the heavenly meaning. The anthropomorphisms in the Old Testament descriptions of God are not to be understood literally, and the absurdities of the law, Origen writes, are to be interpreted allegorically. On the other hand, many historical passages are true and consequently are to be accepted as written. It is typical of Origen that he claims the entire written Gospel is but a shadow of the coming heavenly and everlasting Gospel. Thus, one sees the need for the wisdom of the Holy Spirit in the reading of the Scriptures.

In concluding the final book of *On First Principles* Origen gives a summary of the doctrine of God. Even here he touches on new problems such as the nature and origin of matter. Characteristically, his summary of doctrine is generously documented with Scripture.

Although the later judgment of the Church on Origen was unfavorable, we cannot overlook the recognition he received in his own day nor the influence he exerted for over a century on the theologians of East and West. He produced the first great synthesis of Christian teaching and provided his successors with a method of Biblical interpretation which, if sometimes artificial and arbitrary, was at least consistent and thorough. He was an intellectual who applied all his powers to the teaching office of the Church, in defense of the Gospel and in opposition to the heresies of his day. It is especially to his credit that he dealt with the whole of theology and not merely with one doctrine. Origen represents the coming of age of Christianity as an intellectual force in the ancient world.

THE EXTANT WRITINGS OF JULIUS AFRICANUS

Author: Sextus Julius Africanus (c.160-c.240)
Type of work: Biblical chronology
First transcribed: Third century

PRINCIPAL IDEAS ADVANCED

By studying the genealogies given in the Old Testament in conjunction with Greek and Babylonian Sources, the age of the world from Adam to the advent of Jesus Christ can be accurately set at 5500 years.

The apparent discrepancy between the genealogies of Jesus recorded in Matthew and in Luke is explicable in terms of a twofold manner of recording generations in Israel, the one by nature, the other by law, so that in effect there is no real disparity between the two accounts.

Sextus Julius Africanus, a pupil of Heraclas of Alexandria sometime between 228 and 232, contributed to the Biblical science of chronology in his *Five Books of Chronology* and in his letter to Aristides.

The main facts of his life are known from the *Chronicle* of Eusebius and from his own writings, in which he states that he was attracted to Alexandria by the fame of the teacher Heraclas.

The works ascribed to Africanus, besides the ones already mentioned, are a letter to Origen, in which he sought to prove, by ingenious critical argument, that the story of Susanna in Daniel was forgery; *The Acts of Symphorosa and her Seven Sons,* which is attributed to him in the manuscript, although no other ancient author makes mention of his authorship; and the *Cesti,* ascribed to him by Eusebius, but which may have been written by someone else of the same name.

In the *Five Books of Chronology,*

Julius Africanus undertakes to summarize the events from the cosmogony of Moses to the advent of Christ, and from the advent of Chirst to the reign of the Emperor Macrinus. The chief interest in the fragments that we possess arises from the treatment of the difficult questions of the genealogies of Jesus contained in the Gospels.

The extant fragments of the *Five Books of Chronology* deal first of all with the mythical chronology of the Chaldeans and Egyptians who, according to Julius, in their boastful manner inflate their antiquity and appeal to their astrologers to establish countless cycles and myriad years in their past.

The truth of the matter, writes Julius, is to be found in the writings of the Jews, the descendants of Abraham who, with a modesty and sobriety appropriate to those who were taught the truth of Moses, have correctly informed us that the number of years up to the advent of Jesus Christ is 5500. This figure can be arrived at by adding the ages of those mentioned in the Old Testament genealogies. It then becomes apparent that 2262 years transpired from Adam to Noah and the flood, and that Abraham entered the promised land of Canaan in the 3277th year of the world. From Adam until the death of Joseph, a total of 3563 years transpired. From Daniel 9:24 and other Biblical passages, it is possible to determine that the world will end 6000 years from its creation, in the year 500.

Among the Greeks there is no certain history until the time of the Olympiads, before which time dates are confused and inconsistent. By correlating Hebrew, Greek, and Persian history, it is possible to further ascertain the course of events, and to set the date of the exodus from Egypt, and the date of the exile, as well as the subsequent course down to the very coming of Jesus Christ, the Savior of all.

Such an attempt at chronology, while historically interesting, overlooks the fact that Biblical genealogies are never used in Scripture itself as a basis for chronological calculations. In fact, modern scholarship has noted the fact, overlooked by Julius Africanus, that genealogies have symmetrical forms which suggests the omission of links. They are cast in forms easy to remember and give only such information as is useful to the reader.

Julius Africanus overlooked the fact that many Old Testament genealogies are abridged, and the word "son" frequently means descendant. In spite of the errors that he made, however, the attempt at tracing the history of the world is understandable, at a time when there was no reason to believe that the world is older. His efforts to understand historical sequences by comparing various source materials provided a model for subsequent historical research.

Of further interest is the example of Biblical exegesis in which he suggests the hermeneutic principle that Scripture is to be interpreted by Scripture. In commenting upon Genesis 6:4, where the sons of God are depicted as marrying the daughters of men, Julius Africanus appears to suggest that while it is possible to interpret the expression "sons of God" as referring to angels, it is more likely that it refers to the descendants of Seth, who are called the sons of God because of the righteous men and the patriarchs who descended from him, whereas the descendants of Cain are named the daughters of men, as being destitute of the divine because of their wickedness, which stirred God's indignation.

Julius's letter to Aristides is a famous attempt to reconcile the apparent discrepancies in the genealogies given by Luke and Matthew. Modern scholarship recognizes that the genealogy in Matthew is an arbitrary arrangement in three groups of fourteen, in order to make the divisions come with David and the captivity. In the second group four kings are omitted and Jechonias is mentioned twice. The expression "so all the generations" refers to the generations given in these lists. In the summary statement the generations are reduced to three and Jesus Christ is called the Son of David, who is called the son of Abraham, so that it is readily seen that the word "son" refers to descendant.

The solution to the problem of the apparent discrepancies between Luke and Matthew is worked out in detail by Julius. He rejects the notion that the discrepant enumeration is a mixing of royal and priestly names given in order to show that Christ holds both a kingly and priestly office. Such a device would be both false and unnecessary since every Christian knows that Christ is the high priest of His Father, that Christ presents our petitions to Him, and that Christ is also a supramundane King, who rules by the Spirit those whom He has delivered.

The real reason for the discrepancies, according to Julius, is that the names of the generations in Israel were enumerated in a twofold manner, by nature or according to law. When the enumeration is given by nature, the succession is that of physical offspring; it is given according to law whenever another raised up children to the name of a brother dying childless. Thus neither of the Gospel writers is in error, since the one reckons by nature, and the other by law. Both of the accounts are true, and they come down to Joseph quite accurately, although with considerable intricacy. The same persons are quite justly reckoned as belonging either to their actual fathers or to their legal fathers. Thus, both the genealogies of Matthew and Luke are those of Joseph, since Joseph was the Son of Jacob or of Heli, either by adoption, or simply because Heli and Jacob were either half brothers or brothers. At the death of one of the brothers who was childless, the surviving brother married the widow, who then became Joseph's mother by marriage, so that Joseph was reckoned the son of Heli and of Jacob.

A further work ascribed to Julius, the *Passion of St. Symphorosa and Her Seven Sons,* is of interest in shedding light upon the life of the early Christians in their experience of martyrdom, and although the events portrayed occurred under the persecutions of Hadrian around the year 120, there is no ground to doubt its genuineness, even if it cannot be asserted with certainty that Julius is its author.

The widow Symphorosa and her seven sons refused to sacrifice to the gods in honor of a newly built palace, although they had been given the choice of sacrificing to the gods or themselves becoming sacrifices. When they refused to comply with Hadrian's demands, Symphorosa, whose husband had previously died a martyr's death, was beaten, suspended by the hair, and finally thrown into a river with a stone tied to her neck. Her sons fared no better; they were fastened to stakes, stretched on blocks around the temple of Hercules, and either stabbed to death or cleft in twain from the head downward.

A DECLARATION OF FAITH
(and Other Writings)

Author: Saint Gregory Thaumaturgus (c.213-c.270)
Type of work: Theology, Church practice
First transcribed: c.240-270

Principal Ideas Advanced

God is a triune being, Father, Son, and Holy Spirit, a perfect Trinity which in neither glory, eternity, nor dominion is ever divided from itself.

The Church of Christ is to exercise proper judgment in the readmission of members who have committed offenses in times of persecution; the Church recognizes the distinction between offenses committed under duress and those voluntarily committed because of an evil and covetous heart.

Willful violators of God's commandments whose offenses are particularly heinous are not to be permitted into the public congregation until such time as the Holy Spirit guides the saints in their common judgment concerning them.

Gregory Thaumaturgus, also known by the name Theodorus, was a native of Neocaesarea, one of the most important towns of Pontus. He was born into a wealthy pagan family and was educated in law at such centers of learning as Alexandria, Athens, Berytus, and Palestinian Caesarea. He studied logic, geometry, physics, ethics, philosophy, ancient literature, and theology with Origen, under whose influence he accepted Christianity. In 240 he became Bishop of Neocaesarea and faithfully served the Christian cause until his death about 270.

Gregory was an extremely gifted bishop, deeply versed in pagan learning, and richly imbued with Christian wisdom. His accredited extant writings include a creed on the doctrine of the trinity, *A Declaration of Faith*; a *Meta-*phrase of the *Book of Ecclesiastes*; a *Panegyric to Origen,* in which he expresses his indebtedness to his teacher; and a *Canonical Epistle,* containing penances to be performed by Christians who were unfaithful during the barbarian invasion.

In *A Declaration of Faith*, Gregory affirms his belief in a single God, the Father of the living Word. God the Father is subsistent wisdom and power, the Father of the only-begotten Son, the perfect begetter of the perfect-begotten. There is a single Lord, God of God, the efficient Word, the Power which formed the whole creation. This one Lord is the true Son of the true Father, the Invisible of the Invisible, and the Incorruptible of the Incorruptible, the Eternal of the Eternal. There is also one Holy Spirit, who has his subsistence from God, and is made manifest to men by the Son. The Holy Spirit is the image of the Son, the perfect image of the perfect, the life and cause of the living, the supplier of sanctification, the one in whom God the Father is manifested. God the Son is through all; God the Father is above all and in all; and yet the Father, the Son, and the Holy Spirit are neither divided nor estranged but together constitute a perfect Trinity in sovereignty, eternity, and glory. In the Trinity there is nothing created or in servitude, nor is anything superinduced. There is nothing that was formerly nonexistent. The Son was never wanting to the Father, nor was the Spirit ever wanting to the Son, but without change and variation the same Trinity endures forever.

A Declaration of Faith is significant as a creed in that it is concerned solely with the Trinity.

In his *Canonical Epistle,* written about 258 or 262, Gregory writes of those Christians who ate things sacrificed to idols or offended in other matters during the time of the barbarian invasion. The epistle is addressed to an anonymous bishop who asks Gregory's advice concerning what transpired during the ravage of the Goths in the time of Gallienus (259-267).

Whatever was forced upon Christians while they were in captivity cannot be charged against them. Externals do not corrupt a man, but a believer is corrupted because of what issues from his heart.

Women who were forcibly defiled in their bodies while in captivity are to be received again among the faithful, unless their past lives give evidence that they willingly submitted to such outrage. The damsel in Deuteronomy who was forcibly violated serves as an example for the manner in which the penitent is to be received. Nothing is to be done to punish such a person, since anyone overcome by violence has committed no sin. If in the past a violated woman has lived in utmost chastity, in a manner free of suspicion and purity, she is not to be blamed for falling into wantonness through force or necessity.

In normal times, Gregory continues, the Church of Christ is to bear no one in her midst who is covetous, for covetousness is a great evil. The Scriptures declare that it is not robbery alone that is to be abhorred, but the grasping mind. The disposition to meddle with what belongs to others in order to satisfy the sordid love of gain is sufficiently wicked to give cause to the Church of God to excommunicate such persons from her number. In times of persecution, only the impious, those who hate God, and are of unsurpassable iniquity, would in the midst of woeful sorrow be audacious enough to consider the crisis which brought destruction to all to be the very moment for aggrandizing their private coffers. It seems good, therefore, writes Gregory, that such heinous offences be punished with excommunication, lest God's wrath descend upon the whole people and first of all upon those who bear the responsibility of an office. Unpunished covetousness is such a crime that the wrath of God may descend upon the righteous. The Christian is to have nothing to do with such persons, for he can have no fellowship with such as do the work of darkness. For, if in time of peace it is unlawful to reap gain at the expense of another, whether an enemy or brother, it is even a more heinous crime when adversity strikes, and one steals from another who has been forced to abandon his possessions. Nor is it lawful to retain the property of others on the pretext that it is but just compensation for one's own property that has been lost.

Those who have descended to such depths as to detain by force certain captives who have made their escape are to be treated as men who know not the name of the Lord, says Gregory. And such sinners as have freely enrolled among the barbarians, committing acts of treason against their fellow countrymen, putting members of their own race to death, are to be debarred from the congregation of the Lord, even as listeners, at least until some common decision has been reached by the saints with respect to them.

Those who have invaded the houses of others, or who have taken what the barbarians left behind, and have been tried and convicted, ought not to be permitted into the congregation even as listeners, but if they themselves voluntarily make restitution, they should be put in the rank of the repentant.

Christians who have been faithful ought to demand no reward, nor recompense, nor any acknowledgment. For their behavior was no more than fitting for one who knows the Lord.

Certain other writings attributed to Gregory, *A Sectional Confession of Faith, A Discourse on the Trinity, Twelve Topics on the Faith,* a discourse *On the Soul, Four Homilies, On the Saints,* and *On the Gospel of Matthew* are generally regarded as belonging to other authors of a later date.

The reputation of Gregory made him the subject of legendary lore that was propagated long after his death, and his surname Thaumaturgus, "wonder-worker," testifies that miracles were then regarded as rare.

His address in honor of Origen sheds further light on Origen's character, for Origen is described as one who disclaims any virtue on his own part and extols true piety and faith in the living God as the parent of all justice, temperance, courage, and prudence. The panegyric is one of the most important sources concerning Origen's personality and teaching, and it is a document of the first importance for Christian education in this period.

Gregory's works are of importance, for they show the early attempts of all the Ante-Nicene doctors to work out the formulas of orthodoxy. That they used inept theological phrases, which lack skill and precision, is to be expected when the immensity of their labors and the variety of their works is taken into consideration.

AGAINST CELSUS

Author: Origen (c.185-c.254)
Type of work: Christian apologetics
First transcribed: c.246-249

Principal Ideas Advanced

Christianity is its own best witness or proof, refuting by its practice the arguments of its opponents.

The antiquity of the Old Testament with its prophecies of Christ provides a ground for refuting all charges that the Bible borrowed from pagan religions, and it rules out dependence on the Greek philosophers.

Most philosophical arguments against Christianity can be neutralized by opposing arguments from other schools of philosophy.

The mass appeal of Christianity should not obscure the fact that the leaders of the Church are educated and that the Church requires a long period of catechetical training.

The Holy Scriptures properly interpreted provide a more than adequate defense of Christianity against paganism and philosophy.

Origen's eight books *Against Celsus* rank as the outstanding apologetic work of the first three centuries. The work is the intellectual equal of Augustine's *City of God*. With Origen the Church met the pagan philosophers on fully equal terms. Indeed Origen seems better acquainted with the different schools and systems of Greek philosophy than was his opponent, Celsus.

Celsus wrote his attack on Christianity under the title, *True Discourse* or *True Doctrine* in about 178. The attack was little noticed at the time, and we would probably know nothing of its contents had not Origen preserved a substantial part of it in citations throughout his *Contra Celsum*. It was, moreover, only at the request of his patron, Ambrose, that Origen took note of Celsus and prepared his great defense of Christianity. Indeed, the preface suggests that in the face of false accusations Christianity has always done best to remain silent, for the lives of Christ's disciples are a sufficient witness of Christian truth. The doctrines of Celsus can be recognized as false doctrines by anyone who knows Christianity, Origen argues.

Still, for the sake of the unknowledgeable and the weak in faith, Origen overcame his reluctance and went on to produce eight long books, each averaging seventy-five sections or chapters in length.

The reader of *Against Celsus* is struck immediately by Origen's extensive use of Scripture, both Old Testament and New. Most other apologists made little appeal to Scripture because their pagan audiences were not willing to credit the Bible with authority. Thus, most other apologetic appeals were made to reason and morality. Origen, however, was a Biblical theologian, and he found answers to every question in the Holy Scriptures. He usually interpreted the Bible in three senses, literal, moral, and allegorical, and thus he achieved a great deal of freedom of interpretation.

Besides relying on Scriptures, Origen also made use of his predecessors, the second century apologists, Justin Martyr (c.100-c.165), Theophilus (later second century), and Athenagoras (fl.177). These early apologists used many of the arguments of Hellenistic Judaism in defense of monotheism and the antiquity of Old Testament prophecy. Origen showed a marked advance beyond them, however, in his wide use of the arguments of the philosophers. This use was possible because of the many rivalries among the latter. The Stoics, for example, believed in providence, and their arguments could be used against the Epicureans and Peripatetics who did not. Whatever school of philosophy Celsus turned to, Origen could employ the teachings of its opponents, in all of whom he was well-versed. An incidental result is that *Against Celsus* is a valuable source of information about early philosophy.

Among the general charges against Christianity to which Celsus continually returned were that Christianity is barbarian in origin and a newcomer among religions, that it is for the uneducated and irrational, and that it is disloyal to the Emperor and therefore dangerous to the Empire. It is noteworthy that Celsus did not dwell at length on the old charges of immorality and vice. In fact, he recognized the worth of Christian morals and also that of the Logos doctrine.

The first book of *Contra Celsum* responds to the fairly common accusation that the Christians formed a secret society which engaged in magical and barbarous practices. This charge, Origen writes, reflects an outsider's point of view and is easily enough dismissed. The simplicity of the Christian faith, which offends some philosophers, is really a virtue when this faith is placed in God and not in some man. The person of Jesus serves as an example of wisdom, power, and leadership arising from humble origins, and together with the traditional arguments from prophecy and the Virgin Birth it points to His divinity. At this point in Book I, Origen is considering the objections made by an imaginary Jew whom Celsus introduced in his treatise to present certain traditional Jewish objections to Christianity, but Origen was too skillful an interpreter of the Old Testament to let any literary convention upset his careful analysis and refutation of the arguments advanced by Celsus. Origen employs interpretations developed by his predecessors to meet Jewish polemics, as, for example, that of a double advent, which accounts for the differences between those prophecies which describe Christ as a suffering servant and those which describe Him as a glorious king.

Book II deals further with the arguments of Celsus' Jew. Origen refers to the Jewish-Christians who have not abandoned the Law and the Prophets in any sense. He considers also the Jews' rejection of Christ and denies that this act in any way invalidates Christ, especially since it was already prophesied in the Old Testament. The fulfillment of prophecy becomes the main defense of Christianity in this book. The difficulties presented to the non-Christian mind by the accounts of the Passion of Christ, always a problem for Greeks, are met in this way as well as by comparisons with the Greek myths. The Resurrection also comes under discussion as a traditional difficulty for philosophic minds. As if finally to silence Celsus' spokesman, Origen observes that Jews had a long record of disbelief in God even before Christ and so it is no surprise that they rejected Him.

With Book III the defense against the arguments presented by Celsus on his own commences. Celsus held that the disagreements between Jews and

Christians militate against both. Origen's reply is a summary consideration of the question as to which religion better understands the prophets. The argument that the Church is divided against itself in numerous sects is refuted by reference to the differences among philosophers. Such disputes do not prevent Celsus from trusting in philosophy. Origen is able, moreover, to compare the unity and dignity of the Church to the divisions among pagan religious groups and their unseemly practices and beliefs. The honor paid to Jesus, which Celsus protested, can be shown to be fully deserved by His miraculous works, which excel anything done by pagan deities. The charges that Christianity is for the ignorant and foolish or for the masses, especially for women and boys, are met by reference to the Scriptures where such examples as Solomon and Daniel reveal the greatest wisdom and where Paul's description of a bishop's qualifications shows the true meaning of worldly foolishness and divine wisdom. Nor does the Church appeal to the public indiscriminately. It seeks all men but seeks to educate them in its doctrines and way of life. The Church accepts sinners because sinners are the very ones who need to be saved, but Celsus seems to object to the practice, notes Origen, mainly on the ground that the sinners thereby lose the counsel of philosopher-physicians.

The attack of Celsus which Origen answers in Book IV of *Against Celsus* centers around the Incarnation. How or why should God come down to men? Both Jews and Christians are wrong in expecting such an unreasonable event. This line of thought gives Origen occasion to expand on the divine plan and the gracious nature of God. The use of punishments or terrors to reform men, to which Celsus objects, is justified for the sake of improving the race. Origen explains certain of the actions of God such as the Incarnation as the necessary adaptation of spiritual food for the conditions of men. A considerable discussion of the narratives in Genesis is found in this book, perhaps because Genesis was the Biblical book most familiar to the pagans. Origen uses allegorical interpretation freely, especially for the anthropomorphical descriptions of God. He argues that the legends of the Greeks are more to be scorned than those of the Old Testament. In the end he exposes the irrationality of Celsus in exalting the powers of animals in respect to divination and knowledge of God's ways.

The fifth book opens with a discussion of the worship of heavenly bodies. Celsus argued that since the Christians worshiped God in Heaven, they might as well worship the stars. Origen replies that it is wrong to worship the objects of the Creator which themselves worship Him. The refutation turns next to the doctrine of the resurrection of the body, a doctrine which seemed unreasonable and even undesirable to Celsus; but all things are possible for God, Origen counters, and it is He who determines what is good. To the objection that the Christians depart from the traditional customs of the Jews, which are tolerable because traditional, Origen replies that such customs may often be both impious and evil. Tradition is, or at least can be, simply superstition, which would be unphilosophical to follow. Other topics for discussion are the names of God and the activity of the angels.

Origen demonstrates that names do make a difference and that even some Greeks have believed in angels. He also attributed many of the ideas objected to by Celsus to Gnostic and Jewish-Christian sects; and thus he protected orthodox Christianity.

Book VI of *Contra Celsum* returns again to the problem of education. Origen observes that many of the leaders of the Church have in fact been educated men. Moreover, Christian teaching is not simply Plato misunderstood. Thereafter follows a lengthy discourse on the meaning of numbers and symbols as used in the diagrams of the cosmos by the Gnostics. Out of this discourse emerges the problem of evil and Satan, a problem which is solved, Origen argues, by the New Testament. Origen goes on to explain the relationship of Jesus, the Son, to God, the Father. He follows up this discussion, occasioned by Gnostic cosmogonies which made places for both Satan and Jesus, with an explanation of the creation of the world according to Scripture. Celsus had, however, presented all these matters in order to question the possibility of knowing God, and it is with this question that the next book is concerned.

Book VII looks first at oracles and prophetic spirits that claim to know the will of God. Origen argues that the pagan oracles cannot be compared to the Christian prophets, nor can the latter be judged on the basis of false prophets who have arisen. The Holy Scriptures alone are authoritative. It is these that have prophesied the incarnation of the Word.

At this point Origen expounds his ante-Nicene Christology with its distribution of Christ's activities among the two natures. He tends to equate the soul with the Logos in Christ. He also takes the occasion to clarify the doctrine of the Resurrection again. He argues that Celsus attributed inappropriate ideas and statements to the Christians and that he was not even consistent in his picture of them. The Christians have in effect a direct source of knowledge of God in the Scriptures, and they do not need the philosophical approaches to this knowledge. God has, in addition, spoken to men through Jesus Christ. Origen concludes this book with an attack on images and demon worship.

The final book of *Against Celsus* is essentially a defense of monotheism. Christians cannot serve two masters, Origen argues, and it is misleading of Celsus to describe Christ and God as two gods. The witness of the Bible is that they are one. Naturally any worship of demons is excluded even if they are subordinate to God. Thus, Christians properly honor God when they scorn demons, magic, astrology, and emperor-worship. Nonetheless, Christians are loyal to the state even when they decline to accept public office because their divine services and prayers benefit all mankind.

Origen wrote his apology not merely to refute Celsus but primarily to convert the learned pagans of his acquaintance at Alexandria and Caesarea. It was to such persons that Celsus' arguments against Christianity probably appealed. Origen wanted to prove to them that Christianity was a sound philosophy as well as a sound religion, and that it was not only moral and patriotic but also intellectually respectable. We cannot say who read this work, but the very fact that it has come down to us in its original Greek text would indicate that many copies were in circulation. Certainly no better apology had been prepared for the educated classes prior to this one; and, as it turned out, not many more apologies were to be needed to aid in bringing about, in the next century, the granting of official status to Christianity.

INSTRUCTIONS IN FAVOR OF CHRISTIAN DISCIPLINE

Author: Commodianus (Commodian, fl. c.250)
Type of work: Apologetics
First transcribed: Third century

PRINCIPAL IDEAS ADVANCED

The worship of pagan gods is foolish, for what came into existence and what passes away cannot truly be a god.

Man's salvation is to be found in the keeping of the law of Christ, for He alone has redeemed mankind and will return as the conqueror of the Antichrist, as the judge of the wicked, and as the rewarder of those who have diligently served Him by their works of righteousness.

Little is known about the life of Commodianus, except that he was apparently a North African bishop in the third century. His extant work (which is in Latin verse) reflects the earnestness and piety—and, at the same time, the paucity of learning and theological skill—of a practical Christian whose *Instructions in Favor of Christian Discipline* was written against the pagans. The work is a series of eighty poems, each on a different subject and combined in no particular order.

Commodianus writes that he seeks to instruct those who worship pagan gods; his desire is to supplant ignorance by the truth which he himself found by reading God's word. Eternal life is to be found only in the law of God, which forbids the worship of idols made with human hands. When the Jews were delivered from Egypt, God enjoined them to serve Him alone. The law teaches of the Resurrection and gives hope of happiness in the world.

The many gods that pagans pray to are not gods at all, Commodianus writes. To beautify nature, the true God decreed that angels visit the earth. But the angels that were sent down were contaminated by beautiful women, and hence they were not allowed to return to Heaven. Their descendants, who were said to be giants, made known the arts upon the earth; and when the descendants died, images were erected to them. Since God did allow the demons to be brought back from death, their spirits wander to and fro perverting those who worship them as gods.

The worship of such gods as Saturn, Jupiter, the Stars, the Sun and Moon, Neptune, Hercules, and numerous other gods and goddesses, is sheer folly. Men are seduced by the stories of the poets. Saturn grew old on earth and died. The sun and moon are not to be worshiped; they do not run of their own accord, but were placed in the heavens on the fourth day of creation by the omnipotent Creator who, in His law, commanded that none should worship them.

Man shares the nature of whatever god or goddess he worships. Bacchus, for example, is honored in the midst of drunken orgies. Man is mad to worship the gods of the heavens, gods who were born, who grow old and die. To believe tales about such gods is to believe the lies of a few wicked and empty poets; it is to be the victim of deceit and abominable superstition. A prudent man, says Commodianus, cannot worship a log and call it a deity. To seek what is healthy is to seek the righteousness of the law that brings eternal salvation. To rise again with Christ, man must abandon the wickedness and blindness of the world. The Lord God has permitted demons to wander in the world for man's discipline, but He has ordered that those who forsake the altars of demons shall become dwellers in Heaven.

God will judge those who have chosen the wrong path and who live in wanton gluttony, outside the law, turning their backs upon the God of life, whose desire it is that man will live, not perish in an evil place.

It is mere foolishness, Commodianus writes, to delay in acknowledging Christ, for those who believe in Him will live forever. Whoever believes in Him who was dead will rise again and live for all time, but those who do not believe will undergo a second death; their present joy and luxury will be short-lived; they will suffer the torments of Hell forever. The life of this world is not the true one, Commodianus insists; it is an error to believe that the soul dies with the body. A cruel Hell has been prepared for the wicked. A man does not escape from God when he dies; the dead are not extinct; death is not a mere vacuity. Mortal man is separated from his body, but he is brought back for judgment, to be punished according to his deeds.

Goodness, righteousness, peace, and true patience end in happiness with Christ; an evil mind ends in terrible punishments, in burning fire. Those who are rich in the things of this world ought therefore to humble themselves and to become grateful to God. It is foolish to cling to material possessions and to neglect God's holy law. Whatever a man possesses belongs to God alone, for He made the world and now rules it by His power.

The foolish rich man does not know the time of his departure from this world; he is proud and haughty, and he is uncharitable to the poor; he dishonors God and his fellows. But such an evildoer shall not escape the wrath to come, for his god is his belly, and he is lover of gold.

Both Jews and gentiles should desist from their rejection of Christ, Commodianus writes, for the time will soon come when it will no longer be possible to repent. God Himself has died for us, and Christ will again appear, after the time of the Antichrist. The end of the world will witness the resurrection of Nero, who shall be brought up from Hell. He will reconquer Rome and rage against the Christians. Nero, however, will be conquered by the Antichrist from the East, who will burn Rome, then return to Judea, perform false miracles, and deceive many. Finally, when Christ returns, He will destroy the armies of the Antichrist and convert all nations. Judgment will then take place and the earth will be destroyed by fire.

Commodianus advises that every true believer should live a godly life. Catechumens who fall into error should, when admonished, return to the true faith, leaving all for Christ. The newly converted believer must guard against falling into his old sins and consequently into despair.

The faithful are not to hold their brethren in hatred, Commodianus writes, but are to walk in love, free from strife, shunning all great sins and all evil deeds. The Christian is not to meet force with force. He should even willingly accept martyrdom. Worldly things are to be avoided absolutely; neither the world nor anything in it is to be loved. A believing man is not to live in the pleasures of the world as do the gentiles; his joy is in Christ, and his refreshment is found in giving help and encouragement to the martyr.

The Christian on the path to martyrdom ought to live a godly life, for martyrdom is suited to the blessed and is to be desired only by those who first live well. It is an error to believe that our blood overcomes the wicked one. Only good deeds conquer Satan; if the Christian performs good deeds,

he is already a martyr, and he can feel secure.

The true Christian is to labor in the Lord, to wage a daily war in which he restrains all lust, lives temperately, represses rage. He must be peaceable to all men, a protector of all, a man free from jealousy, without envy, and charitable to everyone.

Ministers are to be an example to the people, Commodianus writes; they are to be submissive to the commands of their Master, always looking upward to the supreme God.

The sick are to be cared for, and food is to be shared with the needy; the hungry and the thirsty are not to be dismissed with mere words. The Christian is to live soberly before his Lord; the women are to conduct themselves in all modesty and chastity, avoiding pomp and vain apparel; men, in meekness and faith, are to serve God in all things. As the servant of God, the Christian has no end other than to please God by doing that of which the Lord approves. Simplicity and meekness are to dwell in his body. When six thousand years have passed, Commodianus predicts, the world will come to an end; the thousand years during which Christ is the ruler will terminate, and Christ will finally judge the wicked and reward the faithful.

ON THE UNITY OF THE CATHOLIC CHURCH

Author: Saint Cyprian of Carthage (c.200-258)
Type of work: Ecclesiology
First transcribed: c.251

Principal Ideas Advanced

The true Church of Jesus Christ was founded upon one man, Peter, in order that its essential unity might be clearly demonstrated; later, all the Apostles were given powers and honors equal to those originally bestowed upon Peter, and they in turn passed on the one office which each possessed in its fullness to the bishops.

The episcopate, therefore, is a single whole which binds the Church into a visible unity, each bishop bearing a responsibility for the entire Church, since the entire Church is present in the one office in which he has a share.

There can be no salvation apart from the Church presided over by the unity of bishops; schismatics and heretics can inherit none of the promises made to the Church, for they have deserted the Church.

The treatise *De ecclesiae unitate* is unquestionably the best known and most important of all the works of the great African martyr-bishop Cyprian. Few attempts to define the nature of the Church have proved to be as widely read and influential as this one. Much of the credit for the popularity which the *De unitate* has enjoyed down through the centuries must be given to the aphoristic style which Cyprian employed with great effectiveness. Such statements as "You cannot have God for your father unless you have the church for your mother" and "He who rends and divides the church cannot possess the garment of Christ" probably account for much of the abiding fame of the treatise as a whole.

In addition to being his most important and best-known work, the *De unitate* is also the most controversial of all of Cyprian's writings. The controversy is due to the fact that the text of the treatise exists in two different forms. In one version—generally called the "episcopalian" or *Textus receptus* —the emphasis is clearly upon the equality of all bishops within the Church. According to the other version, however, the primacy of Peter is stressed in such a way as to suggest that Cyprian recognized the supremacy of the Roman bishop.

In the past, scholarship has tended to divide along denominational lines on this issue, Roman Catholics claiming that the "primacy" text was the original and Protestants claiming that the primacy phrases had been interpolated into the original "episcopalian" text by later champions of papal authority.

More recent scholarship, however, has demonstrated rather convincingly that both versions are genuine, and that historical circumstances in the life of Cyprian were responsible for his issuing the same treatise in two different forms.

The circumstances, briefly, were these: in the year 251, Cyprian was moved to write a treatise on the unity of the Church because of schisms which had occurred not only in his own Church at Carthage, but also in the Church of Rome. The Roman schism, in particular, seems to have been in his mind as he attempted to define the meaning and nature of the Church's unity. In Rome, the presbyter Novatian had had himself consecrated as bishop in opposition to the legitimate bishop Cornelius. For Cyprian it was unthinkable that the same Church could be divided and presided over by two bishops, since the bishop, according to Cyprian, was meant to be the visible symbol of the unity of the Church. Although he seems to have wavered for a time in deciding which of the two men he should recognize as the legitimate occupant of the episcopal office in Rome, he finally decided in favor of Cornelius and then turned all his energies to healing the schism.

In order to impress upon the Romans the necessity for submitting to the one lawful bishop of that city, Cyprian appealed to the Petrine origins of the Church. Peter was chosen as the founder of the Church, he insisted, in order that the essential unity of the Church might be clearly demonstrated. This unity was later represented by the entire apostolic college and then by the successors of the Apostles, the bishops, all of whom were made to share in the one episcopal authority bestowed upon Peter. In every church, therefore, there should be a recognition and zealous preservation of the unity which the bishop personifies, but especially in the Church of Rome where the bishop actually sits upon the *Cathedra* or chair once occupied by Peter, the symbol of the Church's oneness.

It is in this context that the famous statement in the "primacy" text must be understood— "He who deserts the chair of Peter on whom the church was founded, does he trust that he is in the church?" Cyprian's intention in this passage was not to bestow upon the Roman bishop a jurisdiction wider than his own See, but rather to claim for the legitimate occupant of the chair of Peter an exclusive authority over all the Christians in Rome.

A later development in the relations between Cyprian and the Roman Church caused the African to reconsider some of the expressions which he had used in the original version of the *De unitate*. The Church of Rome and the Church of North Africa had different practices with respect to the admission of former heretics and schismatics. Cyprian and his African colleagues insisted upon their rebaptism, whereas the Roman Church did not. Stephan, who succeeded to the Roman episcopate in 254, tried to force the Roman practice upon the North Africans, but he was firmly resisted by Cyprian. To prevent the inference that he himself had previously recognized the right of the Roman bishop to interfere in the affairs of other churches in the original version of the *De unitate,* Cyprian removed the so-called primacy phrases from the treatise about the year 256. The removal of these passages from the text in no way changed Cyprian's basic point of view on the nature of the Church but simply removed the possibility of a papalistic exploitation of the strong Roman orientation of the original version.

In spite of the fact that the *De unitate* was written during one of the most severe persecutions which the Church has ever undergone, Cyprian showed himself to be more concerned about the problems of internal subversion than about external attack. Since the Devil had failed to destroy the Church through persecution, Cyprian noted, he had devised a new method of assault in which the Christians themselves accomplished his purposes by causing dissensions and schisms in the Church.

In addition to schismatics like Novatian (fl. c. 250), one of the most frequent sources of discord and dissension in the Church was the group known as Confessors. These were the Christians who had witnessed to their faith in the face of persecution, many of them undergoing severe torture but without actually being put to death. It was natural that the Confessors should be accorded an exalted position in the Church, but often, as Cyprian discovered, the honors and powers which were bestowed upon them—particularly the power to grant pardon to those who had apostatized during the persecutions—interfered with the established order and discipline of the Church. Cyprian regarded any usurpation of clerical prerogatives by the Confessors as a breach of the unity of the Church and refused to consider the conventicles which formed around the Confessors as expressions of the true Church. The Confessors, like all Christians, were expected to submit to the established authorities and officials of the Church rather than cause discord by presuming to possess powers which belonged only to the clergy.

The passages in the *De unitate* which deal with the Confessors are particularly significant, for they indicate that for Cyprian the unity which he was so anxious to preserve depended mainly upon submission to the visible authorities and officials of the Church. A heroic witness to the faith was completely meaningless unless it was made by one who belonged to the visible organization presided over by a legitimate bishop. Even if a schismatic should be put to death confessing the name of Christ, he could not be saved, for nothing could atone for the great sin of breaking the unity of the Church except a return to the organization which embodied that unity.

For Cyprian, any refusal to conform to the established episcopal structure of the Church was construed as an act of apostasy or adultery. There could be no possible justification for deserting the Church which was presided over by legitimate bishops, since Cyprian held it to be axiomatic that the presence of a legitimate bishop meant the presence of Christ. It was, of course, equally axiomatic that to be separated from the bishop and the unity which he personified was to be separated from Christ.

The motives for leaving the Church which Cyprian most frequently imputed to the schismatics were pride and greed. If the schismatics had been motivated by charity rather than by personal ambition, they would have been willing to submit themselves to the Church and thus preserve its unity. From what we know about the schismatic groups which sprang up in North Africa and Rome in the third century there is no reason to dispute the unworthy and basically selfish motives which Cyprian imputed to them. Thus, it is possible to sympathize, to a degree, with the rigid attitude which he took toward these particular groups. It is not so easy, however, to sympathize with Cyprian's complete identification of the unity of the Church with its visible organization and his conclusion that every protest against and departure from its organization places one outside the saving purpose of the Lord of the Church.

EXTANT FRAGMENTS OF THE WORKS OF DIONYSIUS

Author: Dionysius the Great (c.200-c.265)
Type of work: Theology of the early Church
First transcribed: Third century

PRINCIPAL IDEAS ADVANCED

The notion of an earthly, thousand-year reign of Christ is not supported by Scripture; however, the canonicity of the book of Revelation is not to be rejected, since its deeper meaning is found in a nonliteral sense which underlies its words.

The author of the book of Revelation was not the Apostle John, but an inspired person called John, as can be ascertained by a comparison between the style of both the gospel and the epistles of the Apostle John and the style of Revelation.

It is further alleged that the universe in which we live is not the result of the chance collision of atoms moving in space but is ordered by the providential power of the omnipotent Deity that brought it into being.

For our knowledge of the career of Dionysius the Great, Bishop of Alexandria, we are indebted to the sixth and seventh books of Eusebius's *Historia ecclesiastica* and the fourteenth book of his *Praeparatio evangelica,* as well as to other references in Jerome, Athanasius, and Basil. Only fragments remain of Dionysius's many theological treatises. What remains, however, is of importance to us in that the *Extant Fragments of the Works of Dionysius* provides the historian of Christianity with a valuable account of the life of the Church in the third century.

Dionysius was born of heathen parents. He studied pagan philosophy and later embraced Christianity under the influence of Origen's teaching. In about 232, Dionysius succeeded Heracles as the head of the catechetical school in Alexandria, and he later became the Bishop of that city in about 247, an office which he held until his death, about 265. His tenure as Bishop was far from tranquil, for the period in which he held office was marked by persecution and theological controversy. Dionysius was himself arrested during the Decian persecution and was freed by a fortunate uprising of the populace of a rural district through which he was being transported. During the persecution under Valerian, which began in 257, Dionysius was driven into exile for two or three years. On other occasions he was forced to deal with pestilence and famine as well as civil conflicts.

Dionysius also played a prominent role in the ecclesiastical controversy of his day. He served as arbitrator in a dispute concerning the rebaptism of heretics, and he zealously opposed the Sabellian heresy, although in a manner which later led him to acknowledge his own errors. In all his activities Dionysius displayed an independent spirit of investigation which won him the respect of his contemporaries. He was held in the highest esteem for his learning, moderation, and remarkably productive pen.

The most important of his writings

are his *Treatise on the Promises, A Book on Nature,* and *A Work Against the Sabellians.* Two large abstracts of the *Treatise on the Promises,* written in two books against Nepos, have been preserved by Eusebius.

Nepos was an Egyptian bishop who interpreted certain promises of the Scriptures in such a manner as to lend support to a literal thousand year period on earth that would be replenished with corporeal pleasures. His work entitled the *Refutation of the Allegorists* sought to establish his view of the millennial period on the basis of the New Testament book of Revelation.

Dionysius sharply attacked Nepos's opinion that Christ will establish a temporal reign on earth; at the same time, in a spirit of Christian love, Dionysius expressed his appreciation of Nepos's faith and labors.

The situation in the Church was such, Dionysius declared, that errors had to be opposed, for truth is the primary concern of those who follow Christ. Certain teachers, he contended, held that the law and the prophets are of no importance; they disparaged the gospels and the epistles, and did not concede that the simpler brethren had any conceptions of Christ's appearing in His glory and true divinity, or of our own resurrection from the dead and of our being united to Him at the last day. Such teachers led the people to hope only for what is trivial and corruptible.

Christians ought to be satisfied to accept only that which can be established by the demonstrations and teachings of the Holy Scriptures, Dionysius wrote. What cannot be so established ought neither to be discussed, taught,

nor mentioned, if the harmony of the brethren is to be maintained.

The book of Revelation had been the cause of much dissension, and Dionysius, writing in the third century, mentions that some had set it aside, repudiated it entirely, and criticized it chapter by chapter. The critics of the book, Dionysius reports, denied that John the Apostle was its author and held that it could not be revelation because it is too difficult to understand. It is alleged that Cerinthus, the founder of a heretical sect, sought to give authority to his own notion that Christ will establish an earthly reign, a sensuous kingdom in which bodily pleasures are satisfied. Cerinthus, therefore, attributed his own opinions to the Apostle John, so that in fact the book of Revelation was not written by an Apostle but by a heretic.

Dionysius was, however, unwilling to reject the canonicity of Revelation, although he acknowledged that he was himself unable to comprehend its full import. Many brethren value it highly, Dionysius writes, and it undoubtedly contains much hidden and wonderful intelligence, with a deeper meaning underlying the words. Its authorship is not the work of the Apostle John, the Son of Zebedee and the brother of James, as is evident from a study of its style when compared with the Gospel and epistles of John the Apostle. It was, rather, written by a holy and inspired writer whose name was John. The Apostle John nowhere affixes his name to his writings. Which John wrote the book of Revelation is uncertain, but the fact that its author is unknown in no way disparages its authority or makes it the object of ridicule.

In his *Book on Nature,* preserved in part by Eusebius in his *Praeparatio evangelica,* Dionysius opposes the school of Epicurus, which denied the existence of Providence and insisted that the universe is made up of atomic bodies.

Dionysius argued that it is folly to attribute the universe to an infinite unoriginated matter that holds sway without the aid of divine Providence. To make the constructions of the universe the work of a chance combination of an infinite number of atoms jostling one another in a space of infinite vastness overlooks the analogies even of the small familiar things which come under observation. For no object of any utility, which is fitted to be serviceable, is made by mere chance, but comes into being by design, and is wrought by the skill of the hand, so as to serve its proper use. The notion of chance combinations of atoms is unable to explain the design and order of the world that is experienced by the senses. It is an idle speculation, beyond all observable experience and conception. The Christian is far wiser who confesses to God that the order of the world must be attributed to God Himself. Referring to the atomists, Dionysius writes, "But when they assert now that those things of grace and beauty, which they declare to be textures finely wrought out of atoms, are fabricated spontaneously by these bodies without either wisdom or perception in them, who can endure to hear them talk in such terms of those unregulated atoms, than which even the spider, that plies its proper craft of itself, is gifted with more sagacity."

The body of man and of the universe in all its parts was composed by the providence of an all-wise Father and maker, not by a blind deified nature, Dionysius concludes; the very heavens declare God's glory and show forth his handiwork.

The remaining works of Dionysius that we possess have been handed down to us by Athanasius and Basil and consist for the most part of certain unguarded statements made during the Sabellian controversy, together with letters and a few exegetical fragments.

THE DIVINE INSTITUTES

Author: Lucius Caecilius Firmianus Lactantius (c.240-c.320)
Type of work: Christian apologetics
First transcribed: 304-313

Principal Ideas Advanced

The chief sources of error in human life are pagan polytheism, which ignores or denies the true God, and philosophy, which is undermined by its own contradictions.

True wisdom is found in the religion derived from God the Lord and Father and from Jesus Christ, and this religion rewards man for virtue with the highest good, immortality.

Justice, or true equity, which, together with the true worship of God, was banished under paganism, has been restored by Jesus Christ.

The world looks now toward its own destruction and the judgment of Christ over the virtuous and the wicked in His thousand-year Kingdom.

Lactantius was one of several pagan teachers and writers who became important spokesmen for Christianity after conversion in later life. As an apologist, he employed all the skills acquired as a teacher of rhetoric in the preparation of one of the longest and most eloquent treatises on Christianity up to his day. The *Divine Institutes* was directed to the Emperor Constantine (c.288-337) whom Lactantius later (c.317) served as tutor for Constantine's son Crispus. The work, in seven books, was intended to inform the emperor of the errors of paganism, the injustices done to Christianity, and the nature of true religion and worship. It is really the first systematic account in Latin of the Christian attitude toward life, although it stands in a tradition shaped by the earlier Latin-speaking fathers Tertullian (c.160-220), Minucius Felix (fl.195), Cyprian (c.200-258), and Lactantius' own teacher, Arnobius of Sicca (fl.300). Its distinctive aim was to use a high level of style and language and classical erudition to appeal to literate readers. The success of Lactantius in achieving this aim brought him the epithet, the Christian Cicero, and was to make him very popular among the humanists of Renaissance Italy.

The first two books of the *Divinae institutiones* form a concentrated attack on the errors of paganism. Polytheism is the root of all these errors. It is obvious, writes Lactantius, that there can, logically speaking, be only one God, and the prophets, poets, philosophers, Sibylline Oracles, and Her-

mes Trismegistus (the Egyptian god Thoth) may be adduced as evidence. Homer and Hesiod show us how unworthy the lives of the gods are, and the Stoic interpretations fail to make them more acceptable. If the gods are merely apotheosized men, as seems often to be the case, they do not deserve to be worshiped. Indeed there is nothing about the pagan deities deserving of worship. Their images are made by men, and, if anyone, man should be worshiped as their maker. Since everything in nature and the universe points to God, a right exercise of reason would lead men away from polytheism.

In all this discussion of paganism some reference is made to the Bible in regard to the creation of the world and the fallen angels, but the main body of references is to classical literature and philosophy, of which Lactantius has an excellent command. He openly acknowledges his preference for authorities that will convince an unconverted audience. At the same time he does not hesitate to chastise the pagan writers for leading men into error.

The third book of the *Institutes* takes up the "false wisdom" of the philosophers, another significant source of error. Lactantius stresses, as does the Bible, that truth is superior to eloquence, although he does not hesitate to employ eloquence where appropriate. Insofar as philosophy seeks the truth, it is made up of "knowledge" and conjecture, but the latter is, of course, to be dismissed outright. When the "knowledge" of philosophy is then examined, it is found that the different systems of philosophy contradict or deny one another, thereby disproving themselves completely. Only one philosopher, Arcesilas (c.315-c.240 B.C.); recognized that all other philosophers know nothing. He therefore changed the character of philosophy into complete skepticism by denying even the possibility of knowledge; but here he went too far, Lactantius claims, for truth is possible in dependence on God.

Turning next to moral philosophy, Lactantius maintains that the chief good, the *summum bonum*, must be something peculiar to man and the human soul. It must be something which requires knowledge and virtue to be achieved. He concludes that man's chief good is therefore the immortality promised by religion, and not any physical pleasures or even virtue as such. In respect to achieving this good, philosophy generally errs, and philosophers themselves set bad examples in their lives. (Even his beloved Cicero comes in for Lactantius' censure.) Only divine instruction bestows true wisdom, Lactantius insists. To depend on nature or fortune is simply another mistake of the philosophers, for neither nature nor fortune can reward virtue with immortality as God can. (One should note that Lactantius, in rebuking the philosophers, condemns the foolishness of those who believe that the earth is round.)

With the fourth book the emphasis turns to the positive statement of Christian teaching; namely, "true wisdom" and religion. These two, wisdom and religion, are one harmonious whole for Lactantius. They spring as two streams from one fountain; namely, God the Father and Lord. As proof of this argument Lactantius adduces the antiquity of the Old Testament Prophets, who are also witnesses to God's Son, Jesus Christ, through whom true religion is revealed. The Sibylline Oracles and Hermes Trismegistus are again impartial witnesses to Christ. There follows a discussion of the birth of Jesus as the Word of God and then of the preparations in the history of Israel for His earthly birth. The Incarnation receives a good deal of explanation, for the work is being presented to a pagan audience. The life, miracles, passion, death, resurrection, and ascension of Jesus are also narrated and related to prophecy. In the conclusion to the fourth book, Lactantius explains the union of Father and Son and the dangers of heresies.

The two books that follow, on justice and true worship, are often considered the finest of the entire *Institutes*. In Book V the fundamental argument is that Christianity has suffered unjustly under paganism but that true justice will emerge victorious under Christ. After paying tribute to his predecessors, Tertullian, Minucius Felix, and Cyprian, Lactantius sets forth a general defense against all anti-Christian writings. He recounts the decline of justice under the pagan gods, who gave free reign to all sorts of vices. With Jesus, however, justice is being restored because the real origin of justice is in the true religion or piety which Jesus taught. Since only God by His eternal reward can sustain justice, all men must trust Him. The basic principle of justice for Lactantius is equity. Since equity is no respecter of persons or earthly compensations, the Christians alone can remain just and pious despite afflictions. They alone can practice full equity because they alone trust in God, who rewards them.

A similar moralistic emphasis on rewards is found in Lactantius' discussion of true worship. Religion or worship or service to God is the way of virtue. It is the chief duty of man and leads him to Heaven. The way of vice leads, of course, to Hell. All these things are worked out under the unchangeable divine law. Indeed, virtue apart from God is in vain because there is no reward of immortality attached to it.

There is a second aspect of worship or religion; namely, that directed toward one's fellow man. Here the principle is mercy or kindness which forms the bond of human society. Without mercy, vice and error prevail. Yet even acts of mercy are predicated in large measure on God's rewards. Lactantius appeals to the rich at this point with the argument that the greatest advantage of riches is the ability to do deeds of charity.

The sixth book closes with a discussion of human affections and passions and their right use or application. Above all others, patience is exalted as a Christian virtue. In this connection too, the pleasures of the senses are considered and very nearly condemned as a form of earthly recompense that is enjoyed only at the expense of the heavenly. The note of revulsion at the excesses of pagan society, a revulsion which characterizes most early Christian writers, is sounded quite forcefully by Lactantius. Thus, this sixth book seems less a discussion of worship than an extension of the discussion of religion begun in the fifth book and entitled, "Justice." True and complete religion is just and pious and consist in devoted service to God.

The motif of immortality is continued and expanded in the final book of the *Divine Institutes* on the happy life. The end of the world, toward which Lactantius looks, will bring heavenly rewards for the blessed and hellish punishments for the condemned. After demonstrating that the world must have an end and after exposing the errors of the philosophers in this matter, Lactantius discourses on the immortality of the soul of man, for whom the whole creation exists. Man, in turn, exists or, more correctly, was made to acknowledge and worship God, and for this worship he is rewarded. The pattern of creation is based on the six days of Genesis I, and so the world will come to an end after 6000 years and the 1000-year Kingdom of Christ will begin. The end of the world will be marked, of course, by wars, natural disasters, and false prophets. It will also see a loosing of the Devil and, in effect, two judgment days. One of the most unworthy concepts of Lactantius appears in this book when he declares that the wicked will receive indestructible bodies so that they can endure the torments of eternal fire forever. The *Institutes* closes with an exhortation to virtue.

However eloquent a spokesman for Christianity Lactantius may have been, he was clearly not a theologian. He is obviously ante-Nicene in his Christology. He has no doctrine of or place for the Holy Spirit in his writings. The Church and the Sacraments are hardly mentioned at all. Nor is it surprising that he never occupied an official ecclesiastical position, for he was perhaps sixty years old at the time of his conversion. His zeal to do something for Christianity must, however, be admired. The special talents which, as a layman, he did possess, he gave freely to the writing of the *Institutes*. If this work is often moralistic and theologically superficial, nonsacramental, and even unorthodox, it nevertheless reveals what many people took to be the general intent of the Christian faith. That such a work found a place in the Church of the fourth century is indicated by the preparation of an *Epitome of the Institutes* a few years after its completion. It remains true, on the other hand, that the need for apologetics was lessened after recognition of the Church by the Empire, and the writings of Lactantius do not figure in the great theological controversies of the following generations.

THE INCARNATION OF THE WORD OF GOD

Author: Saint Athanasius (c.296-373)
Type of work: Christology
First transcribed: c.318

Principal Ideas Advanced

Contrary to the opinions of unbelievers, the Incarnation of the divine Word (Logos) was entirely plausible and fitting.

Out of love for men, and in order to uphold the divine purpose, salvation has been accomplished by the same One who created in the beginning.

Through the Incarnation, the progressive sinful degeneration of mankind has been checked, human nature has been restored to the image of God, and the knowledge of God has spread abroad in the world, awakening faith, hope, and love.

The crucifixion of the Incarnate Word was necessary to preserve the consistency of the divine judgment upon man's willful disobedience, but in the Word's death and resurrection, death itself was destroyed.

Athanasius is revered in the history of the Church as the saintly orthodox champion in the long, hard, and eventually successful fourth century struggle against Arianism. The latter maintained that Christ was the incarnation of an intermediate, secondary deity, "like," but not one with, the Highest. The teaching that prevailed was that of the Nicene Creed, that the God united with man in Christ is the same as—"of one substance with"—the ultimate and only God. But between the Council of Nicea in 325, and the Council of Constantinople in 381, the issue was often in grave doubt. During these critical decades Athanasius gave the orthodox party decisive intellectual and moral leadership. Exiled five times, he was by 366 at last triumphant and died seven years later as Patriarch of Alexandria, his native city. From earliest youth Athanasius was no stranger to persecution, having lived through the severe one launched in 303 by the Roman emperor Diocletian. The behavior of Christians facing death made a deep impression on him, as *The Incarnation of the Word of God* shows. Most scholars believe that Athanasius wrote it about 318, when he was barely twenty, and before the outbreak of the Arian conflict.

One of two small treatises (the other being the *Contra gentes*) prepared for the instruction of a recent convert, *The Incarnation of the Word of God* undertakes a "brief statement of the faith of Christ and of the manifestation of His Godhead to us." This purpose, drawing upon what fellow Christians could take for granted, enhances its value as an expression of what the faith was in the Alexandria of that time. The work is not a systematic treatise on all aspects of the Incarnation; the main theme is the redemption of the world by the Incarnate Word; redemption is *theiosis*, deification.

In the companion treatise (the *Contra gentes*), after discussing heathen idol worship and how it arose, Athanasius had sketched the rudiments of the Christian belief in the divinity of the Word (Logos), through whom God the Father creates and governs the universe. Now, he tells Marcarius, the convert whom he is instructing, they must take the further step of considering the Word's becoming man. This mystery, which "the Jews traduce, the Greeks deride, but we adore," was indeed the center of the Christian faith. The belief in a creative, all-governing Word was not exclusively Christian. The uniqueness and the scandal of the Christian claim was that this Word had taken flesh and appeared among us as Jesus Christ, that He had been crucified, had died and been buried, and had risen in the body. It is these things, decried by un-believers as impossible, unfitting, and ridiculous, which Athanasius sets out to explain as altogether possible, appropriate, and necessary.

The indispensable backdrop of the Incarnation is the Christian doctrine of creation. Against the Epicurean theory of purposelessness, the limiting matter of Plato, and the intervening, evil artificer of the Gnostics, Athanasius stresses that the universe was created "out of non-existence absolute and utter," according to the unimpeded purpose of the one sovereign God, acting through His Word, or Image, the Son. Thus, *"the renewal of creation has been wrought by the Self-same Word Who made it in the beginning."* This is a crucial step in the argument, since it establishes the ground for regarding the Incarnation as a rectifying and conserving action, undertaken upon the basis of the original divine purpose. From the beginning, the creation, and man in particular, is God's business. Therefore it is not implausible, but entirely appropriate, that God should undertake to reclaim and restore, by whatever means necessary, that which is originally His.

Created to know and worship God, man's natural mortality was in abeyance so long as he remained centered upon God. But ". . . the will of man could turn either way . . ." and, at the Devil's tempting, turned to violation of the divine commandment. God had warned concerning the forbidden fruit, "in the day that ye do eat, ye shall surely die." (Genesis 2:17). Thus, "men, having turned from the contemplation of God to evil of their own devising, had come inevitably under the law of death. . . . In process of becoming corrupted entirely . . . ," the human race faced extinction. Athanasius' thought is not that God takes vindictive action, but that man, having forfeited the divine presence, deprives himself of the sources of his being. The Author of all being could have replenished man's being, but the irrevocability of the divine judgment stood in the way. Yet what was happening was contrary to God's loving purpose. "It would . . . have been unthinkable that God should go back upon His word, and that man, having trespassed, should not die. But it was equally monstrous that beings which had once shared the nature of the Word should die." In this dilemma is the rationale of the Incarnation.

Three things were needed. First, the divine judgment must be upheld; death must occur in consequence of sin. Second, there must be a renewal of man's being, to reverse the progressive deterioration and to restore the divine image. Third, the knowledge of God must be taught throughout the world. Only the Creator Logos could meet these needs. "For He alone, being Word of the Father and above all, was able . . . to recreate all, and worthy to suffer on behalf of all. . . ." And only He "Whose ordering of the universe reveals the Father . . . [could] renew the same teaching." Since in His divine nature the Word could not suffer or die, He fashioned, from the virgin, a human and mortal body. This assumption of corporeal humanity not only enabled Him to meet the sentence of death in man's stead but also to renew life and health where it was needed, in man's actual, bodily existence. At the same time, the teaching or revealing purpose was served, in that the invisible and universal truth became visibly centered in His personal concreteness.

Athanasius was mindful of the paradox in the thought that the omnipresent Word has become incarnate at a particular place. He explains that the universality of the Word is not diminished by special presence in a human body, nor are the world-governing operations of the Word suspended. The Incarnation does not entail an adulteration of the divine; the Word was in no way changed by the virgin birth. Nor does being in the body defile Him; rather He sanctifies it. It is the same as with His cosmic immanence: "For His being in everything does not mean that He shares the nature of everything, only that he gives all things their being and sustains them in it." Sunlight is not tainted by, but purifies, what it touches. The Word's divinity was not in fact, even within His incarnate existence, held to human limits. By His *ordinary* acts He showed that He was truly in the body, as was necessary. But, Athanasius maintains, by His *extraordinary* acts—miracles showing power over nature, demons, sickness, and death— He proved His divinity.

After explaining its general purpose, Athanasius turns to a more detailed consideration of the death of Christ. It is clear that Christ died for *all*—to pay the debt of the whole race. But two components mingle in the conception of how the Cross accomplishes its result. On the one hand, Athanasius brings into view the surpassing *worth* of Christ as the Incarnate Word, whereby the one death, as it were, has the value of all. On the other hand, we are to think of death itself as being expended and destroyed by union with the Word. Christ, by virtue of His human body, could and really did die; that is, He absorbed death into Himself and swallowed it up: "Thus it happened that two opposite marvels took place at once: the death of all was consummated in the Lord's body; yet, because the Word was in it, death and corruption were in the same act utterly abolished." The death of our bodies still occurs, but no longer under condemnation. Like seeds cast into the earth, we shall rise again in God's good time, and we shall partake in the general resurrection. Meanwhile, we already experience the renewal of life in Christ.

Addressing the circumstances of Christ's death, Athanasius attempts to render plausible even the details. Violence was necessary, because Christ would not have died naturally. The public crucifixion forestalled the ready doubt that might have arisen concerning a resurrection after a private death. The shamefulness was to show that the victory encompassed all, not merely better, kinds of death. It would have been unbecoming for Christ to die by His own hand, nor would it have been fitting for Him to flinch from the aggression of His foes. The fact that His purpose was also to teach by words and deeds explains why the atoning death did not occur earlier in His life. As for the entombment, it was just long enough to establish that natural corruption *should* have set in, and yet not so long as to allow the scattering of the witnesses or the fading of vivid memory. In such reasonings, Athanasius mixes the small and the large; every item of the Gospel story is precious to him.

Special attention is given also to the Resurrection. The Word itself, of course, could not die. Nor, in Athanasius' view, did the mortal body experience corruption. As the instrument through which the sting of death

was suffered and overcome, the body lay for a time under death's sway. But the infinite life of the Word resurged, as it were, through the body; in a mighty demonstration of victory over death, Christ's body was raised as the first-fruits of the general resurrection still to come: "How could the destruction of death have been manifested at all, had not the Lord's body been raised?" But now the fact that death's power has been broken is plain to see in the fearlessness of Christian martyrdom. Men, women, and children who previously shrank from danger now mock at death's impotence. In such valiant faith, Athanasius feels the living presence of the triumphant Christ. "Dead men cannot take effective action. . . ." But "the Saviour is working mightily among men. . . ."

The last third of the book deals with refutation of the Jews and the gentiles. Against the Jews, the basis of argument is the Old Testament. Their own Scriptures show that the characteristics of the expected Messiah correspond to Jesus alone. The Jews say they are still waiting. But for what? What more could they ask than what Jesus has already accomplished? As for the gentiles, Athanasius first focuses upon objections to the idea of incarnation, restating earlier arguments for its plausibility. He stresses the analogy of the Word using the world as His instrument—a thought acceptable to Greeks. But if the whole world, why not a specialized organ in the world? It scandalizes no one that a personality, immanent in the whole body, confers on the tongue a unique expressive role. Should God have used sun or moon for a grander demonstration? But He accommodated himself to our weakness; and, besides, nothing had erred but man. Beyond such considerations, Athanasius appeals finally to what is actually happening. Formerly, every place was full of fraud, magic, madness, and savagery. But now, "where the Saviour is named, every demon is driven out." Christ brings peace, unity, joy, and love throughout the world. He proves his Lordship in that He reigns. In this context occurs the famous utterance: "He, indeed, assumed humanity, that we might become God." It implies, not that essences were blended, but that Christ's victory cre-ated a new situation for all mankind.

From the perspective of later thought, it may appear that Athanasius does not do justice to the full manhood of Christ. Some of his ideas are not fully defined, and his discussion of the Bible is, of course, precritical. But the claim of this small book to a place in the classic literature of the faith is unimpeachable. Besides its immense value as an epitome of the Patristic period, there is an assurance and an enthusiasm about it which illuminates Christ for every age.

ECCLESIASTICAL HISTORY

Author: Eusebius of Caesarea (c.260-c.339)
Type of work: Church history
First transcribed: 324

PRINCIPAL IDEAS ADVANCED

Christianity proclaims the truth of the divine Logos, who was present in creation, who revealed Himself to Israel through the prophets, and who was incarnated in the person of Jesus Christ.

Satan has opposed this truth by hardening the hearts of the Jews, by raising up heresies and schisms, and by stirring up persecutions.

God has defeated the efforts of Satan; the Jews have been punished; heretics have been refuted; and persecutors have been overthrown.

The Church has preserved the truth unchanged from the time of the Apostles.

The recognition of the Christian religion by Constantine marks the beginning of a universal reign of righteousness and peace.

Eusebius explains at the beginning of his *Ecclesiastical History* the method and scope of his work. It is his purpose to bring together memoirs, letters, and various other writings (including state papers) which will preserve a record of the Church's struggles from its beginnings until its official recognition by the Emperor Constantine (c.288-337). Materials are included which record the succession of bishops, important transactions of the Church, the work of evangelists and apologists, and the heroism of martyrs. To round out the story, an account is also given of the opposition which the Church received from the Jews, from heretics, and from kings and emperors. Although Eusebius does not say so, an important part of his purpose was apologetic: to prove by means of historical events that the Church is indeed a divine foundation, and that it is God's providence which has guided it to victory over paganism.

Eusebius begins by pointing out that Christianity is not a novelty. The divine Logos which was incarnated in Jesus Christ was present at the creation of the world, and He revealed His will from ancient times to the people of Israel through Moses and the prophets. The name "Christian" is new, as is also the "new race" which that name signifies. But, he says, "Even if we are clearly new, and this really fresh name of Christians is recently known among all nations, nevertheless our life and method of conduct, in accordance with the precepts of religion, has not been recently invented by us, but from the first creation of man, so to speak, has been upheld by the natural concepts of the men of old who were the friends of God." Eusebius views the story of God's work among men in much the same way as does the author of the Fourth Gospel. He writes, "The light of the truth and the divine Logos himself, which has shown from God upon men by growing up on the earth and dwelling among his own Apostles, was overcoming all things in the might of victory."

But, as John also records, "the light shineth in darkness, and the darkness comprehended it not." From the beginning, says Eusebius, Satan, out of envy, has blinded the hearts of men and stirred up enmity in them against God's truth and against those in whom it is revealed. Thus, the Jews, who in the first dispensation often put to death their prophets, demanded the death of Christ, and afterwards persecuted his followers. Eusebius quotes at length from the writings of the Jewish historian Josephus (c.37-c.95), to show both the wickedness of latter-day Jews and the horrible punishment that was visited upon them as a reward for their iniquity and "their impiety against the Christ of God." God did not permit Jerusalem to be destroyed for a whole generation after the death of Christ because, during that time, James, the Lord's brother, and many other disciples still resided in Jerusalem. But the crime of the Jews against James, when they threw him from the pinnacle of the temple and then clubbed him to death, was the final critical act; and God gave the city over to the horrors of famine, which Josephus so graphically describes.

"Like brilliant lamps," says Eusebius, "the churches were now shining throughout the world, and faith in our Savior and Lord Jesus Christ was flourishing among all mankind, when the Devil who hates what is good, as the enemy of truth, ever most hostile to men's salvation, turned all his devices against the church." The opposition of the Jews had not noticeably slowed down the Church's advance. Therefore, Satan employed "sorcerers and deceivers" in an effort to turn men away from the truth. The first of these mentioned by Eusebius is Simon Magus, who, having professed Christianity in his native Samaria, went to Rome and claimed that he was himself a god. Simon, according to Eusebius, was the "first author of all heresy." From him "there proceeded a certain snake-like power with two mouths and a double head," the gnostic heresies of Saturninus and Basilides. But God's grace "quickly extinguished the flames of the Evil One." Peter's advent at Rome sufficed to bring an end to Simon Magus's pretensions; and against the Gnostics there came into being a band of apologists "fighting with great eloquence" for the glory of the Church, and providing by their writings a permanent refutation of these particular heresies. There were, of course, other heresies besides Gnosticism, and Eusebius records them all, together with the refutations which Christian writers brought against them. In these parts, as elsewhere, Eusebius has rendered an invaluable service for the historian of dogma, preserving extracts and fragments of numerous works which have since been lost.

The third major kind of opposition to the Church was the recurrent persecution of believers at the hands of Roman authorities. Eusebius, who, through his friendship with Constantine, had access to government archives, preserves an accurate record of the state's fluctuating policy toward the Church, and he includes moving accounts written by Christians of the faithfulness and courage of their own martyrs. It is to Eusebius, for example, that we owe the preservation of the record of the Gallic martyrs, most celebrated of whom is the slave girl Blandina. Eusebius contrasts the Church's warfare with that recorded in other kinds of history where men are honored who stained themselves with the blood of countless murders for the sake of patriotism, wealth, and posterity. Our wars, he says, are waged peacefully for peace of soul, for truth, and piety; and our histories are glorious for struggles won over demons and unseen adversaries.

Eusebius suggests that the last and most furious of persecutions against the Church was, in some measure, a punishment drawn by the Church upon itself. Prior to the time of Diocletian (245-313) and Galerius (?-311), the Church had enjoyed unprecedented prosperity; but as a result of greater freedom, pride and sloth entered the Christian fellowship, and envy and strife divided it into factions. Then it was that "the divine judgment" descended. At first the persecutions were mild and sporadic; but when the Church was heedless of these chastisements, God permitted the persecutions to increase, as he did in the time of the prophet Jeremiah. For ten years, persecution raged, rising to unprecedented degrees, until God changed the minds of the rulers and suddenly brought it to an end by afflicting the person of the Emperor Galerius.

Eusebius lived through the final era of the Church's persecutions, and he seems to have been imprisoned at Caesarea, but to have escaped torture. It is believed by scholars that his *Ecclesiastical History* was written during the final years of the Galerian persecution, and that the work was originally intended to end with Book VIII, which records Galerius's Edict of Toleration (311). When persecutions were revived under Maximin (?-314), and later by Licinius (250-324), the work was extended through two further books. In its final form, *The Ecclesiastical History* concludes with Constantine's victory over Licinius, in 323. Constantine, in Eusebius's opinion, was the human embodiment of all that is regal and humane. The *Ecclesiastical History* omits the story, told by Eusebius in his *Life of Constantine,* of the vision in which Constantine saw the shining cross inscribed with the words

"In this Sign Conquer"; but it relates that, after the victory over Maxentius (?-312), a victory which the vision heralded, Constantine erected in the Roman Forum a statue of himself bearing the cross and the words, "By this salutary sign, the true proof of bravery, I saved and delivered your city from the yoke of the tyrant!"

Although Eusebius was inferior to Origen and Augustine in his speculative power, he was nevertheless a competent scholar whose learning was matched by a fine sense of balance and perspective. Through the favor of Constantine he was in a unique position to get from all parts of the Empire whatever materials he needed, and he made good use of his opportunities. It is noteworthy that, while he occasionally cites from sources in which accounts of miracles abound (for example, the apocryphal account of the Apostle Thaddaeus, which was found in the royal archive of Edessa), reports of miracles are almost completely absent from his own work and from the authentic materials which he cites; this is in striking contrast to the practice in the writing of medieval histories and chronicles.

Eusebius was interested, on the one hand, in establishing strict continuity in the development of the Church through the centuries, and, on the other, in preserving the unity of the Christian fellowship in his own day. He was further persuaded that there is no inherent conflict between Christianity and creation, that Christian history represents a victory of Christ over the powers of darkness, and that the Church need not be at odds with society or the state, for the Church continues in this world to insure Christ's victory.

As a historian, Eusebius had no wish to trace any developments within Christianity. From his point of view, Christian truth is eternal, and any alteration of the revelation handed down by the Apostles is the work of the Devil. Eusebius's motive for establishing the succession of bishops in Jerusalem, Rome, Antioch, Alexandria, and other leading centers was mainly to show that the Church in his day was the same as that founded by Christ. For similar reasons, Eusebius was interested in establishing the canon of the New Testament, and he cites the opinions of second and third century writers wherever they bear upon this subject. In Eusebius's day, the four Gospels, the Acts of the Apostles, the fourteen epistles of Paul (including Hebrews, which, however, was sometimes said not to be Paul's), and the first epistles of Peter and of John were admitted without dispute. The remainder were contested by some teachers. It was uniformly agreed, however, that none of the other early writings (such as the *Shepherd of Hermas* and the *Epistle of Barnabus*) was apostolic.

Eusebius's interest in establishing the New Testament canon led him to cite Papias (c. 60-130), whose testimony to the authorship of the four Gospels is of great importance to modern Biblical scholars. Papias relates that he heard from the lips of men who heard it from the Apostles themselves that Mark based his Gospel on the preaching of Peter, and that Matthew "collected the oracles in the Hebrew language." Papias mentions, as one of the sub-apostolic Fathers, the presbyter John of Ephesus. This suggests to Eusebius, as it does to some modern students, the hypothesis that tradition confused this John with the Apostle John, who is also supposed to have resided at Ephesus, and that some of the writings attributed to the Apostle may have been written by the presbyter. Little is known of Papias except what Eusebius records of him, and Eusebius would probably not have mentioned him were it not for the light Papias sheds on Biblical origins. Eusebius describes Papias as "a man of very little intelligence," mainly because Papias took literally the teaching of the Apocalypse that the Resurrection would precede a millennial reign of Christ on earth.

The millenarianism of Papias, the enthusiasm of Montanus, the innovations of Paul of Samasota and Sabellius, and the "puritanism" of Novatian were all regarded by Eusebius as threats to the unity of the Church and its mission in the world. As a bishop of Caesarea (after 313), and as a confidant of the Emperor Constantine, Eusebius labored throughout his life to keep peace and harmony in the Church. The Arian controversy was just beginning at the time when the *Ecclesiastical History* was being completed. In the ecclesiastical counsels which decided the fate of Arius, Eusebius inclined toward a mediating position. Another issue which divided the Church in his day was the question whether those could be readmitted to Christian fellowship who had denied Christ during the persecutions. From the time of Cyprian, this question had been a lively one. Eusebius, as we may suppose, favored the inclusivist position.

Eusebius owed his theological position very largely to the followers of Origen, notably Dionysius of Alexandria (d.c. 264), sometimes called Dionysius the Great. Of his writings,

much esteemed in ancient times, only fragments remain, chiefly from his epistles as quoted by Eusebius. These deal mostly with the issue raised by Novatian, who, with his followers, refused fellowship to Christians who had apostatized during the Decian persecutions, and with the more general question as to whether, as Cyprian (c.200-258) had recommended, apostates be rebaptized before they were readmitted. Dionysius was in favor of tolerance, and he advised that, so far as baptism was concerned, local tradition should be the rule. In Africa, where rebaptizing heretics was a tradition, he advised that it be allowed, for, he says, "I do not dare to overturn their decisions and involve them in strife and contention." Dionysius is also remembered for opposing Sabellius, who, in the third century, brought into controversy the Trinitarian belief concerning God, which was to loom so large in the fourth and fifth centuries. Sabellius taught that the three "persons" of the Godhead are merely three ways in which God reveals himself to men. Against this view, Dionysius not merely insisted on the essential distinction between the Father, Son, and Holy Spirit within the Godhead, but he subordinated the Son to the Father in a way which suggests the opposite heresy of Arianism. However, when Dionysius of Rome protested against the Alexandrian Dionysius' statement, and insisted that the Son is of the same substance with the Father (*homoousios*), the latter agreed to this formulation.

Eusebius closes the *Ecclesiastical History* on a panegyrical note, praising God the King and Christ the Redeemer that the enemies of righteousness have been removed and the whole human race freed from the oppression of tyrants. The major part of the tenth book consists of an oration delivered by Eusebius at Tyre on the occasion of the rebuilding of one of the Christian basilicas which had been destroyed during the late persecutions. In it he draws copiously from the Scriptures, mainly the Old Testament, which prophesy the final triumph of righteousness over iniquity. It seemed to him, as no doubt it did to the majority of Christians in his day, that the new imperial favor which Constantine had shown toward the Church was indeed the goal toward which mankind had been moving since the beginning

of time. For Eusebius, the basilica at Tyre, originally built to worship God, but laid low by God's enemies, only to be raised up again more magnificently than before by God's grace and the munificence of Constantine, was a parable of mankind, and indeed of the whole universe. He writes: "Such is the great temple which the Word, the great Creator of the Universe, hath builded throughout the whole world beneath the sun, forming again this spiritual image upon earth of those vaults beyond the vaults of heaven; so that by the whole creation and by the rational, living creatures upon earth His Father might be honored and revered."

THE CATECHETICAL LECTURES

Author: Saint Cyril, Bishop of Jerusalem (c.315-386)
Type of work: Catechetical instruction
First transcribed: c.347

Principal Ideas Advanced

The candidate for baptism is to present himself before God in true repentance and humility, making sincere confession of his sins, and in the knowledge that there is one God, the Father of the Lord Jesus Christ, who together with the Holy Spirit, is the rewarder of those who diligently seek Him.

At baptism the sins of the believer are remitted; he receives the regeneration of the Holy Spirit, and symbolically he shares in the burial and Resurrection of the Lord.

Cyril, Archbishop of Jerusalem, played an important role in the life of the Church in the fourth century. His writings include the *Catechetical Lectures,* which exemplifies the care bestowed by the early Christian Church upon the instruction and training of converts before admitting then to baptism. The work consists of a series of

twenty-three lectures delivered extemporaneously and probably transcribed by one of the audience. The lectures are divided into two groups; the first eighteen are addressed to persons desirous of receiving baptism, while the last five lectures are addressed to the newly baptized. This work is an important source of information concerning the early liturgy and the local creed of Jerusalem.

Before receiving baptism, Cyril writes, the candidate, being duly registered and admitted, was required to take a course of instruction and begin a course of penitential discipline. The length of the instruction and training varied. Baptism was to be the completion and seal of a spiritual illumination. The candidate was required to confess his past sins and to be truly repentant. Before being baptized he was exorcised, or cleansed of evil spirits. Exorcism, very important in the ancient Church, was applied to all catechumens. The candidate renounced the Devil and his works, made profession of faith, and then was baptized in the name of the Father, the Son, and the Holy Ghost. It was then customary to anoint the baptized with consecrated ointment, and for the baptized then to receive first communion.

Baptism promised the candidate a new birth of the soul, a remission of offences, and the death of sin. The grace of baptism is not bestowed by God upon the hypocrite, Cyril writes, but solely upon the true believer who has put off the bondage of sin. God sees the heart of the candidate and rejects the hypocrite as unfit for His service, but when He finds someone worthy, God readily gives His grace and the seal of salvation. The catechumen is henceforth to be called a believer, for he is now made a partaker of the truth of God.

To be properly prepared to receive the sacrament of baptism, the catechumen must make a sincere confession. The communion of the Holy Ghost is then bestowed in proportion to each man's faith. True confession of sin is followed by forgiveness and pardon,

for God is merciful to those who repent. The Scriptures afford numerous examples of those who have sinned and repented and been saved. The candidate is to take heart and make confession unto the Lord in order that he may receive the forgiveness of his former sins, be found worthy of the heavenly gift, and, together with all the saints, inherit the Kingdom of Jesus Christ.

To be baptized is to be enrolled in the army of the divine King. He that is baptized with water and is not found worthy by the Spirit does not receive the grace in perfection, nor does the virtuous man who does not receive the seal of water enter into the Kingdom of Heaven. With the exception of martyrs, who even without water receive the Kingdom, every man must be baptized to attain salvation.

True godliness, advises Cyril, consists of virtuous practices and pious doctrines. The latter are not acceptable to God without good works, nor does God accept works which are not perfected by pious doctrines. The candidate for baptism must therefore receive instruction in the faith so that he is not spoiled by false doctrine. It is necessary that he understand that God is one, alone unbegotten, the Father of our Lord Jesus Christ, who was begotten God of God, who is in all things equal to Him who begat, and was before all ages eternally and incomprehensibly begotten of the Father. The candidate is to believe that the only-begotten Son took upon Himself a human nature, was born of a virgin, was of two natures, man in what was seen, and God in what was not seen. He was truly crucified for our sins, was buried, rose again from the dead, ascended into Heaven, and will come again to judge the quick and the dead. The candidate is also to believe in the Holy Spirit, the sanctifier of all. He is to keep the faith and thus to be free of condemnation.

Through belief in one God, all polytheism is excluded; by confessing God's triune nature, every heresy is avoided. God cannot be seen with the eye of flesh; His nature is incomprehensible, but it is possible to attain some comprehension of His power from His works. From the Scriptures we know that there is an only-begotten Son of God, a son by nature, not by adoption. It suffices for devotion, writes Cyril, that we know that God is living, that He is good and just, holy and almighty.

The Church glories in the Cross of Christ, Cyril emphasizes, for by the Cross the blind are led into light, sinners are loosed from bondage, and the whole world is ransomed. On the cross the only-begotten Son of God died in man's behalf. The cross was no illusion, Cyril insists; Jesus' passion was real, and He came to it willingly, rejoicing in the salvation of mankind. His Resurrection from the dead was also real, as is attested by many witnesses.

The Christian does not believe in three Gods, but one. The Trinity is not to be separated, Cyril claims, nor is it to be confused. For we know three persons in one Godhead.

The true believer at baptism receives the remission of sins, and the Holy Spirit abides with him. The Christian strives for life eternal, believes virtuously, and receives instruction so that his soul may be prepared for reception of heavenly gifts. When he partakes of baptism, the believer is enlightened by the power of God.

The newly baptized are to be sober and vigilant, Cyril advises, for they are thereafter true-born children of the Church. Once they are baptized, they are ready to receive the more sacred mysteries, for, having renounced Satan and all sin, they have been found worthy of divine and life-giving baptism. The paradise of God is now open to them.

Baptism is not merely the grace of remission of sins, Cyril remarks, nor does it simply minister to us the gift of the Holy Ghost; baptism is also the counterpart of the sufferings of Christ and represents His true sufferings. The candidate is stripped naked to imitate Christ, who was naked on the cross; he is then anointed with exorcised oil, so as to be made a partaker of the olive tree, Jesus Christ, and to ward off the invisible powers of the evil one. The candidate is then led to the holy pool of divine baptism, as Christ was carried from the cross to the sepulcher, and after making the saving confession that he believes in the name of the Father, of the Son, and of the Holy Ghost, he descends thrice into the water and ascends again; this act is a symbol of Christ's burial and Resurrection.

As Christ was in reality crucified, buried, and raised from the dead, so the believer in baptism, if worthy, is crucified, buried, and raised together with Him. And as Christ was anointed with the ideal oil of gladness, with the Holy Spirit, so the believer is anointed with ointment, having been made a partaker and follower of Christ. The ointment with which the believer is anointed is Christ's gift of grace, and it is made fit to impart His divine nature. While the body is anointed with the visible ointment, the soul is sanctified by the Holy Spirit.

The believer is now ready, writes Cyril, to partake of the body and blood of Christ, for after the invocation of the Holy Ghost, the elements of the Eucharist are no longer bread and wine, but the body and blood of Christ.

When the service is near completion, those who have given their lives to Christ, namely, the patriarchs, prophets, Apostles, and martyrs, are commemorated, "that at their prayers and intercessions God should receive our petitions. . . ." The Lord's Prayer is then recited and the benediction pronounced.

Although Cyril's *Catechetical Lectures* is primarily concerned with the preparation for baptism, his declarations of faith in the efficacy of baptism as a result of the divine presence give his work a power of sincerity and dedication which continues to impress the Christian spirit.

THE LIFE OF ANTONY

Author: Saint Athanasius (c.296-373)
Type of work: Hagiography
First transcribed: 357

PRINCIPAL IDEAS ADVANCED

The ascetic life is prescribed by the Scriptures.
Christ commanded men to forsake all and follow Him.
Those who follow Christ must mortify the flesh and fight with demons.
Christ has broken the power of Satan, and those who trust in Christ's name can achieve victory over sin and so attain to peace and joy.

The *Life of Antony* was written by Athanasius at the request of "brethren in foreign parts," probably persons in the West whom the author met during his exile there. Athanasius, who had known Antony personally and embraced many of his ascetic principles, expresses his own satisfaction in being able to pass on some part of what he has heard of the great man and encourages his readers to make inquiries of others. If everyone who has recollections of Antony tells what he knows, says Athanasius, "an account will be had that does approximate justice to him."

Antony was born in Middle Egypt about the middle of the third century of well-to-do Christian parents. As a boy he avoided attending school because he did not enjoy the companionship of other children; hence, he never learned to read or write. He attended church, however, and paid close attention to lessons that he heard. Thus it happened that, when he was about twenty years old, the words of Jesus to the Rich Young Ruler, "If thou wilt be perfect, go sell all thou hast, and give to the poor," impressed him with such force that he disposed of his property, gave his younger sister, who had been left to his care, to be brought up by Christian virgins, and devoted his life to the practice of asceticism.

At that time ascetics were content to practice their discipline within the vicinity of towns and villages, for, as Athanasius notes, "there were not yet so many monasteries in Egypt, and no monk even knew of the faraway desert." Antony profited from what he could learn by visiting these hermits; but in time his peace of mind required him to seek greater solitude, first in tombs which lay at some distance from the village, and later in an abandoned fort in the desert. There he immured himself for twenty years, seeing no one and receiving his store of bread only twice a year.

In his absence Antony's reputation grew. There were reports that he fought with demons in bodily form, and that persons who camped beside his cell were healed of their diseases. Finally men forced their way into his cell and brought him out. It was the first time any had seen him since he had come to the desert; but his body appeared healthy, and the state of his soul appeared to be pure. "He had himself completely under control," says Athanasius, "a man guided by reason and stable in his character."

From this time on Antony did not hesitate to assume the role of a teacher and servant of men; he counseled and healed not only the monks who came to him, but also the general public. He possessed unusual power in prayer, and was gifted with "charm in speaking." As a result of his exhortations, many took up the monastic life, and, in Athanasius' words, "the desert was populated with monks who left their own people and registered themselves for citizenship in Heaven." In 311, during the persecution by Maximin, Antony went to Alexandria and ministered to Christians in prisons and in the mines. He even appeared in the court room, encouraging those who were on trial. Antony wanted to suffer martyrdom, says Athanasius, but "the Lord was guarding him for our own good and for the good of others, that to many he might be a teacher of the ascetic life."

Now it became impossible for Antony to find solitude. He therefore followed a caravan of Arabs eastward almost to the Gulf of Akaba, where he found an oasis at the foot of a high mountain, and "fell in love with the place." Here he made a small garden and raised his own grain, together with a few vegetables which he served to occasional visitors. Respecting his solitude, his disciples were nevertheless solicitous for his welfare, because he was now an old man. Thus, each month someone made the three-day journey to his hermitage to make sure that he was well.

Once Antony made the journey again to visit the cells of those who had taken up their abode in the desert. "As he came to the outer cells, all gave him a hearty welcome, regarding him as a father. And he, for his part, as though bringing them provisions from his mountain, entertained them with his stories and gave them of his practical experience." A new enthusiasm swept the region and Antony rejoiced in the zeal that he found. Again he saw his sister, now grown old in virginity, "herself the guiding spirit of other virgins."

Such, in outline, is the story of Antony's life. A person of ordinary physique, he nevertheless exercised "a great and indescribable charm" over all whom he met. He was never agitated or gloomy, but seemed to radiate in his countenance the joy and imperturbability of his soul. He conversed freely, asking questions as often as he answered them, and he profited from the replies he received. When he was in Alexandria, the multitudes, both pagan and Christian, wanted to touch him, confident that he had power to heal them. He became the national hero of the Egyptians, the "physician of Egypt," (and a forerunner of the religious nationalism which reached massive proportions in the Monophysite controversy during the sixth century). Pagan philosophers who went to see him were astonished at what they found. "For he did not have the rough manner of one who had lived and grown old in the mountains, but was a man of grace and urbanity. His speech was seasoned with divine wisdom so that no one bore him illwill, but rather all rejoiced over him who sought him out."

Athanasius knew Antony well enough to preserve some of the monk's actual sayings: "He used to say that one should give all one's time to the soul rather than to the body"; ". . . he used to say to himself that the life led by the great Elias should serve the ascetic as a mirror in which always to study his own life." He experienced visions and trances, but spoke of these with reluctance, and only to those who sat with him during his ecstasy and afterwards pressed him to tell them what he had seen. The visions which Athanasius reports do not suggest that Antony was a great mystic. On one occasion he heard a voice bidding him go out and look at the skies. Looking up, he saw a frightful, towering figure, whose body reached to the clouds. With his hands the monster knocked down the souls of men as they endeavored to rise to Heaven. He exulted over those who fell, but some passed through his grasp. On another occasion, Antony seemed to see himself carried aloft by angels, but stopped by demons who charged him with faults; these, however, they could not prove, so that the way opened and he proceeded unhindered. Miracles were reported; but Athanasius is careful to say that Antony healed "not by giving out commands, but by praying and by calling upon Christ's name." Thus, when a soldier knocked at his cell and begged him to heal his child, Antony replied, "Man, why do you make all this clamor to me? I am a man just as you are. If you believe in Christ whom I serve, go, and, as you believe, pray to God and it will come to pass."

Unfortunately, Athanasius' firsthand reports on Antony were not sufficient to compose a full-length portrait of the monk; or, perhaps, Antony's sayings were too dry and puzzling to satisfy literary fashions and to serve the purposes of popular edification. In any case, *The Life of Antony* is, in certain respects, Athanasius' own invention.

In order to make some kind of story out of Antony's dreary years in the desert, Athanasius relates them as a kind of *Pilgrim's Progress,* with many exciting episodes in which the saint contended with demons and monsters. Once the Devil masqueraded as a woman; another time he came with his demons and lashed Antony's body so that his friends took him up for dead; again, Antony was surrounded by phantoms of lions, bears, serpents, and wolves; when he first moved to the desert, the Enemy scattered gold along the way in an effort to corrupt him. On each occasion, Antony cited

Scripture verses and pointed to Christ's victory upon the cross, and in this way overcame his tempters. Certainly, there is nothing improbable in the supposition that Antony had such temptations to contend with; but even his Roman Catholic editor concedes that "there is quite too much of it in the *Vita.*"

Athanasius makes abundant use of the ancient literary practice of putting speeches into the mouth of his hero. One of these purports to be the speech which Antony made to the monks on the occasion of his coming back to civilization after twenty years in the fort where he had retired. It is a plausible apology for the ascetic life, concentrating especially on ways of overcoming demonic assaults. Another speech is addressed by Antony to the Neoplationists and contrasts religious truth with philosophical reasoning in a manner which shows considerably more knowledge of Greek thought than Antony is likely to have had. However, it seems fairly probable that Antony was opposed to the influence of Greek ideas on Christian apologetics and theology.

Finally, Athanasius represents Antony as a zealous opponent of Manicheanism and Arianism, heresies that presumably provoked the Bishop of Alexandria more than they did the monk of the Outer Desert. Antony is reported as having said that Arianism was the worst heresy of all, and was the forerunner of Antichrist. "He taught the people," says Athanasius of Antony, "that the Son of God is not a creature nor has He come into being 'from non-existence'; but 'He is the eternal Word and Wisdom of the substance of the Father.' " But obviously these are Athanasius' views; and while Antony may very well have been zealous against the Arians, there is little reason to suppose that he entered intelligently into the debates to which it gave rise.

Antony could neither read nor write. Still, as Athanasius portrays him, he found in the Bible the rule of his life. If, as most Protestants would probably maintain, his was a one-sided and distorted understanding of what the Scriptures require, one need only run through *The Life of Antony* and mark the numerous Biblical citations which Athanasius puts in Antony's mouth to be convinced that the ascetic ideal is, nonetheless, deeply ingrained in New Testament Christianity. "If thou wilt be perfect, go sell all that thou hast. . . . Be not solicitous for the morrow. . . . He that is lazy, neither let him eat. . . . I die daily. . . . Our wrestling is not against flesh and blood, but against principalities and powers. . . ." Such are the principles which guided Antony at each step of his life, sustained him in anxiety, and brought him joy and peace.

Antony's monasticism, as the reader of *The Life* easily observes, was of the hermit variety, and his immediate followers were content so far to emulate him as to live each in his own cell, yet near enough to others that fellowship was possible. It was St. Pachomius (c. 290-346), another Egyptian, who developed the communal monastery surrounded by a wall and ruled over by a superior.

No other monk, however, caught the popular imagination in the same way as Antony did, a fact for which Athanasius' book is largely responsible. The work was translated into Latin almost immediately and made a striking impression in decadent Roman circles, as Augustine remarks in his *Confessions. The Life of Antony* continued to be read throughout the Middle Ages. It was influential, not only in helping form Catholic ideals of piety and in fostering asceticism as a religious alternative to martyrdom, but also in providing a model for medieval hagiography. Meanwhile, the story of Antony's temptations became a perennial source of inspiration to artists and poets.

"The fact that he became famous everywhere and that he found universal admiration," says Athanasius, "betokens his virtue, and a soul beloved of God. For Antony gained renown not for his writings, nor for worldly wisdom, nor for any art, but solely for his service of God. . . that those who hear of him may realize that the commandments can lead to perfection, and may take courage in the path to virtue."

THE LONGER RULES and THE SHORTER RULES

Author: Saint Basil of Caesarea (c.330-379)
Type of work: Ascetical theology
First transcribed: c.358-364

Principal Ideas Advanced

The underlying motivation of the monastic and ascetic life is the love of Christ and obedience to Him through the fulfillment of the Biblical command to love God and neighbor.

One sets himself free to fulfill this double commandment by renouncing the world and its distractions, including property and family, and by joining in a common life with other similarly dedicated persons under a common discipline.

Continence or temperance is the guiding principle for all the regulations of monastic life in harmony with the Scriptures.

The community life of the monastery is oriented around regular public and private prayer and useful work.

Although Basil, Archbishop of Caesarea in Cappadocia (modern Kayseri in central Turkey), is most often remembered as a dogmatic theologian, the influence of his *Longer Rules* and *Shorter Rules* has probably been more widespread than that of his doctrinal writings. The importance of the *Rules* lies in the fact that in them a great theologian supplies the monastic movement with a sound theological basis.

The son of a distinguished family, whose sister had entered upon the monastic life before him and whose younger brother, Gregory of Nyssa (c.330-c.395), became the great mystical theologian among the Cappadocian fathers, Basil the Great was qualified by his classical education, by his travels as a young man among the monks of Syria, Egypt, and Palestine, and by later experience as monk and bishop to set forth the first formal and comprehensive rules for monastic communities.

At the time of his birth Christian monasticism was still in its beginnings, although there had been individual ascetics since New Testament times. The growth of a distinctive monastic way of life came with the end of the persecutions and the formal recognition of Christianity by the Roman empire under Constantine the Great (c.288-337). The earliest form of monasticism seems to have been eremitic, as exemplified by the Egyptian hermit-monk Antony (c.251-356). The communal or cenobitic form appeared, also in Egypt, under the leadership of Pachomius (c.290-346), and the monastery founded by Pachomius at Tabennisi was among those which Basil visited before settling down on the family estate in 356 to found a monastic community. Pachomius and Eustathius of Sebaste (c.306-c.377), a close friend and teacher of Basil who led a monastic movement in lower Armenia, had both given some brief rules to their followers but nothing complete or systematic and nothing firmly based on the teachings of the Bible. The *Longer Rules* of Basil thus met a felt need and came to have a far-reaching influence on the development of monasticism in West and East.

Both the *Longer Rules* and the *Shorter Rules* seem to have been first compiled in that period while Basil and Gregory of Nazianzus (329-389), the orator and preacher among the three Cappadocians, were together at the monastery on the River Iris between 358 and 364, when Basil was elected bishop of nearby Caesarea. The *Longer Rules* is composed of fifty-five discourses, perhaps *extempore* addresses, in question and answer form. The headings or questions do not in every case seem to be original. The first twenty-three chapters form a unit stating the basic principles of monastic life and community organization. Chapters 24-36 deal with more specific aspects of community life such as types of discipline and duties of officers. Chapters 37-42 and 43-55 deal with worship and work, and with the office of the Superior, respectively. It is quite possible that these later sections were added by Basil after he had had more experience in leading the community and sensed the need for them. There are some references which imply that he was already bishop at the time they were written. In any case no doubt has been cast on the genuineness of the *Rules*.

It is especially characteristic of the *Regulae fusius tractatae* that the principles of monastic organization are drawn wherever possible from Scripture. There is a strong emphasis on discipleship, on the love of Christ, as the motive behind monasticism. The primary commandments are the love of God and the love of neighbor. All else is subordinated to the fulfillment of this double commandment. It is for the sake of pleasing God and loving the neighbor that Basil warns against absolute solitude and comes out strongly in favor of communal organization. There is also the need of mutual discipline and correction. This advocacy of the communal life was especially influential on the development of monasticism in the West, and it was essential to the integration of monasticism into the total life of the Church.

Renunciation of the world, which includes the relinquishing of property and complete separation from family and friends, is not an end in itself, nor is it a simple rejection of the world. All the monasteries founded by Basil showed a remarkable concern for the sick and poor in the communities around them. In fact, many of these monasteries were established in the midst of cities or towns and not in the wilderness as in Egyptian monasticism. Renunciation is a release, a setting free from material concerns in order to perform spiritual duties and acts of love. It is the same freedom from material concerns which the guiding principle of continence seeks. All things are to be taken temperately: food, clothing, laughter, and even work. Basil saw the wisdom of moderating the excesses, in particular the abuses of the body, which typified much of Syrian and Egyptian monasticism both then and later. He recognized the different needs of different men in regard to food and other physical necessities, but in regard to the vices of the soul all harmful pleasures were naturally excluded. His rule is a strict one; simplicity and uniformity mark the monastic life.

Many of the *Rules* reveal Basil's great insight into human nature. He warns, for example, against fighting over the lowest seat at the table out of misconceived humility. He recommends distinctive clothing as a means of keeping the brothers up to the standard of a godly life when out in public and faced with temptations. He likewise urges the avoidance of journeys and of contact with relatives from the outside world. All work and duties should be assigned by the Superior according to individual abilities but without respect to individual preferences. The products of the community may be sold outside the monastery, but not for large profits and if possible in the immediate vicinity. In no case are the products of the monastery to be sold at religious gatherings or synods. One of the chapters also discusses the proper relationships with the sisters in the case of double monasteries for men and women. More detailed questions about all these points appear in the *Shorter Rules*.

One of the historically most significant chapters of the *Longer Rules* is the thirty-seventh, which describes the hours or times for prayer. We find here one of the earliest accounts of the eight canonical hours; namely: prime, tierce, sext, nones, vespers, compline, nocturns, and lauds. Each has its particular place and value in the monks' day, and only in the most urgent instances should prayers be missed. At the same time they are not an excuse for idleness and neglect of assigned work, most of which was manual, such as building, carpentry, and agriculture, and could be interrupted for prayers during the day.

One other important aspect of the monastic life is the regular confession of sins to the Superior, often called a physician of souls, or to one of the senior brothers who is suitably qualified by character and experience. With confession goes, of course, correction.

The *Shorter Rules* or *Regulae brevius tractatae* consists of 313 chapters, also in question and answer form, but here the questions are almost certainly original. The questions are of considerable variety, and the whole is not especially well arranged. Some questions may have been submitted to Basil in writing from different monasteries, others may have come from catechism classes, and still others may have been taken down in shorthand at conferences of monastic leaders or Superiors with Basil. In any case, the collection does not seem to have been edited, and it was probably added to over the years of Basil's administration as bishop and founder of monasteries. Among the general concerns dealt with are pastoral care, monastic administration, Biblical exegesis, and liturgical practice. In almost every case we see real situations and practical concerns reflected in the questions and answers, and altogether the many brief chapters of the *Shorter Rules* form a larger work than the *Longer Rules.* Yet they do not set forth a comprehensive system of principles or rules proper as do the more polished chapters of the *Longer Rules.*

The preface of the *Shorter Rules* refers to an all-night meeting of Superiors and thus points to one source of the questions. The first group of chapters deals primarily with questions of repentance, conversion, and the forgiveness of sins, but other chapters near the end of the *Rules* also deal with these topics. The chapters on sin in general and on particular sins and their remedies, which follow, make up a large section, as might be expected. Many of the questions could apply to any Christian, but some arise obviously from the monastic situation. There is one, for example, about being cross or angry when awakened at midnight or before dawn to say prayers. Attention is also given to property, clothing, food, and taxes. One answer is rather amusing. When asked what a brother with nothing of his own except the garment on his back should do for a naked beggar, Basil replies with Scripture, "Let each man abide in that wherein he was called." This verse from I Co-

rinthians 7:20 and one like it from 7:24 are cited several times as a counsel to contentment with one's lot in life.

A great many questions deal with the learning and interpretation of the Bible. These questions often cite for Basil's opinion difficult verses from both the Old and New Testaments. As one would expect, the problems of administering a monastery, especially the double monasteries for men and women, appear repeatedly. In general Basil gives sound and conservative directions, emphasizing always the absolute authority of the Superior. Indeed obedience is the very center of monastic living and takes specific form in self-discipline, in regulated fasting and use of food (one meal a day was customary), and in proper conduct in the workshops, kitchen, and cellar. A central section of the *Shorter Rules* discusses disposition and attitude toward God, others, oneself, and the duties imposed by the community. In all the *Rules* there is only brief reference to priests and to the sacraments, but there is no question that Basil the bishop recognized the place of both.

The lasting contributions of Basil to the development of Christian monasticism emerge clearly from the *Longer Rules* and the *Shorter Rules.* He gave it a foundation of organized asceticism with stated rules. He moderated the extreme austerity and extreme enthusiasm of monasticism in other lands. There was no place for special visions and miracles, but spiritual gifts were not excluded. Although not the first to establish communities of monks, he made the common life the unalterable basis of monastic living. Finally, he brought monasticism into the service of the Church and the larger community. He was the first great monk *and* bishop.

The *Rules* of Basil were taken during his lifetime to the newly organized monasteries of the West and were translated very soon into Latin by Tyrannius Rufinus (c.345-410), a widely traveled churchman from Italy, who either abridged them or used a shorter early version of them. In his translation they were known and used by Benedict of Nursia (c.480-c.550), the father of monasticism in the West and the founder of Monte Cassino. The influence of Basil's *Rules* may be seen in Eastern monasticism to this day, although there was never a Basilian order as such.

THE HYMNS OF EPHRAEM THE SYRIAN

Author: Saint Ephraem the Syrian (c.306-373)
Type of work: Hymnody
First transcribed: c.360

PRINCIPAL IDEAS ADVANCED

The Lord chastens those He loves, is merciful to His children, and is greatly to be praised, for He is exceedingly just, long-suffering, and kind, by whose glory we are healed and brought into His marvelous salvation.

At the birth of the Lord, the glory and majesty of God was revealed; sin and death were conquered, and the doors of Paradise were thrown open.

Saint Ephraem, the Syrian, is one of the earliest Syriac authors whose works remain to any considerable extent. His work is characteristic of Syrian Christianity and was thus little affected by outside influences. Not much is known of Ephraem's life, for there is hardly any trustworthy biographical evidence. He was born in Nisibis in Mesopotamia during the reign of Constantine the Great, was a disciple of St. Jacob of Nisibis, and finally settled in a cell at the Mount of Edessa as a "Solitary." Here he gained a reputation as a saint, an ascetic, a teacher, and a champion of orthodoxy. He wrote voluminously and left a large body of *Sermons, Commentaries,* and *Hymns,* of which many are extant.

The *Hymns* of Ephraem did more than provide the Syrian churches with devotional literature, although the whole of public worship was animated by them. Many of his hymns were controversial and polemical; they were the chosen means by which Ephraem sought to combat error and to teach the truth. Many of the hymns are songs of exhortation, of praise, and of thanksgiving and triumph, but others sought to combat the errors of heretics, errors which had won popularity through expression in attractive tunes that caught the ear and inclined the people to receive false doctrine. The *Hymns* of Ephraem were set to the same tunes, and they superseded the rival hymnody of heresy, so that the day was carried by an orthodox hymnody.

Syriac hymnody is constructed, as is the Hebrew, on the principle of parallelism, in which one thought answers another; but unlike the Hebrew, the clauses of the Syriac are regulated by an equivalence of syllabic measure. A systematic rhyme is missing. The literary value of Ephraem's *Hymns* is not to be compared with the Psalms of David; nevertheless, some do display devotional fervor and human pathos. They differ from the Psalms of David, however, in that whereas the latter render the inner feelings of man in words of simplicity, and rise without effort to utter the things of God, the *Hymns* of Ephraem reflect the somberness of the ascetic, the gloom of the recluse; they express self-reproach, mortification, fears, and sorrow.

Some of the hymns were written about the year 350 during the siege of Nisibis by Sapor, King of Persia. The songs call upon the God who had delivered Noah from the waters of the flood to deliver those oppressed within the walls of the city. The God who gave rest in the haven of a mountain is supplicated to relieve the distressed within besieged walls. The affliction of oppression is recognized as the chastening of guilt and unrighteousness, and yet God is merciful to the wicked, and greatly to be praised. For the Lord is merciful, the hymns declare; He smites the enemy, and rescues the Church from mockery. The Lord forgives us even though our evil deeds outweigh our repentance; the Lord delivers us although we deserve destruction. We ought to sing praises to the One Being, that is unsearchable to us.

No man can complain against the Creator, writes Ephraem, for it is our offenses which cause our troubles. The medicine of salvation is applied to our afflictions. The Son of God heals us, even if our afflictions are like those of Job. The justice of the Lord is to be praised, for He chastises us as a mother rebukes her child; He restrains us from folly, and makes us wise.

Jesus has triumphed over the Evil One and his hosts, Ephraem writes; He resisted the temptations of sin and the Devil and conquered death. He is man and God; His manhood is intermingled with His Godhead. Holy men of old awaited His birth. On the day of His birth the words of the prophets were fulfilled. Immanuel was brought forth by the Virgin in Bethlehem. The True One who came from the Father of truth is blessed; He was sent for our propitiation. He let himself be born, crucified, and buried for our salvation. He sealed our soul, adorned it, and espoused it to himself. He sowed his light in darkness. The clothing of our filthiness was stripped from us; His leaven was mixed in our souls, and our deadness was quickened. Our minds have been enlightened by His doctrine. Our curse has been taken away by His stripes.

Ephraem sings of the Lord: "His Birth flowed on and was joined to His Baptism; and His Baptism again flowed on even to His death; His death led and reached to His Resurrection, a fourfold bridge unto His Kingdom, and lo! His sheep pass over in His footsteps."

Baptism is the wellspring of life which the Son of God has opened, the Father has sealed, and the Spirit has stamped, says Ephraem. The poor are invited to descend to the fountain of life and to be enriched, for the un-searchable Trinity has laid up treasures in baptism.

Besides the hymns of praise and adoration, the controversial hymns by Ephraem are of great interest. The following are typical:

"I have chanced upon the tares, my
    brethren,
That wear the color of wheat, to choke
    the good seed;
Concerning which the husbandmen
    are commanded,
Take them not away nor root them
    out;
And though the husbandmen needed
    not,
The seed waxed stronger than they,
Grew and multiplied and covered and
    choked them."

"I have chanced upon a book of Bar-
    daisan,
And I was troubled for an hour's space;
It tainted my poor ears,
And made them a passage
For words filled with blasphemy.
I hastened to purge them
With the goodly and pure reading
Of the Scriptures of truth."

Further insight into the character and theology of Ephraem and the nature of the verses that he wrote can be gained from his own testament which he wrote in anticipation of his death:

"By him who came down on Mount
    Sinai and by him who spake on
    the rock,
By that Mouth which spake the "Eli"
    and made the bowels of creation
    tremble,
By him who was sold in Judah and by

him who was scourged in Jeru-
    salem,
By the Might which was smitten on
    the cheek and by the Glory which
    endured spitting,
By the threefold Names of fire and by
    the one Assent and will, I have
    not rebelled against the Church,
    nor against the might of God.
If in my thought I have magnified the
    Father above the Son, Let Him
    have no mercy on me!
And if I have accounted the Holy
    Spirit less than God, let mine
    eyes be darkened!
If as I have said, I confessed not, let
    me go into outer darkness!
And if I speak in hypocrisy, let me
    burn with the wicked in fire!"

Ephraem sought no special honor at burial, for he despised all pomp and vulgar ceremony. He wished no luxurious tomb, but counted his body as without import. He declares that he desires to be laid in the cemetery with the broken in heart, "That when the Son of God comes: He may embrace me and raise me among them." His sole hope in this life, he says, and in that which is to come lies in that Firstborn who was begotten according to His nature, and was born in another birth that we may know that after our natural birth, we must undergo a rebirth so that we may become spiritual.

Death has been trampled on by the Lord, Ephraem declares. On the Cross death slew and was itself slain. A bridge has been built across Sheol. The precious pearl of victory awaits the saints. The gates of paradise are open. The Cross has opened them, and the gates of Hell are shut forever!

So Ephraem—like Prudentius (348-c.410), the Latin poet and hymn-writer; like St. Ambrose (c.339-397); and, finally, like Martin Luther (1483-1546)—expressed his Christian faith through his hymnody, and in so do-

ing he exerted a lasting influence on both the content and the expression of the Christian faith.

ON THE TRINITY

Author: Saint Hilary of Poitiers (c.315-367)
Type of work: Theology
First transcribed: Fourth century

Principal Ideas Advanced

The true faith as taught in Scripture is opposed to heretical notions which deny the persons of the Godhead and which assert that since the Son was created, He is not God in the true sense.

Christ is the true and perfect God, neither identical in person with the Father, nor severed from the Godhead; in Christ the fullness of the Godhead dwells.

Hilary of Poitiers exerted an important influence on the growth of Christian doctrine. His work *On the Trinity* was written primarily against Arianism in the Church. The treatise is divided into twelve books which seek to set forth the true faith on the basis of Scripture, in opposition to the interpretations of heretics.

Hilary writes that heretics vary in their errors, whereas the true faith is one. Under the cloak of being loyal to the true God, some tamper with the Gospel by denying the birth of God the only-begotten. Such persons assert that there was an extension of God into man, and that He who took our flesh was the Son of Man, but was not then, nor had previously been, the Son of God. They maintain that there is an identity of begetter and begotten, that in the Incarnation the Father simply extended Himself into the Virgin and was born as His own Son.

The Son and the Father are thought to be mere names or aspects of one divine person, so that there was no true birth of the Son.

Other heretics, Hilary reports, hold that the Son was merely created. They deny that Christ was, even in the beginning, God the Word with God. They cut Christ off from the divine unity, so that, as a mere creature called into being, He could not be said to possess the fullness of the Godhead.

The primary objective of Hilary's work is to refute by the clear assertion of the evangelists and prophets the false opinions of those who deny either that God was born in Christ, or that Christ is God. The true Christian faith does not confess two Gods, Hilary insists, nor yet a solitary God. It holds firmly to the confession that God the Father and God the Son are united, but not confounded. It refuses to allow that Christ is God in some imperfect sense, or that the Father and the Son are identical persons. The very center of saving faith is the faith in God as the Father, and in Christ, the Son of God; faith in Him, not as a creature, but as God the Creator.

The analogies that can be adduced in support of the true doctrine are incomplete and imperfect, Hilary concedes, for there can be no adequate comparison between God and earthly things. The truth is to be found in Scripture. Heresy results when the latter is misunderstood and given some arbitrary interpretation in defiance of the clear meaning of the words. Heresy is found not in the words as they are written, but in the sense assigned; the guilt belongs to the expositor, not to the text. To make the Son an extension of the Father is to make one and the same person both Son to Himself and also Father.

The Church has been commanded to baptize in the name of the Father, the Son, and the Holy Ghost, Hilary continues. All existence owes its origin to the Father. Through Christ, the Father is the source of all; He is self-existent, infinite, eternally anterior to time, which is a dimension of creation. Only the Son knows God. Each of the divine persons has complete and perfect knowledge of the other.

The Son is the offspring of the Father; the Only-begotten of the Unbegotten. There is a distinction, Hilary agrees, for they are Father and Son; but their divinity is not different in kind: both are One, God is God, One God only, begotten of One God unbegotten. Christ and the Father are not two Gods. There is no diversity in nature, for in the living Christ is the life of the living God. The generation of the Son is mysterious. The proper service of faith, Hilary insists, is to confess the truth, as taught by the Gospels and the Apostles. The Christian answer to heresy is that ". . . there is One Unbegotten God the Father, and One Only-begotten Son of God, perfect Offspring of perfect Parent; that the Son was begotten by no lessening of the Father or subtraction from His Substance, but that He Who possesses all things begat an all possessing Son; a Son not emanating nor proceeding from the Father, but compact of, and inherent in, the whole Divinity of Him Who wherever He is present is present eternally. . . ."

Hilary emphasizes the belief that the son of God was born of the Virgin and of the Holy Ghost, for the sake of mankind. Since the Holy Spirit proceeds from the Father and the Son, the existence of the Holy Spirit as a person is not to be doubted. In the Christian confession of faith the Spirit is joined to the Father and to the Son. True wisdom believes what it cannot comprehend. Man cannot comprehend God's nature; he can apprehend it only as it is set forth in the Scriptures. The ineffable cannot be set forth in the limits and bounds of a definition, Hilary affirms.

God the Father and God the Son are one altogether, as Israel had been taught, not by confusion of person, but by unity of substance, writes Hilary. Scripture testifies that God is not a solitary person. God the Son is not God by adoption, or by gift of the name. He is God, equal with true God in power. Unity is to be recognized among the persons. The Arians would make Christ a creature; they are propagators of blasphemy, who deny the words, "This is my beloved Son in whom I am well pleased." Christ is

Son by birth, not by adoption, as is attested by the witness of the Apostles and by the witness of those for whom He performed miracles.

The Arians are blind to the true meaning of Scripture, Hilary insists. In Christ and the Father there is neither one person, nor two Gods. We are given full assurance of the divinity of Jesus Christ, by His name, His birth, His nature, His power, and His own assertions with respect to Himself. The prologue of John's Gospel assures us that in the beginning was the Word, and the Word was with God, and the Word was God. The very essence of the Godhead exists in the Word and is expressed in the very name.

For Christ, to be is to be in God; and it is not to be in God as one thing is in another. Hilary claims that the life and subsistence of Christ is of such a nature that although Christ is within the subsisting God, Christ has a subsistence of His own. Only one divine nature exists. The words, "I and the Father are one, and he that hath seen me hath seen the Father," indicate that the Son who is born is not inferior to the Father. He possesses the divine nature and is therefore nothing other than God. The union between the persons is perfect; it is a unity of nature, an indwelling of the Son in the Father and of the Father in the Son. Christ is one in nature with the Father, but He is not a creature, and He is one in will with the Father. The Godhead is one in nature, although it consists of three Persons.

According to Hilary, the Christian confesses that the only-begotten Son of God was born before times eternal and that He eternally contains in Himself the form and image of the invisible God.

The conclusion reached by faith and by argument, Hilary concludes, is that the Lord Jesus was born and always existed. For God the Father is eternally Father, and God the Son is eternally begotten.

THE LETTERS OF ST. JEROME

Author: Saint Jerome (c.345-420)
Type of work: Pastoral epistles
First transcribed: 370-419

PRINCIPAL IDEAS ADVANCED

When social morality is on the verge of collapse, Christians must undergo rigorous self-discipline in order to save their souls.

Those who wish to undertake the ascetic life should enter a convent instead of attempting to live as hermits.

Work and study, as well as acts of charity and mercy, are as much a part of the ascetic life as are prayer and fasting.

Even after he had undertaken an ascetic life, Jerome could not throw off his passion for literature; but, because of a dream in which he saw himself rejected at the Throne of Judgment for loving Cicero more than Christ, he made a strong resolution to attend more to sacred authors than to profane. Jerome's zeal for languages and learning never abated; and, while his energies were chiefly devoted to translating and commenting upon the Scriptures, he indulged his flair for literary invention by composing and publishing his celebrated *Letters*.

The collection of Jerome's *Letters* which has come down to posterity includes several letters written to Jerome as well as some in which he is merely mentioned. But 117 of Jerome's letters have been preserved, many of which are personal letters, while others are what we should call "open letters."

Ordained a priest, but with no specific priestly responsibilities, Jerome became a spiritual director to a wide circle of devout Romans, especially of the leisure class, during the period of Italy's hastening decline. The *Letters*, which in part are written in the manner of the Latin satirists, give a sorry picture of a society which, though nominally Christian, was really a pagan society in the last stages of disintegration. Jerome's opinion, obviously shared by many of his correspondents, is that serious Christians must undergo rigorous spiritual discipline if they are to save their own souls. He recommends that they break sharply with the customs of the society in which they live, that if possible they remove with their families to the country, and, if they are free from family responsibilities, that they take up the monastic life. Jerome did not introduce monasticism into Italy. On the contrary, he was one of great numbers who were caught up into the movement, the seeds of which had been planted there

by Athanasius (c.296-373). Inspired by the example of the Egyptian hermits, he went to Antioch in the year 374, and he spent five years in the Syrian desert. His purpose was to subdue his youthful passions; but he discovered that physical hardship by itself is not sufficient to discipline the flesh, and that one must find something important to occupy the mind. Having no talent for mystical exercises, Jerome set himself the task of improving his knowledge of Greek and of learning Hebrew, and he spent much time in the study of Scriptures. Upon returning to Rome, he was enthusiastically received into a circle of ascetically-minded Christians, whom he taught to sing psalms in Hebrew and guided in the study of the Scriptures. Then, in 385, with a number of his friends, he left Rome for Bethlehem, where the little community built a monastery and a convent. Here he spent the rest of his life, helping with the community, translating and commenting on the Scriptures, and entertaining a constant stream of visitors from all over the western world.

Like many another seeker after perfection (for example, the English clergyman William Law, in *A Serious Call to a Devout and Holy Life*, 1728), Jerome takes seriously the Scriptural injunctions about the world, the flesh, and the Devil. But, for all his rigor, Jerome is no fanatic, and he does not lose the capacity to suit his advice to the needs of the person at hand. Indeed, he takes his place, along with Benedict of Nursia (c.480-c.547), as one who has helped regulate and moderate the ascetic life.

Jerome's views concerning monasticism, like those of Benedict, are the product of first-hand experience. He requires both monks and nuns to work with their hands, to care for the sick and the poor, to memorize the Scriptures, and to observe stated hours of prayer. He sometimes praises austerities in persons notable for their charity and zeal; but he recommends modest fare and cleanliness as ministering more to a useful life. Knowing the irregularities which overtake most anchorites, he maintains that the discipline of a monastery is preferable for most people. "Do I condemn a solitary life?" he writes to a young man who was contemplating a religious profession; "By no means: in fact I have often commended it. But I wish to see the monastic schools turn out soldiers who have no fear of the rough training of the desert, who have exhibited the spectacles of a holy life for a considerable time, who have made themselves last that they might be first, who have not been overcome by hunger or satiety, whose joy is in poverty, who teach virtue by their garb and mien, and who are too conscientious to invent—as some silly men do—monstrous stories of struggles with demons. . . ."

The most characteristic of Jerome's *Letters* are addressed to members of the circle of Christian friends whom he left behind him in Rome. The reader soon makes the acquaintance of the aristocratic widow, Marcella, who was one of those influenced by Athanasius to profess the monastic life. Her home on the Aventine was a shelter for Christian virgins and widows and the center of the circle in which Jerome was most at home. Many of the *Letters* are in response to Marcella's requests for help in the study of the Bible. Another remarkable woman was Fabriola, the Magdalene of the group, who, as penance for her youthful folly,

sold her lands and gave the money to the poor. Jerome writes: "She was the first person to found a hospital, into which she might gather sufferers out of the streets, and where she might nurse the unfortunate victims of sickness and want." But most celebrated of all was the impetuous Paula, mother of five remarkable children, who led a company of virgins to Bethlehem and established the convent there. Her unmarried daughter, Eustochium, accompanied her in her travels and took her place at the head of the convent upon the death of her mother, to be succeeded in turn by a second Paula, granddaughter of the first. Of the mother, Jerome says, "So lavish was her charity that she robbed her children; and, when her relatives remonstrated with her for doing so, she declared that she was leaving to them a better inheritance in the mercy of Christ." Jerome's letters to these friends are unfailingly kind and courteous, whether he is counseling or consoling, instructing in the Scriptures, or eulogizing departed saints.

Jerome's courtesy sometimes fails him when he is engaged in controversy with other theologians and ecclesiastics. Augustine of Hippo (354-430) wrote in the year 397 to question Jerome concerning the latter's interpretation of the rebuke administered by Paul to Peter, according to Galatians 2:11. Taking the accounts of Paul given in The Acts, Jerome had charged Paul with the same kind of tergiversation with which Paul had charged Peter. Augustine's letter questioning Jerome's interpretation did not get to Jerome, but was transcribed and circulated in the West so that to Jerome it seemed that Augustine was attacking him behind his back. Not for several years were the two great Latin churchmen able to make up their quarrel.

Jerome was even more violent in attacking those with whom he disagreed on principle, notably the partisans of Origen (c.185-c.254), and of Pelagius (c.355-c.425). In theological matters, Jerome may not have had the insight that characterized his work in Biblical exegesis. At any rate, he seems at first not to have detected anything heretical in either of these writers; and when at last he joins issue with them, he does so along established lines. One important issue, however, comes out of these disputes; namely, a clarification of the Church's doctrine concerning the origin of the soul. Jerome distinguishes three possible positions: that men's souls were "created long since" and "kept in God's storehouse"; that "they are formed by God and introduced into bodies day by day"; and that "they are transmitted by propaga-

tion." The followers of Origen held to the first of these views; Tertullian and most of the Western writers held to the third; but Jerome argued for the second view, and the Western Church has generally followed Jerome, in spite of the authority of Augustine, who was inclined toward the third view as better securing the doctrine of original sin.

Many of Jerome's letters were concerned with theological questions, as was, for example, his correspondence with Pope Damasus (c.304-384). Jerome had definite opinions about the proper procedure for translating the Bible. But for the most part he dedicated himself to stressing the value of the ascetic life and the duties of the clergy. His letters are a reflection of the spiritual and intellectual turmoil of his times, and they reveal a passionately spiritual man who demanded as much of himself as he did of others.

PANARION

Author: Saint Epiphanius of Salamis (c.315-403)
Type of work: Heresiology
First transcribed: c.377

PRINCIPAL IDEAS ADVANCED

Heresy is as old as creation and consists primarily of man's tendency to render divine honors to the creature rather than to the creator.

The Church alone has received the genuine tradition of Christ and the Apostles.

The tradition of Christ is contained in the Church's teachings and comprises the only effective antidote against the poison of heresy.

The title which Epiphanius chose for his lengthy work against heresies is suggestive of his conception of the nature of heresy and the means by which it could be overcome. The Greek word *panarion* means "medicine chest."

Epiphanius, in other words, regarded heresy as a deadly poison which would result in spiritual death unless treated by an effective antidote. The "medicine" which Epiphanius held out as antidote was the orthodox tradition of the Church, which, by its very nature, was life-giving and therapeutic.

Few figures in the history of the Church have dedicated themselves so thoroughly to the study of heresy as did Epiphanius. The obvious enjoyment which he derived from identifying and attacking heretical ideas prompted him to see heresies and heretics virtually everywhere he looked. In a number of instances, it would seem that he actually invented heresies and provided them with a history in order that he might further indulge his passion for heresy-hunting. In other instances, he included under the label of heresy certain movements and ideas which, for someone with a more open mind than Epiphanius possessed, would have no place in a Christian catalogue of heresies.

The *Panarion* is generally regarded as the most important treatise written by Epiphanius. It was written in response to a request by two monks for a more detailed study of the heresies which Epiphanius had earlier set forth in his doctrinal treatise, the *Ancoratus*. The *Panarion* is divided into three major sections and considers a total of eighty heresies. The first section deals with pre-Christian heresies and is subdivided, in turn, in accordance with the scheme suggested by Colossians 3:11, into the heresies of Barbarism, Scythianism, Hellenism, Samaritanism and Judaism. Most of what he has to say about Barbarism, Scythianism, and Samaritanism is of little value, reflect-

ing more of a concern for schematization than for historical accuracy.

Epiphanius's identification of the heresies within Hellenism provides an interesting insight into his own intellectual and theological bias, since, for him, the philosophical schools—Platonism, Pythagoreanism, Stoicism, Epicureanism—were the chief transmitters of heresy within Hellenism. At this point, it might be argued, Epiphanius succeeds in displaying not so much the heresy of the philosophical schools, as his own suspicion of classical Greek philosophy. With respect to Judaism, there were, according to Epiphanius, seven distinct heretical sects—the Sadducees, Scribes, Pharisees, Hemerobaptists, Nazarenes, Essenes, and Herodians. Epiphanius's treatment betrays a lack of historical perspective, although the recent discoveries of the *Dead Sea Scrolls* have shown that in some respects Epiphanius's knowledge of first century Judaism was not as deficient as once was supposed.

The second division of the *Panarion* deals with the heretical sects of the second and third centuries, chiefly those of the Judeo-Christians and the Gnostics. Here, Epiphanius is both confused and unfair. Like most of the early Fathers, Epiphanius imputed the basest of motives and a complete lack of moral principles to the leaders of the heretical sects. The chief value of the second division of the *Panarion* is that it preserves the works of earlier writers such as Justin Martyr (c.100-c.165) and Hippolytus (c.170-c.236), whose testimony concerning the heresies of their times is far more reliable than that which resulted from Epiphanius's own independent investigations. A number of writings by some of the early heretics themselves, which otherwise would have been completely lost, are also included in this section and add considerably to its value.

The third section brings Epiphanius's study of heresy down to his own day and includes discussion of such important groups as the Arians, Semi-Arians, Apollinarians, and Pneumatomachi. The fact that he knew these heretical groups intimately makes this part of the *Panarion* much more valuable and reliable than the earlier sections, where his knowledge was often based on nothing more than his own imagination. If the quality of his scholarship improves in this section, however, his narrow-mindedness does not. His attack against the theology associated with the great Alexandrian scholar Origen (c.185-c.254) is particularly indicative of his uncharitable spirit. Epiphanius was incapable of appreciating the rich philosophical orientation of Origen's thought, an orientation which occasionally resulted in some rather bold conjectures on Ori-

gen's part. Rather than acknowledge the great debt of the Church to Origen, Epiphanius chose to concentrate on certain peripheral aspects of Origen's thought and thereby to force Origen into the gallery of heretics. It is important to note in this connection that Epiphanius was not at all an armchair heresiologist. His opposition to Origenism—an opposition prompted by a meeting with St. Jerome in Rome in 392—led him to make a relentless search throughout the Eastern churches for traces of Origen's thought, and he condemned in the most unreasonable fashion anyone who admitted a debt to Origen.

The *Panarion,* sometimes called the "Refutation of all the Heresies," is positively dedicated to the proposition that spiritual health is established and preserved only by correct opinions and beliefs. These correct opinions and beliefs are to be found, Epiphanius claimed, only within the doctrinal tradition of the Church.

FIVE THEOLOGICAL ORATIONS

Author: Saint Gregory of Nazianzus (329-389)
Type of work: Theology
First transcribed: c.380

Principal Ideas Advanced

Because God is its subject, theological discourse can be carried on only within the limits of what is proper for man to say and what is possible for man to know; the mystery may not be treated lightly, and God's nature ultimately remains beyond man's comprehension.

By visible signs and natural law men may know that God exists; but who God is, that which is described by the doctrine of the Trinity, is known only through Scripture and illumination.

The Father, Son, and Holy Spirit, eternally one God, are equal in nature; but they are distinguished in that the Father is unbegotten, the Son is begotten, and the Spirit proceeds.

When we consider the Godhead, or the divine monarchy, what we conceive of is one; but when we consider the Persons of the Godhead, there are three whom we worship.

The *Five Theological Orations* of St. Gregory of Nazianzus earned for him, more than did any other of his works, the honorific title of "Theologian" in the Eastern Orthodox Church. He was noted for his polished style as a writer and orator, his dislike for unrestrained theological speculation, his aversion to the tumultuous life of a bishop, and above all for his contribution to the definition of the doctrine of the Trinity which was accepted at the Second Ecumenical Council held at Constantinople in 381.

Like his two great contemporary compatriots, St. Basil of Caesarea (c.330-379) and Basil's brother, St. Gregory of Nyssa (c.330-c.395), St. Gregory of Nazianzus came from a leading aristocratic family of Cappadocia, a district of Asia Minor. The son of a bishop of Nazianzus, Gregory was educated in Caesarea of Palestine and Alexandria of Egypt. When he was about thirty he was baptized either in Athens, where he was a student with St. Basil, or upon his return to his own country. Much of Gregory's life was spent alternating between able work as a priest or bishop and retreat to the solitude he so dearly loved. Gregory found himself in the center of theological controversy when he was called in 379 to Constantinople to lead the minority of Christians there who held to the faith as set forth by the Council of Nicaea (325). The following year, the Emperor Theodosius installed Gregory in the imperial Church of Santa Sophia in place of the rival bishop Demophilus. Although the Second Ecumenical Council confirmed him as the patriarch of Constantinople, Gregory resigned his office there to administer once again the diocese of Nazianzus before retiring (384) to his estate in Arianzum, where he remained until his death.

The *Five Theological Orations (Orationes* 27-31) were delivered as sermons in Constantinople in 380. The first of the five is introductory and posits, against the excesses of the Eunomians, the limits within which genuine theological discourse may take place. The Eunomians taught a special form of Arianism (which said that Christ was not of the same nature as the Father but was an intermediary between the Father and creation) to the effect that the Son was unlike the Father. The Eunomians were also known for the boldness with which they discussed the most intimate features of God's being. Gregory complains that these talkative dialecticians so delight in strife over words that every marketplace buzzes with profane babblings about that which is most sacred. He maintains that the subject of God is not so cheap that everyone can philosophize about it: discussion about God is only for certain occasions, before certain men, and within certain limits. As in dress and diet, and laughter and demeanor, there is a certain decorum in speech and silence, especially so for Christians because of their reverence for the Word as a title of God. Systematic reflection about God is permitted only to those who have been duly trained, who are skilled in meditation, and who have been or are being purified. Gregory adds that it is necessary to be truly at leisure to know God, for then we have an appropriate time to discern the straight road of divine matters. He says he is not against continual remembrance of God, which is desirable, nor does he want to hinder all talking about God; his objection is to a lack of proper moderation. The reason for Gregory's insistent warning is that ultimately God's nature is incomprehensible to us in this life, and that without these limits in theological discourse ". . . our great mystery is in danger of being made a thing of little moment." (First Theological Oration).

In the second of these orations, Gregory considers how we may know God, whose inscrutability imposes the boundaries explained in the first oration. At the outset, Gregory discloses the method controlling his theological deliberation: ". . . being molded and molding others by Holy Scripture . . . let us now enter upon theological questions, setting at the head thereof the Father, the Son, and the Holy Ghost, of whom we are to treat; that the Father may be well pleased, and the Son may help us, and the Holy Ghost may inspire us; or rather that one illumination may come upon us from the one God, one in diversity, diverse in unity, wherein is a marvel." (Second Theological Oration). Drawing on Exodus 32, Gregory likens the theologian's experience to that of ascending a mount and drawing aside the cloudy curtain by going away from materiality and withdrawing within oneself. Sheltered by the rock which is the Word made flesh for us, the theologian sees only the back parts of God: not the primary and unmingled nature, known exclusively to the Trinity itself, but only ". . . that nature, which at last even reaches to us. And that is, as far as I can learn, the majesty, or, as holy David calls it, the glory which is manifested among the creatures, which it has produced and governs." (Second Theological Oration). The darkness of this world and of the flesh prevents a full understanding of the truth in this life.

Gregory's admonition is not to be used as a starting-point for a quibbling denial of God. For him, we can know by reason that God *is* but not *Who* He is. Our eyes, seeing the beautiful stability and progress of visible things as ordered by natural law and reasoning back from the order of these things to their author, teach us that God exists and that He is their efficient and maintaining cause. Every rational nature longs for God but is unable to grasp Him. Impatient at this disability, the rational creature either fabricates idols out of visible things or attains through the visible order that which is above sight. In the latter case reason, which proceeds from God and is implanted in all from the beginning, enables this ascent. Relying upon all the approximations of reason, however, man still cannot comprehend God: "For how is he an object of worship if he be circumscribed?" (Second Oration).

In the third and fourth theological orations, Gregory sets out to refute his opponents and to state his position on the equality and distinction of the Son in relation to the Father. Some of his adversaries ascribed the name of God only to the Father; others bestowed on the Son a name equal to the one they applied to God but in practice denied

His deity by denying exact equality. Gregory's position is that among the three ancient opinions concerning God, namely, anarchy, polyarchy, and monarchy, the first two were the favorites of the Greeks and led to disorder and dissolution, while the third is the one honored by Christians. However, monarchy, the rule by the one God, is not limited to any one of the Persons of the Trinity: "The Father is the begetter and the emitter; without passion, of course, and without reference to time, and not in a corporeal manner. The Son is the begotten, and the Holy Ghost the emission; for I know not how this could be expressed in terms altogether excluding visible things." (Third Theological Oration). We are not to think of this generation, this begetting of the Son, as an involuntary and natural overflow of goodness. Nor are we to think of the "when" of this generation since it is above all time. The only answer to the question "when" the Father came into being is that "There never was a time when he was not." (Third Oration). (This crucial formula, which is a repudiation of the slogan of Arius, "There was when he was not," is not accurately rendered into English by the phrase used here. The Greek expresses an important subtlety and says literally, "There never was when he was not." Gregory uses this formula so as not to concede the possibility of "time" as a category applicable to the Godhead.) The same is the case with the begetting of the Son and the proceeding of the Spirit. The Son and the Holy Spirit originate from the Father, yet are co-eternal with him since the Father is everlastingly the cause and therefore is not "prior" to the effects. The generation of the Son is without passion because

it is incorporeal, yet it is voluntary since will is not passion.

While all this points to the distinctiveness of the Persons, it also describes their full equality. Countering the viewpoint which insists the uncreated and the created are not the same any more than begetting and being begotten are the same, Gregory preaches that the begetter and the begotten are nonetheless of the same nature, that therein lies the object of the "Father-Son" terminology: the offspring is of the same nature as the parent. The term "Father" does not refer to essence or action; it is a name of relationship indicating an identity of nature. Should "Father" be taken as a term of essence, a Son of the same nature is implied anyway, and if it be taken as a term of action, a Son who is *homoousios* (of the same nature) with the Father is also included.

Gregory recognizes two kinds of Biblical passages about Christ: those witnessing to His divinity and those suggesting His inequality with the Father. The correct interpretation of both sorts, he says, is to apply what is lofty to the Godhead and to that nature in Him which is incorporeal and above all suffering, and to apply what is lowly to the composite condition of Him who for our sakes made Himself of no reputation, who was incarnate, and indeed who was made man and was afterwards exalted. He was incarnate for a cause, and the cause was that we might be saved.

In the fifth theological oration, an oration of particular significance for Greek Orthodoxy, Gregory turns to the campaign against the doctrine of the Trinity waged by another group, the Macedonians. These men rejected the divinity of the Holy Spirit, maintaining instead that He was a creature of the Son. Gregory holds that the Holy Spirit is no strange or interpolated God, as those Macedonians imagine who are so literal in their exposition of Scripture. If ever there was a time when the Father or the Son did not exist, there was also a time when the Spirit did not exist. But if one was from the beginning, then the three were from the beginning. It will not do to call the Spirit God in such a way as to deny His equality in nature with the Father and the Son. If the Spirit is God, then He is consubstantial with the Father and the Son; He is not a creature, nor a fellow servant, nor is any such lowly designation appropriate to Him. The Holy Spirit's distinctiveness lies in His procession, His eternal going forth from the Father by a process of generation which, like the generation of the Son, is beyond human comprehension. The very fact of being unbegotten, of being begotten, and of proceeding gives the name of Father to the first, Son to the second, and Holy Spirit to the third, so that the distinction of the three Persons may be preserved in the one nature and dignity of the Godhead. "When, then, we look at the Godhead, or the first cause, or the monarchia, that which we conceive is one; but when we look at the Persons in whom the Godhead dwells, and at those who timelessly and with equal glory have their being from the first cause, there are three whom we worship." (Fifth Theological Oration).

A final complication dealt with by Gregory is the Macedonian allegation that Scripture is silent about the divinity of the Spirit. On this, he teaches that by God's gracious dispensation the Old Testament proclaims the Father openly and the Son more obscurely, that the New Testament manifests the Son and suggests the deity of the Spirit, and that now the Spirit Himself dwells among us and supplies us with a clear demonstration of Himself. The Holy Spirit's divinity is so marvelous that men could not have believed it without the marvelous precedent of Christ's Resurrection. Of the many things the Savior promised that the Spirit would manifest to His followers, none was greater than the Spirit's divinity. Even if Scripture were silent in this matter, these arguments would still support this doctrine. Yet Gregory goes on to say that in fact Scripture does provide a wealth of testimonies for the divinity of the Spirit.

In the end, Gregory concludes that all images fall short of the subject and that it is best for him, using few words, to abide by the reverent conceptions, to keep as his comrade the enlightenment of the Holy Spirit, and to pass through this world persuading others to worship Father, Son, and Holy Ghost, the one Godhead and power.

HOMILIES ON THE STATUES

Author: Saint John Chrysostom (c.347-407)
Type of work: Sermons on Christian Practice
First transcribed: 387

PRINCIPAL IDEAS ADVANCED

*In a time of civic danger, the Church, like a mother, comforts and strengthens
those who turn to her.*

Christians need have no fear of loss, not even loss of life itself.

*The Christian should lead a life of austerity and mortification; the true ascetic
is one who is pure in heart, reverent toward God, and charitable toward all men.*

*The Christian priest ministers redemption through the sacraments, and per-
suades men to do the will of God by means of the art of preaching.*

Of the extensive body of Chrysostom's writing to be preserved, the most
permanently valuable are his commentaries on Biblical books, and his sermons or homilies. Especially celebrated
are the collection of twenty-one *Homilies on the Statues,* delivered when
Chrysostom was a priest at his native
city, Antioch, prior to being made
Archbishop of Constantinople.

The series takes its name from a
serious political incident which developed during the Lenten season in
which the sermons were preached, an
incident which, to a considerable degree, determined the character of the
sermons. Certain elements in Antioch,
stirred by resentment over a new tax
levy, stormed the Prefect's palace, and,
when repulsed, vented their anger by
overthrowing the public statues of the
Emperor Theodosius (346-395) and
his late Empress, and dragging them
through the streets. The Prefect imprisoned a large number of leading
citizens and brought them to trial.
Meanwhile, the entire population
awaited fearfully the judgment of the
Emperor. Rumor ran wild, and many
inhabitants fled the city under the
impression that the whole population
would be slain and the buildings
razed. The incident, however, came to
a relatively happy conclusion when, on

Easter, it was announced that the Emperor had granted full pardon.

Chrysostom did not take the pulpit
on account of the disturbances. It was
his practice, during Lent, to preach
three or four times a week. Indeed,
the first homily of this series was given
a few days before the seditious acts
were committed. But since the fear
that emptied the forums and market-
places filled the churches, it could not
be ignored. Chrysostom spoke of the
matter at hand, particularly in homilies
two through six. For the rest, he dealt
very much in his ordinary manner
with Lenten topics, giving only incidental attention to the civic concern,
until he came to the final sermon,
which, falling on Easter, coincided
with the news of the city's deliverance.
Various incidents, however, provide
topical interest. Flavian, Bishop of
Antioch, though an old man, traveled
to Constantinople, and was largely influential in moving Theodosius to
clemency. Great numbers of Christian
monks left their cloisters in the desert
and returned to Antioch in order to
share whatever punishment should be
visited upon the citizens. These sacrificial acts, says Chrysostom, demonstrate
the love which the Church has toward
men. He points, by way of contrast,
to the pagan philosophers, who, he
says, forsook the city and hid them-

selves in caves as soon as danger appeared. The *Homilies* also contain vivid and moving descriptions of the brutality of soldiers, the devotion of wives and sisters, and the odd and unpredictable sorts of conduct, sometimes pathetic, sometimes heroic, which sudden stress produces among a people unaccustomed to danger and hardship.

Chrysostom roundly condemns those who overthrew the statues, and he places the Church solidly on the side of Imperial authority. The Church, he says, stands to the Emperor in the same relation as a mother does to the schoolmaster: when the child is punished, she comforts him, and she tries to show him the necessity for the master's severity. His main point, however, is that Christians ought not fear any penalty which the Emperor may choose to impose. As an ascetic moralist, who has himself spent several years in the desert as a monk, Chrysostom argues against the vanity of wealth and position. "We do not live with the austerity that becometh Christians," he says. The Christian, he maintains, should have no fear of what man can do to him: "He who by the aid of virtue leads a life of austerity, and mortification, earnestly longs for death in order that he may be freed from his present labours, and may be able to have full assurance in regard to the crowns laid up in store." Chrysostom presses home his teaching with the aid of such Old Testament stories as that of the destruction of Sodom, Esther's intercession for the Jews, Jonah's mission to Nineveh, the temptation of Job, and the trial of the three young men in Nebuchadnezzar's fiery furnace. To the Socratic (and Stoic) persuasion that no harm can happen to the good man, and the Hebraic confidence that

temporal loss and gain are tokens of divine judgment, he adds the Christian conviction that life on earth is merely preparatory to an eternity of condemnation or blessedness.

The more general topics which Chrysostom deals with in these Lenten sermons are fasting, swearing, and forgiving one's neighbor. Chrysostom is an intrepid expounder of Scripture, as might be expected from the impressive list of commentaries which he wrote, but he uses Scripture to enforce practical, not theological, lessons.

Speaking of fasting, he takes as his text Paul's words to Timothy: "Drink a little wine for thy stomach's sake, and thine often infirmities." Timothy was, on the witness of this text, an abstainer, says Chrysostom; that is, he knew the dangers of indulging fleshly appetites. But Paul assures him that there is nothing wrong in partaking of wine as such, the evil lying in the abuse of a thing that is good. Nevertheless, Paul enforces the need for mastering our desires, inasmuch as he says, "Drink a little."

The practice of swearing is treated more frequently than any other subject. In sermon after sermon, Chrysostom reproaches his hearers with their bad habit of using oaths. We may take this as a commentary on the customs of the times, but it is also a lesson in moral pedagogy, for if a people are severely taken in a fault, it is not enough to preach a single sermon against it; one must preach sermon after sermon, repeating as much as is necessary until a sufficient impression has been made. If one has the wit and imagination of a Chrysostom (whose surname, meaning The Golden Mouth, was given to him because of his eloquence), repetition need never become stale. Chrysostom's most striking text against swearing is that which tells of the curse which King Saul pronounced in the heat of battle against any who should partake of food before victory, and of his son Jonathan's unwitting violation of his father's oath. Another is that of the oath of Herod which led to the death of John the Baptist. Let each of you, Chrysostom enjoins, "taking the head of John, just cut off, and the warm blood yet dripping from it, . . . go home, and think that you saw it before your eyes, while it emitted a voice, and said, 'Abhor my murderer, the oath!' "

Chrysostom takes up the subject of forgiveness in the next to last homily. As the time for Holy Communion approaches, it behooves each one to consider what fault remains that will prevent his participating in the Feast with a good conscience, especially whether he is at odds with his fellow man. "Let no one who hath an enemy draw near the sacred Table, or receive the Lord's body!" the preacher warns; "Let no one who draws near have an enemy! Hast thou an enemy? Draw not near! Wilt thou draw near? Be reconciled, and then draw near, and touch the Holy thing!" He proceeds to give a profound analysis of the violence which resentment does, not to the man toward whom it is directed, but to the man who nourishes it in his breast. "For thou supposest that thou art paying him back the injury; but thou art first tormenting thyself, and setting up thy rage as an executioner within thee in every part, and tearing up thine own bowels." But does someone suppose that it is a weakness to be reconciled to those who have done wrong, and that it will make the wicked man

worse? On the contrary, says Chrysostom, he will become far worse if you remain unreconciled toward him, while if you offer to forgive him, his heart may be touched. "For although he were the vilest of men; although he might neither confess nor publish it openly; yet he will silently approve thy Christian wisdom, and in his own conscience will respect thy gentleness."

Chrysostom's preaching consists mainly in exhorting men to live according to the righteousness of God and to forsake the ways of the world and of their great adversary, the Devil. Protestants will miss in the *Homilies* any pronounced evangelical emphasis, but this does not mean that Chrysostom was lacking in appreciation of the redemptive work of Christ; rather, he stood in the sacerdotal tradition and held that the grace of God is communicated objectively through the sacraments. Readers who are interested in Chrysostom's own reflections on the office of preaching are advised to turn to his *Treatise on the Priesthood*, where, besides magnifying the office of the priest in the Eucharistic sacrifice, where Christ is "laid upon the altar," and the priest stands "praying over the victim," he also places great stress on the "ministry of the Word." Preaching, says Chrysostom, who was trained as a rhetorician before he became a Christian, does not come by nature, but by study and practice. It is an art to be judged by strict canons like any other art, and not by the applause of the masses. The preacher, in Chrysostom's view, is a workman responsible to God, committed with the task of bringing the multitudes to know and obey the will of their Sovereign. It is a particularly difficult task, because the multitudes only half listen, and consequently they readily distort what they hear, for their own purposes. Hence, the preacher must never be swayed by their praise or blame, but must labor in his sermons with a view to pleasing God.

ON THE DUTIES OF THE CLERGY

Author: Saint Ambrose (c.339-397)
Type of work: Christian ethics
First transcribed: c.391

PRINCIPAL IDEAS ADVANCED

Christian virtue is living according to Christ and, consequently, according to what is most in harmony with nature and reason.

The Christian life is balanced and observes due measure; it is not given to the pursuit of extremes in either external affairs and possessions, or in internal states of character.

Whatever is virtuous and whatever is useful to our final happiness are identical.

When *On the Duties of the Clergy* was written about 391 by Ambrose, Bishop of Milan, the Christian Church enjoyed a favored status in Roman imperial policy and was active in formulating its internal discipline. A startling illustration of what could happen in the provision of leadership was the experience of Ambrose himself. He was chosen to be Bishop of Milan in 374 while he was as yet unbaptized (although he had been converted, of course), and only eight days intervened between his baptism and his elevation to the bishopric (at which time he was a catechumen). In addition, his predecessor had been an advocate of Arianism, a theological position which Ambrose vigorously opposed. This change in the doctrinal allegiance of the occupant of the bishop's chair was not a considered product of formal discussion, but a matter of personal perspective on the part of the incumbent.

Clearly, much had yet to be done in the ordering of the ministry when such happenings were possible, and Ambrose's book, *De officiis ministrorum,* was produced as a contribution to one area of concern; namely, the kind of Christian morality that should govern the life of the clergy and, in turn, that of their congregations. The book was written as a practical guide for the young men whom Ambrose was preparing for ordination.

The significance of the work is both in what it has to say and in the time and circumstances in which it was said. Ambrose had had no training in Christian theology or ethics, and he confesses that he had to teach and learn at the same time. His education was that of the Roman governing classes, and, in his case, fortunately, his studies included Greek. With this background it is not surprising that Ambrose turned to Stoic literature for a model when he proposed to discuss the obligations of the clergy. Cicero had written a book, *De officiis*, and this provided a basis from which to work, although the actual occasion on which Ambrose decided to write on the theme was a meditation on Psalm 39.

The work is divided into three books, the first dealing with what is virtuous, the second with what is useful, and the third with a comparison of the two. The fact is, however, that this plan is only loosely adhered to, and there are topics in all the books that do not fit the scheme, and, again, topics that recur throughout the entire work.

Even though the debt to Cicero is obvious, Ambrose did not simply repeat Stoic maxims on moderation, self-control, manly virtue, and self realization. Although by later standards of Christian ethics the book as a whole has its limitations and leaves much to be desired, it is nevertheless a Christian work directed toward "the blessing of eternal life" and not simply toward worldly happiness. Allusions to Scripture are copious, the work of God in history is everywhere emphasized, and the authority of Christ for life-direction is explicitly confessed.

The first duty of any man, Ambrose asserts, is to do what is seemly or suitable, especially with regard to speech. A note of "due measure" recurs again and again; virtue is rewarded. Such an idea seems to be contrary to much of our experience, however, for evil men are often found to be prosperous, and the innocent, like Job, are left in want. But if the conscience of wicked men is taken into account, the picture is different, for the soul of an evil man "is more foul than any sepulchre" and his end is in Hell. Nothing escapes the knowledge of God, the just judge of all, and the end will vindicate the righteous.

The duties of youth are next enumerated in traditional terms; namely, the fear of God, subjection to parents, respect for age, preservation of purity, and, especially, modesty in word and deed. "The movement of the body is a sort of voice of the soul," Ambrose writes. He recalls that he refused to accept among his clergy a person who was arrogant in his gestures. Even the way we walk reveals our disposition. "We ought to be humble, gentle, mild, serious, patient," Ambrose continues; "We must keep the mean in all things, so that a calm countenance and quiet speech may show that there is no vice in our lives."

The principle of due measure has a clear contextual reference. What is virtuous will vary with the occasion in which we act, for we must act suitably and not with a rigid conformity to rules, all of which is abundantly illustrated by Abraham, Jacob, Joseph, Job, and David. These men followed the four virtues of prudence, justice, fortitude, and temperance.

Ambrose then develops the classical quartet of virtues, and he attempts to subsume the many qualities of the good life under these key categories, showing that they are interdependent and all united in piety. He is insistent that good will is as necessary as good external action and that this inner motivation will greatly affect the specific behavior of the Christian man.

His treatment of fortitude, however, reveals the latent difficulty of handling a Christian ethic under a pagan formula. Examples of courage are plentiful in the Old Testament, but the Christian martyrs are eulogized. Again, courage in withstanding temptations of the mind is duly delineated and praised; but love and humility do not fit easily into the Roman admiration for the military virtues, and in Book III Ambrose denies that a Christian should defend himself when attacked "lest in defending his life he should stain his love toward his neighbour."

The second book opens with the thesis, "So great is the splendour of a virtuous life that a peaceful conscience and a calm innocence work out a happy life"; that is, it is most useful to achieve the truly blessed life. Happiness has been variously defined by philosophers in terms of freedom from pain, knowledge, or pleasure, but the Scriptures clearly associate it with "divine things and . . . the fruit of good works." It is a mistake to base happiness on good fortune or to tie it to external possessions. Indeed, some things, such as riches, which are counted good, can be a hindrance to the blessed life; on the other hand, things such as pain, blindness, exile, hunger, slavery, which are thought to be bad, can promote it. What is truly useful is truly godly and serves Christ.

Love is outstanding in its relation to utility. We should labor to be loved by showing moderation, courtesy, honor, and modesty, as Moses and David showed gentleness and affection even to those who had wronged them. Ambrose writes, "It gives a very great impetus to mutual love if one shows love in return to those who love us and proves that one does not love

them less than oneself is loved, especially if one shows it by the proofs that a faithful friendship gives."

Utility is also closely allied to the four cardinal virtues. The man who practices the virtues inspires the confidence of others so that his counsel is sought and he is then able to do the most good.

How wonderful it is "to gain the love of the people by liberality," Ambrose exclaims. This remark is especially pertinent to the clergy, who have opportunity to influence liberality by the feeding of the poor, the redemption of captives, and many other forms of kindness. Due measure, however, has to be observed in liberality for, Ambrose advises, it must be "neither too freely shown to those who are unsuitable, nor too sparingly bestowed upon the needy." Professional beggars, for example, have to be watched: "If anyone were to trust their tale too readily, he would quickly drain the fund which is meant to serve the sustenance of the poor." Ambrose, obviously, had had experience in handling the importunate, and he offers sage advice at considerable length on the administration of church funds. Generosity is a virtue only when it is wise and unostentatious.

If one would learn true wisdom, he must seek the company of wise men, for we become like our companions. Especially ought the young to improve themselves by friendship with the old, as did Joshua with Moses, Elisha with Elijah, Mark with Barnabas, and Timothy with Paul. This is the direct way to be worthy of esteem and to avoid extravagance, dissipation, and destruction. We must study hospitality, defend the weak, and shun avarice, pretense, and adulation.

In one of the most eloquent passages in *De officiis ministrorum*, Ambrose discourses on the occasion when he sold the gold vessels of the church to redeem some captives: "So I once brought odium on myself because I broke up the sacred vessels to redeem captives." But his memorable act, he believed, was according to the spirit of Christ: "It is far better to preserve souls than gold for the Lord." In so acting he followed, he claims, the example of the martyr Lawrence who, when the treasures of the church were demanded from him, brought the poor together: "When asked where the treasures were which he had promised, he pointed to the poor, saying, 'These are the treasures of the church.'"

In the third book the comparison between virtue and utility is discussed. The two are not opposed if they are understood as identical when informed by the Christian spirit. To emphasize this point, Ambrose draws a distinction between ordinary levels of duty and the perfection which the Christian obligation imposes. This distinction led in later ethical theory to the double standard by which one set of duties (the commandments) was expected of laymen and a higher standard of poverty, obedience, and chastity (the counsels) was demanded of the clergy. At this stage, however, the division is at the more elementary level of a comparison between what "the many" count as good, such as saving money or enjoying a banquet, and the self-sacrifice and other-centered ideals of those who are dedicated to Christ. The distinction had been noted in Book I, but it is repeated in Book III, preparatory to an expansion of the "primary" duties of the many. Ambrose is not altogether clear as to the

significance of this duality in duty, for he notes Paul's sayings about being not yet perfect and being already perfect, and he concludes that "There is a twofold form of perfection, the one having but ordinary, the other the highest worth. The one availing here, the other hereafter." What develops in the discussion that follows is little more than a commendation of conduct that serves others rather than the self. To act in such a manner is to be conformed to Christ. We are to be concerned for all who need our help, knowing that we are in a relation of interdependence after the manner of an organism. To act thus is to follow also the law of nature, for "a man who guides himself according to the ruling of nature, so as to be obedient to her, can never injure another." Thus, conscience rebukes us when we are unjust, cruel, and self-centered. Even if we could make ourselves invisible, the upright man will live according to the example of Christ. He will "not hide his person by putting on a ring, but his life by putting on Christ."

By this standard a Christian will never injure another for self-advantage, defraud others in the market, expel strangers in time of famine, or be a party to financial trickery. If a person binds himself with a promise which is subsequently seen to involve what is dishonorable, he is not under any obligation to keep such a commitment. Better that Herod should have perjured himself, than keep his promise to murder John the Baptist. Even for the sake of friendship, which is the guardian of virtue, no one should betray his integrity. It is with a eulogy on friendship that Ambrose concludes his work *On the*

Duties of the Clergy. He has, he says, spoken what will be to the advantage of his readers, and supported his reflections with many illustrations from the past, "So that, although the language may not be graceful, yet a succession of old-time examples set down in such a small compass may offer much instruction."

THE GREAT CATECHISM

Author: Saint Gregory of Nyssa (c.330-c.395)
Type of work: Spiritual instruction
First transcribed: c.395

PRINCIPAL IDEAS ADVANCED

The Christian must avoid not only polytheism but also any monotheism which leads to a rejection of the Trinity.

The doctrine of the Incarnation is central to Christian teaching and may be understood through analogy.

The sacrament of baptism is the first and necessary step in a resurrection to a new, immortal life.

Unless they be followed by righteousness in living, the sacraments are without value.

In *The Great Catechism* by Gregory, Bishop of Nyssa, are found those qualities which caused him to be held in high esteem by his contemporaries and have earned for him an enduring place in the history of the Christian Church as one of its honored founders. The combination of personal sanctity, theological erudition, and zealous defense of Nicene creedal orthodoxy, apparent here as throughout his works, understandably brought to Gregory high praise, leading to his being termed the Father of Fathers and to his being elevated to sainthood. Moreover, Gregory's passionate concerns for the fruit of orthodoxy in righteous living and for the conversion of those outside the faith through carefully balanced and discriminating explanations of Christian beliefs, add to the work an appeal which overcomes the limitations of his historical period and give it an abiding value.

The third son of ten children born to a Christian family of wealth and distinction in the important bishopric of Cappadocia, Gregory, because of delicate health, was educated at home. It is noteworthy that his older sister was extremely devout and established a religious society, and that his brother, Basil, who had studied in Athens and was a student of the great Christian apologist, Origen, was Gregory's most influential teacher. Termed shy and retiring, Gregory remained at home and chose no profession. His religious awakening occurred in a vision which came during a religious service at which he had fallen asleep through fatigue. His sister persuaded him to abandon all secular pursuits and to retire to his brother's monastery, where he devoted himself to prayer and the study of Scripture and of Origen. From his thirtieth year he became increasingly involved in the affairs of the Church. His brother, who had been appointed Bishop of Caesarea in Cappadocia, appointed Gregory bishop in the small town of Nyssa, in western Cappadocia.

Because of his personality and his theological convictions, Gregory found the life of a bishop very trying—so much so, in fact, that he became the object of intrigue and was eventually brought to trial, deposed from his episcopal throne, and banished. With the restoration of the orthodox bishops, Gregory returned to Nyssa but not to happiness, for within a year both his brother and his sister died. From that time onward Gregory enlarged the scope of his labors and received increasingly wider appreciation for his gifts as a teacher and as a great religious spirit. He had been assigned an obscure post, but at his death, about 395, he left it ennobled by his name.

It was not until the end of the nineteenth century that the treatises of Gregory were translated from their original Greek. Among the dogmatic, ascetic, and philosophical works translated and collected in the series edited by Philip Schaff and Henry Wace as *A Select Library of Nicene and Post-Nicene Fathers of the Christian Church,* it is perhaps the apologetic work entitled *The Great Catechism* which reveals Gregory most adequately for the contemporary reader. It is in this manual of instruction

for catechizers, this text for teachers, that Gregory advances his defense and theory of Christianity in terms not so much of the historic arguments based on prophecy or moral considerations as in terms of its truth in the metaphysical sense. In good pedagogic fashion Gregory supplies his readers with a summary of his work, and he indicates the three main topics: the Trinity, the reasonableness of the Incarnation, and the Sacraments.

Gregory begins his discussion of the Trinity by developing the arguments for God based on the presence of design in the world and for God's perfection in unity on the basis of the incompatibility of any notion of imperfection with the notion of deity. The Christian, in combating polytheism, must not so emphasize the unity of God as to fall into the opposite error of Judaism, with its strict monotheistic rejection of the Trinity. In closely reasoned passages which are often intricate and subtle, Gregory undertakes the difficult task of demonstrating both the better logic of Christian belief and the ultimate mystery to which true (Christian) use of logic leads. Gregory meets his logical opponents on their own ground and shows them their errors, yet he does not proceed to present Christianity as a logical system. Careful to insist upon the inherent imprecision of arguing by analogy, and stressing the inability of man to reason by analogy directly to deity, Gregory nevertheless employs this means of argument: "As in our own case we say that the word is from the mind, and no more entirely the same as the mind, than altogether other than it . . . in like manner, too, the Word of God by its self-subsistence is distinct from Him from whom it has its subsistence; and yet by exhibiting in itself those qualities which are recognized in God it is the same in nature with Him who is recognizable by the same distinctive marks."

Here is right reason leading to the point at which the ineffable depth of mystery is reached and for which the doctrine of the Trinity, illogical on a lower level, is the most logical, although paradoxical, expression.

Closely reasoned as they are, Gregory's arguments appear to the critical contemporary reader as open to the criticism that they proceed from premises whose validity has been taken for granted rather than established through careful analysis. When, for example, Gregory proves that God created the world by His reason and wisdom because He could not have proceeded irrationally in that work, the "proof" seems to be nothing more than a statement of what God ought to be. God is defined so as to make it both absurd and impious to "install unreason and unskillfulness on the throne of the universe."

In the section dealing with the reasonableness of the Incarnation, similar lines of argument are developed showing that the Word of God is "a power essentially and substantially existing, willing all good, and being possessed of strength to execute all its will." Gregory explores the implication of the theory of man's having been created from God's superabounding love and in His image as immortal and with the gifts of freedom, independence, and self-determination. Man is thus free to choose against God, as did Adam, who disturbed the divinely ordered harmony between man's sensuous and intellectual natures. Since evil is deprivation of good and has no existence

of its own, God, maker of all substantial things, is not maker of evil. "He who formed the sight did not make blindness," Gregory writes.

Gregory refutes the argument of those who oppose the Incarnation on the ground that the finite cannot contain the Infinite, by referring to the relationship of the human soul to its body. Characteristically he asks "Why may we not, by examples of which we are capable of understanding, gain some reasonable idea of God's plan of salvation?" The question of Incarnation requires a prior consideration of the mind-body problem, which is itself grounded in mystery.

It is the figure of the ransom that Gregory employs to explain the death of the Son of God. The death proves that God's justice impelled Him to offer one who exceeded in value that which was to be ransomed (sinful man). That a description of this sort involves conceiving of God as engaging in a deception upon Satan is candidly acknowledged by Gregory, who sees God's deception as just. God's deception is for good since even Satan will at last recognize God's justice and experience the benefits of the Incarnation.

With strong emphasis on baptism as essential to the sacramental system of salvation, Gregory teaches that in baptism God as Holy Spirit is truly given. Baptism is the first and necessary step in a resurrection to a new, immortal life. Gregory then develops a view of the sacrament of the Eucharist as a transformation of the elements of bread and wine into the body and blood of Christ. Gregory's view is credited as being the first such among the Fathers and as forming the basis for the doctrine of transubstantiation of later medieval theology. Bread and wine are sanctified by the word of God and prayer and become at once, not gradually, the body of God. It is the Eucharist which unites the body of the Christian to God just as baptism unites the soul to God. Bread and wine are thus the antidotes to the poison which human bodies inherited from the Fall.

Gregory ends his treatise to the catechetical leaders with a reminder that for true regeneration it is essential to believe that the Son and the Spirit are not created spirits of like nature with God the Father. The necessity of this emphasis is clear when one realizes that to make one's salvation dependent on anything created would be to trust an imperfect nature which itself needs a savior. The Gospel releases man from the vicious circle of dependence upon other dependents, for it tells us "that the birth of the saved is from above."

For all his insight into the ineffable nature of Christian truth and his emphasis upon the centrality of the sacraments, Gregory's final exhortation reveals a most practical side of his nature and shows how far he was from permitting his high sacramentalism to degenerate into mere magic. If a person is baptized and yet shows no indication that his soul has been washed through better living, Gregory asserts, "though it may be a bold thing to say, yet I will say it and will not shrink; in these cases the water is but water, for the gift of the Holy Ghost in no way appears in him who is thus baptismally born. . . ." Let no one be mistaken, he adds: "If you continue with the characteristic marks of vice in you, it is in vain that you babble to yourself of your birth from above." The seriousness of this condition is made clear when one remembers that the fire of punishment for sin is only a pale suggestion of that torment for which no equivalent may be found in earthly experience.

THE CONFESSIONS OF SAINT AUGUSTINE

Author: Saint Augustine (354-430)
Type of work: Spiritual autobiography
First transcribed: c.397

PRINCIPAL IDEAS ADVANCED

Man's love finds its proper object in God, yet man's temptation is to give his love to finite objects.

Through conversion to faith in God and Jesus Christ, a unification of the self is possible; man acquires insight and power through Christian faith.

The self finds God not through memory or other exercises of the mind but through preparing itself for God's revelation of Himself.

God is the creator; He is not to be identified with His creation.

Time is God's creation; in God Himself there is an eternal present.

The *Confessions*, completed about 397, is surely the best known of Saint Augustine's many works, and it is also perhaps the most synoptic statement of his many-sided mind and life. The title calls attention to the form of the work, which is Augustine's personal address to God. In the presence of God, Augustine discovered his own human personality. His account of his spiritual development is the first of a long tradition of such confessions. Since the book contains accounts of many events of Augustine's life it has often been termed a spiritual autobiography, a characterization which calls for the qualification that the *Confessions* omits many events of Augustine's life and also contains much which is not biography. Yet, the important fact is that the personality of Augustine is clearly delineated in the pages of the *Confessions*.

As the reader reads through the thirteen books of the *Confessions*, he follows Augustine through the changing scenes of his life from his birth and childhood in Tagaste, to his college days in Carthage, to professional posts in Carthage, Rome, and Milan. He also follows Augustine's wanderings among the faiths and philosophies of his time to his baptism into Catholic Christianity in 387. He witnesses Augustine's passionate heart seeking an object worthy of its allegiance. He observes Augustine's adventurous mind seeking an adequate philosophy, probing Manicheanism, Platonism, skepticism, and finally finding truth in Christianity. Yet, most of all, he watches Augustine probing the depths of his anxious and restless self, and coming finally to rest in God.

Augustine's ideas in the *Confessions* are a synthesis of Neoplatonic and Hebraic or Biblical elements. His view of God is similar to the idea of the Absolute One in Neoplatonism, yet the ideas of sovereign will and love are clearly Biblical. Similarly, with respect to man, Augustine's view of the inward depths of personality owes much to Plotinus, yet man for Augustine is basically volitional in nature, and here, once more, his view is Biblical. Again, his view of evil is a synthesis of the Neoplatonic conception of nonbeing and the Biblical conception of rebellion against the sovereign God. As a mortal or finite being, man's love finds its proper object in God. Yet man's temptation is to give this love to objects short of God; it is, in other words, the inordinate love of finite goods. But such objects are unable to sustain this allegiance or love, and so man falls into confusion and nonbeing.

The curtain is raised in Book I upon Augustine's stormy dialogue with God by a characteristic quotation from Psalms 145 and 147: "Great art thou, O Lord and greatly to be praised; great is thy power, and infinite is thy wisdom," which elicits from Augustine the response that ". . . thou hast made us for thyself and our hearts are restless until they rest in thee." These reflections in turn lead onward to the question, so characteristic of Augustine, as to how the finite mind of man can contain the infinite God. The answer here and throughout the work is that only through a paradoxically articulated divine grace and human faith can man know the divine.

Turning to autobiography, Augustine reflects upon his own infancy and childhood. Supplementing recollection and introspection with observation of other human beings and reports of other observers, he speaks of such matters as the origin of speech and the grasping selfishness of infants. In a similar spirit, Augustine recalls the games and pranks of childhood, finding in them an expression of original sin and wickedness as well as the guiding, providential grace of God. He alludes to the austerities of his schooling with its beatings and its full lessons, to his dislike of Greek, and to his intense love of Latin and Roman literature.

Book II continues these juvenile recollections, concentrating attention on the famous prank in which, at the age of sixteen, Augustine and some friends pilfered and then wantonly wasted some pears. Augustine's analysis of this deed emphasizes its wanton and sinful character, leading him to the sort of deep, though often morbid, probing of the self which is recurrent in the *Confessions,* and which is also a salient feature of Augustine's view of the human self.

Book III describes the author's student days in Carthage where, as he put it, "a caldron of unholy loves was seething and bubbling around me." He studied literature and went to the theater. During this period he also encountered Cicero's *Hortensius,* which impressed him deeply as a call to the intellectual and contemplative life. He records his first contact with the Manicheans, who were to hold his attention for the next nine years and to defer his full entrance into Catholic Christianity. Manicheanism was a widely popular faith and philosophy of the ancient world which emphasized both a cosmic and psychological dualism of spirit and matter. The explanation of evil as rooted in matter was attractive to Augustine.

Upon completion of his studies, Augustine took up a career in the teaching of literature and rhetoric, as he tells us in Book IV. His first post was in his home town of Tagaste. During this time he took a mistress who remained with him until shortly before his conversion. He reports also an interest in astrology. A friend's death plunged him into intense grief, leading in the *Confessions* to reflections upon the inordinate love of finite goods, such as human friends. During this time he reports the reading of Aristotle's *Categories* and the writing of his first book, entitled *Concerning the Beautiful and the Apt.*

Book V deals with the year of decision in which Augustine became disenchanted with Manicheanism. Bishop Faustus, a Manichean leader, visited Carthage, and Augustine found the answers to his questions evasive and unimpressive. Renouncing Manicheanism, Augustine moved in the direction of orthodox Christianity, but the way led through skepticism and Neoplatonism. He went to Rome to take a teaching post, only to become the victim of illness. From Rome, with its gay and stimulating life, as well as its disorderly students, he made his way in a year's time to a teaching post in Milan.

Augustine's mother, Monica, followed him to Milan. Here, as elsewhere, his relations to his mother are deeply significant for Augustine's personality and life. These relations constitute a recurrent theme of the *Confessions.* It was she who persistently sought his conversion to Christianity, yet it had been she who had counseled deferring baptism in the fear of postbaptismal sins. It was she who wept on the African shore as his ship departed for Europe, and who subsequently followed him there. It was she who, presumably seeking a more desirable match for her son, led him to break with his faithful mistress.

Surrounded in Milan by a group of friends, Augustine pondered the step of becoming a catechumen of the Catholic Church. One factor of great importance in this step was the eloquent and fervent bishop of Milan, Ambrose. Augustine's admiration for Ambrose was unfeigned and enthusiastic. Still another factor leading to his conversion was his Neoplatonism, which enabled him to think of God as spiritual in nature, in contrast to the corporeal notions of deity characteristic of many faiths of the time. Speaking of the Neoplatonists, Augustine says, "There I read, In the beginning was the word, but I read not the Word was made flesh. . . ." From Neoplatonism Augustine acquired several features of his own system of thought, including notably his penchant for mysticism.

Book VIII describes the event of conversion which, as the *Confessions* clearly asserts, was the climax of Augustine's life. Two of his devoted friends had decided to turn to Catholic Christianity. His own heart in a torment of indecision, Augustine found his way to a Milanese garden where he pondered the course of his life. All at once he heard a voice saying "Take and read." Seeing a Bible, he turned at random to Romans 13:13f., "Not in rioting and drunkenness, not in chambering and wantonness, not in strife and envying, but put on the Lord Jesus Christ, and make no provision for the flesh to fulfill the lusts thereof." Taking this as divine direc-

tion, his course was clear. Conversion meant to Augustine, as it has meant to many others before and since, a new unification of a hitherto unintegrated life, together with new insight and new power.

Augustine resigned his professorship at the end of the following term and retired with several friends to a villa at Cassiciacum, where their days were devoted to contemplation, study, and preparation for baptism. Augustine was baptized April 25, 387, by Ambrose. Soon afterward he turned homeward toward Africa with his mother and his son Adeodatus, presumably to undertake some sort of comtemplative or monastic life. As they paused at Ostia, waiting for passage, Monica became ill and died.

In the shadows of his mother's impending death, Augustine records in Book IX an experience of particularly vivid and personal communion between mother and son. He tells of their exalted and intimate conversation concerning life and death, of her satisfaction that her wandering son had at last come home to Catholic Christianity, as well as of her intimation of impending death. This mystical experience may be characterized as the consummation of the lifelong relation of mother and son.

It is also the end of the autobiographical section of the *Confessions*. Ahead of him, and thus unrecorded in the *Confessions*, lay his years in Africa as monk, priest, and then bishop, and his stormy struggles with the Donatists and Pelagians. Nevertheless, it may safely be said that all the ideas developed in subsequent works are sketched or at least intimated in the *Confessions*.

In Books X-XIII Augustine turns to

reflection on philosophical and theological issues which never ceased to fascinate him, such as the nature and depth of the self, the nature of creation and time, and the relation of God to the world. While his subjects were among the most abstract and technical of all theological study, he continues throughout these books the devotional, confessional style of the earlier books. Also, he continues the deft turn of phrase so characteristic of the *Confessions* and indeed of all his writing, as well as the intensely autobiographical nature of his theological reflection. For Augustine, here as elsewhere, life and thought were bound together in seamless unity. It is worth noting in passing that in this section occurs the famous line which triggered Pelagius's reaction and the Pelagian controversy: "Give what thou commandest and command what thou wilt."

In Book X Augustine turns first to the relation of memory to selfhood, and thence of self to God. Augustine enters what he terms "the fields and spacious halls of memory where are stored as treasures the countless images that have been brought into them from all manner of things by the senses." There follows a notable passage in which these fields and halls of memory are explored in all their vastness and variety and in all their endless spontaneity. Memory becomes a hall of mirrors where, as Augustine says, "I meet myself and recall myself." This analysis of the memory and imagination of man in its depth and transcendence emphasizes once again Augustine's debt both to Neoplatonism and to the Bible.

It is significant to note that Augustine, having plumbed the depths of

mind or self, does not simply find deity there, as would be expected on Neoplatonic assumptions. Rather, he remarks, "I will pass even beyond this power of mine that is called memory — I will pass beyond it that I may come to thee, O lovely Light. And what art thou saying to me?" In this view of the self as being addressed by a God who is beyond the self, the reader sees the victory of the Bible over Neoplatonism in Augustine's thinking.

Earlier in the same book, Augustine, in an often quoted passage, celebrates the transcendence of God. He asks, "And what is this God? I asked the earth and it answered 'I am not he'; and everything in the earth made the same confession." In a similar manner he moves through the whole created universe and receives the same reply, "We are not God, but he made us." So it is that, deeply influenced by the Absolute One of Neoplatonism, Augustine acknowledges as God the Sovereign Will and Love which the Bible celebrates.

According to the Bible, the God who rules the world created it in the beginning. Augustine adds a philosophic idea which translates the Genesis creation story into the language of metaphysics; namely, the concept of creation *ex nihilo*, out of nothing. God also providentially guides the whole course of creation and will eventually bring it consummation. Hence, the themes of beginning and end never ceased to attract Augustine's thought.

Book XI is devoted to an extraordinarily subtle analysis of the nature of time and the relation of time to creation. "What then is time? If no one asks me, I know what it is. If I wish to explain it to him who asks me, I do not know." His analysis of time arrives at the conclusion that time is an aspect of created being, and that, consequently, in the uncreated being of God time has no effective reality. In God and God's consciousness there is no change, no before or after, but only an eternal present. This is, in effect, Augustine's response to the question, What was God doing before He made Heaven and earth? The question turns out to be meaningless for the good reason that, according to Augustine, time was created with the rest of creation. Time or change and the relations of before and after were created when God called the world into being; they have no reality apart from this context.

Yet, as Augustine points out, it is man's mind that perceives and measures time. Indeed, Augustine's treatment of the subject is noteworthy alike for its perception of time's manifold nature and for the candor with which he faces its enigmatic and mysterious aspects.

From time, Augustine moves in Books XII and XIII to the Biblical story of creation and to the philosophic idea which he constructs out of the Biblical story. Augustine's Platonism is apparent in his notions of the unformed matter and primal possibility, which God created first, and out of which he formed all else. In other passages Augustine equates Heaven, which God made, with the Platonic world of intelligible or ideal forms, which subsequently finds embodiment or illustration in the visible or experienced world. Yet Augustine realizes that these interpretations are not the only possible meanings which the Genesis story will bear.

Once the doctrine of creation is raised as a problem, Augustine cannot put it down. The final book of the *Confessions* develops further Augustine's allegorical interpretation of the Genesis story. In his use of allegorical exegesis Augustine was a child of his age. He finds allegories of the Trinity in the Genesis creation story, and he ponders the activity of the Spirit as it broods upon the original chaos. In the firmament he discovers an allegory of the Holy Scripture; in the dry land and bitter sea he finds the division between the people of God and the unfaithful nations, — a theme which was to receive definitive statement a decade or more later in the *City of God*.

The *Confessions* is concluded by a meditation upon the goodness of creation, a goodness which is expressed in the peace which God gives to His people. Truly, the mysteries of God's goodness and power are manifested in His creation, and among His many creatures, most of all in man. St. Augustine's *Confessions* not only summarizes the Christian thought of the ancient or patristic period, but also points ahead to the medieval period, and indeed to the whole subsequent development of Christian thought.

ON THE TRINITY

Author: Saint Augustine (354-430)
Type of work: Philosophical theology
First transcribed: c.400-428

PRINCIPAL IDEAS ADVANCED

Father, Son, and Holy Spirit are one and the same substance and essence; the persons of the Trinity are equal, and God is one.

God is the source of whatever is good.

The trinitarian nature of God is not rare and esoteric; it has myriad counterparts in ordinary experience.

The mind, in having memory, understanding, and will as components, provides a model for understanding the Trinity.

Perhaps no figure dominated medieval philosophy and theology more, or continues to influence contemporary theology so much, as the towering figure of Aurelius Augustinus, Bishop of Hippo. If the *Confessions* is a classic of the religious life and the *City of God* a massive landmark in philosophy of history, then *On the Trinity* is certainly his longest and most important work in philosophical theology. A full appreciation of the brilliance of mind which Augustine exhibits in the work can come only from a reading of the treatise itself, but even a summary examination of his ideas is enough to suggest the remarkable character of Augustine's theological creation.

It is a matter of dispute as to whether the concept of the triune nature of God is actually Biblical or is not really a part of primitive Christian thinking, but there is no question about the fact that after Augustine the problem of the Trinity became a central philosophical and theological issue.

No one can begin theological thought or investigate the nature of God without running into the doctrines Augustine developed here. There is some dispute about the exact origin of trinitarian concepts, but it seems clear that, whatever Augustine did with the ideas, he did not originate them. Trinities are commonplace in Neoplatonic thought and in the *Enneads* of Plotinus, which Augustine probably read, although trinities there are usually characteristic of the lower orders and not of the First Principle. After Augustine the Trinitarian concept is a central part of Christian theological thought.

The work itself is typically Augustinian; that is, it contains a vast collection of philosophical doctrines, interwoven with Scriptural exegesis. To understand *On the Trinity* means to grasp Augustine's blend of psychology, Neoplatonism, theological speculation, Biblical commentary, and philosophical elaboration. Since the work was composed over a long period of time, it is not surprising, particularly in view of its monumental length, that it contains so many doctrines. It is perhaps the best single work upon which to base an understanding of Augustine, since almost every facet of his philosophical, theological, and religious thought is brought to bear upon the central problem of understanding what is apparently a contradictory assertion; namely, that the One is three.

Following the traditional plan of beginning with an exegesis of the relevant Scriptural passages, Augustine, in the first half of the work, attempts to establish (upon a Biblical basis) the crucial point of the *equality* and *unity* of the parts of the Supreme Trinity. Of course, the whole point which makes this lengthy procedure necessary is that the Scriptural passages neither agree with one another nor are clear in their meaning. Some texts are used to argue against the equality of the Son, and Augustine was forced to establish a framework within which to deal with these difficult passages. Philosophical issues are involved in such a discussion, for rational consistency and interpretive standards must be brought *to* the Bible. Since the Bible is not theologically adequate as it stands, philosophy is the catalyst needed to make it so.

Like much of Augustine's work, *On the Trinity* has a polemical quality about it. Augustine begins by arguing against and attempting to refute those who attack the doctrine of the Trinity. Although it is characteristic of Augustine, it is not peculiar to him to have his systematic work generated by a polemical purpose. Religious beliefs, such as the trinitarian doctrine, would not be turned into technical theology if divergent views did not arise within the community of the faithful. Almost all early creeds and much early Christian theology developed in response to philosophical issues involved in religious disputes.

Holy Scripture, Augustine reminds his reader, does not hesitate to use words drawn from actually existing things to describe God and yet He is ineffable. Discussion about Him is difficult and requires that we purge our minds in order to see ineffably that which is ineffable. His thesis is: the Trinity is the one and only true God; Father, Son, and Holy Spirit are one and the same substance or essence. There is an indivisible equality, and yet it is true that the Father has "begotten" the Son. The problem is to understand the unity of the Trinity; that is, how three different forms can be a single being.

Augustine begins his proof by establishing the divinity of the Son. Using the assumption that there is but one God and that what is not creature is divine (there being no ground in between), he argues that since the Son as the agent of all creation is not Himself created He must be uncreated, thus necessarily of the same substance with the Father. The Son, therefore, is equal with the Father, and the working of the Father and the Son is indivisible. Such argument is made necessary, of course, by the accounts in the Scriptures which portray Jesus as born to Mary. This leads Augustine from the issue of the Trinity on to the specific Christian doctrine of the Incarnation, the dual nature of Jesus, so that Augustine can ascribe the creaturely qualities of Jesus to His human nature and thus can preserve the fully divine status of the Trinity's second person.

Since the Son appeared "in the form of a servant" Augustine had to explain how the numerous Biblical passages, most of which portray the human side of Jesus, do not essentially deny the Son's fully divine status. The bulk of his concern is to establish Jesus as fully divine, and all the proof is bent to this aim, His human nature being assumed as evident. Yet the ways of God are so much opposed to those of men that Augustine attempts at great length to explain how Jesus serves as a mediator between man and God, while yet preserving His fully divine status as Son. Nevertheless, Augustine acknowledges that human understanding will always fall at least a little short in any attempt to understand the Trinity, its nature being beyond full rational grasp.

There is no change or accident in God, and yet the Trinity as one substance and three persons must have each person share fully in that substance without losing its personal identity. As individual persons, the Son and the Holy Spirit seem subject to change and relation, but as of one substance with God they are not so subject. The relations between the various persons of the Trinity are difficult to describe, and Augustine admits that there are no terms which accurately express these relations. Every direct statement requires qualification: "Person" seems to be the most desirable term for the constituents of the Trinity, but the three "persons" together are equal to each singly. They are of one essence, with no bulk or interval or unlikeness or inequality. If, however, after this explanation we cannot understand the doctrine of the Trinity, then we must hold it by faith.

As far as the description of any member of the Trinity goes, what is difficult to understand is that whenever each is spoken of in respect to itself, then the persons of the Trinity are not spoken of as three in the plural number, but as one. This leads Augustine on to a discussion of the difficulties of reasoning about God, and of the necessity for the use of the negative method (understanding first what God is *not*), and he recommends trying to understand God through the concept of good, as that Being through which all things are good. There would be no changeable goods unless there were an unchangeable Good, and thus the mind can be led to grasp unchangeableness. The Good, then, is not far from every one of us.

We know what a mind is because we too have a mind, Augustine argues in a manner suggestive of Berkeley and Descartes. Within our own understanding of our self we have the basis for understanding pure concepts, such as righteousness. Where should a man discern himself except within himself? The attempt to understand a difficult aspect of the nature of God drove Augustine back to a search for self-knowledge, in the hope that in this way he could understand both himself and God more fully through the analogies to be found there. Man understands external things through the truth which he discerns and understands within himself. In accordance with Platonic theories of knowledge, Augustine asks: How can you recognize what you find externally if you cannot in some sense know it from within?

Love is a good example. No one can say that he does not know what love is. When a man loves his brother, Augustine argues, he knows the love with which he loves more intimately than he knows the brother whom he loves. And if one knows love he knows the Trinity, since God is love. Love involves three factors: he that loves, that which is loved, and love itself. In love, accordingly, there is a trace of the

Trinity. A kind of trinity also exists in man, who is the image of God: the mind, the knowledge whereby the mind knows itself, and the love with which it loves both itself and its knowledge. Since these three are mutually equal and of one essence, in explaining himself psychologically a man can discover the best mode for understanding the relationships which exist in the Trinity.

When the mind goes further and examines the basis upon which it judges corporeal things, it discovers that particular things are judged according to a form of the eternal Trinity and that this form is discerned by the intuition of the rational mind. Thus, the mind knows God as the source of such truth, and in so far as we know God we are like Him, but not to the extent of becoming equal to Him. An examination of the mind, of its knowing and its judging powers, shows the mind to be like divinity, at least in its trinitarian aspect. For that reason an attempt to understand the Trinity is not an impossibility, since there is a kind of image of the Trinity discoverable in the mind itself.

Since it is absolutely impossible to love things which are unknown, the discovery of man's love for God indicates that at least to some extent man has knowledge of Him. The mind seems to understand itself and to discover, as Descartes insisted, certain truths about itself which it cannot doubt. The mind, we discover, has memory, understanding, and will as its primary components, so that in understanding the unitary action of these capacities we have a mental model for understanding the divine Trinity. In sight also it is possible to distinguish three things; namely, the visible object, the act of seeing, and the attention of the mind. Everywhere he turns, particularly in considering psychological phenomena, Augustine finds images of trinitarian action. Since the mind recognizes its natural affinity to the divine, only the intellectual cognizance of *eternal* things should be called "wisdom," whereas "knowledge" shall mean the rational cognizance of *temporal* things. In rightly understanding and loving its best part, the mind actually loves and understands God in His trinitarian nature. Starting with the creature, Augustine discovered certain trinities, until at last he came to the mind of man and found traces there of the highest trinity which we seek when we seek God. Understanding the human mind means recognizing certain trinities in its action, and understanding the functioning of a trinity is identical with a grasp of God's nature. The undeniable threefold but unified truth—I exist, I love, I understand—leads to as much comprehension of the Trinity as the mind of man, since it is human, although partly divine, can possibly achieve.

THE LIFE OF ST. MARTIN

Author: Sulpicius Severus (c.363-c.420)
Type of work: Hagiography
First transcribed: c.410

Principal Ideas Advanced

St. Martin's life is an inspiring example for all Christians who would draw close to God.

The saint was a virtuous man, able to raise the dead, heal the sick, and give courage and strength to the poor and needy.

He showed his spiritual strength when he resisted the temptations of the Devil, who appeared to him in many disguises.

Sulpicius Severus was born about 363 in Aquitania, and he lived until about 420; thus, he was a contemporary of Augustine and Jerome, and he was acquainted with St. Martin, whose life Sulpicius recounts. The biography of St. Martin is interesting because it contributes to knowledge about the period of which Sulpicius writes, and the work provides an example of one of the most popular forms of Christian literature—the pious biography, in which didactic edification is as important as factual information.

In the biography Sulpicius extols the virtues of Martin, for whom Sulpicius had the greatest affection and the highest respect.

In addition to writing the biography of St. Martin, Sulpicius published a *Sacred History,* which aimed at presenting a compendious history of the world from creation to the year 400. The first part is an abridgment of the Scriptural narrative, but unfortunately it is not without error; the second part deals with events that are not recorded in Scripture, but which are of some value to the historian.

Sulpicius wrote the *Life of St. Martin* so that the life of a most holy man —whom he himself had met—might serve as an example to others who would then also be aroused to divine virtue and to the pursuit of truth, while enlisted in the army of Heaven. Sulpi-

cius claims to have written nothing of his hero except that for which he had certain evidence and knowledge; he claims that he would rather be silent than write anything false.

Martin was born about the year 315 of pagan parents in Sabaria, which was in Pannonia, and he was brought up in Italy in Ticinum. His father pursued a military career, and he opposed his son's service to God. At the age of ten Martin endeavored to become a catechumen; at twelve he desired to live the life of a hermit, and he was already a professed servant of Christ. The government issued an edict, however, which forced the young Martin, as the son of a veteran, to take the military oath, so that for three years prior to his baptism he served in the army. His fellow soldiers held him in the highest esteem, and even in the military service Martin was more a monk than a soldier. He was exceedingly kind, patient, humble, and free of the vices usually associated with the military life; he behaved as a candidate for baptism, was given to good works, aided those in trouble, supported the needy, and kept nothing for himself.

On one occasion, during a severe winter in which he himself had nothing but a cloak, Martin cut his sole remaining garment in two in order to clothe a poor man destitute of clothing. His act of charity was followed by a vision in which Christ appeared to him, arrayed in that part of the cloak which Martin had given to the poor man, and Christ commended Martin for his act of love. The vision did not fill Martin with pride but caused him to acknowledge God's goodness and to seek baptism at the age of twenty.

For two years after his baptism Martin remained in the military. He was released from service only after he offered to face the enemy in battle unarmed, an act which proved unnecessary since, to spare Martin the pain of witnessing the death of others, God caused the enemy to surrender without bloodshed. According to Sulpicius, victory was won because of the piety of a saint.

Upon leaving the military service, Martin sought the company of Hilarius, Bishop of Pictava, who instituted Martin in the office of a diaconate, and appointed him to be an exorcist. After a time Martin was warned in a dream that he should visit his native land in the religious interests of his parents, who were still pagans. Waylaid by robbers along the way, he was set free after his courageous witness to evangelical truth wrought conversion in the heart of the robber who guarded him. As Martin continued his journey, the Devil, who had assumed the form of a man, met him on the way, but he also was quickly put to flight by Martin's piety.

His mission to his mother was successful, but although many others were converted by his example, his father remained a pagan. For a time Martin was persecuted by the Arians, and he was forced to subsist in exile by eating the roots of plants. On one occasion he lay near death from eating poisonous grass, but he warded off the effects by calling for God's help.

Martin, Sulpicius claims, was given the power to perform miracles. A catechumen who died without receiving baptism was restored to life by Martin's earnest prayers. Martin stretched himself at full length upon the dead limbs of the deceased, and perceiving by means of the Holy Spirit that power was present, he raised himself up and waited for two hours without misgivings, whereupon the dead man moved and opened his eyes, for he had been restored to life by the saint's faith.

On another occasion Martin restored to life a slave who had ended his life by hanging himself. Hardly any sick person came to him without at once being restored to health. When Martin kissed a leper, the man was instantly healed. The very threads of his garment wrought frequent miracles upon the sick; sections of his garments drove away diseases from the afflicted when the garments were tied around the fingers or neck of the afflicted. The daughter of a very holy man was cured of a fever when her skin was touched by a letter which Martin had written. The vision of the ailing was restored by Martin's touch, and he himself was healed of grievous wounds by the ministrations of an angel who applied healing ointment to the bruised members of his body.

By miraculous intervention Martin escaped falling trees, the knife of the assassin, and the fury of mobs. He was able to render a procession of men immobile in obedience to his commands. He could order flames of fire to consume idolatrous temples without doing harm to surrounding buildings, and he was so empowered as to be able to turn the fire back when it left its prescribed course. He razed pagan temples to their foundations and he reduced the altars and images of idols to dust, thereby delivering the people from their superstitions. Martin could command serpents to do his bidding, and in all such acts he displayed the piety proper to the distinguished office that he had come to hold as Bishop of Tours.

According to Sulpicius, Martin was in every way distinguished. He established a monastery where some eighty disciples followed his example, spending hours in prayer in their cells, while possessing all things in common, and enduring with humility all temptations and trials. The very angels spoke to Martin, and "As to the devil, Martin held him so visible and ever under the power of his eyes, that whether he kept himself in his proper form, or changed himself into different shapes of spiritual wickedness, he was perceived by Martin, under whatever guise he appeared." The Devil once rushed into Martin's cell with a great noise, holding in his hand the bloody horn of an ox. He sometimes appeared in the form of Minerva, Jupiter, or Mercury.

Martin was often assailed by crowds of demons, to whom Martin did not hesitate to preach. The ruses to which the Devil went in his temptations were truly great. The fiend once appeared surrounded by a purple light, clothed in a royal robe, with a crown of precious stones on his head, and gold shoes on his feet. His countenance was tranquil, so that no one would suspect who he was. Martin, while praying in his cell, was first dazed. The Devil pretended to be Christ, but Martin was not deceived and he detected the impostor, whereupon, "the devil vanished like smoke, and filled the cell with such a disgusting smell, that he left unmistakable evidences of his real character." In Sulpicius' words, "This event, as I have just related, took place in the way which I have stated, and my information regarding it was derived from the lips of Martin himself; therefore let no one regard it as fabulous."

Whether fabulous or not, Sulpicius' biography of the Gaulish Saint Martin (who died about 397, about twenty-three years before the death of his biographer) insures Martin a place in the company of saints whose lives make the Christian ideal both vivid and appealing.

THE CITY OF GOD

Author: Saint Augustine (354-430)
Type of work: Theology of history
First transcribed: c.413-426

Principal Ideas Advanced

Two cities, the city of God and the earthly city, now exist side by side and are inseparable from each other.

Those who believe in the true God may now enter into that heavenly city, al-

though such belief is no guarantee of any preferential treatment whatsoever during this life.

What characterizes each city, and each man within it, is the direction of love, whether it is toward the things of this world (the earthly city) or toward God (the heavenly city).

If any work deserves the title of a classic of Christian literature, it is most certainly Saint Augustine's *City of God*. Critical historians point to it as perhaps the first major philosophy of history, and its influence also spills over into literature, philosophy, and theology. Its size and its scope mark it as monumental, and its doctrines find their way into every sphere. It seeks no less a goal than to define God, man, and the world. To accomplish this goal Augustine chose the city as his metaphorical image because the city was in his day the center and model of culture and political life.

Augustine begins with his most famous distinction: the City of God has a temporal stage here below (journeying as a pilgrim among sinners) and an eternal abode (a blessed goal of perfect peace). Any earthly city is dominated by a passion for dominion, and from such a city the enemies of the City of God come. The unjust, however successful here, will not participate in the joys of the world to come, prepared by Divine Providence. The goods and evils of this life, on the other hand, are divided alike between the just and the unjust. Yet the good and bad who suffer are different even though they suffer the same trials. Though what they endure is the same, their virtues and vices are different. The tide of trouble tests, purifies, and improves the good, whereas it beats, crushes, and washes away the wicked.

Every man deserves some temporal affliction, no matter how good he has been, although the good will escape eternal punishment. The fact that the good often fail to speak out against evil for fear of the loss of some temporal advantage indicates that the good, as well as the bad, love and are attached to an earthly life. As God tested Job before, so the good must now stand adversity as a test of their mettle and of their love of God. Whatever good men lose in this life, it is always possible for such men to preserve their faith, their piety, and the treasures of the interior life. In the midst of adversity, the good man still has more than those who are evil.

Both good and bad men must sooner or later die. Neither has any basic advantage here. Death preceded by a good life is never evil; nothing makes death evil except what is to follow it. This earthly life is a school in which the servant of God is trained for life eternal. Refusing to be enslaved by temporal goods, he uses them as a pilgrim would. Yet as long as it is here, the City of God cannot be sure who belongs to it. Some who appear to be its members here will not be associated in the eternal felicity of the saints. Among even its notorious adversaries here on earth are men destined to be its friends, however little they now know it. On earth the earthly and the heavenly cities are linked and fused together, to be separated at the Last Judgment.

Despite these clear statements about the City of God in Book I, Augustine next turns to a task which diverts him for a considerable share of his work: challenging the view that it was the Christians who were responsible for the barbarian sack of Rome and the wars which desolated the world. Yet even in this practical and apologetic task, his earlier problem returns, since Augustine sees the issue as once again requiring him to justify God's ways to the world and to show how it is possible that good things come to the impious and the thankless while devastation falls upon both the good and the bad. Essentially what Augustine attempts to do is to show that the sack of Rome was due to internal reasons, corruptions which justly brought about this result.

Providence, of course, becomes one of Augustine's major themes. No matter what the apparent force of the evil and demonic powers, Augustine attempts to establish that God's ultimate providential plan can never be set aside. Whatever the apparent present destruction, absolutely nothing occurs outside God's ordaining power. And God's City offers more to those who join it than assurance of God's providential plan; it offers true remission of sins. In such a heavenly city, no longer delighting in immoralities, victory is truth, dignity is holiness, peace is happiness, life is eternity. Plunging into a fairly detailed analysis of important historical events, Augustine seeks to document his thesis beyond doubt, that events were actually not quite as Christianity's enemies conceived them and that the pagans actually worshiped false gods.

In reply to the question of the divine permission of oppression, Augustine replies that a good man, though a slave, is free; but a wicked man, though a king, is a slave. Happiness is actually a gift of God, and the only God men should worship is the one who can make them happy. God orders all things and knows all things before they come to pass. He whose foreknowledge cannot be deceived foreknows what He will choose to do. Some, in order to make men free, will try to give up God, but the fact is that our choices fall within the order of the causes which are known certainly by God and contained in His foreknowledge.

One who does not foreknow the whole of the future is most certainly not God, Augustine says in his most emphatic defense of divine determination. Yet, he adds, human will sometimes prevails—although the power which permits this is God's. How, in view of this strong defense of divine determination in all events, can anyone believe that the laws which govern the rise and fall of political societies would be exempt from the laws of God's providence? Thus the affairs of both the divine and the earthly cities are equally foreknown by God in his eternal plan. Yet the City of God is hated by the lovers of this world, because its ways differ from the ways of the world, and especially since the divine city is not subject to natural death.

The earthly city is given to both believers and unbelievers alike, but the joy of the Kingdom of Heaven God gives only to those who believe in Him; He rules and governs all things. Although His reasons may be hidden, they are never unjust. And it is impossible to reach God and the happiness of His Kingdom through the gods offered for worship by the state, since they are false gods. Since only belief in the true God will bring anyone to the City of God, Augustine gives detailed comparative arguments to document the unsatisfactory nature of the gods of the state. By way of contrast, he describes the qualities of the true God the Christians worship, inviting all to join in this worship and to enter the heavenly City of God while yet bound to the earthly city and its laws.

Books One through Seven are largely Church apologetics, defining the Church in relation to the world and justifying its presence here. When Augustine reaches Book Eight, he turns to philosophical and theological issues, first to the long-standing question of natural theology. Augustine wishes to reconcile and to make compatible the divine truth of Scripture with that of natural theology. Since God is Wisdom for Augustine, a true philosopher, or lover of Wisdom, will actually be a lover of God. Yet not all men who are called philosophers actually recognize their ultimate divine aim. Since theology means the study of the divine nature, genuine philosophers and theologians will find themselves converging on the same goal. From here Augustine goes on to a brief review of philosophy, particularly of Platonism, to justify his point.

The Platonists, Augustine discovers, have in their doctrine come closer to Christianity than has any other school. They posited an immaterial soul and an incorporeal God, premises Augustine takes as central to Christian thought. God's existence is simple and indivisible, and in the mind of man there is a superior form, immaterial and independent of sound, space, and time. Philosophy is a search for happiness, a search which can end only when a love of the good reaches fruition in God. Christians know that from the one, true, and infinitely good God they have a nature by which they are made in His image, a faith by which they know God and themselves, and grace whereby they reach beatitude in union with God.

Insofar as Platonists, or philosophers of any school, hold these truths concerning God, then they agree with the essentials of the Christian view. Augustine considers that his historical review and analysis, demonstrating the essential agreement of Platonism and Christianity, is sufficient to justify his choice of Platonic philosophy as the basis for his discussion of the problems of natural theology. The theories of gods and demons then common were legion, and Augustine uses his Platonism as a critical basis for demonstrating the inadequacy of such theories and for proving the existence of a single, good Deity. In the first ten books Augustine is concerned to refute the enemies of the City of God, but in Book Eleven he begins his discussion of the origin and destiny of the two cities, which, as he has said, are at present inextricably intermingled with each other.

For communication between God and the members of His city presently here, the mind of man is the means, being the most excellent part of man and having nothing superior to it except God himself. By the mind man comes closer to God than by any other means. In order to advance man toward truth, the divine Son put on humanity without putting off divinity, in order to serve as an even more effective mediator between man and God than man's mind alone could be. From here Augustine goes on to discuss the important questions of

144   *Saint Augustine*

creation and time, issues of natural theology which must be settled in order to understand God's relation to both the heavenly and the earthly cities.

Everything, it turns out, revolves around the love of God. Since there is no other good which can make any rational or intellectual creature happy except God, man is made either miserable or happy by this relationship, and thus the cities are defined according to their orientation toward or away from God. God in creation arranged a hierarchy of beings so that, although some beings are higher on the scale than others, there is no being opposed to God. A defect can never be found in the highest good and a defect in any lesser being in the hierarchy cannot be present apart from some kind of good in that being. All natures are good simply because they exist, and each has its own measure of being, beauty, and peace. God having given each being its measure, is never to be blamed for any defect that offends us.

Sin can have no better name than pride, Augustine continues in his famous account of the nature of good and evil, and evil essentially means preferring what is less in the order of being rather than what is greater, turning away from God rather than toward Him. No efficient cause for evil can be found. An evil will is the efficient cause of a bad action, but there is no efficient cause of an evil will. The fault which produces evil begins when one falls away from the supreme Being and toward some being which is less than absolute. God can never be deficient in anything, while things made to be from nothing can be deficient.

The City of God has its origin partly in the body of angels, spiritually like God but lower in order, and partly from mortal men, created by the same God who created angels and who will one day unite the two groups. Following the Biblical account of Adam, Augustine sees the whole human race as taking its start from one man. And once again Augustine runs into the problem that perplexes him so often, the problem of time and its relation to eternity. He wanted to argue against those who hold that the world is eternal, and yet this meant giving an account of the creation of time by an eternal God.

Augustine confesses his inability to settle the problem of time with finality, but he adopts the now traditional view that what was to take place in its own time was already predestined and determined in God's eternity, and it is his co-eternal Word, the Second Person of the Trinity, who essentially serves as the instrument of creation. Augustine, then, begins with a doctrine of creation and inserts change into the eternal plan by the introduction of Jesus in His role of restorer of men and divine mediator. He creates the Christian view of the drama of history, but his announced central purpose is to dispose of the theory of inescapable and eternally repeated periodic cycles of time which cause identical occurrences in different times.

Augustine's aim, thus, is to give a newness to historical events, and yet he relates this newness to a providential order. Each historical event has never occurred before, and there are no unbreakable repetitious cycles in man's history. Augustine believes it possible to have occurrences which are both absolutely new and also part of an eternally ordered pattern of nature. It is quite possible, Augustine is sure, for God to create new beings, hitherto uncreated, and, in virtue of His ineffable foreknowledge, to do this without implying the least change in the divine will. In the first man God created He established the origin of the two cities or societies into which the human race is now divided.

Through sin man fell, that is, turned away from God; and since the direction of affection determines the society, the fall gave the City of Man its origin as a city composed of those whose interests are temporal and not divine. Because of his natural place near the top in the hierarchy of being, man has a tendency to seek his happiness through a knowledge of God, and because of the change brought about by the coming of Jesus Christ into the natural world, the natural direction of man's affections upward has once again been encouraged. In this life the two cities, defined by the direction of the love of the men who compose them, are intermingled and often indistinguishable; but those sometimes hidden men who compose the City of God shall eventually be lifted free and brought to their goal, happiness in the knowledge and love of God their creator.

SEVEN BOOKS OF HISTORY AGAINST THE PAGANS

Author: Paulus Orosius (c.385-?)
Type of work: Apologetics; philosophy of history
First transcribed: 417

PRINCIPAL IDEAS ADVANCED

Pagans who argue that the barbarian invasions are Rome's punishment for accepting Christianity ignore the fact that there was far more destruction and misery in pre-Christian times.

History abounds in calamities because it is the record of man's disobedience and punishment, alleviated only as God intervenes to bring men to repentance.

History is mainly told in terms of the Empires of Babylon and of Rome: Babylon, which ruled the world during the time of Israel, was permitted to perish; Rome, which was established to prepare for the coming of Christianity, has been preserved.

The barbarian invasions are, partly, Rome's punishment for persecuting Christianity, but may also be viewed as a step toward evangelizing the heathen nations.

Paulus Orosius was a young Spanish presbyter who, having escaped the hands of the barbarian invaders of Spain, visited Augustine in Africa and Jerome in Palestine. Augustine thought highly of Orosius' abilities and asked him to write a history of the world which would supplement Augustine's own work, the *City of God*, then only half completed. Orosius complied, and within scarcely more than a year he produced his *Seven Books of History Against the Pagans*. Nothing further is known of the author, but in an age which saw the destruction of many great works of the past, his *History* survived. A bull of Pope Gelasius (494) declared it "a most indispensable work," and helped make it the standard history book through a great part of the Middle Ages. It was translated into Anglo-Saxon by Alfred the Great (c.848-c.900).

Orosius' aim is clearly apologetic. The reader he has in mind is one who, in a world that is officially Christian, has refused to surrender his faith in the pagan gods, and who interprets the barbarian invasions as evidences of the gods' anger at the discontinuance of sacrifices. Orosius attempts to show that the history of the world is one long series of calamities, and that, compared with those which occurred in ancient times, the present disturbances are comparatively mild. The pagan gods, he maintains, never brought any relief from war and disaster, but since the coming of Christ, world conditions have been fairly tolerable because God in His providence was preparing the nations to receive the Gospel, and because as the Gospel spreads it inclines men's hearts to clemency and peace.

As evidence that there is one God who is the author of all things, Orosius appeals to natural understanding and to the teachings of philosophical sects. But, following Augustine, he maintains that "where reason fails, faith comes to the rescue; for unless we believe, we shall not understand." It is, therefore, the Biblical teaching concerning the creation of man, man's abuse of his freedom, and God's redemptive purpose that gives the clue

for understanding human history. Sinful enterprise by itself can never stand; hence, men's grandiose schemes of empire and conquest are foredoomed. But God has not left men to their devices. With a view to bringing them to repentance, He has alternately chastened and blessed them. Such is the uniform experience of the past; and so, according to Orosius, it will continue until the end, except for an intensification of troubles in the last days when Christ comes to claim His Kingdom.

Orosius divides the history of the world into four epochs, corresponding to the Babylonian, Macedonian, Carthaginian, and Roman empires, but he does not find in this division any schema for understanding the human condition, as growing progressively better or progressively worse. For Orosius, the four world empires represent, rather, the four main geographical regions of the world. The East, North, and South each, in turn, tried to rule the world and failed; the West, says Orosius, is now having its turn, and if it also fails, no one should be surprised. The one thing that brightens the prospect is the fact that God has intervened in history with a view to winning men to reconciliation with Himself. But God redeems individuals, not empires, and the most that can be claimed is that, where redemption is effective, some curb will be imposed on sinful man's tendencies to destruction.

Although he recognizes four distinct regimes, Orosius argues that the Macedonian and the Carthaginian were less important than the other two. The main divisions of history are the Babylonian and the Roman world-empires. Orosius remarks that Rome freed herself from the Tarquin kings just at the time when Cyrus overthrew Babylon.

But between the time that Rome began to manage her own affairs and the time that she established her Empire, the Macedonians and the Carthaginians divided the world between them. Orosius proceeds to find certain correspondences between the history of Babylon and that of Rome, the most important being that the Babylonian empire began at the same time as God called Abraham to be the founder of the Israelitish nation, and that the Roman empire began at the same time as God sent his Son into the world to establish the Christian Church. The main difference (and in this, Orosius remarks, the people of Rome have cause to be glad) is that, whereas, in God's providence, Babylon must fall in order for Israel to rise, no such judgment was laid upon Rome. On the contrary, God fostered the rise of Rome through many centuries, and at last He conferred all power upon Caesar Augustus, so that universal peace might smooth the way for those who would proclaim the universal Gospel.

Within this historical framework, Orosius reviews the history of various nations, drawing upon the compendiums in use at the time. He makes no pretense at completeness. "I have," he says, "left out many details . . . and have abbreviated everything, since in no way could I have ever passed through so thick a forest of evils unless I had hastened my journey by frequent leaps." Quite frankly, he writes, he is looking for accounts of human misery. Other historians, he says, "were describing wars, whereas I for my part am more concerned with the miseries caused by wars," it being his design to show "in what way God has punished sinners, in what way He can punish them, and in what way He will punish

them." Those Romans who complain that the barbarian invasions have interrupted their games and circuses ought, he says, to read the history of their own city and see what their forefathers suffered at the hands of Hannibal and, during the civil wars, at the hands of their own compatriots. He suggests that they have been so long freed from care as to regard the slightest anxiety as an intolerable burden. "They are the type of people," he says, "who consider those gentle admonitions by which we all from time to time are reproved, still more severe than the punishments exacted in other times about which they have only heard or read." Even the horrors which attended the destruction of Troy are for them merely pleasant stories to be recited and played.

When, in his seventh book, Orosius writes concerning Christian times, he attempts the awkward task of attaching rewards and punishments to those who favor and those who oppose the progress of the Church. Ten times, he says, the Romans persecuted the Christians, just as, in the time of Moses, the Pharaoh refused ten times to free Israel from its bondage; and, just as the Egyptians were smitten with ten plagues, so the Romans were punished after each persecution. In Orosius' view, the sufferings of his time are part of the punishment for the tenth (Maximian's) persecution; as that persecution was the most severe, so the punishment endures the longest. Orosius further maintains that those emperors since Constantine who defended the Church were rewarded and others were punished. The fate of Julian the Apostate, who perished miserably after trying to restore paganism, offers one example. But Orosius can also point to the Emperor Valens who, when the Goths asked that missionaries be sent to them, sent them teachers of the Arian persuasion. "Therefore," says Orosius, "by the just judgment of God Himself, Valens was burned alive by the very men who, through his action, will burn hereafter for their heresy." On the other hand, the Emperor Theodosius earned the blessing of Heaven. Hopelessly surrounded during his campaign in the Alps, he passed a whole night in prayer and on the following day was marvelously delivered in a battle which destroyed two of his antagonists at once, and brought order and tranquillity to the realm. "Thus Heaven gave judgment between the side that humbly placed its hope in God alone even without the aid of man and the side that arrogantly trusted in its own strength and in idols."

Orosius does not seem to have grasped the notion that Rome's domination of the world had come to an end. He does, however, have a just sense of the political engagements between Rome and the barbarians. In the past, he says, other nations have paid tribute to Rome in order to purchase peace; Rome is now paying tribute to the Goths for the same purpose. He adds that if anyone supposes that the Romans were more tolerable conquerors than the Goths, "his knowledge and understanding are quite at variance with the facts." Orosius also sees a connection between the barbarian invasions of the Roman territory and the evangelization of these peoples. "It would seem," he says, "that the mercy of God ought to be praised and glorified, in that so many nations would be receiving, even at the cost of our own weakening, a knowledge of the truth which they could never have had but for this opportunity."

One of the most remarkable qualities of Orosius' *History* is its catholicity of outlook. Orosius, a Spaniard, rejoiced that he was living in an age in which there was common fellowship between people of different nations. Driven from his own country by war, he found himself warmly welcomed in Africa and in the East. East, North, and South, he said, "all have the same law and nationality as I, since I come there as a Roman and a Christian to Christians and Romans." This, he says, could never have come about as long as polytheism prevailed. It is the work of "One God, Who established the unity of this realm in the days when He willed Himself to become known."

This catholicity of outlook makes Orosius a better historian than he would otherwise have been, enabling him to perceive the distortion which any kind of particularism introduces into men's judgments. The Romans, he points out, say that the world has fallen on evil times because the Goths have been victorious over them; but, in former times, when Rome was victorious, times seemed just as wretched to Carthage and Spain. Orosius concludes that people ought not to attach much importance to the measure of happiness which they momentarily enjoy, but ought to examine the way of life that they have chosen. In speaking of Orosius, Karl Löwith says, in *Meaning in History,* that only in the Swiss historian Jacob Burckhardt (1818-1897) do "we find a similar insight into the fallacy of our comparative judgments and into the correlation of action and suffering as the general pattern of all human history." Löwith adds that, whereas Burckhardt had the task of disabusing his generation of their optimistic impressions, the problem facing

Orosius was to dispel the pessimism of the ancient world, with its theories of cyclical decay, and to argue realistically for the comparative improvement which had taken place in Christian times.

Orosius' own hope, however, does not rest in merely historical prospects. He does not share even the millenarian hopes of Lactantius (d. c.320), but believes that in the last days persecutions will be revived. Just as the Egyptians, when they let Israel go, afterwards tried to drag them back into slavery and in consequence were drowned in the Red Sea, "so, alas," he says, "a persecution by the Gentiles at some future time awaits us while we are journeying in freedom, until we cross the Red Sea, that is, the fire of the judgment with our Lord Jesus Christ Himself as our leader and judge." For Orosius, redemption is transcendent to history, and eschatology points beyond time. This view, which neutralized the apocalyptic urgency of primitive Christianity, henceforth became the outlook of the Catholic Church.

THE ENCHIRIDION ON FAITH, HOPE, AND LOVE

Author: Saint Augustine (354-430)
Type of work: Theology
First transcribed: 421

PRINCIPAL IDEAS ADVANCED

Faith precedes reason, and the role of reason is that of understanding what is previously apprehended by faith.

Whatever is, insofar as it is, is good; being and good are convertible concepts; evil is a privation of the good and is dependent upon the good for its existence.

Original sin accounts for the introduction of evil into the life of man; this sin is defined as pride or self-elevation, and its consequences are ignorance and lust.

Salvation comes to man by the grace of God through faith; this grace is fully manifested in Jesus Christ, who unifies in Himself two natures, divine and human, in one person.

Man is born with a free will, but this free will is corrupted because of the Fall; and man's eternal salvation becomes effectual only through divine predestination.

Love constitutes the final definition of God and the crown of the Christian virtues.

The *Enchiridion* was written by Saint Augustine in response to a request by Laurentius to provide him with a handbook on Christian doctrine. Fulfilling this request, Augustine took as his framework the Apostles' Creed and the Lord's Prayer, and he concluded by showing that the principles of Christian living are to be found in faith, hope, and love. In the compass of these few pages some basic issues pertaining to faith and reason, the nature and origin of evil, salvation and grace, free will and predestination, are stated and discussed.

Augustine begins by clarifying his position on the relation between faith and reason and advances his theory of divine illuminism. In matters of knowledge of divine truth, faith precedes reason. The mind attains knowledge only because there is a prior illumination granted by God Himself. It is made clear to Laurentius that faith, which is itself a gift of God, must provide the starting point. This does not, however, entail a depreciation of reason as was proposed, for example, by Tertullian of Carthage some two hundred years earlier, when he maintained that divine truth is proportional to its rational absurdity. In the thought of Augustine reason plays an important role, and its role is that of clarifying and understanding that which is previously apprehended through faith. The program which he submits is one of faith seeking understanding.

The problem of good and evil, one of the central concerns in the thought of Augustine, is briefly sketched in this compendium of Christian beliefs. The good is defined as a natural harmony or order. The good thus defined is ontologically prior to evil, evil then being understood as the privation of an original good. In the background of Augustine's thought on this point is the Biblical doctrine of creation as well as the Platonic theory of being. Augustine's classical formula, *esse qua esse bonum est,* is at the same time an expression of the Biblical faith that God's creation is good and of the Platonic equivalence of being and

value. It is on this issue in particular that the Augustinian synthesis of Jerusalem and Athens becomes apparent. Every being, insofar as it is a being, is good. All things that exist are good insofar as they have been made by a Creator who is Himself supremely good. However, insofar as existent things are not like their Creator in being supremely and immutably good, their good is subject to a diminution or privation. This privation is precisely what Augustine understands by evil. Thus, evil requires the good as the original reality of which it is a privation. Evil requires a host in which to dwell. So long as a being is in the process of corruption there must be in it some good of which it is being deprived. If perchance this being should be completely consumed by corruption, it would have neither good nor being. Every being, therefore, is good—infinitely good if it remains immune to corruption, finitely good if it is subject to corruption. In any case it remains a good. According to Augustine, there can be no evil where there is no good. The Augustinian relation of good and evil thus provides us with an exception to the logical rule that contrary attributes cannot be predicated of the same subject. Dark and light, black and white, bitter and sweet, beautiful and ugly are contraries which cannot exist at the same time in any one thing. This is clearly not the case with the contraries of good and evil. There is no difficulty involved, for example, in defining man as an evil good. He is good because he is a being; he is evil because part of this being has been corrupted. Evil is not an independent principle. It was thus that Augustine could refute the Manichean heresy (to which he was attracted during the early part of his career), which maintains that good and evil are independent cosmic principles that respectively account for the value and disvalue in human existence.

When we ask how it is that evil as the privation of the good makes its appearance in human existence, the answer must be original sin. This original sin has its locus in the Fall of Adam, in which all mankind shares. In his state of created goodness prior to the Fall Adam had the freedom to sin or not to sin. Attracted by the possibility of infinite knowledge, he transgressed his finite limits and affirmed for himself the knowledge and self-sufficiency which belong to God alone. Adam sought to elevate himself to the level of the Creator. This self-elevation, commonly called pride, is man's original sin, according to Augustine. The Fall of man comes about in that moment in which he seeks to negate his creatureliness and to affirm himself as God. Now the consequences of the Fall are for Augustine extensive in their implications. Ignorance of duty, concupiscence or lust, and the desire for what is hurtful follow in the wake of man's attempted self-elevation, and these in turn introduce error and suffering into the life of man. After the Fall man walks in darkness and loses his vision of the good. He neither knows the good nor is he able to do the good. At the same time, he is caught up in an incessant striving for power and for sensual gratification. The objects of power and sensuality when attained provide no ultimate satisfaction, and thus the soul of man remains turbulent and restless. His life becomes a frustrating cycle of exaltation and depression. His momen-

tary pleasures and passing glory do not add up to happiness. They lead only to insatiable craving. Both the intellect and will of man suffer from this original corruption. This corruption is so pervasive that all efforts on the part of man to deliver himself from his state of perdition are futile. He cannot restore himself by any merit of good works. Before the Fall he possessed the freedom to sin or not to sin, but after the Fall this freedom is trammeled, and all his subsequent actions bear the taint of the original transgression. It is for this reason that man stands in the need of a Savior. God must come to man and effect that restoration which man cannot effect for himself. God extends salvation as a gift. Man is saved by the grace of God through faith.

By virtue of the Fall the creature is separated from the Creator. By virtue of divine grace the unhappy consequences of this separation are transfigured and man is restored. This theme of sin and grace is the pivotal point in Augustine's delineation of Christian doctrine. The emphasis here, as he repeatedly reminds Laurentius, is clearly Pauline. Both the Apostle Paul and Augustine have a horror of any suggestion of a doctrine of salvation by works. This was the central issue in Augustine's controversy with the Pelagians, in whose position he detected a facile deification of man, an attenuation of the reality of sin, and a consequent neglect of the need for divine grace. Augustine's theology of grace has its foundation in the message and person of Jesus Christ. Augustine's Christology, although never explicitly formulated, presents a view of Christ as the Son of God in whom two natures, human and divine, are united

in one person. Just as each individual
man unites in one person a body and
a rational soul, so Christ in one person
unites a divine nature, the Word or
Logos, with a human nature. It is thus
that Augustine's position becomes historically significant as one of the
formative influences which shaped the
Christological formula, *una persona,
duae naturae,* which became normative at the Council of Chalcedon in
451. The saving work of Christ, in
which the grace of God becomes
effectual, proceeds from this unique
event of a unified divine-human
nature. Christ as Logos assumes a likeness of man's human, sinful condition
without Himself committing any actual
sin. He thus remains sinless, but at
the same time He is able to wrest
man from his state of perdition and to
bring about his restoration. This grace,
which becomes manifest in Jesus
Christ, is both prevenient and following. It is clearly stated in the Scriptures,
says Augustine, that the mercy of God
"shall meet me" and that it "shall
follow me" (Psalms 23:6). Grace
comes to the unwilling to make them
willing, and it follows the willing to
sustain them in their continuing life
of faith. Man does not seek God; God
seeks man. In no sense is grace
through faith a human attainment for
Augustine. It is solely the gift of God.

It is within this context of sin and
grace through faith that Augustine's
teaching on free will and predestination must be understood. Although Augustine is concerned to safeguard the
idea of human freedom, this freedom
is a freedom which has not only clearly
defined natural limitations but also a
final limiting condition in the movement of divine grace. In the final
analysis, the will owes its freedom to

God. It is God who prepares the will
for its initial reception of grace, and
it is He who sustains it throughout
the process of redemption. Man's freedom is incurably finite by nature, and
it is fundamentally corrupted by the
Fall. Indeed, after the Fall man's free
will is so impoverished that he can do
nothing without the prior action of the
will of God.

As the thought of Augustine
progresses, it becomes increasingly
evident that predestination takes priority over freedom. This does not mean
that freedom is ultimately denied in
the Augustinian view, but it does
mean that man's free will can operate
only within the wider and ontologically prior context of a creating, governing, and redeeming will of God.
To be sure, in the *Enchiridion,* as
well as in the *City of God,* Augustine submits the distinction between
God's foreknowledge and His foreor-
dination, thus suggesting that God can
foreknow the future state of His
creatures without having foreordained
it. But it remains incontestable, according to Augustine, that after the
Fall the springs of free action are corrupted beyond the possibility of human
restoration and all becomes the work
of divine grace. From this proposition
the doctrine of predestination follows
as a necessary implication. God predestines for eternal salvation those
whom He will. The unavoidable question then arises: What about those who
suffer eternal damnation? Augustine
argues that the will of God is omnipotent and is never defeated, and he
also takes seriously the Biblical assertion that God "will have all men
to be saved" (I Timothy 2:4). How,
then, does one account for the eternal
damnation of some? The apparent con-

tradiction is resolved, argues Augustine, when we understand the Scriptural reference to mean that no man is saved unless God wills it. It does not mean that there is no man whose salvation He does not will; rather, it means that no man is saved apart from His will. And by "all men" we are to understand all varieties of mankind instead of all mankind as a corporate totality. God wills the salvation of kings and subjects, nobles and slaves, learned and unlearned, rich and poor, healthy and enfeebled. God wills the salvation of men from all positions and walks of life. But does he will the damnation of others? Apparently not. Augustine stops short of a doctrine of double predestination, later advanced by John Calvin, in which God predestines some to eternal life and others to eternal damnation. God does not predestine the damned. He leaves them to their own devices, and their fate is a consequence of justice. They receive their just desert. However, He does withhold grace from them, and why He visits grace on some and withholds it from others remains inscrutable to the finite and fractured intellect of man.

Augustine concludes his summary of Christian doctrine with a brief discussion on the centrality of love. Love provides both the final definition of the nature of God and the foundation for Christian ethics. Without love and its manifestation in faith, no important knowledge is possible, and no significant act can originate. Man responds to the creating and redeeming love of God through a resolute love of his neighbor. The motivating principle of Christian action is the love of God and the love of one's neighbor in God. From Christian love follow all the special duties and requirements which constitute the Christian life. Love provides the all-embracing directive for man's ethical existence.

THE COMMONITORY

Author: Vincent of Lérins (d. before 450)
Type of work: History of Christian doctrine
First transcribed: c.434

PRINCIPAL IDEAS ADVANCED

The basis of orthodoxy is Scripture and the tradition of the Church.
The test of orthodoxy when opinions differ is ecumenicity, antiquity, and consensus.
Progress in doctrine must not change the substance of Scripture and tradition.

The formation of orthodox beliefs about the Christian faith reached a high point of concentration in the fourth and fifth centuries. The *Commonitory* of Vincent of Lérins is one of the most significant treatises of that creed-making period when the Church was struggling to decide which among a diver-

sity of opinions were right and orthodox and which were wrong and heretical. Councils debated the issues, especially the doctrines of the Trinity and
Christology, and the fact that various
councils, local and general, continued
to struggle with points of doctrine is
evidence enough that conciliar decisions were not always acceptable to
large groups of Christians. It was a per-
plexing and attenuated condition.

The monk Vincent determined to
record what he believed to be orthodox
and to explain on what grounds beliefs
should be so received. He tells us that
he settled down to his task in a rural
farmhouse outside his monastery and
entitled his work, *Peregrinus' Treatise
on behalf of the antiquity and ecumenicity of the Catholic Faith against the
profane novelties of all heretics.* He nowhere mentions his own name in the
treatise; but there is convincing evidence, which no one disputes, that
Vincent of Lérins was the author, writing under the pseudonym of Peregrinus.

Vincent was certain that what is correct doctrine is based on Scripture, on
"the authority of the divine law," but
he realized Scripture is open to many
interpretations. Everyone quoted Scripture in support of his opinions. Of
course, the councils debated the various interpretations and decided by consensus what formulation should prevail. Could the matter be analyzed further? True, the Scripture rule was a
fixed point, and a council decision was
a historical fact of record, but the conciliar decisions were not arbitrary. Vincent believed that three elements were
present: ecumenicity, antiquity, and
consensus. He does not hold that these
factors were formulated as principles
by the orthodox party, but that they
can be discerned by reflection. Nor

does he hold that all are present to the
same degree when the issues were being debated. All the opinions labeled
heresy by the orthodox, however, fall
foul of one or more of these tests. If
not all accept a position in doctrine,
then clearly the decision cannot be said
to be universal, but it could be claimed
to be the position of antiquity. Indeed
Vincent curiously defines "catholic" or
"ecumenical" as including "almost all
universally." If the minority opinion
claimed antiquity as, for example, in
their support by Scripture, then the
agreement or consensus of a universal
council could be used against them.

This Vincentian Canon, as it is generally called, is applied to various devi-
ant positions in the remainder of the
treatise. The Donatists of North Africa
were out of line with the imperial
Church, and the Arians who at one
time included "almost all the bishops
of the Latin tongue" were out of line
with the ancient faith.

Innovation is the dominant source
of error and the confusion of good doctrine in the illustrations which Vincent
uses. His own explicit aim was to avoid
novelty in his exposition of the faith.
The times in which he wrote were destructive of the old foundations of Roman civilization. The walls of the empire were crumbling; the internal life
of great centers of the Roman tradition
was decaying; monasteries were multi-
plying where men could find a haven
from the confusing and demoralizing
political scene. The great Christological controversies had evoked tremendous party spirit within the churches,
and the Third General Council at Ephesus, 431, was just over when Vincent
wrote in 434. Christendom was stirred
by the conflict between the great sees
epitomized by the battle between Cyril

of Alexandria (376-444) and Nestorius (d.c. 451) at this council. Regional loyalties were strong, and the quest for truth was obscured and embittered by partisan power play. Vincent was a passionate traditionalist who saw nothing but a demonic tendency in innovation. He believed that the time called for conservatism and consolidation as opposed to experimentation and division. The decisions of the ecumenical councils had his vote, and he believed that all Christendom should rally around the most powerful group. Those who refused were spreading "poison"; they were "mad dogs," "pests," "diseased" and "would burn eternally with the devil."

He was not at a loss to explain why God had permitted the heretics to expound their doctrines and often to win considerable support. Plainly, God was testing His people when He allowed them to follow prominent teachers, to build up affection for them, and to form churches under their leadership. Nestorius, Photinus (early fourth century), Apollinaris (c.310-?) are singled out for discussion at length. They had all been involved in the protracted debates on the Person of Christ. It is the work of Origen (c.185-c.254), however, that Vincent deplores most deeply. "My opinion is," he wrote, "that although we are able to adduce many examples of this type of trial, there is almost no instance comparable to the trial brought on by Origen, in whom there were so many features so excellent, so unparalleled, so marvellous, that at first sight one would judge quite easily that credit should be given to all his pronouncements." That most erudite man, however, had been the father of many innovations, and the extent of his influence as a teacher of so many eminent Christians compounded the effect of his mischievous doctrines. Almost as bad as Origen among the Greeks was Tertullian (c.160-c.220) among the Latins. His learning, his literary style, his defense of the truth, were all most wonderful, but his later work was "more eloquent than faithful," Vincent writes, and he regarded Tertullian's views as deserving condemnation.

What may be said, however, about progress in doctrine? Creedal statements formulated by local and general councils were evidence of some sort of advance in belief. Vincent faces this question in section XXII of the *Commonitorium*. Of course, there must be progress, he argues, and it should be "as great as possible." But it must not be a change of doctrine. There is a great difference between altering the substance of the faith by introducing novelty, and making possible a growth of knowledge about the faith. The position, he suggests, is analogous to that of the development of reason in a person as he progresses from childhood to adulthood. The nature is the same, but latent possibilities are developed. In this way ample room can be allowed for clarification, definition, and strengthening of all authentic factors in the Christian religion. There can be new names but no new beliefs. All this progress, of course, must come by way of general consensus. What is new but heretical is sectional, local, and often individual.

The Church as a whole has to guard the deposit committed to its trust. This means guarding Scripture itself against misuse, for it is characteristic of the heretics that they fill their conversation, debates, and books with Scripture-proof texts, sprinkling their poisonous dishes, as it were, with "the perfume of the heavenly law." "We have not the slightest doubt," wrote Vincent, "that the devil is speaking through them." If the Devil uses the heretics, God uses the Church—not, of course, to initiate new doctrine, but to guarantee the correct understanding of the old.

An interesting question has been raised on this section in the *Commonitory* as to the relationship between some doctrines of Augustine of Hippo (354-430) and Vincent. The Pelagian controversy had caused Augustine to develop a belief in divine grace as absolute, being conferred without respect to human conditioning. This view is allied to a belief in a rigid predestinarian view of the operations of the divine will. Vincent, on the other hand, was unwilling to accept either the position of Pelagius or of Augustine and adopted a view which was later called Semi-Pelagian. He claims in section XXVI that it is heresy to teach that "there is a great and special and wholly personal grace of God, so that without any effort, without any zeal, without any industry, though they neither ask, nor seek, nor knock, those who belong to their number have a special arrangement with God. . . ." Augustine is not named, but it is probable that his position in this regard is being condemned by inference. Certainly Augustine would have disagreed with the place given by Vincent to human effort, and probably also with Vincent's reading of what was the content of antiquity in the evaluation of doctrine.

The *Commonitorium* as it has survived consists of one book and the summary of a second. What happened to the second book is unknown, and an ancient editor simply notes that "nothing more of it has survived than the last part, that is, only the summary given below." The summary indicates that the book contained a continuation of the same type of discussion given in the first book.

In the history of Christian doctrine the treatise plays an important part in the development of authority in relation to Scripture, tradition, and the Church. It omits all reference to an authority resting on Apostolic succession, and its criterion may be held to be more negative than positive in that it attempts to define what doctrines may be condemned rather than to single out those which may be developed.

THE DIALOGUES

Author: Theodoret of Cyrus (c.393-c.458)
Type of work: Christology
First transcribed: c.444

PRINCIPAL IDEAS ADVANCED

God the Word is immutable; He became incarnate by taking perfect human nature, not by being changed into flesh; and after the union, He remained unchanged, unmixed, impassible, while preserving unimpaired the nature He had taken.

Theodoret, the author of the *Dialogues*, was probably born in 393; he became a student of theology under Theodoret of Antioch, and in 423 he was consecrated as Bishop of Cyrus (Cyrrhus), where he served until his death. Theodoret was an able administrator and a prolific writer who played an important role in the controversies of his day. Besides the *Dialogues* he wrote numerous exegetical and theological works as well as an *Ecclesiastical History* which continued the work of Eusebius (c.260-c.399).

The *Dialogues*, Theodoret's principal Christological work, was written to vindicate Theodoret's orthodox views and to refute the Eutychian heresy. The latter position held that when Christ became man, He possessed a single nature and His body was not essentially like our own. Nestorius (d.c. 451) had defended the assumption that Christ had two natures. In reaction the Eutychians insisted that there was but one nature in Christ.

Theodoret points out that the orthodox doctrine of the Church insists that there are two natures in Christ, the divine and the human, and that there is no transfer of the attributes of one nature to the other. The natures are not mingled or confounded, but are united in a personal or hypostatic union, so that Christ is but one person. The divine and the human nature are thus inseparably united, not in such a manner as to form a third nature, which is neither human nor divine, but in a manner such that each retains its own properties unchanged, so that there is both a finite and an infinite intelligence, a finite and an infinite will. The properties of the one nature are not transferred to the other. Christ's humanity is not deified, and

His deity is not reduced to His humanity. The union of the two natures is not a mere contact or indwelling, but a personal union which results in Christ's having two distinct natures and one person, so that He is at once both God and man.

The *Dialogues* consists of a series of discussions between Orthodoxos and Eranistes. The former represents Theodoret's understanding of the Apostolical decrees, whereas the latter is portrayed as the innovator of new doctrines.

The first part of the *Dialogues* seeks to show that the Godhead of the only-begotten Son is immutable; the second, that the union of the Godhead and the manhood of the Lord Christ is without confusion, and the third contends for the impassibility of Christ's divinity.

To attain the proper view of the nature of Christ, says Theodoret, it must first be recognized that Holy Scripture teaches that the Father, the only begotten-Son, and the Holy Spirit are one substance. What is predicated of the divine nature is common to the Son, to the Father, and to the Holy Ghost, but what is said of a particular hypostasis, a particular person of the Trinity, does not apply to the Holy Trinity. The term "God," for example, is common to the entire Trinity, but the name "Father" denotes the hypostasis to which it is proper. The names "Son," "Only Begotten," and "God the Word" do not denote the Holy Spirit or the Father, and the words "Holy Ghost" do not denote the Father or the Son but denote the hypostasis of the Spirit. Some terms are thus common to the Holy Trinity and some peculiar to each hypostasis. The term "immutable," however, is common to the Trinity as a whole, since it is not possible for a part of the substance to be mutable and a part immutable. The Father, the Son, and the Holy Ghost are immutable; thus, even though the Son became flesh, one cannot predicate mutation of His immutable nature. On the other hand, it is undeniable that when the Word was incarnate, it was not so simply in appearance; Jesus was not in reality God without flesh. The Son took upon Himself the seed of Abraham, and He wrought the salvation of mankind. The divine Word was made flesh, not by a mutation in His immutable nature, but by taking on a human nature. He who was born in Bethlehem was God; He was not God only, but also man; after the flesh He was an Israelite, a son of David, a man, and the eternal God.

The Holy Scriptures are the only source of true doctrine, Theodoret claims. The Scriptures clearly teach that the Son did not take an angelic nature, but the nature of a man. God was manifest in the flesh. The divine nature is not visible, but the flesh is visible. Through the visible the invisible was seen. When Jesus healed the sick, gave sight to the blind, and walked upon the sea, the almighty power of the Godhead was displayed. The Lord Christ had a body which He offered as a sacrifice, but His immutable nature did not undergo mutation into flesh. A body was prepared for Him by the power of the Holy Spirit, so that he was born of the Virgin Mary. In His humanity Jesus Christ is of the seed of David; in His deity, He is the immutable Son of God. As God and the Son of God, Jesus Christ was clad in the glory of the Father, and He shared the divine nature with Him. The one who in the beginning was with God and was God, the Creator of the world, took upon Himself the form of a servant, and He became God clad in human nature, so that He could accomplish the salvation of men. He was made in the likeness of man, and He acted and suffered as a man.

The divine Word is and was and will be immutable, but when He took man's nature, He became man, so that it is necessary to confess both natures, the divine and the human.

Two errors are to be avoided, Theodoret warns. The one confounds the hypostases, instead of recognizing three; such was the error of the Sabellians; the other error is to divide the substance and to introduce three substances instead of one; such was the error of the Arians.

Scripture teaches that there are three hypostases and only one substance. The man Jesus is the one Mediator between God and man; He is the Mediator because He does not exist as God alone. If Christ had not shared our nature, He could not have accomplished the work of redemption. Within Himself he unites distinct qualities, the Godhead and manhood. These two distinct natures are not to be confounded. In His divine nature He has neither beginning, nor end; He is eternal and co-eternal with the Father. Yet He is truly man. The Incarnation is real. Both qualities are proper: existence from the beginning, and generation from Abraham and David.

In Christ, says Theodoret, the two natures are not confounded, but unimpaired. Both His divine attributes and His human qualities are proclaimed in the Scriptures. When we speak of the two natures each must be carefully distinguished, so that we recognize that some attributes belong to the Godhead and some to the manhood. However, when we speak of the person, what is proper to the natures is to be applied to the person, and both sets of qualities, the divine and the human, are to be ascribed to the Savior. The same being is to be called both God and man, both the Son of Man and the Son of God, both David's Lord and David's son, both Abraham's creator and Abraham's seed.

Each nature has its own properties, but the two natures are united in one person.

It is to be noted further, Theodoret concludes, that God the Word did not taste death or suffer. The divine nature is immutable and incapable of suffering. What is repugnant to the divine nature is impossible to it. Our Savior *as a man* underwent the passion; *as God* He remained incapable of suffering.

TOME

Author: Saint Leo I (c.400-461)
Type of work: Doctrinal epistle
First transcribed: 449

PRINCIPAL IDEAS ADVANCED

The Apostles' Creed and the Scriptures clearly attest to the fact that although Christ was truly human as well as truly divine, but He was one person.

As a result of being deceived by the Devil, mankind had incurred guilt and the loss of immortality.

By secret counsel, God devised the mystery of the Incarnation to ransom man from the power of the Devil.

Only one who is both God and man could pay man's debt and restore what he had lost.

The *Tome* of Leo I, "Leo the Great," is a long epistle, addressed by Leo, Bishop of Rome, to Flavian, Bishop of Constantinople. The letter contains Leo's theological opinions concerning the problem of the divine and human natures in the person of Christ. The occasion of the epistle was the controversy raised by the Abbot Eutyches (c.378-454), who had been condemned and excommunicated by a Synod at

Constantinople on the charge of denying the humanity of Christ. Eutyches addressed a circular letter to all the Metropolitan Bishops, and thereby succeeded in winning the support of Dioscurus, Bishop of Alexandria, who, in turn, persuaded the Emperor to call a General Council at Ephesus, in 449. Leo, who did not attend the Council in person, sent three legates, bearing his *Tome*. But the Council, dominated by Dioscurus, refused the *Tome* a reading and declared Eutyches exonerated; indeed, it went so far as to excommunicate both Flavian and Leo. Matters were reversed only with the ascension to the throne of a new emperor, who summoned another Council, at Chalcedon, in 451. Here, Leo's *Tome* was received with general satisfaction, and it provided the substance of the formula which the Council adopted and which since that time has been regarded in the West as stating the orthodox doctrine concerning the Person of Christ. The Council of Chalcedon, besides annulling the proceedings of the Council at Ephesus, deposed Dioscurus, and raised the See of Constantinople to second place, after Rome, in order of precedence.

In his *Tome,* Leo censures Eutyches for indulging in speculation rather than applying his thoughts to Scripture, or even to the Apostles' Creed. The latter, says Leo, is decisive, inasmuch as it simultaneously declares that Jesus is the only Son of God and that He was "born of the Holy Ghost and of the Virgin Mary." As Son of God, He shares from eternity the power and glory of His Father, but as the Son of Mary, He had His beginning in time, and took upon Himself our passible nature, to make it his own. This birth in time, says Leo, took nothing away from nor added anything to His divine nature, but it added to our nature that by which alone mankind can conquer sin and death.

From the Apostles' Creed, Leo turns to the Scriptures. Eutyches had said that "the Word became flesh in such a way that Christ, born of the Virgin's womb, had the form of man but had not the reality of his mother's body." But the plain intention of Scripture,

says Leo, citing Isaiah's words about the son of the virgin and Paul's declaration that Christ was the "seed of David according to the flesh," is that, although God "gave fruitfulness to the Virgin, the reality of His body was received from her." Thus, the flesh which the Word took was that same flesh into which God had breathed the rational spirit when he formed man in the Garden of Eden.

Leo knows that caution is needed, however, lest in reproving Eutyches's error he seem to support the opposite error of Nestorius (died c.451), who was condemned in 431 at the Synod of Ephesus. Nestorius had complained against a teaching very similar to that of Eutyches, and in his insistence on the separation of the divine and human natures in Christ, he had said that it was wrong to speak of Mary as "the Mother of God." His words were taken to mean that Christ was not properly God, but "a man, energized by the Logos of God."

In his *Tome,* therefore, while arguing for the genuine humanity of Christ and its distinctness from His divine nature, Leo specifically notes that "in the Lord Jesus Christ, God and man are one Person." Accordingly, it is permissible to say that Mary is "the Mother of God," and that "the only begotten Son of God was crucified and buried," even though Christ's birth and death occur only in His human nature and do not affect the divine.

Leo explains the necessity for the Incarnation as a means of ransoming man from the power of the Devil. Having himself fallen under divine sentence, Satan sought revenge against his vanquisher by using deception to corrupt man. But Satan failed to reckon with the immutability of God's purpose, which cannot be turned aside. By a secret counsel God devised a "hidden mystery" by means of which to restore man to immortality and endow him with those divine gifts of which Satan had deprived him. Following this divine stratagem, God would become man, to pay man's debt and bear man's punishment, yet He would do so without compromising His divine power or glory.

The marvelous paradoxes of the Gospel, says Leo, all follow from this mystery, as the lowliness of manhood finds in Christ a meetingplace with the loftiness of divinity. In His human nature, the Redeemer suffers; in His divine nature, He performs miracles. He that is laid in a manger is heralded by angels; He whom Herod strives to kill is adored by the Magi; He who submits to be baptized by John is saluted as the Son of God by a voice from Heaven; He who is grieved to tears for His dead friend, Lazarus, bids the same friend step forth from the tomb; He who hangs with pierced hands on the cross opens the gates of paradise to the dying thief. At all times, Christ is fully human as well as fully divine. Even after the Resurrection, when He appears inexplicably through closed doors and breathes upon His disciples the Holy Spirit, He partakes of bread and fish, and He urges those who doubt to touch the wounds of His passion, so that they may be convinced that He is no spirit but flesh and bone.

Leo charges that, in denying the true humanity of Christ, Eutyches has made void "the mystery whereby alone we are saved." Peter, when he confessed, "Thou art the Christ, the Son of the living God," affirmed that the selfsame person was both Son of God and Christ. Neither of these truths,

says Leo, profits to salvation without the other. There is equal danger in believing either that Christ is only God or that He is only man. Eutyches, in affirming the former, has left man without salvation, since it is by the suffering which Christ endured in the flesh, and by the water and blood that flowed from His wounded side, that the Church lives and that mankind is cleansed of its sin.

The *Tome* of Leo is a polemic rather than a speculative work, intended to persuade its readers to favor Flavian's judgment condemning Eutyches and what came to be known as the Monophysite heresy. Leo, however, was a great statesman, and he rightly perceived the importance to the Church of arriving at a firm doctrinal position on so central a matter. In declaring that two natures, divine and human, are indissolubly united in Christ, yet in such a manner that divinity is not changed by Christ's passion, nor humanity absorbed by his divinity, Leo was only restating the position generally held in the West from the time of Tertullian. But his formulation of the crucial issues has classic strength and simplicity. Leo's declaration that two natures (*naturae*) were united without confusion in one person (*personam*) seems, indeed, to have provided the key terminology for the orthodox doctrine of the "hypostatical union." For, although Leo wrote in Latin, his distinction is obviously preserved in the Greek of the Chalcedonian Creed, which declares the Savior to be "one and the same Christ, Son, Lord, Only-begotten, in two natures (*physesin*), inconfusedly, immutably, indivisibly, inseparately; the distinction of natures being by no means taken away by the union, but rather the peculiarity of each nature being preserved and concurring in one person (*prosopon*) and one substance (*hypostasin*), not parted or separated into two persons, but one and the same Son and Only-begotten, divine Word, the Lord Jesus Christ."

Protestant scholars make a point of observing that Leo's treatise could not become the Rule of Faith for Christendom until it had been confirmed by a general Council, and that there is no suggestion at this date of the doctrine of papal infallibility, even on the part of so stanch an advocate of the Petrine supremacy as was Leo. It must be acknowledged, however, that Leo dissented from that action of the Council of Chalcedon which raised the See of

Constantinople to seeming parity with that of Rome; and it is a glaring fact that, behind the theological controversies concerning the person of Christ, a momentous struggle for power was going on, in which the claims of Alexandria, Antioch, Constantinople, and Rome were being challenged. Leo, called by his successors, "The Great," did more than any of his predecessors to establish the dominance of Rome. But Leo was also a forceful preacher and an effective writer; he has been designated *doctor ecclesiae*. His sermons have supplied many lessons now found in the Roman breviary, and his *Tome* was read in medieval monasteries during the Advent season.

THE BAZAAR OF HERACLIDES

Author: Nestorius (died c.451)
Type of work: Christology
First transcribed: c.451

PRINCIPAL IDEAS ADVANCED

The Incarnation is the union of God and man, the nature (ousia) of each being complete and remaining distinct from the other.

The two natures are united in one prosopon, *so there is one Son, the Lord Jesus Christ.*

The prosopon *of the man Jesus and that of God are the same and they are both present in the one* prosopon *of Jesus Christ.*

Jesus Christ is born of the Virgin Mary, but God the Word is not born, and does not grow, suffer, or die.

Mary is not theotokos, *God-bearer.*

There are not two Sons, or two Christs.

The *Bazaar of Heraclides* is the exposition and defense in dialogue form of Nestorius's Christology. The English translation by G. R. Driver and Leonard Hodgson is made from the

Syriac translation of about 535. It contains a detailed and repetitious statement of and argument for Nestorius's position, together with extended accounts of his treatment by the Council of Ephesus (431), of the turpitude of Cyril of Alexandria (d.444), and of the later persecution of Flavian (d.449), Bishop of Constantinople. Nestorius makes charges of violence and political maneuvering to put him in a false light at Ephesus. In his argument against Cyril he cites Scripture, the "three hundred and eighteen" of Nicaea, and many of the Fathers to give support for his own doctrine. He charges Cyril with deceitfulness, contradiction, hypocrisy, confusion of thought, and heresy. It is a heated polemic. Nestorius reveals not only a passionate earnestness but also logical acumen and constructive power. He, like others of his time, so far identified correct rational belief with Christian faith as to hold that doctrinal heresy meant damnation.

The charge against Nestorius was that he would not confess the Virgin Mary as "Mother of God," *theotokos* or God-bearer. Back of this phrase, in its acceptance or rejection, lies the whole problem of the Person of Christ. All agreed that there is One Lord Jesus Christ. All agreed also that Christ is God and man, human and divine. The critical issue was one *what?* and two *what?* This also involved the problem of *how* the two are united in the one. The trinitarian formula already approved employed two terms, *ousia* and *hypostasis:* God is three *hypostases* in one *ousia*. At first used as synonyms, *ousia* is now reserved for the essential nature of God, and *hypostasis* designates the three names for God in Christian faith; Father, Son, and Holy Spirit. Nestorius, however, usually assimilates *hypostasis* to *ousia*, although once or twice equating it with his own favorite term *prosopon*. For him the *ousia* or nature is the inalienable and incommunicable essence of God, and likewise of man. God is one *ousia*, man is another *ousia*. He rejects any teaching, such as that of Apollinarius (c.310-c.390), which replaces an element in human nature with one of the divine *ousia*.

How then are the two *ousiai* or natures united in the One Lord Jesus Christ? Nestorius uses the word *prosopon* to designate the One. He rejects "hypostatis" or natural union because this means to him two *ousiai* in one *ousia*, and this he scorns as irrational and impossible. It is this error with which he charges Cyril of Alexandria. To say, as Cyril did, that the eternal Word of God is the One Lord Jesus Christ means to Nestorius two things that are false and disastrous: (1) that the eternal Word who is God is "passible," that in His own nature He is born in time (Mary is *theotokos*) and grows and suffers and dies, and (2) that since the Son thus suffers as the divine *ousia*, the human *ousia* is wholly obliterated. Thus Christ is God but not man, and the whole claim to salvation in Christ is undermined.

Nestorius's own position is easily, and by him endlessly, stated. There are two *ousiai*, each complete, and the two are wholly distinct from each other. Each *ousia* has its nature and attributes which are inseparable from it. For the purposes of this doctrine, the most important difference between the natures is that one is passible and the other impassible. But each *ousia* also has a *prosopon*. The *prosopon* is not merely appearance or countenance. It is act, manifestation, role, and "dispensation." Granting, as he sometimes does, the distinction between *ousia* and *hypostasis*, Nestorius argued that each *ousia* has its own *hypostasis* and *prosopon*.

It is possible for each *ousia* to give its own *prosopon* to the other *ousia,* and to receive the other's *prosopon* in return. This is possible because the two *prosopa* are really identical. In Incarnation there is thus the one *prosopon* which is at once the *prosopon* of God and the *prosopon* of man. There are two *ousiai* or natures and one *prosopon.* This Nestorius calls the prosoponic union of God and man in the One Lord Jesus Christ.

The distinction between the impassible Deity and the passible humanity is preserved. Christ, who is the *prosopon* of God as well as of man, suffers in the flesh, the human *ousia.* He also is born in the flesh of Mary. He grows from childhood to manhood. Nestorius never tires of quoting Gregory of Nazianzus (329-389) as saying, "He who begins and gradually advances and is brought to fulness is not God, although on account of the manifestation which [took place] gradually, he is so called." But all this Christ does in His human nature. In His divine nature He does not suffer nor was He born of the Virgin Mary, for the Eternal Word cannot suffer and begin in time. A radical distinction is made between God the Word, which is the divine *ousia* solely, and Christ, or Lord, or Son, who is the union in one *prosopon* of the human and the divine *ousiai.* Nestorius does confess that Christ was born of Mary, but not that God the Word was born. He does say that from the conception by the Holy Spirit, the two *ousiai* were united in prosoponic union. He even grants that God the Word "passed through" the Virgin Mother, but not that He was born.

Nestorius repeatedly denies that he teaches "two Sons" or "two Christs."

There is one Son, one Christ. And this one Son or Christ is God; He is also man, for He is made or composed of two *ousiai,* each of which is complete and distinct from the other. He will no more grant the two Sons than He will surrender the two natures. And each nature includes separately and distinctly all the attributes of the *ousia.* However, the human nature can and does take the divine *prosopon,* and the divine nature the human *prosopon.* Since the two *prosopa* are the same, this requires no change. It is exchange without change. The divine *ousia* has the divine *prosopon* by nature, and the human *prosopon* by union, as Nestorius repeatedly asserts.

The open question never adequately discussed by Nestorius is the nature of the *prosopon.* He does distinguish it from *schema,* or surface appearance. He also distinguishes it from will, which is an attribute of nature. It does not seem to have a merely functional meaning, although it clearly includes that. References to "dispensation" seem to involve the active role of God in history through the Incarnation. But there is no clear recognition of these questions or any attempt to answer them. Nestorius has a formula for which he finds support in Scripture, in the Creed, and in the Fathers. He even claims that Cyril himself says the same thing essentially, although Cyril also contradicts it. He felt that this formula was logically sound and of the greatest theological importance. Apparently his death came just after or perhaps before the end of the Council of Chalcedon which, although it repudiated Nestorius, to a large extent vindicated his argument; union of two natures in one *hypostasis* has more than a superficial resemblance to Nestorius's prosoponic union. The difference, and it is an important difference, lies in the fact that according to Chalcedon there is no human *hypostasis,* but only that of the Eternal Son; while with Nestorius there is a complete human nature, and the one *prosopon* of the union is as truly the human *prosopon* as it is the divine.

The open question with Chalcedon is that of the absent human *hypostasis,* and the question has been answered by the doctrine of impersonal humanity (*anhypostasia.*) The open question in Nestorius's thought is the manner of union of two *prosopa* which though the same belong equally to two numerically different and distinct *ousiai.* Nestorius never seemed to be aware of this theoretical problem, nor of the need to provide some theological or Scriptural basis for the affirmation that something in man is identical with a corresponding something in God. There is no suggestion, for example, that this might be the *imago dei.* The identity is simply affirmed.

THE DIVINE NAMES

Author: Dionysius, the Pseudo-Areopagite (fl. c.500)
Type of work: Philosophical theology
First transcribed: c.500

PRINCIPAL IDEAS ADVANCED

The names given to God cannot represent Him literally, for He is nameless; since the understanding and contemplation of God's actual nature is not accessible to any being, names for God must be used symbolically.

The Supreme Godhead is celebrated by every name while yet remaining nameless, although some names are applied properly to His unity and others only to His differentiated aspects.

The highest name is "Goodness," although the Trinity surpasses this name, as it does all names, since God is the nonexistent source of all existence.

The vast influence of Dionysius' masterpiece, on *The Divine Names,* is not understandable without some knowledge of its history. The author follows the practice of attributing his writing to a more famous personage, in this case to St. Paul's Athenian convert Dionysius the Areopagite. The actual author remains unknown, but the important point is that until the sixteenth century the Church accepted the writings as having been written by the early Dionysius. Thus, for centuries the theology of the Church reflected the views of an unknown author who initiated the greatest falsification in the history of Christian thought. Since the influence of Proclus seems present, the treatise is now dated as having been composed about the end of the fifth century. The author may have come from Syria, where speculative mysticism abounded, and he was widely read in the Eastern Church. Scotus Erigena's translation in the ninth century began a series of important commentaries in the West.

The Pseudo-Dionysius begins with the assumption that no proper concept of God can be formed or expressed in speech. Since the Godhead is beyond comprehension, every doctrine concerning God's nature must be derived from or be in harmony with Holy Scripture. The One, as Dionysius calls God, is beyond utterance and surpasses the reach of words; yet man must do his best to discourse about God. The ineffability of the One is due partly to the fact that the One is beyond existence; it is the *cause* of existence while itself not existing. This paradox results from the attempt to understand God by the use of names.

As a Christian theologian, Dionysius must meet the problem of the Trinity. It is clear, however, that Dionysius prefers unity to trinity as an ultimate concept, although he attributes a Trinitarian nature to his Godhead as a natural expression of its supernatural fecundity. It is generally agreed that the doctrine of God's fecundity is not one which became orthodox in Christianity, since the doctrine of the Trinity must remain as an inexplicable expression, an outpouring of a nature essentially beyond distinctions.

Symbolism is obviously highly important to a doctrine such as this, for no literal term or statement can in the nature of the case be wholly accurate. Since the Divine Being transcends all being, He obviously transcends all knowledge; He may be symbolized by terms but not grasped by them. On the one hand, we use the negative method and deny attributes as being inappropriate to God; on the other hand, we draw upon the whole of creation in an effort to characterize God properly. Like the Scriptural writers, Dionysius celebrates the One by every name while yet calling it nameless. Such a transcendent cause must both be nameless and, in some sense, the source of the meaning of all names.

The difficulty of these concepts, and the apparent contradiction often involved in their use, led Dionysius to label all such discussion of names (including this particular discussion) as esoteric. Those uninitiated into these matters should not become involved in the discussion of them, or else mockery and laughter will result. This brings to light the most difficult and also the most important characteristic of this subject; namely, that the study of the divine names requires new methods of thinking and the abandonment of conventional modes of logic. One must not despair when little progress is made or when the task appears to be impossible. The difficulty of the subject dictates that any outcome will be a compromise subject to objections, especially from those not used to such problems.

The first and perhaps most important distinction which Dionysius learns from his study of the names applied to the Divinity is that those names which are properly applied are applied not partially but to the whole, entire, full, and complete Godhead. Names not fully proper, then, can be detected when it becomes evident that they refer only to some special aspect, rather than to the Godhead fully and completely. Such partial application tends to split the Godhead, and the importance of maintaining unity indicates that any term which tends to apply only partially cannot really be a proper term for divinity. The aim is to exclude the confusion of all distinctions in the Deity.

Theology, then, has two methods: that of using names which fail to make distinctions and that of using names which reveal differences; properly understanding God means to keep the attributes which belong to each class separate. Undifferentiating names (for example, excellent, divine, knowing) belong to the whole Godhead and may be applied equally to any aspect of it; differentiating attributes (for instance, Father, Son, and Spirit) can neither be interchanged nor held in common. Undifferentiating attributes indicate the ineffable, hidden, unknowable Permanence, but differentiating attributes are emanations or manifestations. Undifferentiating attributes without any confusion are yet wholly commingled. Differentiating attributes indicate the passage of the Divine Unity into multiplicity. Divine things, even those revealed to us, are known only by such communications.

The ultimate nature of Divinity, what it possesses in its own original being, is beyond mind, beyond all being and knowledge. The originals of what the creature perceives as divine manifestations are only images, while the originals in the divine nature transcend and exceed the grasp of creatures. For instance, how Jesus was born in human form is beyond expression in language or grasp by the mind. That Jesus took man's substance is a mysterious truth which we have received, particularly mysterious in view of the fact that in spite of His assumption of the substance of man He maintained His full divine existence. The undifferentiated Godhead became differentiated without loss of unity.

Actually the Godhead is beyond even the distinction between unity and plurality, although it is the source of both and has unity as an undifferentiating name. In divine things the undifferentiated unities are always of more might than the differentiated attributes. Dionysius declares, furthermore, which name among the class of the undifferentiating names is most important, and it is not surprising that Dionysius should designate Goodness as the highest name. Dionysius notes here that it is increasingly difficult to gain knowledge about Divinity as one attempts to become more specific, but he continues in spite of this, arguing that such knowledge of Divinity as is possible must not be disregarded.

As one familiar with the Platonic tradition might expect, in beginning with the first and crucial attribute, Goodness, Dionysius uses the analogy of the sun. As the sun, through no choice of deliberation, but by the simple fact of its existence, sends forth its rays, so the Good sends forth the rays of its undivided goodness upon all things, according to the receptive powers of each. All things are endowed with soul and life, including even those things without soul or life. In beginning to speak thus more concretely about Divinity and its specific functions, Dionysius is forced into an appropriate negative method as he expresses characteristics in a transcendent manner by negative images.

Even the nonexistent shares in the Beautiful (Dionysius' second name) and the Good; for even what is nonexistent shares in the Beautiful and the Good, since by negation of all attributes nonexistence is ascribed superessentially to God. Here we see the beginning of the tradition which ascribes nonexistence to God as the most perfect way of preserving His perfection. All that has being comes from the Beautiful and the Good, including all those things which have no substantial being. Because of this, even "yearning" can be ascribed to God, since both yearning and its object have their pre-existent roots in the Beautiful and the Good.

In one sense, Divinity is the cause and producer and begetter of the thing signified, and yet, in another sense, it is the thing signified itself. There is but one simple Power which itself moves all things to be mingled in a unity, starting from the Good, going on to the lowest of the creatures, and returning through all the stages to the Good. But what about evil? The Good cannot produce things which are not good. Evil has less being than what is nonexistent and actually is further removed from the Good. Evil only destroys and debases; it is productive only by means of the action of the Good. If the Good were entirely removed, nothing would remain, neither the good nor the partially good nor the absolutely bad.

Actually both good and evil must have another origin or cause. Following Neoplatonic principles, Dionysius argues that no duality can be an origin; some unity must be the origin of all duality. Yet it is absurd to suppose that two entirely opposed things can owe their birth and their being to the same thing. This would mean that the origin was not unified, but divided, double, self-contradictory, and discordant. Such a situation in Divinity, for a Neoplatonist who treats unity as basic, is intolerable. Thus

Dionysius' main problem is to give an account of evil and its origin such that evil becomes a part of and is not opposed to the Good.

Dionysius describes evil as a warping, a declension from right condition, a failure, a weakness or a loss of the power which would have preserved perfection. Evil things are so in a negative way, only in so far as they do not exist. In desiring evil one actually desires that which is nonexistent, the perfection which is absent. The only evil in anything lies in its inability to fulfill its natural functions. Since all things that have being are from the Good, matter must also come from the Good and in that sense cannot be viewed as evil. What is good comes directly from the one Universal Cause; evil comes from the many partial deficiencies. God knows evil only under the form of good. Evil is merely a weakness and deficiency of Good. Hence evil can have only an accidental cause and mode of existence. Evil exists nowhere simply as evil.

When Dionysius turns to the traditional term "being," he is forced to conclude that God is not existent in any ordinary sense, although in a simple and indefinable manner He embraces and anticipates within Himself all existent things. Just as all number pre-exists indivisibly in the number one, and this number contains all things in itself under the form of unity, so God is all things in that He is the cause of them all, and holds them together while He anticipates in Himself all beginnings and all fulfillments.

Hence, although all attributes, all the divine names Dionysius has discussed, can be affirmed of God, He is no one thing. He provides the limits of all things and yet He is a boundless infinitude, in a manner transcending all opposition between the finite and the infinite. Going out to all things, He remains in Himself. Not only is God so overflowing with wisdom that there is no limit to His understanding, but also He transcends all reason, intelligence, and wisdom. In seeking to understand the divine names, the human intellect is caused to transcend its intellectual nature. We are transported wholly out of ourselves and given unto God. Here is both the end of Dionysius' investigation of the names applicable to Divinity and the beginning of his mysticism.

ON THE HOLY TRINITY

Author: Anicius Manlius Severinus Boethius (c.480-c.524)
Type of work: Systematic theology
First transcribed: Before 524

PRINCIPAL IDEAS ADVANCED

The Christian belief in the unity of the Trinity is founded on the absence of difference and therefore of plurality in the Godhead.

Theology is that branch of speculative science which is abstract, dealing not with motion or matter but with that pure form which is Being itself and the source of all being; namely, the divine substance which is its own essence and which gives form and therefore being to everything.

Father, Son, and Holy Spirit are not identical, but there are not three Gods because predicates of relation affect neither the divine substance nor the divine unity.

The qualities attributed to God, such as justice, goodness, and greatness, are substantial or even supersubstantial because to be God is to be just or good or great, and these qualities may be ascribed to any one or to all the persons of the Trinity.

Boethius has been called by some the last Roman and the first scholastic and by some more a pagan philosopher than a Christian theologian. His theological tractates, of which the treatise *On the Holy Trinity* is representative, argue convincingly against his paganism but do not dispel the basically philosophical interests of the author. Boethius was a philosopher, and his self-appointed life work, although never finished, was the complete translation of Aristotle and Plato into Latin, together with commentaries that would reconcile their differences. His greatest contribution to the culture of the Middle Ages lay in the parts of this task which he did complete. It was he who established the Aristotelian philosophical terminology of medieval thought, the so-called *quinque voces* (five voices) of genus, species, difference, property, and accident. The importance of these terms is evident in his treatment of the Trinity.

Boethius lived in an age of change,

at the end of the classical world in fact, when the historical focus was shifting from the Mediterranean to western Europe and from the Romans and Greeks to the Germanic tribes. The Church had settled its central doctrinal problems at the great ecumenical councils or, in the West, by reference to the writings of Augustine (354-430), bishop of Hippo and the greatest of all Latin theologians. Theological creativity was on the wane, and an age of commentaries was commencing. Even Boethius acknowledges his indebtedness to Augustine in his essay *On the Holy Trinity*.

Boethius came from one of the eminent patrician houses of Rome. His father and father-in-law had served as consuls, and he himself was consul in 510 and saw his sons in this office in 522, although they were still minors. It must be remembered, however, that he lived under the kingdom of the Ostrogoths in Italy, who preserved the ancient Roman offices only as a semblance of legality and continuity. Boethius became a trusted adviser of Theodoric (c.455-526), the king of the Ostrogoths and an Arian. Politics, however, became his undoing; he was put in prison and executed by Theodoric for defending Albinus, an ex-consul, accused of treasonous relations with the Byzantine emperor. It was in prison that Boethius wrote his most famous work, *The Consolation of Philosophy*, which became one of the most widely read books of the Middle Ages. Because it contains nothing specifically Christian, the impression long prevailed that Boethius himself was not really a Christian. The short but lucid exposition *On the Holy Trinity*, together with his other theological treatises, provides evidence against that impression.

On the Holy Trinity consists of but six chapters and a preface on the difficulty of the subject. It is dedicated to Boethius' father-in-law, Quintus Aurelius Memmius Symmachus, an ex-consul and a Roman patrician. The first chapter states the belief of Christianity in the unity of the persons constituting the Trinity. Each person is God, but there are not three Gods. The cause of this union of the Trinity is the absence of difference. It was the Arians, Boethius claims, who argued for value distinctions within the Trinity and so converted it into a plurality. The author introduces a discussion of genus, species, and number as expressions of sameness and difference.

The second chapter continues the discussion of terms and method just begun. Boethius divides speculative science into three branches: physics, mathematics, and theology. The first deals with motion and is not abstract. The second deals with forms, not motion, and is also not abstract. Theology deals neither with motion nor matter and is abstract. Physics uses scientific concepts; mathematics, systematic ones; and theology, intellectual ones. Theology studies that form which is pure and not the image of any other form, which is Being and the source of being because everything owes its being to form and not simply to matter. The divine substance is form without matter; it is one, not the substate of anything.

The third chapter of *On the Holy Trinity* declares that there is only one divine essence without distinction according to accidents or substantial differences. To call the Father God and the Son God and the Holy Spirit

God does not create three Gods or a plurality, for this is a case of concrete rather than of abstract enumeration. To mention the sun three times does not produce three suns, and to call a sword also a blade and a brand does not make three swords. So it is with the three persons of the Trinity, among whom there is no difference. Still Father, Son, and Spirit are not identical although the same, and therefore number is involved.

Before clarifying the question of number, Boethius takes up in his fourth chapter the application of particular predicates or qualities to God. There are ten universally predicated categories: substance, quality, quantity, relation, place, time, condition, situation, activity, and passivity. Depending on their subject, they may denote substantial attributes or accidental ones, but when applied to God, they have a very different meaning. God is really a supersubstantial substance, and His qualities are substantial and not accidental. One sees this fact best with examples such as justice and greatness. To be God is to be just and to be great. To be a man is one thing, and to be a just man is another, not necessarily the same. Man may be great but not greatness itself. God, however, is identical with justness and greatness. In regard to the other categories, such as time and place, God is unique. God is everywhere, yet not in every place, because He does not occupy and is not contained by any place. He is eternal; He is in fact sempiternity or always present, always eternal. The categories of time and place as well as those of condition and activity are unlike those of substance, quality, and quantity because they are not substantial, but accidental. Hence, they are not simply applicable to God, who is not an ordinary subject; He is wholly substance.

The category of relation, however, has a special connection with the persons of the Trinity, and it is the topic of the fifth chapter of *On the Holy Trinity*. Because the category of relation has nothing to do with substance, predicates of relation, such as Father and Son, cannot alter or change their subject. In fact, the relation already belongs to or inheres in God's substance. There is no real difference in the subject, God, but only a difference of persons. There is no spatial separation in the Trinity and no essential or substantial differences.

In the final chapter, Boethius concludes that the divine substance preserves the unity and that the divine relations bring about the Trinity. He observes, moreover, that only terms of relation can be applied singly to each person of the Trinity because only these do not affect the substance of their subject. Thus, Boethius establishes the point expressed by the original title of his work: *The Trinity Is One God Not Three Gods*.

This treatise with its systematic explanation of the Trinity according to Aristotelian categories is representative of its age. It undertakes a task which each generation seems to find necessary, the task of comprehending the mysteries of faith and of giving them a rational exposition. Boethius continues this discussion in another essay directed to an unidentified John the Deacon. It is entitled *Whether Father, Son, and Holy Spirit May Be Substantially Predicated of the Divinity*. His conclusion is negative.

Each person of the Trinity is a substance, and the three are one substance. All predicates of substance such as justice, truth, goodness, omnipotence, and greatness must, of course, pertain to all three. Predicates such as Father, Son, and Spirit, which obviously pertain only to one person, are relative and not substantial, as the treatise *On the Holy Trinity* had already indicated. They are not predicated substantially of the divinity. But beyond this observation, Boethius affirms that even the Trinity is a relative predicate because it cannot be predicated substantially of each person.

These theological discussions of Boethius rest on dogmatic conclusions that were already established. The limits of discussion were already set. The degree of creativity possible to any writer on such topics was thus correspondingly restricted. In this respect Boethius could not be expected to produce something epochal. Still, his tractates are important to us as pointing the way into a new era of theology, the medieval and scholastic.

THE RULE OF ST. BENEDICT

Author: Saint Benedict of Nursia (c.480-c.547)
Type of work: Monastic rule
First transcribed: c.528

PRINCIPAL IDEAS ADVANCED

The communal life is essential for those who will undertake the way of perfection.

The discipline of the body is secondary to the discipline of the will through humility.

The worship of God is the main vocation of men, but manual labor and study are also important duties.

The Abbot is the vicar of Christ to his monks, and in submitting without murmur to his commands the monks work out their salvation.

The monastery is a congregation to which the monk attaches himself for life.

Christian monasticism, which originated in Egypt, was planted in Italy by Athanasius (293-373), whose *Life of St. Antony* stirred in many souls a resolve to undertake the life of abnegation. In the following century barbarian invasions provided additional incentive for men and women of all ages and rank to abandon civilian life either to join a religious community or to wander about begging hospitality. But, lacking leadership and adequate motivation, the movement rapidly became a scandal. Undisciplined individuals in ill-administered communities brought dishonor to God and ruin to their own lives because, as Benedict complains, they had no law, but called holy whatever suited their own will and fancy. Benedict himself, as a young man, undertook the hermit's life until his reputation for holiness led a nearby monastery to make him its ruler. His attempt to bring order to the monastic community was a failure, but, persuaded of the value of communal living, he went forth to organize several new communities in line with his ideals.

The *Rule of St. Benedict* is a full account of those principles and practices, derived from various sources, by which Benedict converted Western monasticism into a vigorous and wholesome institution, suited to play a historic role in preserving and propagating Christian civilization. His rule is to a considerable extent based on earlier rules of John Cassian (c.360-435) and St. Basil, as mediated to the West in the Latin version of Eastern monasticism.

Benedict considered the communal life essential for all who undertake the way of perfection. The life of a hermit, he writes, represents a higher attainment; yet it is not to be entered upon in the initial enthusiasm of conversion, but only after one has learned discipline by the help of others in a monastery. In principle, the rules which Benedict lays down for his monks constitute merely a beginning. They are the "least of rules" and have been "drawn up for beginners," he writes. When men have learned to live by them, they should desire to advance to higher degrees of perfection. In practice, however, as Benedict was astute enough to see, few monks will ever be able to dispense with these "instruments," and it is ordinarily assumed that those who enter the community are wedded to it until death.

According to Benedict, what man chiefly needs to achieve salvation is for his will to be humbled and tempered to obey the commands of Christ. Bene-dict speaks of monastic life in various terms: as a "school of the Lord's service" where men may overcome their habits of sloth and self-will; as a "workshop" where they are employed day and night with "instruments of the spiritual art," in order by the labor of obedience to return to Him from whom in disobedience they have departed; and as a training camp, where hearts and bodies may be drilled and accoutered to fight for Christ, the King. In contrast to oriental monasticism, which traces man's evil or ignorance to his body and hence views deliverance in terms of physical self-discipline and contemplation of reality, Benedict traces man's evil to pride and rebellion, and he views asceticism and contemplation merely as aids in the nurture of holy wills and affections.

Because Benedict does not regard materiality as the source of evil, he is more lenient than his Eastern counterparts in matters pertaining to the body. His monks are never deprived of food or sleep, and penance does not take the form of physical torture or privation. (An exception is that corporal punishment is recommended for boys.) In matters pertaining to the will, however, Benedict gives no quarter. Those who enter the monastery surrender everything to Christ, even the control of their own bodies; and this surrender means, in effect, that they yield absolutely to the will of the Abbot in all things. Such obedience is not acquired immediately, and satisfaction must be made for every fault. But the purpose of the satisfactions is to overcome pride and obstinacy, and punishment is designed accordingly. For example, an offender may be asked to prostrate himself at the door of the Oratory as the brethren pass in and out; or, for lighter offenses, he may have to take his meals apart from the brethren.

Taking as his text the Scriptural passage which says "Everyone that exalts himself shall be humbled, and he that humbles himself shall be exalted," Benedict charts the way of perfection in terms of twelve degrees of humility. They are: to keep in mind the fear of God and eternal punishments; to delight not in self-will but in Christ's service; for the love of God, to submit to one's superiors; to bear hardships without complaining; to confess one's evil thoughts and secret sins to the Abbot; to be content in the meanest circumstances; to think oneself the least worthy of men; to do nothing but what the rule and custom of the monastery direct; to maintain silence except when questioned; to refrain from laughter; to speak gently and soberly; and, at all times, to demonstrate humility by one's outward mien and conduct. By ascending these degrees of humility, beginning with fear of God, the monk will arrive "at that love of God which, when perfect, casts out fear." Then, his mind being conformed to Christ, the monk will no longer think of punishment or reward but, purged of vice and sin, he will rejoice in virtue and in love, and the Holy Spirit will dwell with him.

If this aspect of the *Rule of St. Benedict* seems unduly somber, let us remember the moral collapse which had accompanied the fall of Rome. Benedict's counsels were admirably suited for the rehabilitation of "tyrannical souls" (to use Plato's expression) which had overthrown all discipline and needed to be rebuilt from the ground up before they could be restored to the dignity of sons of God

and workers in his Kingdom. Only to this extent is the *Rule of St. Benedict* somber, that it reprobates the base condition to which man has reduced himself. The condemnation does not extend to human nature or to creation generally. On the contrary, Benedict reaffirms the fundamental Hebraic conception of creation and man's place in it, and the major part of his program is what we may call a kind of occupational therapy, consisting of three parts: worship, labor, and study.

"The Divine Office," which Benedict also calls "The Work of God," is the major employment of the monks, in terms of importance, and consists in eight daily services of worship. Here, as for nearly all his rules, Benedict is able to cite Biblical authority, notably Psalm 118, as numbered in the Vulgate, where we read, "At midnight I arose to give praise to Thee," and again, "Seven times in the day I have given praise to Thee." The former text is the authority for what is called the Night Office; the latter for the seven day services: lauds, prime, tierce, sext, none, vespers, and complin. The *Rule* contains detailed instructions as to when these services are to be conducted, varying according to the seasons of the year, and what psalms, readings, and allelujahs shall be used. It further is explicit in requiring full and prompt attendance on the part of all the monks, and correct and intelligent performance of all parts of the service.

The services of worship, however, ordinarily require only five or six hours out of the day. Benedict provides for two work periods between services, one in the morning, one in the late afternoon. Another period, in the morning, is set aside for reading and study.

From sext until none (two-thirty or three p.m.), the monks are free to read or rest. The day ends with complin, after which complete silence is enjoined.

The monks regularly keep fast through the morning and have only noon and evening meals. On Wednesdays and Fridays, however, they fast until three o'clock. Their fare is simple but adequate. They each receive daily a pound loaf of bread, which is served with two cooked dishes and, when available, a fresh fruit or vegetable. A moderate amount of wine is allowed, but, except for the sick, no meat. A separate table, with special dishes, is provided for the Abbot, and guests are entertained there. The *Rule* provides detailed instructions concerning dress and sleeping quarters. No hardships are intended in any of these details, but at every turn the monk is reminded that he has no property which he can call his own, and no choice in what shall be appointed to him from the common possession.

No attempt is made toward achieving equality. On the contrary, it is a principle with Benedict that the Abbot must have in view the individual needs of each of his monks, both physical and spiritual, and it is part of the lesson of humility that other brethren should not murmur when, for example, the Abbot exempts an older monk from certain duties that are beyond his strength. An elaborate and self-contained establishment, such as the monastery was intended to be, requires a chain of authority and a distribution of responsibility. The Abbot must use great discretion in selecting the dean in charge of the divine office, the readers, the porters, and the cellarers. Furthermore, consideration must be given to whether a particular monk can assume special rank without being overcome with pride.

Within the provisions stipulated by the *Rule*, the Abbot exercises absolute control over his monastery. He is enjoined, whenever important matters come up, to assemble the monks and hear the opinions of old and young alike; but the decision is his alone. He is Christ's vicar, so far as his monks are concerned, and that is why they call him "Abbot," from the Aramaic word *Abba*, or Father. His actions must, of course, be answered for at the Judgment Day, and therefore he must avoid all favoritism and injustice, must govern by example as well as by the preached word, and must not hold back from such punishment as has to be imposed.

Benedict did not organize a monastic "order," in the medieval sense of that term, with many houses under a single administration. He thought of each monastery as an independent congregation, to which the monk attaches himself for life. The election of an abbot was left to the monks themselves, to be decided by a majority vote, although as a safeguard, lest a community fall upon evil ways, Benedict urged that the bishop of the diocese or abbots of nearby monasteries, or other Christians, take a hand in restoring discipline. His rule, although not original, and owing much to Eastern monasticism, provided the ground plan for Western monastic practices, and it has been a charter to which Western reformers have again and again had occasion to appeal.

PASTORAL CARE

Author: Saint Gregory I (c.540-604)
Type of work: Pastoral counseling
First transcribed: c.590

PRINCIPAL IDEAS ADVANCED

*The office of pastor is a burden which most men are advised not to assume.
The care of souls is "the art of arts," and those who undertake it may do either
great harm or great good.*

*Men's needs differ widely, and the pastor must have the skill to deal with each
according to his particular circumstances.*

While living in the spirit, the pastor must enter compassionately into the experience of those living in the flesh.

Historians are unstinting in their praise of Pope Gregory I, known to history as Gregory the Great. When he came to office, civil administration in Rome had completely broken down. Gregory raised armies, negotiated with barbarian invaders, and fed the populace; he also reformed certain abuses within the Church and promoted missionary activity. For these labors he was well prepared, having devoted all his life to Christian work and public service. Still, when by popular acclaim he was elected to be Bishop of Rome, he sought to avoid the office. This hesitancy on his part brought reproof from one of his fellow churchmen. In reply, Gregory composed the treatise *Liber regulae pastoralis* (Pastoral Rule), better known in English, since the time of Alfred the Great, as *Pastoral Care* from the phrase with which the book begins, "The burden of pastoral care. . . ."

The book deals with two main topics: first, the bearing of the office of pastor on the salvation of the incumbent; second, the bearing of the office of pastor on the salvation of those entrusted to his care. Gregory breaks the topic into a multitude of special exhortations, which resemble brief sermons or meditations on Biblical texts. Gregory, who belongs to the medieval rather than to the Hellenistic age, draws his material almost exclusively from the Scriptures. He did not make use of the classical authors in his writings, and although his Latin is celebrated for its simplicity and strength, he was not trained in the rhetorical tradition. Moreover, his work is only partly influenced by patristic learning. For the most part, in support of nearly every point he wants to make, Gregory uses a Scriptural citation. Some of these are direct applications of prophetic and apostolic sayings; others are pointed illustrations drawn from Biblical history; others, however, are oblique conclusions arrived at by the free use of allegory, as, for example, when he applies to the pastor the Mosaic directions against offering blemished animals as sacrifices.

Gregory demands that each one who entertains the thought of entering upon the office of pastor subject himself to profound self-examination. The responsibility which a physician takes upon himself, who holds in his hands the life and health of his patients, is a light one in comparison with that of the minister to men's souls. Gregory especially warns against undue eagerness to teach on the part of those who have a merely intellectual knowledge of salvation: "They hasten to teach what they have learned, not by practice, but by study." Those who are precipitant in undertaking the office of pastor are, he says, like a woman who gives birth before her time: ". . . they are filling not a home but a sepulchre."

The office of pastor is fraught with danger to those who minister as well as to those ministered to. Among the perils mentioned by Gregory is the tendency which a pastor has to neglect his own spiritual life when he is burdened with the cares of others. Any man who enters public life is subject to special temptations; a man who in private life knows quite well his limitations will, upon being exalted to office, invariably become conceited. The fact that his orders are executed promptly and that his subjects praise everything he does leads him astray. The danger is even greater in the case of the pastor. "The human mind," says Gregory, "is prone to pride even when not supported by power; how much more, then, does it exalt itself when it has that support!"

But, in spite of the dangers, there are those who ought to become pastors, who incur guilt if they refuse the office out of self-regard. There is a false humility, says Gregory, as well as a genuine humility. Vices frequently masquerade as virtues, and what appears to be humility may be sloth or even a kind of perverse pride. Those who hold back when they ought to serve do an injury to those

persons who stand in need of their help.

Gregory acknowledges that some good men have desired the office of preaching while others no less worthy have been driven to it by compulsion. Isaiah, for example, volunteered: "Lo, here am I, send me." Jeremiah, on the other hand, was reluctant to go when commanded: "Ah, Lord God, behold, I cannot speak, for I am a child." Moses, says Gregory, admirably filled both parts, "who, though unwilling to accept the supreme rule of a great multitude, yet obeyed." But those who accept so great a responsibility must be clear in their hearts that it is not "the glory of that honor," which they seek, but "the ministry of a good work." When Paul said, "If a man desireth the office of bishop, he desireth a good work," he placed the emphasis where it belongs, says Gregory, who goes on to explain that in Paul's time the bishop would ordinarily be called upon to endure the tortures of martyrdom.

Gregory accepts the principle, common to the New Testament and to classic social thought, that men are unequal in ability and therefore in what is expected of them. The pastor, according to Gregory, must be spiritually superior to those who are committed to his care. He must live with his eye fixed on things spiritual, yet he must be compassionate toward those who are entangled with things carnal. Thus, Jacob saw the angels ascending and descending; thus, Moses frequently went in and out of the tabernacle. The pastor cannot sympathize with the trials of others without himself being assailed by temptations. Yet, if he trust in God and combine self-discipline with love for men, he need not fear for the health of his soul.

After these exhortations which bear upon the pastor's self-rule, Gregory turns to the practical problems which the pastor meets as he deals with different sorts of men. Gregory's considerable experience and keen intelligence brought him to the conviction that if the Christian teacher is to help instead of to harm those to whom he ministers he must be constantly alert to special demands of different kinds and classes of men. Gregory's method consists in giving directives by reference to opposites, such as poor and rich, joyful and sad, wise and dull, kindly and envious, slothful and hasty, quarrelsome and peaceable. There are forty of these combinations. Some of them represent differences in external conditions, health, or temperament; others represent differences of character and purpose. As far as possible, Gregory wishes to lay down rules. For example, the poor are to be offered consolation and encouragement; the rich, to be reminded of the dangers of pride. But Gregory is not unmindful of the fact that classificatory systems often break down in individual cases, and he recognizes that there is no single way of dealing with either poor or rich. Nathan wisely did not chide David, but very subtly led him to see the iniquity of his way.

The care of souls, according to Gregory, is "the art of arts," and it requires a special kind of practical skill. The pastor does not always need to be strictly candid with those whom he is trying to help, says Gregory. For example, when dealing with persons who are hardened to their faults, it may be necessary for the pastor to feign a despair that he does not actually feel. On the other hand, in order to make progress with the fainthearted, it is often wise to skirt their faults and to praise their virtues. Sometimes the pastor can best help the haughty by pretending that he needs them to help him, as when Moses won over his kinsman Hobab by asking him to be his guide.

Gregory is keenly aware of sins of the spirit, especially the faults of self-deception. Speaking of kindly-disposed persons, he points out that frequently their benevolence is merely that of spectators. He observes that abstemious persons are likely to be impatient and proud, and he admonishes that in order to be pleasing to God, the man who fasts must bestow on the poor what he subtracts from his own nourishment. Special dangers, he remarks, attend "those who prosper in their pursuit of temporal things." They come to respect the means to living and to lose sight of the things men live for, and thus they need to be reminded of the words of Solomon, "The prosperity of fools shall destroy them."

Gregory tried always to keep the affairs of man in the perspective of eternity. He viewed men's sins as affronts to God, and he trusted in God's pursuing grace to reconcile men to Himself. On the other hand, he stressed the need for men to respond to God's call, and the importance of human instruments in bringing men to repentance. If Protestants find his book lacking in any respect, it will probably be because Gregory thinks of sins in the particular ("We shed streams of water from our eyes when we weep for each sin separately, for the mind does not grieve for all sins equally at one and the same moment . . ."), rather than of sin as a condition of the heart. Thus he was inclined to look for "an-

tidotes" to particular faults, and to pre-
scribe penances. Still, the personal
counselor, whatever his religious de-

nomination, has much to learn from
this wise and holy man.

THE LADDER OF DIVINE ASCENT

Author: Saint John Climacus (c.570-c.649)
Type of work: Monastic guide
First transcribed: c.640

PRINCIPAL IDEAS ADVANCED

Thirty steps representing the thirty unknown years in the life of Jesus reveal the progress necessary to attain spiritual perfection.

Beginning with the most important, renunciation of the world, one progresses through obedience toward repentance.

Silence is necessary, as is simplicity and solitude, for one who would achieve heaven on earth, a godlike dispassion, and perfection.

Although little is known except by conjecture about St. John Climacus, and in spite of the fact that no definitive text of his masterpiece exists, *The Ladder of Divine Ascent* or *Ladder of Paradise* has penetrated into numerous cultures and languages. In fact, it is not too much to say that it is one of the few definitive classics of the contemplative life, having provided inspiration for numerous monastic disciplines and still profoundly influencing many of those who seek religion through renunciation of the world. Much of the ground John Climacus covers is similar to that of a fifth century ascetical compilation known as the *Book of the Holy Men*, a collection of sayings attributed to the Desert Fathers. The idea of a ladder, with its thirty steps leading to spiritual perfection, may have been inspired by the Biblical account of Jacob's vision of the ladder.

Particularly in Orthodox monasteries,

the influence of this work has been constant and decisive. Simeon the New Theologian, (949-1022) one of the outstanding figures in Byzantine monasticism, acknowledged his indebtedness to Climacus, and Climacus was of fundamental importance in the development of the Russian ascetical tradition. The purpose of the work was to guide the monks in their new life and, as traditional, was written in response to a request from a group of monks for a written guide, by one who himself claimed only to be a continual learner.

Following a long tradition, Climacus begins with a discussion of God, and he classifies people according to their relationships to God. God belongs to all free beings; to the faithful and unfaithful, the just and unjust, the pious and impious—just as the sun and the weather are for all. There are various ways of relating oneself to God, but the monk is one who loves as a mourning soul. Both asleep and awake he is unceasingly preoccupied with death. For him withdrawal from the world is voluntary hatred of vaunted material things and a denial of nature for the attainment of what is above nature. Since the monk's life is a contest, Climacus often compares the monk's state to that of the physical athlete. The monk must renounce all attachment to things, and a good foundation for his detachment is continence, fasting, and temperance.

The life of the solitary is a difficult one. In fact, it is so difficult that the most difficult problems of such a life are hidden from those outside of it, to whom it often appears easy. If others knew the difficulties of the monk's existence, few would renounce the world, since usually one renounces the world to escape difficulties. Very few men are ready to leave the world's advantages for what in fact are even greater difficulties. But a man troubled by his sins may eventually hate even his own flesh, and he may detach himself from the world and count it a disgrace to worry about anything that cannot help him in the hour of death. He who retains an attachment to anything visible, writes Climacus, is not yet detached from grief.

The monk renounces all business, all association with secular people and with parents; if he is victorious in these detachments, he receives rewards which the world cannot offer. If these rewards could be purchased in any other way, there would be no need for asceticism or solitude. Yet those who sail the spiritual seas know that the harbor of asceticism provides safety from worldly pressures, although it also exposes one to dangers of its own. Certain temptations are removed by removing oneself from the world, but new temptations come with the ascetic life.

Exile is the monk's state. Exile is separation from everything in order to keep the mind inseparable from God. Detachment is excellent, but exile is her mother. Exile involves running from places of sin as from the plague, and never looking back for fear of becoming useless. The family is left and the monk gains a new life—the remembrance of death. The solitary lives in a place which lacks opportunities for comfort and ambition, but provides the conditions for humility. Men who live in solitude are the warriors and athletes of Christ. The exile of the body and will must always precede obedience, the virtue which is most important to the monk's life.

Obedience, the absolute renunciation of one's own life, is clearly expressed in bodily actions and in the mortification of the limbs while the mind remains alive. Nor is obedience any less necessary at the end of the monk's life. Obedience is distrust of oneself, however good one may be, and perfect trust in one's superiors right up to the end of life. A man may question and examine before he enters on such a life, but once the arena has been entered, he must no longer judge his superiors. The temptation to judge his superiors is more difficult to resist than the natural temptations of the flesh.

Monastic discipline aims at the separation of body and spirit. If the monk learns to control his wandering mind in his distracted body, then amidst the actions and movements of his limbs he can practice mental quiet; in the midst of commotion he will be unmoved in soul. When he opposes discipline, when in conversation he tries to establish his own opinion, then he should recognize that he is sick with the Devil's disease, disobedience. From obedience comes humility, and from humility comes dispassion. It is not without peril for a monk to leave a group and attempt the solitary life on his own, since to do so is to be without the guidance of a spiritual superior, without the aid of the example of obedience.

Let the monastery be your tomb before the tomb, Climacus advises the monk. Constantly wrestle with your thought, and whenever it wanders, bring it back to you. Unbroken reflection is proper only to an angel, but the monk must strive to approximate it.

A servant of the Lord is the one who in body stands before men, writes Climacus, but who in mind knocks at Heaven's door with prayer. It is the Devil's prompting if anyone seeks to achieve any spiritual virtue prematurely. But keep at it, brother athletes, Climacus exhorts the monks; keep running fearlessly! The contemplative's steps lead to a new way of life, a life very much opposed to ordinary secular ways, a life with its own spiritual rewards and special difficulties.

The love of God sends a man into exile, and then obedience is born of self-condemnation. The thought of death is a constant aid to temperance, while solitude helps to establish chastity. Fasting quenches fleshly burning, and contrition wards off shameful thoughts. To win dependency, unceasing prayer is necessary, and to cure oneself of anger one must learn to love indignity. Detachment from the things of the senses will gradually lead to contemplation of spiritual things. Visible pride can be cured by grim condition, while quietness and solitude work against vanity. However, the only thing to do if one is with others is to seek dishonor. Only humility can destroy spiritual enemies.

Such are the items of advice John Climacus passes on to the monks as a guide for them in pursuing a spiritual life. The thirty steps leading to spiritual perfection for the solitary correspond in number to the thirty unknown years in the life of Jesus. Climacus points out that the solitary life is best pursued among a community of like-minded men, where authority can guide and a good community can excite mutual fervor among its members. Till the monk's very last breath, Climacus writes, the man who desires to attain the ultimate spiritual goal must never give up hope. Spiritual perception is a property of the soul itself, and through these thirty steps a dedicated man can be brought to perfect vision.

ECCLESIASTICAL HISTORY OF THE ENGLISH NATION

Author: Saint Bede ("The Venerable," c.673-735)
Type of work: Church history
First transcribed: 731

PRINCIPAL IDEAS ADVANCED

The defeat of the British peoples at the hands of the English invaders was a punishment for their sins.

When the British failed to preach the Christian gospel to the English nations, God sent missionaries from Ireland and from Rome.

Although the Irish missionaries were saintly men and zealous evangelists, they were mistaken in certain matters of worship and discipline.

The official recognition by the English of Roman ecclesiastical order has opened a new era of peace and godliness.

Bede, often called "the father of English history," was a priest and monk at the Benedictine monastery at Jarrow, which he entered as a student at the age of seven and from which he never had occasion to depart except for short visits to nearby churches and religious houses. Although Jarrow was a new monastery, its founder, Benedict Biscop (628-690), had brought back from Rome a good library and a chanter. Bede says, "I wholly applied myself to the study of Scripture, and amid the observance of monastic discipline, and the daily care of singing in the church, I always took delight in learning, teaching, and writing." A list of his writings includes, besides the *Ecclesiastical History,* numerous Biblical commentaries, lives of saints and churchmen, and treatises on the arts and sciences. The latter, in particular, were widely influential, not merely in England but also in France, prompting Continental scholars, such as Professor Étienne Gilson, to place Bede alongside Cassiodorus (c.485-c.580) as an important source of medieval learning.

In his *Ecclesiastical History of the English Nation,* Bede wrote with conscientious regard for the truth. His conception of history differs from that of the modern critical historian in that he was content merely to cite his sources, but he was aware of the importance of sources, and he tells us, in general terms, the authorities upon which his work rests. For information concerning the centuries prior to the coming of Augustine to Kent, he depended upon books written by others; for the critical years during which Roman Christianity was establishing itself on the island, he drew upon documents—such as the correspondence between Gregory I and Augustine—obtained for him from Canterbury and from Rome; for more recent developments, he made a point of consulting "men of good credit" from different provinces. "I humbly beseech the reader," he says, "that if he shall find anything set down other than truth in this that I have written, he will not impute it unto us, as the which have endeavoured with all sincerity to put in writing to the instruction of our after comers such things as we have gathered by common report, which is the true law of history."

Bede was English and his sympathies were wholeheartedly with the invaders who, beginning about 450, had gradually wrested the better part of the island from the hands of its native British inhabitants. The British, under Roman occupation, had accepted Christianity; and Bede quotes with appreciation the story of one of their martyrs, St. Alban, who was beheaded during the Diocletian persecution. But on the whole he regards them as a weak and indulgent people, unable to govern either their land or their passions once the Romans had withdrawn. The conquest, he says, was "God's just revenge of the wickedness of the people," like that which He executed on the Jews at the hands of the Chaldees.

Modern historians point out the comparative savagery of the English conquest of Britain and that, unlike the Gothic occupation of the Mediterranean provinces, it held no quarter for the vanquished. The Britons were either killed, driven back to remote portions of their island, or forced to emigrate across the sea, and a pagan and barbaric race took their place. As a result, the dispossessed had little opportunity, and no inclination, to impart to the newcomers any of the refinements of civilized life. More particularly, as Bede notes, "they never took care to preach the word of faith to the folk of the Saxons or English which inhabited the land along with them." But, says Bede, God's hand was with "his people which he foreknew to be saved," that is, the Anglo-Saxons; and in good season he "provided for the said folk much more worthy heralds of the truth, by whom they might be brought unto His faith."

This is the point at which Bede's story begins in earnest. The fact is, heralds came to the invaders from two directions. In the year 565, the Irish priest Columba founded a monastery at Iona, west Scotland, from which in succeeding generations Irish missionaries evangelized the northern portions of the Island; and in the year 596, the missionary Augustine (d.604), came from Rome, and established a church and monastery at Canterbury, in the south. Of the two "heralds of the truth," Bede's sympathies are all with those who came from Rome. Still, he tells with admiration the story of the rival missions.

One of the best known parts of Bede's *History* is the account ascribed by the author to "the tradition of our elders," of how Gregory the Great (c. 540-604), before he was made pope, saw in the slave market boys "of white skin and comely countenance and hair also of excellent beauty." Asking from whence they came, and being told they were called "Angles," he replied, "Well are they so called, for they have too an angel's face, and it is meet such men were inheritors with the angels in heaven." Gregory then asked the pope for permission to go as a missionary to this people; and, although he did not receive permission, when he became pope soon after, he sent Augustine to carry out the work.

Augustine arrived at Kent with a company of some forty persons, including interpreters. His arrival was smoothed by the fact that Ethelbert, the Kentish king, had married a Frankish princess who was a Christian and who had a chaplain with her. Augustine was courteously received, and at length he brought the king to embrace the Christian faith, who henceforth supported their mission with his possessions, although he "would force none to become Christian, . . . for he had learned from the masters and authors of his salvation that the service of Christ must be voluntary and not forced."

Bede records that Augustine tried to establish fellowship with the leaders of the British Christians, and he did succeed in meeting several of them in conference. Besides asking that they acknowledge him as the representative of the Universal Church, he required that they undertake three things: to change the date of celebrating Easter, to follow the Roman custom in baptism, and to join in preaching the Gospel to the English. When the Britons refused to acknowledge his authority, Augustine said that "if they would not have peace with brethren, they should have war with enemies." This threat was fulfilled, says Bede, when many monks and priests of the Britons were slaughtered by the pagan king Ethelfrith at Chester. Thus, "these heretical men learnt by the vengeance also of temporal death, that they had despised the counsels of eternal salvation offered to them."

The fortunes of Christianity were advanced by the marriage in 625 of Edwin, king of Northumbria, and the daughter of the Christian King Ethelbert. Among the influences contributing to Edwin's conversion was the counsel of the pagan priest Coifi, who avowed to him that there was no value whatsoever in the religion of his fathers and advised him to accept the new one "if you shall find after good examination that these things which be now newly preached to us be better and of more power." To this counsel the king's nobles agreed, one of whom compared man's life to the flight of a sparrow through a warm hall in the dead of winter. While it is in the hall, the sparrow does not feel the storm, but "after a very short space of fair weather that lasteth but for a moment, it soon passeth again from winter to winter and escapeth your sight." So, said the nobleman, is the brevity and

uncertainty of our life on earth: "Wherefore if this new learning hath brought us any better surety, methink it is worthy to be followed." Coifi, the priest, then recommended that they curse and burn the temples and altars of their old religion, and that they all embrace the Gospel. The king agreed, and he and all his people were baptized.

About the time of Edwin's conversion, other Northumbrian princes, living in exile among the Irish, were also converted to Christianity. Oswald, Edwin's brother, was one of these. When he came to the throne of Northumbria, wars had caused the Christian party to take flight. The new king, therefore, turned to Ireland for reinforcements, and Aidan, a monk from Iona, was sent. Bede describes Aidan as "a man of marvellous meekness, godliness, and sobriety, and one that had the zeal of God, though not fully according to knowledge." He notes that Aidan had to preach to the Saxons by an interpreter, and that, on occasion "there was a gracious and pleasant sight seen, when the bishop . . . was preaching the Gospel, and the king himself was interpreter of the heavenly word to his aldermen and thanes." The Island of Lindisfarne was given to Aidan for the founding of a monastery, and during his time Christian missions flourished under the eager Irish brethren.

Irish Christianity had enjoyed two centuries of independence from Roman interference, during which several differences of practice had grown up. The main difference was that the Irish Church was administered by the abbots of large monasteries, whereas in Italy and France the Church was under bishops who acknowledged the authority of the pope. But overlying this important issue were minor differences, which loomed much larger in the eyes of the people. One of these had to do with the style of tonsure worn by the clergy and another with the date of the celebration of Easter. Inevitably, as more of the English embraced Christianity, and as the warring nations learned to live together in peace, the rival ecclesiastical parties came into conflict. The issue was formally joined by King Oswy of Northumberland, at Whitby, in 664. Bringing together representatives of the two groups, he proposed "that it behoved those who were united in serving God to keep one rule of living and . . . to search out what was the truer tradition." Colman spoke for the Irish, and Wilfrid for the Romans. Bede records their arguments at length. What decided King Oswy in favor of the Romans was Wilfrid's argument that Peter had received from Christ the keys of the Kingdom of Heaven. "I will not gainsay such a porter as this," Oswy said, "lest it may be, when I come to the doors of the kingdom of heaven, I find none to open unto me, having his displeasure who is proved to hold the keys thereof." His nobles consented, and "abandoning their former imperfect usage," says Bede, "hastened to change over to those things which they had learned to be better."

The Synod of Whitby opened the way for the Roman archbishop, Theodore (c.602-690), to carry through the work of standardizing the English Church. Arriving in England in 669, he toured the country, reorganized the monasteries after the Roman rule, and brought local bishops under his authority. A forceful leader, he not merely brought peace to the Church but also helped to unify the nations, so that, in

Bede's words, "there was never since the English first came to Britain, any time more happy than at that present; when they both had most valiant and Christian kings and . . . the desires of all were wholly bent to the late joyful tidings of the kingdom of heaven." Theodore was himself a scholar, "fully learned in profane as well as in holy literature," and he did much to encourage learning by bringing books and scholars to England. "The proof whereof is," says Bede, "that even to this day some of their scholars yet living have as good knowledge of the Latin and Greek tongues as of their own in which they were born."

Such is the main story which Bede sets himself to tell. But Bede follows his sources into many curious byways, and he permits himself to interject matters of interest along the way. He quotes at length letters from popes and abbots designed to clarify doctrinal matters. Most of his written sources, where they deal with heroes of the faith, abound in tales of miracles; Bede records all of these. A book came into his hands which related the visit of Arculf, a bishop of France to the Holy Land. Bede condenses its description of Bethlehem, Jerusalem, and Hebron, and gives them a place in his book.

One passage, of great interest to students of English literature, is the account which Bede gives of the minstrel, Caedmon, who never having learned to play the harp or sing, dreamed that he was commanded to sing the praises of creation, and he discovered to his amazement that in his dream he had the gift of making verse. On rising, he remembered what he had sung in his sleep, and, mentioning it to the authorities, he was encouraged to take the monastic habit and to receive instruction in Christian teaching. Thereafter, says Bede, "whatsoever of the divine writings he learned by them that expounded them, he set it forth after a little time with poetical language, put together with very great sweetness and pricking of the heart, in his own, that is to say, the English tongue." Bede, who writes in Latin, makes no attempt to reproduce the poems, for, he says, "songs, be they never so well made, cannot be turned of one tongue into another, word for word, without loss to their grace and worthiness." But he testifies to the power which they had to turn men's lives toward God, and he adds that, though many of the English tried their hand at writing religious poems, none could match the cunning of Caedmon.

Bede was one of the favored generation which profited from the civil order and cultural enrichment which Archbishop Theodore introduced. The fact that he could live a full lifetime in peaceful pursuits only a century after the landing of Augustine on Kentish shores is by itself remarkable, not to mention the gentle humanity of his person, his love of poetry, and his knowledge of ancient authors. Bede was a celebrated teacher, whose students numbered in the hundreds. One of his disciples, Egbert (d.766), was later Archbishop of York, and founder of the celebrated cathedral school of York, where Alcuin (c.735-804), founder of the school of Paris, received his training.

The *Ecclesiastical History* by which Bede is chiefly known, besides being invaluable to historians, will probably continue to stand in the first rank of literary works because of its simple, unaffected style, and its sure handling of the picturesque and the dramatic. It was translated into Old English by Alfred the Great (849-899). The first modern translation was made by the learned Oxford scholar, Thomas Stapleton (1535-1598).

THE FOUNTAIN OF WISDOM

Author: Saint John of Damascus (c.675-c.749)
Type of work: Christian philosophy and theology
First transcribed: After 742

PRINCIPAL IDEAS ADVANCED

All knowledge of being can be treated under the five universals and ten categories of Aristotle, properly defined.

All heresies spring from four archetypes: Barbarism, Scythism, Hellenism, and Judaism.

An accurate exposition of the orthodox faith is grounded in the teaching of the Fathers, the Scriptures, and natural reason or philosophy.

Some books open up new periods in the history of thought, some bring periods to a close, and a few both end one period and begin another. The

Fountain of Wisdom falls in the last category. It marks the end of the patristic era and the beginning of Greek scholasticism. It is the summary of more than six hundred years of Christian theological development and the model for theological handbooks throughout the Middle Ages and, in some respects, down to the very present.

John of Damascus (Yanah ibn Mansur ibn Sargun) was the son of a Christian official in the court of the Caliph at Damascus. He himself became Logothete, or chief representative of the Christian community before the Caliph, until in about 715 he entered the monastery of St. Sabas near Jerusalem. It was under the protection of Islam that he wrote his attacks against the iconoclastic Byzantine Emperor Leo III, the Isaurian (717-740), and it was under his Arabian name of Mansur that he was anathematized by the iconoclastic council of 753. The iconclastic controversy, which lasted from 725 to 842, is reflected at many points in the *Fountain of Wisdom*.

The *Fountain of Wisdom* (*Fons scientiae*) is composed of three parts: the "Philosophical Chapters or Dialectica," "On Heresies in Epitome," and "An Exact Exposition of the Orthodox Faith." In no case does the Damascene claim originality. Indeed he disclaims it, and his use of sources is quite evident and sometimes clearly specified. The work was dedicated to a friend from the monastery, Cosmas (born c.700), who in 743 became Bishop of Maïuma (modern Gaza). Apparently Cosmas had asked John to write such a *summa theologica*. John's previous writings included a work on moral theology based on the fathers, the *Sacra parallela,* disputations with such heretical sects as the Manicheans, Nestorians, and Monophysites, and the *Life of Barlaam and Joasaph,* a Christianized version of the story of Buddha.

The first part or "Philosophical Chapters" of the *Fountain of Wisdom* was intended to present the best of Greek philosophy, but it consists mainly of the definition of terms. As such it is still valuable to the student of Greek theology. Foremost among the terms discussed are the Aristotelian universals: genus, species, difference, accident, and property. In providing definitions for these terms John was forced to treat also the questions of being, priority, division and subdivision, and definition and description. Then, after defining his terms and his method, he compared, contrasted, and related the terms to one another.

Having defined the universals, the Damascene then took up the categories: substance, quantity, relation, quality, time, place, position, state, action, and passion. In connection with these terms there is a useful discussion of such specifically theological concepts as hypostasis, enhypostaton, and anhypostaton, as well as, of course, hypostatic union. The last named term is of particular significance in understanding the dogma of the two natures and one person of Jesus Christ. Altogether the philosophical chapters are sixty-eight in number and are followed by an appendix on expressions used in the description of the natural world, such as "seasons" and "heavenly phenomena."

The sources for the philosophical chapters besides Aristotle's *Categories* include the *Introduction to the Categories of Aristotle* or *Isagoge* of Porphyry (c.232-303), a Neoplatonist philosopher, and the *Commentary on the Isagoge of Porphyry* by Ammonius Hermeae (fl. fifth century), a Greek philosopher and commentator on Aristotle. To these sources John of Damascus added a good deal of his own analysis of terms, especially of the theological ones.

The second part of the *Fountain of Wisdom* lists and describes more than one hundred different heresies. The Damascene believed that they all came originally from four parents or archetypes: Barbarism, Scythism, Hellenism, and Judaism. The first eighty chapters are taken verbatim from the *Panarion* of Epiphanius (c.315-403), a zealous defender of orthodoxy in his position as Bishop of Salamis. Unfortunately, only his summaries or table of contents are reproduced by John and not the excerpts from heretical writings, which are still of great value. To the last of these eighty heresies, the Massalians, there is added material from another, now unknown, writer, so that this chapter is now the principal source of information on that sect.

The next twenty chapters, 81-100, are from another unknown author, who perhaps had already borrowed the material from Epiphanius and thus provided almost the entire catalog of heresies in finished form to John of Damascus. In any case these twenty chapters deal with heresies from the time of Nestorius (died c.451) to that of the Greek emperor Heraclius (575-641). The discussion of the Monophysite heresy in Chapter 83 is one of the longest in the catalog and includes quotations from John Philoponus, the Grammarian (fl. sixth century), a Christian philosopher at Alexandria.

The final three chapters, 101-103, represent the direct contribution of John of Damascus. Here he attacks the Ishmaelites or Saracens on such grounds as the deficiency of the Koran and the worship of the famous Black Stone at Mecca. There is a short chapter against the Christianocategori (accusers of Christians) or Iconoclasts, and a chapter on the Aposchistae (makers of schism), apparently perfectionists who had separated themselves from the Catholic Church. This part of the work concludes with a doxology and a confession of faith.

Looked at as a whole, the heresies are grouped in roughly chronological order, although some, those of the Donatists, are out of place. There are groupings of Samaritan heresies, Jewish heresies, heresies of the Gnostic sects, of the Jewish-Christian sects, of Marcion and his followers, Christological heresies, and heresies against the discipline of the Church. Probably nowhere else could one find such a variety of heresies cataloged in such brief compass.

The third part of the *Fountain of Wisdom*, sub-titled "On the Orthodox Faith," is usually divided into four books. The first of these books discusses the Godhead in unity and trinity. The topic is, of course, one that occupied the attention of the Christian Church for well over three hundred years, until the definition of the Council of Nicaea (325) was reaffirmed by the Council of Constantinople in 381. John of Damascus was very respectful of the limitations of human reason in describing or defining the Godhead. He states that he will in no case exceed the teachings of the New Testament and the Church Fathers. His favorite Father, whom he cites most often in all four books, is Gregory of

Nazianzus (329-389), whose five sermons delivered in Constantinople in 380 and known as the *Theological Orations* have been a primary theological source for his successors. It is noteworthy that John nowhere cites any ante-Nicene Fathers. Apparently their orthodoxy could never be certain enough to satisfy him because they had no standard such as the Nicene Creed to which to conform. There is little place for proofs of the existence of God in the Damascene's theology. Only one proof is given. More important to John are the relationships between the three Persons, their unity and their distinctions. He is careful to note that some things are described or affirmed as if God had a body or a human nature. These expressions are all symbolical or figurative as are many of the names of God. In this connection the treatise on *Divine Names* by Dionysius the Pseudo-Areopagite (c.500), an anonymous Greek theologian, is a useful source.

The second book concentrates on the First Person of the Trinity, God the Creator. Beginning with the invisible creation, John maintains among other things that evil spirits foretell the future by guessing at events, while angels actually foresee them by the grace of God. Within the visible creation man is of the greatest interest. Some fifteen chapters are devoted to a description of man, his emotions and feelings, his senses and faculties, and his activity, be it voluntary or involuntary. This book concludes with the already venerable problems of providence and predestination. For his teaching on creation the Damascene turns especially to the Syrian theologian, Nemesius of Emesa (fl. c.390), who wrote *On the Nature of Man,* and to the Cappadocian theologian and bishop, Basil of Caesarea (c.330-379), who delivered a series of homilies on the six days of creation.

With the third book, "On the Orthodox Faith," John of Damascus moves into the realm of Christology where, as in the doctrine of the Trinity, only long years of debate had made dogma a reality. The problems here center around the Incarnation and the relationship of the two natures, divine and human, in the one person of Jesus Christ. Much of the presentation retains the polemic tones of the Nestorian, Monophysite, and Monothelite controversies of previous centuries. It is in discussing the two natures and one person that the categories of Greek philosophy as outlined in the first part of the *Fountain of Wisdom* are most prominent. Quantity, number, action, and difference all enter into the understanding of the Second Person of the Trinity in his Incarnation. John does not hesitate to divide Jesus' earthly activities between the two natures, but the real key to His person is the hypostatic union of God and man. This union can hardly be explained. The attempt to find suitable analogies, such as the red-hot knife which both burns and cuts always, falls short. Leontius of Byzantium (died 543), an anti-Monophysite theologian, and Maximus Confessor (c.580-662), who was one of the first to recognize the dangers of Monothelitism, are important as sources for this third book together with, as always, Gregory of Nazianzus.

The fourth and final book of this last part of the *Fountain of Wisdom* begins with Christology but moves shortly into a discussion of various aspects of faith and practice. There is a significant chapter on Mariology as well as on the veneration of saints and relics. John defends the cult of holy images almost as strongly as he does the Bible. He brings his book to a ringing conclusion with the doctrine of the bodily resurrection.

It was in his treatment of the somewhat miscellaneous and not then dogmatically defined theological topics of his book that the Damascene made greatest use of the Scriptures. The Fathers themselves had not said enough on these matters to be really helpful.

The *Fountain of Wisdom* is an impressive work for its very comprehensiveness. There had been others, such as Origen (c.185-c.254) with his *De Principiis* or Gregory of Nyssa (c.330-c.395) with his *Catechetical Discourses* or Theodoret (c.393-c.458) with his *Compendium of Divine Teachings*, who sought to propound the Christian faith in systematic form, and they may have served John of Damascus as models. They were, however, clearly overshadowed by John in the ability to synthesize and comprehend the many-sided teachings and traditions of the Church. All Greek theology up to his day, but no Western or Latin theology, was drawn upon for the *Fountain of Wisdom*. It is little wonder that this writing enjoyed considerable influence throughout the Middle Ages and was even translated into Latin in the twelfth century for the use of Western scholastic theologians.

SELECTED WRITINGS ON THE SPIRITUAL LIFE

Author: Saint Peter Damian (1007-1072)
Type of work: Ascetical theology
First transcribed: Eleventh century

PRINCIPAL IDEAS ADVANCED

Human learning, especially grammar and dialectic, is useless and even harmful, the only profitable studies for the spiritual man being the Holy Scriptures, commentaries, homilies, and martyrology, while logic is so far from being applicable to divine things that God is able to bring it about that an event which has occurred in the past has not occurred.

The monastic and preferably the eremitic way of life aiming at the peace of contemplation has three stages of ascetic ascent: the mortification of the flesh, in which fasting is fundamental while other modes of chastisement including flagellation may be employed; the discipline of the spirit, consisting in solitude, silence, and stability; and prayer, public and private, accompanied by tears.

Since reason has no legitimate function except as a handmaid to faith and since the life of nature is rejected unless swallowed up in grace, the state has no reality apart from the Church, temporal power being delegated to the emperor by the pope.

St. Peter Damian, born in Ravenna in or about January 1007, studied and taught in schools of northern Italy until in 1035 he entered the monastery of Fonte Avellana. Damian, himself a model of monastic rigor, was prominent as a leader of the reform movement in the eleventh century. His "Liber Gomorrhianus," dedicated to Pope Leo IX, frankly depicted the moral degradation of many of the clergy, while the "Liber Gratissimus" recommended a moderate solution to the problem of the validity of simoniacal orders. During the pontificate of Stephen IX (1057-58), Damian was elevated to the cardinal-bishopric of Ostia, probably as a result of the influence of Hildebrand.

Damian is known as an anti-dialectician, an opponent of worldly learning, particularly of grammar and philosophy. He writes in *The Book of "The Lord Be with You"*: "I spurn Plato, the searcher into the hidden things of nature, who set a measure to the movements of the planets, and calculated the courses of the stars; Pythagoras, who divided the round world into its regions with his mathematician's rod, means nothing to me; I renounce the much-thumbed books of Nichomachus, and Euclid too, round-shouldered from poring over his complex geometrical problems; the rhetoricians with their syllogisms and the cavillings of the sophists are useless in this matter. Let the gymnasts shiver in their nakedness for love of wisdom, and the peripatetics seek truth at the bottom of a well." Damian proceeds to scorn the inventions of crazy poets, the melodramatic adventures of pompous tragedians, the poisoned stream of scurrilities flowing from the noisy lips of comedians, the satirists' bitter banquets of insidious slander and the skilled speech and skilled argument of the orators. He desires instruction from the simplicity of Christ and asks to be taught "that of which the unskilled throng of dialecticians knows nothing."

In "On the Perfection of Monks," Damian angrily assails the monks "who follow the rabble of grammarians, who, forsaking spiritual studies, desire to learn all the follies of worldly skill, who, despising the rule of Benedict, love to apply themselves to the rules of Donatus." He compares such men with one who deserts the chaste spouse lying upon the bridal couch of faith to consort with the harlots of the stage. In his "De ordine eremitarum," Damian enumerates as volumes suitable for a monastic library the Old and New Testaments, a martyrology, sermons of the Fathers, allegorical commentaries on Holy Scripture by Gregory, Ambrose, Augustine, Jerome, Prosper, Bede, Remigius, Amalarius, Haimon, and Paschasius Radbertus. In the "De sancta simplicitate," human knowledge is rejected as harmful and useless. The serpent in Eden was the first grammarian, teaching Eve to decline "God" in the plural. The almighty God does not require grammar to draw men to Himself, since in the beginning of redemption, He did not send philosophers and orators, but simple men and fishermen. The jawbone of an ass by which Samson killed a thousand Philistines is interpreted allegorically to mean the tongues of humble and simple men, by whose preaching the humility of Christ is inculcated.

The opusculum "On Divine Omnipotence" uses philosophy against itself. In it Damian joins issue with St. Jerome, who had denied that God could make the past not to have occurred. God is shown to be able to do many things which He does not will, and His will is proved to be the cause of the existence of all things. Nothing can prevent Him from raising up a fallen virgin, either with respect to the plenitude of merits or to the integrity of the flesh. If it is objected that God is able to destroy Rome, but not to bring it to pass that Rome has never existed, the reply is made that the same reasoning would have to apply to the present and to the future as well as to the past. So far as the order of discourse is concerned, contingency is excluded from the present and the future as well as from the past. But such dialectical considerations have no application to God. Damian writes: "That which is from the argument of the dialecticians cannot easily be adapted to the mysteries of divine power; that which has been invented for the benefit of the syllogisms . . . let it not be obstinately introduced into divine law and let it not oppose the necessities of its inference to the divine power." Dialectic must remember that her position is that of a handmaid subservient to her mistress.

The spiritual writings of Damian inculcate the ideal of the contemplative life, and a severe course of ascetic exercises is recommended as the means to such a life. In the writing "On the Perfection of Monks" he declares that rest is the whole end of the monastic way of life and renunciation of the world. The images of divine illumination and spiritual marriage are employed to express the excellence of the contemplative state. Worldly knowledge is a hindrance rather than a help to this goal: "Who lights a lantern that he

may see the sun, or candles that he may behold the glory of the stars?"

The ascetic life as an ascent towards contemplation has three stages: the mortification of the flesh, the discipline of the spirit, and prayer. The enjoyment of the end is not an automatic effect of the ascent of this ladder, but a gift freely given by God. The Augustinian note of dependence on the grace of God is stressed in Damian's "Sermon on the Holy Spirit and His Grace." Without the grace of the Holy Spirit no man, however hard he struggles and strives, can rise to good works or bring forth fruit pleasing to God. Our souls must then seek this Spirit without ceasing, if they are to receive the gift of grace.

Perfect mortification is achieved when the greedy gullet is kept in check, the wanton tongue compelled to be silent, the ears shut to scandal-mongering, the eyes forbidden to look upon unlawful things, the hand bound for fear it should strike cruelly, the foot lest it should wander idly, and the heart withstood for fear it should envy the prosperity and happiness of another. Mortification is pursued not only as a means to contemplation but in imitation of Christ and as penitential suffering. In defense of flagellation, Damian writes: "I scourge both flesh and spirit because I know that I have offended in both flesh and spirit."

Severe rules for fasting are laid down. Bread, water, and salt are all that are needed in a perfect fast. The hermits at Fonte Avellana had a staple diet of bread and vegetables, while cheese, fish, and eggs were permitted. Meat was forbidden and wine used only in exceptional cases. Damian justifies these rigors of fasting as destroying the desires of our gullets and extinguishing the flames of lust. Yet he denies that he is condemning anything which God has made.

While fasting is fundamental in physical mortification, other forms of self-inflicted suffering are also to be employed. In the opusculum "De laude flagellorum," Damian defends the practice of flagellation, by appealing to the example of Christ and the Apostles. Since it is not likely that we will receive such treatment at the hands of others, if we are true disciples of Christ, we will inflict these chastisements on ourselves. Damian's influence led to the spread of the practice of flagellation. At length he found it necessary to dissuade some whose zeal led them to recite the whole Psalter once or more, scourging themselves throughout: "Wherefore . . . we have decreed that no one in the hermitage shall be compelled to use the discipline; and if holy zeal urges anyone to this he is permitted to scourge himself for the course of forty psalms, and no more, in any one day."

The second stage of the ascetic's progress, the discipline of the spirit, consists of solitude, silence, and stability. Solitude is best cultivated in the life of the hermit. Chapter Nineteen of *The Book of "The Lord be With You"* concerns the merits of the solitary life and contains an eloquent panegyric on the hermitage. While the monastic life is admitted to be good, the eremitic (hermitic) is to be preferred. The corrupt state of many of the monasteries of the day no doubt

encouraged this preference for the solitary life. Damian regarded the monastery, even at its best, as a place of preparation for the desert.

Solitude is insufficient if unaccompanied by silence and stability. Silence is necessary because undisciplined tongues empty the soul of the strength of heavenly grace and weaken its healthful vigor. Unnecessary conversation leads to frivolous gossip and slander. Stability is no less important. Instability is a disease that deprives its victims of the benefits of the active and of the contemplative life. Restless pacing up and down within one's cell is itself a symptom of inner instability. Damian's journeys on papal business prevented him from fulfilling his own precepts in this matter.

The third stage of contemplation is prayer, both public and private. Prayer should be joined with tears of compunction. Tears that come from God bring assurance of the certain forgiveness of sins. Tears of spiritual joy bring with them the savor of divine contemplation. This water has its source in fire, for he who wishes to abound in these flowing streams must first kindle in his heart the fire of divine love.

Damian espoused a view of the relation between Church and state of one piece with his view of faith, reason, nature, and grace. For him the emperor derives his authority from the pope. The civil order has no reality apart from the spiritual, even as reason has no value apart from faith and nature no claims apart from grace.

MONOLOGION

Author: Saint Anselm of Canterbury (c.1033-1109)
Type of work: Scholastic theology
First transcribed: 1076

PRINCIPAL IDEAS ADVANCED

The existence of God may be demonstrated by rational proofs.

In its attempt to understand the nature of God, reason encounters certain rational antinomies, the chief of these being that God is at one and the same time a unity and also a trinity of Father, Son, and Holy Spirit.

Although God is ineffable, and all affirmations about Him are to be taken figuratively, man must believe in the triune God, for the human mind is made in order that it may believe in and love God.

The proofs show that God is that absolute good in whose goodness all relative goods participate; He is that self-subsisting being to whom all contingent beings owe their existence; and He is that single being in relation to whom all other beings are inferior.

Anselm of Canterbury was born at Aosta in northern Italy, most likely in the year 1033. In his middle twenties he left for France, where he traveled and where eventually he became a Benedictine monk after having studied under the famous Lanfranc at the monastery of Bec. For approximately thirty years he was an official of Bec, first as prior and later as abbot. He spent the last years of his life as primate of the English Church, having succeeded his old master Lanfranc in 1093 as Archbishop of Canterbury. These last years were stormy and unhappy ones for Anselm because of the widespread rejection in England of the claims of papal supremacy. He died in Canterbury in 1109.

Anselm ushered in the movement known as Scholasticism, which was to reach its zenith in the thirteenth century. Scholasticism took its name from its association with the monastic and cathedral schools of the eleventh and twelfth centuries—such schools as Bec,

Laon, Chartres, and Notre Dame de Paris. Later, in the thirteenth and fourteenth centuries, some of these schools developed into such universities as Paris and Oxford, which became models for numerous later universities.

Anselm's work marks the transition from a tradition of heavy dependence upon the authority of the Scriptures and of the Fathers of the Church, in the direction of a much larger role for reason. He assumed that the traditional doctrines of the Church were the content of faith, and the act of faith itself was understood by him to be essentially a surrender of the will to the teachings of the Church. Still, reason is necessary for the explication and clarification of beliefs. Augustine's maxim *Credo ut intelligam* (I believe so that I may understand) was adopted by Anselm. The emphasis, however, was placed differently by the two men. Augustine was impressed by the necessity of believing before attempting to understand, whereas Anselm was impressed with the desirability of going beyond belief to understanding.

Anselm's decision to apply the methods of logic or "dialectics" to theological questions was not in itself novel, but his results reversed the predominantly heretical theological direction of other employers of the method. Berengar of Tours (c.999-1088), for instance, denied that the bread and wine were materially changed into the body and blood of Christ. The consecration of the elements adds to the elements—which remain bread and wine—the presence of the heavenly Christ, whose reality is wholly spiritual. Roscelin of Compiegne (Roscellinus, d. c.1125), afforded another example of the unorthodox possibilities of the dialectical theological method. He attacked the doctrine of the Trinity by declaring that either the Father, Son, and Holy Spirit are identical, or they are three separate Gods. As will be evident below, in the *Monologion* Anselm is attempting to show, in opposition to Roscelin, that reason supports the doctrine of the Trinity.

The *Monologion*, which was probably Anselm's first work, was written at Bec in 1076 in response to the urging of students who desired a wider audience for the thought of their mentor. In the *Monologion* (or Soliloquy), Anselm is concerned to demonstrate by rational proofs the existence of God, and other doctrines of Christianity which relate closely to the theistic affirmation. He employs three arguments for the existence of God.

The first argument begins with the premise that all men seek to enjoy those things which they consider good. When things are compared to one another, they are seen to be more or less good. There must, therefore, be an absolute good by which they are judged and in whose goodness they all participate. Since all good things possess their goodness through it and not through themselves, it alone is good through itself and is therefore the greatest good. That which is supremely good is also supremely great. There is, therefore, something which is the greatest and best of all things that are, and it is this "something" to which we give the name God.

The second proof runs as follows: Everything which exists has being either through something or through nothing. But from nothing, nothing comes. Everything, therefore, is through something. This something is either one or many. If the something is many, then all of the many are through a single thing, or each is through itself, or they are through each other. If all of the many are through a single thing, then all things owe their existence ultimately to that one thing. If each owes its existence to itself, then there must be a single power of existence which accounts for each thing, so that ultimately there is a single source of being. It would be absurd to hold that things owe their existence to one another, for that would mean that the same things are both the causes and the effects of one another. There is, therefore, a single thing to which all other things owe their being. This thing alone is not dependent upon something else for its being. All things that are good or great exist through this self-subsisting being. It is, therefore, supremely good and supremely great. Such a being is God.

The third argument is based upon the inequalities in the levels of being of the various kinds of reality. The horse has a higher nature than wood, and a man belongs to a higher level of being than a horse. It would be unreasonable to conclude, however, that there exists nothing whatsoever which has no superior, for such a conclusion implies an infinity of kinds of being. There is, therefore, some reality which is superior to all other realities.

That reality which is inferior to nothing is either one, or it consists of several essences, all of equal degree. But if there are several such realities they owe their equality to a single cause. This cause would be either the very essence of their natures or something external to their natures. If the cause is the essence of their natures, then they are essentially one. But if the cause of their superiority is something other than themselves, then they are inferior to the order of being represented by their cause. In any event, then, there can be no more than one being which is superior in excellence to all other beings. There is, therefore, a single being which is the greatest and best of all existing things. This supremely great and good being is through itself, and all other things are through it. This supreme being is through itself, not in the sense that it *makes* itself, but in the same way in which a light shines of itself. All other things are made by it.

Anselm's argument continues by affirming Augustine's teaching that all things in the created order were made of nothing. They pre-existed, not in the form of some shapeless material, but only in the mind of their Creator, just as an object of art pre-exists as a conception in the mind of the artist. And just as the artist's mental conception of a work of art can be reduced to words, so the creative activity of God is through a kind of inner speech. This inner speech of the supreme essence, by virtue of the fact that it is strictly within the Godhead, may be identified with the supreme essence itself.

Because the supreme being is better than any other nature, any quality which is absolutely better than its contradictory can be attributed to it. Thus the supreme being (or God) must be living, wise, powerful, true, just, blessed, and eternal. These attributes may also apply to human beings. The difference is that all God's attributes are essential to Him; God would not be God without these attributes. Man, however, receives these attributes from beyond himself. God, on the other hand, has not received them from an external source. We may not correctly say God *has* life, or justice, or eternity. Rather, he *is* life, justice, and eternity. His attributes and his essence are identical. God *is* justice as such, goodness as such, truth as such, being as such. Moreover, because of the unity of the divine essence, all of God's attributes constitute in reality but a single attribute.

Having powerfully stated the foregoing conception of God, Anselm then turns to an enumeration of the difficulties inherent in the conception. If God is eternal, then He must be simple, not subject to change or decomposition. But does not eternity also mean that God is distributed over infinite points of time? And does not divine omnipresence mean that God is distributed over all points of space? Still, to interpret God's simplicity as meaning that He is nowhere in time and space would be equivalent to denying his existence. Anselm proposes that the two extremes of God's simplicity (or eternity) and His omnipresence be reconciled by asserting that God is both omnipresent and eternal but not limited by time or space.

Another serious difficulty which Anselm acknowledges arises because there is nothing accidental or nonessential in God; in God there is no change. Every substance, however, has accidents or nonessential qualities. Hence God is not a substance. He is beyond all substance. At this point in his argument Anselm displays hesitation and apprehension, and he declares that although the term substance does not apply to God in the usual way, still, no better term can be applied to God, who not only most certainly exists, but is also the highest form of being.

The theological antinomies thus far described are minor compared to the most formidable and completely irresolvable antinomy of all: the doctrine of the Trinity of Father, Son, and Holy Ghost in the unity of the divine essence. The Word (or God as Son) is God insofar as He is thought or conceived by Himself. The Holy Spirit is the bond of love between God and the Word. The Holy Spirit is God's love for the Word and the Word's love for God, or God's love for Himself.

Having thus explicated the meaning of the Trinity, Anselm confesses, in seeming discouragement, that "the mystery of so sublime a subject transcends all the vision of the human intellect." He affirms, nevertheless, that the truth of the Trinity, although inexplicable, is supported by the balance of logical evidence. Still, the Supreme Essence in itself is ineffable, and all affirmations about it are to be understood figuratively, not literally. The surest approach to knowledge of God is to reflect upon that which most nearly resembles God; namely, the human mind. The more intently the rational mind attempts to know itself, the more surely will it ascend to knowledge of God. Human rationality is given in order that man may distinguish between good and evil and thus love the good and hate the evil. The mind is made in order that it may love the supreme good above all lower goods. But in order for the mind to be able to love God above all other goods it must strive for understanding of God. God is triune in nature, so that belief in the Trinity is necessary in order for one to be able to love God. Belief in God and love of God constitute a living faith which will be manifested by good works. The triune God alone ought to be worshiped in love and loved in worship, for He alone is the source of happiness and the refuge from adversity.

PROSLOGION

Author: Saint Anselm of Canterbury (c.1033-1109)
Type of work: Scholastic theology
First transcribed: c.1077-1078

PRINCIPAL IDEAS ADVANCED

Everyone must grant that God is to be understood as a being than whom no greater can be conceived.

A being than whom no greater can be conceived must be conceived of as existing in reality and not merely in thought, for that which is conceived of as having real existence is greater than that which is thought of as only a concept.

Because God cannot be thought not to be, He necessarily exists.

God is at one and the same time compassionate and passionless, just and merciful, sensible and incorporeal, omnipotent and unable to do wrong, unified in being and existing as the Trinity of Father, Son, and Holy Spirit.

The *Monologion*, Anselm's first writing designed to demonstrate the existence of God, was long, complicated, and uneven in the quality of its logic. Anselm was painfully aware of these deficiencies, and he resolved to formulate a brief, lucid, and irrefutable single argument for the existence of God as the supreme good. The product of this effort was the *Proslogion, or, Faith Seeking Understanding,* written about 1077-1078.

The alternative title to the book— *Faith Seeking Understanding*—indicates Anselm's conviction that although reason or "dialectic" is not the source of faith, faith seeks to go beyond belief to understanding. It would seem to follow, then, that the purpose of his argument is to nurture faith from its simple form as belief to its more mature form as understanding. But within the text of the *Proslogion* itself there are suggestions that the argument may also lead from nonbelief to belief in God. As we shall see below, Anselm's lack of clarity in defining the intention of his argument has opened the way for wide disagreement among his interpreters.

The first chapter of the book consists of an eloquent and moving prayer in which Anselm acknowledges that man "has lost the blessedness for which he was made, and has found the misery for which he was not made." He implores God for a restoration of the blessedness which comes with understanding, for "I desire in some measure to understand thy truth, which my heart believes and loves. For I do not seek to understand in order to believe, but I believe in order to understand."

The second chapter—consisting of but a single paragraph—contains Anselm's famous "ontological argument," one of the most discussed and disputed passages in the history of speculative thought. Anselm affirms not only that God exists, but also that God "is a being than which none greater can be thought." Even the Psalmist's fool, who said in his heart, "There is no God" Psalms 14:1; 53:1), knows what is meant by the expression "a being than which none greater can be thought." The fool understands immediately, too, that a "being than which none greater can be thought" exists at least in his understanding. If anyone continues to reflect upon the meaning of the foregoing definition of God, he will also understand that the being than which a greater cannot be conceived cannot exist merely as an idea. For if such a being actually exists only as an idea, it cannot be thought of as existing in reality, and yet that would be greater. In short, the very idea of a perfect being necessitates the actuality of such a being. One cannot understand what the term "God" means and think of God as not being. Since God cannot be thought not to be, He necessarily is.

Anselm's argument is based upon the presuppositions of Platonic realism, which pictured the relationship between thought and reality as such that whatever is necessitated in thought is also necessitated in actuality.

Before turning back to the historically significant part of the *Proslogion* which centers around the ontological argument, it should be indicated here that the bulk of this brief book consists of a discussion and defense of the seemingly contradictory attributes applied to God. Thus Anselm attempts to demonstrate that there are no contradictions in affirming that God is compassionate and passionless, just and merciful, sensible and incorporeal, omnipotent and incapable of doing wrong, eternal and in all places and all times, unified in being and existing as a Trinity of Father, Son, and Holy Spirit.

Anselm's ontological proof has never ceased to fascinate and challenge speculative minds, and few of the chief theological and philosophical minds of the Western world since the twelfth century have failed to respond in one fashion or another to the argument.

One of Anselm's worthiest adversaries was a contemporary Benedictine monk, Gaunilo, who lived and studied in the abbey of Marmoutier near Tours. In a brief and tightly argued treatise wittily entitled "In Behalf of the Fool," Gaunilo—while not denying God's existence—contends that Anselm's argument does not refute atheism. If it were true, writes Gaunilo, that God cannot be thought without His actual existence being understood, then no argument for God's existence would be necessary, for God's existence would be a proven fact as soon as one's understanding possessed the concept of God. And yet, he points out, Anselm distinguishes between having a thing in mind as an idea and the later idea of the actual existence of the thing.

The most frequently cited and most graphic part of Gaunilo's refutation centers around the case of the imaginary isle of bliss. Suppose, he argues, that someone should describe an island whose qualities far surpass the qualities of any other island, and then should conclude that such an island necessarily exists because it is perfect. Once one conceives of a perfect island, the island must exist in reality as well as in thought, else it would not be a perfect island. Such a conclusion, reasons Gaunilo, is no less absurd than the argument that God's existence is necessitated by the idea of God as perfect being.

How telling Gaunilo's blows are against Anselm's argument has been a matter of dispute for many centuries. It is fair, however, to point out that Gaunilo missed the main point of Anselm's argument, as Anselm himself indicates in his reply to Gaunilo's treatise. Only of God, replies Anselm, can it be concluded that it is impossible to conceive of His nonexistence. God alone is Being itself. Of God alone can it be said that to exist is part of His essence. Thus the nature of God's existence is sharply distinct from that of islands or any other kind of finite reality.

After Gaunilo's attack Anselm's ontological argument attracted hardly any notice until the thirteenth century. It enjoyed varying degrees of acceptance from such theologians as William of Auxerre (d.1231), William of Auvergne (c.1180-1249), Alexander of Hales (c.1170-1245), and St. Bonaventura (1221-1274). This mood of sympathy was broken by St. Thomas Aquinas (1225-1274), in whose thought there was a new emphasis upon the experience of the senses as the starting point for proofs of the existence of God. St. Thomas was to become the key thinker of the thirteenth century, and because of the continuing dominance of his thought in the Roman Catholic Church, his adverse verdict on Anselm's argument was enough to insure that the argument would not become central in Roman Catholic natural theology.

Thomas examines Anselm's argument in a number of places, including both of his chief works, *Summa contra gentiles* (I, 10-11) and *Summa theologica* (I, 2, i). In another source, *Quaestiones disputatae de veritate* (10, 12), he contends that there are three opinions regarding the question whether the idea of God is a first principle whose invalidity cannot even be thought. The first opinion is that belief in God does not rest upon such an idea, nor can God's existence be proved. God's existence can only be believed. The second opinion is that the mind does not know of itself that God exists, but His existence can be demonstrated from evidence external to the mind and known by the mind. The third opinion is that of Anselm and those who agree with him; namely, the opinion that the mind is persuaded of God's existence by the very idea of God.

Thomas rejects the first opinion as false, but he accepts each of the latter two as true in a certain sense. It is true only for one who has had direct knowledge of God that the idea of God requires the existence of God. Such experience, however, is extraordinary. The ordinary ways of knowing God both give indirect knowledge. One way is faith, and the other is rational demonstration of God as a necessary inference from particular facts known directly. For one whose experience is limited to these ordinary channels of knowledge it is not true that the existence of God is known to the mind from the idea of God.

The ontological argument of the French philosopher René Descartes (1596-1650) is significant both because he regarded it as a clarification of Anselm's argument and because Immanuel Kant (1724-1804) was responding to the Cartesian form of the argument when he formulated what is widely regarded as a cogent refutation of all forms of the ontological proof.

The clearest statement of Descartes' argument is found in his *Discourse on Method*. Descartes argues that if one has in mind the idea of a triangle, the idea implies the conclusion that the three angles of the triangle must equal two right angles. Still, there is nothing in this argument which necessitates the actual existence of a triangle. The idea of a perfect being, on the other hand, includes existence as intrinsic to the very idea, just as the idea of triangle necessitates the conclusion that the angles of the triangle are equal to two right angles.

The form of the Cartesian argument is very similar to that of Anselm's proof. The difference is that Descartes saw the proof as resting on purely rational grounds. Anselm, on the other hand, indicates through the devotional tone of the *Proslogion* that the logical exercise contained in the ontological proof was an expression of his Christian faith which was already assured of the existence and goodness of God.

In the *Critique of Pure Reason,* Immanuel Kant argues that the ontological proof is invalid. Using the Cartesian form of the proof, he says that the argument defines God as *ens realissimum,* the most real being, or the subject of all predicates which necessarily belong to absolute being. Kant rejects the traditional contention that existence is so related to God that God would not be God without existence. The conception of God is fundamentally the same whether God is conceived of as existing or not, just as a hundred dollars in one's imagination have the same fundamental predicates as a hundred dollars in one's wallet. Because existence is not a predicate which is intrinsic to absolute being, the ontological argument has no validity.

Although directed specifically against Descartes' version of the ontological proof, Kant's refutation has had the historical effect of widely discrediting all forms of the ontological proof, particularly in philosophical circles, notwithstanding such powerful philosophical defenders of the proof as Georg W. F. Hegel (1770-1831).

In recent years there has been a revival of interest in Anselm's argument, particularly in theological circles. This new interest has been generally attended by the claim that the so-called "proof" of Anselm is actually a form of theological affirmation rather than a philosophical argument. Thus, it has been contended that the *Proslogion* is an essay in mystical theology in which Anselm reduces to rational terms the import of his mystical vision of God. The Protestant Swiss theologian Karl Barth argues in much the same fashion by contending that the ontological argument was not a proof but rather an expression of a faith already held. Paul Tillich, the German-American Protestant theologian, contends that the ontological argument is valid as an analysis of the unconditional element which is necessarily present in all thought as the basis of the distinction between truth and falsity. Anselm's thought takes a wrong turn, however, says Tillich, in identifying this unconditional element with a "highest being." God is the Ground of Being rather than the highest being.

We have seen that historically the *Proslogion* has been interpreted sometimes primarily in terms of its element of *ratio* (reason) and has been judged by such interpreters as mainly of philosophical importance. Other theologians have been more impressed by the element of *fides* (faith) and thus view the work as essentially theological in significance. That the *Proslogion* has had such a history of interpretation points to the fact that in it the conjunction of *ratio* and *fides* remains ambiguous.

CUR DEUS HOMO

Author: Saint Anselm of Canterbury (c.1033-1109)
Type of work: Scholastic theology, soteriology
First transcribed: 1098

Principal Ideas Advanced

The necessity of the Incarnation can be proved by the use of reasoning alone, apart from any reference to a knowledge of Christ.

Man is a rational being whose purpose is to find happiness in fulfilling the will of God; man's sin is that disobedience wherein he witholds from God the honor that is due Him.

It would not be fitting for God to remit sins unless punishment is inflicted or satisfaction rendered, since this would introduce irregularity into God's Kingdom; but punishment would incur the ruin of man, and satisfaction cannot be rendered by one who already is under the obligation of total obedience.

Man must pay a debt to God, which only God is able to pay; therefore out of love for His creature and in congruity with His own nature, God wills to become man in order that the necessary satisfaction can be rendered.

The God-Man, who is the incarnate Son of God, offers up His sinless life to pay the debt of sinful mankind and to restore the Father's honor; since the Father cannot allow this deed to go unrewarded and yet the Son needs nothing, the reward accrues to the advantage of those for whom the Son died.

Anselm, Archbishop of Canterbury from 1093 to 1109, has been called the father of scholastic theology, since his systematic explication of the Christian faith and use of the dialectical method set a pattern for the great systems of theology that developed among the Schoolmen of the twelfth and thirteenth centuries. His *Why God Became Man (Cur deus homo)* is considered the classic presentation of the "Latin" doctrine of the atonement, and many scholars believe it is his greatest work. In it he set out to "prove" the rational necessity of Christ's incarnation and death, but although he thought the sheer reasonableness of his argument should be compelling for unbelievers, he insisted that the proof was not meant to establish faith but was rather to serve as an example of "faith seeking understanding."

In opposition to the "Greek" tendency to think of Christ's death as God's ransoming of mankind from the Devil, Anselm elaborated an understanding of the atonement within the context of the relationship between God and man. He sought to express the unfathomable depth of God's love and, at the same time, to suggest the horrendous character of man's sin. In his doctrine he introduces two ideas which have been very influential in the subsequent history of soteriology. The first is his theory of satisfaction, the source of which has been attributed to feudal custom and Germanic law, but is more likely to be found in the medieval church's practice of penance. The second is his notion of the absolute necessity of the atonement, and here we need to distinguish between that necessity which is grounded in the nature and will of God himself, and the rational necessity of Christ's incarnation and death; that is, the mode of salvation that Anselm intends to prove by the logic of reason, without appeal to what Christians believe about Christ.

Why God Became Man is written in the form of a dialogue or debate between Anselm and a friendly interlocutor named Boso, whose duty it is to raise and pursue the questions of faithful inquirers as well as unbelievers. The chief question to be answered is stated in this fashion: "For what reason or necessity did God become man and, as we believe and confess, by his death restore life to the world, when he could have done this through another person (angelic or human), or even by a sheer act of will?" Anselm divided the work in which he attempted to answer this many-faceted question into two parts. In the first he intended to answer the objections of unbelievers who deem the Christian faith to be contrary to reason, and to prove by necessary reasons alone the impossibility of any man's being saved without Christ. In the second he wished to show that man was created for the purpose of enjoying a blessed immortality, that it is necessary for this purpose to be achieved, but that the achievement depends upon God's becoming man and undergoing, as God-Man, all the things that Christians believe concerning Christ.

The first charge that unbelievers bring against Christians is that they dishonor God by affirming that he descended into the womb of a woman, was born, grew, and lived a genuine human life, dying on a cross between thieves. Anselm answers by pointing to the following parallelisms: as death came by the disobedience of man, so life is restored by the obedience of man; as sin had its beginning with a woman, so the Savior from sin ought to be born of a woman; and as the Devil conquered man by tempting him to eat of a tree, it is fitting for the Devil to be vanquished by man's bearing of suffering on a tree. Boso admits the beauty of this arrangement, but asserts that for unbelievers such talk sounds like pure phantasy. What they require are sound reasons why God either ought or could condescend to such things as Christians proclaim. Anselm retorts that surely it is reason enough when one considers that the human race, the creation so precious to God, was totally ruined; that it was not fitting for God's purpose for man to be thwarted; and that this purpose could not be achieved unless the Creator himself delivered the human race. When Boso asserts that it would be easier for man's mind to accept the notion of deliverance if it were accomplished by a being other than God, such as another Adam created completely new and sinless, Anselm explains that if man were saved from eternal death by any being other than God, he would then be adjudged the servant of that being rather than of God, and thus would not be restored to his original dignity.

Boso now poses another question often asked by unbelievers: Why is it that Christians speak of their salvation as a "redemption," since it is hard to imagine any bondage so captivating that God could not free man without going to the extreme of shedding His own blood? If Christians answer that

God redeems them both from sins and His wrath and from Hell and the power of the Devil in order to purchase back for them the Kingdom of Heaven, unbelievers merely inquire why God does not do all this by a simple command, or in some other way. If God cannot accomplish redemption by a simple command, is He omnipotent? If He could and yet chose to do it the hard way, is He wise? Does God come down from Heaven to defeat the Devil because the Devil has a just claim on man?

Confronted with this line of questioning, Anselm first makes clear that the Devil has no rights whatsoever vis-à-vis man. If it can be said that man suffers justly in his bondage to evil, then his punishment is a just judgment permitted by God in His incomprehensible wisdom, not a right given to the Devil. As for why God chose to redeem man in the way that He did, the sheer fact that this represents God's will, which is never irrational, should be sufficient reason. However, for the sake of those who contend that God's stooping to lowliness and suffering is contrary to reason, Anselm explains that in the Incarnation the divine nature of the God-Man undergoes no debasement, since divine nature is intrinsically impassible, that is, incapable of suffering. The Lord Jesus Christ is true God and true man, one person in two natures, and the humiliation refers to God's bearing the weakness of the human nature, which in turn is thereby exalted. Boso concedes the impassibility of the divine nature, but asks whether it is just for the Man whom God calls his "beloved Son" to be condemned for the sake of the guilty. Anselm replies that the idea that God the Father compelled this Man to suffer death is mistaken. It is rather the case that Christ voluntarily chose death in order to effect the salvation of sinful mankind. It is true that Christ was "obedient unto death," but this obedience is not demanded of Him by the Father, since this Man did not sin. Instead, it is an obedience by which the Son maintained justice congruent with the will of God, who was unwilling to restore the human race unless man performed a great act, equal to the Son's death. The Son, then, exercises the free obedience of a rational being, and the Father takes pleasure, not in the Son's suffering, but in His choice, which both honors the Father and effects salvation.

In his further exploration of the ground on which God forgives sins, Anselm points out that there would be no sin if angels and men rendered to God His due, which is the subjection of their every inclination to God's will. Sin is the withholding of the honor that man owes God, and, considering the contempt involved, it will not suffice merely to restore what is taken away. The restitution must be greater, corresponding to the magnitude of the dishonor, and this payment is the satisfaction that every sinner ought to make to God. It would be unseemly for God to remit sins without requiring satisfaction or punishment, since this would introduce disorder into His Kingdom, and the way of satisfaction is preferable to the ruination that would result from punishment. The difficulty is that no man is able to render satisfaction commensurate with his sin, since even his total obedience is only what every rational creature owes God already. The debt that man owes calls for the payment of something that is more than the whole world and all that is not God. Only God could pay such a debt, and yet the payment is required of man. Of necessity, then, salvation calls for the work of a God-Man.

For our sake and by grace God becomes man, and if we speak of a "necessity" here, we must understand that it is a necessity freely accepted in accordance with God's own changeless goodness, which desires to complete the purpose for which man was created; namely, the attainment of blessedness in the enjoyment of God. The God-Man is both perfect God and perfect man; the integrity of each nature is preserved, and yet the two natures meet in one person. The person of the Son of God takes into unity with Himself the manhood of the race of Adam, a man born of a virgin. Because man is meant to be immortal and suffers death only because of sin, this God-Man, who does no sin, is not obliged to die. On behalf of the race of Adam, however, He chooses to lay down His life in order to satisfy the debt that sinful man owes to God. This death of the God-Man in His human nature, freely undergone and yet with the divine wisdom and power that comes from the Incarnation itself, is an offering so precious that it far outweighs the sins of the whole world. An infinite dishonor is overcome by an infinite satisfaction. This self-giving of the Son to the Father merits a reward, and yet the Son needs nothing. Therefore, it is only just that the Father grant the Son His desire; namely, that His reward be assigned to those for whom he became man and for whose salvation He died.

Thus Anselm claimed to have shown by necessary reasons the necessity of the God-Man for the accomplishment of salvation, and his argument is said to corroborate the truth of the Old and New Testaments. The atonement is understood in a way that emphasizes God's mercy and, at the same time, maintains His justice.

THE STEPS OF HUMILITY

Author: Saint Bernard, Abbot of Clairvaux (1090-1153)
Type of work: Contemplative theology
First transcribed: 1129-1135

PRINCIPAL IDEAS ADVANCED

To learn the way to humility, one can first learn the twelve steps by which one moves from humility to pride; the order may then be reversed.

One moves from humility to pride by the following twelve steps: curiosity, frivolity, foolish mirth, boastfulness, singularity, conceit, audacity, excusing one's own sins, hypocritical confession, public defiance, assuming the freedom to sin, and habitually sinning.

One attains humility by ridding oneself of these vices.

Humility makes self-knowledge possible through reason; compassion makes knowledge of others possible through love; and contemplation makes knowledge of God possible through purity.

Thus, humility is necessary if one is to ascend to love and truth.

Saint Bernard states in the preface to *The Steps of Humility* that he is bold enough to write the work only because he has been urged to by others. To write from his own motives and to satisfy his own desires would be a violation of the virtue he intends to describe. Yet the first eight chapters do not concern the twelve steps to humility themselves, but the various steps toward truth. Thus, as is quite common in contemplative or mystical works, the treatise centers around a theory of knowledge. The work is neither purely ethical nor contemplative. Before the ethical and religious virtues can be discussed, an elaborate theory of knowledge must be developed. Humility is related to truth, Bernard writes, since humility is the way that leads to truth.

Knowledge of truth is the fruit of humility, for the achievement of humility clears the mind and makes unclouded vision possible. Truth is concealed from the proud and revealed to the humble. But what is humility as a virtue, and how does it prepare the way for truth?

Humility, Bernard tells us, is that which makes a man, thorough self-examination, contemptible in his own sight. (Once again the Socratic goal of self-knowledge as the means necessary to clear vision reappears, here connected with the ethical condition of self-contempt.) In self-contempt one understands oneself truly, thereby achieving the Socratic goal, but not in the Socratic way. Without humility, Bernard's contention is, no man can understand himself thoroughly, and without self-

knowledge a grasp of truth is not possible. Thus, humility has its rewarding consequence.

The ascent to truth, it turns out, requires taking the twelve steps which lead to humility. (The number twelve is often important in Christian writings, perhaps because the number of Christ's disciples was twelve.) Humility, it is true, is bitter and purging, but it yields love, which is sweet and consoling, and contemplation, that solid and strengthening condition which so many mystics sought. Truth is to be found in three forms; in ourselves, in our neighbors, and in its own divine nature. Thus, we are instructed to seek truth first in ourselves and in our neighbors before attempting to see it in itself. Having attained self-knowledge, we can then purify our vision by brotherly love and thus prepare ourselves to enjoy the contemplation of truth in its own nature. Only if we develop compassion within ourselves for our brother can we hope to understand him, just as pure truth is seen only if the seeker after truth himself has a pure heart.

How is the mercy necessary for an understanding of our neighbor to be developed? Observe, we are told, what we are and that we are wretched indeed; thus we learn to be merciful; we cannot know mercy in any other way. No one can be merciful who is not himself meek. What is pride but love of one's own excellence, and what is humility except contempt for one's own excellence? Love of self deceives any man who judges himself, and thus humility is necessary to clear self-vision. Whoever wants to know truth must first rid himself of pride; after attaining humility he can then come to the first step of truth, self-knowledge.

The first step of self-knowledge leads to the second step of truth, for one learns about himself only by becoming contemptible in his own sight, a situation which makes him value mercy more than justice. When this happens, then one is ready to seek mercy from others, to learn the needs of others from having discovered one's own. From one's own miseries one learns to commiserate with others who are miserable, and thus to know them —which is the second step necessary to truth. We ascend the first of the three steps toward truth (self-knowledge) by the toil of humility. We climb to the second step (knowledge of others) by the emotion of compassion, and then on to the third (knowledge of God) by the ecstasy of contemplation.

Reason is what we use to examine ourselves, to achieve the first step of truth. Love is the means we use to sympathize with and to know others, and this entices us to the second level of truth. Purity lifts us to invisible heights, snatches us to the third and final stage of truth. Humility and love form a finally perfected soul, one in which neither the will resists reason nor reason dissembles truth. Bernard will climb the ladder of humility until, clinging to truth, he comes to the fields of love. Thus, humility is not really the ultimate virtue and goal but only the necessary means to achieving a vision of truth and a capacity for love. Yet the way that goes up also goes down, and the steps may be traveled in either direction, toward pride and a loss of ability to love, or toward

humility, purity of vision, and depth of love.

Thus, an amazing and simple discovery is made. The way to humility, love, and truth is neither far off nor mysterious. Men have naturally and easily taken the twelve stages of the descent to pride. But the way down is also the way up. All that one who desires humility needs to do is to reverse the process by which he descended to pride; the twelfth step of pride is the first step toward humility. By ridding oneself of the vices which led to pride one can finally attain the state of humility. It is important, then, to understand how one descends to pride.

The first step toward pride is *curiosity*. It is through becoming curious that the humble man first begins to go astray. Neglecting the examination of himself, the man who is descending to pride begins to amuse himself by contemplating others; no longer interested in the self-examination by which he might make his faults known to himself, he turns his attention to what others are doing.

Curiosity, innocent in itself, leads to a fall from truth, because what one first observes out of mere curiosity, one may then go on to covet unlawfully and finally to aspire to possess for oneself. Furthermore, a soul made frivolous by its wandering eyes is no longer sobered by self-examination and is subject to extremes, first exalted to the pinnacle of pride, then plunged into the depths of envy.

The second step toward pride is *frivolity*, since the proud always seek what is cheerful and avoid what is gloomy. A proud person likes to make jokes and is easily and quickly moved to laughter. The third step of pride is *foolish mirth*; a person given to mirth thinks only of what pleases him, without regard to whether it is proper. Having descended thus far he can no longer restrain his laughter or conceal his foolishness.

The fourth step of pride is *boastfulness,* the habit of speaking constantly, not to edify anyone but to display one's learning. This base aim is not easily detected, but often a boastful person can be recognized by his volubility, by his using more words than he needs to convey his meaning. This fourth step is closely associated with the next, *singularity,* or egotism, the habit of calling attention to and dwelling upon oneself. *Conceit* is the next phase, the vice of believing all one says to be true, approving fully of one's own way while ignoring one's own motives. When praise is heard the conceited man ascribes it not to the ignorance or benevolence of the speaker, but to his own merits.

Will not the man who thinks himself superior to others be more forward than others? Probably, and the seventh step is logically that of *audacity.* The audacious man cannot confess his wrongs; he has come to think himself incapable of wrong and cannot tolerate his being thought so. To accompany audacity there is an eighth step, *excusing one's own sins.* Yet even worse than this is the ninth step, *hypocritical confession,* and this is an even worse state in which to be, since a false and proud confession is much more perilous than a willful and stubborn defense. Such a man is not at all like what he confesses himself to be; his interior is full of deceit. He condones his guilt by presumably confessing it; he conceals his guilt by presumably revealing it—thus, he compounds his sins.

As might be expected, pride eventually shows itself as *public defiance.* At this tenth step the individual becomes shameless and brazen, and the more he becomes so, the more he is driven on down to further defiance. What Bernard discovers now is that the first and early steps toward pride involved contempt of brethren, which then broke over into contempt for masters. This brings the sinner to the ultimate depths, to contempt for God. What began in secret, covered and appearing only in camouflaged forms, is now openly directed toward God Himself. The last restraint is gone, the last pretense fallen.

When even God is no longer feared we have reached the eleventh step, *assuming the freedom to sin.* Initially, fear of God held pride back; now the proud man is allured into satisfying his own desires, for he is made confident by a freedom that respects not even God. As lust awakens, reason is lulled to sleep and habit becomes binding. At the twelfth and final step toward complete pride he now allows himself to do whatever he pleases. He denies the existence of God, to whom he might be responsible. Astutely, Bernard observes that only the highest and the lowest fly without hindrance or exertion, the highest because they are so disciplined as to be above all law, the lowest because they recognize no external restraint. Truth makes the one secure; blindness is the security of the other. The fear of God is lost and contempt of God is incurred. *Habitual sinning* is the twelfth and last step of pride.

Bernard modestly claims to know more about the way going down than the way going up, and he did not think it proper and consistent with his goal of humility to attempt to describe the way upward toward humility. Yet if the way of descent in pride is carefully examined, the way upward to humility may be found as the reversal of that descent. In the descent he has described, Bernard hoped that his reader would find the steps leading to humility, and that, by ascending them, he might read them better within himself than in Bernard's book.

SOLILOQUY ON THE EARNEST MONEY OF THE SOUL

Author: Hugh of St. Victor (c.1096-1141)
Type of work: Mystical dialogue
First transcribed: Unknown; probably about 1133

PRINCIPAL IDEAS ADVANCED

A dialogue between a man and his soul reveals the gift which, when recognized, will direct the soul toward a true love of self, identical with a love of God.

True self-esteem is ultimately better for the soul than all the ephemeral objects to which it is presently attracted, since the soul is the object of divine love, and, in fact, God has already presented the pledge of His love (the earnest money given at the time of betrothal).

The nature of true self-esteem consists in seeking for the Supreme Good, to be achieved through self-examination and contemplation.

Although *The Earnest Money of the Soul* is not Hugh of St. Victor's chief work, nor his longest, in brief compass it presents an excellent sample of his famous mysticism, a mysticism thoroughly and rationally founded. This famous soliloquy on love attempts to reveal where true love is to be found and how it ought to arouse in the heart of the reader a desire for heavenly joys, which come through zeal in spiritual meditation. The work reveals Hugh's debt to Augustine and the Neoplatonic tradition.

Hugh begins by asking his soul what it loves above all things, and he declares that he knows already that love is the very life of the soul, and that without love the soul could not exist. Is it the beautiful things of the universe, Hugh asks, which the soul loves most? Most men's appetites are inflamed by beautiful things, and their number is infinite. The soul replies that it cannot love what it has not seen, and that it has been unable to find among visible things anything which ought to be loved above all else. His soul is in suspended animation; it cannot exist without love and yet it is not able to find a true object for its devotion among the visible things of beauty in this universe.

Man, the second person in the dialogue or soliloquy, now suggests to his soul that the reason it is unhappy is that, while attracted by a desire for temporal goods, the soul cannot find here a love of those things which are eternal. At least, however, from the soul's dissatisfaction with the temporal world's beauties, it has learned to direct love to a better object. The most important step has actually been made: through recognizing that it is not temporal beauties which the soul seeks, the soul has been prepared to be separated from all finite things willingly, if only a greater beauty can be found.

Yet, how, the soul asks, is it possible to love that which is not visible? And if temporal goods do not satisfy, and the invisible cannot be loved, then surely the soul is in a miserable state! No one can be happy without love, for unhappiness means not having what one esteems. To this Man replies that if he esteems the visible world, why not esteem himself instead, since as man he surpasses all visible beauties. The eye sees all but does not see itself.

Love, it is agreed, must have an object; it never permits itself to be solitary. Love ceases to exist if it does not pour forth the ardor of its affections, and yet the object of love must be upon something equal in station to itself. If a man recognizes first his own dignity, then he will not attach himself to things inferior, for fear of injuring his love. Thus, the soul learns that it must not, in fact cannot, seek a love that is either solitary or degrading, for should it do this its love will cease. The goal is now known: seek a love that will be yours alone and also one that is especially worthy.

Hugh compares love to fire. What is put upon it should burn with a pure flame, not with smoke or stench. What is put upon love is crucial to the person, since through love one is transformed into a being like the one to whom the lover is joined by affection. Since this is true, one must choose the object of his love carefully, knowing

that it not only can, but necessarily will, change him in its process.

Then Man suggests to his soul a startling thesis: that the soul has a betrothed but does not know it. He is the most comely of all, but his face has not been seen. Could his face be seen, the soul would lose all doubts about its own fairness. For one so beautiful must have been attracted by an equal beauty, so that one can learn of his own soul's loveliness through discovering the beauty of the unseen one betrothed to the soul without its knowledge. How can such a loved one not be seen? Because he is absent. Thus, one is able to prostitute oneself to some shameful pleasure and never blush, scorning his wholly devoted love because it is unseen.

Next the soul is asked to consider the pledge money, proof of his devotion, which the unseen lover has given. If this could be seen, then perhaps by his very gift he could be recognized, known in his gift while yet remaining unseen. Learning this, perhaps the soul could see with what affection it ought to love him and with what zeal and diligence it ought to preserve itself unsullied for him. Now the problem is faced: What is the pledge money this unseen lover has given, how is it to be discerned and what does it tell the soul about its lover and itself?

To answer its question the soul is instructed: Look at the universe. Everything in it, the soul is told, serves the soul's needs. The pleasures and the needs are met by what nature provides. Nature is directed with one accord to the soul's service. Who does this? The gift is plain to see, but the giver is hidden. Each soul accepts the benefits bestowed, but few know their benefactor. When all of nature is taken as a gift to the soul, it indicates the greatness of the love of the giver—and the not inconsiderable worth of the receiving soul. By this gift of all of nature's benefits, two things are revealed: one who loves generously and one (the soul) worthy of being loved so greatly.

This being understood, the soul is free to love the benefits of nature, yet each one is seen in a new life, as a gift of promise, as earnest money of the betrothed, as the offering of a true friend. Nevertheless, the hardest part is still ahead, for it is easy to begin to prefer the gifts to the giver. Instead, the soul must constantly accept every gift nature has, but only as a token of an unseen lover. What is the rule? Honor him who gives, respect yourself, and honor his gifts for his sake. When the soul does this, its vision is changed and it sees every benefit of nature, everything it has received, as the pledge of a lover's devotion. Best of all, in such a love there is nothing which can cause sadness.

With all this, the soul still continues to question. The soul loves the giver now, but similar gifts are given to others. The soul loves the giver, yet the soul is not the giver's sole delight. How can a soul glory in such a privilege, if it is possessed in common not only with the brutes but with all living things?

Man replies to his soul's doubts: not all gifts are shared equally by everyone. Some gifts from the soul's betrothed are given in common with others, some are given as one of a special group, and some are given to the soul as the soul's alone. And here the soul wonders what would make it happy. Would it be happy if the world had been given to it alone, or is the problem not in the exclusiveness of the gift after all? Whether directly or indirectly, everything has been given to the soul and is at its disposal.

What about evil? Is the soul's gift diminished because in temporal goods both the good and the wicked participate in the same way? The Neoplatonic answer is given. The evil live for the sake of the good, not for their own sake, and they are permitted to live among the good in order to stimulate the lives of the good by their association. The lives of the wicked are a constant warning; the lives of the virtuous are the consolation of the soul. It would be good to delight in this love alone, but it is much more blessed to delight in it in the company of the many good men in this life, since a thing is known better through sharing. Such love, which is at once the love of all and the complete love of each is neither diminished by participation, nor exhausted by use, nor aged with time.

Is it possible to explain how this love can be present both in spirit and in reality to each of those whom he loves? Creation, the gift of life, comes to all and yet is fully present in each, and we do not have a mere colorless existence, but one which is beautiful and fair. We men have more of the glory of existence than do other creatures, since we have been raised to the level of the Creator's own likeness. When one considers all he has been given, beginning with existence itself, one must return His love. Instead, the soul often deserts its Lover and squanders its affections on others.

The most important argument, however, remains: Not only has existence been given as a gift by the soul's Lover, but also He has permitted Himself to be humbled in order to redeem man. This is the central Christian teaching. In creation He is exalted; in redemption He is brought low. He came down among men, took on their mortality, suffered His passion, conquered death, and restored mankind. Defiled by its own wickedness, the soul has by His grace been made beautiful again. What happens at this realization is the familiar phenomenon of conversion. The soul is indeed changed, turned now from its vague and uncertain infatuations, won over by the demonstration of so great a love; now it is turned toward its one true Love.

Immediately upon such a realization the soul's only question is how it can prepare itself by the use of the font of baptism, the basin of regeneration in which the soul may wash away the stain of past sins. Confession ends the dialogue, and the soul thanks God, whom the soul now recognizes as its true Lover, in virtue of all the gifts He has given in token of His affection. The soul has been given earnest money, actual demonstrations of God's undivided love, and because of these gifts the soul is now enabled to recognize its Spouse. From now on the soul will seek to keep itself untouched, undefiled and pure, without a stain, for Him. If once the soul was a harlot, vainly chasing pleasures in the world, now it has become a virgin. His love is bestowed on many, but it embraces each one individually. God's countenance cannot be seen, in answer to the soul's early question, but His presence can never be escaped. Now the soul takes God as its exemplar, desiring only to become more and more like Him. And if God loved the soul enough to demonstrate His affection when the soul was repulsive, how much more will He desire it when it has begun to be beautiful? Love Him only, pursue Him only, take Him only, and possess Him only.

KNOW THYSELF

Author: Peter Abelard (1079-1142)
Type of work: Christian ethics
First transcribed: Twelfth century

Principal Ideas Advanced

The human race shares in the punishment, but not in the guilt, of Adam's sin.

Certain weaknesses of the human mind make man prone to sin, but guilt is incurred solely in consenting to the suggestions of these weaknesses.

By reason, man is able to decide what is good; desire in itself is not sinful, but sin lies in the consent to desire.

God alone can correctly estimate the extent of a person's guilt; confession is not for the purpose of receiving absolution, nor is penance a sacrament.

Peter Abelard's *Know Thyself* (*Scito te ipsum*) was probably written a few years before the condemnation of some of his ideas in 1140 (or 1141) at the Council of Sens. In spite of the condemnation, Abelard's ethical views —which find expression in *Know Thyself*—had an important influence on medieval moral thought.

The divergence of Abelard's point of view from the theories then current provoked the opposition of William of St.-Thierry (c.1085-c.1148) and St. Bernard (1090-1153). Traditional Augustinian orthodoxy held that by the fall of Adam, mankind had been brought into a condition of sin and misery in which all men share the very guilt of Adam's first sin. Of himself, apart from divine grace, man is incapable of performing any good act. What is right and what is wrong is fixed by the eternal law of God. To sin is to fall away from what is good. Sin must be atoned for by penances so that the sinner may be restored to the life of grace.

For Augustine, sin had two causes. We sin because we do not know what we ought to do, or because we do what we know we ought not to do. The first is the sin of ignorance; the second is the sin of weakness. Sins are divided into two groups, grave (mortal) and light (venial), and appropriate penance is to be applied in each case.

Abelard's own view departed from the accepted view in several respects, the chief of which lay in his denial that mankind has contracted the guilt of Adam's first sin. Original sin refers solely to the punishment to which we are liable through the guilt of our first parent. Anyone may escape damnation by exercising his own will in good works. The human mind does

have certain defects or qualities which dispose a man to good or bad actions. Defects of mind do not make man guilty, however, but only incline him to consent to what he ought not to do, or to leave undone what he ought to do. Such consent is sin, for it displays contempt of the Creator. To sin is to despise God; it is not to do for God what we believe we should do for him, or not to renounce what we think we should renounce on God's behalf.

Frequently we err, Abelard concedes, but we do so not because of an evil will. To consent wrongfully is to commit sin, but sometimes sin is committed without an evil will. Our weaknesses make us prone to sin, but they do not make us guilty; we are guilty only when we consent to the suggestions of our weaknesses. It is our task to master and to direct those defects which dispose our minds to evil. The Christian life is thus characterized by struggle, writes Abelard. We strive in a contest to obtain a victor's crown. Our opponent is our own evil will, over which we must triumph by subjugating it to the divine will.

God weighs our intention rather than the deed, Abelard declares. The deed itself adds nothing to our merit, no matter whether it proceeds from a good or an evil will. A man is not better or worse because of what he does. To give in to our desires is vicious, but we are not meant to be wholly without desire. It is not sinful to desire a woman, but it is sinful to consent to the desire. The good man conquers his desire, but he does not extinguish it; if he is not enticed into consent, he does not commit any sin.

We consent to what is sinful when we do not draw ourselves back from an evil deed, and are ready, if the opportunity is offered, to perform it. Anyone who has the intention to commit an evil deed is guilty before God as much as if he were caught in the act. Hence, the act of sinning does not add anything to guilt or to damnation before God; sin is not increased by the doing of an action. The soul is marred by nothing except what is of its own nature; namely, consent.

When certain acts which ought not to be done are committed under force or by ignorance, they are committed without any sin, Abelard writes. To consent to a covetous desire is, however, to be guilty of sin, though there be no sequel to this intention. A transgressor is, therefore, not one who does what is prohibited but one who consents to what is prohibited.

Whether a person actually gives money to the poor, or whether a sense of charity makes him ready to give alms, makes no difference to the merit of the intention. The opportunity may not be present although the will to be charitable is there. Actions which are right and actions which are wrong are done by good and bad alike; good men are separated from bad solely by their intention.

Abelard insists that it is the spirit of the action, the intention, and not the deed, which determines the virtue of the doer. The same action may be done from different motives: for justice by one person, for an evil reason by another. A diversity of intentions may cause the same act to be performed from different motives and hence to acquire different moral values.

Just as to wish is not the same as to fulfill a wish, writes Abelard, so to sin is not the same as to carry out a sin. In the first case, it is by the consent of the soul that we sin. In the second case, we fulfill in deed that to which we have previously consented. Frequently, we are led through three stages in the commission of sin: suggestion, delight, and consent. We are first led by the suggestion of something within us, and if we know already that such a deed is pleasant, our imagination is held in delight and we are thereby tempted in thought. At this point our desire ought to be repressed, says Abelard, and we ought to obey the command of God. If, however, we continue and give our consent to such delight, we are guilty of sin. By penitence we can here gain pardon, but we may in fact pass on and actually commit the sin.

Abelard insists that the spirit in which a thing is done rather than the action itself is what God considers. God weighs the guilt in our intention accurately. God sees where no man sees, and when he punishes sin he regards the will, not the work. It is because we consider only the deed, which we can see, and not the will, which we cannot see, that we frequently punish the innocent and acquit the guilty. God tries the heart and discerns our intentions.

According to Abelard, every sin is of the mind alone, for it is only in the mind that there can be contempt of God. Nevertheless, it is still possible to speak of spiritual sins, which proceed from the imperfection of the mind, and of carnal sins, which proceed from the weaknesses of the flesh.

By reason, a person is able to decide what is good, and he may consent to or refrain from the tendencies of his mind. It is from good intention that good action arises. An intention is good when it is right in itself; an action is good, not because it contains some good within it, but because it issues from a good intention. The same act, performed at different times by the same person may, because of the diversity of intention, be good on one occasion and bad on another.

An intention is good not simply because it seems good, writes Abelard, but because it is such as it is estimated to be; that is, because what it aims at is really pleasing to God. It is, however, not possible to say that the persecutors of Christ sinned in the sense that they had contempt for God, or consented to that which they ought not to have consented to. Since there is no sin except that against conscience, those who did not believe in Christ and who rejected the Christian faith because they believed it to be contrary to God, did not sin. The ignorance of those who crucified Christ freed them from the possibility of real guilt. Those who persecuted Christ may be said to have sinned in action only (*per operationem*), but if they had acted contrary to their conscience and had permitted Christ to go free, they would have sinned in will and hence more grievously.

We need have little fear of God's holding us guilty of a fault when we do not violate our conscience, Abelard assures his readers; if we do not rightly know our evil deeds to be sinful, or if we do not really wish to do them, then such acts are not to be called sins.

It is, of course, possible to speak loosely and to call every unsuitable act, as well as infidelity, by the term "sin," even though no contempt of God appears. Properly speaking, however, sin is that which can never come about without personal guilt, and the latter cannot occur without intention. Infidelity, disbelief in the gospel, the rejection of Christ, and refusal of the sacraments involve exclusion from eternal life for those who are rationally full grown, even though such acts arise less from malice than as a result of ignorance.

The sinner may be reconciled to God by passing through three stages of penance: compunction, confession, and satisfaction. Penitence is grief of mind for what is done amiss. In some cases, Abelard writes, penitence arises from love of God for His kindness and is therefore fruitful; in other cases penitence is motivated by fear of some penalty. Where there is heartfelt contrition or true penitence, sin does not persist. The love of God which evokes our grief does not permit vice. We are immediately reconciled to God by our repentance, and we receive pardon for our former faults. Wherever there is true penitence, proceeding solely from the love of God, there is no sin, and no contempt of God remains. By inspiring penitence God renders the sinner worthy of divine forbearance. Hence, the sinner is not damned so long as he remains repentant.

Although the repentant sinner may by circumstances be prevented from coming to confession, he is in no danger of damnation if he dies with contrition on his lips. Ordinarily, however, the penitent confesses his sins to another person, as a sign of humility and true contrition and as a means of securing the prayers of others. The priest who hears the confession of the penitent is, however, unable to give absolution in a sacramental sense. A bishop may wish to increase or to diminish the punishment of a fault without moderation and discretion; he may wish to extend punishment indefinitely. In fact, however, Jesus' promise to the Apostles which gave them the power to remit sins was addressed to them alone, and not to all their successors indiscriminately. For unless the verdict of the bishops is in accordance with divine justice, writes Abelard, it is without validity.

In forgiving the penitent not every penalty is remitted by God. Many who sorrow for sin have died before they were able to offer penitent satisfaction. Such will give satisfaction in purgatory.

Confession is not always needed, however, says Abelard; it may be deferred or omitted altogether if the penitent feels that his confession would do more harm than good.

There are many priests without faith and discretion, Abelard claims. Confession to such men may be not merely useless but also dangerous, for such priests are not worthy of being heard in their petitions to God; they are ignorant of canon law and know no moderation in their prescription of penance. But although such priests are of no use to the penitent, the latter need not despair, provided repentance towards God has preceded confession and the receiving of penance. If less penance is imposed than the sin warrants, God will correct the error with punishment in purgatory. By fasting, prayer, and the denial of the flesh we can, however, escape such future punishment and give present satisfaction for sins.

In spite of the fact that much of Abelard's thought was condemned at the Council of Sens, his teaching exerted its influence upon medieval ethical theory, for it caused later theorists to lay stress upon the notion of motive *(intentio),* and it produced the practical test of deliberateness in judging the degree of guilt in mortal sin. However, the practical effect of Abelard's emphasis on intention was that the distinction between good and evil *acts* was obscured. Abelard's development of St. Augustine's suggestions concerning intention suffers from a lack of the sense of proportion which made Augustine's Christian ethics more immediately applicable to the problems of men.

POLICRATICUS

Author: John of Salisbury (c.1115-1180)
Type of work: Christian social philosophy
First transcribed: 1159

Principal Ideas Advanced

Instead of being surrounded by competent and industrious officials, the prince is surrounded by courtiers, who use philosophy to disguise the falsity of their position.

The true commonwealth is like a living body, with the clergy as its soul, the prince as its head, office-holders as its eyes, hands, and stomach, and the people as its feet.

The well-being of the whole depends upon each performing his proper function; in particular, the functions of the clergy and of the magistracy should be kept distinct.

The prince should be guided by the law of God, and he should respect the liberty of his people and seek their peace and prosperity.

The Plenitude of God's Goodness and Wisdom is mirrored in the just society.

The *Policraticus*, which was dedicated to Thomas à Becket (c.1117-1170), at that time chancellor to King Henry II, combines a satirical account of contemporary court life with a serious account of the nature of a Christian commonwealth. The author, although an Englishman by birth, studied for many years abroad, and is an admirable representative of the Christian humanism of the twelfth century renaissance. Personally acquainted with such diverse persons as Peter Abelard (1079-1142), Bernard of Clairvaux (1090-1153), and Pope Hadrian IV (c.1100-1159), he was, at the time when he wrote the *Policraticus*, secretary to Theobald, Archbishop of Canterbury.

The full title of the work is *Policraticus, sive de nugis curialium et de vestigiis philosophorum*, which means, literally, "Policraticus, or Concerning Follies of Courtiers and Remnants of Philosophers." While scholars disagree on the significance of the term "Policraticus," the obvious purpose of the work was to expose the evils to be found in the class of men which surrounded kings and bishops. Court life demeans those who enter upon it. To succeed as a courtier, one must combine the appearance of "philosophy and goodness" with all manner of folly and vice. But, says John, the courtier-philosopher is a monster, a kind of hermaphrodite, who "deforms womanly beauty with a harsh and bristly countenance, while he pollutes and defiles manhood with womanish weakness." He continues: "The court casts out philosophy utterly, and the true philosopher will in no wise participate in the follies of a court." John hurries to add that this need not be the situation, and that a wise ruler changes the complexion of his court. Nevertheless, he is quite explicit about court life in his day, both in England and in Rome. The pope, he says, is in an impossible position because of his court. He cannot administer justice if he accepts gifts; but he cannot achieve anything unless he offers gifts; and in order to have the means to offer gifts, he must accept them.

In the course of his book, John comments on numerous practices which, in his opinion, are hindrances to the welfare of the commonwealth. Among the targets of his wit are hunting, gambling, licentious music and drama, fortunetelling, and astrology. He complains, for example, that soldiers think only of "cutting a fine figure with clothes of brighter hue than others, and in so squeezing and twisting their linen or silken garments as to make them cleave as close to the body as a second skin." Interested in "the arts of pleasure" rather than in valor, they "would be more certain to capture the stronghold of Thaïs than that of Hannibal." Addressing himself expressly to Becket, he says, "I shall not forbid you to dress in raiment of gold, to dine daily in splendid state, . . . to do as is customary to do in these degenerate days, while remaining upright yourself, and to mock a world that mocks you with its allurements. For you are too great a man to be caught in its tentacles." But not many, he avers, are thus able to rise above temptation.

But John's commentary on the manners of his time is only one aspect of his work. Like Erasmus and Thomas More, who were to speak for Christian humanism in the sixteenth century, John of Salisbury has a well-articulated moral and political philosophy. John is an eclectic, who combines the skepticism of the Academics with the Ciceronian ideal of a just man, one completely formed in knowledge and virtue and able to express himself eloquently. He borrows, as suits his need, from Horace and Vergil, Lucian and Petronius. But underlying his whole philosophy is the Platonic and Augustinian conception of virtue as discipline and happiness as the harmonious subordination of the parts within the whole, according to the will of the Creator.

John's criticisms of ecclesiastical and political abuses presuppose his conception of a Christian commonwealth or republic in which the economic, civic, military, and ecclesiastical orders all work together to produce a society in which men and women can live justly and at peace with God and their fellows. Thus, at least from one point of view, politics should subserve morality and religion. From another point of view, morality and religion are the substance of a true polity; for, according to John, the well-being of the community is assured if each member performs the duty which God has assigned to him.

John elaborates his conception of the ideal state after the analogy of the human body, a figure widely used both by Christian and pagan authors. He says that, since the end of the commonwealth is the service of God, the soul of society is the priesthood. The head, which is responsible for governing the body, is the prince. The heart, "from which proceeds the initiation of good works and ill," is the Senate. The eyes, ears, and tongue are the governors and judges. The stomach and intestines are the fiscal officers. The hands are the soldiers and police. The feet are the artisans and husbandmen. In order for any part of the state to function well, all parts must work together harmoniously. The rulers must reverence God, must be informed, and must be trained for their particular tasks. They must remember that, being few in numbers, they exist for the advantage of the multitudes. The people, for their part, owe obedience and service to their superiors in return for protection and succor. John cites with appreciation Vergil's lines in the *Fourth Georgic,* concerning the political constitution of the hive of bees. He adds, "Then and then only will the health of the commonwealth be sound and flourishing when the higher members shield the lower, and the lower respond faithfully and fully in like measure to the just demands of their superiors, so that each and all are as it were members one of another by a sort of reciprocity, and each regards his own interest as best served by that which he knows to be most advantageous for the others."

John of Salisbury borrows his exposition of the body-politic from a treatise which he believes to have been written by Plutarch, called "The Instruction of Trajan," explaining that where the pagan author referred to "gods" he has substituted the singular "God." Thus, in all innocence, a medieval author and statesman conceives the Christian religion as taking the place of the ancient civil cultus, and the Church as performing a normal function in organized human society. The ancient Christian apologists, such as Tertullian (c.160-c.220), begged for a state without religious ties, within which Christians might enjoy the same civil rights as others. Augustine of Hippo (354-430), although he was thankful for a Christian emperor and was willing for the Church to receive material assistance from the state, nevertheless thought of the Church as belonging to a higher order than the state, and as seeking a different end. In John of Salisbury's view, however, Church and state are one body, and the priesthood and the magistracy are merely responsible for different functions of the common life. This view, of course, persisted after the breakup of the Middle Ages, into Protestant times, and by many people is not thought incompatible with the formal separation of Church and state. Washington Gladden (1836-1918), for example, advocating the "social gospel," argued that the human community is an organism, of which the Church is a normal part.

The supremacy of the priestly hierarchy over the prince is represented by John, as it had been previously by Bernard of Clairvaux, under the figure of the two swords. Like Bernard, John urges the Church to disengage itself from political matters, and, at the same time, he warns the state to quit interfering with the affairs of the Church. He maintains that both the material sword and the spiritual sword were given by Christ to the Church, and that the prince receives his power from the hand of the priest. But it is no part of John's claim to propose that the Church select the ruler or direct him in the administration of his duties. Rather, he maintains that the prince stands under the law of God, and must have sufficient learning to be able to discover for himself what that higher law demands. John argues that there are certain laws which have force among all nations; to see how these apply, the prince is advised to study the Code of Justinian. Other laws are inscribed in the Holy Scriptures, which the prince ought to read every day, particularly the book of Deuteronomy.

John holds that kings receive their offices from God, as part of God's general providence over mankind. He hesitates to say that they owe their position either to heredity or to popular election; for men sometimes come to the throne in devious ways, and piety demands that all kings be obeyed. Sometimes, he says, God imposes unjust and tyrannical kings upon a nation as a chastisement, in which case it behooves men to cry out to God for deliverance. God's law stands supreme, however; and if a tyrant commands men to do what is unlawful, they should refuse to obey him. In extreme cases, it is lawful to kill the tyrant. Here John puts in a word for "liberty," which, he says, is second only to virtue, "if indeed liberty can ever properly be severed from virtue." Liberty consists in "judging everything freely in accordance with one's individual judgment, and does not hesitate to reprove what it sees opposed to good morals." In order to have liberty, however, men must cultivate tolerance. "It is the part of a good and wise man to give a free reign to the liberty of others and to accept with patience the words of free speaking, whatever they may be."

Underlying John of Salisbury's conception of the state is something of the prejudice shared by Stoics and early Christians against all political authority. If men cultivated virtue, he says, reason and charity would so far prevail that princes and monarchs would not be necessary, or, at least, their rule would be no burden. John does not suppose that, in man's sinful condition, society can ever be rid of government. His desire is, however, that the prince will, above all men, be governed by moral considerations, will never seek his own interest above that of others, will embrace his subjects as brethren, and, when he has to correct them, will temper his strength with kindness. In short, John is committed to the ideal of a state founded on the goodwill of its rulers and the piety of its people, rather than on the distribution of power. It was this ideal which Niccolò Machiavelli (1469-1527) opposed in his book, *The Prince*.

John sees the ultimate duty of man in the light of the First and Great Commandment; namely, that God "is to be loved by all men alike and worshiped with all their heart, and all their soul, and all their strength." It is by love rather than by understanding that man draws near to God in this life, says John of Salisbury. For, the Divine Being can never be grasped by human intelligence so long as it is burdened with the body. But God can be loved, in two ways: directly, "by affection, which is a disposition of the mind," and indirectly, "by the display of works." Thus, according to John, the whole round of human activity may become a reflection of God's wisdom and goodness. Men have different characters and offices, with different virtues and obligations, but some portion of God's goodness is present in each of them. Just as the ray of the sun emits a red color when it falls on a carbuncle, and azure on a sapphire, so God's goodness appears in some men as prudence, in others as fortitude, and in others as temperance or justice. Only thus can the Divine Plenitude reveal itself to us here on earth: "But, in time to come, when through His grace we shall look upon Him face to face, and see Him as He is, then He will be all in all." Then also, says John, God shall be visible in the company of his elect "in such fulness of majesty that they shall lack nothing of any grace, and He alone shall be visible in them, and they shall be reckoned in His name, their true substance being preserved entire and without any changefulness of nature."

BENJAMIN MINOR

Author: Richard of St. Victor (died c. 1173)
Type of work: Mystical theology
First transcribed: c.1160

Principal Ideas Advanced

Man's highest good is the mystical contemplation of God.

Man's preparation for contemplation can be learned from the spiritual (allegorical) interpretation of the Biblical story of Jacob's family.

Man's preparation consists in progress in the virtues and the proper use of the senses, imagination, and reason.

The way to the higher knowledge of God is by way of self-knowledge, which can be gained only with the help of Christ, laborious effort, meditation, and prayer.

The highest form of contemplation lies beyond man's efforts and reason.

We know nothing about Richard's youth except that he was a native of Scotland and a very young man when he entered the abbey of St. Victor (near Paris), the most renowned of all the houses of the Canons Regular of St. Augustine. He served as prior from 1162 to 1173 and was greatly influenced by a previous prior, Hugh of St. Victor (c.1096-1141), whom he may have known personally. St. Victor sought to continue the early medieval tradition of monastic piety, with its emphasis on asceticism, contemplation, and the "Sacred Page." Unlike the Cistercian abbey of Clairvaux, however, it was open to every kind of learning, and it did not hesitate to employ the dialectic that was becoming increasingly characteristic of the learning of the schools.

Hugh and Richard mark an important turning point in the history of Christian mysticism. Mysticism in the West, where it was universally known as "contemplation" in the early Middle Ages, had been decisively shaped by Augustine of Hippo (354-430), John Cassian (c.360-435), and Gregory the Great (c.540-604). This Augustinian-Benedictine tradition remained essentially unchanged to the time of Bernard of Clairvaux (1090-

1153). Mystics of this Western type experienced the reality and presence of God, and entered into union with God; they described their experiences; but they did not develop a "science" of contemplation. Both theology and contemplation remained inextricably linked to the Bible and to the experiences of devout men and women.

Hugh and Richard stood in this tradition, but they modified it considerably. It was through these two Victorines that the mysticism of Dionysius "the Pseudo-Areopagite" (apparently a Syrian monk writing around 500) entered the mainstream of Western spirituality. Its impact there, largely mediated by Hugh's commentary on Dionysius' *Celestial Hierarchy*, may be compared to that of the recovered Aristotelian corpus on Western thought. It promoted a growing systematization of mystical theology, and here Richard led the way. He described the soul's preparation for contemplation in *Benjamin minor*, contemplation itself in *Benjamin major*, and the fruits of contemplation in *Four Degrees of Passionate Charity*.

Richard's passion for unitive comprehensiveness and hierarchical constructions is clearly Dionysian. His most famous classification, the *sex gen-*

era contemplationis, occurs in the *Benjamin major.* Here he distinguishes (1) contemplation which is purely imaginative; (2) contemplation that is imaginative, but in a rational manner; (3) rational contemplation that speculates with the aid of the images of visible things; (4) purely rational (nonimaginative) contemplation; (5) suprarational contemplation; (6) seemingly contra-rational contemplation. This scheme is reflected in many medieval treatises on contemplation, including *The Mind's Road to God (Itinerarium mentis ad deum)* of St. Bonaventura (1221-1274).

Richard is distinctively Western in his psychological (experiential) interest. Man's ascent to contemplation is by the elevation of both heart and mind to God; in fact, it is the unification of man's "higher powers," (through concentration on the Supreme Unity) that facilitates (and is facilitated by) the mystical union with God. When later theologians argued over the relative priority of the will (love) and the intellect (knowledge) in the mystical ascent, neither side was completely justified in invoking Richard's authority in its own behalf. Where Richard is very clear is in his conviction, against that of Dionysius' first translator into Latin, John Scotus Erigena (c.815-c.877), that God can be known by created beings.

Benjamin minor is principally an allegory on the family of Jacob (Genesis 31:1-24; 35:16-20; Psalm 68:27). Jacob represents man as a rational spirit; Rachel, "the teaching of truth"; that is, reason producing "right counsel"; Leah, "the discipline of virtue"; that is, "ordered affections" producing "holy desires." Bilhah, Rachel's maidservant, stands for the imagination; Zilpah,

Leah's maidservant, for sensation. The order in which these four women bear sons to Jacob represents the pattern of man's preparation for contemplation. First come the sons of Leah: the fear of the Lord (Reuben), sorrow for sin (Simeon), hope for forgiveness (Levi), and love of righteousness (Judah). Bilhah's son Dan represents a combination of the imagination with reason, while Naphtali represents the imagination in conjunction with intelligence. Richard distinguishes here between reason and intelligence, assigning to the latter the capacity to transcend the corporeal world. Zilpah's son Gad represents abstinence; Asher represents patience. Leah's son Issachar represents the joy of inward sweetness; her son Zebulon, the hatred of sin; and her daughter Dinah, shame. Rachel's first-born son Joseph represents the supreme virtue of discretion. Rachel (reason) dies in giving birth to Benjamin (contemplation).

Richard sees a radical dichotomy between the worlds of body and spirit. Within the latter there is a triad of spirits, human, angelic, divine. To these correspond the traditional three heavens and three types of knowledge: faith, reason, contemplation. Man may (actively) ascend to the first two heavens; to the third heaven he must be (passively) carried. (See II Corinthians 12:3.) Richard likens true self-knowledge to a great mountain that towers over all the learning of this world, including Plato's and Aristotle's. He identifies it with the Mount of Transfiguration and asserts that we can ascend it only when truth itself, Jesus Christ, is our guide. The three disciples He chose represent work, meditation, and prayer, without which the ascent is also impossible.

He writes: "Would you see Christ transfigured? . . . Would you see and recognize Moses and Elias without any sign? Would you understand the law and prophecy without a teacher or commentator? Climb this mountain, learn to know yourself. Would you have the privacy of the Father's secrets? Climb this mountain, learn to know yourself."

The shining garments of Christ stand for a new type of teaching that is to be obtained only at the top of the mount of self-knowledge. They pertain to heavenly things, just as Christ's ordinary garments, that is, His ordinary teachings, pertain to earthly things. (See John 3:12.) At the top of this mountain, Christ can be believed only when He authenticates Himself by being met by Moses and Elias; that is, by the literal and spiritual sense of Scripture; for the Devil himself transfigures himself into an angel of light. Rachel dies and Benjamin is born when the Father's voice is heard; the disciples fall to the ground; senses, memory, and reason fail, and the soul is in ecstasy.

Richard is typical of the mainstream of medieval spirituality when he insists on ethical (ascetic) prerequisites for contemplation, the radical distinction of body and spirit, the subjective approach to God ("Know yourself"), and the possibility of a higher knowledge (Christ's shining garments). Richard does not indicate here whether he would keep this higher knowledge from the masses, or, with the Western homilectic tradition, utilize it for spiritual edification. In his emphasis on ecstasy Richard seems to follow Dionysius and to reverse the dominant tendency of Western spirituality, which had learned, beginning with St. Augustine, to recognize the reality while discounting the importance of ecstatic raptures. The earlier Middle Ages had not been greatly exercised over the possibility of mistaking the Devil for Christ, but this concern of Richard's was bequeathed to much of subsequent mysticism. His distinction between *speculatio*, in which man is active, and *contemplatio*, in which man is wholly passive, also proved to be very influential. It marks the beginning of a tendency to posit a radical discontinuity between ordinary spirituality ("acquired" contemplation) and mystical experience ("infused" contemplation). In requiring the corroboration of any "shewing" (*revelatio*) by both the historical and spiritual sense of Scripture, Richard shows himself a willing disciple of Hugh, who had insisted that the spiritual meaning of Scripture not be divorced from the historico-literal. While Richard wants to follow Hugh, it is plain that he (unlike his contemporary Andrew of St. Victor, who died in 1175) is no friend of the letter: "Therefore . . . let him show the authority of the Scripture, not only figuratively but also openly. It is a lovely and joyful spectacle when in the revelation of truth, clear reason presents itself at this point, and both the historical and the figurative reading concur in supporting that revelation. . . . Moses and Elias appear with the Lord on the mount, and they appear in majesty, not in the obscurity of the letter in the light of the spiritual understanding."

This Scriptural attestation is needed, however, only when the "showing" pertains to heavenly things: "If Christ teaches me about external things or about my own interior life, I accept him easily, as in those things which I can prove by my own experience."

In England, the *Benjamin minor* appears to have been the most popular of Richard's writings, and the unknown author of *The Cloud of Unknowing* (a fourteenth century mystical treatise) his most faithful disciple.

On the Continent the *Benjamin major* was valued more highly, and its direct influence extends into the sixteenth century, when Catholic mystical theology was definitively formulated by the Spanish Carmelites Teresa of Avila (1515-1582) and John of the Cross (1542-1591).

TREATISE ON THE FOUR GOSPELS

Author: Joachim of Fiore (c.1132-1202)
Type of work: Eschatology; philosophy of history
First transcribed: 1202

Principal Ideas Advanced

To the enlightened understanding, the Bible foretells the end of the Church age in the year 1260.

The history of mankind unfolds in three stages: the first reveals God the Father; the second, God the Son; the third, God the Holy Spirit.

The clerical Church is limited to the age of the Son; the monastic orders are the true forerunners of the age of the Spirit.

Joachim, Abbot of Fiore (or Flora, or Flore), carried on the monastic revival which had previously been championed by Bernard of Clairvaux (c.1090-1153). Dante speaks of him in the *Paradiso* as "endowed with prophetic spirit," and he places him next to the great Franciscan, Bonaventura (1221-1274). But only within the last century have historical scholars begun to appreciate the scope of Joachim's influence, and, even more belatedly, to publish his long-neglected writings. The *Tractatus super quatuor evangelia,* which was published in Rome in 1930, is the first of several such works scheduled to be issued in modern critical editions. Some of Joachim's works were printed in the six-

teenth century, but the *Tractatus,* which is a lengthy fragment left incomplete at Joachim's death, has been handed down only in manuscript copies.

All of Joachim's writings develop essentially the same body of ideas, a kind of apocalypticism which made bold to prophesy that history was about to enter upon a new paradisiacal age. Millenarian expectations had been repressed in the official teaching of the Church, largely through the influence of Augustine, who taught that the thousand-year reign of Christ spoken of in the book of Revelation was the age of the Church. But among diverse groups the idea remained popular that, just as on the seventh day God rested from creating the world, so, at the end of six thousand years of history, the human race would have rest. Joachim gave a new and powerful expression to these perennial hopes, by means of a system of interpretation which presumably enabled him to discover Biblical allusions to his own times.

Joachim's understanding of the Scriptures came to him as a sudden insight while he was studying the Revelation. "Suddenly," he says, "the eyes of my spirit were enlightened, and the fulfillment of this book and the harmony between the Old and the New Testaments was revealed to me." The hidden truth given him in this way was that, just as the Mosaic dispensation had been replaced by that of Christ, so the Christian dispensation must henceforth give way to the dispensation of the Holy Spirit. Using allegorical methods, traditional in the Roman Church, Joachim developed his views in three books: *The Harmony of the Old and New Testaments, An Exposition of the Apocalypse,* and *The Psaltery of Ten Strings.* In his *Treatise on the Four Gospels* he undertakes to carry out the same scheme on a more impressive scale. Joachim's use of the allegorical method does not impress historical scholars as original —except, as his editor Ernesto Buonaiuti says, "quantitatively." What mainly distinguishes Joachim's commentary from other allegorical works is that instead of finding doctrinal and moral teachings hidden beneath the historical meaning of the text, Joachim found prophecies.

Joachim had the same kind of problem which faces anyone who wishes to comment on the four Gospels synoptically. He found that the four Gospels form a single narrative covering Christ's life until the Galilean ministry; but, upon observing that the first three Gospels do not record the Jerusalem visits which are mentioned in the fourth Gospel, and that John, for his part, does not detail the Galilean work, he had to break up his commentary into different books. Of the three books completed, the first deals with the birth narratives, the baptism and temptation, and Jesus' early preaching, through the story of the wedding at Cana. The second book takes up the early Galilean ministry as recorded in the first three Gospels, printing the accounts, where they diverge, in parallel columns. The third book follows John's account of Jesus' ministry in Judea and Samaria, breaking off in the middle of John's fifth chapter, after the healing of the lame man at the pool of Bethesda. The omissions, transpositions, and other seeming discrepancies between the Gospels do not appear to have disturbed Joachim, nor does he go out of his way to harmonize them. He was convinced that the Gospels were not written according to men's wisdom, but were dictated by the Holy Spirit, who wishes through them to convey something more than the literal story of Christ's life on earth.

As is true of many present-day "students of prophecy," Joachim often finds his truth in out-of-the-way places. Matthew's account of the genealogy of Christ, which most readers skip, interests him because it enables him to set a date for the termination of the Church-age. Matthew mentions that there were fourteen generations from Abraham to David, fourteen generations from David to the Babylonian captivity, and fourteen generations from the Babylonian captivity until Christ. Added together, this gives the figure forty-two, which appears often in the Scriptures. For example, Elijah prayed that Israel should suffer drought for three and one-half years, that is, forty-two months; and the woman in Revelation is forced to dwell in the wilderness for 1260 days, or forty-two months. Now, the fact that both John the Baptist and Jesus began their ministries at the age of thirty suggests that, when the Holy Spirit says "generation," he means thirty years. All of this reminds Joachim that he is living in the fortieth generation after Christ's birth, and that only two generations remain before the dispensation of the Church reaches its end.

The fundamental framework of Joachim's system is presupposed in the *Treatise,* and it is supplied in the current edition in the form of footnote citations from his earlier works. Briefly, Joachim maintains that history is divided into three ages, corresponding to the three persons of the Holy Trinity. Each age has its forerunners and its leader (*Dux*). The first age, which was prepared by Adam and Abraham, began with Moses and "revealed God the Father in his glory"; the second, which was announced by David and Uzziah, began with John the Baptist, and "made known the Son to the Christian people"; the third, which numbered among its predecessors Paul, Antony, Benedict, and Bernard, will begin with the coming of "that Elijah" who is foretold in the closing verses of the Old Testament, and will "belong to the Holy Spirit, who, during this age, will be shown in his glory even as the Father was in the first, and the Son in the Second."

Once having discerned this scheme in Scripture, Joachim claims, the reader who possesses "spiritual understanding" is able to find it on almost every page of the four Gospels. For example, Elizabeth, the mother of John the Baptist, conceived a child after being barren for many years. The time of her barrenness stands for the first era, the age of the Mosaic law and the synagogue; the time during which she carried the future prophet in her womb stands for the second era, the age of Christ and the Church; the time when she was delivered of a son stands for the beginning of the third era, the advent of Elijah and the age of the Spirit. Joachim uses great freedom in interpreting his symbols. On one plane of interpretation, John is the herald of the Christian era; on another, he symbolizes the Elijah that is to come.

A further example of Joachim's exegesis is his interpretation of the wedding at Cana, when Jesus turned the water into wine. Those who read with only historical understanding are puzzled by the words, "On the third day." The third day of what? No connection is apparent. Those who read with spiritual understanding, however, recognize at once a reference to the third period of history, "in which the peace of God is given to the Church, so that it may contemplate him as King, and be united in marriage with him to whom it has been betrothed." In the narrative itself, the bridegroom stands for the ecclesiastical hierarchy; the bride, for Christian believers during the Church-age; the mother of Jesus, for the monastic orders within the Church; and Jesus, for the Holy Spirit, who shall abolish the sacrament of water-baptism and substitute for it baptism by the Spirit.

We have mentioned the fact that Joachim was trying, in his own day, to carry on the monastic revival which had begun with the founding of the Cistercian order about 1075, and had proceeded apace under Bernard. The movement represented a strong protest against the secularism of the Church, and had, in addition, many social and economic implications. Its advocates did not view it as a withdrawal from the world, but as entering upon a new and more promising way of life, in which feudal restraints and social inequalities were abolished. Joachim describes the monastic movement as preparing the way for the age of the Holy Spirit, in the same way as the Davidic monarchy and the Levitical priesthood prepared the way for the age of the Church. From Joachim's point of view, the Church, with its sacraments, its hierarchy, and its scholastic teaching, is a transitional moment between the dispensation of the Father and that of the Spirit. The institutional Church is still in bondage to the letter of the Law, and thus it beholds God darkly, as in a mirror. The monastic orders, however, represent a serious effort to enter into the spirit of Christ, and, dispensing with worldly compromises, to live according to the perfect will of God. Joachim does not deny the validity of the clergy or the sacraments, nor does he hold that the new age is already realized in monasticism. He maintains, however, that when the new Dux appears, he will set aside both the feudal and priestly orders, and establish an order in which the spiritual way now pursued by the monks will become the way of life for all men.

Besides writing and preaching, Joachim was active in monastic reform.

His own ascetic principles were too severe for the monastery of Corazzo, in Calabria, of which he was the abbot, and he withdrew, with a few companions, to form a new abbey high in the mountains, under a rule which he himself drew up. From this abbey, known as St. John of Flore, other houses sprang up, and, in 1204, after Joachim's death, the "Order of Flore" was approved by Pope Innocent III. But Joachim's teaching spread rapidly outside his own order. There is ground for believing that he influenced Francis of Assisi (c.1182-1226), whose formal activity began about the year 1210; and it was among strict Franciscans, or Spirituals, that he found his most zealous disciples. One of these, a young teacher at the University of Paris named Gerard of Borgo San Donnino, wrote a book in 1254 called *The Eternal Gospel*, in which he pronounced that the age of the Holy Spirit would begin on schedule in 1260, and that the Franciscan Spirituals were the agents to bring it in. The controversy raised by this book resulted in disciplinary measures that dampened the Joachite movement within the Church; but the influence of the movement continued among fringe groups, such as the Fratricelli, and even in secular movements, such as that of the Roman revolutionary, Cola de Rienzo (c.1313-1354). Scholars argue that the optimistic, anarchistic, and egalitarian principles which were in this way disseminated throughout Europe have influenced social and political revolutions to this day. (See, for example, Karl Löwith, *Meaning in History*, 1949, Appendix I, "Modern Transfigurations of Joachism.")

Whether the Christian "hope" is this-worldly or other-worldly is still debated. (One needs but to recall discussions prompted by the meeting of the World Council of Churches at Evanston, in 1954.) Interestingly, apocalypticism, in this period of world wars, has come to be associated with an other-worldly eschatology. This was not true in the case of Joachim. Although he believed that divine manifestations would usher in the millennial age, he thought of it not as the termination of history, but as its fulfillment. The true successors of Joachim, therefore, are not those who set dates for history to end, but those who look for God's Kingdom to be realized here on earth.

According to the Augustinian world-view which governed the theology of the Middle Ages and continued to be the standard for the Reformation Churches, God stands outside His creation, and He intervenes only to save His handiwork from ruin; the contradiction between God's righteous demands and man's fallen conditions is accepted as normal and as not to be resolved except in eternity. Joachim of Fiore challenged these assumptions, and he thus prepared the way for the more modern view, which finds God progressively at work in nature and history.

Professor Löwith cites as an example of Joachim's influence the Enlightenment philosopher, Lessing, whose *Education of the Human Race,* 1780, profoundly influenced both French and German social and political thought. Lessing developed the idea of history as unfolding in three stages, stating that the Jewish and Christian dispensations must be superseded by a "new eternal gospel." Lessing believed that the new age would be introduced by reason and education; still, he maintained that it would come as a linear development out of the Judeo-Christian revelation. Referring to Joachim and his followers, he said, "Perhaps this doctrine of three world-ages was not at all an empty whim of these men; . . . they maintained the same economy of the same God, or, to let them speak my own language, the same plan for a common education of the human race. They only hastened it too much, believing that their contemporaries, who had just grown out of their childhood, could suddenly be made into adults, worthy of the third age, without proper preparation and enlightenment."

RETRACING THE ARTS TO THEOLOGY

Author: Saint Bonaventura (Giovanni di Fidanza, 1221-1274)
Type of work: Mystical theology
First transcribed: c.1250

Principal Ideas Advanced

The various forms of knowledge may be divided into four levels of illumination and then subdivided, according to distance from divine wisdom.

As each level and branch of knowledge is dissected, however, traces of divine similitude become evident, indicating that each has and discloses a divine origin.

Thus, each form of knowledge is directly relevant to and an assistance for theology, since, properly analyzed, all levels disclose a divine element and thus retrace their origin to God.

When it is placed beside Thomas Aquinas's *Summa theologica*, Bonaventura's *Retracing the Arts to Theology* may seem insignificant. Small it is, but unimportant it is not. In fact, what is so instructive about this little work is to see how much can be accomplished in so short a space. Moreover, like most of Bonaventura's works, this one is intricate in detail, encompassing a great deal in a short space and shaped into a very compressed form.

Now, in the twentieth century, it is interesting to see that Bonaventura opens his treatise with what afterwards became Kierkegaard's favorite Biblical passage, from the first chapter of James: *Every good and perfect gift is from above, coming down from the Father of Lights.* The metaphor of light is characteristic of those who, like Bonaventura, follow the Neoplatonic tradition. In fact, this Scriptural passage is central to Bonaventura's doctrine here, since it would not be possible to trace all of the arts to a theological source unless a divine light actually took various forms and appeared in many modes and levels. Divinity transcends normal natural modes, but it nevertheless is completely immanent, present behind and discernible through every order of nature.

Bonaventura begins with what is essentially a division of the sciences and the branches of philosophy, by distinguishing each as a form of light. First, there is an external light or the light of mechanical art, followed by a lower

light of sense perception. Then there is the inner light or the light of philosophical knowledge. And finally there is the higher light or the light of grace and of Scripture. The lower light illumines artifacts, while the second reveals natural forms to us, and the third discloses intellectual truth. The fourth and last concerns saving grace, and this is the most crucial to man. Bonaventura, it is true, does not develop these analogies in detail. A sketch of related structures always seems to be sufficient for him.

The first (external) light, since it concerns artifacts, deals primarily with things exterior to man and intended to supply the needs of his body. As such it is servile and of a lower nature than philosophical knowledge. Since there are seven mechanical arts, this external light has seven subdivisions, and these taken together are sufficient for man's consolation, comfort, sorrow, or delight. Following this light, so important to man's basic needs, is the lower light of sense perception. This begins with a material object and needs the aid of corporeal light. In its turn, sense perception has five divisions, corresponding to the five senses. The sensitive life of the body actually partakes of the nature of light.

The investigation of intelligible truths is the third light, the light of philosophical knowledge. It is an inner light, since it inquires into inner and hidden causes, through inherent principles of learning and natural truth. Philosophy is, of course, subdivided into three divisions, rational, natural, and moral. Philosophy involves discerning the causes of being (in physics), grasping the principles of understanding (in logic), and learning the right way of living (in moral or practical philosophy). As a result, philosophy enlightens man as to the truth of life, the truth of knowledge, and the truth of doctrine. Physics, mathematics, and metaphysics are all combined in this general division, considering in turn generation and corruption, abstracted forms, and the ideal causes, leading back to one first principle, God.

Most important of all, of course, is the fourth light, illumining the mind for the understanding of saving truth. This is to be found in the light of Scripture. Such a light is properly called higher, since it leads to truths beyond reason and as such is not to be acquired by human research. It comes down from above, by inspiration from the Father of Lights. In a literal sense, this light is one, although in a mystical sense it has a threefold spiritual meaning; allegorical, moral, and anagogical. By these three means we are taught what to believe concerning Divinity, how to live, and, finally, how to be united with God. This divides men into doctors, preachers, and contemplatives.

There will, however, one day come a twilight, when all knowledge will be destroyed, followed by a day which knows no evening, the illumination of glory. All of the branches of knowledge are ordained as a means to a knowledge of Sacred Scripture. All illuminations of all knowledge are to be brought back, or traced to, the light of Sacred Scripture. As we discern this, we discern the Word be-

gotten from all eternity as itself the medium of all perception. As the sense object is seen in perception by means of a similitude, so God has connected from all eternity a Similitude or Offspring. Through Him (Jesus) the minds of all who receive that similitude of the Father through faith are brought back to God.

Perhaps the best example of the similarity between divinity and sense perception can be seen in the delight one takes in sense perception, for in this we can see a similarity to the delight of the soul when it unites with God. In this way and in others, the Divine Wisdom actually lies hidden in sense perception, as in fact it does in all of the various forms of knowledge. As the artist produces a work according to a similitude in his mind, to take a further example, so the Invisible becomes visible and takes flesh in Christ. And most certainly, carrying the parallel further, the divine wisdom can also be found in philosophy, since the speaker begets words from mental concepts, following the same procedure of God in begetting the Eternal Word.

All natural philosophy, because it discloses primarily the various relations of proportion, duplicates the Word of God begotten and become incarnate. Since God is above, it is necessary that the apex of the mind itself be raised aloft, thus indicating in the process of philosophy the natural goal of the mind for union with God. What all of this analysis discloses most clearly, Bonaventura concludes, is how the wisdom of God lies hidden in all knowledge and in all nature. To discover divine knowledge hidden in the various forms of nature and levels of knowledge is the central meaning of retracing the arts to theology.

In this sense all divisions of knowledge are "handmaidens of theology," a phrase much objected to and much misunderstood. The divisions of knowledge "serve" theology by showing themselves to be, upon careful dissection, forms of divine light. Theology uses material and terms from every branch of knowledge precisely because every form of knowledge actually discloses, to an astute observer, its peculiar form of divine wisdom through the divine analogies to be discovered on every level. The way to illumination is wide, not narrow, since not one but every possible branch of knowledge is actually capable of leading a keen mind through itself to God Himself.

In everything perceived or known God lies hidden within: this is Bonaventura's amazing discovery and his central message to the reader. The fruit of every science is that through it faith may actually be strengthened, rather than diverted and diminished. It takes a discerning mind to discover this divine element present in every form of knowledge, but that it can be done makes every mode of knowledge an avenue to God and an aid to theology. For theology we need not go far afield from man's ordinary pursuit of knowledge but simply gain the discernment to discover how every level of knowledge may be traced directly to God.

The four lights described by Bonaventura form the basis of a complete theory of knowledge, a cosmology, and a metaphysics, and all four unite to form a theology. All the arts, all the branches of science, all the activities of men are accounted for here, and each becomes a step leading the mind further upward, toward its theological goal of divine union. God has left His traces in every facet of the natural world and in men themselves, and a careful mind may discover the divine light in all things and, retracing it to its divine origin, be led by the arts to theology. Each form and level remains distinct and independent, yet each serves to raise the mind farther on its way toward God.

This brief treatise by Bonaventura must be looked on as only a sketch. Bonaventura has compressed his whole system of philosophy and theology into one brief essay. In its simplicity, however, the account is in some ways more suggestive than a more elaborate and detailed discussion could ever hope to be. There is no question that Bonaventura belongs to the Platonic tradition, and writers of this persuasion have always suggested and sketched possible theories in a tentative fashion.

Viewed in this way, it is easier to understand why no evidence whatsoever is offered to support the theory. If illumination is a way to knowledge, the mind cannot be forced or coerced. A suggestion can be made, a hidden factor pointed out, and then the listening mind is free to discern or not to discern the qualities outlined for it. Thus, the theory serves as a verbal platform for consideration. The attempt is to raise the mind to new perception by means of the theory; in this case, the effort is to discern the divine presence implicit in every natural phenomenon and fundamental to every art and inquiry.

SUMMA CONTRA GENTILES

Author: Saint Thomas Aquinas (c.1225-1274)
Type of work: Christian apologetics
First transcribed: c.1258-1260

PRINCIPAL IDEAS ADVANCED

Theology has the two-fold task of expounding truth and refuting error.

The truth of the Christian doctrine of God, of creation, and of providence can be established by reason and probable arguments.

The truth of the doctrine of the Trinity, the Incarnation, and the atonement must be accepted by faith, but can be defended and explained by reason.

The highest good for man is the beatific vision, for attaining which both faith and reason are necessary.

According to tradition, the *Summa contra gentiles* was composed at the request of the Dominican order (of which Thomas was a member) with a view to the needs of its missionaries in Spain, where the influence of Islamic and Jewish philosophy was strong. But in Thomas's day the influence of such non-Christian thinkers as Maimonides (1135-1204), Avicenna (980-1037), and Averroës (1126-1198) was not limited to Spain, for European scholars generally were dependent on Moslem transmitters and interpreters for their knowledge of Greek science and philosophy. In the *Summa contra gentiles* Thomas, who was second to none in his mastery of Aristotle, brought Christian faith and pagan learning together, not as enemies, or even as strangers, but as natural counterparts and allies, although unequal.

Citing a text from *Proverbs* in which Wisdom declares, "My mouth shall meditate truth, and my lips shall hate impiety," Thomas explains that the truth which Wisdom seeks is that truth which is the origin of all truth, pertaining as it does to the first prin-

ciples of all reality. It is the same truth which Aristotle made the subject of his *Metaphysics*, but it is also the same truth which was incarnate in the person of Jesus Christ. But, says Thomas, it belongs to one and the same science both to establish the truth containing its subject and to refute opposing errors. Hence, the two-fold task of theology.

That the *Summa contra gentiles* is intended primarily as a work in theology and not in philosophy, follows from the distinction which Aquinas makes between these two sciences. The task of philosophy, he says, is to know things according to their own natures; that of theology is to know things in their relationship to God. Furthermore, the procedure of philosophy is to begin with those things which are best known to man and then to proceed toward those things which are least known; that of theology, on the contrary, is to begin with that which, although least known to man, is inherently the most intelligible. In other words, philosophy starts with the knowledge we have of the creature and progresses toward knowledge of the

Creator, whereas theology starts with the knowledge of God, and considers creatures in the light of what we can know of Him.

A glance at the outline of the *Summa contra gentiles* is sufficient to show that it is primarily a theological work. There are four books. In view of the fact that the adversaries he had in mind were not Christian heretics, but Jews and Moslems who would not be convinced by an appeal to Scriptural authority, Thomas devoted the first three books to proving as much of the Christian faith as can be shown to be true by demonstration and probable argument. The fourth book expounds the truth of revelation, and covers those parts of the Christian faith which cannot be discovered by reason. In Books One to Three, as well as in Book Four, the argument begins with our knowledge of God and explains the world in relation to Him, first, as owing its existence to God, and second, as finding its fulfillment in God. Book One treats of God as He is in Himself; Book Two treats of the derivation of the creatures from God; Book Three treats of the creatures insofar as they are ordered toward God as their end. Book Four recapitulates the order, but on the plane of revealed knowledge: first, of the Trinity, then of the Incarnation, then of the sacraments, and finally of Heaven and Hell.

Many philosophical issues are raised in the course of the work, but they are subordinated to the theological plan. Ordinarily, they are introduced with a view either to showing that reason leads to the same conclusions as faith or to helping the mind comprehend what has been apprehended by faith. But occasionally the situation is reversed, and faith is able to further the interests of philosophy by correcting philosophy when it has gone astray and by answering questions which are philosophical in nature but which cannot be answered by reason alone. For example, the question whether the world is or is not eternal is a philosophical question to which reason cannot find the answer. Both Greek and Islamic philosophers made the mistake of inferring that it is eternal, but the Christian learns from Scripture that this answer is false. He could know it no other way than by revelation. But having received the true answer, the Christian perceives that the alleged arguments for the eternity of the world are not sound. Thus, the *Summa contra gentiles,* while mainly theological, is also a contribution toward Christian philosophy.

The reader, therefore, must be on guard against the popular notion that, for Thomas, whatever rests on reason is philosophy, and whatever rests on authority is theology. He must also disabuse himself of any notion that Thomas was more certain of the truths of reason than he was of the truths of revelation, and that he conceived it as the task of the theologian to justify revelation in terms of reason. Thomas had a moderately high opinion of man's reason, and he had an unlimited belief in the complete rationality of the universe. But these assumptions, particularly the last one, partake of the nature of religious faith, whether or not the faith confides in any authority. Actually, Aristotle and his Moslem interpreters held the same assumptions without connecting them with the God of revelation. Thomas took the further step of identifying the Intelligence which made the world with the God of the Bible. He concluded from this that reason and revelation cannot conflict, and that if reason seems to lead to conclusions contrary to those of revealed truth, some error is present in the use of reason. What private doubts Thomas may have entertained will never be known, but it seems probable that those are correct who say that, for Thomas, the question was not whether faith is compatible with what we know by reason, but whether reason is compatible with what we know by faith.

In this connection, the manner in which Thomas uses the proofs for the existence of God is instructive. We might have expected to find the Christian philosopher exerting himself at this point, bringing all his resources to bear upon the proof that God exists. The least he could do would be to distinguish between Aristotle's Unmoved Mover, who was supposed to determine the motions of the uncreated universe by the sheer force of its attraction for rational creatures, and the God of Moses, who gives existence to every creature and sustains it by His will and power. As a matter of fact, Thomas did nothing more than repeat, with careful analysis, the proofs which lay at hand in Aristotle and in the Arabian commentators. The explanation lies in the distinction Thomas makes between essence and existence and in his contention that only the existence of God is demonstrable. The proofs, then, as he understands them, tell us only that nature presupposes the existence of a being which is perfect in precisely those respects in which nature is imperfect. At this point, faith steps forward and joins hands with reason, saying, "This is the one we call God." Similarly, throughout Books One to Three, Thomas fol-

lows reason as far as it appears to him to lead; then, characteristically, he concludes each chapter with a Scriptural quotation or statement of faith from one of the doctors of the Church. In contrast, the procedure of Book Four is to cite the authorities at the beginning only afterwards and to adduce the reasons, to clarify meaning, and to answer objections.

Aquinas's theology, in this way, maintains a balance between faith and reason. The Platonic philosophy which the earlier Middle Ages took from Augustine saw no necessity to limit the claims of reason. Anselm (c.1033-1109), for example, who stood in that tradition, believed that reason can penetrate even the highest mysteries of faith, such as the necessity for the Incarnation and for the atonement. His celebrated ontological proof of the existence of God rested on the assumption that man's knowledge of God is implicit in the knowledge of the creature. But in the thirteenth century that tradition was challenged. That age saw great advances in many fields of knowledge, stimulated in large part by the recovery of Greek philosophical and scientific writings, with their Arabic commentaries and glosses. For the Church, the choice was either to resist the new learning or somehow to accommodate it. Inevitably, many saw no possibility other than open conflict. Some eagerly embraced the doctrine of the two-fold truth, which was connected with the name of Averroës; namely, that reason and revelation are irreconcilable, and that the latter, although necessary for the ignorant masses, has no value for the learned. Others, identifying Aristotelianism with pagan thought, took their stand firmly on faith and minimized the validity of reason. Thomas, together with his teacher Albertus Magnus (c.1200-1280), sought a middle ground. Both Thomas and Albertus Magnus affirmed that reason supports faith, but they claimed that the earlier tradition had been mistaken in supposing that reason can penetrate the mysteries of the divine being and of man's salvation. Thomas wrote voluminous commentaries on Aristotle's works nearly as rapidly as they were translated into Latin. Albertus was especially interested in the new sciences of nature. The Christian, these men maintained, had cause only for rejoicing at the new frontiers which had been opened to the Christian world, nor need faith suffer at any point. On the contrary, the more we know about the nature of things, they argued, the more we see the truth of God's revelation; and, in particular, the more exactly we understand the nature of man, including the limits of his understanding, the more clearly we see the inability of man's unaided reason to come to ultimate truth and to the blessedness which depends on possessing that truth.

Although Thomas departs from the traditional Augustinian position when he denies that the mysteries of the faith are fathomable by reason, he avoids going to the opposite extreme of maintaining that there is complete disparity between our reason and God's hidden essence. Following Aristotle, he maintains that human knowledge is dependent upon the senses; we arrive at intelligible truths only by abstraction from our sensible experience of the material world. For this reason, we cannot directly apprehend the divine essence. But indirectly, through what we know about nature, we can come to some knowledge of God. What we must remember is that there is a gradation of being and a dependence of the lower upon the higher, such that something of the perfection of the higher must be discernible in the lower. Thus, what we know about the world does not hold true of God exactly, but a certain proportionality between the creature and the Creator makes it possible for us to apply our intelligible notions to God indirectly, by way of analogy. In this way we can speak with some confidence of God's intellect, His will, His life, His love, His blessedness.

In Book One, where he discusses the nature of God, Thomas rarely clashes head-on with his infidel opponents. Important differences in principle are involved, but they are not the broad issues of popular controversy. These latter issues appear when, in Book Two, the discussion turns to the subject of creation, and Thomas, in defense of the Christian faith, is obliged to uphold the doctrine that God created the world out of nothing, that He created it freely, and that He created it at a particular point in time. The groundwork for Thomas's replies has, of course, been laid in Book One. Since, as he shows there, God alone is self-existent, the creature must depend entirely upon His will and power. Moreover, since there is nothing outside Himself for Him to consider, it follows that God's will is determined only by His knowledge of Himself and is therefore free. As to the world's having a beginning, there is, Thomas asserts, no conclusive evidence on either side, and hence the matter can be decided only on the basis of Scripture.

Another controversial issue between the Christians and the Moslems concerns the nature of the human soul and its relation to the body. Here Thomas takes issue with Plato, as well as with Averroës. Plato had maintained that the intellect is related to the body simply as mover. Averroës, who professed to follow Aristotle, maintained that there is one intellect which enlightens all men, but that it is united to no man's body. Thomas musters a great display of learning in favor of what he considers Aristotle's view; namely, that each man's intellect is his own, and that it is united to his body not accidentally, as mover, but essentially, as its entelechy or form.

Book Three is a consideration of the world, and especially of man, this time in relation to God as final cause. No vigorous polemics are found here, but numerous perennial topics are discussed, among them the nature of evil, man's felicity (whether it consists in willing or knowing), man's present incapacity for happiness, the problem of divine foreknowledge and the efficacy of second causes (including man's will), the laws of nature and the moral law, sin and its rewards, and the necessity for grace if man is to reach the end for which he was created. This part of the work corresponds to the *Purgatory* of Dante's *Divine Comedy*. It is a kind of *preparatio evangelica*. But Thomas was careful to state that none of the demonstrations of the first three books can be expected to convert men to Christianity. At best they show that in a world where there is so much evidence of divine wisdom and love, it is reasonable to ask whether God will not somewhere have raised man from his deeply unsatisfactory condition. Like Virgil in the *Purgatory*, Reason leads man up the mountain of human striving, but it cannot take him past the gates into Paradise.

Book Four is written from the perspective of one who stands beyond the gateway which divides reason and revelation. Reason is henceforth employed for the purpose of making revelation more comprehensible and of defending revealed truths against the attacks of pagans and heretics. Thomas explains that this book is written only for the consolation and edification of believers, not with a view to convincing unbelievers. On the contrary, he has a word of reproof for over-zealous protagonists who, by attempting to demonstrate things that are beyond reason, actually confirm men in their unbelief by leading them to suppose that Christians rest their faith on bad reasoning.

Thomas does not permit us to confuse reason and faith. Reason and faith are separate ways of knowing God, each disclosing something of Him that is not given by the other. Faith, of course, is the higher of the two, inasmuch as it enables man to lay hold of the means by which the soul is prepared for the perfect vision of God in the life to come—a vision which is another way of knowing God, distinct alike from faith and reason. But although faith is necessary to the beatific vision, it is not sufficient, except in conjunction with the other virtues. The recipient of grace is enabled to turn to God, but the turning must be his own, as well as the progress which he makes toward sanctification. To this end, reason is of the utmost importance—not merely the practical reason by which man is enabled to know God's law, but also the theoretical reason by which he contemplates God's truth. The latter is an incentive to godly living, because it moves the soul to admiration and reverence. But, in addition, it is its own reward, for contemplation of the divine is the highest good. According to Thomas, each being tends toward that which perfects it, and that which perfects human intellect is divine truth.

THE JOURNEY OF THE MIND TO GOD

Author: Saint Bonaventura (Giovanni di Fidanza, 1221-1274)
Type of work: Mystical theology
First transcribed: 1259

PRINCIPAL IDEAS ADVANCED

The soul of man can ascend to a mystical vision of God by passing through six stages in which it beholds God outside itself, through His traces and in His traces; within itself, by His image and in His image; and above itself, by contemplating God's essential traits and by reflecting on the Trinity.

By sense and imagination, reason and intellect, intelligence and the illumination of conscience, and by the aid of divine grace, the soul can at last pass over into God through the transports of contemplation.

The Journey of the Mind to God (*Itinerarium mentis ad Deum*) is the work of Saint Bonaventura, the Seraphic Doctor of the thirteenth century. Although the book is very short, it contains a system of Christian metaphysics, illustrates a philosophical method, and is representative of the Christian experience which culminates in a mystic vision of God.

The soul ascends to God by passing through a series of stages or steps. Since beatitude, the fruition of the highest good, is above us, it can be attained only if our hearts are elevated by a higher power. Divine help comes to those who seek it humbly in prayer.

The human mind has three aspects; the first, animality or sensuality, refers to the external body; the second, spirit, looks inward into itself; the third, mind, looks above itself. Since each of these aspects is twofold, there are six stages of the soul's powers, implanted in us by nature, by which we pass through the six stages of ascension into God. We mount from the depths to the heights, from the external to the internal, from the temporal to the eternal, through the powers of sense, imagination, reason, intellect, intelligence, and the illumination of conscience (synteresis).

Contemplation is unattainable without meditation, holy conversation, and devout prayer. Man was created for contemplation, but because of his sin he sits in the shadows and does not see the light of Heaven unless he is reformed by divine regenerating grace, imparted through Jesus Christ, the Word Incarnate. The first rung in the ladder by which we mount up to God is attained by reference to the whole sensible world, which as a mirror reflects the Creator's supreme power, wisdom, and benevolence.

The bodily senses serve the person who in contemplation sees things in themselves, in weight, number, and measure. From these traces of God's power one can rise to an understanding of the power, wisdom, and immense goodness of God as a living, understanding, spiritual, incorruptible, and immutable being. The senses enable the believer to consider the world in such a way that he discovers its origin, course, and terminus; they serve the rational inquirer by enabling him to discern the potential excellence of things.

The second stage of the ascent of the soul involves contemplation of God not only *through* sensible things but also *in* sensible things, to the degree that God is in them by essence, potency, and presence. God can be contemplated in all things which enter our minds through the bodily senses.

The doors of the five senses permit this world, the macrocosm, to enter the soul, the microcosm. Objects in the sensible world are shadows, echoes, and pictures—the traces and reflections of God. Sensible things are exemplifications set before our minds; through sensible things, which we see, we may be carried to the intelligibles, the divine ideas, which we do not see. The invisible things of God are signified by whatever inhabits the sensible world, because God is the origin, exemplar, and end of all created things; every effect is the sign of its cause, and the exemplification is the sign of its divine exemplar.

From the contemplation of God in and through his traces we have recourse in the third stage to the mirror of our mind, where the divine image shines. Here with the eye of reason, we become aware of a threefold power of the soul, the contemplation of which leads us to behold the image of the blessed Trinity.

The first power of the soul known to reason, that of memory, enables us to retain and to represent things present, past, and future, things corporeal and temporal, things simple and eternal. Since memory makes possible the retention of temporal things, it is the image of eternity whose indivisible present extends to all time. Memory is not formed solely from without by images (phantasms), but also from within by receiving simple forms from above and retaining them in itself. From its retention of the eternal principles and axioms of the sciences, memory has an undying light present to itself by which it remembers unchangeable truths. The operations of memory thus disclose that the soul itself is the image of God.

The second power of the soul known to reason is that of the intellect, which is concerned with the meanings of terms, with propositions, and with inferences. Since our intellect is conjoined with eternal truth, it knows with certainty under the guidance of the divine light.

The third power of the soul that reason knows is the operation of will found in deliberation, judgment, and desire. When we deliberate as to what is better, we can do so solely by reference to the best, so that the idea of the highest good is involved. Our deliberative faculty in judging involves an appeal to divine laws, and our desire for happiness is not fulfilled unless we attain the best and ultimate end.

The soul is thus so close to God that

memory leads in its operations to eternity; intelligence leads to truth; and the power of will leads to the highest goodness. Memory, intelligence, and will are consubstantial, coequal, and coeval. Thus, the mind, when it considers itself, rises through itself as through a mirror to the contemplation of God as the Father, Word, and Love; the Triune God; three persons coeternal, coequal, and consubstantial —one God.

The fourth level of contemplation of God as the First Principle is found within ourselves. By turning away from the sensible world, the mind can return to itself as to the image of God. It is, however, impossible for a fallen creature to enter into himself in order to delight in the Lord in Himself, unless he loves and has faith in the Mediator between God and man, Jesus Christ.

Since man is a fallen creature, the reflection of God in the image of the mind must be reformed, repaired by the gifts of grace, by the theological virtues of faith, hope, and love. By faith the soul recovers spiritual hearing and vision—hearing to receive the lessons of Christ, vision to behold the splendor of His light. The soul is illuminated by hope and perfected by love. The spirit is thus able, through its conformity, to mount upward to the heavenly Jerusalem.

By the reformation of the image through the theological virtues and through the delights of the spiritual senses, our soul is made hierarchical; that is, purged, perfected, and illuminated. God is then seen to be all in all through the contemplation of Him in the minds in which He dwells.

Man's mind, inhabited by the divine wisdom, is thus made the temple of the Holy Spirit, without whom no man can know the secrets of God.

God is contemplated not only outside us and within us, but also above us. He is seen outside us through His traces and inside us through His image. He is seen above us through His light.

There are two ways by which contemplation of the invisible and eternal things of God is possible. The first way provides the fifth stage in the soul's ascent; it involves contemplation of God's *essential attributes*. The divine unity is reflected in its primary name, which is *Being*. To contemplate the invisible traits of God insofar as they belong to the unity of His essence, the soul must concentrate on Being itself. When Being is contemplated with the illumination of eternal light, the mind understands that Being itself cannot be derivative. Lacking nonbeing, Being-itself has no beginning or end; it is eternal, most simple, most actual, most perfect, and one to the highest degree.

Since Being is most pure and absolute, that which is Being is simply first and last; Being, therefore, is the final cause and origin of all. Because Being is eternal and most present, it encompasses and penetrates all duration. Because it is most simple and greatest, Being is entirely within and entirely without all things; therefore, it resides in an intelligible sphere whose center is everywhere and whose circumference is nowhere. Because Being is most actual and immutable, it causes the universe to move. Because it is most perfect and immense, Being is within all, though it is not included in all; it is beyond all, but it is not excluded from all; it is above all, but it is not transported beyond all; it is below all, and yet it is not beneath all. Because Being is most highly one and all-inclusive, it is all in all, even though all things are many and it is only one. Being contains all power, all exemplary causality, and all communicability. It is omnipotent, omniscient, and all-good; from it and by it and in it are all things. To see this perfectly is to be blessed.

The second way the soul looks above itself to contemplate the invisible and eternal things of God, the sixth stage, is by reflection upon the most blessed Trinity, upon the properties of the persons of God. In the fifth stage of contemplation, Being is seen as the root and name of the vision of the essential traits of the Deity; in the sixth stage, it is the name *Good* which is the principal foundation of the contemplation of the divine emanations of the Trinity.

Since the Good is self-diffusive, the highest Good is the most self-diffusive. The greatest diffusion exists where it is actual, intrinsic, substantial, hypostatic, natural, voluntary, and perfect. In the highest Good there is a production which is actual and consubstantial, a hypostasis as noble as the producer. The Father, Son, and Holy Spirit constitute the greatest Good, the greatest diffusion. By contemplating the purity of goodness, the soul may see by the highest communicability of the Good that a Trinity of Father, Son, and Holy Spirit is necessary.

It is necessary that there be in the Trinity the greatest communicability and, therefore, the greatest consubstantiality, the greatest configurability, and

the greatest coequality, coeternity, and cointimacy.

When we contemplate the Goodness that excells all goodness, the properties of the Trinity are manifest. We behold in wonder a plurality of hypostases, a unity in essence and in form, in dignity, in eternity, in existence and illimitability. For we wonder not only at the essential and personal traits of God in themselves, but on the sixth stage of our ascent we behold the miraculous union of God and man in the unity of Christ's person, the Eternal joined with temporal man. The most simple is here joined with the most composite. Communicability exists with individuality, consubstantiality with plurality, configurability with personality, coeternity with production, and cointimacy with mission—for the Son was sent by the Father, and the Holy Spirit by both.

The stages of the soul's ascent to God, as described by Bonaventura, reach their perfection on the sixth level when man comes to the point of beholding in the first and highest principle and the Mediator of God and men, Jesus Christ, those properties of which the likeness cannot in any wise be found in creatures and which exceed all the insight of the human intellect. Here the soul passes over into God through elevation. If this passage of the soul is perfect, all intellectual operations are abandoned, and the whole height of our affection is transferred and transformed into God in a mystical and secret manner, which no man knows unless he has received this mystic wisdom through the revealing power of the Holy Spirit.

SUMMA THEOLOGICA

Author: Saint Thomas Aquinas (c.1225-1274)
Type of work: Scholastic theology
First transcribed: c.1265-1274

PRINCIPAL IDEAS ADVANCED

Man's knowledge is mediated through the senses; whatever knowledge man has of divine things must be by inference from knowledge of material things.

God is the Supremely Real, who in knowing Himself knows all truth, and in willing Himself wills all good.

Such truths as are contained in the doctrines of the Trinity, the Incarnation, and the Resurrection must be known through revelation.

The world process is a double movement, flowing out from and returning to God, who is Himself unmoved.

Christianity is the complement of civilaztion, revelation an extension of reason, and grace the perfection of creation.

Thomas Aquinas's *Summa theologica* is a theological omnibus, written for the beginning student rather than for the accomplished scholar. It is a veritable "question box," in which unprofitable puzzlers take their place alongside the set questions of theological instruction. Because it is an introductory work, controversial matters are not pursued to the length they are in other of Thomas's writings. Nevertheless, partly because it was written after his various commentaries and earlier summas when Thomas was at the height of his powers, and partly because an intelligent "abridgment" of an increasingly unwieldy mass of theological material was overdue, the *Summa theologica* soon achieved authoritative standing. Modern readers will find many questions discussed which have ceased to be live issues since the thirteenth century, but they will also find classic discussions of such perennial questions as divine providence, human freedom and responsibility, and the moral law.

In the history of systematic theology, the *Summa theologica* would be a landmark if for no other reason than for the order it imposes on its material. Prior to its appearance, theological handbooks had followed the scheme of Peter Lombard's *Sententiarum libri quatuor* (c.1150), even when they were not directly commenting on that text. Thomas, for the first time, divides and orders the subject according to logical principles. Part One, theology proper, treats of the divine essence, of the Trinity, and of creation and providence. Part Two, moral theology, comprises two divisions, each as extensive as either of the other parts. The first (*prima secundae*) deals with the foundations of ethics; the second (*secunda secundae*) is an elaborate treatise on the virtues and the vices. Part Three, Christology, deals with the person and work of Christ, with the sacraments, and with the future life. The last part of the discussion of the sacraments and the whole of that on the future life was compiled after

Thomas's death by his disciples, and is known as the *Supplement*.

The outline of the *Summa theologica*, which is anticipated in the slightly earlier *Summa contra gentiles*, is an outgrowth of Thomas's efforts to give theology its rightful place among the sciences. The thirteenth century saw the rise of the first European universities, with separate faculties of law, medicine, arts, and philosophy. It is no mere chance that this departmentalization of knowledge coincided with Europe's rediscovery of Aristotle, who not only left masterful treatises on a wide variety of subjects, but also argued on principle that each subject requires to be treated in its own way. For example, Aristotle distinguished between the theoretical science of physics and the practical science of ethics; above both of these, he placed philosophy, which he also called theology. Thomas Aquinas, who accepted the new outlook and willingly appropriated Aristotle's conception of science, believed that theology needed to set its house in order. The boundaries between philosophy and theology needed to be more clearly drawn, with principles laid down which should govern the relations between reason and faith.

Having devoted many volumes to commenting on Aristotle's work, Thomas yielded to none in his technical mastery of the new philosophy. But *Summa theologica* is a theological work, and philosophy is here put at the service of Christian doctrine. An important instance is the use Thomas makes of Aristotle's theory of knowledge. According to the Augustinian view, which had prevailed in earlier scholasticism, man's intellect is able, by divine illumination, to possess im-

mediate knowledge of supernatural reality. Not so, says Thomas, following Aristotle: man's knowledge, in this life, is always mediated through the senses, and whatever knowledge he has of divine things must be by inference from or by analogy with his knowledge of material things. It follows that what man can know about God by reason alone is strictly limited. He can know, as Aristotle showed, that there must exist a First Cause over nature, and he can know, by the "negative way" of abstracting from the imperfections of the creatures, something of the perfections of the Creator; but he cannot know anything of God's internal life, nor His purposes toward creation. Such truths as are contained in the doctrines of the Trinity, the Incarnation, and the Resurrection could not be known if God had not revealed them. Nevertheless, according to Thomas, once these truths have been revealed, reason can make them intelligible. Thomas considered himself a faithful Augustinian in all matters of essential Christian truth. The new task, as he saw it, was to preserve Augustinian theology by bringing it into its proper relation to the rest of human knowledge. For this purpose, it was necessary to subject Christian wisdom itself to the discipline of "the Philosopher" (as Thomas called Aristotle).

Thomas's devotion to Aristotle, however, did not affect his even more fundamental commitment to the Neoplatonic world view, transmitted to Western thought partly through Augustine, and partly by Islamic and Jewish philosophers, but most directly, as far as Thomas is concerned, through the writings of the sixth century Greek theologian who wrote under the name of Dionysius the Areopagite, who was in Thomas's day believed to be the convert of Paul mentioned in The Acts of the Apostles. Like the Neoplatonists (and Aristotle too, for that matter) Thomas saw everything as having its source and destiny in God. His theology is not the least anthropocentric, nor geocentric, nor even Christocentric. It is theocentric, in the fullest sense of the word. We are to study, says Thomas at the beginning of the Summa, God as he is in himself, God as the beginning of things, and God as the end toward which all things move. Christ is introduced as "the way to God." This, in Thomas's view, is the sum of theology.

Again, God, in Thomas's system, bears a much closer resemblance to the "Form of Forms" in Aristotle's philosophy, or to the One of Neoplatonism, than to the God of the Bible. God is the Supremely Real, who in knowing Himself knows all truth, and in willing Himself wills all good. In Aristotelian fashion, Thomas explains God's will as the natural inclination of God's intellect toward the Reality which it contemplates; and with Augustine he equates these principles with the three Persons of the Trinity.

In his doctrine of creation, Thomas modifies what, for the Neoplatonists, is essentially a necessitarian scheme, by insisting on the freedom of God's will. Nonetheless he explains creation much as the Neoplatonists did by urging that it was the perfection of God's goodness which made him want to increase the good by creating a counterpart to himself, a sort of "moving image of eternity" (as Plato put it), which will be as perfect as divine wisdom can devise. Called into being out of nothing, the created world will not have the simplicity and unity that belongs to

the Creator; rather, its order will be that of an organism in which the whole is achieved by means of the differentiation of its parts. Accordingly, within creation there will be degrees of perfection and imperfection depending on the distance by which the creature is removed from the divine similitude. At the one extreme will be pure angelic intelligence; at the other, inert matter. Critically situated on the border between matter and intelligence is man, through whose composite being the whole world is in a manner represented.

It is essential to Thomas's conception of God that the creation involves no alteration or diminution of the divine Being, and that the eternal tranquillity of the divine life is not disturbed by the rebellion and sufferings, or by the redemption and glorification of man. In his terminology, the divine activity toward the world is a real relation as far as the creature is concerned, but ideal only (secundum rationem tantum) as far as God is concerned. Human history is the working out on the plane of man's existence of the world plan which God saw would bring the most good into being. That there must be sin and suffering, that men must endure the penalty of eternal damnation, that Christ must die in order that any might merit eternal blessedness—all these were included. How else could divine mercy and justice, wisdom and love be made fully known? Thomas does not hold back from the full Augustinian doctrine of predestination. God's foreknowledge and His election are presupposed in everything that takes place; specifically, it is by His decree that some receive grace and others are passed by.

Thomas's doctrine of grace is closely

connected with his Aristotelian view of human nature. According to this view, the perfection of any rational being comes only with the full knowledge of God; but man, because his knowledge is mediated through the senses, is not able by nature to behold God. Hence, when God created man, He supplemented man's natural powers with a supernatural gift of righteousness and holiness. Had our first parents continued to obey God, they need never have died but, after a time, would have been translated to eternal bliss. When they disobeyed, they lost the supernatural gift without which no true happiness is possible to man; but in addition, they brought upon themselves the stain of guilt, liability to punishment, and the corruption of their natures. This is the sad and guilty condition of the race which God visits with the gift of salvation. First, it is necessary that the sinner's will be rehabilitated by an infusion of grace into the soul, so that he may seek after God, abandon his evil ways, and receive the remission of his guilt. Faith is thus created in him, followed by the other virtues which then make it possible for him to pursue the way of salvation provided in Christ and made available through the instrumentality of the sacraments.

It is worth noting that Thomas considers God's grace and man's justification in the second part of the *Summa*, instead of after his discussion of the person and work of Christ, where the Reformers are accustomed to consider it. He treats of grace, together with law, as one of the principles or dispositions by which God in His providence leads mankind to beatitude, and he follows it with his treatise on the virtues: first, the theological virtues (faith, hope, and love); second, the cardinal virtues (prudence, justice, courage, and temperance). In this way, Thomas succeeds in emphasizing the relevance of grace to man's moral and civil life, but at the cost of making the work of Christ seem almost an afterthought. Luther's concern to link justification directly to the work of Christ arose out of a desire to avoid the latter consequence, although some might charge that he lost precisely the advantage that Thomas gains.

In his treatment of the person and work of Christ, Thomas follows the general path outlined by St. Anselm of Canterbury (c.1033-1109) in his book, *Cur Deus homo* (*Why God Became Man*); but, where Anselm had sought to demonstrate the necessity of God's Incarnation and passion, Thomas is content to show that the plan which God adopted is in accord with the divine nature and the way most suitable to our human situation. Prominent among the reasons he brings forward is that the infinite majesty of Christ's divine person and the sinlessness of His humanity makes His death especially appropriate as a recompense for our guilt. Other reasons emphasize the utility to man, limited as he is to sensible evidences, of having the Word of God made flesh for strengthening his faith and instructing him in virtue. Thomas is careful to explain that the coming of the Son and of the Holy Spirit into the world for man's salvation does not introduce mutability into the Eternal Godhead, since, like creation, Christ's presence is simply a manifestation in the world of divine wisdom and power. Thus, the union of a human nature to the person of the eternal Son does not alter the divine nature; but within the universe it makes every difference that the Son of Mary is effectively the Second Person of the Godhead. So with the Holy Spirit, who takes men's hearts for His temple: the power of God's Spirit works in a new way in the elect, restoring and enabling their wills; yet He does so without Himself undergoing any change.

In his doctrine of the sacraments Thomas stresses the point that the sacraments do not merely signify holy things; they are also instruments by which the benefits of Christ's passion are made effective in the lives of men for their sanctification unto eternal life. That divine grace should be ministered through corporeal signs is especially suitable because, as we have seen, man's thought and activity are by nature geared to sensible objects, but especially because, in his fallen condition, man is abnormally under the domination of material things. Thomas holds that the effective power of grace is contained in the sacraments themselves, if they are performed according to the intention of the Church; grace does not depend either upon the mind of the priest or upon the intention of the recipient, notably in the case of infant baptism; but mature persons of sound mind must will to receive the grace of Christ if the sacrament is to be effective in them.

Thomas's achievement is significant in that it effected synthesis of the Christian doctrine of salvation with a world view which owes its origins to non-Christian thinkers. The legitimacy of this kind of undertaking has been questioned repeatedly in the history of the Church. Is there any continuity between Christ and the world? Thomas, as we have seen, gives the affirmative answer. Christianity is continuous with creation; revelation is a supplement to reason; redemption is a moment in the universal drama; Christ is the center of world history; and the Church is not so much a challenge to civilization as its complement. Thomas is favorably disposed toward civilization wherever he finds it. The ancient Greeks and Romans, with no other resources at their disposal than those which make up man's natural endowment, rose to admirable heights. So did the Jews and the Arabs, with their partial and marred revelation. But, if non-Christians have achieved so much in science, art, law, and philosophy, how much more ought Christians to achieve under the economy of grace! There can, and should, be a Christian philosophy, a Christian art, a Christian morality, all built upon broadly human foundations, but corrected at some points and extended at others in virtue of the supernatural light of revelation.

SERMONS AND TREATISES

Author: Johannes Eckhart (c.1260-c.1327)
Type of work: Mystical theology
First transcribed: c.1300-1327

Principal Ideas Advanced

Union with God, interpreted at times as intimate communion of two selves, but more often as complete ontological fusion of being, is asserted as the highest goal of man's life.

The path to God, beginning with a movement from the external to the inner world, and ascending by degrees to its goal of union, is proclaimed.

The eternal birth, or birth of God, or God's Son in the soul, which is the goal of life, produces as by-products many good works as well as a new and altogether affirmative sense of human worth or dignity.

Despite the acknowledged significance of Meister Eckhart's writings, questions and disagreements hamper our study of him and his work. For this, Eckhart himself is in part responsible, for he regarded himself as a popular teacher and preacher rather than a writer. Thus, the *Treatises,* which include *Talks of Instruction, The Aristocrat,* and his *Defense,* appear to have been addressed to specific situations which have long since perished. His powerful and popular sermons may well have been delivered from notes rather than manuscript, thus raising unanswerable questions as to what he actually said and how much of the writing attributed to him is actually his.

A few facts concerning his life have been established. Johannes Eckhart was born at Hochheim near Gotha about 1260, the son of a steward in a noble's castle. As a youth he entered the Dominican Order and attended school at Cologne. He was made prior of his order at Erfurt, and then provincial vicar of his order in Thuringia. The *Talks of Instruction* appear to come from this early period. He seems also to have studied and preached at the College of Paris around the year 1300. Returning to Germany, he rose to higher posts in the Dominican Or-

der. He was in Paris again from 1311 to 1314. Returning home, he gained a wide reputation as a popular preacher and teacher, first in Strasburg and then in Cologne. His sermons seem to come from this period of his life.

From 1321 to his death he was embroiled in charges of heresy. Popular mystical movements were spreading in Germany at this time, to the great distaste of Heinrich von Virneberg, archbishop of Cologne. In 1325 a charge of heresy was made against Eckhart, but he was formally cleared, perhaps because the investigator was also a Dominican. However, the archbishop, who was a Franciscan, persisted, and a second examination of his writings was made by two Franciscans who emerged with a formidable list of errors. Eckhart responded with his *Defense,* stating poignantly, "I am able to err, but I cannot be a heretic, since one has to do with the intellect and the other with the will." He was summoned to answer charges at the archbishop's court in Cologne early in 1327. Shortly afterward, an appeal to Rome was denied. He seems to have died soon thereafter. A papal bull of 1329 specifically refers to him as dead.

It is easy to classify Eckhart as a mystic, but less easy to give a precise and significant meaning to the term as here used. Indeed, the word *mysticism* is notorious for its elasticity of usage. The broadest reference is to religious or quasi-religious phenomena in which immediacy of knowledge is emphasized. The term *intuition* is often applied to such processes of immediate awareness or knowledge.

Other interpretations of mysticism add to this minimum definition one or more of the ideas which cluster about the term, such as the unity of man with God, experiences of ecstasy or rapture, the ascent of the soul to God, the absolute oneness of God, the idea of God as absolute or self-subsistent being, and the idea of emanation. These ideas also tend to group themselves in a historic tradition, which in the West includes such figures as Plato, Plotinus, Dionysius the Areopagite, and Scotus Erigena. Eckhart's writings show familiarity with many of these ideas, figures, and influences. It is also important to remind oneself that the whole ethos of medieval Christian thought and life was mystical in the primary sense noted above; Eckhart, like any man, was a child of his age.

Yet upon his influences Meister Eckhart placed the stamp of his own strong and intense personality and mind. His mysticism was the result of his own highly individual and deeply subjective religious life. Thus it is that as a result of Eckhart's influence, mysticism in the West has come to mean a form of inner individual experience that not only resists any logical or rational demonstration but also withstands or opposes it. Eckhart's mysticism was Eckhart's own intense, personal, and self-justifying religious vision.

It is for this reason that without seeming to renounce either one, Eckhart's mysticism moves beyond both traditional Christian religion and traditional Western philosophy. He used the terminology of traditional Christianity, and there is no reason to question his sincerity. Eckhart lived and died believing himself to be a loyal Catholic Christian. Yet upon closer inspection almost all the old traditional words received at his hands a new and altered meaning. Sometimes the altered meanings are not far from the old, but at other times, incompatibilities arise.

A similar point may be urged for Eckhart's relation to philosophic tradition. He frequently alluded to Plato and Aristotle, and he used what superficially appears to be a traditional terminology. Upon closer scrutiny, however, some or all of these terms are altered to serve as the vehicles of Eckhart's own unique intuition and message.

Whether one begins his journey into mystical theology by studying self or God does not matter, Eckhart tells us, for man and God are ultimately aspects of a single seamless unity.

It is important to point out that Eckhart nowhere taught a simple equation between deity and any actual or empirical human soul, or indeed between deity and all human souls or all being. For Eckhart there is, to be sure, from the beginning "a blood relationship" between man and God; we are His children, and it is our proper destiny to realize or fulfill this relation. In another metaphor, according to Eckhart's teaching, man rises by degrees to a relation sometimes characterized as intimate communion with God, but more often described as one in which all distinctions are left behind in the fullness of ontological union.

The beginning of this path to God

consists in coming to realize the clear and sharp difference between inner and outer world. Man must leave the world of things and creatures behind and enter the inner castle of the soul. He must, as Eckhart wrote, get beyond time and space. Just as inwardness is good, so conversely, concern with externalities or creatures is evil or sinful.

In many ways Eckhart's inwardness recalls that of Augustine and other previous mystics. Yet Eckhart lacks the guidance which Augustine received from Christian orthodoxy. Where Augustine in the inner recesses of his soul heard God speaking to him in Christian or Biblical tones, Eckhart found a darkness (or, paradoxically, he sometimes says a light) in which all distinctions are lost in total unity. So it is that Eckhart, along with many mystics before and since, identified God with this inward reality.

To achieve this inwardness man must have a pure heart, the complete absence of ulterior motivation. One must want God solely for God's sake, and not for any ulterior reason. The self or mind so conceived is asserted to be free. Indeed, by freedom of mind or self Eckhart meant precisely the capacity to shake oneself free of all attachment to finite things. Such a process is alternatively characterized as disinterestedness, as a losing of the self, and as a reducing of the self to nothingness. For Eckhart the virtue of humility, frequently recommended to his hearers, carried a similar meaning. Preaching from Biblical texts which command man to conform his will to the divine will, Meister Eckhart bade his hearers to lose themselves by getting beyond all finite things whatsoever. Perfection he defined not as per-

fect conformity to the will of God, but as emancipation from all finitude.

As a further step along this path, Eckhart called his followers to transcend the inner divisions or agents of the soul, thus realizing the soul's inner unity. The soul, he said quoting Aristotle, is "between one and two." By this course of introspection he sought to make it one. So it is that the mind or soul, emptied of detailed contents, achieves an inward autonomy which Eckhart never tired of calling the state of the spiritual aristocrat. It is a state of contemplative bliss beyond all motion and desire. In company with mystics of all times and places, Eckhart made it clear that this state must be directly experienced to be known. It grew directly out of his own experience, and the goal of the *Sermons* is to communicate it to his hearers. In this connection, it must be noted that there is in Eckhart not a trace of bizarre and aberrant emotionalism, which has been mysticism's frequent accompaniment.

The path of the soul to God has necessarily been intimated in this sketch of the soul's nature. While he spoke in detail of this path, or this relation, Eckhart had no unified or systematic formulation; he used, rather, a variety of metaphorical suggestions. His writings have at least one reference to six stages of ascent of the soul to God, by analogy with the growth of the human soul from infancy through childhood to a maturity in which he is at peace with himself and the world, and thence onward to a final and sixth stage in which he is transformed "in the divine eternal nature, having full perfection." He spoke analogously of three kinds of knowledge, sensual, intellectual, and aristocratic or mystical, in which "the soul communes with God face to face as he is." The intellect is described as that which in unity and vision sees "beyond the idea of God and truth until it reaches the *in principio*, the beginning of beginning, the origin or source of all goodness and truth."

By far the most frequent metaphor of Eckhart for the relation of the soul to God is that of birth—the eternal birth, the birth of God, or the Son in the soul. His exposition of the birth of the Son in the soul is an excellent illustration of Eckhart's interpretation of Biblical texts to fit his own meaning. In a Christmas sermon on the text, "Where is he that is born King of the Jews?" he asked where this birth takes place, and he responded that it takes place eternally in the essence or core of the soul. This process of eternal birth in the soul may be described as the emergence in the human mind of that awareness so greatly prized by mystics of all times and places, of unity with God. As already noted, this was sometimes interpreted by Eckhart as intimate communion, but more often, as complete ontological fusion.

To facilitate this consummation, the soul must be humble and passive to God. It must cultivate the ignorance which is beyond knowledge. It must cultivate forgetting, self-losing, and contemplating "the stillness."

Another recurring metaphor for the relation of God to man is Eckhart's repeated assertion that God pours His grace, indeed, that He pours Himself into the soul. In fact, Eckhart goes further, asserting that "God must give himself," that this pouring occurs necessarily. Such assertions make clear the similarity of Eckhart's thought to that of Plotinus, with its idea of emanation. Like Plotinus and Plato, Eckhart uses the metaphor of light. He speaks of the sparks of God in the soul, of grace coming from God to man like the light emanating from the sun. The culminating mystical experience is also characterized as an experience of illumination and light. By these and other metaphors, Eckhart's sermons called man to the high destiny of unity with God. Repeating, but reformulating, a familiar Christian quotation, Eckhart asked, "Why did God become man? So that I might be born to be God. Yes— identically God."

Nowhere is Eckhart's ambivalent relation to the Christian tradition more apparent than in his view of the God who is the object of man's search. "God," said Meister Eckhart, "is being" —an assertion traditional enough in both Christianity and philosophy, but luxuriant in its variety of meaning. Had not Plato and Plotinus declared deity to be self-subsistent reality? Indeed, had not the Lord in Exodus replied to Moses' question regarding His name with the revealing words "I am that I am," and had not Aquinas just a generation before Eckhart brought these two meanings together in his great synthesis? So it was that Christianity asserted that God possesses in Himself the fullness and perfection of being which men as mortal creatures have only partially and unperfectly.

If it be asked how Eckhart's interpretation of absolute or supreme being departs from traditional interpretations, the answer lies in his view of the nature of Absolute Being and of the relation of this being to human or finite reality. The deity of Christianity is a personal God, while that of Meister Eckhart is an impersonal absolute unity which transcends all relations. As he specifically asserted in the title of one sermon, "Distinctions are lost in God." This distinctionless deity was apparently what Eckhart had in mind in his repeated distinction between God and Godhead. In other sermons he spoke of going beyond God to God, or beyond God to Unity. Truly, God is for Eckhart a fullness of being which surpasses our human comprehension. He, or rather It, is like a blinding or dazzling light in whose brightness all human distinctions are lost.

Eckhart's view of deity, while basically impersonal, is nonetheless affirmative in tone. As to its impersonality, in contrast to the view of man's conforming his will to God, Eckhart's view is one of impersonal contemplation of absolute reality. While there are some negative aspects of this vision, its dominant tone is affirmative. Eckhart spoke of God as darkness as well as light, sometimes of both as paradoxically juxtaposed. He repeatedly recommended humility and self-negation, and he charged his hearers to transcend the world of things. Yet on balance his vision is overwhelmingly affirmative in character. There is relatively little asceticism and no outright negation of the world's reality and significance. In style and temper Eckhart was more yea-saying than nay-saying. In contrast to the negative character of much mysticism, this affirmative temper of Eckhart's vision must be judged as, in part

at least, the result of his own personality.

The practical fruits of Eckhart's view are similarly affirmative. While the goal of mystical unity is beyond all action, there are many clearly moral phases in this road to perfection. Eckhart is hostile only to those works which are prompted by ulterior motives or which beget self-righteousness. Indeed, it is justifiable to put aside contemplation in order to give food to a sick man. The spirit of Eckhart's thought is clearly one of respect for, and affirmation of, human personality.

In the case of the professional religious life, while he points out that no set of works is a sufficient or valid guarantee of perfection, he is actively hostile only to works of hypocrisy. The religious life is, again, part of the road to perfection. Here, as in the case of morality, one must keep the contemplative and active life in balance as one seeks the goal beyond. It was a bold new path that Eckhart blazed and walked. It was the result, as we have argued, of his own intense and individual subjectivity. Its impact was to be felt for centuries in the new emphasis on individualism and subjectivity. In this respect Eckhart is often spoken of as a precursor of modern times. His "God is Being" recurs from Spinoza to Hegel and Tillich. His mysticism of individual subjectivity has been a lure and a threat to religious thought ever since his time.

ORDINATIO:
OXFORD COMMENTARY ON THE SENTENCES OF PETER LOMBARD

Author: Johannes Duns Scotus (c.1264-1308)
Type of work: Religious metaphysics
First transcribed: c.1302-1304

PRINCIPAL IDEAS ADVANCED

The human intellect can know God through natural reason, for knowledge of the infinite need not itself be infinite.

Since God is the first cause, the final end, and the supreme nature, He is infinite and He necessarily exists.

There is but one God, for no two Gods could both be infinitely knowing, infinitely good, and infinitely powerful.

The human intellect can know some certain truths without any special illumination.

The belief in a general resurrection of mankind cannot be demonstrated by reason; such a belief rests on faith alone.

Duns Scotus's *Ordinatio* is described by Allan Wolter, editor and translator of Scotus's *Philosophical Writings* (1962), as the subtle doctor's "most important work. . . ." The *Tract Concerning the First Principle* (*Tractatus de primo principio*), which is regarded by many scholars as Scotus's most effective statement of his natural theology, is said by Wolter to have been derived from the *Ordinatio*. The alternative title, *Oxford Commentary on the Sentences of Peter Lombard*, is perhaps the more familiar title. Wolter's edition is particularly interesting in that it contains both the original Latin and the translated passages, and it extracts from the monumental *Ordinatio* those questions concerning the nature and existence of God and the immortality of the human soul which are most likely to be of concern to Christian scholars who are interested in the development of Christian theology.

The *Ordinatio* is a final draft, checked by Scotus, of a report of Scotus's lectures at Oxford (c.1302-1304) in commentary on the *Sentences* of Peter Lombard (c.1100-1160). The work is devoted primarily to the exposition of Scotus's own views concerning the nature and existence of God.

Duns Scotus was a theologian in the Franciscan tradition; he was renowned for the extreme subtlety of his thought; hence, the descriptive name, "Doctor Subtilis." In his philosophical thinking Scotus drew heavily from the views of Aristotle and Augustine (354-430), and he placed himself in opposition to many of the ideas presented by Thomas Aquinas (1225-1274). Aquinas placed almost complete reliance on reason in his effort to know God, but Scotus argued that love and the will are more important than reason both in understanding God and in relating the soul to the divine. Scotus is important for his brilliant and early defense of the doctrine of the Immaculate Conception, the doctrine that Mary was without original sin. He is noted also for his view that God did not need to assume human form in order to save man after the Fall; according to Scotus, the Incarnation was not forced upon God, for God is eternally free.

Scotus describes metaphysics as "the transcending science," as that study which goes "beyond" (from *meta*) the "science of nature" (*physica*). Since questions concerning the existence and nature of God are questions which demand inquiry beyond the natural realm, the study of God (theology) is necessarily metaphysical. Of all the transcendental attributes or predicates, none is more fundamental or common than "being." Being is the "first object of the intellect," writes Scotus, because it has both primacy of commonness and primacy of virtuality; that is, everything either has being or belongs to that which has being.

Like Aquinas, Duns Scotus presented his theological findings in question and answer form. The present edition of the *Ordinatio* follows Scotus's discussion of metaphysics with the theologian's discussion of the question *"whether the intellect of man in this life is able to know God naturally."* Scotus then presents arguments advanced by Aristotle to the effect that since God is not a sense object and since He is infinite, He cannot be known, and Scotus also refers to Gregory's opinion that the mind must contemplate only what is beneath God.

Introducing his argument in opposition to these claims, Scotus argues that since even negative conceptions (that is, conceptions as to what God is *not*) are meaningful only if they ad-

mit of rephrasing as positive ideas, a positive conception of God is possible if any conception is possible. The question to be considered is rephrased as follows: "Is it possible by natural means for man's intellect in the present life to have a simple concept in which concept God is grasped?"

After referring to the opinion of Henry of Ghent (d. 1293), Scotus presents his positive argument. In opposition to Henry's view that God cannot be known "through something incidental to Him," Scotus argues that any knowledge of God which is possible through consideration of some attribute must finally end with a "quidditative notion of God"; that is, with a notion of *what* it is that exhibits the attribute. In opposition to Henry's opinion that God is known in a general way only by analogy, Scotus maintains that God can also be conceived "in some concept univocal to Himself and to a creature."

Scotus then considers Henry's arguments in support of the conclusion that God can be known in a *most* general way, a *less* general way, and the *least* general way. These ideas are rejected, and Scotus argues that God is not known in His essence, that God can be known by concepts which apply to Him and not to creatures, and that God is known through intelligible species.

Returning to the claims made by Aristotle and Gregory, Scotus argues that the intellect can abstract from sense experience and in that way transcend such experience, that knowledge of the infinite need not itself be infinite, and (in opposition to Gregory) that knowledge of what is beneath God may be useful, not as a terminal object, but as suggesting some intelligible feature of the divine.

Scotus next considers the question, "Among beings does one exist which is actually infinite?" Various arguments are cited which have in common the claim that the supposition of an infinite being is either self-contradictory or incompatible with the existence of finite beings. Scotus's counter argument proceeds from a demonstration of the existence of such relative properties as primacy and causality to the conclusion that an infinite being exists since the relative properties in question can belong only to an infinite being.

The first of Scotus's conclusions in regard to the triple primacy of God is that "Among beings which can produce an effect one is simply first. . . ." Such a being cannot itself be caused, he then argues, but if such a being is not caused, it must exist "of itself." Three similar points are made in regard to the final cause, the ultimate end. Finally, the primacy of pre-eminence is established by the following three points: ". . . some eminent nature is simply first in perfection. . . ."; ". . . the supreme nature cannot be caused"; ". . . the supreme nature actually exists." God as the first cause, final end, and supreme nature possesses a triple primacy; such a being necessarily exists, concludes Scotus, because nothing incompatible with its existence can exist.

Scotus then argues from the relative properties of God to His absolute properties. If God is the first cause, the final end, and the supreme nature, He must be intelligent, endowed with will, and possessed of a knowledge of all things. A being capable of infinite causality, making reference to infinite knowledge, and unlimited in intelligence must be an infinite being. But it has already been established that a being which possesses triple primacy necessarily exists; therefore, God, as that being which has triple primacy and is infinite, necessarily exists.

Scotus then writes, "I ask whether there is but one God?" He considers a number of minor arguments advanced in support of the claim that there is more than one god, and he refers to the view that the unicity of God is to be accepted only on faith. In opposition to those who deny God's unicity (His status as the sole God), Scotus offers seven proofs, based on natural reason, of God's unicity. The proofs are based on the attribution to God of infinite intellect, infinite will, infinite goodness, infinite power, absolute infinity, necessity of existence, and omnipotence. A summary of Scotus's argument based on God's infinite intellect will indicate the subtlety of Scotus's thought: If there were two Gods, A and B, then A, as possessed of an infinite intellect, would know B perfectly. But if A does not know B's essence, A does not know B perfectly. And if A knows B's essence, the knowledge is posterior to B's essence; as posterior, A's knowledge could not be God's knowledge. Therefore, there cannot be two Gods.

Scotus asks whether the human intellect without "the special illumination of the uncreated Light" can know any "certain and unadulterated truth." Quotations from Augustine support the negative view, but Scotus argues for the positive answer by critical opposition to an opinion advanced by Henry of Ghent. Scotus claims that Henry's opinions lead to skepticism, and he rejects Henry's three points, which follow: (1) Infallible and certain knowledge cannot be abstracted from the mutable; (2) The soul, which is itself changeable, cannot be corrected by the mutable; (3) There is no way of distinguishing the true from what appears to be true. Scotus's corresponding rejoinders are as follows: (1) Not all sensible things are constantly in motion, and in any case it is possible to know immutable natures by contemplation of mutable things; (2) Although the soul is changeable in that it can move from error to truth, it need not, when in error, be corrected from the outside; the soul has the power of self-correction, particularly when it is dealing with logical matters; (3) Although the imagination may be unable, in dreams, to distinguish the true from what appears to be true, the intellect, which uses intellectual entities and not sense images, cannot suffer from this difficulty.

The question concerning the possibility of certain knowledge is answered in the affirmative by reference to the intelligible which reflects the divine intellect. Special illumination is not needed since the ideas themselves, as influenced by the divine intellect, provide assurance to the intellect of man.

The final question given in Wolter's selection from the *Ordinatio* is as follows: *"Can it be known by natural reason that there will be a general resurrection of mankind?"* Scotus, whose ability to generate rational arguments is clearly shown throughout the *Ordinatio,* reveals his intellectual honesty as he uses rational proofs in support of the conclusion that natural reason alone *cannot* support the belief in a general resurrection. He considers both *a priori* and *a posteriori* arguments for general resurrection, but he concludes that no proof is entirely satisfactory.

Scotus's discussion and rejection of *a priori* proofs begins with the Aristotelian point that the intellective soul is essential to man. It is then argued that the intellective soul is immortal, but although Scotus supposes that there is some reason for believing the soul to be immortal, he concludes that there is no way of demonstrating the truth of the immortality of the soul. Arguments advanced by Aristotle are carefully appraised, but Scotus finds them to be inadequate. The third proposition on which *a priori* proofs are built is the proposition that "the human soul will not remain outside the body forever." In criticizing this proposition, Scotus suggests that if the soul is immortal and immaterial, it is more likely that it remain outside the body than that it will rejoin the body.

Scotus notes that the desire for resurrection is a natural desire, but he does not agree with those philosophers who maintain that "A natural desire cannot be in vain" (Averroës, *Metaphysica*). He also considers the *a posteriori* argument that if virtue is to be rewarded, men must be resurrected; but he finds no natural reason for supposing that there is a ruler who works to achieve a balance of rewards and punishments. He gently suggests that "the good act is itself sufficient reward for anyone," and he quotes with approval Augustine's remark (in the *Confessions*) to the effect that inordinate desire brings its own punishment.

Scotus concludes that the belief in resurrection must be maintained by faith alone, and he refers to the view presented by Augustine (in *De trinitate*) that the belief in the immortality of the human soul is maintained not by reason but by Christ's injunction, "Do not be afraid of those who kill the body but cannot kill the soul."

Thanks is given to God for faith which "has made us most certain of those things which pertain to our end and to eternal life. . . ." With refreshing and elevating candor Scotus, the subtle doctor, concedes that there are divine truths which escape the natural reason of man. The faithful spirit of the Franciscan expresses itself in the midst of some of the most ingenious exercises of the intellect to be found in the writings of the medieval theologians.

DE MONARCHIA

Author: Dante Alighieri (1265-1321)
Type of work: Christian political philosophy
First transcribed: c.1313

PRINCIPAL IDEAS ADVANCED

The well-being of the world necessitates that mankind be ruled by a common government headed by a single Prince who is best able to actualize the whole capacity of the intellect, promote universal peace and freedom, establish justice, and rule mankind in a manner patterned after God's rule of the Universe.

The office of monarchy has rightfully been appropriated by the Roman people, for they are the most noble, were aided by miracles, were victorious over all contestants, and exercised jurisdiction over all humanity in pronouncing judgment upon Christ.

The Roman Monarch derives his power directly from God and not from the successor of Peter, the keeper of the keys of the Kingdom of Heaven.

Dante Alighieri, frequently referred to as the spokesman of the Middle Ages, exerted his influence upon the religious, philosophical, and political spheres of Western society. The emphasis of the *De monarchia* is political, but its effect upon subsequent questions of the relationship between the Church and state are indeed difficult to estimate.

The *De monarchia* is divided into three books. The first considers whether temporal monarchy is necessary for the well-being of the world; the second, whether the Romans rightfully appropriated the office of monarchy; and the third, whether the authority of the Roman monarch derives immediately from God or from some vicar of God.

In writing the *De monarchia* Dante was motivated by a love of truth and a love of his fellow-men, not by any cynical desire for personal power. By temporal monarchy, the Empire, Dante understood a single principality which extends over all peoples and has authority in all temporal matters. His work is an expression of his concern over the pretenses and failures of the

Papacy, and the book reflects the dying phases of the contest between the Roman Empire and the Papacy.

The purpose of the universal monarchy is not to promote the self-interest of the ruler, writes Dante, but to secure the well-being of those who are ruled. God makes nothing without a purpose, so that human society as a whole has an end, conformable to the proper function of the human race as a whole; namely, to actualize continually the entire capacity of the intellect, primarily in speculation, but secondarily in action. The human race can accomplish its work most freely and readily when it enjoys the calm and tranquillity of peace, for then the individual can grow perfect in wisdom and knowledge, and what modifies the individual affects humanity as a whole. The beatitude of humanity is best attained where universal peace prevails, for then the human race may fulfill its proper office.

The necessity of temporal monarchy, writes Dante, can be gainsaid by no force of reason or authority; on the contrary, it can be proven by the most powerful arguments. For when several things are ordained for one end, one must regulate or rule and the others submit to such regulation. The happiness of the individual depends upon the rule of the intellect over his other faculties, and the tranquillity of a city depends upon the direction and government of a king, but the well-being of the world requires a universal monarchy or Empire. Since the whole human race is ordered for one end, it is fitting that the leader be one, and that he be called Emperor or Monarch.

The order which is found in the parts of the human race should also be found in the human race as a whole. The individual, the family, the village, and the city are included in kingdoms, and the latter should be ordered to one Prince or Principality, to one Monarch or Monarchy.

With relation to certain parts, mankind is a whole, but with relation to a certain whole, mankind is a part; that is, in relation to particular kingdoms and nations, mankind is a whole, but in relation to the universe, mankind is a part. The several parts of humanity can correspond to the whole of humanity through the one principle only, that of submission to a single Prince. Humanity can correspond to the universe, or to its Prince, who is God, through one principle only, the submission to a single Monarch. Monarchy is necessary to the well-being of the world because the relation of kingdoms and nations to the Monarch should be patterned after the relation between humanity and God. Men are made in God's image, and God is one. God intends that everything should represent the divine likeness insofar as this is possible. Since God is a unity, writes Dante, the human race should dwell in unity, and this it does when it is subject to a single Prince, whose rule is, therefore, most in accordance with the divine intention and constitutes the best disposition of mankind. As the sons of Heaven, men ought to follow in the footprints of Heaven. The entire universe is controlled by a single mover, God; thus, the human race is best ordered when its movements are controlled by a single Prince.

A supreme judge is necessary to settle disputes, Dante adds. When strife is a possibility, there must be judgment, or imperfection could then exist without a perfecting agent. If a single Prince were not present, disputes between rulers would be interminable. The rule of the Prince is, however, not to be thought of as that of an arbitrary dictatorship. The world is ordered best when justice is pre-eminent in it. The Monarch is the person in whom justice dwells to the highest degree. The Monarch is to be free of avarice and to be filled with the love which, scorning all else, seeks God and the good of man. Love makes justice thrive. The Monarch is the universal cause of peace and well-being, and the good of men is to be loved by him above all others.

The human race is best ordered when it is most free, Dante claims; freedom is the greatest gift that God has given to men, and it is under a monarchy, not a democracy, oligarchy, or tyranny that man is most free. The aim of an upright government is liberty, that men may live for themselves, not for the sake of the ruler; the Monarch is the chief servant of all. His laws are not ordered for his own sake, but rather for the sake of the ruled. As the person best adapted for ruling, the Monarch is the best director of other man, for he is to possess the highest degree of judgment and justice and is, therefore, perfectly qualified, or especially well qualified, to rule.

What a single agent can do is better done by one than by many, Dante insists. Every superfluity is displeasing to God. Minor decisions concerning individual cities are not to issue from the Monarch directly, for the Monarch is to concern himself with general matters pertaining to all peoples, so that they may be guided to peace by a common government. That Monarchy is essential for the best disposition of mankind and for the well-being of the world is further evidenced by the fact that Christ Himself willed to be born in the fullness of time when Augustus was Monarch, during a period of unity.

The people of Rome have appropriated the office of Monarchy by right, Dante claims; since their rule is in accordance with the will of God, their rule is to be accepted. The rule of the Roman people, who have taken to themselves the office of Monarchy, is not by usurpation but by right, since the Romans are the noblest of men and thus deserve precedence before all others. The Roman Empire was aided by miracles, Dante points out, and thus it must have been favored by God. In subduing the world, the Roman people had the good of the state in view. Nature has set the Roman people apart in the world and has endowed them with the qualities suitable for universal sovereignty. God has decreed that the Empire belongs to the Romans, as is evident from their being victorious over all other contestants, whether nations or individuals. And, finally, the fact that Christ was born when He was, and that He died under Roman jurisdiction, offers conclusive evidence that the authority of the Roman Empire is just and extends over all humanity. For, if the Roman Empire did not exist by right, the sin of Adam was not punished, Christ did not suffer under a lawful judge, and His penalty was not punishment—consequences which are all obviously false.

The sole question that remains for Dante is to determine whether the authority of the Roman Monarch is derived from that of the Vicar of God, from the Church, or whether it proceeds directly from God. His answer is of consequence for subsequent developments in the relationship between Church and state.

The principle to be kept in mind in deciding this issue, writes Dante, is that God does not will what is counter to the intention of nature. The traditions of the Church, the papal decrees or Decretals, are unquestionably inferior to the Scriptures. Temporal power does not receive its existence, strength, or function from spiritual power. The latter does provide the grace which enables the temporal power to fulfill her function more perfectly. Since no vicar divine or human can be co-ordinate with the authority of God, the successor of Peter is in no way coequal with divine power, at least not in the operation of nature.

From the fact that Peter had the power to bind and to loose spiritual things, it does not follow that he has the power to bind and to loose the laws and decrees of the Empire, Dante claims. Those things that belong to the Church no one can rightly possess, unless granted them by the Church. However, the ruling temporal power does not belong to the Church. The Church has its own foundation, and the Empire has its own foundation. Christ is the foundation of the former, but human right is the foundation of the Empire. The Empire consists in the indivisibility of universal Monarchy; to apportion it would be to destroy it, and to destroy the Empire is contrary to human right. The Emperor cannot rightfully relinquish temporal jurisdiction.

Dante insists that imperial authority is not derived from ecclesiastical authority, although certain pontiffs, priests, and others, moved by their zeal for Mother Church, erroneously hold to the contrary. The Empire had power before the Church existed, and what was then nonexistent could not have been the source of the Empire's power.

The Church has received its power from God, not from nature. "The usurpation of a right does not make a right." The Church cannot give what it does not possess; what is contrary to the nature of anything cannot be a power of a thing, and the power to confer authority over the kingdom of our mortal life is contrary to the very nature of the Church. The nature of the latter is its informing principle, which is to be found in the life of Christ, comprised in His teaching and deeds. Christ disclaimed before Pilate any power of a ruling king when He said that His Kingdom was not of this world. As an exemplar of the Church, Christ had no temporal charge over His temporal kingdom.

Dante's answer, then, is that the authority of the Empire is directly derived from God who is the immediate source of its power. The Monarch of the world sustains an immediate relationship to God, the Prince of the Universe. For man alone occupies a middle place between the perishable and the imperishable, and as a mean shares the nature of the extremes. Man shares both natures and is ordained to two ends, the one perishable, the other imperishable. The first is concerned with temporal happiness; the second with life everlasting. Man attains his twofold end by diverse means: the one by moral and intellectual virtue; the other by faith, hope, and charity; the one by reason, the other by revelation. In accordance with his twofold end, man requires a twofold directive agent; the Supreme Pontiff to lead him to eternal life by means of revelation, and the Emperor to guide him to temporal happiness by means of philosophic instruction. The Monarch and the Pope are to rule independently under God.

The authority of the Monarch descends without mediation from God, the fountain of universal authority.

Caesar ought to honor Peter, since human happiness is ordered to everlasting happiness, but the Monarch and the Pope have different spheres, and the Monarch has been set over the earthly sphere by God, who is alone the Ruler of all things spiritual and temporal.

THE DIVINE COMEDY

Author: Dante Alighieri (1265-1321)
Type of work: Allegorical poem
First transcribed: c.1320

PRINCIPAL IDEAS ADVANCED

Dante wakes to find himself in a dark wood, where he is confronted by a gay leopard, a savage lion, and a gaunt wolf.

Virgil becomes his guide through Hell; passing through Hell-Gate and the Vestibule (where the uncommitted spirits dwell), Virgil and Dante arrive at Limbo (where the unbaptized and the virtuous pagans wander forever), and then descend to witness the horrors of Hell: the circles of the Incontinent, the circles of the Violent, and the circles of the Deceitful.

In the frigid depths of Hell stands Satan beating his wings and, with his three mouths, devouring Judas, Brutus, and Cassius.

Reversing their direction at Satan's thigh bone (for they are then in the center of the earth), Virgil and Dante begin their ascent to the surface of the world.

Dante travels with Virgil to the top of Mount Purgatory; he then is accompanied by Beatrice through the heavenly spheres, and he finally comes into the presence of God.

Dante's title for his masterpiece was simply *Commedia,* a title chosen to indicate the triumph of God's love throughout the created universe. It was Boccaccio who, some forty years after Dante's death, spoke of the poem as "divine"—an epithet which has seemed so appropriate that it has become part of the title itself.

The poem is an allegory, as Dante himself explained to his patron, Can Grande della Scala. According to Dante, the poem has four levels: the literal, the allegorical, the moral, and the anagogical. Taken as a story, the *Divine Comedy* is an account of an imaginary pilgrimage which Dante made through Hell, up the mountain of Purgatory, and outward through the celestial spheres into the very presence of the Triune God. Taken as an allegory, it portrays the Christian's deliverance from sin and his ultimate beatitude. A scholar of encyclopedic range, the author describes his travels in terms of the best scientific learning of his day, and he enlivens his narrative with a wide range of historical and legendary personages. In effect, he has created a universal drama around the theme of man's Fall and redemption.

As the poem opens, Dante has lost his course and finds himself in a dark wood. The light of God quiets him, but his way is suddenly barred by a gay leopard, a savage lion, and a gaunt wolf (probably the symbols of incontinence, violence, and fraud). From his distress Dante is rescued by the poet Virgil, who explains that he has been sent, through the prayers of Dante's beloved Beatrice, to lead him to the gates of Paradise. Together they descend into the earth's interior, which is hollowed out like a great funnel outlined by concentric circles narrowing as they approach the earth's center. Sins of incontinence are punished in the upper circles, for such sins are regarded as less vicious than sins of violence and fraud. The uppermost circle is Limbo, where the unbaptized and the virtuous pagans reside; they experience no torment other than the sadness that attends a life without the hope of Christ. It is otherwise with the lustful, the gluttonous, the covetous, and the wrathful, who populate the next four circles; they have turned from the good to sell their souls for vanities, and thus they are condemned to be blown by the wind, to wallow in cold mud, and to roll great rocks—in various ways working out their futility and meanness. It is even worse, however, with those who, instead of merely mistaking the good, have turned with violence against it—whether in their own persons, or in the persons of their neighbors, or in the person of God: the murderers, suicides, blasphemers, and perverts. Lower still are those whose wickedness comes from abusing the highest human faculty, the understanding. These are the fraudulent and the malicious, a vast company ranging from seducers and flatterers to false friends and traitors. At the frozen bottom of Hell, visible only from his loins upward, is the monstrous figure of Satan. Dante and his guide have to climb past his shaggy figure in order to travel upwards through the other half of the earth's interior so that they may continue their journey to Purgatory.

As Dante imagines it, Purgatory is a mountain situated on an island in the watery hemisphere opposite to our own. The souls of believers do not ordinarily arrive there by traveling through Hell, but are conveyed across the sea by a heavenly boatman. Dante and Virgil see various groups which have not yet been allowed to pass through St. Peter's gate and to begin their progress up the mountain. They are persons who died in grace, but because of indolence, or neglect, failed in their lifetimes to prepare their souls for death. In fact, the gate is rarely opened, because entrance into Purgatory, as well as progress up the mountain, depends entirely upon the will of man, and perverse loves are hard to overcome.

Dante, upon entering the gate, has seven P's inscribed upon his brow—one for each of the cardinal sins (Latin: *peccata*): pride, envy, wrath, sloth, avarice, gluttony, and lust. The lower stages of the climb are the most difficult; but as he mounts, one after another of the P's is erased, and his feet move with less and less effort. The mountain is, essentially, a school in virtue. At each grade, the scholar is instructed by a series of sculptures which represent the virtue strived for and its opposite vice. For example, the proud are instructed by carvings representing the humble attitudes of the Virgin Mary, of King David, and of Emperor Trajan, and by a corresponding series representing the ruinous pride of Satan, of Saul, and of the general Holofernes. The proud themselves bear heavy stones to correct their postures; they beat themselves, and recite a version of the Lord's Prayer which magnifies the distance between God and His creatures.

Reaching the top of the mountain, Dante must bid farewell to Virgil, who, representing Reason, has brought him as far as he can come. He is welcomed to the Garden of Eden by a pageant of heavenly creatures symbolizing the Old and New Testaments and the theological virtues. There for the first time Dante beholds his beloved, Beatrice, who, as a symbol of Revelation, is to be his guide into the presence of God.

Dante's journey into Heaven begins without his being aware of it. As he and Beatrice mount with the speed of lightning, Beatrice explains to him that the native instinct of the soul draws it straightway to God as soon as every hindrance is removed. Their journey takes them through the ten spheres recognized by Ptolemaic astronomy, each of which represents a grade of spiritual achievement. The spheres this side of the sun's orbit represent respectively the blessedness of those weak in faith, in hope, and in love. The spheres of the sun and of those planets beyond it represent the blessedness of those who excelled in prudence, fortitude, justice, and temperance. Beatrice must explain to Dante that, although the absolute will of each of the Blessed is fixed towards its one true good, the conditioned will may deviate more or less. For example, the will of certain nuns was to keep their vows; but when they were forced to marry, they yielded rather than resist to death. So it happens that souls are unequal in glory, but without any being on this account discontent or desiring a higher place.

Dante visits each sphere in turn, passes through the sphere of the fixed stars, where he discourses with Peter, James, John, and Adam, and through the Primum Mobile, where dwell the angels and archangels. Dante comes at last to the Empyrean, the true Heaven of the Redeemed; and finally, in the company of St. Bernard, who replaces Beatrice as his guide, Dante is brought into the very presence of God and of Christ, where his sight undergoes alteration:

"O splendor of God through which I saw the lofty triumph of the true kingdom, give me power to tell *how* I saw it!

"There is a light up there which makes the Creator visible to that creature who, only in seeing Him, has its peace."

In the depth of the Eternal Light Dante beholds, first of all, the unitary scheme of all creation. Next, "three circles of three colors and of one dimension" appear to him, the second reflecting the first, and the third reflecting the other two. Finally, and most wonderfully of all, within the second circle there seems to be depicted "our image within itself and of its own color." The vision fades; the poet's powers fail:

"As one who in a dream sees clearly,
    and the feeling impressed remains
    afterward, although nothing else
    comes back to mind,

"So am I; for my vision disappears almost wholly, and yet the sweetness caused by it is still distilled within my heart."

Even so bare an outline must suggest how closely Dante's allegory is interwoven with his narrative. This account cannot convey anything of the vividness of hue or richness of texture which Dante's masterly use of concrete images gives to the whole. Dante stands in the tradition of the Hebrew prophets. His vision of the Eternal does not detract from, but rather enhances his perception of things temporal. *The Inferno*, particularly, brings fresh, clear vision to bear upon the weakness, passion, and ignominy of men. We are shown the guilty in all their hatefulness, and are forbidden to sympathize with them as they languish in torment. At the same time, it is impossible for us to be indifferent to their ruin. Dante writes as one who cares.

Personal tragedies bear heavily upon him. For example, Ser Brunetto Latini (d.1294), whom he finds in the circle of the Sodomites, was once his teacher, a gentle and paternal man, who is still interested in Dante's literary progress. Their meeting is tender. Dante acknowledges his eternal gratitude to Brunetto and breathes the wish that he were yet among the living. But inevitably the older man, swept along by the fatality which attends his choice, must be off with his company in torment.

With even livelier interest, Dante follows the affairs of his native Florence, torn in civil strife and betrayed by Papal intrigue. From this center, his thought extends throughout the whole of Italy and of the Empire. He is vexed and saddened at the decay of the Church, and at the growing international anarchy, for which he can see only one remedy—that the Church shall restrict itself to matters spiritual and support the rights of the Emperor in the temporal domain. (See Dante's *De monarchia*.) So deep and abiding are Dante's convictions in these matters that he carries them to the very threshold of Eternity: there in the sphere of the Fixed Stars, Peter denounces the ruling pope, Boniface VIII, in terms which cause Beatrice to blush.

The close connection between the literal and allegorical aspects of the *Divine Comedy* is best understood if we think of the work as a stylized account of the author's own spiritual biography—a kind of confession. The interested reader should refer to Dante's earlier works, *The New Life* (c.1292), and *The Banquet* (c.1307), where he informs us of his youthful aspirations, of certain delinquencies into which he fell, and finally of his recovery through the study of philosophy. Following the conventions of courtly love, Dante makes his Beatrice the symbol of all that is good. Dying while in the bloom of youth, she left him desperate and adrift, until, as he is content to believe, she led him to philosophy in order to save him from perdition. The image of the Dark Woods and of the three beasts is transparently Dante's own condition when, in his middle years (the setting of the poem is 1300, when Dante would have been thirty-five years old), he set his face toward Heaven. Philosophy, in the person of Virgil, can do no more than bring him back to the angel whose gracious presence first lifted his thoughts toward things eternal. She reappears, therefore, as the symbol of revelation, by whom, when his soul has been freed from sin, he is to be led to his spiritual fruition. From the allegorical point of view, the punishments of Hell are a figurative account of the author's (and every Christian's) experience with temptation and sin, as the disciplines of Purgatory are quite explicitly an account of the measures by which the soul works out its salvation. Perhaps, in like manner, we are justified in concluding that the description of the beatific vision of Paradise is an expression of a mystical experience vouchsafed to Dante, comparable to that experienced by St. Paul, of which the Apostle said that he "beheld things not lawful to utter." In any case, the *Divine Comedy* deserves a place in the literature of mysticism, though it belongs to the class which Dean Inge (*Christian Mysticism,* 1899) calls "Nature-Mysticism," rather than to the speculative kind; that is to say, it realizes God in His creation and by means of natural symbolism instead of retreating from sense and imagination into the recesses of the soul.

The theological and philosophical framework of the *Divine Comedy* are adapted by Dante from Thomas Aquinas's great synthesis of Aristotle and Augustine. Thus, Dante cites Aristotle's *Ethics* and *Physics* as his authority for the divisions of Hell. But

Thomas did more than make Aristotle an acceptable authority in the Church. It was he, more than any other, who committed Catholic theology to the distinction between the realms of nature and grace. According to Thomas, the realm of nature, including man, is intelligible to reason without the aid of revelation. Ethics and politics, therefore, do not require special revelation any more than astronomy or medicine. But because God has created in man a capacity for fellowship with himself, supernatural gifts are needed to bring him to perfection. Thus, according to Thomas, nature must be supplemented by grace, and reason by revelation. These are the theological assumptions underlying Dante's poem. Reason is sufficient to lead the soul to the very gates of Paradise, but, in order to find its way to the Empyrean and the objects of its love, it must have revelation as its guide. In like manner, a distinction should be observed between the offices of the Emperor and the Pope. Law and politics have not to borrow wisdom from the Church, to which is committed rather the ministry of supernatural grace.

Modern Protestants, while reading the *Divine Comedy,* cannot forget that they are reading a Catholic work: Thomas's distinction between nature and grace was repudiated by the Reformers, as well as, even more emphatically, the doctrine of Purgatory and of the intercession of the Saints. However, there is in the *Divine Comedy* a complete absence of crude supernaturalism, and no Protestant was ever more outspoken than Dante against the corruptions of the hierarchy. Standing at the threshold of the Italian renaissance, Dante represents the heights of Christian humanism, which, if it had been able to triumph within the Italian Church, might have preserved the unity of Western civilization by averting the Protestant revolt, on the one hand, and the rise of anti-Christian humanism on the other.

THE LITTLE FLOWERS OF SAINT FRANCIS

Author: Unknown
Type of work: Hagiography
First transcribed: In Italian, c.1322 (probably earlier in Latin)

PRINCIPAL IDEAS ADVANCED

Saint Francis and his companions were holy men, practicing the Franciscan virtues of love of poverty, simplicity, humility, charity to the poor, compassion for all sufferers, and joyousness in the Lord—ideas which are illuminated and extolled in this tribute to the founder of the Franciscan Orders.

The Little Flowers of Saint Francis is a collection of anecdotes, mostly very brief, concerning Saint Francis and the first generation of Franciscans. It is not an academic biography of the saint or a history of the early years of the Order which he founded, for there is no historical truth in it. Yet it is unmistakably authentic. The truth it conveys is to be found, not in the events of its narrative, obviously legendary, but in the vivid and convincing impression it gives in its totality of the most Christ-like of saints.

The historical Francesco Bernardone, born in Assisi in 1181 or 1182, was the son of a prosperous merchant. His childhood was uneventful; his education was mediocre, even by twelfth century standards. He idled away his early youth in the company of the *jeunesse dorée* of Assisi, but though pleasure-loving and gay during those years, he was never dissolute, and he was always generous to the poor. When he was about twenty years old he suffered an illness which prevented him from carrying out his intention of becoming a soldier, and which was also the occasion for a change of heart. Thenceforward he led a devout and ascetic life, spending more and more time in solitary prayer, and devoting himself to service of the poor and sick, especially the lepers.

In 1209 he became convinced of his mission to preach, and he began to gather disciples; when their number had grown to twelve, he conducted them to Rome, where he succeeded in obtaining the verbal approval of Pope Innocent III for their way of life. Thus was founded the Order of Friars Minor. They were granted the use of the half-ruined Chapel of Saint Mary of the Angels, called the Portiuncula, on the plain below Assisi. They repaired the chapel and built for themselves shelters of branches; the little Portiuncula with its cluster of huts was to become the headquarters of the Order.

The aim of the friars was to live the

life of Christ as closely as possible, with no rule but the Gospels. In complete poverty and simplicity they went in pairs among the people, preaching, tending the sick, earning a bare subsistence by manual labor or, failing employment, begging their bread. They accepted only enough to satisfy their daily needs; they slept in barns or on the porches of churches; they owned nothing. The zealous preaching of the friars, their sincere humility, and their practical charity brought about a strong religious revival in Umbria. In 1212, Saint Clare, under the direction of Saint Francis, founded the Second Order, for nuns, the Order of Poor Clares.

The Franciscan Order grew with a rapidity which astonished even its founder. As recruits flocked in, many friaries were founded up and down Italy, then throughout Europe. Francis himself traveled to Dalmatia, France, Spain, Egypt, and Palestine. As the foundations multiplied and the number of friars grew to the thousands, the initial simplicity of life, guided by Francis's own counsel and example, had to give way to a more complex organization, similar to that of the other orders. During Francis's stay in Egypt and Palestine, from 1219 to 1220, there began internal struggles in the Order and divisions into parties; the dissensions were to become very grave after Francis's death. He hurried home when the news of the troubles in the Order reached him. At an extraordinary general chapter at the Portiuncula in 1221 he resigned as Minister General, giving as the reason for his resignation that the Order had grown beyond his powers of administration. In that same year he also composed his Rule and founded his Third Order, an order for laymen who wished to practice Franciscan virtues without entering the First Order.

In 1224, Francis underwent an experience which was for him the culmination of his many years of asceticism and contemplative prayer practiced in solitude, and which for his brothers in the Order marked him as a saint even before his death. He went up Mount Alverno with a few companions for forty days of fasting and prayer, terminating on September fourteenth, the Feast of the Holy Cross. On that day Francis had a vision of a Crucified Seraph flying toward him from the rising sun. The vision filled him with rapture, but when it ended he felt sharp pains in his hands, feet, and side; there on his own body he found the marks of the Passion of Christ. Though the stigmata became a constant torment to his body, he accepted them with spiritual joy; in spite of the suffering they caused him, and in spite of nearly total blindness, he continued to work at the revision of his Rule and other provisions for the welfare of his three Orders. He died in the Portiuncula on October 3, 1226. In 1228 he was canonized by Pope Gregory IX.

In the years immediately following the death of Saint Francis, the Friars Minor increased rapidly in numbers and spread all over the world; they entered the universities, where they challenged the supremacy of the Dominicans; they became prosperous and powerful. Meanwhile, the disagreements within the Order, becoming more acute, resulted in the formation of three parties: the Spirituals, who demanded literal observance of the Rule with a return to the way of life of Saint Francis and his first disciples; the party at the other extreme, composed of those who wished to abandon Franciscan poverty and simplicity of life; and the Moderates, who worked for a compromise. The quarrels of the three parties were not pacified until Pope Leo X, in 1517, divided the Franciscans into two branches, completely independent of each other: the Conventuals, allowed to own property as other Orders do; and the Observants, who observe the Rule closely in poverty and all other matters.

I Fioretti di Sancto Francesco is of anonymous authorship and uncertain date; what is evident is that it was written in the Italian of Tuscany of the fourteenth century. Scholars agree that its anecdotes were culled and translated from earlier Latin works. Its immediate source is the *Actus sancti Francisci et sociorum eius,* in turn compiled from earlier sources between 1322 and 1329. The *Fioretti* was compiled by several hands, perhaps in large part by Frate Ugolino di Monte santa Maria; it is possibly original in part. In spite of derivative subject matter and mixed authorship—circumstances usually unfavorable to high literary quality—the *Fioretti* is a minor literary masterpiece by virtue of its sincere simplicity and candor of tone, the winning naïveté of its narrative, its lively style, and the freshness and purity of its language, all of which qualities, except the last, come through translation unimpaired.

Chapters 1 to 38 retell the legends of Saint Francis and his companions; Chapters 39 to 53 recount anecdotes of the friars of the Province of the March of Ancona. Added to the *Fioretti* proper are "Five Considerations on the Stigmata," an account of how the stigmata were imprinted upon Saint Francis, and of their conse-

quences for him and those who came to know about them in spite of his efforts at concealment. This account is followed by a report of the circumstances of the death of the Saint, and a rehearsal of the testimony to the authenticity of the stigmata. Some editions add also "The Lives of Brothers Ginepro and Egidio."

Consideration of the contents makes it clear that the *Fioretti* was composed by members of the Spiritual Party in the Order. The chapters concerning Saint Francis stress his love of poverty, his humility and simplicity, his devoted service to the poor, and his compassion for lepers, whom he tended with his own hands. The particular attention given the friars of the March of Ancona would follow naturally from the fact that the Spirituals were dominant in that Province. Furthermore, there is evidence of hostility—tempered by charity—toward the other parties. In Chapter 38, Saint Francis learns by divine revelation that Brother Elias (who became the head of the party of relaxation) is damned, but in answer to the earnest prayers of the Saint, the sentence of damnation is revoked. In Chapter 48, a friar has a dream in which he sees Brother Bonaventura (Saint Bonaventura, the most distinguished leader of the Moderates) attacking with claw-like nails brother John of Parma (one of the Spirituals); Saint Francis comes to the defense by cutting off the talons.

The chief interest of *The Little Flowers of Saint Francis* for modern readers lies in the inspired selection of anecdotes which show the Saint in his unique moral beauty of character. He is tender without sentimentality, gentle to all—even to his enemies—and strong beneath his gentleness. His humility and self-abnegation are the fruit of constant self-discipline; his love for his fellow men is practical, direct, and down-to-earth. He is always "joyful in the Lord, gay and pleasant," as his Rule enjoins.

The charming legend of his preaching to his "little sisters, the birds" is well known. Just as appealing is the story of the "simple, innocent, chaste" wild doves, captured and taken to market, whom Saint Francis rescues out of pity; in their gratitude they remain with him, domesticated and obedient.

The episode of the taming of the Wolf of Gubbio illustrates the Saint's forbearance toward malefactors and also his practical good sense. He offers the Wolf a reasonable bargain: if "Brother Wolf" will stop attacking the townspeople they, for their part, will feed him daily. Saint Francis gives charity to robbers because sinners are reformed by kindness rather than by rebukes. The personality of the beloved Little Beggar of Assisi stands forth from these pages in all its spiritualized humanity.

DE CORPORE CHRISTI

Author: William of Ockham (c.1300-c.1349)
Type of work: Sacramental theology
First transcribed: c.1324

Principal Ideas Advanced

Truth concerning the sacrament of the altar must be apprehended by faith; that is, by acceptance of the teachings of the Bible and the Roman Church.

The Eucharistic dogma of the Church embraces the doctrines of the real presence, transubstantiation, and the integrity of the body of Christ in every particle of the consecrated element.

The common opinion that the accidents of the bread inhere after consecration in the "quantity" of the bread as in a substance is to be rejected.

William of Ockham's surname comes from his native village in Surrey, England. Many alleged details of his life and writings continue to be doubtful. We are able, however, with considerable assurance to divide his literary career into two great periods. The earlier of these two periods finds Ockham in Oxford. It begins with his commentaries on the four books of Peter Lombard's *Sentences,* and ends with his two treatises on the Eucharist, *De sacramento altaris* and *De corpore*

Christi. Both treatises (which in printed editions have usually been treated as one work) were apparently written shortly before Ockham left for Avignon (probably in the late summer of 1324), where he had been called to defend himself at the court of Pope John XXII (1249-1334) against charges of heresy that had been made against him by a former chancellor of Oxford University, John Lutterell (died 1335).

The *De corpore Christi* constitutes

Ockham's answer to the hostile criticism that he knew had been aroused by certain statements concerning the Eucharist that he had made in his *Sentences* commentary. The answer is two-fold. In the prologue and the first seven chapters he spells out the Church's doctrine of the Eucharist, and he explicitly embraces it as his own. In the remaining chapters (VIII-XLI) he systematically develops his own contribution to the theological understanding of this doctrine, which consists primarily in a detailed philosophical discussion of the notion of quantity in relation to the ecclesiastical doctrine of transubstantiation.

The Eucharist is presented as a memorial of Christ's giving of Himself "on the altar of the cross," and as a daily mystical immolation of Christ in behalf of men, who err daily. Agreeing that it is improper to seek to investigate the "unspeakable loftiness" of this sacrament, Ockham professes his intention to limit his assertions to the positive doctrine of the Roman Church, and he explicitly submits his speculations (made "only for the sake of practice and of inquiring into the truth") to "the correction of all the skilled, orthodox Catholics who are interested." Noting that Pope Innocent IV (Pope, 1243-1254) had excused ignorance even of clearly revealed truth provided that it was accompanied by "implicit faith" in the teachings of the Church, Ockham pleads for similar consideration in the case of one inquiring into areas that are determined neither by Scripture nor by approved doctors.

The Eucharistic doctrine of the Church is presented under three heads: the "real presence" of the body of Christ in the sacrament, the transubstantiation of the bread into the body of Christ, and the integrity of the body of Christ in every particle of the sacrament.

Although the very body that was born of the Virgin, that suffered, died, rose again, and ascended into Heaven, that now is seated at the Father's right hand, and that will come again to judge the living and the dead, is contained under the species of bread, "it certainly is not seen by us with the bodily eye" (as Ockham was to be officially charged with teaching), but is mentally (*mente*) believed to be present by the faithful. The real presence is a truth that cannot be demonstrated by natural reason, but can be known only through faith. But it is clearly taught in Scripture and it is confirmed by "the eminent Doctors, the Holy Fathers, the most illustrious expositors of the divine scriptures" approved by the Roman Church; and Ockham presents several of their statements that have passed into the canon law of the Church.

The doctrine of transubstantiation is not to be found expressly in the Bible; "but this doctrine is believed to have been divinely revealed to the Holy Fathers, or to have been proved from passages of the Bible by a diligent and skillful examination." (This statement marks a modification of Ockham's earlier position that this dogma was not contained in Scripture, and rested solely on a post-Apostolic revelation received by the Church.) Three opinions are traditionally distinguished: (1) that the same substance which initially is bread becomes the flesh of Christ; (2) that the substance of the bread ceases to be, and the body of Christ begins to be, though the accidents (taste, color, weight, for instance) of the bread remain; (3) that the substance of the bread remains, together with the body of Christ, under the species of bread. Ockham says that the second opinion "seems to be the determination of the Roman Church" and its approved doctors. (Actually the more ancient and common opinion is the first, which was also held by Thomas Aquinas, c.1225-1274.) Aquinas held that the third opinion involves a contradiction, while John Duns Scotus (c.1264-1308) and Ockham deny this. Ockham had been attacked by Lutterell for stating that the third opinion would give rise to fewer intellectual difficulties than the second. Here he points out that this was only a hypothetical consideration, not intended to undermine the position of the Church. But he indirectly defends this speculation by saying that the position he shares with Scotus "seems to me more probable and more in accord with theology, because it rather exalts the omnipotence of God. . . ." Transubstantiation, properly speaking, produces only the body of Christ. But in a wider sense it might be said to include Christ's divinity, soul, blood, or corporal accidents, insofar as these are united with His body. (Elsewhere Ockham had labeled Christ's body the *terminus formalis* and the other facets of His personality the *termini per accidens*.)

That the whole body of Christ is present in the whole Host, and in every part of it equally, is proven by patristic authorities, by the consideration of the absolute power of God (which is said to be known frequently to supersede the natural order of things), and by such analogies as the "rational soul" (*anima intellectiva*, which is said to be equally in the whole body and in every part of it) and the presence of an angel (which is said to be a definitive presence in whatever place it happens to be, and in every part of that place).

The problem to which Ockham addresses himself is posed by the apparent conflict of the ecclesiastical dogma of transubstantiation with the Aristotelian science that was generally accepted in his time. According to this science, a thing consists of a substance (an essential nature) and accidents (accidental, or variable, properties) that inhere in the substance. According to the doctrine of transubstantiation, which was made an official dogma at the Fourth Lateran Council (1215), the substance of bread is changed into the body of Christ, while the accidents of the bread remain. The problem is: Wherein do these accidents inhere after consecration? It was universally agreed that they do not inhere in the body of Christ, for that would mean that the identical body of Christ might be moist in one place, dry in another, and mildewy in a third. The common opinion (shared by Thomas Aquinas, the *doctor communis*) was that the accidents now inhere in the "quantity" of the bread; and this "quantity" was defined as an absolute accident concretely (*realiter*) different from the other accidents, and from the substance. Ockham's argumentation is one sustained attack on this opinion.

Ockham describes quantity as extension, circumscriptive presence, involving a quantum, and, following John of Damascus (c.675-c.749, the great systematizer of Eastern Orthodoxy), as "having part separate from part." Quantity is not an absolute term, but a connotative term; that is, it stands, not for some entity "quality," but for some other entity, and indicates that that entity is a quantum. Ockham applies his famous principle of economy, often referred to as "Ockham's razor" (*"frustra fit per plura quod potest fieri per pauciora"*), to cut off "quantity" as a separate entity. Quantity, therefore, is not simply another accident; rather, it may be predicated of accidents. Quantity may also be predicated of substances; thus, the body of Christ is a quantum insofar as it has part separate from part; that is, the eye is not the foot, but separate from it. Now the absolute power of God is able to create causes without their natural effects, natural effects without their proper (secondary) causes, substances without accidents, and accidents that do not inhere in any substance. The absolute power of God is also able to cause to be present definitively (noncircumscriptively, nonquantitatively, not having part separate from part) a substance that is properly a quantum, and that without accidents; this is precisely how the body of Christ is present in the Eucharist as a result of transubstantiation. Now quantity may refer to the subject or to the predicate of a proposition. Subjectively (*a parte subiecti*), Christ's body may be a quantum, and present as such in the Eucharist (*quantitas corporis Christi est in sacramento altaris*). But predicatively (*a parte praedicati*), Christ's body is not quantitatively present in the Eucharist (*haec tamen est falsa, "substantia corporis Christi est in sacramento altaris quantitas"*).

The *De corpore Christi* may well be regarded as one of a long line of medieval attempts to implement the motto of Anselm of Canterbury (c.1033-1109): *Fides quaerens intellectum;* I believe in order to understand. Ockham's starting point is the authoritative doctrine of the Church. As a theologian (and this aspect of Ockham's work has not been accorded proper recognition in the traditional presentation of Ockham), he seeks to incorporate the implications of dogma in the logical framework of systematic thought. That is to say, he tries to enlarge the philosophical horizon by means of the data of revelation; to synthesize, as it were, the realms of nature and super-nature that were sharply distinguished in Thomism. This "synthesis" deprives man of the relative security of a universe functioning largely by means of natural law, which was only occasionally interrupted by miracles. Ockham's universe is moment by moment directly dependent upon the will of God, whose radical freedom poses an ultimate threat to man's existence. Ockham's doctrine of the Eucharist serves as a stark reminder of this wholly nonanalogical relationship between God and man. It magnifies the miraculous character of transubstantiation. For the conclusion of Ockham's argumentation about quantity is that the accidents do not inhere in "quantity," nor in anything else, but remain suspended, sustained only by the naked power of an omnipotent God.

A recent study (Erwin Iserloh, *Gnade und Eucharistie in der philosophischen Theologie des Wilhelm von Ockham,* 1956) has charged Ockham with giving a very limited and one-sided treatment to the Mass, and with divorcing the doctrine of the Eucharist from the experiential realm of personal participation. It may be said in Ockham's defense that he apparently understood his own work as a contribution on a particular point to a traditional Eucharistic doctrine which he accepted. At the same time, it must be conceded that there is little in Ockham's discussion of the Eucharistic mysticism that had transformed the Mass, during the high Middle Ages, from a mere cultic act into a personal religious experience. Ockham deals with certain authoritatively given data, and he approaches them, not from the perspective of his own Christian experience, but from the point of view of Aristotelian science. Ockham recognizes two religious authorities: the Bible and the Church. His whole Eucharistic theology in a sense grows out of the recognition of the Church's ability authoritatively to define dogma.

Ockham's views continued to arouse opposition. John Wycliffe (c.1329-1384) was not the only critic of Ockham. But Ockham's views were increasingly accepted, and when John Huss (c.1369-burned in 1415) was tried for heresy at the Council of Constance (1414-1418), his Ockhamist prosecutors Peter d'Ailly (1350-1420) and John Gerson (1363-1429) indicated that only the Ockhamist theory fully corresponded to the official dogma of the Church.

In the sixteenth century the Catholic position on transubstantiation seems to have been largely understood in Ockham's terms, both by the Protestant Reformers and by Catholic apologists. The authoritarian and logical approach, which seems to have largely dominated the Eucharistic theology of the period between Ockham and the Reformation, may have helped to prepare the way for the large-scale reaction against transubstantiation in the sixteenth century. At the same time, Luther (who was well acquainted with Ockham and with such Ockhamist writers as Peter d'Ailly and Gabriel Biel, c.1420-1495) found in them theoretical support for his doctrines of consubstantiation, the real presence, and the ubiquity of Christ's body.

Ockham's stay in Avignon lasted almost four years. A commission of six (including Lutterell) was appointed to try his case, and reported seven articles (out of fifty-one) explicitly heretical and thirty-seven false. Pope John XXII expressed his agreement with the report but never proceeded to a formal condemnation; nor did any succeeding pope. During this period at Avignon Ockham's fate became closely intertwined with that of Michael of Cesena (died 1342), general of the Franciscan Order, to which Ockham belonged. Cesena was in disfavor with the pope because of differences over "apostolic poverty," which the Franciscan general upheld and the pope condemned. Ockham became involved in the struggle, and in May, 1328, he fled with Cesena from Avignon. Both joined the forces of Emperor Louis the Bavarian (died 1347), whom John had excommunicated. Ockham spent the remainder of his life (1329-1349) in Munich, and he devoted this second period of his literary activity to political writing, treating the respective power of pope and emperor, the position of the pope in the Church, the heresies of Pope John, and other topics of this kind. When Pope Clement VI (1291-1352) laid down terms for the readmission of

Ockham and his party to the favor of the Church, no mention was made of any nonpolitical errors on Ock-

ham's part. Whether Ockham accepted Clement's terms and died officially reconciled to the Church is not known.

THE ADORNMENT OF THE SPIRITUAL MARRIAGE

Author: John of Ruysbroeck (1293-1381)
Type of work: Mystical theology
First transcribed: c.1346

PRINCIPAL IDEAS ADVANCED

God's supreme command to man is the command to "see"; neglect of this command entails eternal perdition.

The purpose of man's life and labors is to meet Christ in love.

The life of God, Trinity in Unity, is an eternally simultaneous movement and rest; man can participate in this life on various levels.

Even at the highest level, where man rests in the Godhead, he is not purely passive, but active in contemplation and fruition.

Man is essentially united to God in that he exists ideally and vitally in God prior to his creation in time; this unity is the first cause, but not the efficient cause, of man's highest beatitude, which consists in his return to this unity through vision and love.

Grace, the moral code, and the authority of the Church and of the Bible are never transcended; they form the foundation of true spirituality.

John of Ruysbroeck takes his surname from his native village, located some three miles southwest of Brussels. At the age of eleven he left home and thereafter lived with his uncle, a canon of the collegiate church of SS. Michael and Gudule. After his own ordination he ministered at the same church for a quarter century. In 1343 he retired with his uncle and another canon to the nearby forest of Soignes, where they founded the priory of Groenendael and accepted the rule of the Augustinian canons. Ruysbroeck's saintliness and wisdom became known far and wide. Groenendael grew and became a center of spiritual life for the

whole lower Rhine region. The great German preacher John Tauler (c.1300-1361) and the promoter of the *devotio moderna,* Geert de Groote (1340-1384), were among his friends that visited Groenendael. Of Ruysbroeck's eleven literary works, three were completed before his departure from Brussels, and several others, including *The Adornment of the Spiritual Marriage,* were probably begun there. The latter work was completed at some time prior to 1350. It is Ruysbroeck's most systematic work.

As Ruysbroeck stands at the head of the vernacular prose writers of the Low Countries, so he stands at the center of its spirituality. The spirituality of the Low Countries had imbibed the affective warmth of Bernard of Clairvaux (1090-1153). This warmth is clearly reflected in the writings of the two outstanding mystical writers before Ruysbroeck, the Cistercian Beatrice of Bethlehem (died 1268) and the Beguine Hadewijch of Antwerp (probably first half of the thirteenth century). Near the end of the fourteenth century the spirituality of the Low Countries divided into two streams, both of them greatly influenced by Ruysbroeck. The ascetic line was represented at Groenendael by John of Schoonhoven (died 1431) and is generally associated with the *devotio moderna,* the Brethren of the Common Life, and the canons regular of Windesheim. The more speculatively interested mystical line includes such men as John of Leeuwen (at Groenendael, died 1374); Denis (of Leeuwen, or of Rijkel) "the Carthusian" (1402-1471); the Franciscan Henry Herp (died 1477); and the Benedictine abbot Louis de Blois (1506-c.1566).

This indigenous spirituality was promoted by the *Rijmbijbel,* a vernacular version of the entire Bible in rime, and other translations of the poet Jacob of Maerlant (c.1235-1300).

A second major influence, more specifically formative for Ruysbroeck's mysticism, was the school of Meister Eckhart (c.1260-c.1327), which is sometimes identified with the movement known as the Friends of God, or more generally with German mysticism. It combined Plotinian, Augustinian, Dionysian, and Thomistic elements in a manner that did not always satisfy the guardians of orthodoxy. Heresy proceedings were brought against Eckhart himself, and in 1329 Pope John XXII condemned several of his theses. Eckhart's followers responded to this condemnation by avoiding the exceptionable phrases and generally emphasizing their doctrinal and moral orthodoxy.

A third potent influence in the spirituality of the Low Countries was the teaching generally associated with the Brothers and Sisters of the Free Spirit. This doctrine, variously described as antinomian, quietistic, or pantheistic, had made great inroads especially among the Beguines, and proved hard to eradicate. It derived largely from Amalric of Bena (died c.1204), a master in the University of Paris who was officially condemned in 1209, and Ortlieb of Strassburg (born c.1200); and more remotely from the Arab philosopher Averroës (1126-1198). Ruysbroeck is said to have carried on a campaign against this type of mysticism and its outstanding representative, one Bloemmardinne (Heilwige Blommaerts, died 1335), a woman of good birth and of outstanding reputation both for personal sanctity and miraculous powers, who had founded a *beguinage* in Brussels. Ruysbroeck was always careful to dissociate himself from this type of spirituality, and in his largely apologetic *Book of Supreme Truth* denounces its adherents rather vehemently. Throughout his writings, as in his life, Ruysbroeck displayed a deep concern for moral virtue, which he regarded as fundamental for all true spirituality. Ruysbroeck's efforts to prove himself orthodox were successful. He is the only major representative of the Eckhartian school whose writings have never been put on the Index, and in 1909 he was officially beatified.

Ruysbroeck bases his exposition on the four parts of the verse, "Behold, the Bridegroom cometh, go ye out to meet him" (Matthew 25:6). "Behold" indicates a divine command to see; men who "neglect this command and remain blind are all damned." The remark "the Bridegroom cometh" indicates the various times and manners of the coming of Christ, the Bridegroom; the bride is human nature. The injunction "go ye out" indicates the response that is required of men. The phrase "to meet him" indicates "the purpose of our labour and of all our life; that is to say, the loving meeting with our Bridegroom." Both the vision and the three-fold movement of divine coming, human response, and divine-human encounter take place at three different levels.

Book I is devoted to the "active life," which is the common life of virtue and religion that is necessary for salvation. Vision is here shown to depend on three factors: the light of divine grace, the voluntary conversion of the will, and the cleansing of the conscience through perfect contrition. The coming of the Bridegroom is said to be threefold: in the Incarnation, in a daily coming with graces and gifts (a special instance of which is Christ's coming in the sacraments), and at the Last Judgment. From the "loving observation" of the Bridegroom's coming, there arises in the human heart a yearning to follow Christ in His virtues; this going out takes place in charity and righteousness, which together lay the foundation of all the other virtues, humility. To meet Jesus, it is necessary with Zacchaeus (Luke 19:2-4) to climb the tree of faith, which "grows from above downwards, for its roots are in the Godhead," and

whose twelve branches are the twelve articles of faith; to "come down quickly" (Luke 19:5) means "nothing else than a descent through desire and through love into the abyss of the Godhead, which no intelligence can reach in the created light. But where intelligence remains without" (here Ruysbroeck is quoting the mystical theologian Hugh of St. Victor, c.1097-1141), "desire and love go in."

The second level (Book II) is that of the "interior life," to which Ruysbroeck devotes some two-thirds of his treatise. Grace shines more brightly here; the conversion of the will encompasses also the unification of all of a man's powers, and the heart is cleansed from "all distracting images and attachments." Man is naturally sustained by three unities: the essential unity of his being, by which he exists, eternally one, in God; the active unity of his higher powers (memory, understanding, will) in the soul considered as spirit; and the vital unity of his bodily powers in the soul considered as the forming principle of the body. Now in the interior life Christ comes (1) in the unity of the bodily powers, as "driving and drawing" these powers toward Heaven, by heat and cold, weal and woe, hope and despair; (2) in the higher powers as strengthening, enlightening, and enriching the spirit in many ways, abundantly pouring Himself into man and demanding a response wholly transcending creaturely powers; (3) as "an inward stirring or touch in the unity of the spirit, wherein are the higher powers of the soul." Man's going out on this level includes beholding and glorifying God in the celestial hierarchies of His saints and angels; offering intercessory prayers for sinners and for souls in purgatory; instructing, reproving, serving, and praying for all good men; and peacefully possessing the unity of His spirit. The essential union of the human spirit with God, though "the first cause of all holiness and all blessedness," of itself "neither makes us holy nor blessed." Thus Ruysbroeck writes, "And so we have need of grace, which casts out sin, and prepares the way, and makes our whole life fruitful. And this is why Christ always comes into us through means, that is, through grace and multifarious gifts; and we too go out towards Him through means, that is, through virtues and diverse practices . . . for without the mediation of God's grace and a loving turning to Him in freedom, no creature shall ever be saved."

It is precisely in this respect the quietists are said to err: "Now mark this: when a man wishes to possess inward rest in idleness, without inward and desirous cleaving to God, then he is ready for all errors; for he is turned away from God, and inclined towards himself, in natural love, seeking and desiring consolation and sweetness and everything that pleases him . . . they believe themselves to be free, and to be united to God without means, and to be above all the customs of Holy Church, and above the commandments of God, and above the law, and above every work of virtue which can in any way be done. . . . They are empty of every virtue; and indeed so empty, that they will neither praise nor thank God. They have no knowledge and no love, no will, no prayer, no desire; for they believe that all that they could pray for, and desire, is already possessed of them. . . . And therefore they would be free, and obedient to none; neither pope, nor bishop, nor parson . . . sometimes . . . they are so cunning that one cannot vanquish them on the ground of reason. But through Holy Scripture and the teaching of Christ and our Faith, we may prove that they are deceived."

Ruysbroeck regards as similarly perverted the conviction of those who believe that "God works all their works" and that therefore they cannot sin.

The third level (Book III) is that of the "God-seeing life." Here the contemplative becomes the Light by which he sees. The eternal coming of the Bridegroom which he now experiences is the perpetual generation of Christ in the human spirit, which has now died to itself and entered the darkness of fruition. His going out is now in "contemplation and fruition, according to the way of God," for it is the will of God that men should return in a supernatural manner, through vision and love, to the eternally generated image in which they have their ideal being prior to their creation in time. The meeting at this highest level is a loving embrace, in the essential nudity and unity of the Godhead. "This is the dark silence in which all lovers lose themselves."

Attacks on Ruysbroeck's orthodoxy have always centered on Book III of The Adornment of the Spiritual Marriage. Henry of Langenstein (died 1397), formerly professor of theology at Paris and Vienna, and John Gerson (1363-1429), chancellor of the University of Paris and a mystical theologian of some stature, were the most prominent of his critics. In two letters (1399 and 1408) to the Carthusian Bartholomew Clantier, in a sermon preached at his university (1399), and in his treatise *De mystica theologia* (c.1402), Gerson seeks to connect certain teachings of Ruysbroeck with those of the condemned Amalric of Bena. Specifically, he objects to Ruysbroeck's conception of a super-essential union of man with God as the return of the rational creature to its primal archetype or exemplar in God, where the contemplative becomes the divine Light in which he sees God. Gerson was answered by John of Schoonhoven in two treatises, in which he explains that Ruysbroeck was not speaking of the union of identity (*per identitatem realis existentiae*) subsisting between the Father and the Son (John 10:30), nor of the moral union (*per consensum et conformitatem voluntatis*) common to all believers in the state of grace (Acts 4:32), but of that union in which the soul is melted by love and in a manner dies to itself (Galatians 2:20). Bernard of Clairvaux, Hugh of St. Victor, Gilbert of Holland (died 1172), and Thomas Gallus (died 1246) are the authorities he cites for this kind of union. The return of the rational creature to its ideal principle is also interpreted as a return by love, not by a reversal of the process of creation. With Bernard, the supposed author of the *Epistola ad fratres de Monte Dei* (actually William of St. Thierry, died 1149), he distinguishes between "being what God is" and "being God." That this distinction furnishes the key to the proper understanding of Ruysbroeck's conception of supreme beatitude is borne out by a statement in *The Book of Supreme Truth:* "This blessedness is essential to God, and super-essential to all creatures; for no created essence can become one with God's essence and pass away from its own substance. For so the creature would become God, which is impossible; . . . yet all loving spirits are one fruition and one blessedness with God without distinction; for that beatific state, which is the fruition of God and of all his beloved, is so simple and one-fold that therein neither Father, nor Son, nor Holy Ghost, is distinct according to the Persons, neither is any creature." The union is the one Christ prayed for: "That they all may be one; as thou, Father, art in me, and I in thee, that they also may be one in us . . ." (John 17:21).

THEOLOGIA GERMANICA

Author: Unknown. Attributed to an anonymous Teutonic Knight, sometimes known as "the Frankfurter"
Type of work: Mystical theology
First transcribed: c.1350

Principal Ideas Advanced

Since sin is nothing but disobedience or self-will, salvation, which is nothing but obedience or ceasing from self-will, must be wrought in the person who sins.

Freedom is self-surrender to God; self-assertion is the most miserable bondage; freedom from the law does not mean license.

To know and believe in Christ means to know and believe in the Christ-life; man's union with God is primarily a union with the will of God.

The *Theologia Germanica* was first published in 1516 by the German Reformer Martin Luther (1483-1546), who had come across it, without title or indication of authorship, and in incomplete form. Luther published two more editions in Wittenberg in 1518, and two further editions were published the same year in Augsburg and Leipzig; the treatise acquired its title, "German Theology" (sometimes written *Theologia Deutsch*), in that year. In all, some one hundred editions have been printed in Germany alone, and translations have been made into many languages.

The best manuscript, which dates from 1497, was discovered in Würzburg in the middle of the last century. It indicates that the author had been "a Teutonic Knight, a priest, and a warden in the house of the Teutonic Knights [an order founded in Jerusalem in 1118] in Frankfurt," who was also a Friend of God, and that he wrote against the Free Spirits. These Free Spirits may be defined as adherents of the more extreme branch of medieval mysticism, which pushed its understanding of God as immanent to the point of pantheism and antinomianism. The group seems to have flourished especially in the thirteenth century.

The Friends of God, a fourteenth century movement that flourished all along the Rhine and in Southern Germany, represents a conservative reaction against these excesses. Meister Eckhart (c.1260-1327), superior-general of the German Dominicans and a professor in Paris and Cologne, whose personality and writings form the foundation of the movement, and his greatest disciples, John Ruysbroeck (1293-1381), Henry Suso (c.1295-1366), and John Tauler (c.1300-1361), were all loyal churchmen. By disciplining their mystical experiences and speculations with Christian dogma and the common morality, they produced a literature which is regarded by many as the finest flowering of mysticism. German mysticism enriched and molded the German language; it largely determined German spirituality; it provided the foundations of German classical philosophy; and it cast a certain conservative hue over German social life.

The *Theologia Germanica*, written in the middle or second half of the fourteenth century, is generally regarded as the epitome of Eckhartian mysticism. Permeated by great moral earnestness, not to say rigorism, it sets forth simply and clearly the message of the Friends of God. It has not enjoyed much ecclesiastical approbation. Luther wrote in 1516 that he had never seen a more wholesome theology, but in his later years he came to repent his initial enthusiasm for the little book. The French Reformer John Calvin (1509-1564) categorically rejected it. Calvin's adversary Sebastian Castellio (1515-1563), the most prominent advocate of religious toleration in the sixteenth century, liked it well enough to translate it into Latin, as did the German rational-spiritualist Sebastian Franck (c.1499-c.1542). The book was placed on the Index by Roman Catholic authorities in 1621. It was revered by German and French Pietists. Forgotten by the Enlightenment, it has again found a goodly number of readers in the nineteenth and twentieth centuries.

According to the *Theologia Germanica*, God is the only substance and goodness. No created being has substance or goodness in itself, but only as it participates in God. Man can dispose himself for greater participation by renouncing whatever is not God, and the disposed man will get his reward. The renunciation of will, wisdom, love, desire, and knowledge means that God is acknowledged as the author of all these goods. To claim any of them for oneself is to touch God in His honor. Nothing is to be loved, nothing is to be the object of human satisfaction, but God. God may be considered in three ways: as Godhead, that is, as pure transcendence, without name, manifestation, knowledge, or will; as God, that is, as a being with personal distinctions, knowing, loving, and revealing Himself to Himself, not actively, but substantially; and as man, that is, as a being incarnate in Christ or in any man who has come to be a partaker of the divine nature, as pure love to all creatures, joined to a profound grief over their sins. God as man never resorts to force. The partakers of the divine nature are the poor in spirit, who are also the heirs of the Kingdom of Heaven.

Sin is defined as self-will, a turning from the unchangeable good to the changeable. Any willing "without God" is self-will. The Devil fell by claiming "for himself to be also somewhat." The message is clear: "For the more a man followeth after his own self-will, and self-will groweth in him, the farther off is he from God, the true Good, for nothing burneth in hell but self-will. Therefore it hath been said, 'Put off thine own will, and there will be no hell.' " Ownership derives from self-will; there is no ownership in Heaven. Sin does not exist substantially, in God; hence, the all-embracing love of God does not extend to sin.

Salvation is described in the *Theologia Germanica* in moral and psychological terms. The only cure for disobedience is obedience, and it must be effected in the one who disobeyed: "But how shall my fall be amended? It must be healed as Adam's fall was healed. . . . Mark this: man could not without God, and God should not without man. Wherefore God took human nature or manhood upon himself, and was made man, and man was made divine. . . . So also must my fall be healed. I cannot do the work without God, and God may not or will not do it without me; for if it shall be accomplished, in me, too, God must be made man. . . ." As Adam's obedience "fell and died" when he disobeyed God, so disobedience "fell and died" in Christ's perpetual obedience. The new birth that is necessary to enter the Kingdom of God (John 3:3,5) is nothing other than the birth of obedience. When Christ says that "No man cometh unto the Father but by me" (John 14:6), what is meant is that the only way to God is by following Christ's example; that is, by complete obedience. "No man can come unto me, except the Father which hath sent me draw him" (John 6:44) means that only as men catch a glimpse of the Eternal Goodness do their souls conceive "a longing to approach unto the Perfect

Goodness, and unite herself with the Father." This longing grows in proportion to the degree of completeness of the revelation.

The Frankfurter propounds a very characteristic view of freedom. God cannot exercise His will in Himself, since He is immutable; but He delights to exercise it in the creature: "Therefore the will is not given to be exerted by the creature, but only by God, who hath a right to work out His own will by means of the will which is in man, and yet is God's. And in whatever man or creature it should be purely and wholly thus, the will would not be exerted by the man but by God, and thus it would not be self-will, and the man would not will otherwise than as God willeth; for God himself would move the will and not man. . . . That which is free, none may call his own, and he who maketh it his own committeth a wrong. Now, in the whole realm of freedom, nothing is so free as the will, and he who maketh it his own . . . doth a grievous wrong. . . . But he who leaveth the will in its freedom, hath content, peace, rest and blessedness in time and in eternity. . . . Furthermore, mark ye that where the will enjoyeth its freedom, it hath its proper work, that is, willing. And where it chooseth whatever it will unhindered, it always chooseth in all things what is noblest and best. . . ."

Men enlightened by God live in the freedom of disinterested love, says the *Theologia Germanica*; they are motivated neither by "the fear of pain or hell" nor by "the hope of reward or heaven." There is a sense in which those who are "led by the Spirit of God" (Romans 8:14) are "not under the law but under grace" (Romans 6:14). They are free from the law in that the Christ-life is greater than the requirements of the law, and includes them.

The opposite view is the "false freedom" of the Free Spirits or Free-Thinkers. A preface included in the 1497 manuscript indicates that the *Theologia Germanica* "teaches . . . especially how and whereby the true and rightful Friends of God may be recognized and likewise the unrightful and false Free Spirits who are most harmful to Holy Church." The Free Spirits identify nature with God, while the *Theologia Germanica* identifies nature with the Devil; all things are to be loved only in One, the transcendent One in all things. Since "all deception beginneth in self-deception," the free spirits lack the sense of sin; they suppose that "it standeth quite well with them." Hence, they are guilty both of spiritual pride and high-mindedness and of a false, lawless freedom. They think themselves superior to "custom, order, measure, fitness, and the like" (which are, however, divinely ordained), and hence free to violate them. He who is poor in spirit, on the other hand, sees that these things are necessary, because "he cometh to see and understand aright, how that all men are bent upon themselves, and inclined to evil and sin, and that on this account it is needful and profitable that there be order, customs, law and precepts, to the end that the blindness and foolishness of men may be corrected, and that vice and wickedness may be kept under, and constrained to seemliness." Men naturally resemble the Evil Spirit more than they do God; for every man truly possessed with the Spirit of God, there are a hundred thousand or more possessed with the Evil Spirit.

Reason (perceiving, cognition) and will are the creature's highest gifts, and they cannot be separated. Faith (belief) precedes (experiential) knowledge. To know and understand Christ is to know and understand His life, and to believe in Christ is to think the Christ-life best of all. Love is defined as the practical pursuit of its object, by action conformable to the latter. Hence, when the *Theologia Germanica* claims that there is no true knowledge of God without love, what is meant is that the knowledge of God is practical. The true light and reason teach the soul to love only the perfect good, and for its own sake; love for the sake of a reward is an especially false kind of love.

Self-knowledge is praised as the highest art. But the real ideal of the *Theologica Germanica* is the Christ-life: to be to the Eternal Goodness what his own hand is to a man. Though the Christ-life be the most bitter of all, it is to be desired above all things; such a life cannot be attained by book-learning, but only by forsaking "this and that," the world of the many and the particular. Men endowed with considerable reason are in danger, in fact, of mistaking their own reason for the true light of God. The Christ-life is primarily a union of man with the will of God, and it requires submission to all things. Man's will must come to be wholly at one with God's, by a union which "standeth not in any man's powers"; the individual will must cease to be separate from God's, but it must not relinquish its distinct identity. This union with God's will becomes a permanent condition of the "inner man" and can be broken only by self-will. Such a view does not imply that a man should not be touched at all by "outward things." Perfection is not to be looked for at once: John Tauler says that some take leave of types and symbols too soon. Three stages in the ascent of will are recognized: purification, enlightenment, union. Time is portrayed as the "outer court" of eternity; Paradise is "all things that are"; Hell and Heaven may be experienced in this life; and it is possible (according to "St. Dyonysius") to "cast a glance into eternity" now. Christ was able to look with the right eye of his soul into eternity while looking upon the things of time with the left; but in other men the "left eye" must utterly cease to function if the "right eye" is to become operative. In expressing these views, the *Theologia Germanica* describes and fosters the Christian way to the sinless life.

THE DIALOGUE OF CATHERINE OF SIENA

Author: Saint Catherine of Siena (1347-1380)
Type of work: Devotional meditations; mysticism
First transcribed: 1370

Principal Ideas Advanced

Through proper self-knowledge the soul learns of its complete dependence on God.

True knowledge of God lies beyond human understanding and takes place in the mystical experience of the beatific vision.

Suffering is integral to the religious life, for it follows when the soul discerns its distance from God and it encourages the proper attitude of contrition.

God made of Christ a bridge by which fallen man may travel the road to Heaven.

The subtitle is uncommonly helpful for understanding *The Dialogue of St. Catherine*: "The Book of Divine Doctrine given in person by God the Father, speaking to the mind of the most glorious and holy virgin, Catherine of Siena, and written down as she dictated it in the vulgar tongue, she being the while entranced and actually hearing what God spoke in her." There are difficulties here for the modern reader to whom seraphic virgins, states of ecstasy, and mystical dialogues are unfamiliar, but once the reader learns something of the cultural milieu in which Catherine moved, it is possible to approach the work with some expectation of satisfactory understanding.

In Catherine's day the dominant religion was Roman Catholicism and the saintly or holy person was a familiar type in her society. Thought to be especially close to God, the saintly person was considered to be free from some aspects of fallen humanity; the prayers of such a person were considered especially efficacious, and the holy one was often accepted as a bearer of revelation, sometimes in the form of divine judgment against persons in high places as well as low.

Siena, an ancient walled city set on three hills in the mountainous north-central region of Italy, had suffered a disastrous loss of some eighty thousand of its population by plague the year after Catherine's birth in 1347. Catherine's twin sister died at birth, and only twelve of her twenty-four brothers and sisters reached maturity. She passed her childhood in the midst of her large family, all of whom lived in one small house. It is told that at the age of five she experienced levitation; at six she was vouchsafed a vision of Christ on His throne wearing papal vestments and papal crown; and at seven she dedicated her virginity to Christ. So grief-dispelling was her presence even as a child that she received the affectionate name of Euphrosyne. Becoming a member of the Dominican Third Order at sixteen, she spent three years in her house in religious seclusion and severe asceticism; subsequently she ministered to the sick and poor, and she sought the conversion of the rich. It is in keeping with her spirit of self-renunciation that Catherine prayed successfully for invisible stigmata; thus, she suffered the pain of Christ's wounds, but did not bear their marks.

Catherine's life was cast into a time of turbulence. The Church had fallen upon evil days in that the moral state of both the secular clergy and the papacy was generally acknowledged to be at a disgracefully low level. The pope himself had moved to Avignon, France, and his prestige was in serious decline. It was openly preached that the Roman Church was about to face a destructive end from which the devout should flee. Heretical movements were mounting. It was these conditions to which Catherine was destined to minister. The *Dialogue* with which we are here concerned, however, deals not with Catherine's political ideas, but rather with her fundamental religious convictions.

Catherine has been praised as having a permanent and foremost place among the guides of humanity. She dwells in her work on the sheer beauty of the soul in the state of grace as contrasted to the ugliness of sin. Throughout this extraordinary book it is not so much the teaching, which consists principally of the basic Roman Catholic creeds, but the remarkably sustained elevation of tone which is impressive.

The *Dialogue* is divided into four treatises of unequal length; the first, on divine providence, covers twenty-four pages; the second, on discretion, covers a hundred—as does the third, on prayer; the last, on obedience, runs to fifty-three pages.

The treatise on divine providence is introduced with an account of the soul rising in mystic ecstasy to ask God for help: first, for the self; second, for the reformation of the Holy Church; third, for men in general and particularly for the rebels against the Church; and, finally, in all things both worthy, general, and specific. Through proper self-knowledge the soul learns the humbling lesson that no one exists in and for himself, but only derivatively

from the Eternal Truth or God. Proper self-knowledge dissipates narrow self-love and permits one to gain the knowledge of God which is beyond all human understanding. A natural accompaniment of this ineffable love of God is grief, for one soon becomes aware of one's own sin and of the sins of the world. Pain and suffering are to be borne in patience, for through the virtue of love, suffering leads to satisfaction and reward not only for one's self but for others also. It is not suffering, however, which is effective in the spiritual realm but the contrition which accompanies it.

God's grace is sometimes shown in His allowing men to know the world in order to see its instability. Indeed, Catherine reports God as saying that "the eye cannot see, nor the tongue relate, nor the heart think, how many are the roads and ways which I use, through love alone, to lead them back in grace, so that My truth may be fulfilled in them." Similarly, from the divine perspective the injustice practiced by the wicked man makes even more evident the justice of the man who bears injustice humbly and with undiminished faith. When a man receives injury from his neighbor, he proves his patience.

The treatise on discretion deals with that virtue of true knowledge which the soul should have both of itself and of God. Parables are given to show how love, humility, and discretion are united, how penance and similar works are merely means and are not of the essence of the soul, how God made of Christ a bridge by which fallen man could travel the road to Heaven, and how those that ignore the bridge are as trees of death whose fruits are sensuality, avarice, injustice, and error. Those thus damned are deprived of the vision of God; their conscience gnaws at them increasingly like a worm; they see the Devil; and they experience a fire which burns but does not consume since the soul, being spiritual, cannot be consumed as a material thing. In contrast, the blessed ones rejoice in God and experience the beatific vision.

In the treatise on prayer Catherine continues her presentation of the tenets of Roman Catholic orthodoxy, and she offers advice regarding what must be done in order for the full meaning of the tenets to be realized in the life of the individual. When the question is asked in the divine soliloquy about the way in which imperfection is lost and perfection acquired, the answer follows immediately: "By perseverance seasoned with the most holy faith." Even if vocal prayer is imperfect it should be practiced lest one fall into the worse state of idleness. Catherine speaks from the depths of personal experience of perseverance, and often her asceticism may be discerned. When, for example, God is discoursing on the glory of His charity and mercy, which are extended to the unjust as well as the just, He adds that He often gives "more to the sinner than to the righteous man, because the righteous man is able to endure privation, and I take from him the goods of the world that he may the more abundantly enjoy the goods of heaven." If there is in some an invincible ignorance, there must surely be in others an invincible faith, and Catherine's faith is such. When desolation, suffering, and persecution are interpreted as proofs of God's mercy and love and become causes for praise, it is clear that here is a faith forged in the crucible of personal experience and validated in the mystical union which lies beyond human understanding. It is to descriptions of the various phases of the mystic state that the remainder of this section is dedicated.

The final treatise on obedience makes explicit what has been implicit throughout: attainment of the state whereby one is able to receive the glorious divine vision depends upon one's unquestioning obedience. The perfectly obedient soul "passes by the assaults of the devils, mortifying and macerating his flesh, stripping it bare of all pleasures," for it clothes itself with the "labors of the order in a faith which despises nothing." The obedient soul remembers not "the injuries, pains, or blows inflicted upon her by his superior in the order, but calling him humbly, turns to him without anger, hatred, or rancour, but with meekness and benevolence." The pains of the present, after all, are scarcely comparable to the joys which will come to the obedient person later in Heaven. A recapitulation of the major themes brings the work to a close on an exalted note of mystical rapture.

Though Catherine will be remembered for her activities in the politico-ecclesiastical sphere, for her published prayers, and for her nearly four hundred letters which have been ranked as equal to the work of Petrarch for beauty and significance, it is her *Dialogue* which shows most clearly her claim to spiritual greatness.

THE REVELATIONS OF DIVINE LOVE

Author: Lady Julian [Juliana] of Norwich (c.1342-after 1413)
Type of work: Mystical theology
First transcribed: 1393

PRINCIPAL IDEAS ADVANCED

Although man sees some things as good and others as evil, God sees all things as good.

Christians must embrace the sufferings of Christ in order to receive the bliss of Heaven.

Man's sin and Fall is part of God's eternal purpose, and in the end men shall see why God ordained it.

God does not blame Christians for their sins, but pities them for their sufferings; yet more profound than His pity is His joy in the bliss which they shall have in Heaven.

In revealing these truths, Christ designs to teach Christians to rejoice in the great love which binds them to Him.

An early copyist prefaces the *Revelations of Divine Love* with the following statement: "Here is a vision shewn by the goodness of God to a devout woman whose name is Julian. She is a recluse at Norwich and is living yet in this year of our Lord 1413." We know little more than this concerning the name and circumstances of the author, who would have preferred to remain unknown, even as to the identity of her sex. On the other hand, Julian tells explicitly the date and the hours on which she received a series of visions, and she offers a great deal of information concerning her physical and mental condition during the visions. These details are germane to her purpose, because they attest the actuality of what Julian maintains was a true revelation which God gave to mankind through her. Julian believed in the truth of the Scriptures and the teachings of the Church, but she was convinced that out of His love for the elect and His desire to be known of them, God had revealed additional truths to her.

Julian relates that, as a young woman, she prayed for three things. The first was that she might have the knowledge of Christ's passion that was given to those who, like Mary Magdalene, were present at the Crucifixion. The second was that she might experience grievous sickness in her own body, so as to know all the temptations and sufferings of the dying, yet without bringing about the departure of her soul. The third was that she might receive "three wounds" in her life; namely, "the wound of true contrition, the wound of kind compassion, and the wound of earnest longing for God." She had asked that the sickness come when she was thirty years of age —and so it happened. For six days she hovered on the brink of death. On the seventh, she gradually lost all feeling in her body. When the priest held the crucifix before her, her sight began to fail and everything grew dark except the image of the cross. Then she thought of obtaining the "wounds" that she had previously desired, especially to know the suffering of Christ. Suddenly the revelations began. It was four o'clock on the morning of May 8, 1373 when the revelatory experiences began, and three in the afternoon when they ended.

During the fifteen revelations, Julian had no pain, but after they were ended, her sickness came over her again. When the priest spoke to her, she said that she had "raved during the day," and that the cross which he held before her seemed to bleed. The priest laughed at first, but was later convinced; Julian, feeling that she had betrayed God's revelation to her, was smitten with guilt. That night she dreamed that the Devil appeared to her; but, on waking, she thought of the truths which had been revealed to her and she was comforted. Then, on the following day, came the final vision, in which her soul appeared to her as a city, with Christ dwelling in its midst. "Know it now well," she heard Him say, "that it was no raving that thou sawest today. But take it and believe it and keep thee therein, and comfort thee therewith, and trust thereto; and thou shalt not be overcome." So the visions ended. But Julian continued over a period of twenty years to have "lightings and touchings" by means of which she saw further meanings in her visions. Thus, her book contains, besides vivid descriptions of her "shewings," long discussions of the truths which they were meant to convey.

Julian's description of her visions is complicated by the fact that she discerned three kinds of awareness present during each of "shewings":
bodily sight, verbal understanding, and ghostly sight. By her bodily sight she beheld the crucifix that hung before her transformed into the likeness of the suffering Christ, His face soiled with blood and spittle, and contorted with pain. But while this vision continued, many things passed through her understanding concerning Christ's godhood and manhood, and concerning God's love for the world. At the same time, she had "a ghostly sight of his homely loving," that His love encloses us like a garment and that "he is to us everything that is good." Julian says that she cannot show the ghostly sight as fully as she would like, and must trust that God will help her readers to "receive it more ghostly and more sweetly than I can or may tell it."

The visions fall into four unequal groups. The first twelve have as their focus the passion of Christ, in which, as Julian considers it, is shown the height and depth of God's goodness, and the nothingness of the world outside His love and care. "I saw God in a point," she declares; "the sight, I say, was in my understanding, by which I saw that he is in all things." In this moment it was showed to her that, although man sees some deeds as good and others as evil, God sees that all is good, for "everything that is done is so in virtue of God's doing." Julian says the pain of these visions was such "the grumbling and frailty of the flesh" made her want to look away. She had, as she puts it, "an offer in my reason; it was said to me, as though by a friend: 'Look up to the heaven to his Father.'" But through faith she answered, "Nay, I cannot for Thou art my heaven." For, as she explains, she would rather have endured endless pain than enter Heaven other than by Him. Her devotion was soon rewarded. At the point when it seemed that Christ's life could endure no longer, His countenance changed. "This change in him changed me," she writes; "and I was as glad and merry as it is possible to be." Suddenly she understood that in our present life we are "on his cross, dying with him in our pains and our passion." When His countenance changes, this life is ended, and we are with Him in heaven.

The thirteenth revelation seemed to Julian the answer to a question which had long troubled her, for it had seemed to her that not pain but sin is the cause of all distress. "Thus in my folly, even before this time, I often wondered why the beginning of sin was not prevented by the great foreseeing wisdom of God; for then—or so it seemed to me—all would have been well." In this vision Jesus said, "Sin must needs be, but all shall be well. All shall be well; and all manner of thing shall be well." How this could be remained a secret, which prompted Julian to distinguish between those things which God wills to make known to us, and those which He hides in Himself. Nevertheless, she found "a mighty comfort" in the assurance that "in the last day" He would "make all well that is not well." Several consolations were given her in the meanwhile. One was that in all her visions of Christ she saw nothing of sin but only of pain. Another was the assurance that God sends suffering to His children, not because they have offended Him, but to prepare their souls for greater bliss.

One question which Julian wanted answered was never settled; namely, what happens to Satan and to men who die outside the faith of the Holy Church. While protesting that she is an orthodox believer, she finds it impossible to understand how "all manner of things should be well" if part of creation is damned. "But," she says, "I had no other answer to the difficulty in this shewing of our Lord's, except this: 'What is impossible to thee is not impossible to me; I shall save my word in all things—I shall make all things well!' "

The problem of sin has other aspects which troubled Julian. The most vexing, because of its practical importance, is the conflict which she presumed to exist between the teachings of the Church that sin deserves to be punished, and the disclosures of her revelations that God is love and that there is no wrath in Him. "If I take it thus, that we are not sinners or blameworthy," she writes, "then it seemeth as though I should err in failing to acknowledge the truth. But granted this truth—that we are sinners and blameworthy, good Lord, how may it then be that I cannot see this truth in thee, who are my God and my Maker?" The question seemed to her so basic and so important ("I need to know, as it seemeth to me, if I am to go on living here, for the knowing of good and evil"), that she cried with all her strength to God for help. In answer, God showed her a parable of a lord and a servant. The servant is shown as standing reverently before the lord, loving him and wishing to do his will; and the lord, returning the love, sends the servant to work in his field. The servant goes, but falls into a ravine and is hurt. Being able neither to rise nor to find any comfort, he forgets his master's love for him, and thinks only of his misfortune. Meanwhile, the lord, who knows what has befallen the servant, has two thoughts. The first is of great "ruth and pity" for the hurt that has come to his servant. This he shows on his countenance. His second thought, "more inward and ghostly," is of "joy and bliss" for the reward which he intends to bestow upon him. For the servant is not to blame for the condition into which he has fallen. As he lies in the ravine, he is "as lovable and as good inwardly as he was when he stood before his lord." Therefore, says the lord, because he has endured harm and evil for love of me, it is proper "to give him a gift that is better and more worshipful to him than his own wholeness should have been."

The interpretation of this parable was not given to Julian all at once. She took it at first as referring to Adam, the father of the race. Afterwards she saw that the "ruth and pity" which appeared outwardly was for the falling of the creaturely Adam, but that the "joy and bliss" which appeared to her ghostly sight was for the falling of His eternal Son. In this manner, Julian found an answer to her question. Looked at through the eyes of the flesh, while God does not blame us for our sin, nevertheless He appears to rue it and to pity our condition. Looked at through the eyes of the spirit, God does not even consider what we are at present but only what, in view of our love and faithfulness, we shall be; in this aspect, He does not view us as progeny of Adam but as members of the body of Christ.

In her efforts to expound the relationship of the spiritual elect to Christ (for Julian simply says that she received no revelation concerning the damned), the author elaborates the conception of the Motherhood of God, and particularly of Christ. "I beheld the working of all the blessed Trinity," she says; "in which beholding I saw and understood these three properties: the property of the Fatherhood, and the property of the Motherhood, and the property of the Lordship—in one God." God is our Father in that we have our being from Him, our Mother in His mercy toward us, our Lord in the grace with which He strengthens us. She goes on to explain, in line with her quasi-Platonic conceptions of man's constitution, that Christ is our Mother in a twofold sense: our higher, substantial part is grounded and rooted in Him, but so also is our lower, sensual part. It is in the lower part that man falls and suffers pain; this is the part of Christ that endures the anguish of the cross. In his higher part, man neither sins nor suffers pain; this is the part of Christ that is eternal, in union with whom the elect shall enjoy eternal bliss.

In the interval which preceded Julian's final revelation, her sickness had returned, she had in a manner been false to her vision ("I raved"), and she had been frightened by a nightmarish vision of the Devil. The final revelation was to her ghostly eye, showing her her own soul "so large as it were an endless world, and also as it were a blessed kingdom," in the midst of which sat Christ in His majesty, "comely of person, and tall of stature, the greatest bishop, most awful king, Lord of highest honor." It was then that the words were spoken which confirmed that her visions were "no raving," and encouraged her with the promise "thou shalt not be overcome." Here, she says, is the true comfort for Christians, not that they shall escape trouble and travail and distress, but that they shall not be vanquished. Sin, she goes on to say, will continue to vex the believer as long as he lives on earth; nor is anything more contrary to God than sin, which cuts us off from His blessed sight, and leaves us as dead for the time. But although we lose our vision of Him, He never loses sight of us. "In falling and in rising we are preciously kept in the same love. For," says Julian, "in the beholding of God we fall not, and in the beholding of ourselves we stand not. And both these be truth, as I see it. But the beholding of our Lord God is the higher truth."

This tension between the higher and the lower, which refuses, on account of the faith in the Incarnation, to deny the reality of pain and of sin while nevertheless affirming the transcend-ence of love and bliss, is character-istic of the best in Christian mysticism, or, more strictly, "apocalypticism." For Julian does not claim to be the pos-sessor of any spiritual art by which she has access to divine life. On the contrary, she considers that the reve-lations granted to her were a minis-tration of Christ's love, who intends it as a favor not just to her but to her "even-Christians." "For," she explains, "I saw truly and understood in our Lord's meaning that he shewed it be-cause he will have it known more than it is. In which knowing he will give us grace to love him and cleave to him. For he beheld his heavenly treasure with so great love on earth, that he willeth to give more light and solace in heavenly joy, in drawing our hearts from the sorrow and darkness which we are in."

THE CLOUD OF UNKNOWING

Author: Unknown
Type of work: Mystical theology
First transcribed: c.1375

Principal Ideas Advanced

Meditation on God's works of creation and redemption, although useful in early stages of the soul's preparation, must be covered in a cloud of forgetting before one can begin the mystical ascent.

The task of the mystic is to bring his understanding to a halt in a cloud of unknowing, and wait in that state for God to show Himself.

The soul that has achieved union with God becomes perfect in love and par-takes in the work of redeeming fallen creation.

The *Cloud of Unknowing* is a psy-chologically penetrating essay of prac-tical advice ostensibly addressed to a young monk who, having entered upon the life of an anchorite, wants to know how to achieve perfect union with God. Because the youth is with-out much learning, the author of the

Cloud of Unknowing undertakes to answer his question by replying in plain English. The author was a scholar, versed in the mystical writings of St. Augustine (354-430), Dionysius, the Pseudo-Areopagite (fl. c.500), and Richard of St. Victor (died c.1173). He ably transcended his learning, and he wrote from personal experience of the way he wanted to commend. Nothing is known about him other than what his writings disclose; namely, that he was a "clerk" in the Northeast Midlands of England in the second half of the fourteenth century.

The *Cloud of Unknowing* is in the tradition of the "negative theology" of Pseudo-Dionysius. Man's part in drawing near to God consists in emptying his mind of every thought. When he has brought his reason to a standstill, he must wait for God to disclose Himself. The experience of union is momentary and indescribable, but it is powerfully efficacious for man's redemption. We read: "This is the work of the soul that most pleaseth God. All saints and angels have joy of this work and hasten them to help it with all their might. All fiends be mad when thou dost thus, and try for to defeat it in all that they can. All men living on earth be wonderfully helped by this work, thou knowest not how. Yea, the souls in purgatory are eased of their pains by virtue of this work. Thou thyself art cleansed and made virtuous by no work so much."

The familiar distinction between the active and the contemplative life, symbolized by Martha and Mary in the Gospel narrative, is preserved in the theology of the *Cloud of Unknowing.* When Jesus said of the sister that sat at His feet, "Mary hath chosen the better part," he had reference, says

the *Cloud of Unknowing,* to the higher part of the contemplative life. For the contemplative life starts where the active life ends, with meditation or mental prayer, in which the soul thinks of its sin, of Christ's mercies, of saintly men, or of the joys of Heaven; but meditation is useful only to bring the soul to that state of humility and obedience from which it can begin its ascent into the divine presence. The actual work of perfection requires that the mind rigorously empty itself of the very thoughts which are the staple of meditation. Every thought of God and of His creatures must be trampled down and covered with *"a cloud of forgetting."*

So far, the ascent is the work of man. By a travail that is hard and wearisome for the beginner but is lighter for those who have some practice, the soul must bring itself into "a darkness, and as it were a *cloud of unknowing,* thou knowest not what, saving that thou feelest in thy will a naked intent unto God." Beyond this, however, man's efforts are of no avail. Man can bring himself neither to see God by the light of understanding nor to feel Him by the sweetness of love. But if he keep himself in this darkness, smiting upon the cloud with "a sharp dart of longing love," it may be that God will favor him and perform his gracious work: "Then will he sometimes peradventure send out a beam of ghostly light, piercing this *cloud of unknowing* that is betwixt thee and him, and show thee some of his secrets, the which man may not and cannot speak. Then shalt thou feel thine affection inflamed with the fire of his love, far more than I can tell thee, or may or will at this time. For of that work that pertaineth only to God dare

I not take upon me to speak with my blabbering fleshly tongue."

The author has a carefully developed theology, basically orthodox, of which, however, only fragments are stated in the *Cloud of Unknowing*. One interesting feature of his system is his conception of time as made up of a finite number of instants, in each of which the heart experiences a "single striving." Man's responsibility is to love God perfectly in each fleeting moment: "Look not forwards and let the backwards be." In his fallen state, however, no man can do this. He can barely heed one instant in a hundred; and how can he make satisfaction for the times he has lost? For help, says the author, he must turn to Jesus, who, "by his Godhead is maker and giver of time," and "by his Manhood is the true heeder of time." Love, the author continues, knits man to Jesus and through Him to the blessed angels and all the saints, who, by "heeding of time" make satisfaction for the time which others have lost. "But," warns the author, "I cannot see who may truly claim fellowship thus with Jesu and his just Mother, his high angels and also with the saints, unless he be such a one as doth that in him is, with the help of grace, in heeding of time."

The fourteenth century witnessed the rise of numerous religious parties. The most outstanding example in England was that of the followers of Wycliffe (c.1329-1384), who are censured in the *Cloud of Unknowing* as being "fleshly living men of the world, which think the statutes of Holy Church over hard for them to amend their lives by," and who "burst up and blaspheme all the saints, sacraments, statutes, and ordinances of Holy Church." But the author is less concerned with these open heretics (as they seemed to him) than he is with pseudo-mystical practitioners within the Church who lead astray persons which were never suited to contemplation. "I tell thee," he says, "that the devil hath his contemplatives as God hath his." Such idle contemplatives are always yearning for "bodily showings," straining to turn their eyes inward, or to soar upwards into planetary spheres, failing, says the author, to comprehend the indifference of spirit to spatial distinctions, or that "nowhere bodily is everywhere ghostly." The *Cloud of Unknowing* contrasts the bizarre behavior of such false mystics with that of the true mystic, who, in virtue of the meekness and charity which he receives in union with God, becomes more "seemly" and "favorable" in the eyes of men than ever before.

Although it stands in the tradition which denies the possibility of knowing God through the reason, and demands that the soul forget every creature as well as every divine manifestation within creation in order to wait upon God, the *Cloud of Unknowing* is not in the least morbid or world-weary in temper. Admittedly, when one is in the *cloud of unknowing,* the feeling of his sin makes him loathe himself, but, according to the author, it never makes him desire "to un-be." "He liketh right well to be, and he giveth full heartily thanks unto God for the worthiness and the gift of his being, although he desire unceasingly for to lack the knowing and the feeling of his being." When, in perfect charity, he is "oned unto God," he does not lose his being: "For although it may be said in a manner that in this time God and thou be not two but one in spirit, nevertheless thou art beneath him . . . in nature." Moreover, that divine love which binds the soul to God comprehends every creature: "For charity meaneth nought else but love of God for himself above all creatures, and of man for God even as thyself." The proof thereof, writes the author, is that the Christian who has tasted of heavenly bliss no longer has preferences among men; he does not prefer kin above stranger, or friend above foe: "All men, he thinketh, be his friends, and none his foes."

TIIE FOLLOWING OF CHRIST

Author: Gerard [Geert de] Groote (Gerardus Magnus, 1340-1384)
Type of work: Devotional manual
First transcribed: c.1380

PRINCIPAL IDEAS ADVANCED

The main concern of a Christian life is to follow Jesus Christ and to deny the self.

The transitory world is a source of misery and must be renounced in favor of allegiance to the eternal world.

Constant self-examination is necessary to guard the soul from engagement with illusory pleasures and the temptations of the Devil.

Adversity and anxiety are the lot of man in this world and can be met and overcome only by those who follow the way of the Cross, for it is only through such humiliation that man receives eternal life.

Very few books on the devotional life have attained the eminence of *The Following of Christ* by Gerard Groote, the founder of a late medieval religious order commonly known as the Brethren of the Common Life. The book is the spiritual diary of this Netherlands spiritual leader. The work was written during various periods of Groote's life, and it covers a variety of topics. It is not unified in the formal sense as a planned treatise would be. The sections are separate in both time and subject matter so that the parts can be perused in any order agreeable to the reader without any loss of value. Such unity as the book possesses comes from the reflective devotional attitude of the author as he follows Christ according to his understanding of the significance of the Christian life.

While the volume is believed by many scholars to be correctly ascribed to Gerard Groote, the work has also been widely circulated under the title *The Imitation of Christ* and credited to Thomas à Kempis (c.1380-1471). What happened seems to have been that Thomas was assigned the task of editing the manuscript of the founder of his order and produced two editions, the first in 1427 and the second in 1441. In neither does he name the author, no doubt assuming his name to be known by those who would use the diary. But he closes the second edition with the historical note in Latin, "Finished and completed in the year of our Lord 1441 by the hand of brother Thomas van Kempen at Mount Saint Agnes near Zwolle." In this way his own name became associated with the book. Actually some of it was from the pen of the editor, for some liberties were taken with the manuscript both by way of arrangement of the contents and by additions to the text. In this enlarged form it was distributed widely even before the invention of printing, and since that time it has had phenomenal circulation and has been translated into many languages to the great benefit of all who value the development of the life of the spirit. [A separate account of the work as credited to Thomas à Kempis also appears in this volume.]

There are three distinct parts in the original version of Groote. Book One, under the title *De imitatione Christi,* was in the hands of many as an aid to monastic devotion shortly after the author's death in 1384. The twenty-five short chapters can be divided into three sections: the first, written by Groote as a layman; the second, after he entered the monastic life; and the third, a detached series of admonitions.

The concentration of thought is on the elevation of the mind in the light of the teaching of Christ on self-denial. It is this spirit of submissive obedience that matters in religion, far more than learning in the usual disciplines of education. The author himself was a man of great accomplishments as far as erudition was concerned and had been professor of philosophy and theology at Cologne. Hence, there is no encouragement

given to ignorance as the parent of devotion. The question is rather that of assessment of the degrees of value to be placed on different kinds of knowledge. In the light of the fact that man's life is lived by the mercy and under the judgment of God, then all that makes the soul pleasing to its Divine Creator takes precedence over all that is merely pleasing to one's fellow man: "Right knowledge is not to be blamed; but a good conscience and a virtuous life are always to be preferred." Pursuit of this perspective leads to a drastic re-evaluation of the place of all temporal goods in life. Not only self-renunciation but restriction of association with other people and material things as an aid to interior discipline seems to be indicated. "It is a very great thing to live in obedience, to be under a superior and not to be one's own master," writes Groote. In this mood Gerard Groote entered the Carthusian monastery at Munnikhuizen on the Rhine.

The remaining eight chapters of Book One appear to be notes made while Groote was a novice. They place in high regard the life of seclusion and self-mortification. Contrasts with the world outside the monastery are frequent, and the many temptations to be avoided are the subject of the author's proverbial style of wisdom. Talkativeness, inquisitiveness, criticism of others, envy, and self-will are all snares to the devout by which he can lose his soul. Complete submissiveness to the community is difficult but obligatory: "You must learn to break your own will in many things, if you wish to live in peace and concord with others." This is the opposite of an ideal of aggressive self-assertion in the competitive world of commerce where the financial profit and loss account is the criterion of success or failure. The attention in monastic devotion is on the self, but not in its aggrandizement. It is self-abnegation in the belief that all the transitory world is vanity and vexation of spirit, and all that matters is the cultivation of contemplation on the eternal.

This fundamental point of view comes out clearly in the admonitions which end Book One. The great company of martyrs "hated their lives in this world, that they might keep them into life eternal." Groote weaves this theme in and out of his reflections; he sees the history of the Church as a story of toil and struggle against clever devices of evil to embroil the virtuous man in temporal affairs. Every moment must be made subject to the needs of others, and regular self-scrutiny is encouraged lest some wickedness penetrate the citadel of the soul. "Prepare yourself as a man to fight against the wickedness of the devil," he counsels. "Bridle your immoderateness and you will easily conquer every inclination of the flesh." Every person is to suit the discipline of the soul to his own needs and opportunities. Since men have different problems to overcome, flexibility must be permitted and even encouraged in all spiritual exercises.

The medieval theme of contempt of the world is never missing from these chapters, and the negative emphasis on what a virtuous man will not do is the subject of sentence after sentence. "It is truly a great misery to live here on earth," Groote writes; or again, "For to eat, to drink, to watch, to sleep, to rest, to labor and to satisfy all the needs of nature is truly a great misery, unhappiness and affliction to a devout man, who would fain be released and freed from all sin." Clearly, unless such an attitude is balanced by a compensating joy and satisfaction in obedience to Christ, Groote points out, it can be morbid and destructive of Christian regard for others outside the monastery who do not have the leisure to pursue intensive periods of self-examination and must attend to the business of mundane commerce. It could also be taken as a denial of the wisdom of the Creator in providing the world for man's habitation. At times Gerard Groote himself appears to lose this balance and to be too contemptuous of the temporal order.

Book Two opens with a quotation from the Gospels, "The Kingdom of God is within you," and this is understood as a reference to the interior life of each individual. "Learn to despise exterior things," the author admonishes, "and to apply yourself to interior things"; thereafter absorption in the affairs of earth are condemned in particular after particular. The heart that desires peace must follow Christ in suffering, misunderstanding, adversity, and humiliation: "Had you but once penetrated deep into the heart of the sweet Jesus and tasted only a little of his burning love, you would not be anxious about your own weal or woe; but you would rather rejoice when humiliation comes upon you, for the love of Jesus makes a man despise himself." True strength is inner strength; true security is found only in unqualified humility and obedience; true joy will come when the Cross is changed to a crown in the final consummation of union with Christ.

In the second part of Book Two the author composes a dialogue between Christ and the devout Christian and further develops the theme of disengagement from the world through indifference to the things which concern many other men. Interpreters of this section have seen in it an occasional reference to Groote's own trials when he became a preacher in the diocese of Utrecht, after he was advised not to complete his monastic vows. His public utterances on the love and goodness of God, and his caustic denunciation of the morals of the clergy, brought crowds to listen. The bishop, however, was not happy about the outspoken preacher and in 1383 stopped his troublemaking by withdrawing his license. Protests went unheeded, and an appeal was finally made to Rome for redress of the wrong, but no answer came before Gerard Groote's death in 1384.

It was during the period of his fame as a preacher of what is called the "Modern Devotion," that some others of like mind gathered round him, and the community of the Brethren of the Common Life was founded, through which educational work was done all over Europe.

The Following of Christ concludes with a series of admonitions in preparation for holy communion. It was in this section that Thomas made considerable changes, perhaps not always for the better, and it is here that the Roman Catholic allegiance of the author is most prominently expressed. Much of this Third Book would be impossible as a guide to devotion for those influenced by the Reformation. The fervency, sincerity, and humility of Groote are deeply impressive, however, and in this all Christian people can be at one when confronted with the claims of discipleship.

TRIALOGUS

Author: John Wycliffe (c.1329-1384)
Type of work: Polemical theology
First transcribed: 1382

Principal Ideas Advanced

God, man, and the universe are intelligible and necessary.

The Bible contains all truth and is the sole authority in religious matters.

Moral virtue and man's acceptation in God's sight are one and the same, and depend upon grace.

The wealth of the clergy and the mendicancy of the friars are contrary to the teaching of Scripture.

Transubstantiation and the "treasury of merit" are heretical conceptions.

Generally speaking, John Wycliffe (or Wyclif) was known to his contemporaries as a peerless scholastic, to the fifteenth century as an archheretic, and to the Protestant reformers as the *doctor evangelicus*. The

Enlightenment appreciated Wycliffe's anticlericalism; the nineteenth century hailed him as the "morning star of the Reformation," and the twentieth century has reacted by portraying him as a much less admirable figure. The definitive study of Wycliffe's thought, as contained in his very extensive writings, remains yet to be made.

The *Trialogus* was completed after Wycliffe's censure by the Blackfriars Council of 1382 and before his first apoplectic stroke later on in the same year, which left him an invalid. It represents his final convictions, and comprehends both his essential philosophic positions and his main reformatory concerns. The work consists of four books, and is written in the form of a "trialogue" among the champion of truth, Alithia; its adversary, Pseustis; and the judicious Phronesis, who represents Wycliffe's own point of view.

Book I ("*De Deo*") deals with the nature and attributes of God and with the ideas in the mind of God. It includes a discussion of the Trinity, which Wycliffe proceeds to prove by natural reason. Just as we reason from the perception of motion to the First Mover, he writes, so we can reason from the perception of the trinal nature of the soul (*memoria, ratio, voluntas*) to the trinal nature of the Deity that created it. For Augustine (354-430) does not regard this trinity of powers in the soul as three powers that inhere accidentally in it but as three distinct entities (*tres res*), any one of which is essentially the soul, just as any one of the three divine Persons is essentially God. But if God's self-intellection is a personal reality, His intellection of extrinsic objects is not a personal reality, but a necessary truth; namely, the intelligi-

bility of objects, which logically precedes their producibility; otherwise God would be able to produce an object which He did not understand, and thus to act unwisely (*non sapienter*). But how, then, could God create man wise (*homo . . . sapiens*)? Hence, Augustine rightly asserts that it is impossible to make a wise man apart from these exemplary ideas. These truths are formally distinct from each other and from God, but essentially they are God. For the "subtle evangelist" says that "whatever was made was life in him" (a common medieval reading of John 1:3,4: "*quod factum est in ipso vita erat*"); namely, in Him who said, "I am the way, the truth, and the life" (John 14:6). Ignorance of this metaphysic and of these eternal truths or ideas is wholly due to ignorance of the language arts (*artium sermocinalium*); namely, grammar and rhetoric; while, more generally, an erroneous understanding of Holy Scripture (which, according to Augustine, contains whatever truth there is) is due to ignorance of grammar and logic.

Book II ("*De mundo*") deals with the unity and necessity of the world, time and eternity, primary matter, psychology, the theory of knowledge, the doctrine of angels, predestination, and astronomy. Of special interest is Wycliffe's rational proof of the immortality of the soul, since this doctrine was not given the status of dogma in the Roman Church until 1517, when it was affirmed by the Fifth Lateran Council.

Book III ("*De virtutibus peccatisque et de salvatore*") in some respects seems to move in the direction of Reformation thought. Wycliffe's conception of faith, however, is wholly traditional. He defines faith as the "supernatural and habitual apprehension of truths to be believed." He recognizes that "faith" sometimes refers to the act of believing, the habit (*habitus*) from which the act proceeds, or the truth that is believed; and he distinguishes between unformed faith (*fides informis*) and faith that is formed by love (*fides caritate formata*). Love is the supreme virtue, the wedding garment without which no one shall be admitted to the celestial wedding of Christ and His Church. The love of God is understood as the love of His law, and all sin is attributed to ingratitude, but also to unbelief, for as long as a man is mindful of God he does not sin. All sin is to be avoided; if God Himself commanded a man to sin, it were better to disobey God than to sin. Nevertheless, "through the infinite compassion of God, the fall of man . . . has been made to subserve the introduction of a greater amount of good than would have resulted from his continuance" in the state of innocence. Man is incapable of moral virtue as long as God's grace is absent, and since the meritoriousness of a man's work depends on divine acceptance of it, a man cannot know his moral status apart from a special revelation. Nevertheless, "the grace of predestination, or final perseverance, cannot fall away from any one." There is only one mortal sin: final impenitence. God alone can punish or remit sin; hence, "prelates in granting indulgences, commonly blaspheme the wisdom of God." Men ought to be mindful of the commandments of the Lord, rather than of "the bulls of the pope, and the pretensions of the religious orders," writes Wycliffe. To disdain the au-

thority of Scripture is equivalent to disbelief in Christ. The veneration that is accorded to the saints ought to be given to Christ.

It is especially in Book IV ("*De signis*") that we encounter Wycliffe the reformer. He attacks the avarice of the clergy, the lethargy of the laity, and the noxiousness of the friars, all in the process of subjecting the reigning sacramental theory and practice to a searching critique.

Just as the Old Testament assigned no source of revenue beyond the tithe to the priests and Levites, so Christ and the Apostles taught by precept and example that the clergy should be content with the provision of its bare needs. By turning their back upon the institution of Christ, the clergy has accumulated tremendous wealth. Temporal lords (to whom Christ showed six distinct favors in His lifetime) by endowing the Church have begotten Antichrist. From the time of Constantine, the secular power has been diminished by the usurpations of the papacy. To restore to the secular lords their full power would mean the end of wars, greater freedom for the preaching of the Gospel, and an increase in the number of those who "wing their way to heaven." Wycliffe suggests that a gradual recovery by the Crown of the wealth of the Church should not be difficult, since title to the large benefices passes to the Crown upon the death of the incumbent, until the installation of his successor.

Wycliffe is no less opposed to begging friars than to rich priests. By begging, the friars deprive the needy and violate the law of nature, the commandment of God, who said, "There shall be no needy man nor beggar among you" (Deuteronomy 15:4, Vulgate), and the counsel of Solomon, who said, "Give me neither poverty nor riches." The friars' main defense, that Christ Himself practiced mendicancy, is answered by the allegation that Christ was not asking as a beggar for what was another's, but as a lord for what was His own. But mendicancy is only one of the faults of the friars. They also, writes Wycliffe, "have fallen into a radical heresy, for they pretend expressly in . . . letters, that the individuals to whom they grant them, shall be made partakers of merits from themselves after death." In thus making merchandise of their pretended merits, the friars even go beyond the popes, for the latter insist on contrition as prerequisite for the validity of an indulgence, while the friars do not. "Yet we know that God cannot remove the guilt of the sinner unless he be truly contrite." The whole notion of a "treasury of merits," Wycliffe insists, is "rude blasphemy."

The Friars make a simoniacal use of the office of preaching, Wycliffe continues, for they abuse their privilege of hearing confessions, neglect the evangelical law of brotherly admonition, and teach Eucharistic heresies. While they pose as Christ's poor ones, the friars, Wycliffe calculates, cost England 60,000 marks annually for the support of some four thousand of them. These "false brethren" err in subjecting themselves to some rule other than the rule of Christ, and in teaching men to rely on their pretended merits rather than on "the graciousness of Christ."

Wycliffe discusses each of the seven sacraments recognized by the Roman Church and expresses his dissatisfaction with the way they are understood and administered. For him, "Christ, in his own person, is a sensible sign, and as it seems to me, the sacrament of sacraments." In the sacrament of matrimony, the essential thing is that there be genuine (not merely verbal) consent, an actual being-joined-together by the Lord. The sacrament of holy orders no longer follows the New Testament pattern, which identifies the office of bishop and presbyter, and recognizes deacons only as a second order. Wycliffe reinterprets the sacrament of penance so as to make contrition (its essential element) a feeling that is perfected by oral utterance to God alone ("confession") and private confession to a priest ("satisfaction"). Auricular confession, said to be the invention of Pope Innocent III (1160-1216), should be made optional, as not essential to salvation. Modern bishops cannot claim Peter's authority to bind and loose, since they resemble Peter neither in spiritual power (to work miracles) nor in lowliness and holiness of life. Confirmation and extreme unction lack a proper scriptural foundation, he claims, and together with baptism and all the rest they are encumbered with unauthorized ceremonies.

The most detailed discussion is devoted to the sacrament of the Eucharist. For a thousand years, Wycliffe says, until Satan was loosed (see Revelation 20:1-8), Rome was in agreement with the "ancient doctrine" that the bread, which Jesus said was His body, truly is and remains bread. Wycliffe writes: "Mice . . . have an innate knowledge of the fact, that the substance of bread is retained, as at first; but these unbelievers, who deny this ancient doctrine, have no such knowledge. . . . What, I ask, could move our Lord Jesus Christ, thus to take away the power of judgment from his worshippers? In no way doth it redound to their good, nor can it be established by reason or Scripture, that it is necessary for men to be so deceived; for bread and wine, retaining their old form, would be a fitter representation of the body and blood of Christ, than an accident without a subject. . . ." "Quantity," being itself an accident, cannot serve as the subject. Nor can accidents exist *per se*. "And so Antichrist, in this heresy, overturns grammar, logic, and natural science; and, what is more lamentable, destroys the meaning of the Gospel. . . . The reason why men fall into this heresy, is that they disbelieve the Gospel, and embrace in preference the papal laws and apocryphal sayings. . . ."

When the sacramental bread is said to be the body of Christ, Wycliffe continues, this is to be taken as a figure of speech. For "the body of Christ . . . remains above in the skies, stable and unmoved, so that it has a spiritual existence in the host, but not of the dimensions, nor according to the other accidents appertaining thereunto in heaven. Hence it seems to me that the body of Christ, and so Christ in his humanity, may extend spiritually to every part of the world."

The body of Christ is then present "corporeally, substantially, and essentially" only in the (improper) sense in which the fullness of the Godhead is said to be dwelling in Christ bodily (Colossians 2:9). The sacrament is consummated "whenever Christ operateth with a man"; hence, a duly ordained priest is not absolutely necessary for the consecretion of the element, nor does his proper intention necessarily assure effectuality.

Wycliffe seems to represent the "intellectualistic" approach to theology that is usually associated with Christian Platonism and, in Latin theology, with Saint Augustine. Wycliffe's doctrine of the ideas represents this understanding of being as ultimately necessary and intelligible. His doctrine of God, man, sin, and salvation clearly reflects an awareness of the reality of the chain of causation which seems to be the peculiar characteristic of one strain of late-medieval Augustinianism. His great predecessor here was Thomas Bradwardine (c.1290-1349), who died as Archbishop of Canterbury. Both Bradwardine and Wycliffe represent a "conservative" reaction against the developing Ockhamism of their time. While Wycliffe and William of Ockham (c.1300-c.1349) agreed in their opposition to papal pretensions and to certain common scholastic views (for instance, that "quantity" is the subject of the accidents of the Eucharistic bread), their theological orientation was fundamentally different. Wycliffe recognized but one source of authority, the Bible, and would subject all ecclesiastical practices and pronouncements to the rule of Scripture; he identified moral virtue and merit in the sight of God, making both absolutely dependent upon the presence of infused grace; and he saw as one the totality of what God can (or could) do and what God in fact does do (or rather, has done from all eternity).

The boldness with which Wycliffe pressed the claims of Scripture and reason upon the ecclesiastical establishment, especially in his denial of transubstantiation, eventually cost him the support of politically powerful men. One by one, his followers within the University of Oxford were induced to recant. The Lollards, who drew their inspiration from Wycliffe, failed to maintain the high Augustinian theology of their master. Wycliffe found an apt disciple in John Huss (c.1369-1415) in Bohemia, and was condemned together with Huss by the Council of Constance in 1415. Some historians have seen in the English Reformation the realization of Wycliffe's ideals. Others have noted a certain theological kinship to John Calvin (1509-1564). Still others consider him the pioneer of English Nonconformity.

ON ECCLESIASTICAL UNITY

Author: John Gerson (1363-1429)
Type of work: Polemical theology
First transcribed: 1409

PRINCIPAL IDEAS ADVANCED

As the Church is essentially one in Christ, it has the right to promote its outward unity and to procure for itself an undoubted vicar of Christ.

Equity (divine and natural law) is to override positive law; the interests of the Church are to override all other interests.

The Church (represented by a general council) is superior to all its members (including the pope), for that which cannot err is superior to that which can err.

John Gerson was born December 14, 1363, as Jean Charlier in the French village of Gerson, near Rheims, the son of devout, poor peasants. He rose to become one of the best known and respected men of his time, and one of the most important figures in the later Middle Ages. Educated at the University of Paris, he earned his doctorate in theology and in 1395 succeeded his former teacher Peter d'Ailly (1350-1420) as chancellor of the university. He still occupied this position at the time of the Council of Constance (1414-1418), where he represented the university, the archdiocese of Sens, and the kingdom of France. One of the leading figures at this council, he must share the responsibility for the death of John Huss (born c.1369) and Jerome of Prague (born c.1370), who were burned as heretics in 1415 and 1416, respectively. The accession to power in France of the faction of the duke of Burgundy, which had been repeatedly censured by Gerson for the assassination of the duke of Orleans, prompted the chancellor to go into exile in Germany and Austria. In 1419 he found refuge in a Celestine monastery in Lyons, where he died in 1429.

Gerson was one of the most noted preachers of his time, whose spiritual fervor, reminiscent of Bernard of Clairvaux (1090-1153), found expression in a moving eloquence that was widely admired. A leading theologian of the nominalist (Ockhamist) school, he was at the same time a pillar of ecclesiastical orthodoxy. A moralist and counselor of the Christian conscience, he became known as the *doctor consolatorius*. As an educational reformer, he sought to infuse the warmth of Christian mysticism, particularly as it had been developed by the school of Saint Victor, into the scholastic curriculum. He is best known, however, as a leader of the conciliar movement, and as one of its important theorists.

Conciliarism, in brief, was the theory that the Church as a whole is superior to any and all of its members, including the pope, and that it exercises this authority through representative general councils. Late-medieval conciliarism had its roots in certain canonistic traditions, which were first gathered into a system by the Dominican John of Paris, who died in 1306. Marsiglio of Padua (c.1275-1342) and William of Ockham (c.1330-c.1349) were noted conciliarists, but their interest centered more in the Church as the collectivity of the faithful than in the general council as representing it. The outbreak of the Great Schism in 1378 gave considerable impetus to the spread and elaboration of conciliarism. Two German professors at the University of Paris, Conrad of Gelnhausen and Henry of Langenstein, wrote important conciliarist treatises during the early period of the schism, urging the calling of a general council in order that it might be determined who was the legitimate pope. In the 1390's two new approaches were proposed. One was to withhold recognition from both claimants until all reasonable doubts could be dispersed. This approach was intermittently adopted by the kingdom of France, Church and state collaborating in a manner that was to become the characteristic of Gallicanism. The other approach was to seek to persuade both pontiffs to abdicate. This approach, known as the *via cessionis*, was supported by the University of Paris and its chancellor, Gerson. It led directly to the Council of Pisa, which was called by cardinals of both obediences for the express purpose of ending the schism. The council opened its sessions on March 25, 1409. On June 5 both reigning popes were deposed, and the council proceeded to elect a new pope, Peter of Candia, who assumed the name Alexander V (reigned 1409-1410). Neither Benedict XIII (reigned 1394-1417) nor Gregory XII (reigned 1406-1415), however, surrendered their claims to the papal office, so that there were then three popes. Conciliarism had actively asserted itself; it did not triumph until the Council of Constance obtained the abdication of Gregory XII and effectually deposed Benedict XIII and John XXIII (antipope: 1410-1415), the successor of Alexander V. Its triumph was short-lived, however, as the new pope, Martin V (reigned 1417-1431), and his successor Eugenius IV (reigned 1431-1447) exerted every effort to undermine the supremacy of the general council over the papacy, which had been solemnly affirmed in the decree *Sacrosancta* of 1415. The victory of the papacy in this struggle may be dated from 1439, when Eugenius, having succeeded in "translating" the Council of Basle first to Ferrara and then to Florence, obtained the consent of the leaders of the Greek Church to reunion and the proclamation of his own supremacy.

Gerson's treatise *De unitate ecclesistica* was composed immediately after the chancellor had addressed the English delegation on its way to the Council of Pisa (January 20, 1409). It reflects the stage of conciliarist thought at this point of time, and purports to answer certain objections urged against the *via cessionis*. It is concise, and arranged into twelve propositions.

In Proposition I Gerson strikes a note that is now considered to be the keynote of late-medieval conciliarism: the interdependence of unity and reform in the Church. Gerson connects them by asserting that "the unity of the Church has been hampered by the sins of her sons; the remedy is their reform." It is evident, however, that Gerson here uses the term "reform" in a sense different from that of more radical conciliarists, such as Dietrich of Niem (c.1340-1418), who had specific constitutional and administrative reforms in mind. Gerson appears to think of reform in the traditional individualistic sense of a spiritual and moral rebirth, a turning from sin and a returning to Christ. While all conciliarists after the outbreak of the Great Schism sought both the unity and the reform of the Church, it seems appropriate to make a distinction among them. The "moderate" conciliarists, men like the cardinals Peter d'Ailly and Francis Zabarella (1335-1417), were not basically anti-papal at all; their main concern was the ending of the schism, and for that reason they looked upon the council as primarily an emergency measure for the restoration of the virtually absolute papal monarchy. The "radical" conciliarists, such as Dietrich of Niem and Matthew of Cracow (died 1410), recognized in the Roman curia the primary source of ecclesiastical corruption and decline, and were therefore more interested in reform than in the restoration of a single papal headship. At this time Gerson still belonged to the "moderates."

In Proposition II Gerson affirms that the essential unity of the Church always remains in Christ, the head of the Church, in whom all are one. But as divine and natural law enable any corporate body to procure its outward union, so the mystical body of Christ, the Church, has the right, through a general council, to procure for itself an undoubted vicar of its true head. Such a vicar is not really essential to the unity of the Church, for from time to time the Church is left without one, as at the death of a pope. Legal principles, therefore, are to be cast aside in favor of the theological principle of expediency, which requires the sacrifice of the interests of both contestants to the interests of the Church as a whole (Proposition III). Both contestants owe all that they are to the Church; hence they should be ready to offer their all, even their own lives, for her well-being. To surrender the primacy is not to abandon the flock, but to unite it (Proposition IV).

According to Gerson, the general council is not bound by all the provisions of positive law, but can proceed on the principle of equity. The application of this principle *doctrinaliter* belongs above all to those learned in theology, and only in a secondary way to those skilled in canon and civil law (Proposition V). If the two contestants refuse to abdicate, they should be condemned, and a new pope chosen, provided that the entire council approves the choice of two-thirds of the cardinals, or the greater and wiser part of them (Proposition VI). The alleged rights of both contestants are vitiated by their contrariety to natural and divine law (Proposition VIII). The Church should go back to the state it occupied before the outbreak of the schism; papal pronouncements made since then should be held in abeyance. If both contestants submit their abdication to the council, they are to be assured of sufficient security and rank (Proposition IX).

In Proposition X Gerson asserts that to affirm that one has completely fulfilled his duty in seeking the unity of the Church is rather to remain obstinate in one's error. Though he refuses to anticipate a conciliar decision as to whether this is actually the case now, he does not hesitate to say that circumstances may arise in which it would be permissible to withhold obedience from a duly elected pope, to coerce him even to the point of imprisoning him, or to maintain neutrality. For the pope is subject to the whole Church as one capable of error is subject to what can never err. Gerson here seems to maintain the infallibility of general councils. Conciliarism generally opposed the infallibility of the Church to the fallibility of the pope, but some leading theorists like William of Ockham, Conrad of Gelnhausen, and Peter d'Ailly distinguished the Church from its representative body, the general council, and attributed infallibility only to the former. Gerson does not seem to make the distinction.

When Gerson asserts that the conciliar program expresses only the common obligation of all Christians (Proposition VII), he reflects the general tendency of the later Middle Ages to emphasize the role of the laity in Church affairs. The Fourth Council of the Lateran (1215) had set the pattern for the councils of the later Middle Ages in aiming at the representation of the whole Church: the general council was no longer exclusively an assembly of bishops, but it included lower clergy and laymen. Ockham had insisted on the widest possible representation of laymen—even women—and had laid down the pregnant principle that all in authority have the right and duty to participate in the process of legislating for the Church. Peter d'Ailly advocated this Ockhamist position at Constance because of the abnormal situation, and asked that titular bishops be excluded from the suffrage, while doctors of theology and of civil and canon law be admitted on the ground that they exercise authority over their pupils. Gerson specifically commends King Charles VI of France (reigned 1380-1422) for concerning himself with the affairs of the Universal Church, as indicated by his open letter *Pax ecclesiastica* (1408), in which he threatened once again to withdraw obedience from Benedict XIII.

In Proposition XI Gerson asserts that it is not necessary to determine absolutely which of the contenders is the true pope. Those who are in doubt may do conditional penance. Just as a legitimate pope would be sinning in failing to promote the unity of the Church, so his opponents may be pardoned if they were always prepared to obey the Church and the truth that was known to them. In this proposition we catch a glimpse of that concern for the conscience which earned Gerson the title *doctor consolatorius*. We also see a principle enunciated which, though not originated by the late-medieval nominalists, was greatly developed and extended by them: the principle of implicit faith. Earlier it had been held that laymen (including the ignorant lower clergy, according to Pope Innocent IV) were not required to know Christian doctrine beyond a very few fundamentals, provided they affirmed that they believed implicitly whatever the Church believed. Heretical beliefs were held by Innocent IV to be harmless in laymen, so long as they were not aware that their beliefs differed from those of the Church. From the time of Ockham on, professions of implicit faith became common even among theologians.

If it seems unlikely that a new pope will be universally accepted, Gerson concludes, then the cardinals should make some other provision. They might, for instance, adopt the proposal of the Council of France (probably the Fifth French National Council of 1408) that there be no election if either of the present claimants should die. The cardinals assembled at Pisa notoriously failed to heed this warning, and consequently simply added a third claimant of the papal throne.

One can trace fluctuations in Gerson's conciliarism. Noteworthy is an initial burst of enthusiasm, expressed in several sermons of 1391 and 1392, and in the theses he defended in connection with his obtaining of the master's degree, in 1392. At that time Gerson did not hesitate to violate the royal injunction against public discussions of reunion, and perhaps even advocated its repeal in the presence of the king. When the university voted in favor of the "subtraction" of obedience from the Avignon pope (1395), it was over the opposition of the chancellor. Gerson saw in such a move an attack upon the traditional constitution of the Church that would at the same time aggravate the divisions in the ranks of the faithful. The "subtraction" was nevertheless made effective throughout France in 1398. Gerson continued his opposition, writing in defense of Benedict XIII, and in 1403 witnessed the restoration of obedience to the Avignon pope. Thereafter his attitude towards the papacy hardened, and by November, 1406, he was affirming the propriety, despite provisions of canon law to the contrary, of general councils not presided over by the pope or a papal legate. From the election of the supposedly conciliatory (Roman) Pope Gregory XII (November, 1406) to the latter's abandonment of the policy of reconciliation by the creation of new cardinals (May, 1408), Gerson was again counseling moderation. Then followed the period dominated by the prospect of the Council of Pisa, and from then on Gerson's conciliarism becomes increasingly radical. His sermon *Ambulate dum lucem habetis* (1415) may have saved the Council of Constance after the precipitate flight of (the Conciliar) Pope John XXIII. His treatise *De potestate ecclesiastica*, read at Constance on February 6, 1417, is one of the most comprehensive expressions of the conciliarist theory of ecclesiastical authority. Gerson envisaged a permanent subordination of the papacy to the general council, in the spirit of the decree *Frequens* adopted at Constance in the same year.

Conciliarism may be interpreted as an intermediate stage between the internationalism of the medieval Church and the ecclesiastical nationalism that was to emerge more strongly in the fifteenth and sixteenth centuries. Whereas in the earlier stage the control of religion had been mainly in the hands of the ecclesiastical hierarchy, and in the later stage came to be increasingly in the hands of the state, for a brief period the leadership of the Western Church was assumed by the universities, above all by Paris. From the beginning of the Great Schism until well into the sixteenth century, the University of Paris was the head and heart of the conciliar movement. Even after its defeat by the papacy, conciliarism survived as a potent influence in many universities, notably Paris, Vienna, Erfurt, Cracow, and Cologne.

Gerson seems to have been aware of a certain connection between Conciliarism and higher learning, between the university and the general council. This connection apparently revolves around the concept of equity, which dominates his *De unitate ecclesiastica.* As the ordinary hierarchical order of the Church is superseded by the authority of the Church as a whole, exercised through a general council, so the ordinary canonical laws are superseded by the principle that underlies all laws, the principle of equity. In Proposition V Gerson finely distinguishes between the determinative and the doctrinal application of equity. The former, a quasi-judicial function, belongs to the council. The latter, a teaching function, belongs primarily to scholars learned in theology, and secondarily to those skilled in canon and civil law. In the sermon *Vivat rex* (1405) Gerson specifically defended the right of the university, as the "Mistress of Truth," to proclaim the truth and to uphold the faith. In the sermon *Pax hominibus* (1409) Gerson stressed the cosmopolitan character of the university and deduced from it a duty to seek universal peace and unity.

TREATISE ON THE CHURCH

Author: John Huss (c.1369-1415)
Type of work: Church theory
First transcribed: 1413

PRINCIPAL IDEAS ADVANCED

The pope and the cardinals do not constitute the Church; the true Church is made up of the body of the predestinate in Heaven, on earth, and in purgatory.

Christ, not the pope, is the head of the Church; since the pope can err, he is to be obeyed solely when his teachings and life conform to those of Christ and the Apostles.

The spiritual power to retain and to remit sins is given to the Church, but neither pope nor priest can absolve except when absolution has first been given by God.

John Huss, the author of the *Treatise on the Church,* was burned as a heretic, on July 6, 1415, for the views written in the *Treatise.* The work is Huss's defense of views he acquired from John Wycliffe (c.1329-1384), from whom Huss draws heavily, particularly in the early chapters. The book was written in answer to a document signed by eight doctors belonging to the theological faculty of the University of Prague. The document called for the absolute submission to the commands of the pope and other ecclesiastical superiors. The work of John Huss, like that of Wycliffe, is protestant in opposition to the accredited ecclesiastical system of Rome. It is a work of first importance among works on the Church, and it was to be a forceful influence a century later during the troubled time of the Reformation.

The Church, as Huss conceives it, is one throughout the world. The bond of its unity is predestinating grace. The Holy Catholic Church is the totality of the predestinate, present, past, and future. The Church universal is one, but it is divided into the Church *militant*, the predestinate now waging war against the flesh, the world, and the Devil; the Church *dormient*, the number of the predestinate suffering in purgatory; and the Church *triumphant*, the blessed at rest in Heaven, who kept up Christ's warfare against Satan and have finally triumphed.

The visible Church is a mixed body made up of predestinate and reprobate. Christ alone is the head of the universal Church. The universal Church is not constituted by the pope and the cardinals, nor is the Church limited to that body over which the apostolic see has jurisdiction. The Roman Church is a part of the Church militant, and as long as the pope and his college follow Christ, it is in dignity its chief part, but no partial church can be the Holy Catholic Church. It is noteworthy that the Roman Church was in the past properly called a company of Christ's faithful, living under the obedience of the Roman bishop, just as the Antiochian Church was called the company of Christ's faithful, under the bishop of Antioch.

The visible Church is not inerrant, Huss claims, and the pope and his college of cardinals may be soiled with wickedness and sin. Unless the lives of the prelates are in accordance with the teachings of Christ, their authority is not binding. The foundation of the Church is the faith upon which the Church is built, not a faith in popes, but a faith in the Rock, Jesus Christ.

A Christian must believe explicitly and implicitly all the truth that is in Scripture, not the sayings of the saints which are apart from Scripture; nor should he believe papal bulls, except insofar as they are founded on Scripture. God cannot deceive or be deceived; the pope may deceive and be deceived.

Huss writes firmly that Christ, not the Roman pontiff, is the head of the Church. When, in Matthew, Christ says: "On this rock I will build my church," the term "rock" does not refer to Peter, nor to the Papacy, but to Christ himself. Christ alone is the chief foundation of the Church. Peter never was, nor did he claim to be, the head of the Holy Catholic Church. Christ appointed Peter as Captain and Shepherd because of the pre-eminence of virtues which fitted Peter to rule the Church. Peter excelled in faith, humility, and love. The person who is called to be Peter's vicar and who shares the faith and virtues that Peter had is his true vicar, but if he walks in opposite paths, then he is the legate of Antichrist and is at variance with Peter and Jesus Christ.

With respect to the power-authority of Christ, given to His vicars, as expressed in the words, "I will give unto thee the keys of the kingdom of heaven," the power to bind and to loose sins, "and whatsoever thou shalt bind on earth, shall be bound in heaven, and whatsoever thou shalt loose on earth shall be loosed in heaven," Huss notes that such power is spiritual. It is, however, not given to a person, but to the whole Church militant. The vicar of Christ is not able to absolve or to bind, to forgive sins or to retain them, unless God has given remission previously. The ignorant believe that the priest first binds and looses men, and then God follows, but God's act of binding or loosing is absolutely first. The power of remitting sins and retaining them is, therefore, simply a declaratory power. The priest can absolve from sin only when such absolution has previously been granted by God. (Huss declared himself opposed to the practice of granting indulgences.)

Every vicar of Christ may in fact err even in those things which concern the faith. God alone knows infallibly whose sins may be remitted, and God alone cannot be moved by a wrong motive in binding or loosening. The vicar that refuses to impart absolution to one truly penitent cannot truly refuse absolution to one whom God has already absolved.

No one is saved unless he is meritoriously subject to Jesus Christ, and it is the latter who is the true and sole Roman Pontiff, for He is the head of the universal Church and of every particular church. The pope at Rome is not the head of the Church or even necessarily the vicar of Christ. On occasion the Roman bishop has been unlettered,

a heretic and antichrist; that is, a pope living contrary to Christ. The pope may be the vicar of Christ and may be so to his profit, if he is a faithful minister predestinated unto the glory of the head, Jesus Christ.

The accepted notion that the pope is the head of the Church and that the college of cardinals is the existing body of the Church, is rejected by Huss because that notion is not known by the bodily senses, discovered by infallible intelligence made known through revelation, or laid down in sacred Scripture.

It is not necessary for salvation for Christians to believe that anyone is the head of any church whatsoever unless the evangelical life and works of the claimant plainly establish him as Christ's vicar.

It is, moreover, erroneous to hold that the college of cardinals is the body of the Church, for the college by itself does not include all the predestinate, the true Body of Christ. Christ is the head of the Church and each of the predestinate is a member.

No one truly occupies the place of Christ or of Peter, unless he follows Him in his life, nor does any person otherwise receive procuratorial power. The vicarial office demands the conformity of life and authority to the power of Him who appoints. When a pope is humble, when he pastures the sheep on the Word of God, when he is meek, patient, chaste, and solicitous in the service of the Church, then he is the vicar of Christ, so far as the outward senses can determine. If he lives otherwise, however, the pope is the vicar of Antichrist. No pope is the manifest and true successor of Peter if the pope lives at variance with the principles of Peter. Nor are the cardinals the manifest and true successors of the college of Christ's other apostles, if they do not live as did the Apostles and keep the commandments of Jesus Christ.

The government of the Church need not be carried on by the pope and the cardinals. God is able, without assistance, to rule His Church. In fact, for three hundred years the Church was so ruled. In those early centuries, the office of the apostles consisted solely in good living, in teaching, in baptizing, and in healing; the regimen of the apostles was free of pomp and luxury. God is in fact able to bring His Church back to its pristine state by taking away the government from the pope and the cardinals and giving it to others.

The prelate who is proud, who lives in luxury and greed, who does not feed the sheep, but oppresses them and scatters them, is neither to be followed nor obeyed. The standard of ecclesiastical judgments is the law of God.

According to Huss, the Scriptures are the norm of our behavior; they are, however, to be explained solely as the Holy Spirit requires, not according to human fancy. The opinion of no man, including that of the pope, is to be held if it plainly contains falsehood or error, as it surely does when it contradicts the Scriptures. Obedience should be rendered to the pope and the cardinals only as long as they teach the truth according to the law of God.

A man cannot be morally virtuous if he does not obey God, but when obedience is rendered to man, rather than to God, then it is evil obedience, so that everyone obeying evilly is disobedient to God. He who commands ought only to command things in agreement to the law, and the person who obeys ought never to act contrary to the will of God.

The faithful disciple of Christ ought to consider how a command emanates from the pope, whether it is the express command of Christ's law or of any Apostle. If the command of the pope is the command of Christ, the believer ought to obey humbly and reverently. However, if the believer knows that what the pope commands is at variance with the teachings of Christ or is detrimental to the good of the Church, then the believer ought to resist it lest he become a partner in crime.

When a superior of the visible Church commands that preaching be restricted to cathedrals, parochial, or cloistral churches, and that chapel services cease, such a command is contrary to that of Christ, and it is not to be obeyed. The believer can appeal to the true head of the Church, to Jesus Christ. For He is superior to any pope in deciding a case; He cannot err, nor deny justice, nor can He condemn where there is no demerit.

If the pope puts aside the law and a devout profession of the Gospel, and gives heed to human tradition—if he abandons the manner of life followed by Christ, and becomes secular in his interest, then to rebel against such an erring pope is to obey Christ the Lord.

Work that is commanded by a pope or other prelate for which there is no reason or utility to the Church of Christ ought not to be performed. We ought to realize by faith that God never commands us to do anything which is neither meritorious nor profitable to salvation. No one should obey man in anything, Huss insists, even the least thing, if it is opposed to the divine commands. As we must obey what is lawful, so we must resist our superiors when they walk contrary to the commands of Christ. Inferiors and laics ought to examine and to judge intelligently the commands of superiors, for no human decree is valid or to be observed unless it can be seen to exemplify a divine commandment of Christ.

The believer who disobeys in a state of grace without committing mortal sin need have no fear of the excom-munication of man. For no judge can excommunicate a man unless the man himself has already excommunicated himself by his offenses. Only those who depart from the Lord's commandments are truly excommunicated. Whoever excommunicates another falsely for temporal gain is himself in danger of true excommunication. The true believer need not fear excommunication, suspension, nor interdict; he need fear only that he become unfaithful to the teachings of Jesus Christ.

THE IMITATION OF CHRIST

Author: Thomas à Kempis (c.1380-1471)
Type of work: Counsels on spiritual life
First transcribed: c.1418

PRINCIPAL IDEAS ADVANCED

The aim of the true Christian should be to imitate, insofar as it is possible, the model given to him in the person and in the life of Christ.

To achieve this aim means to discover the spiritual, the inner life, to turn completely away from the affairs of the world and our own outwardly directed desires.

Humility, contrition, self-discipline, and a willingness to submit to spiritual authorities, are all necessary if one is to achieve the goal of the imitation of Christ's life, reconciliation with God, and spiritual peace.

The unspoken assumption of Thomas à Kempis's *Imitation of Christ* is that the Christian is expected to attempt to follow the life of Christ. Christ's life ought to be of first consideration for all who desire enlightenment and freedom from spiritual blindness. Whoever wants to understand the words of Christ must, if he desires success, strive to make his whole life conform to that of Jesus. Discoursing learnedly on the Trinity is beside the point, if one lacks humility, Thomas asserts; for a true Christian it is better to feel contrition than to be able to define it.

The model life is the contemplative one. Its aim is to despise the world and to draw near daily to the Kingdom of Heaven, to withdraw one's heart from the love of visible things, and to direct one's affections to things invisible. Of what use is knowledge without the fear of God? A man who is humble pleases God more than does an intellectual who charts the courses of the stars but neglects his own soul. On the other hand, a man who truly knows himself realizes his own worthlessness and does not take pleasure in the praises of men. An inordinate desire for knowledge, Thomas advises us, should be restrained, for such desire leads to anxiety and deception. There are many things which matter little whether they are understood or not. In fact, it really is not wise to busy oneself with anything except what furthers salvation.

Unless one's life is more holy than the average, Thomas advises, the more complete and excellent one's knowledge the more severe will be God's judgment. A genuine understanding and a humble approval of oneself is, actually, the best and most valuable of all lessons. No one has a harder goal or a fiercer struggle than the man who strives to conquer himself. At best, knowledge will contain an element of obscurity, just as all perfection in life is accompanied by some imperfection; and a humble knowledge of oneself is a safer road to God than a long study of the sciences. However, it is not learning itself that is to blame, for in itself it is worth while, but a sincere conscience and a holy life are always preferable.

On the Day of Last Judgment one will not have to account for what one has read but for what he has done, Thomas continues. If one chooses to be great rather than humble, he will simply perish in his own conceit. As far as action is concerned, the problem is that evil told about someone is believed more easily than if the report were good, and the problem in the self is that a man who is not perfectly dead to self

is easily tempted and overcome even in small matters. True peace of heart comes only from resisting the passions, not from yielding to them, and whoever puts his trust in men or in any creature, Thomas warns us, is being very foolish.

To want to go to other places and constantly to desire change is what unsettles many. These desires represent opinions, Thomas asserts, and if God is to dwell among us, sometimes our own opinions must be sacrificed for the sake of peace. Public gatherings lead to a discussion of worldly affairs, and this is a hindrance since, even with the best intentions, it quickly corrupts and ensnares us in vanity. Any outward consolation, such as these discussions, may be an obstacle to inner and divine consolation. How can anyone be at peace as long as he meddles in affairs other than his own? If only we can become completely dead to self and be free from inner conflict, then we can savor spiritual things and come to deserve an experience of heavenly contemplation. Even the outward observances of religion, if relied upon, deter genuine devotion.

The happiest fact of all, however, is that the man who could root out one fault each year would soon become perfect. Even trouble speeds us on our way toward this goal, since it compels a man to search his own heart. If only men could place such complete trust in God, Thomas exclaims, that they would no longer need the comfort of men, that would be ideal. Temptations, although troublesome, are to be preferred to too smooth a life, since through temptations we are humbled, cleansed, and instructed and thus brought to depend more on God. Since we are born with an inclination toward evil, temptation comes from our own nature and will be with us as long as we live. Yet the beginning of all evil temptation is an unstable mind and a lack of proper trust in God.

Disciplining ourselves in various ways, says Thomas, is the only way that we can hope to live in peace and harmony with others. Yet discipline is not limited to the rigors or form of the monastic life. Only the transformation of our way of life and a complete mortification of the passions can make us truly religious followers of the Christian way of life. Solitude and silence help. Whoever wants to live an inward and spiritual life must withdraw from the crowd. No man can live in the public eye without risking the loss of his soul. In silence and quietness a devout soul can make progress. Too much freedom is a detriment. Discipline the senses and examine yourself strictly, Thomas advises, since the more strict the self-examination the more cause for sorrow.

No happiness will be found until men turn to God. Since everyone, including king and pope, has trouble and anxiety, his lot is the happiest who is able to suffer for the love of God. The inner life is greatly hindered by the body, but that difficulty is simply something man must put up with in this life. What can be done is to discipline the body with penance, in order to enjoy a sure hope of salvation. Keep yourself a stranger, Thomas urges, and be a pilgrim on earth. It is better to learn to endure a little now, in order to avoid more grievous trouble, and he who really loves God will not fear death or punishment or judgment or Hell. Nevertheless, the fear of Hell can act as a restraint against sin, even if the love of God does not. The stricter we

are with ourselves, the greater will be our spiritual progress.

After having given these counsels in the spiritual life, Thomas à Kempis turns to consider the inner life. Here is the most important area for concentration, since all true glory and beauty, he is sure, are really to be found within the soul. The inner man never becomes wholly immersed in outward affairs, and so it is easier for such a man to understand himself. If the inner life is rightly ordered, a man is not troubled by the strange and perverse ways of others. All good things turn to the advantage of the inner man, since a discontented or restless man is tormented by suspicions. Simplicity and purity are the most important qualities to develop in the inner life, since simplicity reaches out after God while purity is able to discover and to enjoy Him. Any man who turns wholly toward God loses his sloth and becomes transformed into a new creature.

To become interior and devout is our goal, Thomas avers, but this cannot be reached until each man refrains from criticism of others and pays attention to his own faults. This is what we all must do if we really desire true peace and union with God. Set everything else aside and attend to yourself, Thomas urges. Yet not even the self is our ultimate aim or value, since the soul that loves God will come to regard all things other than God as worthless. True and lasting glory involves nothing of worldly glory. And neither external praise nor blame disturbs a man who has achieved great tranquillity of heart. Everything else must be surrendered for the sake of the love of Jesus. But if any man should forget and turn aside to worldly things, he will soon cause

Jesus to leave him and he will lose His grace.

Pride is to be avoided and contrition desired, and any consolation or contemplation which leads to either ought to be avoided. Seeking comfort is a sign of self-interest, and any self-centered man is really mercenary. Pure love of Jesus is free from all self-interest and self-love. Yet the problem is, and Thomas à Kempis freely recognizes it, that man is not by nature inclined to chasten the body and to bring it into subjection. A life of contrition is in a sense a dying life, since certain natural instincts are starved. The discipline of self cannot really be achieved by man's own strength without divine assistance. Yet there is no better way than contrition, no way more comfortable, to achieve salvation.

Turning to the means to achieve inward consolation, Thomas à Kempis advises us never to think ourselves to be anything because of our own good deeds, but instead to remember our sins with deep sorrow. Leave the examination of God alone and consider rather how much good we have left undone, Thomas advises. Love is our greatest asset and guide in achieving inward consolation, since it is born of God and is free and unrestrained. Humility is also necessary here, and in fact is much more necessary and desirable than a great store of learning coupled with vain complacency. Self-interest as a motive is often hidden, and as long as it exists, even in a secret form, it will be nothing but a hindrance and a burden.

Obedience is a key quality here too. Any man who is unwilling to submit freely and willingly to his superior shows that his lower nature is not yet under his control. It is hard, Thomas à Kempis agrees, to subject oneself to the spiritual authorities of the temporal Church for God's sake, and yet it is absolutely necessary to achieve grace. Since what is impossible by nature can be made possible by grace, obedience is an issue of no little import. And the man who hangs on to life and self-assertiveness gets little for his reward, since life is subject to so many sorrows and calamities. The sacrifices necessary to achieve inward consolation are well worth it.

Our mind should seek to rest in God above all things, remembering God's blessings. Four things will bring us peace: possessing less rather than more, regarding ourselves as lower than others, praying to have God's will fulfilled through our acts, and always doing the will of others rather than our own will. Curiosity brings only evils, whereas a mind free from such desires is excellent above all else. Self-love only hinders our search for God and trouble actually helps us find Him. There is no loss at all involved if we forsake creatures in order to find the Creator. God is fully gracious to those who love Him.

A surrender of the self, in the way Thomas à Kempis describes, will bring us freedom of heart, he is sure. No longer will a man thus free be over-anxious. If man has no personal goodness of which to boast, then his peace does not depend upon himself or upon any man, but upon God alone. Distractions can be avoided, distractions of outer things which would take away inward consolation. Man's trust should be entirely in God, in times of peace and in times of trouble as well. Grace cannot be granted to the worldly minded, but through the imitation of Christ, by following His way of suffering and self-denial, all men can turn their minds from the worldly toward the inner life, and place their hopes and trust in God alone.

OF LEARNED IGNORANCE

Author: Nicholas of Cusa (Nicolaus Cryfts or Krypffs, c.1401-1464)
Type of work: Mystical theology
First transcribed: 1440

Principal Ideas Advanced

Since from God there is an outflow of all things, the question arises as to how the creation returns to unity with its Creator.

In God there is a reconciliation of contraries, but such a situation places God beyond rational grasp, so that knowledge of this fact is a learned ignorance.

The basis of the understanding of God is usually mathematical, for it is by reference to quantities that one can grasp the various features of God as constituting both the maximum and the minimum in such a manner that reason is necessarily transcended.

Since number includes all things that are capable of comparison, Nicholas of Cusa (Nicolas Cusanus) argues in *Of Learned Ignorance* that number is a fitting framework for discussion. Yet the subject he proposes to discuss is the most difficult of all: the divine nature; here the best efforts yield only ignorance. It is nevertheless beneficial, Nicholas's thesis runs, to understand why we are necessarily ignorant about the divine. The better a man knows his own ignorance, the greater his learning will be. If we are to deal with ignorance as our greatest learning, then we will have to determine the precise meaning of the "maximum" or "greatest." If the term "maximum" means that nothing greater can exist, then being and the maximum are identical. Furthermore if all things are united with the maximum because it is the maximum, then the minimum also coincides with the maximum, since nothing can be placed in opposition to the maximum.

The maximum is Nicholas's name for God, and the study of Him is above reason; to the minimum Nicholas gives the name Jesus. In the discussion of these ultimate concepts and in the attempt to reconcile their apparent opposition, one must take all terms symbolically rather than literally, since the foundation for learned ignorance is the truth that the absolute is beyond our grasp and can only be indicated. A finite intellect cannot by means of comparsion reach the absolute truth of things; the intellect can never grasp any truth with such precision that the truth could not be comprehended with infinitely greater precision. All we know of truth, then, is that the absolute truth is beyond our final reach. Ontological truth is unobtainable in its entirety. The better we learn this lesson of ignorance, writes Nicholas, the closer we draw to truth itself.

The simple absolute maximum is greater than our powers of comprehension, and nothing in existence can be greater than it. On the other hand, the minimum is that which cannot be less than it is. But neither can the maximum be less than it is. Thus, Nicholas argues, it is evident that the minimum is identical wtih the maximum. The maximum quantity is infinitely great, while the minimum is infinitely small. Therefore, the minimum is as much a superlative as the maximum. Furthermore, distinctions exist only for things susceptible of "more" and "less"; and, since distinctions cannot exist in the absolute maximum, the maximum is above any form of affirmation or negation. Being without distinction, the absolute maximum is all things while yet being none of them. The absolute is at once the maximum and minimum of being.

The basis for learned ignorance is that there is no difference between the two affirmations (1) that God is light and (2) since God is light at its highest, He is light at its lowest. This paradox is beyond our understanding, which is fundamentally unable by any rational process to reconcile contradictories. Nicholas claims that the discovery of God's paradoxical nature forces us to admit our ultimate ignorance, not because we know nothing, but because what we do discover about the divine nature we are unable to reconcile rationally. Yet an absolute maximum is intelligible, able to be named. It remains ineffable, beyond our comprehension, only because the intelligible attributes we learn are rationally irreconcilable. Number is still our best

aid here, for Nicholas does not leave understanding at this point of ignorance, which is the beginning, not the end of learning. For number too, it is one and the same thing to call a number infinite and to say that it is the minimum.

Unity is a minimum, Nicholas continues, a simple minimum that coincides with the maximum. Unity cannot, therefore, be a number, although it is the principle of all number. Considering number led Nicholas to the conclusion that absolute unity (following the Neoplatonists) is a most fitting attribute of God; but the divine unity is of a special kind, concerning which intellectual difficulties arise. God's unity is such that He is actually all that is possible. God, consequently, is infinite unity. Number, since it is a being of reason, owes its existence to our power of comparing and distinguishing. The reality of number is limited to the reality it has in the mind. Therefore, number could not exist if it did not necessarily proceed from unity. Number and unity and God are thus linked in a necessary and yet ultimately baffling way—baffling not because we cannot discern these basic relationships but because we cannot fully reconcile that which we so clearly discern.

Nonbeing and minimum being are identical with the maximum, since nothing can stand in opposition to it. All that can be said or thought, Nicholas concludes, can be exhausted by the following propositions: it is, or it is not; it is, and it is not; it neither is nor is it not. Here the problem is posed at its extreme. Nicholas feels obligated to assert every possible form of being and nonbeing as applied to the maximum in order to preserve its ultimate status as the maximum. Yet doing this leads to assertions which seem not reconcilable. The name "maximum" must mean that being in this highest, although indescribable, way is predicated of it more than of any being that can be described. The problem is that the ultimate description requires so many statements that God remains indescribable.

Nicholas then proposes unity, equality, and connection as a trinity which is at once a unity. Such a three-in-one is required in order that from unity, eternality, and equality, we shall be able to see how diversity, inequality, and changeableness arise. Strangely enough, such a concept of unity is not itself a simple notion. We have a connection of unity only when we grasp that each thing is a unity, that unity itself is all things and that, as a consequence, each thing within unity is also all things. There is, then, only one correct way of understanding the Supreme Unity and that is as a trinity. Unity at its highest and most perfect understanding necessarily presupposes these co-relationships: intelligent being, intelligible object, and act of understanding. Thus, the correct concept of unity must be as a three-in-one. Unity, in fact, is a trinity, for nondivision, distinction, and connection all have their origin in unity and constitute its essential meaning.

The mathematical parallel has led to new ways of reasoning about God, which in this context do not seem out of order. New modes are valid and possible, which in no way correspond to the simple, natural order. In this setting, a new mode of reasoning does not seem out of order. The examples which number provides, when number is correctly interpreted, lead to a new

truth and understanding. Following this path, the reader experiences a wondrous delight and advances in the new way of learned ignorance. Reasoning about God requires learning new forms, modes of reasoning which deny normal ways of thought. The grasp of these new ways which bypass simple understanding enables one to realize in what respect learning is necessarily a learned ignorance, a learning incapable of final statement or full reconciliation with pedestrian norms.

Symbolism, of course, is necessary in such a novel situation. No image can reproduce divine nature accurately enough to rule out another image more faithful and precise. Mathematics furnishes some good examples of precise imagery, and in fact mathematical symbolism is necessary where things divine are concerned. Symbols are a necessary approach to things divine, and mathematical signs supply a certain indestructible certitude. From here Nicholas goes on to explore certain mathematical relationships between the finite and the infinite, and particularly the way in which the potentialities of the finite are actualized in the infinite. Mathematical examples assist one in rising to the intelligible order, and then what is impossible in the material order is seen as not only possible but as absolutely necessary in the divine order.

An infinite line is the infinite actualization of all that is potential in a finite line; this mathematical analogy indicates to us the way in which the maximum is the infinite actualization of all that is simply and absolutely possible. Mathematical symbols and analogies help one to see what otherwise could not be seen easily or directly; in the maximum, absolute possibility it-self and infinite actual existence are perfectly identified. No intelligence comprehends God and yet, through the knowledge gained by such mathe-matical comparisons and considera-tions, He is known. Intelligence can be learned in this respect; it is igno-rant only in that it discovers its own final inability ever to comprehend God. Sciences are inadequate to comprehend His nature, and in this respect wisdom finally is ignorance and pretentious language is meaningless.

God can be approached by remov-ing all that has participated being, but the difficulty is that when one does this there seems to be nothing left. Once one mentally removes all that has participated being, such an entity is hard to grasp, and yet exactly what seems nothing to the intellect is the incomprehensible maximum. God ac-tually encompasses all things, even contradictories, just as a circle en-compasses all that exists and all that does not exist. The circle is a crucial theological figure, Nicholas argues, and he claims that all theology is cir-cular and lies within a circle. Even the terms of the attributes are truly con-vertible. Infinity seems to make attri-butes equal and to embrace contradic-tories.

Nicholas, of course, is quite partial to the method of negative theology. Such a method is absolutely indispensa-ble, he argues, since without it no thinker could reach high enough or be able to reach to God as ineffable. In theology negative propositions are true, and affirmative ones are inade-quate. Of the negative ones, those are more true which eliminate greater im-perfections from the infinitely perfect. Through negative theology we are in

a position to see that absolute truth ex-ists, though we are still unable to com-prehend it. Degrees cannot be admit-ted in the infinite; absolute equality is predicable of God alone.

God is the opposite of nothing, Nicholas asserts, with being as an in-termediary. Thus, it becomes clear that Nicholas's method of "learned igno-rance" actually yields some quite ex-plicit statements about God, even though He is beyond comprehension. The creature comes from God, yet it cannot add anything to Him who is the maximum. The plurality of things is due to the fact that God is nothing. The universe for Nicholas is only a re-stricted form of maximum; the uni-verse is infinity contracted to the rela-tively infinite. Absolute unity admits no plurality, whereas the unity of the universe does. In the universe iden-tity consists in diversity, just as unity consists in plurality. Universe means universality; that is, a unity of distinct things. The entire universe was brought into being by a simple emana-tion of the restricted maximum from the absolute maximum.

Apart from God every being is lim-ited, and there is no potency, form, or act which is not God. Only in their fi-nite state is it true that the forms of things are distinct. In the absolute the forms are not many and distinct but one. One infinite exemplar is all that is needed and one alone suffices. Our ig-norance that is learning has shown that in God identity is diversity. Nicho-las incorporates the doctrine of the Trinity and of the Holy Spirit in ex-traordinarily abstract discourse, and in his third and last book he interprets the person of Jesus in abstract and di-alectical categories. Nicholas believes fully that God is not comprehensible, and yet out of his considerations as to why this is true he nevertheless develops a complete theology, and he thereby wrests learning from his ignorance.

THE SCALE OF PERFECTION

Author: Walter Hilton (d. 1396)
Type of work: Devotional guidebook
First published: 1494

PRINCIPAL IDEAS ADVANCED

The achievement of a mature and deeply satisfying Christian experience requires serious effort and self-discipline.

The scale or ladder to the heights of authentic Christian love and devotion is one which must be climbed one step at a time.

The ascent to Christian fulfillment involves both God's grace and man's deliberate and often arduous effort.

Whether one practices an active or a contemplative Christian life, he must avoid emotional extremes; he must demonstrate a love of truth, and he must pay attention to the practical demands of life.

In the practice of the devotional life, one must turn not to Rome or to Jerusalem, but to his own inner soul.

The *Scale of Perfection* is the chief work of Walter Hilton, who occupied a central position in the small group of English mediaeval mystics which included Richard Rolle (c.1295-1349), Julian of Norwich (c.1342-after 1413), and the anonymous author of the *Cloud of Unknowing.* Hilton, about whom little is known, was an Augustinian canon of the Thurgarton Priory, near Southwell in Nottinghamshire. In *The Scale of Perfection* Hilton produced a devotional guidebook which reflects the varied demands made on him as an official of a religious order composed of men who devoted themselves not only to meditation but also to land and property management. His book circulated in numerous manuscripts for over a century before it was printed in 1494. No less a student of English mysticism than Evelyn Underhill observed that probably no other work of its kind has so wide and enduring an influence.

Intent upon maintaining unswerving orthodoxy at a time when Lollard and Wycliffe followers were being combated, Hilton relies most heavily upon the Bible, especially the Psalms and St. Paul, and upon St. Augustine (354-430), St. Bernard (1090-1153), St. Bonaventura (1221-1274), and Richard of St. Victor (d.c.1173). The influence on Hilton of the mystical theology of Dionysius the Pseudo-Areopagite (fifth century), with its stress on the paradoxes of mystical experience, is also easily discerned. Hilton, however, makes no attempt to impress his readers with erudition or to pose as an exceptionally pious man. Nor does he claim for himself the heights of mystical rapture. He observes that while his subject is the contemplative life he does not himself "have it in feeling and in working as I have it in saying." Hilton demonstrates a greater concern for truth and for common sense practicalities than for the bizarre and the emotional: "It sufficeth to me for to live in truth principally, and not in feeling."

The Scale of Perfection is not a storehouse of esoteric wisdom for initiated souls, but "a way-book for the soul traveling in spirit to Jerusalem." In his book Hilton checks the natural desire of the ardent beginner for special experiences and consolations, warns against the religious formalism which stresses religious practices as the end and not as the means to the devotional life, and expresses a common sense attitude in respect of physical austerities: "Rather use best meat and most costly if it less hinder the keeping of the heart than to take only bread and water, if that hinder him more." It is not surprising that Hilton has been praised for his sanctified common sense.

The *Scale* (or ladder) presents the difficulties on the road to that perfect flowering of the interior life of love and prayer to which in a greater or lesser degree every authentic Christian is called. The image of the ladder, a very common one in mystical writings, is used. Man must take one step at a time on the way, the gradual ascent doubly conditioned by God's grace and man's deliberate and arduous striving. As Evelyn Underhill observes in her discerning introduction to the 1923 edition of Hilton's masterpiece, the underlying theological structure is the concept of man's soul, which is not only the image of God, but also a reflection of sin, which has impressed upon the mortal soul another pattern or "dark image." The goal of the spiritual life is the restoration of the soul to its proper status by a remaking or reformation which will obliterate the false or dark image.

The book is addressed generally to those who crave the deeper consciousness of reality and feel the impulse to a more complete consecration. It is written in particular to a recluse in her cell, who is dedicated to the life of prayer. Hilton prepares the reader for a deep analysis of motive, for the gradual awareness of the self-deceiving tendency to rationalization within the spiritual life. What helps man most to God, says Hilton, is attending to God and not to the self. Man needs to concentrate his whole will and feeling on this goal, the attending to God, as the true goal of the spiritual quest.

There are two manners of life, Hilton declares, the active and the contemplative. The active consists in love and charity exercised exteriorly by good or "corporal" works. The contemplative is reflected in perfect love and charity. Within the contemplative there are three sections on the scale of perfection. On the lower section one knows God, yet it is the knowing of God as one knows water, unsavory and cold, before the miracle of wine, when cold reason is changed into spiritual light and burning love by the gift of the Holy Ghost. The next section on the scale of perfection is affection, the knowing of God by feeling. The rung of affection may be brief, "a little tasting of the sweetness of the love of

God," or prolonged on a higher level through spiritual exercise. The highest section is reached when one both knows and feels the knowing and perfect love of God. A man begins the contemplative life on earth, but full perfection, beyond the highest level of knowing and feeling, is reserved for Heaven. No living man can have the height of the contemplative state continually and habitually.

The knowing of God by man comes not by the sound of ear, sweetness of mouth, nor through any bodily sensation, writes Hilton. The knowing and feeling extends beyond the physical so that man may know and feel what is the length of the endless being of God, the breadth of the wonderful charity and goodness of God, the height of His almighty majesty, and the bottomless depths of His wisdom. The contemplative life demands that man conform his soul to God. Three means are known that can bring a soul to contemplation: the reading of holy Scripture and good books, spiritual meditation, and diligent prayer with devotion. One needs to have humility, firm faith, resolute will and purpose to seek after God. Right humility requires man to put out of his heart all imprudent looking into other men's actions. It drives one wholly to behold oneself as if there were nothing other than God and the self. A trivial sin in oneself is considered more grievous than a mortal sin in another, if a man possesses right humility within himself.

The necessity of prayer within the contemplative life is constant. Prayer is not the cause for which God has given grace, but it is a way or means by which grace freely given comes into the soul. When man awakes out of his sleep, he should whisper the prayer

of the spirit, not of the body, a prayer free from all fleshly thoughts and affections. Prayer is an ascending of the desire of the heart to God by withdrawing it from all earthly thoughts. There are various prayers: the vocal prayer of the individual, the prayers of the Church, the vocal prayer which comes from the affection of the heart, the prayer which is only in the heart, a prayer without speech which brings great rest and quietness of soul and body. Prayer is not voice or reason, but it is in the great stillness of voice and softness of heart. In order to rid prayers of vain thoughts, man must mentally make and frame between himself and God a full purpose and intention to serve God with all the powers of his soul by his present prayer. He must *begin* and *do* as well as he can.

There are no specific rules for spiritual meditation, Hilton warns. However, a period of deep sinful awareness is necessary for everyone, followed by a meditation on Christ's humility in His humanity. This meditation brings about the union of spiritual insight with devout affection, the opening of the spiritual eye to the humanity of Christ, *the fleshly love of God*. Temptations are not to lead men away from spiritual meditation, but to encourage the development of a more complete trust in God. The temptation which comes from God develops within man the full willingness to suffer and abide in His will.

Man should know the measure of his spiritual gift. Hilton compares the man who seeks spiritual knowledge to the hound that runs after the hare and grows very weary when he sees only other hounds. When the hound sees the hare (for himself) he will not spare himself until he has caught it.

So it is for man when he sees his own soul, when at last he glimpses the prize rather than the many souls around him. Man must enter into himself, know his own soul (the fairness and foulness of it) and its powers. From this insight comes the desire for spiritual work in order to recover again that dignity and nobleness which one has lost.

Nothing else but the name of Jesus is spiritual health for spiritual illness, declares Hilton. The three powers of the soul: memory, will, and understanding, call into man the remembrance, the sight, and love of the most blessed uncreated Trinity which is God. Man in the contemplative life seeks his lost image. This is done by speaking the name Jesus, which is all goodness, endless wisdom, love and sweetness, joy, glory, everlasting bliss, God, Lord, and salvation. One is to desire Jesus with such devotion that one's thought is set upon nothing else. Such a contemplative person feels no stirring of vain-glory, or self-love, or any evil affection. Then he observes by what manner of prayer, meditation, or exercise of devotion he has found the greatest and purest desire for Him and the most feeling of Him. Then he is to use this kind of prayer, meditation, spiritual exercise on the scale (ladder) to perfection. One ought never to cease from the spiritual desiring and loving of Jesus while he lives, Hilton declares.

The contemplative life is to seek, and to seek is to suffer. One must not turn to Rome or to Jerusalem, but one must turn within. Jesus seeks to find His image reformed within man; otherwise, He is a stranger. Steps to the conforming of the image within to the image of Jesus are (1) to cease for a time all physical work, (2) to detach one's thought from all the bodily senses, (3) to seek one's soul, the dark and ill-favored image, and (4) to think about the soul's image. The soul is the nought within; it is the darkness of conscience and a lacking of the love of God and light, the nothingness which *is* emptiness, darkness, and heaviness.

When a man comes home each night to a disorderly home and a chiding wife, he finds no comfort within; so the soul finds no comfort in itself, but only the disorder of spiritual blindness and the great chiding of guilty or fleshly thoughts. Thus, the soul, like the man, grows weary and retreats. However, advises Hilton, this is the moment when the soul must stay and suffer the pain of its discomfort. The soul must abide therein, face the darkness, and hate and loathe it, for within this darkness is spiritual peace which one will not find with all one's seeking unless one passes through the nought and experiences spiritual travail. The nought is the image of a false, inordinate love of oneself, from which spring the seven deadly sins: pride, envy, anger, sloth, covetousness, gluttony, and lechery. In order to defeat these sins, man must face the nought within himself.

Out of this encounter comes humility, the knowing of oneself and the ability to separate the sin from the sinner. True humility hates sin and truly loves the sinner. A man can hate sin only when he has faced the truth within himself. He is humble who truly knows himself as he is, for humility is truth. The humble man loves himself and his neighbor only in God or for God: "Leave thy prayer for thy neighbor, take time and find God in his need, listen and feed his speech in its need."

The scale of perfection is the journey to Jerusalem: "I would fain be at Jerusalem." Enemies appear along the journey attempting to destroy the desire for the love of Jesus. Some cry that the right confession has not been made and that there is further need to ransack the soul. Yet the task has already been done. Hold on the way and think only on Jerusalem, Hilton writes. Others will say that man is not worthy of God's love, yet it is because of unworthiness that one seeks God's love. Dangers of sickness, madness, fancies, melancholy, poverty or bodily mishap, and of secret temptations and illusions will come, making the one desire for the love of Jesus seem futile. Then attacks of men will come, attempting to make the traveler hateful and angry. Later, enemies will try flattery—but think only on Jerusalem, Hilton advises, and maintain this sole desire (love of Jesus) through prayer and spiritual exercises. One is not to tie himself to habitual devotions which never alter in their pattern. Meditation is a means and not an end.

The soul moves through faith, the gracious imagination or spiritual knowledge of God, to feeling, the faith and imagination of Jesus in His manhood, and finally to the spiritual feeling of the Godhead in unity with humanity. One knows God in two ways: first in imagination and then in understanding. The latter is the beginning of contemplation proper. Understanding is the gate to Love uncreated (God). Through it one sees that the Father makes the soul, the Son re-

deems it, and the Holy Ghost justifies it. One cannot love God by sheer might. It is a great folly, Hilton declares, for a man of his own head or willfulness to press or strain himself too much in spiritual matters: "And then is the soul more suffering than doing, and that is pure love." The opening of the spiritual eye, however, requires both the grace of the Holy Ghost and the will of human effort. The opening of the spiritual eye brings purity of spirit, spiritual rest, inward stillness, peace of conscience, elevation of thought, loneliness of soul, a lively feeling of grace, and a meekness of heart.

Advice is given by Hilton to the practical man who is engaged in the "mixed life," being neither purely active nor solely contemplative. He is to exercise and use the desire for God: (1) by rising in the night after sleep to pray, (2) by calling out good thoughts and meditations wherein he feels the greatest ease and pleasure, (3) by thinking of his own sins and then of the sins of all Christian brethren (one may make of another man's sins a precious ointment to heal one's own sin *if* one thinks with compassion and deep sorrow), (4) by thinking of the humanity of Christ, His birth, passion, and works, and (5) by thinking of the virtues and the Saints, the holiness of the Lord, the blessed Lady, the power, wisdom, goodness, mercy of God, and the real miseries of this life. Again, advice is given to use discretion in devotions, to take them moderately. No man suddenly becomes supreme or perfect in grace.

ENCHIRIDION MILITIS CHRISTIANI

Author: Desiderius Erasmus (c.1466-1536)
Type of work: Christian ethics
First published: 1503

PRINCIPAL IDEAS ADVANCED

The true Christian life is a warfare against the evils of ignorance, ignoble desire, and weakness of purpose; the battle is waged not so much between men as within man himself.

The greatest defense against evil is faith in and imitation of Christ, reinforced by prayer and enhanced by knowledge of Scripture and other sources of ancient wisdom.

In order to achieve the victory of eternal life over eternal torment a Christian should march along level ground, not climbing to unreal heights of complete protection by divine grace or sinking into a pit of despair because the battle seems overwhelming.

The highest expression of religious devotion is found not in the formalities of ritual, in the vain and subtle disputations of Scholastic theologians, in the veneration of saints and relics, or in the opinions of the crowd, but in the practice of virtue motivated by inward piety; the highest pleasure is the happiness derived from a pure conscience.

Desiderius Erasmus was a man of diverse talents and contrasting moods, who, perhaps more than any other prominent individual of his era, reflected in his personality and his writings the tensions of the Western world during the early sixteenth century.

Hans Holbein (1497-1543), German painter, captured the serious and gentle mood of Erasmus in an unpretentious portrait displayed in one of the small rooms at the Louvre. In this portrait Erasmus is seen with pen in hand and manuscript before him, his face revealing a deep and placid concentration intent on a serious task before him: an attitude characterizing the emotional tone and ideas expressed in his *Enchiridion militis Christiani* (*Manual of the Christian Soldier*).

Another glance at a different mood of Erasmus might reveal a cynical sneer reminiscent of the satire in *The Praise of Folly* or a whimsical smile depicting the light humor found here and there in various stories collected in the *Colloquies*. Although there is righteous indignation and typical Erasmian sarcasm expressed in the *Enchiridion*, its overtones are generally sober, and its ideas are presented in a straightforward manner.

Erasmus's life was devoted to scholarship and religious reform. In the *Enchiridion* this Renaissance scholar projects those tenets of Christian Humanism which exalt ancient literature and ask for a return to the simple piety of early Christianity, untarnished by centuries of ritualistic and linguistic corruption. He uses the framework of the *Enchiridion* to support one of his

322 *Desiderius Erasmus*

chief concerns: an enlightened, reformed, theologically purified Church.

Erasmus focuses on the individual as
a means to this restoration, and his *Enchiridion* provides guidelines for the
life worthy of the name "Christian."

Erasmus suggests, therefore, that the
ideal of an enlightened, reformed, theologically purified Church worthy of
its head (Christ) will be achieved
only if each member of the body
(Christians collectively) becomes enlightened, reformed, and enabled to understand theology at its source (the
Scriptures).

Pacifist though he was, Erasmus
uses the analogy of warfare for this
treatise. The Christian life is a warfare
against the forces of evil, especially the
evil tendencies within the individual.
"Enchiridion" means both "dagger"
and "manual," and the author employs
the term in both senses.

Erasmus maintains that each Christian is a soldier who must arm himself
with a "dagger" and carry it at all
times to ward off the forces which prevent him from leading a life of virtue.
The "dagger" is fashioned of rules of
conduct which will aid his offensive
and defensive positions. These rules
also comprise his "manual."

The *Enchiridion* contains thirteen
chapters, with Chapter 8 enumerating
twenty-two such rules or "weapons." In
the opening chapters Erasmus chides
Christians who are lukewarm in the
struggle against the vices which engulf
man. Citing the battle-scarred Job of
Hebrew tradition, Erasmus reminds his
readers that all life is beset by turmoil
for the righteous as well as the wicked.
It is a man's soul which is at stake in
the warfare, and the struggle involves
not only man's integrity, but also his
eternal life.

Erasmus uses the term "soul" in different ways. He speaks of the "soul-
body" or "spirit-flesh" divisions often
used in Pauline description of man's
battle with himself and the world, and
in other instances he uses a three-fold
division of "spirit-body-soul," acknowledging the thought of Origen (c.185-
c.254), head of the Catechetical School
at Alexandria. Using the latter three
categories, Erasmus makes the soul an
interacting agent between the other
two: "The spirit renders us gods; the
flesh, animals; the soul makes us men."

Erasmus was appalled at the lack of
concern on the part of some Christians
who did not behave as if they were
fighting under a banner of Christ at
all. He describes them as men who
become greatly concerned if they
break an arm or have a fever but do
not seem to understand the gravity of a
sick soul (here "soul" means higher
faculties producing sympathy, virtue,
intelligent decision): "You see your
brother suffering indignities, yet your
mind is not in the least moved. . . .
Why at this point does your soul feel
nothing? Surely because it is dead.
Wherefore dead? Because God, its life,
is not present. Where God is, there is
love."

"Know thyself," Erasmus says, as others before him said. A man can never
contend successfully with the evil
around him until he understands and
can conquer himself.

In his discussion of self-knowledge
and self-mastery, Erasmus dips into Platonic and Stoic philosophy for several
analogies likening individual man with
a political state. Reason, the "king,"
must govern all "lower classes," the
base passions, such as envy, lechery,
lust. The "nobles" are affections such

as piety, love, and mercy, which help the "king" rule a harmonious "state."

If the Christian is to rule himself, he must guard against three main enemies: (1) blindness, which leads to ignorance, (2) the flesh (ignoble desire), which incites his base passions against his reason, and (3) infirmity, which causes him to waver in the path of virtue.

If a person is ignorant, he pursues the worst instead of the best. In order to clear his vision he must investigate what should be shunned. If a person knows what is best, he still faces the onslaught of harmful desire, which renders his reason ineffective. In order to overcome this desire, he should hate evil thoughts and love good ones. Even if he knows what is best and loves good thoughts, his infirmity may cause him to stumble, especially if virtue eludes him and he is caught in a snare of boredom or temptation.

What is the best defense against evil? Faith in Christ. Erasmus means an active faith involving conduct, even martyrdom if necessary. A Christ-like man is one who follows the teachings of Christ: "Set before you Christ as the only goal of your whole life, to whom alone you dedicate all zeal, all efforts, all leisure and business. Indeed, think of Christ not as an empty word, but as nothing else than love, simplicity, patience, purity—in short, whatsoever he has taught."

If Christ is to be more than an empty word, the Christian soldier must fortify his defenses by an *understanding* of Christ, and in order to gain that understanding, he must turn first of all to the Scriptures. But the Christian also must seek other avenues of enlightenment to help him understand the Scriptures. For those avenues he should turn to those most prepared to speak authoritatively on Scripture, especially to those who are concerned with the spiritual meaning and not merely the letter: Paul (d. c.65), the Apostle; and the Church Fathers, especially Origen (c.185-c.254); Ambrose (c.339-397), Bishop of Milan; Jerome (c.342-420), translator of the Vulgate Bible; and Augustine (c. 354-430), Bishop of Hippo, who are in a better position to speak authoritatively than are modern theologians who follow such men as John Duns Scotus (c.1264-1308), Scholastic theologian. Such men as Duns Scotus, Erasmus contends, often speak *about* the Scriptures without having undertaken a careful study *of* them.

Erasmus would have the student trace his quest for understanding still further by directing him to the Greeks and Romans and other extra-Biblical sources which provide examples of virtue worthy of imitation: "Nor ought you to despise pagan authors, for they too are often good moral teachers."

The revelation of divine wisdom neither begins nor ends with Christ, but reaches its perfection there. For philosophical guidance Erasmus especially recommends the Platonists, "for the reason that in very many of their opinions and in their way of speaking they approach as closely as possible the prophetic and gospel pattern."

The Scriptures, the commentators, and the classical writings are best understood in their original languages, Erasmus claimed, thus advancing another Humanistic idea. Erasmus did not write for the common man, and the unsophisticated soldier (John, the German, who may or may not be fictional) to whom Erasmus dedicates the *Enchiridion* would have found many of the classical references difficult to appreciate.

Knowledge is not always sufficient protection against evil. Knowledge must often be fortified with prayer, for "pure prayer . . . is a citadel inaccessible to the enemy." The two are necessary complements, for knowledge helps one pray intelligently, and prayer helps subdue passions which knowledge can not always conquer unaided.

Man may be the highest of creatures "for whose sake alone God fashioned this wonderful machine of the world," says Erasmus, but he reminds man, lest he be overelated, that whatever has made him beautiful, great, or famous, is a gift from God, but whatever has made him sordid is his own doing. The Christian soldier should therefore beware of being haughty after victory, for the underlying credit belongs to God in the struggle against the Devil (the vices which plague man).

Erasmus warns the soldier that the consequences of following the Devil cannot be compared with the consequences of following God. The former path brings eternal death (which is not the fire of Hell, in Erasmus's view, but everlasting mental torment), and the latter path brings immortal life.

Erasmus cautions that sudden death for one who is a slave to the Devil could result in an eternal death. The soldier, however, should not give up the fight because of its rigors and the possibility of defeat; moreover, he should not put down his weapons in utter dependence on the protection of God. Salvation is a co-operative effort.

Erasmus had a firm belief in free will, and his views of the nature of man and his destiny were semi-Pelagian; that is, he believed that man is capable of exercising free will to

choose the good, which aids his own salvation, although he is dependent upon God's gift in the atonement by Christ to erase the taint of original sin.

Indeed, it is a man's ability to choose the good over the evil which determines his skill as a Christian soldier. Erasmus acknowledges the difficulty of living in society, with all the mundane pressures and conflicts which are presented by demands of family, friends, enemies, in addition to the human desires for recognition, comfort, and pleasure; nevertheless, Erasmus asks, "What is this that the miserable call pleasure?", and declares that "the true and only pleasure is the joy of a pure conscience. The most elegant banquets *are* enjoyed in the study of the Holy Scriptures. The most pleasing songs are the psalms of the Holy Spirit. The most joyous fellowship is the communion of saints. The highest delights are in the enjoyment of truth. Only purify your eyes, your ears, your palate, and Christ will become sweet to you."

The Christian must withdraw from the demands of the world and his own mundane drives and live "in Christ." By this thesis Erasmus does not mean that it is necessary for the Christian to live *away* from society or mystically to withdraw himself while in the *midst* of society ("monasticism is not godliness, but a kind of life, either useful or useless to anyone depending on one's habit of body and of temperament"), but it is necessary for him to live subject to the standards of Christ and not to the standards of the world: "If you are in the world, you are not in Christ." Erasmus does not mean by this statement the geographical world, for he characterizes the world as false ambition, evil desire, harmful delights;

that is, as whatever is detrimental to a virtuous life.

Erasmus would say to anyone seeking praise that he should seek God's praise, not the praise of men, which is fickle, because men may retract whatever honor they have bestowed. Honor comes only from true virtue, Erasmus maintains, and honor granted by men is perilous and tentative: "Think how blessed is the tranquility of a modest and private life, removed from all clamor of pride. On the other hand how thorny, how full of care, perils, pains, is the life of the powerful! . . . How complete the crash from the heights!"

A Christian, therefore, should not be influenced by the opinions of the crowd. Christ is the archetype of opinion and behavior, and Erasmus suggests that it is far better to imitate Christ's behavior than it is to revere His image; it is better to practice the virtues of the saints than to visit their shrines or touch their relics; it is far better for a Christian to reconcile himself to a brother he has injured or to one who has injured him than merely to recite platitudes about Christian love.

Do not retaliate an injury, says Erasmus, for this increases the pain; sometimes by leniency the injury can be cured, and a former enemy then becomes a friend.

This sentiment of reconciliation exemplifies one of the gentle and serious moods of Erasmus, "Prince of the Humanists," who was to find himself several years after writing the *Enchiridion*

involved in the midst of religious controversy which made many of his former friends enemies as he tried to work for reform within a unified Church when the breach became "irreparable."

Many of the sentiments expressed in the *Enchiridion* may have been influenced by the training Erasmus received under the Brethren of the Common Life during his early school days at Deventer. He respected the sincere piety of the Brethren, although he deplored their lack of enthusiasm for classical learning.

Another source of inspiration may very well have been a man whom Erasmus admired a great deal, Jehan Vitrier (c.1454-?), Prior of the Franciscan monastery at St. Omer, where he composed at least a portion of the original manuscript.

The *Enchiridion* was written in 1501 and first published at Antwerp in 1503 among a collection of other works entitled *Lucubratiunculae* (which could be translated "little works composed at night"). Later editions were entitled *Lucubrationes* (which could be translated "studies by lamplight"). The *Enchiridion* appeared in at least seven more Latin editions after the original, the last one being issued in 1540, and it was translated into English, French, German, Dutch, Czech, and Spanish.

At first the *Enchiridion* was not very popular, but later, especially after the translations appeared, it enjoyed greater popularity for a number of years, and then its fame diminished.

THE PRAISE OF FOLLY

Author: Desiderius Erasmus (c.1466-1536)
Type of work: Christian satire
First published: 1511

Principal Ideas Advanced

Not wisdom but folly dominates the life of man.
Folly leads both to self-deception and to the deception of others.
There are different forms and degrees of folly, from the amiable self-deception which makes life livable and pleasant, to the hypocrisy that covers the greatest evils.
The folly of Christian faith and devotion is the true wisdom.

Erasmus says that he wrote *The Praise of Folly* (*Moriae encomium*) in seven days while a guest in the home of his friend Sir Thomas More (1478-1535). It was published two years later in Paris and was at once received with acclaim even by many who were the obvious victims of his satire, including Pope Julian II. Translation into many languages soon followed. The first English translation was made in 1549 by Sir Thomas Chaloner. The one most commonly used today is from the pen of John Wilson and appeared in 1668. Quotations herein are from that translation.

The Praise of Folly is the most famous work of what was known as "Fool Literature" which had its distinguished beginning in Sebastian Brant's *Narrenschiff*, published in 1494. Such writing represents the license and indulgence once granted to the "Court Fool," now transferred to the higher levels of culture. With Erasmus it is the rational mind of the humanist and scholar at work exposing the hypocrisies and ridiculing the pretensions of men in all walks of life, including even the most honored and powerful of men. But Erasmus wrote with such a light touch, and "folly" is so frankly commended in his book by the Goddess of Folly herself, that a sophisticated society could take his criticism in good part and enjoy laughing at itself. In any case there is no hint that anyone is expected to do anything about the reign of the Goddess of Folly other than to laugh with her at the role of folly in the affairs of men.

The Goddess, who appears as the speaker throughout, starts with an account of her place among the gods, and with references to the more ribald side of their lives. Even the highest of the gods must lay aside their dignity to beget their children, she says. All are indebted to her, indeed, for being born! She is the giver of the pleasures of life. Youth is valued because it has not yet learned wisdom, and old age is blessed by a return to childishness. The gods that are most popular are Bacchus, Pan, Venus, and Flora, all of whom bring pleasures and gaiety into the lives of men. Folly has the advantage over wisdom in that wisdom comes from reason, while folly is the fruit of passion. And the joy of life is derived not from reason, but from passion, not from wisdom but from folly.

Wisdom is limited to the head; passion has its domain in all the rest of the body. In all the enjoyments of life— sex, feasting, delight in children, friendship, and matrimony—we indulge in foolish praise and flattery. Folly sweetens all human relations. Even a wise man must flatter himself; self-love is a necessity.

Taking war as "the very root and matter of all famed enterprises," in spite of the fact that everybody loses more than he gains by it, Folly shows how inept and useless the philosopher is. For war is "manag'd by Parasites, Pandars, Thieves, Cut-Throats, Plowmen, Sots, Spendthrifts and such other dregs of mankind, not Philosophers." The wise man has no place in public affairs or in the life of cities. Politicians use flattery and deceit to control the people. It is tyrants who are deified, so the man of wisdom and prudence is useless. On the other hand, folly leads men to attempt great things and to achieve them. Men, like actors, play roles in life; they are inwardly quite the opposite of what they appear to be. Life is a comedy in which we all change our roles at will; we could not get along otherwise.

The prudent man would make himself odious if he were to point out the miseries and hypocrisies of men. The Stoic is cold and unfeeling, having no passion (folly); he cannot properly take the part of a ruler; he is a failure as a husband, and impossible as a guest. It is better to be a "middle fool."

There are so many ills in life, says the Goddess of Folly, that wisdom would lead men to suicide. But by the help of folly everyone eagerly seeks life, and delights in it, even the old and infirm. Philosophers say that all these miseries are good because they are part of man's condition, but the philosophers are mistaken. Science is of the Devil, and the imposition of laws and the rules of grammar on man is an evil thing. The happiest ones are those who follow nature (folly). Among all the professions those who come nearest doing this are the physicians and the politicians. It is best to live like the flies and the birds; that is, according to nature.

The Goddess quotes Homer and Pythagoras on the misery of man, who by seeking wisdom tries to go beyond what nature has made him. Fools are the happiest, the Goddess declares. It is said that princes will not listen to wise men because wise men speak the truth. "And yet this is found by experience among my Fools," the Goddess says, "that not only Truths but even open reproaches are heard with pleasure; so that the same thing which, if it came from a wise man's mouth might prove a Capital Crime, spoken by a Fool is receiv'd with delight."

The Goddess takes her cue from the logicians and makes a distinction between two kinds of madness, "the one that which the vengeful furies send privily from Hell, as often as they let loose their Snakes, and put into men's breasts either the desire of War, or an insatiate thirst after Gold, or some dishonest Love, or Parricide, or Incest, or Sacrilege, or the like Plagues, or when they terrifie some guilty soul with the Conscience of his Crimes; the other, but nothing like this, that which comes from me, and is of all things the most desirable; which happens as oft as some pleasing dotage not onely clears the mind of its troublesome cares, but renders it more jocund."

Among those who follow folly's better way the Goddess mentions hunters with their ridiculous ritual of dismembering a buck, gamblers with their passion for dice, and fortunetellers and others who use magic charms and prayers to secure success or to avoid certain evils. Some saints "are good for one thing, others for another. And some there are that are good for more things than one; but chiefly, the Virgin Mother, to whom the common people do in a manner attribute more than to the Son." This is all from folly; "whereas if some scurvy Wise fellow should step up, and speak things as they are, as, To live well is the way to die well; the best way to get quit of sin is to add to the money thou giv'st, the Hatred of sin, Tears, Watchings, Prayers, Fastings, and amendment of life: Such or such a Saint will favor thee, if thou imitatist his life;—these, I say, and the like, should this Wise man chat to the people, from what happiness into how great troubles would he draw 'em?"

Men make claims to nobility and diligently trace out their ancestry; each nation and city prides itself on its greatness. But any serious attempt to get back of these opinions destroys the joy of life, says Folly. Happiness comes through thinking things beautiful and costly even though they are neither. The Goddess Folly removes cares. There is no formal worship of her, but all do her service.

So much for the common folk. Erasmus now turns to the "Wise men." He writes with feeling on this theme. He lists the pedantry, the contentiousness of grammarians, poets, rhetoricians and writers of books, and he points to their mutual praises, and to their attacks upon one another. Even the learned indulge in some of this. He pays his biting respects to the advocates, to the

philosophers with their speculations about natural phenomena, and to the divines with their fine distinctions and the subtleties of their theology: "As, whether there was any instant of time in the generation of the Second Person; whether there be more than one Filiation in Christ; whether it be a possible proposition that God the Father hates the Son; or whether it was possible that Christ could have taken upon Him the likeness of a Woman, or of the Devil, or of an Ass, or of a Stone, or of a Gourd; and then how that Gourd should have preach't, wrought miracles, or been hung on the Cross . . . ."

The arraignment of the professional divines is followed by a pertinent reference to the Apostles and to the simple and genuine account they give of faith and love, of the Eucharist and baptism, of worship and the meaning of spirit, and of grace. Erasmus declares, through his Goddess, that they confuted the heathen not by syllogisms, but by their good lives and miracles. Some of the divines see their folly, but most of them are happy in it and pursue their fine definitions and their judgments upon things heretical or questionable as though the whole of the faith rested upon their doings.

The monks and those who profess their religiosity come in next for similar treatment: "most false in both Titles, when both a great part of 'em are farthest from Religion, and no men swarm thicker in all places than themselves." They are all absorbed in the small matters of their dress, their names, the details of their rites and prayers, the distinctions between themselves, and between themselves and others. "In a word," says Folly, " 'tis their only care that none of 'em come near one another in their manner of living, nor do they endeavor how they may be like Christ, but how they may differ among themselves." The sermons of these religious men are derided for both matter and method. Use of far-fetched analogies, proving of doctrines by analysis of words or finding a theological meaning in the first letters of a formula, and other devious and meaningless performances are held up to ridicule. These men add to their strange logic the arts of rhetoric in equally dubious fashion, and they exaggerate the modulations of voice which they have learned from teachers of elocution. The parting comment of the Goddess on these people shows that even Folly cannot be proud of their performance: "But I willingly give over these Stage-players, that are such ingrateful dissemblers of the courtesies I have done 'em, and such impudent pretenders to Religion which they ha'nt."

Princes and "Court-Lords" are subjected to severe treatment by the Goddess. If a prince took to heart the great responsibilities that rest upon him, and if he realized that his character and conduct affect so much the lives of all men, he would be overwhelmed by his duties and would henceforth live a life of rigorous discipline. But, as a matter of fact, the prince leaves all these cares to the gods and devotes himself to the hunt and to all kinds of frivolous and costly formalisms. The "Court-Lords" are interested only in their pleasures and fine clothes, in their feasting and entertainments, and in rivalries for the favors of the prince.

Cardinals and bishops are much the same, declares Folly. Instead of living the lives of devout men and giving themselves to the care of the faithful, they are busy with the increase of their own wealth and dignity. Popes would do well to imitate their Master, to live simple lives, and to give themselves wholly to the care of their flock. But actually they are absorbed in the glories of their office and in their titles and ceremonies. They are always given to war, Folly insists; "Nor are they destitute of their learned flatterers that call that palpable Madness Zeal, Piety, and Valor, having found out a new way by which a man may kill his brother without the least breach of that Charity which, by the command of Christ, one Christian owes another." The real care of the people is passed on by the popes to the bishops, by the bishops to the parsons, by the parsons to the vicars, by the vicars to the mendicants, who finally give it over to the monks.

The Goddess now returns to her argument that folly is better than wisdom, and she quotes classical writers to prove it, while providing examples from life. The last part of the satire moves into the realm of Scripture. Here another distinction is made implicitly in the nature of folly. The book begins, as will be remembered, with Folly's quoting the pagan gods and citing their conduct as support for a kind of folly that releases gods and men from the ordinary decencies and moralities, and frees them to indulge their natural desires. But now a new meaning of folly is gained from the Christian faith. For example, St. Paul's words are quoted: "God hath chosen the foolish things of this world," and "It pleased God by foolishness to save the world." Even the authority of Christ is invoked: ". . . Christ gives Him thanks that he had conceal'd the

Mystery of Salvation from the wise, but revealed it to babes and sucklings, that is to say, Fools." Christ is called the Lamb of God, and His disciples are His "sheep, than which creature there is not any thing more foolish. . . . And Christ himself, that he might better relieve this Folly, being the wisdome of the Father, yet in some manner became a fool, when taking upon him the nature of man, he was found in shape as a man; as in like manner he was made Sin, that he might heal sinners." "To speak briefly," Folly declares, "all Christian Religion seems to have a kind of allyance with folly."

The treatise closes with an account of the "madness" of the spiritually minded few who seek in this life the experience of things eternal. These fools have found the true wisdom, and are indifferent to the worldly satisfactions and enjoyments that most men seek. They have a foretaste of future happiness. Here Erasmus, in his proper person, exclaims "But I forget myself and run beyond my bounds."

AN OPEN LETTER TO THE CHRISTIAN NOBILITY OF THE GERMAN NATION

Author: Martin Luther (1483-1546)
Type of work: Polemical theology
First published: 1520

PRINCIPAL IDEAS ADVANCED

The Romanists have surrounded the doctrine of papal supremacy with three "walls" of supporting arguments by which they frustrate all attempts to reform the Church through the temporal powers, the Bible, or a council.

The Romanists contend that the "spiritual estate" is superior to all temporal authority, that the pope alone has the authority to interpret the Bible, and that only the pope may call a council.

In the Christian Church baptism confers upon all members the same basic status and responsibilities, so that the right to interpret the Scriptures and to call reforming councils belongs to all Christian believers.

The Christian princes and noblemen of Germany must take the initiative in wresting German political and religious life out of corrupt papal control, and in reforming German religious practices and institutions.

Luther's *Open Letter,* or *Address,* appeared in German under the title *An den christlichen Adel deutscher Nation von des christlichen Standes Besserung.* It was the first of the three so-called "Reformation treatises" of 1520, all of which Luther wrote in response to his conviction that his break with the medieval Church was irreconcilable and that he had the duty of assuming the leadership of the mammoth task of reforming Christendom.

Luther's opposition to the medieval Church increased steadily after his initial dramatic act of nailing to the doors of the Church of All Saints in Wittenberg his famous ninety-five theses on October 31, 1517. His protest against the abusive sale of indulgences was to assume minor importance in comparison with his questions about other features of the Church. Between October of 1518 and June of 1519, Luther investigated with intense scrutiny the evidences for the claim of absolute papal authority, a claim which he himself firmly upheld when he first raised questions about indulgences.

Papal claims to absolute authority were based largely upon a collection of documents now known as the Pseudo-Isidorian or False Decretals. The collection dates from the middle of the ninth century and purports to be the work of a certain Isidore Mercator. The Decretals included decisions of popes and councils from the first century through Gregory II in the eighth century. They had been regarded as authentic for over six and a half centuries. Luther discovered, to his indignation and amazement, that many of the documents were forgeries. Both disturbed and relieved by his discovery, he was forced to come to a quick conclusion on the question of papal authority when he was challenged to debate the subject with John Eck, a theologian who taught at the University of Leipzig.

Eck was a clever and brilliant debater, and he accomplished his purpose of leading Luther into declaring himself in agreement with certain heretical views which the Church had definitely condemned. Specifically, Luther was led to acknowledge agreement with certain views of the Bohemian reformer John Huss (c.1369-1415), who had been condemned and sentenced to death in 1415 by the Council of Constance. Eck was able, at the end of the debate, to point to Luther as a heretic who not only rejected the pope's authority but who also seemed to reserve to himself the right to agree or disagree with councils of the Church.

After an initial melancholy reaction to the Leipzig debate, Luther's spirits quickly rallied, and he faced up to the deep division of outlook which separated him from the supporters of the papal claims. In the three treatises of 1520 Luther undertook to make clear to himself and to the public the ground on which he stood.

The *Open Letter* is closely related to a tract which was published on June 26, 1520, bearing the title *The Papacy at Rome: A Reply to the Celebrated Romanist at Leipzig*. The concluding paragraph of the tract contains in germinal form the argument of the *Open Letter*, which was composed in June but which did not appear in print until the middle of August. While Luther was at work on the *Open Letter* the bull of excommunication which formally banished him from the Church was signed by Pope Leo X.

In the *Open Letter* Luther writes as a German who is outraged at the exploitation of the German people by the greedy and luxury-loving pope and the enormous entourage which made up his splendid court. Luther had come to the conclusion that the only hope for lifting the burden of Roman oppression off Germany and restoring the life of the Church to Biblical foundations was through the initiative of the newly elected emperor, Charles V, and the German princes and nobility who ruled the relatively autonomous German provinces. The *Open Letter* was a challenge to these men to assume the initiative in reforming the Church.

The Romanists, or defenders of papal supremacy, have frustrated all attempts to reform the Church, claims Luther, by erecting "three walls" around themselves. When under pressure from civil or temporal powers, they argue that the spiritual power is superior to the temporal. When they are confronted with Scriptural evidences that the Church has fallen into corruption, they respond with the argument that the pope alone has the right to interpret the meaning of the Bible. When threatened by a council, they reply that only the pope may call a council. Luther assaults the three walls one by one.

The distinction which the Romanists make between the "spiritual estate" (consisting of pope, bishops, priests, and monks) and the "temporal estate" (consisting of princes, lords, artisans, and farmers) is completely false, says Luther. All Christians belong to the same estate and have the same basic status in the Church. A cobbler who is a baptized Christian believer is no less a member of the spiritual estate than a bishop. Ordination does not confer upon priests any special graces but simply designates them as set apart to do a particular kind of work in the fellowship of Christians. If a pope or bishop or priest fails to do his task properly, he is as deserving of public censure and civil punishment as is a dishonest or incompetent cobbler or tailor. Baptism ordains every Christian to responsibility for the Word of God and for the well-being of the Church. Baptism, then, is the warrant which grants to the Christian princes and

nobility the right and the obligation to reform the life of the Church.

The second wall, writes Luther, is even less substantial than the first. He points to the irony of the claim of the papists that the pope alone is authorized and competent to interpret the Scriptures even though many of the popes had been ignorant of the Bible and had contradicted it grossly in the conduct of their lives. Luther further argues that canon law contained many heretical and unchristian ordinances which reveal ignorance or disregard of the Bible. Luther ironically suggests that, since the Romanists claim that the Holy Spirit never leaves them, the Bible is really not needed and might as well be burned.

The right and ability to interpret the Scriptures belongs to those who possess the true faith and are imbued with the spirit and mind of Christ. Every Christian has the duty to understand and defend the faith and to rebuke all errors, no matter by whom they are committed.

The third wall falls of itself, claims Luther, once the other two are leveled. Just as all Christians have the duty to judge papal behavior by Scriptural standards, just as much so is it the right of all Christians to use councils as a method of insuring the spiritual health of the Church.

Luther points out—and historical evidence supports him—that the Council of Nicaea (325) was called by the Emperor Constantine I and not by the bishop of Rome, and that later emperors likewise called councils. On the basis of the priesthood of all Christian believers, he contends, it is the duty of those who are in a position to do so to call a free council to deal with the papacy and its manifold abuses.

The critics of the papacy should not be deterred by any threats or by excommunication, for God does not give to the pope the power to excommunicate those who are doing their Christian duty.

Having made his case for the legitimacy of the initiative of the German princes and nobles in calling a reforming council, Luther goes on to enumerate in great detail the abuses with which such a council should deal. His bill of indictment is a vivid account of conditions in the German Church and of the economic, political, and social consequences and implications relating to those conditions.

The center of corruption in the Church, affirms Luther, is the pope, with his insatiable appetite for opulence and splendor. Surrounding the pope are the cardinals, who appear to be fully employed in collecting and enjoying the revenues from the richest convents, benefices, and endowments in Europe. The papal court is enormous, including three thousand secretaries and numerous other functionaries, all of whom are waiting eagerly for more German benefices to fall open, even though they have no intention of performing the ecclesiastical duties theoretically connected with the benefices. More German money goes annually to the papal court than to the German emperor.

Rome systematically robs Germany through the system of *annates*, whereby the holder of a benefice must turn over to the pope one half of the first year's income. The system of *annates* was set up about a century before, supposedly as a way of financing a war against the Turks, but the money has never been used for that purpose.

Some of the most shameless methods of raising money, Luther goes on, are those connected with the granting of ecclesiastical exemptions from the requirements of ecclesiastical and moral laws. For appropriate sums monks are permitted to leave the cloistered life, priests may gain permission to marry, and bastards are declared legitimate.

Luther's list of corrective measures is long and specific. He calls for the German princes and noblemen to take command over the system of Church revenues and to abolish entirely the *annates*. He also calls for complete jurisdiction of civil authorities over all temporal matters, with the pope's authority limited to the affairs of the Church. Then, striking an unusually forceful blow at papal power, he demands a German national church, with its own ecclesiastical council as the final court of appeal.

Turning to a long list of less radical proposals, Luther continues his assault upon the corrupt practices and institutions of medieval Christendom. Pilgrimages should be discouraged because they are inducements to immorality and shirking of work. The large number of mendicant orders should be reduced so as to cut down on the number of vagrant monks. All convents and nunneries should be thoroughly inspected, and nuns who wish to return to the world should be permitted to do so. Holy days—which have become numerous—have become occasions of debauchery and drunkenness. Sunday alone should be observed as a special religious day. Endowed masses should be forbidden. Canon law should be abolished, partly because the pope himself disregards it and perverts its meaning, and partly because the Bible is a sufficient guide for the Christian life.

Turning from reforms relating directly to the Church, Luther next directs his attention to economic and social questions. He deplores the luxury and ostentation in dress of the richer classes of Germany. Garments made of wool and flax and other common materials are suitable for everyone. The Germans are foolish to let their money flow out to foreign lands for luxury items of food and dress when Germany is bountifully supplied with the necessities of life. In general, Luther was suspiciously opposed to the economic trends which betokened the end of the old feudal agrarian economy and heralded a new economy based upon money and trade. Thus he speaks out against the great trading companies which reaped enormous profits by securing monopolies in the staple articles of commerce.

Of all the works which make up the enormous corpus of literature which came from Luther's pen, none had such an instantaneous and dramatic effect as did his *Open Letter*. He appealed to German national pride, and his religious proposals were such that their adoption would clearly strengthen the hands of the German civil rulers at the expense of the pope. The emperor Charles V decided to stand by the papacy, but enough of the German princes responded to Luther's appeals that his movement gained sufficient political protection to guarantee its wide success in Germany. Although it would be a mistake to interpret the Protestant movement as fundamentally political in significance, it is nonetheless true that it both aided and benefited from the tide of nationalism which was rising in Europe in the sixteenth century. The *Open Letter* exemplifies the spirit of both movements, for Luther was writing both as a proud German and as a man motivated by deep religious convictions.

THE BABYLONIAN CAPTIVITY OF THE CHURCH

Author: Martin Luther (1483-1546)
Type of work: Polemical theology
First published: 1520

Principal Ideas Advanced

The elaborate system of sacraments by which the Roman Church enslaves its members cannot be justified by reference to the Bible.

A true sacrament must have been instituted by Christ, must include a promise of a specific spiritual benefit or grace, must include an outer sign or symbolic act, and requires faith on the part of the recipient.

Only baptism and the Lord's Supper qualify as true Christian sacraments.

The Roman Church has corrupted the Lord's Supper by withholding the cup from the laity, by the doctrine of transubstantiation, and by teaching that the Mass is a sacrifice which man offers to God.

It is a spiritually beneficial practice for one to confess his sins to a Christian brother and to receive comforting assurance of divine forgiveness, but the Roman sacrament of penance places the emphasis upon the penitent's contrition and works of satisfaction rather than upon God's forgiveness.

Confirmation, marriage, and ordination may be regarded as Church rites, but they are not sacraments.

In the conclusion of his *Open Letter to the Christian Nobility* Luther wrote: "Ah well, I know another little song about Rome and about them. If their ears itch for it I will sing them that song too, and pitch the notes to the top of the scale." His *Babylonian Captivity of the Church,* published on October 6, 1520, is the "little song" which Luther had in mind.

The *Babylonian Captivity* contrasts with the political tone of the *Open Letter.* Whereas the *Open Letter* assaults the theoretical foundations of the vast temporal power of the papacy, the *Babylonian Captivity* strikes at the sacramental system, the theological and religious heart of Roman Christianity. In attacking the sacramental system and theology of Rome, Luther also set forth his own sacramental theology. The *Babylonian Captivity* sums up and expands upon conclusions which Luther had reached in shorter earlier writings on the sacraments. It stands as the most influential of his theological writings.

In the preface to the *Babylonian Captivity* Luther expresses a spirit of truculence and self assurance which indicates the depth of his breach with Rome and his firm intention to reform the Church. He expresses regret at his previous caution in dealing with the subjects of indulgences and the papacy. He suggests that the booksellers burn his writings on these two subjects. He is now ready to affirm categorically that indulgences are nothing but deceitful tricks and that the papacy represents nothing more than the greed of the Roman bishop.

Luther opens his assault on the Roman sacramental system by denying that there are seven sacraments. He vacillates somewhat on the question of how many sacraments he accepts, suggesting initially that there are three (baptism, penance, and the "bread" or Lord's Supper). He also affirms that in the strictly Scriptural sense there is only one sacrament—Christ—who is available to man under the three sacramental signs of baptism, penance, and the Lord's Supper. His final conclusion, however, reached after careful examination of each of the Roman sacraments, is that "there are strictly speaking, but two sacraments in the Church of God—baptism and bread. . . ." It was this last view which Luther continued to espouse and which almost all Protestant bodies adopted.

Luther's criteria for determining the validity of a sacrament are as follows: A sacrament must, first of all, have been instituted by Christ himself. Second, a sacrament must include a promise of a specific spiritual benefit of grace. Third, a sacrament must include a sign or symbolic act. Fourth, a sacrament requires faith on the part of the recipient, faith here being understood as grateful acceptance of the promise of God which is symbolized and conveyed by the sacrament.

The most extensive section of the

Babylonian Captivity consists of Luther's examination of the Eucharist or Lord's Supper, on which subject he had already published, in 1519, his *Treatise on the Blessed Sacrament.* Through their perverse interpretation of the Eucharist, contends Luther, the papists hold in captivity and subjection the members of the Church. The first perversion is the refusal to permit the laity to drink the consecrated wine as well as to eat the bread, which refusal suggests that only the priests may partake of the entire sacrament. Luther refers to the Biblical passages which describe the Last Supper (Matthew 26, Mark 14, and Luke 22) and concludes that anyone who receives the Lord's Supper is entitled to both the bread and the wine. He cites the writings of Cyprian (c.200-258), Bishop of Carthage, as evidence that the laity in the early Church received both elements.

The second papist perversion of the Lord's Supper is the doctrine of transubstantiation as the form of stating the miracle of the real presence of Christ in the elements of bread and wine. Transubstantiation is the doctrine that the accidents, or qualities, of bread and wine which are evident to the senses (such as color, taste, odor) remain, but the substance or essence which can only be thought but not sensed is miraculously changed into the body and blood of Christ. Luther describes this doctrine as an invasion of Christian theology by Aristotelian philosophy, and he urges an interpretation of the Eucharistic miracle based upon the Christian doctrine of the Incarnation. Human nature does not have to be transubstantiated in order for it to be the dwelling place of the Godhead, and neither do bread and wine have to be transubstantiated in order for them to bear the real physical presence of Christ. Thus the Eucharistic bread and wine remain bread and wine in every way.

A third error which has crept into the Roman understanding of the Lord's Supper, Luther contends, is that the Mass—of which the Lord's Supper is the center—is regarded as a good work and sacrifice. In actuality, says Luther, the Mass is the promise or testament which Christ left behind at His death. It is the promise of the remission of sins. Man's appropriate response to this promise is faith, or trust in the promise. To make it clear that the Mass is the medium through which the Church communicates Christ's promise of the remission of sins, the priest at Mass should speak out loudly and clearly, and in the language of his hearers rather than in some strange liturgical tongue. The Mass is not a gift or sacrifice which the priest offers up to God; it is, rather, God's gift of his Son for the remission of man's sins.

Baptism, contends Luther, has remained essentially uncorrupted. Its basic meaning is its communication of the divine promise of salvation. This promise is complete in baptism, and does not have to be ratified or reinforced through good works or holy vows. To assume that baptism must be supplemented is to show one's lack of faith in God's promise as expressed by baptism. The application of water to the body is the outer sign of one's acceptance of the promise of God. Baptism signifies death and resurrection, the dying of the old life of faithlessness and the rising of the newly justified man. The newly regenerated man is secure in God's promise of redemption and thus is free from all threats and terrors from human sources, and free, too, from anxiety about the elaborate requirements which the papists have falsely identified with Christian responsibility.

Baptism is the basis of the equality of all Christians. The functions of priests and monks "differ no whit in the sight of God from the works of the rustic toiling in the field or the woman going about her household tasks, but . . . all works are measured before Him by faith alone. . . ."

Having emphasized the importance of faith in the heart of the recipient of a sacrament, Luther recognizes that he must face the queries of those who ask if infant baptism is of no effect since the infant is incapable of faith. Falling back upon a position stated by Thomas Aquinas (1225-1274) and going back to St. Augustine (354-430), Luther contends that the faith of those who present the infant and witness his baptism is capable of effecting changes in the infant.

It is in order at this point to recognize that Luther adhered to a realistic view of the Lord's Supper and baptism. That is, he regarded those sacraments as being genuine vehicles of divine grace which effected objective changes in the lives of the recipients.

Luther accuses the papists of having completely abolished the proper understanding of the sacrament of penance. Instead of assuring the guilty consciences of men of the forgiveness of Christ, the Church tyrannizes its faithful by constantly reminding them of its own power to forgive or damn.

The Roman Church's division of penance into contrition, confession, and satisfaction introduces further perversion. By teaching that contrition precedes faith in the promise of divine forgiveness, they make forgiveness a reward for human merit rather than a free gift of divine grace. Thus the Church encourages men to trust, not in God's mercy, but in their own contrition.

The man-centered character of penance is further emphasized in the importance attached to satisfaction. Tortured consciences are driven to pilgrimages, fasts, vigils, and scourgings. The fact that the Church gives absolution or forgiveness prior to satisfaction helps to keep the emphasis on satisfaction. If absolution came after satisfaction, as it properly should, then one could expect Christians to devote more attention to faith and the living of an amended life.

Although he eventually comes out with a list of sacraments which omits penance, Luther strongly endorses private confession because it is morally and spiritually salutary. Confession does not, however, have to be to a priest. It is fit to confess one's sins to any Christian brother, for the lips of any Christian may speak the message of comfort and reassurance which constitutes the faith of the Church.

Confirmation is not a sacrament, contends Luther, but it derives historically from the practice of laying on of hands, as when Christ blessed young children, and the Apostles imparted the Holy Spirit, ordained elders, and blessed the sick. Despite its indirect New Testament antecedents, confirmation is not a sacrament, for it contains no word of divine promise to which faith may respond.

Luther rules out marriage as a sacrament because, like confirmation, it contains no word of divine promise. Marriage is a universal human institution which preceded Christianity, so that there are no grounds for arguing that it is a special means by which the grace of Christ comes to man.

Quickly dispensing with the sacramental question relating to marriage, Luther goes on at length to discuss various social and personal questions related to marriage, and in these passages he reveals a great depth of experience as a counsellor. He castigates the elaborate regulations of the Roman Church which defined eligibility for marriage, particularly those rules specifying "hindrances." Can anyone justify, Luther insists, a rule which forbids any relative of a deceased husband, even to the fourth degree, from marrying the widow of the dead man?

Luther's permissiveness in regard to marital matters takes such a radical form in the *Babylonian Captivity* that many editions of the book leave out those sections. Impotence of the husband is a just reason for annulment of a marriage, contends Luther, and yet to seek such an annulment through the legal processes might bring painful embarrassment. In such a case it is permissible for the wife, with the husband's consent, to bear children by another man and to convey the public impression that the children belong to her legal husband. If the husband should refuse his wife such permission, says Luther, "rather than allow the woman to burn or to commit adultery, I should counsel her to contract a marriage with another and flee to distant parts unknown." Luther is to be understood here, not as an advocate of sexual license, but as one struggling with desperately acute human problems which he knew about through concrete instances.

The sacrament of ordination, says Luther, is an invention of the pope, not of Christ. It receives no mention in the New Testament. In a sense, baptism is ordination, for "as many of us as have been baptised are all priests without distinctions. . . ." Ordination, in the more narrow meaning, is "nothing else than a certain rite of choosing preachers in the Church." As far as the Scriptures are concerned, one who performs for a while the tasks of the ministry may then become again a layman, since he is a minister by virtue of the tasks which he performs and not by virtue of ordination.

Luther traces the sacrament of extreme unction to the practice reported in James 5:14f. of anointing the sick with oil. Still, Christ did not institute the practice, and nowhere in the Bible does one read of any rite which fits the description of extreme unction. The intent of the rite described by James, and by other Biblical writers, was clearly to restore the health of those who were ill, not to prepare a dying man for death.

We end up, then, says Luther, with only two sacraments—baptism and the Lord's Supper—which meet all the requisite criteria.

Luther ends the *Babylonian Captivity* by an oblique mention of his own excommunication, which had been signed in Rome several months earlier but which had yet to be published in Germany. He humorously refers to the *Babylonian Captivity* as "a portion of the recantation I shall make," and promises that his pen will shortly produce other "recantations."

A TREATISE ON CHRISTIAN LIBERTY

Author: Martin Luther (1483-1546)
Type of work: Soteriology
First published: 1520

PRINCIPAL IDEAS ADVANCED

Through faith (trust) in God as revealed in Jesus Christ the soul of the Christian achieves complete freedom from all adversities which may affect the body.

The gift of divine justification makes the Christian free of any necessity of making himself worthy through ceremonial, legal, and moral works.

One who regards his own works and merits as necessary for his salvation thereby shows his distrust of the absolute sufficiency of the mercy and goodness of God as manifested in Jesus Christ.

Although completely free from any necessity to do anything for his own salvation, the Christian will subject himself to whatever discipline is required in order to express his faith in God and his concern for his fellow men.

The justified Christian will love his neighbor without any thought or hope of reciprocation, just as the Christian himself is the beneficiary of the free and unconditional love of God.

The man of faith will not interpret his liberty as license to disregard all ceremonies and routines, but he will despise only that ceremonialism which expresses a lack of faith in God.

Published in both German and Latin in November of 1520, Luther's *Treatise on Christian Liberty* was the last of his three "Reformation treatises" of 1520. Absent from *Christian Liberty* is the polemical tone of the *Open Letter to the Christian Nobility* and the *Babylonian Captivity of the Church.* The book is deeply devotional and contemplative and exhibits the more strictly religious aspects of the many-sided personality of Luther.

Luther concluded the *Babylonian Captivity* with the promise of *Christian Liberty,* but the immediate occasion of the fulfillment of the promise was his agreement to make a conciliatory gesture toward Pope Leo X. The agreement was the fruit of the arduous labors of Karl von Miltitz, a German diplomat who represented Pope Leo.

Miltitz was sent to Germany originally to bring Luther to Rome, but he became convinced that the only hope of ending the dispute between Luther and the papacy was by handling the matter in Germany. At Miltitz's suggestion Luther and Leo X had written conciliatory letters to one another in March of 1519, but neither letter reached its destination. Luther's debate with John Eck in Leipzig (June, 1519) seemed to end all hope of a settlement, but Miltitz persisted in his peacemaking efforts, even after a papal bull of excommunication was on its way to Luther in the summer of 1520.

Late in August of 1520 Miltitz attended at Eisleben a meeting of monks of Luther's order, the Augustinians, and urged them to try to persuade Luther to write the pope a letter assuring the pope that his attacks had not been directed against the pontiff personally. Luther agreed to this plan, even though he had no confidence that any positive results would come of it.

In October Luther had yet to write his letter to Leo, when Miltitz arranged a meeting with the former. Luther again promised to compose and send a letter, accompanied by his written version of the dispute which had been raging then for almost three years. The historical account of the dispute—in very brief scope—was included in the letter, and the accompanying treatise was *Christian Liberty*. Whether Leo actually ever received Luther's letter and the accompanying treatise is not known.

Luther's tone in the letter is respectful, but there is nothing in it to indicate an attitude of submission or contrition. Although he denounces the Roman curia, he is careful to exempt Leo X from the charges which he levels at the curia. He pictures Leo X as an essentially good and innocent man surrounded by a corrupt and conniving court, as one who "sittest as a lamb in the midst of wolves, like Daniel in the midst of lions, and, with Ezekiel . . . dwellest among scorpions." He ends the letter with a reference to *Christian Liberty* as a sample of the kind of study in which he "would prefer to be more profitably engaged, as I could be if your godless flatterers would permit me, and had hitherto permitted me." It is difficult to believe that Leo X, who was a man of humanist outlook, would have been other than contemptuous of Luther's

letter and indifferent to *Christian Liberty.*

The subject of *Christian Liberty* is the paradoxical relationship between liberty and bondage in Christian experience. Luther states this relationship in two propositions: "A Christian man is a perfectly free lord of all, subject to none. A Christian man is a perfectly dutiful servant of all, subject to all." The first part of the treatise is an exposition of the first proposition, and the second part expands upon the second proposition.

The freedom of the Christian man is an inner liberty which belongs to man's soul, not to his body. No kind of misfortune which affects the body can harm the soul, and the soul receives no benefit from any adornment or chastisement of the body.

The liberty and health of the soul depend upon one thing alone, the Word of God which is contained in Jesus Christ. The soul which possesses the Word of God is rich and needs nothing else for its well-being, for this possession confers liberty, wisdom, peace, righteousness, and joy. Without the Word of God the soul is smitten.

The Word of God may be appropriated only by faith. No amount or quality of works will bring the reward of the Word of God. One cannot trust (have faith) in both his own works and in the Word of God. (By "works" Luther has in mind, it is clear, primarily the elaborate set of requirements spelled out in the sacramental system and the canon law of the Roman Church.) Faith alone justifies man.

In a slightly mystical passage very likely inspired by Johann Tauler (c.1300-1361), Luther describes the union of the soul with Christ as analogous to the union of husband and wife in marriage. The soul and Christ claim one another, so that the man of faith may claim for his own all that belongs to Christ, and Christ claims for Himself all that belongs to the man of faith. Christ's victory over sin, death, and Hell now belongs to the Christian. Christ the Bridegroom, rich in all spiritual graces, bestows all that He has upon the poor wicked soul who is joined with Him in faith.

Just as Christ is King, so every Christian is king, lord over all circumstances, completely secure against all harm to his soul. Just as Christ is priest, so every Christian is a priest, bearing Christ to his brothers, praying for them, and ministering to their needs. Some Christians ought to be set aside for full time public ministry to their brothers, but these ministers are not fundamentally distinct from their lay brethren. There is no justification for any Christians' lording it over their brethren.

Turning to the Christian's responsibility for proclaiming the Gospel, Luther insists that it is not enough to recount the acts and sayings of Christ. The point of preaching is to move men to faith in Him, "that He may not only be Christ, but be Christ for thee and for me, and that what is said of Him and what His Name denotes may be effectual in us."

Turning from the inner man or soul, whose freedom is secured through faith in Christ, Luther turns next to the outward man. In this section of his treatise Luther expounds the meaning of the second basic proposition of his work: "A Christian man is a perfectly dutiful servant of all, subject to all."

Faith is completely sufficient for the nurture and well-being of the inner man, the soul. But in his earthly existence man is also a body, and he is set in the midst of other men. Thus the Christian may not take his ease in the life of faith. He must subject his body to the discipline necessary to make it conform with and express the faith of the inward man. The outward man lusts for the world and for its own advantage, so that the soul must seek to keep the body in check. The works involved in these efforts are not, it is important to note, attempts to justify oneself, efforts to gain salvation. They are the products of a justification already given by God and not the means to the achievement of justification. "Good works do not make a good man, but a good man does good works. . . ." Faith alone makes a man good, and only unbelief makes him evil.

Good works are expressive not only of faith in God, but also of love for the neighbor. Just as Christ did not live for Himself alone, so the Christian, as long as he is in the body, lives for other men. Thus he disciplines his body that it may be a more effective instrument of his love for his fellow men. The life of faith, then, produces acts of service to the neighbor, performed not in order to save one's soul, but out of joyous gratitude that one's salvation is already assured through Christ. Nor does the Christian do good to his neighbor in order to enjoy the gratitude or reciprocating deeds of his neighbor. Just as God bestows his blessings upon men without considering their deserts, so the Christian, too, gives himself unconditionally in service to his fellow men. Just as God gives himself freely to man in Christ, so the Christian is to be a Christ to his neighbor.

St. Paul, who taught a similar doctrine of Christian liberty, and whose writings deeply influenced Luther, quickly discovered (I Corinthians: 5, 6) that libertinism is likely to emerge as a perverted understanding of Christian liberty. Luther warns against such a misunderstanding of his doctrine. Some, he says, will want to show that they are Christians and free men by despising the traditional ceremonies and traditions of the Church. The Christian, however, shows his faith by avoiding both libertinism and fastidious ceremonialism. He will oppose anyone who misinterprets liberty as providing opportunities for contempt towards tradition rather than for service for one's neighbors. And he will also oppose the ceremonialist who, in his trust of ceremonies, has neither faith in God nor concern for his neighbor. But one must be patient and kind to the ignorant and timid multitudes who are held captive by the ceremonial requirements of the Church. Ceremonies are indispensable to the life of worship. But, like all works, they must be expressive of faith in God rather than objects of faith. Thus ceremonies are not to be despised, but uncritical trust in them is to be despised.

Christian Liberty contains the classic expression of the theme of justification by faith, a theme often identified as the heart of Luther's theology and as his basic religious insight. What, precisely, is intended by the phrase "justification by faith"? "Justification" is righteousness or goodness. Luther understood righteousness as a condition of the will, an attitude. He was at pains to avoid identifying righteousness with external works or behavior. The moral and religious quality of the will, he believed, depends upon the object and the strength of its trust and allegiance. The truly righteous (justified) man has trust (faith) in the goodness of God rather than in his own capacity for goodness. The goodness of God as manifested in Jesus Christ is absolutely sufficient for man's salvation. Christian faith, then, is a trustful acceptance of God's gift of Himself in Jesus Christ. It is the acceptance of one's own forgiveness. To try to merit this gift by performing righteous deeds is to exhibit a lack of confidence in the goodness of God.

To state that justification by faith is Luther's revolutionary insight can be misleading inasmuch as both "justification" and "faith" are processes within man. Luther's concern was to correct what he regarded to be the basic fault of medieval Christianity, its man-centered character. Justification he understood as God's work through Christ, and he taught that faith, man's appropriation of the divine gift, depends completely upon the divine initiative. Thus faith is possible only because of grace, and faith is, indeed, a gift of grace.

The basic theme of Luther in *Christian Liberty* was not new but was, rather, a powerful restatement of a theme prominent in the thought of St. Paul and St. Augustine. In one crucial respect Luther's thought in the *Christian Liberty* has closer affinity with that of St. Paul than with St. Augustine's ideas. Like Paul, Luther emphasizes faith as the proper response of man to God, and love as the proper response of the Christian to his neighbor, whereas Augustine had emphasized love (*caritas*) of man for God as well as for neighbor. Luther's affinity with Paul underscores the radically

theocentric and Christocentric character of the thought of both men. Each
was reluctant to affirm that man was
capable of loving God as God loves
man, and each pictures the Christian
as the channel which conveys divine
love to other humans.

In the *Open Letter* and the *Babylonian Captivity* Luther had tried to indicate the anthropocentric character of
medieval piety. *Christian Liberty* is designed to pilot the Church back to a
theocentric-Christocentric base for its
life.

LOCI COMMUNES RERUM THEOLOGICARUM

Author: Philipp Melanchthon (1497-1560)
Type of work: Systematic theology
First published: 1521

Principal Ideas Advanced

*Self-love is original sin, a native propensity within man that taints all his so-
called good deeds, so that all men are truly sinners—as the evidence from the
study of the mind and from Scripture abundantly shows.*

*Sin pertains to man's inner being, to his heart, his emotions, and it is impos-
sible for man to obey the two commands to love God and neighbor, for self-love
tyrannically dictates man's actions.*

*Man stands condemned, knowing that he must keep the law but unable to do
so until the grace of God brings forgiveness of sins and turns his heart from himself to God and neighbor.*

*Man remains a sinner, even after receiving grace, for he does not cease to be a
human being, but he is consoled in knowing that his sin is not imputed to him;
and the knowledge of a God who forgives and cares for him temporally and
eternally makes him relatively less selfish in his actions.*

*Man cannot make himself righteous; meritorious works are a pretense and a
delusion.*

The *Loci communes* of Philipp
Melanchthon was the first systematic
statement of Protestant theology. It appeared in April, 1521, antedating John
Calvin's *Institutes* by fifteen years.
Melanchthon sought to draw a system of doctrine solely from the Scriptures, a goal which in his day was
radically new in theological science.
In doing so, he disparaged the commentaries of the scholastic theologians
as "silly, insipid, and impious," for

they were rooted in the thought of
men rather than in the Word of God;
and he heaped scorn on ancient philosophers, particularly Aristotle, for "ego-
tistic" principles of morality, doubt,
and criticism, which bar the way to
Christ and render truth elusive. The
Bible, and especially Paul's letter to the
Romans, provides man with the truth
about his nature and destiny, Melanchthon believed.

Melanchthon joined the faculty of

the University of Wittenberg in 1518, and under the influence of Martin Luther developed a love of Scripture that made all other writings seem inferior. He wanted even his own book to be only a guide to and in no way a substitute for the Bible. From Scripture he drew his three principal topics of sin, law, and grace, and under these he subsumed free will, vows, love, hope, baptism, penitence, confession, customs, and government. He sought to arrange and relate the ideas in Scripture so that they could be easily understood. This practice gave his work a freshness in contrast to arid scholastic disputations and a practicality in view of the Protestant emphasis on the Bible as final authority, but it prevented him from using the tools of philosophy to explore his ideas. Melanchthon sensed this limitation and in subsequent editions he deliberately curtailed or omitted many of his tirades against philosophy.

Under his first topic, "Sin," Melanchthon held that man cannot of his own free will perform works that will merit justification before God. The Bible teaches that all men are sinners and that a bad tree bears bad fruit; good works born of man's free will are impossible for his will is already bound. Scripture, Melanchthon argued, teaches that all things happen by necessity or according to divine predestination, and hence there can be no freedom of the human will. Melanchthon's language was unfortunate at this point, for he meant that man because of his sinfulness cannot do meritorious works, not that he has no power to choose. In later editions and writings he emphatically rejected determinism.

A study of the mind also shows that man's reasoning faculty is controlled by the will or emotions, Melanchthon declared, for one cannot choose to love or not to love, to hate or not to hate. Emotions must overcome emotions, for reason lacks the power to do so; since sin is rooted in the heart, in the inner emotions of man, man is not free to do good works and thus to merit the grace of God.

In the heart of man, Melanchthon wrote, as the Bible and the study of the mind both witness, sits original sin, a native propensity, an inborn impulse, an energy, a self-centeredness that vitiates all altrusim. Self-love turns all concern for others or for God into an oblique or direct love of self, so that the two basic commandments, to love God and love neighbor, are shattered. As long as this self-love is uncurbed, man can produce only shadows of virtues. "All men according to their natural powers are truly sinners and do always sin," Melanchthon claimed. To say that man's "good" works merit righteousness is but to deceive and to deepen man's spiritual blindness, for every attempt to merit righteousness is motivated by a love of self. Holy works, pilgrimages, veneration of relics, vigils, and fasts become self-love in disguise.

Law, both natural and divine, Melanchthon declared, was given to man that he might be aware of his sinfulness. In addition to the natural laws of self-preservation and reproduction which man shares with animals, man possesses a law of conscience which tells him that he ought to love God, ought to refrain from injuring his fellow man, and ought to share all things. This is the natural law, or light, that is implanted in every man, a law inscribed on the soul of each man, to rule and shape character, although it is often barely apprehensible.

By the sharing of all things Melanchthon did not mean communism, for he believed that the best way to share and to serve was for each man to possess and manage a portion of the common property, and that the established ways of buying, selling, and contracting were the best practical means for achieving this. These imperatives in natural law have their parallels in Scriptural commands to love God, love neighbor, and love by serving.

But self-love in man's heart makes it impossible for man to keep the law except in an external manner, for he loves God in order to gain merit for himself; he injures others thinking he can promote himself; and he uses his share of the common property for his own rather than for the public good.

The divine law demands obedience which man cannot render. From this circumstance man knows he is condemned, lost, helpless. At this point, Melanchthon maintained, the Gospel consoles man by revealing God's benevolence and willingness to forgive sins, and by imparting the gift of the Holy Spirit to man's heart to turn it from love of self to love of God and neighbor. Man does not totally escape his natural propensities, however; they remain as long as he is in this world, but man's feeling of gratitude and joy for the revelation of divine benevolence makes praise to God and service to man rather than self-concern the center of motivation.

Even so, this feeling of gratitude is not man's doing; it is the product of faith, beholding the divine mercy promised in Christ. "Faith is the constant assent to every word of God; a thing that cannot be done except the

Holy Spirit of God renews and illuminates our hearts," Melanchthon wrote. In the state of faith man knows that he cannot merit righteousness by keeping the law, but he keeps the law and does good works and praises God out of joy and gratitude for the mercy that God has revealed.

Melanchthon then applied these ideas to various questions that had arisen. Since the Gospel bestows salvation gratuitously, without regard to our "meritorious works," is man free to do as he pleases? No, because the Spirit that reveals this to man is the Spirit of love in which all law is summarized. Man keeps the law because the will of God is the law, and the Holy Spirit is but the living will of God active in man. Christian liberty means that the Christian keeps the law but keeps it spontaneously from the heart—in fact, that he would do what the law enjoins even if there were no law. The law is not abrogated; it is fulfilled on a different level of motivation; man cannot dispense with the demands of law, for he is never fully possessed by the Spirit, and the flesh in this life is never fully crucified. Man needs constantly through the law to be made aware of sin and to hear the consolation of the Gospel. Melanchthon indicated in this a process of sanctification after justification.

The sacraments are signs; they do not justify. They do not merit righteousness. The sacramental signs of baptism and the Lord's Supper have been divinely given as tokens of God's grace. There is no Scriptural basis for any others. Baptism signifies a passing through death unto life, the submersion of the old man and the awakening of the new; faith alone justifies. The Lord's Supper is a sign to confirm our wavering consciences and to certify to us the Gospel and the remission of sins.

In keeping with Romans 13, Melanchthon accepted magistrates as stewards who carry the sword and guard civil peace, their power deriving from God. If a magistrate's commands are contrary to the word of God, they are not to be obeyed; but otherwise they are to be obeyed, even when that which is ordered is tyrannical, for love demands that tyranny be suffered if it cannot be changed without public disturbance and sedition. Melanchthon applied the same rule to ecclesiastical magistrates saying that they are not to be heard when they command something contrary to Scripture, and they are not to be obeyed if they command something outside of Scripture so as to bind consciences, as in the case of celibacy and forbidden meats, even though these commands themselves are not evil. Christian love enjoins one to suffer if necessary to avoid offense and injury, but in the presence of Pharisees demanding observances one may violate human traditions to show that it is no sin to do so; thereby one asserts the liberty of Christians that results from justification by faith.

Again and again Melanchthon lashed out at those who without grace feign good works and pretend that they are meriting God's love, calling them howling Pharisees, whitewashed sepulchres, Roman tyrants, sophists, and theologasters. Melanchthon believed that justification was the work of God through faith; he could not delegate any portion of justification to man's merit.

Martin Luther (1483-1546) praised the *Loci communes* saying it should be placed in the Canon. Johann Eck

(1486-1543), Roman Catholic theologian, answered its unorthodoxy in 1525 with *Enchiridion locorum communium adversus Lutheranos*, and Johannes Cochlaeus (1479-1552), Catholic theologian, branded it as "heretical, abominable, and putrid."

For a hundred years it was used as a textbook in dogmatics in Lutheran seminaries, and it was made required reading at Cambridge University in England. Two of Melanchthon's students, Victorinus Strigel (1524-1569) and Martin Chemnitz (1522-1586), wrote commentaries on it.

The *Loci* went through many editions. Georg Strobel, Church historian, traced it through three basic periods. In the first period, 1521-1525, eighteen Latin editions appeared. In the second period, 1525-1535, numerous Latin editions came from the press, showing by their changes that Melanchthon was actively enlarging, amending and revising. In the third period, 1535 on, still more Latin versions appeared with changes, especially in 1540. The earliest German translations were done by Georg Spalatin, the first one appearing in 1522; from 1526 to 1536 Justus Jonas was the chief translator, and in the third period, Melanchthon undertook the task.

The various editions contained significant changes. Melanchthon depended heavily on the writings of Paul, particularly on Romans. In his emphasis on justification by faith he made statements about free will which seemed to lean toward determinism: "The Spirit teaches that all things happen necessarily according to predestination." In later editions Melanchthon clearly rejected determinism as something that would lead to fatalism. In subsequent editions, Melanchthon changed many such sentences and phrases so as to emphasize man's ethical responsibility, changes which later involved him in controversies over synergism, controversies concerning exactly how much man does or does not do in the process of salvation. Melanchthon maintained that man at least accepts or rejects the mercy of God, although such is not even a possibility without the Word and the Spirit first drawing and inviting man. Melanchthon also altered the vicious remarks about philosophy which he made in his zeal to combat work-righteousness. He later saw the usefulness of philosophy in developing ethics and maintaining the common welfare.

Three hundred years after it was first published, Philip Schaff, Church historian, aptly described the *Loci* as marking an "epoch in the history of theology." The influence of this masterful work continues to be felt in modern theology.

THE BONDAGE OF THE WILL

Author: Martin Luther (1483-1546)
Type of work: Polemical theology
First published: 1525

PRINCIPAL IDEAS ADVANCED

Erasmus is in error in holding that man is endowed with a power to change the desires of his will in matters that pertain to salvation.

Free will is a term which applies solely to God, for apart from the spirit of God man is unable to do what is good.

Arguments based upon Biblical injunctions to choose between life and death fail to support the notion of free will, since they simply tell man what he ought to do; they in no way imply that man has the ability, apart from God's grace, to do what he ought.

Other arguments seek to support free will by distorting clear passages of Scripture by allegorical interpretations, thereby ignoring the fact that the doctrine of free will ultimately denies the omnipotence and foreknowledge of God.

The *Bondage of the Will* is Martin Luther's answer to Erasmus's *Diatribe on Free Will* (1524). Luther begins by recognizing no authority other than the Scriptures. The Church can decree nothing that the latter do not contain. The Scriptures are neither obscure nor ambiguous, and yet the Spirit of God is necessary before they can be understood and believed.

Luther accuses Erasmus of inconsistently holding that our will is both active and passive in the acquisition of eternal salvation. Erasmus held that it is irreligious and idle speculation to seek to determine the role of the will in matters pertaining to salvation. Luther, on the contrary, argues that it is both possible and important to discover the role of "free will" and its relation to the grace of God. The question of free will is a wholesome part of Christian doctrine, Luther insists. To know what free will is, it is necessary to know what the human will does and how God's will is related to the human will.

Luther's basic thesis is *"that God foreknows nothing by contingency, but that He foresees, purposes, and does all things according to His immutable, eternal, and infallible will."*

What we do may appear to be contingent, writes Luther, but in reality, with respect to the will of God, what we do is done necessarily. The term "necessarily" does not properly connote compulsion, but the necessity of immutability. The will, whether divine or human, does not act by compulsion but by willingness and desire. Our corrupt will is of itself, apart from divine grace, unable to do good. Man's salvation is beyond any power that he has; it depends solely upon the will of God. Before the Spirit of God works in us we do nothing to gain our salvation. The evil that a man does apart from the Spirit of God is done not against his will, as by violence, but spontaneously and with a desire for doing evil.

The "free will" that Luther denies is the alleged freedom that a man has to do what is good, in the sense of meriting salvation. Man is not free to change the bent of his desires; he cannot change a corrupt will, which loves that which is evil, into a will that desires and loves that which is good. Such a change is effected solely by the Spirit of God. When the latter is at work in a man, his will is changed, so that without compulsion it desires and craves what is good.

The term "free will" in its fullest sense is applicable to God alone, Luther writes, for God alone does what He will on earth and in Heaven. Man may be said to exercise free will in the use of his goods and possessions, if it be remembered that his acts are overruled by the freedom of God; but in matters related to his salvation, man has no free will, for he is in bondage and slavery either to the will of God or to the will of Satan.

Luther seeks to establish the validity of his own position, first by refuting the arguments advanced in support of free will, second, by meeting objections to his own arguments, and third, by contending for the grace of God against free will.

In support of free will Erasmus contends that the human will is able to apply itself to, or to reject, things which lead to eternal salvation. The human will is thus thought to possess a power or faculty to choose or to refuse the words and works of God that lead to salvation; that is, to choose or refuse the Gospel and the law. Luther, on the contrary, maintains that Erasmus's position ascribes to the will what is beyond its capacity and comprehension. Apart from the Holy Spirit no man knows, believes in, or desires eternal salvation. To endow the will with the power to work salvation is to ascribe divinity to it, for the power of God alone can will not to sin and to embrace the law and the Gospel. Free will is and remains a divine term because it signifies a divine power.

Once the will has lost its liberty, it is compulsively bound to the service of sin and cannot will any good; the term free will then becomes an empty term;

that is, it fails to designate any actual faculty of man.

Advocates of free will may seek to base their view on such a passage of Scripture as Ecclesiasticus 15:15-18, in which it is written that God made man from the beginning and left him to his own counsels, enjoining him to keep His commandments, and presenting him with a choice between life and death.

Such a passage in no way suggests free will, writes Luther, for it militates against free will, in that it subjects man to the precepts and will of God. Such a passage in no wise asserts free will, he claims, since it does not teach that man has the power to keep the commandments of God.

Nowhere in the Scriptures is man told that he is able to keep the commandments; he is rather constantly reminded of his impotency. Such expressions in Scripture as, "If thou wilt," ". . . if thou hear," ". . . if thou do," do not state what man can do, but what he ought to do.

To the objection that man is mocked if he is told to choose when in fact there is but one course of action open to him, Luther replies that such injunctions are given so that a man might better see his own impotency. The words of the law do not assert the power of the will, but they teach man what he ought to do and they make man aware of his own sin. Such words as "choose," "keep," and "do" in the Scriptures convey the precept to be kept; they do not describe any power of man.

Imperatives in Scripture prove nothing concerning human ability, Luther claims, for imperatives simply enjoin what ought to be done and what ought not to be done. To interpret them otherwise would be to assert that free will can do all things without grace.

It is a part of man's blindness and misery that he believes himself to be free, when in fact the words of the law show us only what we ought to do but cannot. What ought to be is not the same as what has been; what is exacted is not the same as what has been performed; and what is required is not the same as what has been rendered.

The Biblical expression "I desire not the death of a sinner" offers divine mercy to the world. Such mercy is received by those who are touched by the law and know their sin. That some are touched by the law and others unaffected is wholly attributable to the secret will of God.

It is, therefore, necessary to distinguish between God preached and God hidden, between God's Word and God Himself. God wills many things that are unknown to us. What and why God wills is unknown. When we speak of God preached, writes Luther, we can say that God desires that man should be saved, but it is hidden from us why God does not change every human will. The secret will of God belongs to God's incomprehensible nature.

With the coming of Christ into the world, writes Luther, grace was offered; if man will believe, he is given the opportunity of becoming a child of God, and yet the believer is led to such faith, not by free will, but by the Spirit of God, for all things take place from His immutable will.

To seek to evade the force of the arguments against free will, it is necessary, Luther claims, to interpret the teaching of Scripture allegorically. To call God into question is to demand that God cease to be God. For God is that being for whose will there is no cause or reason to be assigned in terms of which God's acts can be judged. There is no rule or standard outside God. Nothing is superior or equal to God's will; the divine will is itself the rule of all things. God's will would no longer be the will of God if it acted by any rule or standard, or from any cause or reason outside God. What God wills is right not because He is bound by some standard or rule, but simply because He wills it.

Moreover, Luther continues, we could not believe the promises of God unless what He promises takes place of necessity. What God foreknows must take place of necessity, or God would otherwise be deceived in what He foreknows. The free will of man is thus incompatible with the prescience and omnipotence of God. To grant God's foreknowledge and omnipotence is to grant that whatever we do is done by His omnipotence. What we do we do, not because of free will, but because God brings about whatsoever comes to pass according to the counsel of His infallible will.

In the case of Judas's betrayal of Christ, for example, Judas willingly betrayed Him, without any compulsion or force, but this willingness on the part of Judas was foreknown by God and immutably decreed to take place.

The necessity of which Luther speaks is not a necessity of force with respect to the act, but a necessity of mutability in reference to the time. The question is not whether Judas was willing or unwilling to become a traitor, but whether or not God infallibly predetermined by His decree that at a certain time Judas should will to betray Christ. Judas did not have it in his power to will not to become a traitor. To deny this is to render the immutable foreknowledge of God mutable.

Before man is regenerated into the new creation of the Kingdom of the Spirit, man does nothing and tries to do nothing to become a part of that Kingdom. It is the Spirit alone that regenerates and causes men to persevere as members of His Kingdom.

By the law man gains a knowledge of sin, Luther writes; man is cast down and afflicted, not to be delivered by the law or by himself, but only by the redeeming love of Christ. Free will does not move a man to the righteousness of God, for God alone can draw a sinner unto Himself. God alone can justify a sinner, and this He does freely, not because the sinner has any merit of his own. God's grace comes by the purpose of God, by divine election and not by any endeavor of our own.

If salvation were dependent upon man, instead of upon the grace of God, no one would be saved, and all would perish together. If we believe, however, that Christ redeemed us by His blood, we must also believe that the whole man was lost. Because of original sin, nothing is left in man devoid of the Spirit; apart from God, man cannot turn to what is good, but must turn towards evil. It is to God alone that the judgment of righteousness belongs; the potter has power over the clay.

Luther's *Bondage of the Will*, as an extreme but consistent answer to Erasmus's faith in the freedom of the human will, is an important contribution to the Augustinian tradition within Protestant thought.

ON THE ERRORS OF THE TRINITY

Author: Michael Servetus (1511-1553)
Type of work: Systematic theology
First published: 1531

PRINCIPAL IDEAS ADVANCED

The orthodox doctrine of the Trinity, that there are three persons in one substance in the Godhead, leads to tritheism and is to be rejected in favor of the Scriptural doctrine that there is one God who manages Himself in different dispositions or dispensations.

Christ is the Son of God, equal with the Father in power rather than in essence; God the Father is alone God in nature.

The Holy Spirit is not a third person of a triune God, but is rather an activity or disposition of God, a divine impulse that works in us.

The doctrine of the Trinity has led to sophistical quibbling; the doctrine arises out of Greek philosophy rather than out of the Scriptures, and it is largely responsible for the alienation of the Jews and the Mohammedans.

Michael Servetus, Spanish scholar, scientist, and physician, influenced the religious thought of the Reformation by the publication of *De trinitatis erroribus libri septem* (1531), and his *Dialogorum de trinitate libri duo* (1532). His last work, *Christianismi restitutio* (1553), for which he was condemned, was at once so utterly destroyed that its historical influence was negligible.

Both the Reformers—Calvin in particular—and the Roman Catholics condemned the views of Servetus and approved of his execution at the stake on October 27, 1553. In 1553, Servetus's views served as the fountainhead of subsequent anti-trinitarian tendencies which culminated in Unitarianism.

Servetus's *Dialogues on the Trinity,* published a year after his *On the Errors of the Trinity,* differs from the earlier work in tone, but the *Dialogues* does not disavow the position taken in the *Errors.* The latter intended to point out the errors in the traditional doctrine of the Trinity and to reformulate Biblical doctrine in a manner more compatible with reason and piety.

The *Errors* is divided into seven books. The work shows evidence of a carefully considered plan, and yet it is frequently repetitious and crude. The substance of Servetus's argument is set forth in Book One; the remaining six books take up certain aspects in more detail and with considerable repetition.

Servetus admits that Jesus is the Son of God and that He is God, but he does not admit the orthodox view of the Trinity. The orthodox doctrine of the Trinity, embodied in the Nicene, Constantinopolitan, and Athanasian creeds, insists that the terms Father, Son, and Spirit are not expressive of relations within a single person, but are personal designations. The word *hypostasis,* "person" in English, is used to indicate that the Father, Son, and

Spirit express necessary and eternal relations in the Godhead. The three persons are a trinity in unity. The persons are not to be confounded, nor is the substance to be divided. The three persons of the Trinity are one substance, equal in glory, majesty, and power.

Servetus also speaks of Christ as equal with God, but he claims that Christ's equality is in power, not in nature or essence. Jesus, according to Servetus, was not a hypostasis, but an actual son. The first point to be made is that Jesus Christ is a man. The discussion of the Trinity should not begin with the Word, but with the man, Jesus Christ. Many texts of Scripture and the early writers of the Church clearly attest that Christ was a man, and His miracles clearly show that Jesus was the Christ.

The second point, according to Servetus, is that Christ is the Son of God; the almighty power of the Word of God overshadowed Mary, so that Jesus is the real Son of God by nature, not an hypostasis. God is called the Father of Jesus Christ, just as earthly fathers are the fathers of their own sons. He is the Son of God by nature; others are sons by adoption. The sense in which Christ is the Son of God is higher than the sense in which men become sons of God through faith in Christ.

The third point, continues Servetus, is that the Scriptures clearly prove that Christ is God. He is man according to the flesh, but in the spirit He is divinity. The notion that the human nature shares its properties with God, the *communicatio idiomatum,* is a sophistical quibble. God has in fact shared the fullness of His deity with a man and has given Christ a name above every name. God was in Him in singular measure; the real Christ is complete in divinity. God does not share any of man's imperfections, but He shares His full deity with Christ. Christ is God in appearance, not in nature, but by grace. It was given to Him to be God by way of privilege. The Father alone is God by nature. The expressions "God and Christ," "Christ and God," indicate that Christ is a being distinct from God. The Father alone is the invisible God. God and Christ are distinct beings, and yet the word "God" can be used in a sense in which it can be said that Christ is very God. Before all time Christ was in the Spirit of God. The equality which Christ had while He existed in the form of God, He had by reason of the authority or power that God gave Him. His equality is an equality of power. The Old Testament use of the word "Elohim" for beings less than the supreme God serves as an indication of the nature of the deity of Christ. As the Word of God, Christ came down from Heaven; He is not a second God, but He was made equal to God in power.

Christ is not one in nature with the Godhead. God does not consist of two beings in one nature. To admit a metaphysical equality is not the intention of Paul when he says in Philippians 2:6 that Christ, being in the form of God, thought it not robbery to be equal with God. If Christ were the second person of the Godhead by nature, how could he be said to have the appearance of deity? Christ existed in the likeness of God, was equal to God in power, not in nature or essence; since He bore the humble form of a man, it was not robbery for him to be on an equality with God. He did not neglect the work that His Father had appointed Him to accomplish, nor did

He seize a kingly tyranny over the world.

The notion of three beings in one nature is the work of philosophical imagination, Servetus insists. The Holy Spirit regarded as a third separate being leads to a practical tritheism, and even if the unity of God is insisted upon, such a plurality of gods is no better than atheism.

The Scriptures know of no such nonsense. "For by Holy Spirit it means now God himself, now an angel, now the spirit of a man, a sort of instinct or divine inspiration of the mind, a mental impulse, or a breath. . . ."

In Book Two of his *Dialogues on the Trinity,* Servetus retraced the statement that the Holy Spirit is an angel. The Holy Spirit can be said to be created, only in the sense that God created a new *disposition* in Himself. The Scriptures mention the existence of God the Father, and of the Son, but the Holy Spirit is mentioned not as a separate being, but as an activity of God, as an in-breathing or in-working of God's power.

God disposes or manages Himself in three different ways, writes Servetus. The Father is the whole substance; it is from Him that three wonderful dispositions or aspects shine forth; the Father, the Son, and the Holy Spirit are not three by virtue of any distinction of being in God, but simply through a disposition or dispensation of God in various forms of deity.

The traditional orthodox view of the Trinity is a delusion, Servetus insists; a trinity in one being cannot be imagined; the notion of three beings is a pure phantasm, and what cannot be understood ought not to be received. Nothing can be in the mind which is not in the senses first. Since no one has ever had a sensation of three beings constituting a single nature, to conceive of a multiplication of beings without conceiving of a multiplication of essences or natures is impossible. The orthodox doctrine of the Trinity cannot be proven from Scripture or established by logic. The Scriptures clearly teach but one God, and one Christ, His Son. The admission of three persons is the admission of three entities, of three substances—in effect, a plurality of Gods.

According to Servetus, the doctrine of the Trinity has given rise to countless ridiculous subtleties which are wholly foreign to the Mohammedans, though Mohammed holds Christ and the Apostles in the highest honor. It has prevented the Jews from believing that Christ is the Messiah promised in their law. The doctrine of the Trinity is due to the introduction of Greek philosophy into the doctrine of the Church, whereas the latter should be founded on the belief that Jesus Christ is the Son of God.

Christ is the Word of God, a disposition or dispensation in God by which He has revealed His will to us. The Word God uttered at the creation of the world is the Christ who became flesh and is the Son of God, descended from Heaven. Christ is God's voice become flesh. The world was created by the Word, not by a being. In Christ there is the whole nature and essence of God. Christ is in the Father, just as the voice is in the one that speaks; the Father and Christ are one, just as the ray and the sun are one light.

Before creation, the Word existed and was begotten when first God uttered it; afterwards it was incarnate in Jesus, God's Son. The titles ascribed to Christ ascribe high praise to Him, but they do not mean that He was an abstract being. He is rather the wisdom of God that came forth from God. The Word was a disposition, an aspect, of God at the beginning of the world; the Word was never the Son. God is above all distinctions of time, so that God and the Word existed causally before the world. The Word is a disposition of God above all distinctions of time; it is not the Son. To believe that Jesus is the Christ is the very essence of Christianity; it is the belief which ensures our salvation.

The Scriptures never pay attention to natures, says Servetus, but only to appearances and dispositions. The differences between the persons, or dispositions, are to be judged in the manner of their appearing. God is manifested in three different persons or dispositions. In Christ the real image of God is manifest. When the Word became flesh in Christ, it ceased to exist. Since Christ has ascended to God, Christ is as really in God as the Word was with God before. The Word is in no way identical with the Son. The Word prepared the way so that the glory of Christ could be manifest. Christ is the very image of the substance of God, but the substance of God has nothing to do with the divine nature. The substance of the Father is the Father's way of subsisting. The essence of God is mingled with the angels, for God is the essence of all things, and all things are in Him. Christ is the disposition of God which wrought everything in the world. In Himself God is incomprehensible; He is known solely through Christ, by faith and not by philosophical speculation.

Servetus's views represent a radical departure from Christian orthodoxy; their positive contribution to the Reformation is that they provoked a violent negative reaction, which necessitated that the Reformers unequivocally affirm their belief in the basic Christian doctrine of the Trinity, as confessed by the Holy Catholic Church.

A DIALOGUE OF COMFORT AGAINST TRIBULATION

Author: Saint Thomas More (1478-1535)
Type of work: Spiritual direction
First transcribed: 1534-1535

PRINCIPAL IDEAS ADVANCED

Tribulation is part of the just man's life; the only basis for comfort is faith in God's promise to reward the believer in Heaven.

Much of the anguish of tribulation is in the mind.

Suffering is medicinal; bearing it patiently, the Christian makes payment for his sins, and even lays up a store of merit.

Pagan philosophers have many helpful things to say for our consolation, but lack the one thing needful; namely, the hope of reward in Heaven.

Sir Thomas More, whom Henry VIII had raised to the position of Chancellor of the realm on account of his liberal outlook, fell from the royal favor when he opposed Henry's resolve to divorce Catherine. Afterwards, having been imprisoned in the Tower for refusing to swear the Act of Supremacy, he was executed on the charge of treason. He wrote *A Dialogue of Comfort Against Tribulation* during his imprisonment; his intention was to console his family.

Unlike the celebrated *Utopia* (1516), which was written in Latin, the *Dialogue of Comfort Against Tribulation* was written in colloquial English. The author amuses himself by representing the work as having been written in Latin by a Hungarian, and as having found its way into English as a translation from the French. The *Dialogue* purports to be a series of conversations between an elderly Hungarian gentleman, Anthony, and his young nephew, Vincent, at a time when Hungary is about to be invaded by the Turks. Anthony, a man of learning and broad experience, having twice been a prisoner in Turkey, is near death. The thought of his dying at the time of the Turkish peril is a special trial to his children and friends, because it has become their custom to lean on him for advice and comfort. At Vincent's request, therefore, Anthony undertakes to call to mind such things as he has read and thought which may be of use to his family in laying up "a store of comfort" in their hearts "as a treacle against the poison of all desperate dread that might rise on occasion of sore tribulation."

The patriarchal tone of the work reflects the actual situation between More and his family, who, as is shown in Holbein's painting "The Household of Sir Thomas More," lived surrounded by his children and grandchildren. That was during the happier days of which Erasmus wrote, "In More's house you would see that Plato's Academy was revived again, only, whereas in the Academy the discussions turned upon geometry and the power of numbers, the house at Chelsea is a veritable school of Christian religion." In prison, appointed to martyrdom, his modest wealth confiscated by England's Grand Turk, Sir Thomas was able to do little for his loved ones except point their thoughts to God. "For," as Anthony says to Vincent, "God is and must be your comfort, and not I. And He is a sure comforter, that (as He said unto His disciples) never leaveth His servants in case of comfortless orphans: not even when He departed from His disciples by death, but both as He promised, sent them a comforter, the Holy Spirit of his Father and Himself, and made them also sure, that to the world's end He would ever dwell with them Himself."

The comfort to which More directs his reader is uncompromisingly Christian. Tribulation, he argues, is a normal part of the just man's life, and loss of property and bodily injury are not great disasters. Those who think that such difficulties are important are governed by imagination rather than by exact understanding. In reality, every man is a prisoner under sentence of death, with no certain hold on this world's good, and with no security from bodily harm. Such being man's condition, his only comfort is in God, who, by his Word, has promised to reward men in heaven. The root and origin of all comfort, therefore, is the faith that the Scriptures are God's Word. Those who truly believe will be able "to command a great mountain of tribulation to void from the place where it stood in our heart," but those of little faith "shall be scant able to remove a little hillock."

More understands very well the mental anguish into which men are often plunged by adversity. There are, he says, those who refuse any kind of comfort. He describes the vacant-eyed dullness of persons who are so overwhelmed with their sorrow that they lie in deathly lethargy, refusing to think of anything, and thereby gradually lose all memory and understanding. Another sort respond with frenzied impatience and are so poisoned and antagonized by their loss that one hardly dare speak to them. Both kinds, says More, are guilty of mortal sin: the former of sloth, the latter of anger. When, in contrast, the believer finds that he is able to seek and find consolation in God, he receives a fresh impression of that divine favor which Christ has visited upon us, and he finds comfort in the mere fact that he is able to desire comfort.

More deals at length with delusions and morbid obsessions, especially with those which come to a man in the night. When cut off from normal human intercourse, as a prisoner is likely to be, man loses his perspective, and he easily falls prey to fears and scruples which at other times he would not entertain. The temptation to despair and to self-destruction is particularly to be reckoned with, and suicide often appears to the distempered mind to be a religious duty. In such an hour, says Thomas, besides calling upon God for help, one must resist the call

of death by the use of reason; the prisoner must tell himself "that a great part of this temptation is in effect but the fear of his own fancy." The devils, he says, are not themselves able to throw us down, even though, like people calling to a man when he is walking across a high bridge, they may arouse destructive fears in one who would otherwise walk safely.

More stresses the fact that tribulation is usually more mental than physical. This is especially the case with that form of tribulation which is common to every righteous man, and never far from him; namely, temptation. Trouble is more difficult to bear when it is avoidable than when it is unavoidable; religious persecution is troublesome to conscience because such persecution is usually avoidable. The Turkish peril, concerning which Anthony speaks in the *Dialogue,* was of this kind. So was More's own tribulation. He was, his biographer tells us, soundly rated by his wife for obstinately lying in prison when he had only to yield to Parliament and be restored. More's reply was, "Don't you think, Mistress Alice, that this place is as near to heaven as Chelsea?" To her petulant reply, he answered, "Suppose I were to go back to my house in Chelsea, how long do you think we would live to enjoy it?" "Possibly twenty years," she said. "Twenty years!" said he; "Why, if you had said a thousand years it would have been something, and yet he would be a very bad merchant that would put himself in danger to lose eternity for a thousand years; how much the rather, as we are not sure of it for one day."

More's counsel to those who are threatened with loss or harm for the sake of the Gospel is to make themselves familiar with what they must face and "to appoint with God's help in their own mind before hand, what thing they intend to do if the very worst fall." Most of the terrors which cause men to flee are imaginary, and if such terrors be pondered and weighed by the reason, they are not as fearful as they seem at first.

It was no part of More's plan, however, to deny the actuality of affliction and pain. On the contrary, he takes as one of his main sources of comfort the medieval doctrine that merit is acquired by suffering. Through God's grace, he says, every tribulation is "either medicinal or more than medicinal." Tribulation is "medicinal" when we suffer for our sins; the more we suffer in this life, the less we have to suffer in purgatory. Tribulation is "more than medicinal" if it has no connection with our sin but is sent to prove a man's patience and to increase his merit. More permits Vincent to raise the Protestant objections against penance and purgatory, and, generally, against the whole doctrine of merit. In reply, Anthony says that he can see no very deep difference between the Lutherans and the Catholics on the matter of faith and works. "Like as we grant them that no good work is ought worth to heavenward without faith, . . . so this one thing or twain do they grant us again, that men are bound to work good works if they have time and power, and that who so worketh in true faith most, shall be most rewarded." But he says that great damage is done by preachers who emphasize faith so strongly that people are encouraged to neglect the obligations which Christ lays upon His disciples, especially the duty to fast. As to purgatory, it would

be a consolation to Anthony were he able to believe that the Protestants are right, but he declares that he dare not go against the received interpretation of the Scriptures from the days of the Apostles down to the present time.

Because Sir Thomas stands at the threshold of the English renaissance, it may be surprising to find him so deeply committed to the traditional Christian viewpoint. One might have thought, from reading *Utopia,* that he was ready to embrace a kind of minimal faith, composed of the best elements in paganism. But that work seems to have been more a satire on the times than an expression of his positive convictions. The *Dialogue* is, nevertheless, an unmistakably Renaissance work. The very fact that Christianity is something to be discussed and reasoned about instead of merely taken on authority is itself enough to put the work in a new category, and the dialogue form shows More's enthusiasm for the classical revival. The author also shares the new interest in fables and folk tales, and he brightens the tone of what might otherwise be a somber work with several humorous tales which could have appeared in Chaucer or Erasmus.

More's familiarity with pagan philosophy is abundantly evident. But his considered judgment is that the natural reasons which pagan philosophy adduces are not able to give sufficient comfort of themselves, because they neglect the special point which is not only the chief comfort but is also that without which all other comforts fail; namely, "the referring the final end of their comforts unto God." "We shall therefore," he says, "neither fully receive these philosophers' reasons in this matter, nor yet utterly refuse them: but using them in such order as shall beseem them, the principal and the effectual medicines against these diseases of tribulation shall we fetch from that high, great, and excellent Physician, without whom we could never be healed of our very deadly disease." Thus, with all its echoes of Seneca and Plato, particularly of the

Phaedo (the dialogue in which Socrates bids farewell to his friends), the true original of More's *Dialogue* is found in St. John's Gospel, chapters fourteen to seventeen, in which Jesus takes His departure from His disciples and promises never to leave them comfortless.

THE INSTITUTES OF THE CHRISTIAN RELIGION

Author: John Calvin (1509-1564)
Type of work: Systematic theology
First published: 1536, 1539, 1559

Principal Ideas Advanced

The knowledge of God and the knowledge of man are inseparable, for knowledge of man's imperfection leads to knowledge of God's perfection, and knowledge of God's perfection is prerequisite to self-knowledge.

The redemption of lost humanity is to be sought in Christ alone, without whom the knowledge of God as creator is useless.

The moral law promulgates the rule of God's righteousness.

Faith is the origin of repentance; justification is obtained exclusively by the righteousness of Christ.

God's eternal decree alone has determined the eternal destiny of every person.

Baptism testifies to man's purgation; the Lord's Supper testifies, by analogy, to man's redemption.

John Calvin's *The Institutes of the Christian Religion* was published in 1536, but it did not receive its final form until 1559. Calvin's *Institutes* was the first attempt to systematize the theology of the Reformed churches of the Reformation; it is still unsurpassed as a theological treatise.

The two main topics of Calvin's treatise, the knowledge of God and the knowledge of man, are inseparable topics, for—Calvin insists—no one can survey himself without realizing that

his own existence is a subsistence in God. Knowledge of man's ignorance, unhappiness, depravity, and corruption leads to the perception that in the Lord alone and in His perfection can true wisdom and happiness be found. Yet, on the other hand, Calvin writes, true self-knowledge must be preceded by the contemplation of the perfect nature of God.

In Calvin's opinion, it is not sufficient simply to have the notion that there is such a being as God. God requires us to know that we owe everything to Him, that He is the source of all good, that we are subject to His authority, and that we must love and obey Him.

The knowledge that God requires of us is not to be sought in man alone. Such knowledge is natural to man, since man has an innate sense of deity, but man needs a source of truth which will direct him to the Creator of the world, and he finds it in the Scriptures, which are self-authenticated, carrying with them their own evidence of authority. The believer's conviction that the Scriptures are the Word of God is produced not by the testimony of the Church, nor by rational proofs, but by the inward witness of the Holy Spirit.

What is taught in the Scriptures concerning the nature of God is sufficient to overthrow all idolatrous beliefs and practices, Calvin claims, for the Scriptures teach that there is one God, one divine essence, in which there is a trinity of persons. Each person is a subsistence in the divine essence, related to the others, yet distinct from them by reason of an incommunicable property.

The *Institutes* places considerable emphasis on the absolute sovereignty of God. God is described as an omnipotent creator, a governor by providence who allows no event to occur which is not an expression of His divine will. The Calvinistic claim that it is only through the grace of God, working on the souls of those whom He has predestined to be redeemed, that any men are saved, is a further expression of the conviction that God, by His divine will, directs everything that happens in nature and in the course of human affairs. God wills those acts by which men express their freedom and are responsible: such a view may be paradoxical, but it is consistently Calvinistic.

Calvin asserts that the Scriptures acquaint us with ourselves by informing us of the original state at our creation, and of our state after Adam's Fall. Created in the image of God, man's soul was endowed with a mind capable of distinguishing the good from the evil and of discovering by the light of reason what ought to be pursued or avoided. In his primitive state of perfection, man possessed reason, understanding, and the necessary prudence and judgment to regulate his earthly life and to attain eternal happiness with God. He also possessed a free will, upon which his choice depended, so that, if he had chosen, "he might have obtained eternal life."

Calvin writes that since the sin of Adam we have fallen from our original state of integrity and that to know ourselves we must be aware of our present state of misery. Adam's sin of disobedience obliterated the divine image and resulted in the loss of wisdom, strength, sanctity, truth, and righteousness, not only for himself, but for his posterity, so that his every descendant is born with the contagion of sin and is defiled and polluted with innate depravity. The entire human race is involved in Adam's guilt and corruption and is, therefore, justly condemned in the sight of God.

In his present fallen condition man is despoiled of freedom of will and is subjected to the miserable slavery of sin. Man is now destitute of all rectitude, Calvin writes, for man has of himself no power for the pursuit of righteousness. Apart from the special grace that is bestowed only upon the elect in regeneration, man cannot perform good works. His natural gifts have been corrupted and his supernatural gifts have been taken away. Man's reason is incapable of attaining spiritual wisdom; that is, he cannot know God; nor can he know God's favor towards men, a favor on which salvation depends; nor does man know the way by which he ought to regulate his life according to God's law. Nevertheless the common grace of God sometimes restrains sin in the unregenerate, who are often "invested and adorned by God with excellent talents." (Here Calvin refers, as Dante did, to those who might be called "virtuous pagans.")

The human will is by nature so entirely vitiated and depraved that everything it produces is evil, Calvin claims. When destitute of grace, men are in slavery to the corruption of their own evil desires and are not moved toward what is spiritually good. The will, rather, is subject to the dominion of sin and is in bondage. Whatever good men enjoy is from God, and whatever evil they suffer is from themselves. Everything that is the product of man's corrupt nature deserves condemnation, for having been corrupted by the Fall, man now sins voluntarily, not reluctantly, not under external constraint or compulsion, but with the strongest propensity of his own disposition. Such necessity in no way precludes voluntary bondage to sin; all men are under voluntary servitude.

The sole remedy for such bondage, Calvin suggests, is to be found in divine grace. It alone can correct the depravity of man's nature. It is God who begins the good work in men, by bending their hearts towards righteousness, and by confirming them to perseverance. The will is then created anew, converted from evil tendencies to good.

Whatever is good in the will is the work of grace alone, a work performed only by God; man's salvation is entirely gratuitous. God's grace is not bestowed upon all men, writes Calvin, but solely upon the elect, not on the basis of any merit, lest any should boast. The direction of the human will towards what is good is from the very first dependent upon the will of God, and the perseverance, the subsequent constancy of the elect, is likewise due to that selfsame grace, so that all ability that a convicted sinner has is derived from grace alone.

The entire human race perished in the person of Adam until God appeared as the Redeemer in the person of His only begotten Son. The redemption of lost humanity is to be sought in Christ alone, without whom the knowledge of God as creator is useless. Knowledge of God, without knowledge of the Mediator, Jesus Christ, does not afford salvation. Christ responds to the faithful of all ages, including the faithful during the Old Testament times. The Law was in fact given to encourage the people of Israel during the period of hope for salvation by the Messiah.

The Law, writes Calvin, is like a mirror in which man beholds his impotence and his iniquity, and the consequences of both. The moral law remains in full force for the faithful, for it promulgates the rule of God's righteousness and makes men attentive to His will, by enjoining them to obedience.

In Old Testament times the Law tended to excite in the faithful an expectation of the Christ that was to come; yet it is only in the Gospel that Christ is clearly revealed. The saints of the Old Testament were, however, partakers of the same inheritance, and they hoped for the same salvation through the grace of the one Mediator, Jesus Christ. For Christ was the pledge of the Old Covenant as well as of the New.

According to Calvin, the Old Testament differs from the New Testament, in spite of this basic unity. For in Old Testament times man's celestial inheritance was exhibited under the figures of terrestrial blessing; the Old Testament was promulgated without the efficacy of the Spirit; it was a covenant not of liberty but of bondage; it denoted the Law, rather than the Gospel, and it dealt with a single nation, rather than with the nations of the earth.

The fullness of man's redemption was accomplished by Christ becoming man in order to fulfill the office of Mediator. Jesus the Christ is truly God and truly man, asserts Calvin. Christ assumed a real humanity; and invested with flesh, the Son of God became also the Son of man, not by a confusion of substance, but by a unity of person. The divine and the human natures constitute the one person of the Mediator; each nature retains its own properties, and yet together they constitute a single Christ, who as redeemer fulfills a threefold office, that of prophet, priest, and king. As a prophet, He reveals the will of God for our salvation, by His word and spirit; as a priest, He offered himself, once and for all, as a sacrifice to satisfy divine justice, and by continually interceding for us, He reconciles us to God; and as a king, He rules and defends us, subdues us to Himself, and conquers our mutual enemies.

As our redeemer, by His death, resurrection, and ascension to Heaven,

Christ has procured our salvation. He alone merits the grace of God.

How then is the grace of Christ received? Our enjoyment of Christ and of all His benefits, Calvin answers, depends upon the secret and special operation of the Holy Spirit, who works faith in us, and unites us to Christ, illuminates our minds, and renews our wills.

It is by faith, Calvin writes, that we who are the adopted sons of God enter into the possession of the Heavenly Kingdom. For faith consists in a knowledge of Christ, not in reverence for the Church; it is a knowledge of the benevolence of God towards us. The knowledge of faith exceeds that of the understanding; it is an acknowledgment, a persuasion of the veracity of God; it consists more in certainty than in comprehension. It places the goodness of God beyond all doubt and uncertainty, for we apprehend that salvation and everlasting life is obtained. Faith grafts us into the body of Christ.

Faith is the origin of repentance, for the latter can arise only when a man knows himself to be of God, and does turn from sin and seek new obedience. Repentance is properly followed by confession of sin to God alone. There is no need of confession to a man, nor of further satisfaction or indulgences for the remission of sin. Believers ought to present themselves as living sacrifices, and be transformed, and take up the cross, always remembering that it is by faith alone that they are justified. The justification of the sinner is an act of God whereby God esteems him as a righteous person and remits his sins through the imputation of the righteousness of Christ; however, this in no way implies that justification is not accompanied by good works. Justification is obtained exclusively by the righteousness of Christ.

Man is never saved by his own righteousness, writes Calvin, but if he is regenerated by the Spirit of God, he will devote himself to true holiness. The entire life of the Christian should be an exercise in piety, for the Christian is called to become holy. The Christian is at liberty with respect to the yoke of the law, but he yields voluntarily to the will of God, without necessarily being under obligation with respect to things which are in themselves indifferent.

The principal exercise of faith is to be found in prayer, for nothing is revealed to us that is to be expected from God, for which we are not commanded to pray. To pray properly, the heart and mind should be suitably composed, free of all external cares; we should pray for no more than God permits. Our petitions should reflect a real sense of our indigence; they should be offered without distrust, and without any sense of our own merits, while at the same time the petitioner recognizes that it is Christ alone, not the saints, who is able to intercede for him at the throne of Grace.

Salvation is not offered to all, but only to some, Calvin writes; for some are predestined to salvation, others to destruction. God gives to some what He refuses to others. God's eternal decree has determined the destiny of every person; some are foreordained to eternal life and others to eternal damnation, without any consideration of merit, solely upon the basis of His gratuitous mercy. The voice of the Gospel is addressed to all men, but the gift of faith is bestowed only upon a few.

The validity of election does not depend upon human consent, Calvin insists. The elect are effectually called to salvation, and the reprobate are appointed to be instruments of God's wrath; being devoid of the Spirit they can do nothing except what deserves His curse.

To maintain the preaching of the Gospel, God has deposited His treasure with the Church. He has given His authority to His pastors and teachers to promote the unity of the faith, and He has instituted two sacraments to nourish and support the faith.

The Church is universal or catholic in that it includes all the elect of God, the dead as well as the living, the Church invisible, as well as the Church visible. The latter is to be found wherever we find the word preached purely and the sacraments administered as Christ instituted them.

The government of the Church is ordained by God. To edify the Church, its ministers must themselves study and proclaim the Word of God as it is contained in the Scriptures. The Church has no authority, however, to make laws which bind the consciences of men in those respects in which they have been set at liberty by Christ.

The Church has no power of the sword, no authority to punish or coerce; its jurisdiction is spiritual, and to this end it must maintain discipline, consisting of private and public admonitions, and in extreme cases, of excommunication.

The Christian faith is supported by the preaching of the Word and by the sacraments, the latter being an outward sign by which the Lord seals the promises of His good will in our consciences and gives us support in our weaknesses.

Two sacraments and two only present us with a clear exhibition of

Christ: baptism, which testifies to our purgation and ablution; and the Lord's Supper, which testifies to our redemption.

As a sign of initiation, baptism admits us into the Church. Baptism is proposed to us by the Lord as a token of our purification; it shows our mortification in Christ and our new life in Him, and it testifies that we are so united to Him as to be partakers of all His benefits. Baptism of infants assures them of God's pardon, although no man will be saved by baptism alone, for God must first have elected to save the soul and thereby have endowed it with the faith which makes baptism efficacious.

In the Lord's Supper the bread and wine represent the nourishment that we actually receive from the body and blood of Christ. The sacrament provides us with the assurance that the body of the Lord was once offered as a sacrifice for us, and His blood was once shed for us, for our salvation. The corporeal objects themselves undergo no metaphysical change, but they conduct us by analogy to the realm of the spiritual. When bread is presented as a symbol of the body, we are led to the comparison, that as bread nourishes the physical body, the life of the soul is sustained by the body of Christ; likewise as wine nourishes and refreshes the physical body, so the advantages of the remission of sin are conferred on us by the blood of Christ.

The elements of the Sacred Supper are signs of the working of Christ's spirit; their efficacy is not a function of man's power. According to Calvin, Christ "pours his life into us . . . not by putting before us a vain or empty sign, but offering there the efficacy of his Spirit, by which he fulfils his promise." Only those who are faithful to Him enjoy the fruits of His Spirit, but the Spirit is what gives the sacrament its efficacy. There is also the suggestion that the elements signify not only Christ's Spirit, but also His body: "If it is true that the visible sign is offered to us to attest the granting of the invisible reality, then, on receiving the symbol of the body, we may be confident that the body itself is no less given to us. . . ."

Calvin's *Institutes* is more than a standard work of theology. It provided the confessional foundation for the Reformed (in distinction from the Lutheran) branch of Protestantism, including English and American Puritanism. Its influence has, therefore, penetrated the cultures of many of the Western nations.

A SHORT AND CLEAR EXPOSITION OF THE CHRISTIAN FAITH

Author: Ulrich Zwingli (1484-1531)
Type of work: Reformed theology
First published: 1536

Principal Ideas Advanced

The faith of the Zurich Reformation has been falsely accused of departing from the ancient Christian truth.

Sacraments are signs and symbols of holy things and are to be reverenced only because they commemorate what has already happened; sacraments cannot remit sins or confer blessings.

The Lord's Supper witnesses to the birth and passion of Christ to both believers and nonbelievers; the body of Christ is eaten only spiritually.

Included within the visible Church are the elect and non-elect; the elect are also members of the invisible Church.

Ulrich Zwingli, a leader of the Reformation in German Switzerland, inaugurated a new phase of the Protestant movement when, in 1519, he began his duties at the Cathedral in Zurich. On that New Year's Day he announced that he would discard the traditional practice of expounding on the appointed Scriptural texts and begin his preaching with the first chapter of Matthew and proceed through the New Testament. The new pastor was departing from the old ways. The essay *A Short and Clear Exposition of the Christian Faith* was designed as a summary statement of his work; it was written in 1531 at the end of his career.

Zwingli was born in 1484, in the village of Wildhaus in Switzerland. His education was received at the Universities of Basle, Berne, and Vienna, where he came under the influence of the humanists. His study of classical philosophy, of Greek and Roman history, and of the mode of thought and expression he learned from Erasmus (c.1466-1536) carried through his life's work. He studied Erasmus's Greek edition of the New Testament with such diligence that he was able to recite the body of Pauline literature by memory.

The Swiss and German Reformation movements had common bonds. Though Zwingli did not attribute his own work to that of the German Reformer, he did say that Luther gave him the courage to preach what he learned from Paul. The sole authority of Scripture, the denial of celibacy, the reduction of the number of sacraments, the centrality of the doctrine of justification by faith, and the rejection of medieval ecclesiastical organization were ties which united these two early leaders of the Protestant Reformation. But there were differences. Zwingli was turned to the Reformation by study and reflection; he did not undergo the same struggle of soul that Luther had experienced in his early days. And Zwingli's Swiss patriotism led him along paths which were foreign even to Luther's loyalty to Germany, for Zwingli was engaged in political activities and looked for the establishment of the Kingdom of God on earth, which would be visible in the "elect" at Zurich. Zwingli was willing to take up arms to defend the Church, and unlike Luther he did not regard the use of force as a prerogative only of civil rulers.

Above all else, it was Zwingli's use of the Bible which gave the distinctive character to the Zurich form of the Reformation. In Zwingli's opinion, current practices of the Church, such as celibacy, fasting, and the veneration of images, had no Biblical foundation and therefore could not be binding. In carrying out the "restoration of primitive Christianity" Zwingli was led to abolish the Mass and curtail other practices; the reform in Zurich was clearly more puritanic in nature than that stemming from Luther.

Zwingli's reform was vigorous. Other towns followed his lead and with the increasing evidence of support for him the lines of separation with Catholic dominated regions became sharp. Armed conflict ensued.

At Marburg in 1529, the Lutherans and Zwinglians sought to find ways to unite their respective groups. The central and continuing point of conflict of these two branches of Protestantism concerned the Lord's Supper. Luther insisted on the real physical presence of Christ in the sacrament, and he could not tolerate Zwingli's assertion of only the spiritual presence. No union of the groups was effected. Zwingli returned to Zurich to deal alone with the political and military circumstances which his reform had produced. In the Battle of Kappell (1531) he was killed while carrying the chaplain's banner.

A Short and Clear Exposition of the Christian Faith was published by Heinrich Bullinger (1504-1575) in 1536, some five years after Zwingli's death. The essay was designed to state the Zurich Reformer's position on theological, social, and political matters to Francis I. The division between the two major branches of the Reformation over the Lord's Supper had already occurred, and Zwingli found himself in an increasingly hostile environment. He hoped to win Francis and even the entire French country to the Reformed faith. The essay itself dealt with the essential points of controversy and did not intend to be a complete resumé of the faith; it offered a summary of Zwingli's position on a number of topics with which he dealt at more length elsewhere.

A humanistic thread runs throughout his essay. It was characteristic of Zwingli to use Scripture as the basis for any doctrines which were specifically Christian, though he was not unwilling to derive added support for such doctrines from non-Christian literature; he argued from reason and the testimony of speculative philosophers when he dealt with issues which were common to philosophy and theology. In his outline of his position on the doctrine of God, he cast his discussion more in philosophical than Biblical terms. When he dealt with the theme of Church and state, examples from Greek and Roman history were corroborated by Biblical references. When he discussed eternal life, he was mindful of the interests of Francis I, a well known patron of the Renaissance. In the life to come the faithful will commune not only with Abraham, Moses, Isaiah, David, Peter, and Paul, but also with Theseus, Socrates, Aristides, Antigonus, Numa, Camillus, and the Catos and Scipios. This assertion of the final salvation of some of the "heathen" marked a clear separation of Zwingli from other phases of the Protestant Reformation and offered evidence of the type of reform characteristic of those so greatly influenced by the humanists. Zwingli wrote, ". . . there has not lived a single good man, there has not been a single pious heart or believing soul from the beginning of the world to the end, which you will not see there in the presence of God."

Zwingli is most noted in the history of Christian thought for his position on the Lord's Supper. In this essay he summarized his earlier tract entitled, "On the Lord's Supper" (1526). He defined a sacrament as a sign and symbol of holy things. In the Lord's Supper the body and blood of Christ are eaten spiritually, not naturally and literally. According to Zwingli, "the papist teaching that the body of Christ is eaten in the same form and with the same properties and nature as when he was born and suffered and died is not only presumptuous and foolish but impious and blasphemous." The discussion of the papist doctrine had been central in the debates of the time, and Zwingli took pains to point out to Francis that his position was not heretical: ". . . we never taught a single word that we have not taken from Holy Scripture or the Fathers." The risen body of Christ is at the right hand of God, Zwingli argued; Christ's body cannot be in more than one place (as the papists and Luther, Zwingli argued, had suggested); therefore, Christ's body cannot be present at the Lord's Supper. The humanity of Christ or the body of Christ is not eternal and is not omnipresent, Zwingli added. With numerous Biblical references, Zwingli asserted that ". . . as regards a natural, essential, and localized presence the humanity is not here, for it has left the world. Hence the body of Christ is not eaten by us naturally or literally, much less quantitatively, but sacramentally and spiritually." If the body of Christ is literally present, then the Christians are open to the charge of cannibalism. But in the New Testament we learn

that "Ministering women used to honour the body of the Lord by washing and anointing it, not by feeding upon it."

Another distinctive aspect of Zwingli's doctrine of the Lord's Supper centered around his understanding of the sacrament as offering "historical faith." He wrote, "All celebrations, monuments and statues give historical faith, that is, they remind us of some event, refreshing the memory like the feast of the passover amongst the Hebrews or the remission of debts at Athens. . . ." The celebration of the sacrament is of benefit even to the unbelievers. "For whether they receive it or not, it testifies to all that which is of the power of the sacrament, the fact that Christ suffered. But only to the faithful and pious does it testify that he suffered for us." The Lord's Supper does not give faith; faith is presupposed. Those who take the sacrament without faith do not participate sacramentally. If one does partake as a public act without faith, then the judgment which will rest upon that individual will be more severe than that passed on the impious unbeliever.

In summary, Zwingli wrote, "Therefore whether we like it or not, we are forced to concede that the words: 'This is my body,' cannot be taken naturally or literally, but have to be construed symbolically, sacramentally, metaphorically or as a metonymy, thus: 'This is my body,' that is, 'This is the sacrament of my body,' or, 'This is my sacramental or mystical body,' that is, the sacramental and representative symbol of the body which I really assumed and yielded over to death."

On one other major point Zwingli sought to clear up what had been charged against him. The Protestant reformers had frequently been accused of minimizing "good works." In writing to Francis, Zwingli likened the discussion of faith and works to the duties of subjects to kings: "Supposing someone has performed a great service for your majesty, but not sincerely. Do you not say at once that you owe no debt of gratitude to the one who performed it because he did not do it from the heart? . . . The same norm and standard applies in relation to good works. The source of works must be faith." Some of the more extreme forms of the Reformation were tending to an antinomian position, and Zwingli took care to dissociate himself from that movement. To him, the intent of the "work" is primary; faith comes first, and works issue from that. The works in themselves have no bearing on one's relation to God; man is justified by faith.

The tenor of the essay is defensive and apologetic. Zwingli was attempting to state his understanding of the Christian faith in terms which were compatible with the beliefs of Francis, though there is no evidence that he was at all successful. The essay serves as an excellent, though brief, summary of Zwingli's position on the central issues of the Swiss Reformation.

FOUNDATION OF CHRISTIAN DOCTRINE

Author: Menno Simons (1496-1561)
Type of work: Apologetics; Church order
First published: 1539

PRINCIPAL IDEAS ADVANCED

Christians must not merely believe that God forgives sins; they must be converted from their worldly living.

Baptism does not regenerate a man, but it is a sign that he has been converted from the world and lives according to the will of God.

The Lord's Supper is not a sacrament, but a memorial of Christ's death, and a loving fellowship; it is a rite to to be partaken of only by those who live godly lives.

By strict discipline, the Church is to be kept pure from all false doctrine and practice, and those who do not live godly lives are to be excluded from its fellowship.

The followers of Christ, being peaceable and nonviolent, will aways be the victims of the world, which follows Antichrist.

Magistrates ought to obey Christ and further His righteousness, but without resorting to tyranny and unnecessary force.

Before he became a leading Anabaptist, Menno Simons was a Catholic priest, with a superior education which included knowledge of the Church Fathers, both Greek and Latin. Shortly after his ordination, in 1524, he began to be troubled by the kind of doubts Protestants were raising against the sacrifice of the Mass, and he started to restudy the Scriptures. His enlightenment, according to his own testimony, was gradual; and he began to be recognized by some as an evangelical preacher while still within the Catholic Church. Even after he had been persuaded of the Anabaptist position, which may have been as early as 1531, he did not break with the Church. Instead, he opposed the excesses of the more radical Anabaptist sects, such as the followers of John of Leiden, against whom he wrote a booklet in 1535. Later that year, however, the horrors perpetrated against Anabaptists in his native Friesland became such a personal burden that he resolved to renounce the Catholic Church publicly (January 30, 1536).

After a brief retirement, Menno Simons joined the moderate Anabaptist group which had been founded in Zurich in 1525 and had followers in Netherlands, and he was ordained an elder in 1537. In constant personal danger, he preached and organized churches in Holland, Northwest Germany, and Holstein, writing extensively on the controversies which rent the church at that time. His *Foundation of Christian Doctrine* (first published in the dialect of the Baltic coastal regions), which was written with a view to exhibiting the Biblical foundations of the Dutch Anabaptist Brethren, later called the Mennonites (the followers of Menno), was his most widely read and influential work.

The fundamental idea set forth in the *Foundation* is the need for followers of Christ to live holy lives. In enforcing this demand, Menno and the Brethren believed that they were merely continuing the true Church of Christ and His Apostles. "Ours is no new doctrine," says Menno; "It is the old doctrine which was preached and practiced in the church for more than 1,500 years, the doctrine by which the church was begotten, is being begotten, and will be begotten to the end." Christ came calling men to repent of their sins, to cast themselves upon the promises of God, and to turn from the ways of the world. Menno Simons made it clear that those who follow Christ will have to sacrifice possessions and loved ones, and bear grievous afflictions from wicked men and from the Antichrist. But most of those who call themselves the representatives of Christ, Menno argues, whether they be Catholic, Lutheran, Zwinglian, or members of Corrupt Sects (Menno's designation for the radical Anabaptist groups), have never repented of their sins or turned their backs on the world. Of the Protestant preachers of justification by faith alone, he writes, "They preach nothing but the grace, the favor, the mercy, and the love of God before their covetous, proud, showy, impure, drunken, and impenitent church, little realizing that the whole Scriptures testify that such folk cannot inherit the kingdom of God."

Menno's insistence upon adult baptism is closely connected with his conviction that those who confess Christ must repent and be converted. The practice of infant baptism has, he says, no justification in the Scriptures, and is contrary to the command of the Gospel, "Go ye into all the world, and preach the gospel to every creature; he that believeth and is baptized shall be saved, but he that believeth not, shall be damned." Menno considers the usual arguments for infant baptism, such as the one based on Paul's comparison of baptism and circumcision. Paul, says Menno, is referring not to the circumcision of the flesh but to the circumcision of the spirit; hence there is no argument here for the baptism of infants, but the very opposite. For the Mennonites, the washing with water does not confer regeneration, but symbolizes the change that takes place in the hearts of believers when they confess Christ and declare their obedience to Him. Menno writes, "For the testimony of Jesus they are prepared to forsake their homes, possessions, lands, and lives, and to suffer hunger, affliction, oppression, persecution, the cross and death for the same; yes, they desire to bury the flesh with its lusts and arise with Christ to newness of life. . . . Therefore we are buried with him in baptism into death; that like as Christ was raised up from the dead by the glory of the Father, even so we also should walk in newness of life." Menno docs not deny that the grace of Christ saves infants, but he insists that they are saved without being regenerated. For regeneration to take place, there must be a hearing of the Word, then a sincere believing; afterwards, Christ is put on and the Holy Spirit is given. It is of some interest that during the time of Menno, Anabaptists did not practice immersion, but affusion. Menno speaks of baptism as "a handful of water."

Similar concern is manifested by Menno concerning the Lord's Supper. The Catholic teaching that Christ is sacrificed anew upon the altar, and that whenever the priest pronounces the words of consecration over the bread and wine, the Lord, "willing or unwilling . . . must descend and land on their idolatrous hands," Menno could only regard as an abomination, an invention of Antichrist, analogous to Aaron's golden calf. There is no hint of such a thing in Scripture, he says, not even of the teaching that the Holy Supper is a sacrament endowed with power to forgive sins. On the contrary, Christ ordained it to be a memorial of His atoning death, a fellowship of love among the redeemed. Only those who eat and drink inwardly, by faith, are true partakers of the feast; and those who come to the table with impenitent hearts eat and drink damnation to themselves. Menno laid great stress upon what is now called "close communion," and in the interests of a pure Church he enforced a rigid ban or excommunication against backsliders, except when they gave evidence of repentance. He also stressed the necessity for true believers to shun all contact with those who preach Romish doctrine, since these not only do not have the truth but are in the service of Antichrist.

Menno's general theological position is not very different from that of Luther and the other Reformers. He takes his stand flatly on "the whole Scriptures, both the Old and New Testament," which he commonly refers to as the Word of God. Through the Scriptures, and through the Word Incarnate, God has called men to repentance and salvation, says Menno; those who do not obey it will not be able to stand before the judgment seat, while those who humbly seek God's will therein have an infallible rule for this life and that to come. While he would not give the creeds or councils any authority independent of Christ and the Scriptures. Menno nevertheless agreed with "the twelve articles" (that is, the Apostles' Creed), and with the ancient symbols which set forth the doctrines concerning the Trinity and the person of Christ.

What chiefly distinguishes the doctrine of the Mennonites and other Anabaptist groups from the Reformation churches is an emphasis upon blamelessness of conduct which would seem to some Lutherans and Calvinists a kind of legalism. Menno affirmed, with the Reformers, the doctrine of original sin, the necessity of Christ's death as an atonement, and the need for men to be regenerated by the power of the Spirit. He further agreed that Christians cannot, in this life, achieve perfection, because of the weakness and sinfulness of the flesh. But he gave more emphasis than the Reformers to the ethical standards of the Gospel, particularly to those passages which insist that in order to follow Christ men must take a stand against the powers of this world.

Closely connected with the demand for purity of life is Menno's doctrine concerning the Church. None of the leaders of the Reformation had abandoned the Catholic idea of the Church as an objective, supernatural institution by means of which divine grace is made available to men, irrespective of the subjective intention of its ministers. Such discipline as they enforced was meant to keep the Church true to the principles of its institution. In contrast to this notion of an "inclusive" Church, the Mennonites reaffirmed the principle of an "exclusive" Church, gathered out from the midst of the world and set apart to holiness. Menno was aware of the distinction between the Church "visible" and the Church "invisible." He believed that the same frailties which keep the individual from achiev-

ing perfection make it impossible to have a Church in which there are no hypocrites. Nonetheless, says Menno, every effort must be made to keep the visible Church "irreproachable in life before the world, so far as man, who is able to judge only that which is visible, can see."

The relation between the Church and the world must, in Menno's view, always be one of more or less open hostility. The forces of Christ and of Antichrist are at war, and shall be until the end of the world. Moreover, as Christ must suffer at the hands of His enemies, so those who are His disciples must expect to suffer. Persons who love houses and lands and the approbation of men more than they love Christ are not His disciples. No compromise, therefore, may be made with the powers of this world in the interests of security and worldly well-being. The Gospel, moreover, forbids the Christians ever to use force. In opposition to the "corrupt sects," notably the Münsterites, who appealed to the example of the Old Testament and sought to establish the Kingdom of Heaven by the sword, Menno emphasizes the difference between the Old Covenant and the New, and he insists that the Gospel demands nonresistance. "Iron and metal spears and swords we leave to those who, alas, regard human blood and swine's blood about alike," he says.

Menno and his followers were, in fact, the victims of cruel and persistent persecution, and part of the practical aim of the *Foundation of Christian Doctrine* was to enter a plea for toleration. Like Tertullian in his *Apology*, Menno tries to clear away popular misapprehensions concerning the beliefs and practices of the Brethren. They are, he insists, not causing any harm to anybody; they are quiet, law-abiding citizens, fully aware of their obligation to obey the civil authority in all matters which do not contradict the commands of the Word, and willing to suffer evil rather than to perform it. If they have to lay down their lives, they will do so; but they cannot do so without protesting that injustice is being done, and reminding the authorities that they are fighting against God. Menno fails, however, to arrive at a clear conception of the "secular" state, uncommitted with respect to the principles of any religion. Because the state owes its authority to God, he conceives that it is obliged to enforce Christian morality and to prevent the propagation of false religion. "This," he says, "is the task to which you are called: namely to chastise and punish, in the true fear of God with fairness and Christian discretion, manifest criminals, such as thieves, murderers, Sodomites, adulterers, seducers, sorcerers, the violent, highwaymen, robbers, etc. . . . also to restrain by reasonable means, that is without tyranny and bloodshed, manifest deceivers who so miserably lead poor helpless souls by hundreds of thousands into destruction. . . . Whether the deceivers are priests, monks, preachers, baptized or unbaptized, it is your task to restrain them so that they may no longer retract from the power of the almighty majesty of God . . . nor introduce such ridiculous abuses and idolatry under semblance of truth as has been done until now." In this way, he says, without force or bloodshed, and in all love, rulers and magistrates "may enlarge, help, and protect the kingdom of God."

Menno writes with the fervor, and with much of the flavor, of a Biblical prophet. His thought and expression are saturated with the language and imagery of the Scriptures. He is strong in his denunciation of sin and hypocrisy in all classes, but he is without rancor or impatience. He expresses the confidence that, having made the great renunciation, he is on Christ's side; he declares himself filled with the same joy and peace that is manifest in the writings of the Apostles, with whom he hopes for the imminent return of Christ and the end of the world's woes.

THE NECESSITY OF REFORMING THE CHURCH

Author: John Calvin (1509-1564)
Type of work: Protestant polemics (polemical theology)
First published: 1544

PRINCIPAL IDEAS ADVANCED

Christianity consists primarily of the knowledge of the proper worship of God and of the source of salvation.

Sacraments and Church government are of secondary importance; their function is to preserve the aforesaid knowledge.

The religious establishment prevailing in Europe prior to the Reformation was marked by the extinction of the aforesaid knowledge, and by the corruption of the sacraments and of Church government.

Protestants have not separated from the Church; they have restored it.

The prevailing abuses and divisions cannot wait to be settled by a general council; secular authorities must restore the unity of the Church by bringing the religion of their territories into conformity with the aforesaid knowledge, which finds its locus in Christ.

From the time of the first publication of his *Institutes of the Christian Religion* in 1536, John Calvin was recognized as an authoritative and effective spokesman for the Protestant Reformation. Always laboring for harmony and a common front on the part of the churches of the Magisterial Reformation, he frequently noted the debt owed by these churches to the pioneering work of Luther, though his own views proved to be more congenial to the non-Lutheran or Reformed churches.

It was Calvin's intention to advance the Reformation by supporting the views of Luther and by establishing continuity with the Church Fathers. There are many instances of his skillful use of passages from Gregory, Augustine, Cyprian, and other Fathers of the Church; and there are many avowals of his concern to advance the ideas of Luther.

The Necessity of Reforming the Church is a "supplicatory remonstrance" presented to the Emperor Charles V (reigned 1519-1555) and the estates of the Empire assembled at the Fourth Diet of Spires, in 1544. Calvin wrote it at the instance of Martin Bucer (1491-1551), the Strasbourg reformer. The work is at once an apology for what had been accomplished by the Reformation up to this point, and a challenge to the emperor, the princes, and the free cities to preserve and extend these accomplishments.

This appeal to the secular power to reform religion differentiates the Magisterial Reformation from the Radical Reformation, which tended for the most part to discountenance such "interference," and from the reform-minded Catholics, who tended to look to a general council or to existing ecclesiastical institutions to effect the work of reform. Calvin's coolness to the idea of a general council reflects a second stage in the evolution of Protestant thought on this subject. The enthusiasm for a council, which had been expressed by Luther and others, had been dampened by years of delay and by the political complexion which the conception of a council had assumed, as well as by second thoughts on the likelihood of a general council being guided solely by the Holy Spirit and the authority of Scripture.

Basic to Calvin's argument is his definition of Christianity as the knowledge of the proper worship of God, together with the knowledge of the source of salvation. Sacraments and Church government are given a secondary place, as being not ends in themselves, but means for the preservation of this two-fold knowledge. Calvin contends that this two-fold knowledge was lost amidst the corruption of the sacraments and government of the pre-Reformation Church.

Calvin defines proper worship as being basically the recognition of God as "the only source of all virtue, justice,

holiness, wisdom, truth, power, goodness, mercy, life, and salvation; in accordance with this, to ascribe and render to Him the glory of all that is good,
to seek all things in Him alone, and in
every want have recourse to Him
alone." Worship includes prayer, praise,
thanksgiving, adoration, and obedience,
all directed solely to God himself. God
abominates, says Calvin, all impure
worship, such as prayer and adoration
directed to the saints, ceremonialism,
or "will-worship," which proceeds from
man's fertile imagination rather than
from the will of God.

Calvin claims that the Reformation
has rebuked idolatry (which includes
for him the veneration of saints, images, and relics), and has inculcated a
spiritual worship. Will-worship (see
Colossians 2:23) has been curbed:
extra-Scriptural practices have been
abolished, while divinely-ordained rites
(such as baptism) have been given a
spiritual meaning. Prayer has been reformed: the saints have been displaced
by Christ as man's intercessor; the uncertainty that pervaded late-medieval
piety has been replaced by confidence;
an unknown tongue (Latin) has given
way to the vernacular.

Calvin argues that the proper knowledge of the source of salvation involves
three steps: (1) the sense of individual wretchedness, (2) the knowledge
of Christ's mediatorial work, and (3)
the personal assurance of salvation in
Christ. He sees such knowledge obscured by the scholastic interpretation
of original sin as "little more than ex-
cess of bodily appetite and lust," an
interpretation which neglects "blindness and vanity of intellect . . . and
. . . inward depravity of soul." The
knowledge is obscured also by the attribution to men of an imaginary free-

will, and by the teaching that men are
justified by faith plus works, a view
which deprives men of the certain assurance of the divine favor, and hence
of all true confidence.

The Reformation is credited with restoring the true knowledge of salvation.
It has recovered the conviction that
man cannot save himself. His free will
consists only in spontaneity, not in ability to do the right in his own strength.
Such a doctrine of the will, says Calvin, inculcates in men true humility
and true gratitude. Good works are accorded due praise, but Calvin affirms
as Protestant convictions the beliefs
that man's acceptance before God does
not depend on good works but solely
on the gratuitous divine mercy, that
there are no works of supererogation,
and that men's good works are acceptable to God only in Christ.

The "pollution" of the sacraments in
the pre-Reformation Church is said to
consist in the addition of five spurious
sacraments to the two instituted by
Christ, and in the corruption, both in
form and meaning, of these two. Calvin insists on the distinction between
"mysteries instituted by Christ" and
pertaining to eternal life, and human
ceremonies, no matter how wholesome
in themselves. With respect to the two
genuine sacraments, he insists that the
elements be always accompanied by
the word, that is, by an intelligible explanation, so that men's hearts and
minds might be directed to Christ.
Transubstantiation is rejected as contrary to the words of Christ and as
"abhorrent to the very nature of a sacrament," which requires a visible symbol of the spiritual truth signified, not
"some empty phantom that mocks the
eye." The elevation and adoration of
the consecrated bread are likewise re-

jected as unscriptural corruptions. The sacrifice of the Mass has been replaced by a genuine communion, where both clergy and laity partake of both the bread and the cup. The use of the vernacular makes the service understandable to all.

With respect to Church government, Calvin alleges that the pastoral office had fallen into dissuetude and that the episcopal succession had been interrupted long ago. In the true Church all rulers are teachers, but the pre-Reformation clergy was notorious for its failure, even its inability, to teach. There can be no episcopal succession, says Calvin, where there are no canonical elections; the pre-Reformation Church was notorious for its indifference towards the life and doctrine of its candidates; the people were deprived of their rightful voice in episcopal elections; the rights of the clergy were usurped by the bishops, and the rights of the episcopate by the pope. The Roman "episcopate" stands condemned not only by its failure to preserve the truth of God, but also by its enmity to that divine truth.

Calvin lays it down as a Reformation principle that civil laws ought to be carefully obeyed, but that God is the only legislator for the conscience. Human traditions were odious to the Reformers on two main grounds: some, impossible of being fulfilled, led men to hypocrisy and despair; others "made the commandments of God of none effect." The Reformation consequently abolished such "human traditions" as abstinence from meat on Fridays, clerical celibacy, and compulsory auricular confession.

Calvin proceeds to deal with some eight basic charges made against the Reformation by its opponents. To the charge that the Reformers have disturbed the peace of the Church, Calvin replies that this charge has always been brought against men of God. But when the prophet Elijah was thus charged, he replied that not he, but the sins of Ahab and his house were the real troublers of Israel (I Kings 18:18). Christ Himself was a stone of stumbling and a rock of offense to His countrymen (Romans 9:31-33).

To the charge of undue rigor Calvin replied by admitting that in the life of the Church there have always been some blemishes which it is necessary to overlook. But the abuses prevalent in the papal church of the sixteenth century were too serious to be overlooked. The idolatrous veneration accorded to images and saints, the people being deprived of religious services in their own tongue, the honor of man's salvation being divided between Christ and the sinner, the selling of sacraments and other rites, the keeping of the cup from the laity in the Lord's Supper (contrary to the explicit command of the Lord), the fancied transmutation of bread into the body of Christ, the loss of a teaching ministry and of liberty of conscience—tolerance extended to such abuses as these would be criminal indifference, Calvin writes, an insult to Christ and a neglect of the Church's fatal wound.

When it is said that the time is not auspicious, or that the condition of the Church is so desperate as to make attempts at reformation mere futile gestures that aggravate the pain, Calvin replies that "the restoration of the Church is the work of God, and no more depends on the hopes and opinions of men, than the resurrection of the dead, or any other miracle of that description. Here, therefore, we are not to wait for facility of action, either from the will of men, or the temper of the times, but must rush forward through the midst of despair. . . . What the success will be it is not ours to inquire."

Were the results of the Reformers' efforts all bad, Calvin claims, what they did would still remain the work of God. But the results have not been bad. Idolatry, superstition, and error have been curbed. Many pious persons testify that through the teachings of the Reformers they have for the first time found peace of heart and mind. Men of vicious lives have been converted. Taken all in all, Calvin boasts, the adherents of the Reformation exceed the best of the Papists in "innocence, integrity, and true holiness."

Calvin ridicules the charge that the Protestants lack discipline. He compares the clerical discipline of Rome, which allows children twelve years old to be made archbishops, which tolerates nonresidence and pluralism and every kind of personal defect, with the teaching ministry of the Reformation churches. For the laity, there is no discipline in the Roman Church as long as its authority is unreservedly acknowledged; in many of the Reformation churches, on the other hand, excommunication is used as an effectual check on the religion and morals of the people.

When it is said that Protestant lords have expropriated the wealth of the Church, Calvin professes himself unwilling to defend all that has been done along this line. Yet he calls attention to the fact that what was called the wealth of the Church was largely used to feed an idle clergy that either labored to no purpose or else perpetrated sacrilege. In a better age, he notes, poverty was deemed the glory of the clergy. While the revenues appropriated by Protestant princes are used in part for secular purposes, the remainder is used to support "true ministers, who feed their flocks with the doctrine of salvation." In many cases monasteries have been supplanted by hospitals or schools.

To the "last and principal charge" of schism Calvin replies by distinguishing the name of "church" from the reality, and accusing the papal party of making a specious use of the name. The Prophets of the Old Testament and the Apostles of the New, he avers, also had trouble with the "church" of their day. While they did not forsake the divinely approved worship of this pretended church, yet they did not share in any idolatry. Protestants likewise have not forsaken the true Church, but have rather returned to it. Since the Church is essentially above all the body of Christ, Calvin insists that care be taken not to separate the body from its head. The body denies the head when it refuses to acknowledge sound doctrine; that is, the Gospel. For since, according to Ephesians 2:20, the Church is built upon the foundation of the Apostles and Prophets, a well-ordered Church is uniformly distinguished by two marks: the preaching of sound doctrine and the pure administration of the sacraments. Moreover, the true Church is one that "from incorruptible seed, begets children for immortality, and, when begotten, nourishes them with spiritual food (that seed and food being the word of God) and which, by its ministry, preserves entire the truth which God deposited in its bosom." The unity of the Church, therefore, which Calvin asserts to be held in sacred esteem by the adherents of the Reformation, is a unity that is based on union with Christ, and attested by a common consent to "sound doctrine."

Pastors are mere ministers and witnesses of the truth of God, and hence to make the unity of the church dependent upon obedience to them, rather than upon the truth which they are to proclaim, is to substitute the means for the end. To make the unity of the Church dependent upon submission of the pope is unreasonable: "I deny that See to be Apostolical, wherein nought is seen but a shocking apostasy—I deny him to be the vicar of Christ, who, in furiously persecuting the gospel, demonstrates by his conduct that he is Antichrist—I deny him to be the successor of Peter, who is doing his utmost to demolish every edifice that Peter built—I deny him to be the head of the Church, who by his tyranny lacerates and dismembers the Church, after dissevering her from Christ, her true and only Head."

Calvin writes that he is not averse to the reformation of the Church by means of a general council. But since the various nations of Christendom are too busily engaged in making war, or in other secular pursuits, and since the pope is doing all he can to prevent the meeting of a general council, this approach to reformation is not a promising one. Since, moreover, Calvin continues, a council approved by Rome would turn out to be a council controlled by Rome, and since the evils rampant in the Church threaten at any moment to bring about the "breaking up of the whole Church," which, according to Calvin, would be "the most miserable thing of all," it is up to the German princes to reform religion in their lands, before it is forever too late. Calvin notes that heresies like Donatism and Pelagianism were dealt with by provincial synods. Though the bishops should be taking the lead in working for reformation, Calvin writes, their failure to do so does not discharge the princes from their obligation, which derives from their possessing the means to effect it.

A DISPUTATION OF THE SACRAMENT OF THE EUCHARIST

Author: Peter Martyr Vermigli (1500-1562)
Type of work: Sacramental theology
First published: 1549

Principal Ideas Advanced

In the sacrament of the Lord's Supper the substance of the bread and wine is not altered.

The body and blood of Christ are spiritually present and are joined sacramentally to the bread and wine; they are received by faith, hence only by believers.

The life of Peter Martyr Vermigli has recently been aptly characterized as that of an ecumenical reformer. (J. C. McLelland, *The Visible Words of God; An Exposition of the Sacramental Theology of Peter Martyr Vermigli*, Edinburgh and London, 1957.) Certainly Peter Martyr's labors in behalf of the Reformation knew no national boundaries. Born in Italy, probably in Florence, he enjoyed at least the beginnings of a classical education before entering the Order of Augustinian Hermits. He continued his studies in the monastery and was able to attend lectures at the University of Padua, then a famous center of Aristotelian studies, where he obtained the doctorate in divinity. A successful preacher and administrator, he found time to teach himself Greek and Hebrew in order to further his study of the Bible. During a three-year stay at Naples he came under the influence of the "Evangelical Catholic" Juan de Valdez (c.1500-1541) and subsequently distinguished himself as a vigorous monastic reformer. In 1541 he became prior in Lucca. His educational and disciplinary reforms led to the establishment of a Reformed congregation which survived for several years. It was at Lucca that he first administered the communion in an evangelical manner. He was forced by impending persecution to flee the city in 1542.

He was warmly welcomed in Zurich, in Basle, and in Strassburg, where he succeeded Wolfgang Capito (1478-1541) as professor of theology. Here he won the lifelong friendship of the reformer Martin Bucer (1491-1551), who encouraged him to deepen his knowledge of the Church Fathers. While generally in theological agreement with Bucer, Martyr deplored the latter's tendency to use ambiguous language in order to obscure differences among Protestants concerning the Lord's Supper.

In 1547 King Henry VIII of England (reigned 1509-1547) died, and though initially it was resolved to make no major changes in religion during the new king's minority, certain steps were taken to advance the cause of the Reformation in England. One of the most important of these steps was the invitation extended almost immediately to Peter Martyr to become Regius Professor of Divinity at Oxford. He was soon recognized as the chief instrument of Archbishop Thomas Cranmer (1489-1556) in making the Anglican Church truly Protestant.

The accession of Mary the Catholic to the English throne (1553), forced Martyr to return to Strassburg. Here he continued for three years as professor of theology, but under heavy pressure from the Lutheran party, who finally procured an order from the senate ordering him to avoid certain issues and to "restrain his zeal" on others. Rather than submit to the curtailment of his academic freedom, Martyr accepted a call to become professor of Hebrew in Zurich.

During this last period of his life, Martyr was invited to take part in the Colloquy of Poissy (1561), held before the Queen-Regent of France (Catherine de Medici, 1519-1589), like himself a native Italian. He was instrumental in rallying support for his disciple and successor in Strassburg, Jerome Zanchius (1516-1590, another Italian), who was under heavy attack from the Lutherans.

Of all Martyr's "ecumenical" labors, his work in England appears to have been most fruitful. The University of

Oxford had not taken kindly to Protestantism, and Martyr often seemed to be fighting a lonely battle, in which he was mainly sustained by the support of Archbishop Cranmer and the young King Edward VI (1537-1553). The opposition seized upon Martyr's exposition of I Corinthians 10:16,17. Martyr was challenged to a disputation about the nature of Christ's presence in Holy Communion, and though his challenger fled the country, the traditional point of view was defended by three scholars of the University. The commission in charge of the debate, headed by the king's tutor, Richard Cox (c.1500-1581, chancellor of the University and later Bishop of Ely) did not render a formal decision, though Cox in his closing remarks highly commended Martyr. The disputation took place on May 29, 30, 31 and June 1, 1549. Martyr had the proceedings printed the same year, and an English translation was published soon afterwards.

In his opening statement Martyr defends disputations in general on the ground that they do not necessarily lead to strife and discord, and that Christ and the Apostles did not hesitate to enter into disputations. He notes that the common people are greatly addicted to the traditional view of the Lord's Supper, which he is combatting with his three theses:

"1. In the sacrament of the Eucharist, there is no transubstantiation of the bread and wine, into the bodie and bloud of Christ.

"2. The bodie and bloud of Christ is not carnallie and corporallie in the bread and wine; nor, as others speake, vnder the shewes of bread and wine.

"3. The bodie and bloud of Christ is sacramentallie conionied to the bread and wine."

He calls attention to the fact that, in deference to the usage of Scripture, he has used the terms "carnallie" and "corporallie" rather than their scholastic equivalents "substantiallie" and "reallie." He defines the sacramental conjunction as "a most effectual signification" that must be clearly distinguished from a "mere" signification, which he associates with the Anabaptists, the Marcionites, the Valentinians, and the Manichees.

The opening statement of his first opponent, Dr. Tresham (a canon of Christchurch), invokes against Martyr's theses the authority of the Gospels and of St. Paul, the consent of the whole world and perpetual usage, the "great authoritie of our holie mother the church" expressed in its decrees against men like Berengar of Tours (c.999-1088) and John Wycliffe (c.1329-1384, Oxford scholar and reformer), the testimony of "the right catholic fathers" properly interpreted, and the official pronouncements of the government of the present king.

The disputation of the first day revolved around certain arguments from the Bible and the Church Fathers that can be summarized in three points. (1) Martyr argues from the fact that Scripture nowhere teaches a change of substance, but rather refers to the bread as bread even after its consecration, to the conclusion that the substance of the bread remains. He supports this conclusion by citations from Origen (c. 185-c.254, head of the Catechetical School in Alexandria), Epiphanius of Salamis (c.315-403, Metropolitan of Cyprus), John Chrysostom (c.347-407, patriarch of Constantinople), Augustine of Hippo (354-430, greatest of the

Latin fathers), Cyril of Alexandria (died 444, widely regarded as the best writer on Christology in the Eastern Church), Pope Gelasius I (reigned 492-496), and Pope Gregory I (reigned 590-604). His opponent replies that transubstantiation is implied in Jesus' words, "This is my body," and that the Scripture passages cited by Martyr must be interpreted figuratively. (2) Martyr invokes the authority of Cyprian (died 258, Bishop of Carthage) and of Theodoret (c.393-c.458, Bishop of Cyrrhus), who used the analogy of the two natures in Christ to illustrate the co-existence of true bread with the true body of Christ in the Eucharist; Irenaeus (c. 130-c.200, Bishop of Lyons) is cited as using the analogy of men's bodies, which without change of substance, were changed into immortal bodies through partaking of the Communion. (3) From the fact that Christ's (literal) body was created, Martyr argues to its restriction to one locality at any one point of time; namely, since the Ascension, to Heaven.

During the course of the second day's disputation, Martyr spelled out his doctrine of analogy, which is regarded as central, not only for his eucharistic theology, but for his theology as a whole: "In all sacraments there ought to be an analogie or proportion observed and kept betweene the sacrament and the matter of the sacrament. . . . Seeing therefore the Eucharist hath for the matter of the sacrament both the bodie of Christ, and the mysticall bodie; ye which by transubstantiation take awaie the bread and wine, ouerthrowe the analogie, which consisteth therein; that even as we be naturallie nourished by bread and wine, so by the bodie and bloud of Christ, we are nourished spir-

ituallie, both in the outward and inward man. And as concerning the mysticall bodie, therein dooth the similitude stand; that even as bread and wine consist of much gathering and pressing togither, that is to saie, of manie graines of corne, and manie grapes; so the mysticall bodie standeth of manie members, which growe vp togiether in one."

Martyr calls attention to the fact that a sacrament is, by definition, a sign. Augustine, Tertullian (c.160-c.220, earliest of the great Latin Fathers) and Jerome (c.342-420, author of the authoritative Latin version of the Bible) are cited as teaching a figurative interpretation of the saying, "This is my body."

On the third day, Martyr defined his position with respect to the problem of authority in religion. He acknowledges the inward authority of the Holy Spirit and the outward authority of Holy Scripture. The Church Fathers do not possess an independent authority of their own: "Trulie I will not contemne the fathers, naie rather I will attribute much to them, when they speake according to the scriptures. . . . [Yet since] I see that manie are addicted vnto them superstitiouslie, which perpetuallie crie out; The fathers, the fathers, and doo thinke them to be euermore against vs, I thought it good to shew such men, that they make most of all for vs." His attitude towards Church councils is similar.

Martyr proceeds to show that in the sacrament there are two kinds of eating, proper and metaphorical, and two kinds of nourishment, natural and spiritual. He approvingly cites Irenaeus to the effect that by the second kind of eating, that is, by embracing the body and blood of Christ in faith, men's minds are "filled with the spirit and with grace; secondlie, our bodie is renewed, that it may from daie to daie become a fit instrument for the spirit, and so made more capable of the blessed resurrection." It is no "feined flesh" that is received, but the true body of Christ. Nor is the sacrament absolutely indispensable: ". . . for both with the signes and without the signs, while we consider in our minds Christ crucified for vs, and his bloud shed for vs, and doo so beleeue, we are truelie made partakers of him: but yet the signes being ioined therewithall, which the holie Ghost vseth as instruments, for the better printing of faith in our minds, we are verie much holpen. For we be verie slacke vnto diuine things, and therefore we haue need of outward sacraments."

On the fourth day Martyr summarized his arguments. In support of the first of his three theses he notes that (1) Augustine said that we are made partakers of Christ's body and blood in baptism, yet there is no transubstantiation there; (2) Paul said: "Ye are the body of Christ" (I Corinthians 12:27), and there is no transubstantiation here, though upon reflection Christ will be found to be more intimately joined to His people than to the sacramental bread; (3) transubstantiation by analogy supports the Marcionites, who attributed only the appearance of a human body to Christ; (4) transubstantiation involves a miracle wholly unknown to the Fathers; namely, the preservation of accidents apart from their proper substance; (5-7) if transubstantiation were a fact, then Christ ate Himself when he partook of the Last Supper, and many other absurdities follow that require a multitude of miracles in order to be explained. In support of his second and third theses Martyr points out that (1) there is no advantage to be derived from a Christ hidden in the signs that is not abundantly vouchsafed by Christ in Heaven; (2) Jesus Himself "confuted the carnall eating of his bodie" in dealing with the Capernaites (John 6:22-65); (3) Augustine called the sacraments visible words, and Jerome agreed with him that we eat the flesh of the Lord by means of the word; (4) men are cleansed in Christ's blood every time they turn to him in faith and repentance; (5) Scripture knows only two comings of Christ, not a third in the sacraments; (6) the definition of a sacrament as a visible signs of an invisible grace agrees far better with "signification" than with transubstantiation; (7) truths of Scripture should be interpreted in a simple way that will be conducive to faith and that will not necessitate a multiplication of absurdities and "miracles." Since eating the body of Christ is an act of faith, it is evident that unbelievers do not receive the body and blood of Christ in the sacrament.

Martyr was to publish several more works dealing with the nature of Christ's presence in the Lord's Supper, notably the eight-hundred-page *Defensio . . . adversus Gardinerum* (1559). John Calvin (1509-1564), the mastermind of Reformed Protestantism, regarded his work on the subject as definitive. It should be noted, however, that Martyr's position is actually closer to that of Ulrich Zwingli (1484-1531), the Reformer of German-speaking Switzerland, and closest to that of Thomas Cranmer. Martyr and Cranmer share with Zwingli the denial of a substantial presence of Christ in the sacrament. They also share with him

—and with the Catholic tradition before the late-medieval ascendancy of the view that the Mass is a literal sacrifice, propitiatory for the living and the dead—the understanding that the Lord's Supper is above all a eucharist, a sacrifice of praise. Martyr expresses it thus: "The substance of our sacrifice is, a giving of thanks for the bodie of Christ given vpon the crosse. And by reason of this giving of thanks, faith and confession, the fathers said, that the bodie of Christ is offered in the supper."

Cranmer beautifully elaborates his conception in his rendering of the prayer *Supplices* in the First Book of Common Prayer, which was introduced in the English churches some eight days after the conclusion of Martyr's Disputation. The prayer supplicates God "to accept our sacrifice of Prayse and thanks-geuinge . . . and here wee offre vnto the (O Lord) oure self, oure souls, and bodyes, to be a reasonable, holy and liuelie sacrifice vnto thee."

When Cranmer wrote *A Defense of the True and Catholic Doctrine of the Sacrament* in 1550, the doctrine he defended was essentially the same as Peter Martyr's.

THE DECADES

Author: Johann Heinrich Bullinger (1504-1575)
Type of work: Sermons on Reformed doctrine
First published: 1549-1551

PRINCIPAL IDEAS ADVANCED

The Holy Scriptures of the Old and New Testaments are the sole rule of faith and practice, from which we learn what we are to believe concerning God, and what God requires of us.

From the Scriptures we learn the content of true faith: that God is our creator, sustainer, and the redeemer of fallen humanity by means of the sacrificial death of His Son, Christ Jesus.

By faith in Christ, without works, we are freely justified, pardoned, and forgiven of our sins, and are made righteous so that the fruits of righteousness, good works, are then brought forth.

The Church of Rome is not the true Church; the latter is inwardly constituted by true believers and is visibly found wherever the Word of God is faithfully preached and the sacraments of baptism and the Lord's Supper are properly administered.

Johann Heinrich Bullinger was born in 1504 in a small town near Zurich and was educated at the University of Cologne, from which he received a Master's degree in 1522. Bullinger was intimately acquainted with Ulrich Zwingli (1484-1531), and he was very much influenced by the latter's view of the Eucharist. In 1531 Bullinger was appointed to the pulpit of the Cathedral of Zurich to fill the vacancy left by the death of Zwingli. Bullinger occupied this important post until his death in 1575. His publications were voluminous and frequent; his pastoral, ecclesiastical, and civil activities were many, and his home was ever open to befriend refugees from countries ravaged by religious persecution. His moderation and sincerity were eminently conspicuous during his long unsuccessful efforts to effect a reconciliation between the Lutherans and the Church of Zurich on the question of the sacraments. He did manage to reach an agreement with John Calvin (1509-1564) and Guillaume Farel (1489-1565) on the Lord's Supper, thereby uniting the churches of Zurich and Geneva on the issue.

The *Decades* consists of five groups of ten sermons, published in English in four volumes. The first and second decades were published in Latin in 1549, the third and fourth in 1550, and the fifth in 1551. There have been three editions of the English translation of the *Decades*; namely, in 1577, 1584, and 1587. The sermons were widely read, and they exerted considerable influence outside Switzerland, especially in the Church of England, during the reign of Queen Elizabeth, where the sermons were required reading for those studying to be preachers.

The fifty sermons of the *Decades* cover the whole range of Reformed doctrine and practice. They are marked by a strict adherence to the Scriptures of the Old and New Testaments, by doctrinal content, by clarity, and by Reformation piety. They successfully combine doctrinal exposition with devotional meditation, controversy with charity, predestination with responsibility, and the law with grace.

Bullinger shared with the Reformers the conviction that the Scriptures and the Scriptures alone constitute the sole infallible authority in all matters pertaining to faith and practice. Several sermons are devoted to this theme. According to Bullinger, every doctrine of the Christian faith, every rule as to how to live rightly, well, and holily, and all true and heavenly wisdom are to be derived from the testimonies and determinate judgments of the Word of God, and from no ecclesiastical body.

The *verbum Dei*, the Word of God, signifies the very speech of God and the disclosure of God's will; it was first uttered by Christ, the Prophets and Apostles, and then registered in writings which are rightly called holy and divine. The Word of God declares truly that God is just, good, pure, immortal, and eternal, so that what He has declared in His word is also to be received as true, just, without deceit, without guile or error, and as holy, pure, good, immortal, and everlasting.

Since God alone is truth, Bullinger writes, and since the Word of God is truth, it is God who is the beginning and cause of His Word. From the beginning of the world, God revealed Himself to the world by speaking to men in a voice easily understood by men. He spoke to Adam, to Abraham, to Moses, and to the Prophets.

Bullinger tells how holy men of old taught their children what God had revealed: that of His natural goodness, He desired men to know the truth and to be like God Himself, holy, happy, and blessed. For this reason, in the beginning God created man in His image, so that man, too, could be good, holy, immortal, and the blessed partaker of God's good gifts. Man did not remain in this happy condition, for because of the influence of the Devil, and his own disobedience, man fell into sin, death, and misery, thereby changing his image into that of the Devil.

Because of His infinite mercy, God did not leave man in the state of sin and misery into which he had fallen, but He began anew the work of salvation, by which man is restored and set free from the bondage of sin and is once again made like unto God. To accomplish this work of redemption, Bullinger writes, God appointed the Incarnate Word, and by this taking of flesh, He united man to God. Finally, by dying in the flesh, God Himself cleansed, sanctified, and delivered mankind. By giving man His Holy Spirit, God made him once again similar in nature to Himself; that is, absolutely blessed and immortal. There remains, moreover, a great day of judgment, in which, though all men are gathered together, yet the righteous alone will receive the reward of Heaven, whereas the wicked will be consigned to eternal perdition.

God is the God of all men and of every nation, Bullinger claims. God has revealed His Word so that all men can come to a knowledge of the truth and the benefit of salvation. God has revealed Himself to men in order that they may know of Him and be saved; by faith in Christ, men might know who He is, and by what means salvation is possible.

Every point of true godliness is taught us in the Holy Scriptures, Bullinger insists. Nothing more is needed, neither the traditions of men, nor the inventions of deceivers.

Bullinger states that it is erroneous to believe that the Scriptures are so dark that they cannot be read by laymen, and he claims it is equally false to affirm that men have no need of exposition. It is God's will that His Word be understood. The difficulties that the Scriptures contain can be overcome by study, diligence, faith, and by skillful and proper means of interpretation. The Scriptures are difficult only to the unlearned and the malicious, not to the zealous and the godly reader. To the later they are plain and most assuredly certain.

A holy exposition of Scripture is, however, most profitable to the godly, Bullinger writes. The Scriptures are not to be corrupted by foreign expositions, nor by introducing human fantasies. They must never be expounded in a way that is contrary to the articles of Christian belief, nor must their exposition be repugnant to the love of God and our neighbor. The Scriptures are to be expounded with zealous heart, after earnest prayer, in a manner that takes note of the occasion upon which something is spoken, and of what precedes, what follows, and of when it was spoken; and of what order, to whom, and by whom it was uttered.

Bullinger agreed with the other Reformers, with Luther, Calvin, and Ulrich Zwingli (1484-1531) that the Scriptures cannot be properly interpreted in a manner that denies the true faith. For, with them, Bullinger held that it is by faith alone that a sinner is justified. To the mind, faith is a most evident seeing; to the heart a most certain perceiving of things invisible and eternal. Faith is a steadfast assuredness of conscience, which embraces Christ as He is offered in the Gospel; faith is a gift of God, poured from Heaven into man, by which he is taught with an indubitable persuasion to lean wholly on God and His Word. The latter contains God's promise of eternal life and of all good things in Christ; it contains all things that are to be believed.

The beginning and cause of faith is God Himself, who inspires faith in our hearts by his Holy Spirit, writes Bullinger. To implant faith, God uses ordinary means; namely, the preaching of His Word. By sending His Holy Spirit into our hearts and minds, God causes us to believe what we have learned to believe from the teaching of His word. True faith is not an irrational acceptance of everything possible; it is ruled and bound to the Word of God; it bends toward God and leans on His Word alone. The object and foundation of true faith is God and His Word alone. The Word holds that God in Christ promises life and every good thing through Him. True faith is ignorant of all division, Bullinger insists; it is the true knowledge that maketh us wise. To have faith is to believe that all the words of God are true, and that God has a good will towards all mankind, not only in general but towards the individual believer. Thus, each Christian believer believes that the soul is immortal, that our bodies rise again, that the faithful will be saved, and that unbelievers will perish.

Faith makes us happy and alive, Bullinger asserts; it joins us to God, and it justifies without works. To justify is to acquit from judgment and to lift the sentence of condemnation. To justify is to remit offenses, to cleanse, to sanctify, and to give life everlasting. Justification is the absolution and remission of sins; it is the washing away and forgiveness of sins, the deliverance from condemnation.

Justification means to be adopted by God as His sons. Before the judgment seat of God, when our condemnation was to be pronounced, Christ took our sins upon Himself, and by His sacrifice on the cross, He purged us of our iniquities, so that upon Him God laid our fault and punishment. The pain and offence of our sin have been taken away by Christ; with His stripes, we are healed. The pain, punishment, and correction were laid upon our Lord. Whoever believes in the only-begotten Son of God partakes of His righteousness, is justified by Him, absolved from sin, and made heir of everlasting life.

Bullinger describes faith as a gift of God's grace, containing within it the promise of righteousness. Our own merits and works have no place in justification. Our works are never perfect, but our salvation is assured by God's free gift. It does not follow from the fact that the faithful are justified by faith without works, that faith is utterly destitute of good works, for wherever there is faith there are good works. After the faithful are justified and made righteous, they bring forth the works of righteousness. True faith is in fact the very wellspring and root of all virtues. From it springs peace of conscience, patience, hope, and charity, the fulfilling of the law, which contains the very sum of good works.

The content of true faith is summarized in the Apostle's Creed, Bullinger writes; the works that it produces are summarized in the love of God and the sincere love of one's neighbor, in the keeping of the moral law as found in the Ten Commandments.

The believer who unfeignedly turns to God in an act of repentance and who humbly acknowledges his sins in true confession to God is forgiven by Him, who alone is to be adored and worshiped.

Christ alone is the intercessor and advocate with the Father; the saints are not to invoked, nor does the Church stand between God and man. The Church, says Bullinger, is the whole company of the faithful, those who are triumphantly in Heaven, and those who are militantly on earth; it is not identical with its visible institutional form. The true Church, the invisible Church, is made up of true believers, and is free of heretics and hypocrites.

According to Bullinger, the visible Church of God on earth has two special and principal marks, the sincere preaching of the word of God, and the lawful use of the sacraments of Christ, of which there are two, baptism and the Lord's Supper. The upstart Church of Rome is not the Church, Bullinger insists, for the Church of Rome has departed from the true Church, and thus no longer bears its marks.

A DEFENSE OF THE TRUE AND CATHOLIC DOCTRINE OF THE SACRAMENT

Author: Thomas Cranmer (1489-1556)
Type of work: Reformation theology
First published: 1550

PRINCIPAL IDEAS ADVANCED

The Lord's Supper is a sacrament to be observed in the Christian Church in accordance with the teaching of the New Testament.

The Roman doctrine of transubstantiation is a perversion of the Apostolic and patristic tradition.

Christ is truly present in the Lord's Supper spiritually and wholly but not substantially or corporeally.

Repentance and faith on the part of the communicant are necessary to effective reception of the elements.

Because the Mass is so prominent and central in Roman Catholic religious observances, it was inevitable that all who supported the Reformation movement found themselves involved in a discussion of its revision. The title of Thomas Cranmer's first book devoted to the subject suggests the context in which he worked: *Defense of the True and Catholic Doctrine of the Sacrament of the Body and Blood of Christ.* Cranmer's treatise did not propose to set forth a position that was new in Reformation writing, but to clarify his own position as Archbishop of Canterbury and to support the main lines of criticism of the Roman position. The work established Cranmer's reputation as a competent theologian, despite bitter criticism by rival thinkers.

The plan of the book is simple and

straightforward. It is divided into five parts dealing in succession with the true observance of the Eucharist, the central error of the doctrine of transubstantiation, the nature of the presence of Christ in the bread and wine, the reception of the elements, and the nature of the sacrifice involved.

All the Reformers made much of Scriptural exegesis in order to demonstrate how far removed from Apostolic teaching the history of doctrine had travelled, and the Archbishop made ample use of previous studies. He was widely read and did not allow his administrative duties to rob him of his theological research interests. His industry therein is manifest. Especially to be marked is his competency in the use of patristic literature. It might not be too much to say that he set an example and tone which influenced Anglican scholars thereafter. To be able to demonstrate that Roman doctrine had departed from the teaching of the Church Fathers as well as from Scripture was a telling device of debate when tradition counted heavily in settling points of dispute. Another line of defense involved the use of arguments of reason, by which Cranmer hoped to expose the contradictions and absurdities of the doctrine being examined. "The papistical doctrine," Cranmer averred, "is against all our outward senses." The point, of course, is not that all the tenets of religion must be validated by sentient experience, for Cranmer acknowledged freely that faith claimed matters to be true which were unseen. What was in question was the sheer incredulity with which reason confronted the claims made for Eucharistical transsubstantiation, the miraculous change of bread and wine to the body and

blood of Christ. The substance of the elements of the sacrament was changed, it was said, while the accidents, or characteristics, remained the same. The explanation rested on Aristotelian metaphysics. The separation of substance and accidents was a metaphysical divorce, which Cranmer believed to be utterly irrational, as indefensible as it was unnecessary for a true doctrine of the Lord's Supper. Thus, he writes: "And although all the accidents, both of the bread and the wine, remain still, yet, say they, the same accidents be in no manner of thing, but hang alone in the air, without anything to stay them upon." Cranmer could not accept change which did not involve change of the accidents or sentient qualities.

It was Cranmer's contention that the real presence of Christ was in the elements, but the body of Christ was not present substantially. He was far from supporting a theory of bare signs or mere symbols. The body of Christ is in Heaven, he contended, and it will return only at the last day. The real presence is not to be equated with the historical presence in the incarnate life of Jesus before His crucifixion.

It was absurd to Cranmer that the body of Christ should be said to be masticated and torn by human teeth like a piece of corporal flesh in a cannibal feast. On this he animadverts at length in his answer to a criticism by the Bishop of Winchester, Stephen Gardiner (c.1490-1555). Cranmer claims for his own opinions that they hold "that Christ is present in His sacraments, as they teach also that He is present in His word, when He worketh mightily in the hearts of the hearers." The body of Christ is truly present but sacramentally, not organically, and not in such a manner that the body of Christ is really two, one in Heaven and the other on the altars of the churches.

It would be saying too much to claim that Cranmer is always intelligible in these distinctions on which he wrote at great length in his treatises on the Eucharist. However, his point that the historical Incarnation is to be distinguished carefully and clearly from the sacramental presence is one which Cranmer affirms most persuasively.

The real presence is in the sacrament whether discerned by the recipient or not, Cranmer contends. When the elements of the sacrament are taken by the faithful, they are efficacious in spiritual benefits; when they are taken by an unworthy person, they are figurative only and do not convey grace. A helpful analogy is suggested by consideration of the fact that during His earthly ministry God was present in the person of His Son, but was not always recognized and received as such. Faith is necessary to discern the truth. The spiritual state of the recipient is a necessary factor in the action, and this subjective condition must be accorded full significance together with the objective divinely promised deed and action. Worship is not to be directed to the bread: "All that love and believe in Christ Himself, let them not think that Christ is corporally in the bread, but let them lift up their hearts unto heaven and worship Him sitting there at the right hand of His Father." The tendency is thus always to keep close to the common thrust of Reformed doctrine that the Christ who comes in the sacraments is the same Christ who comes in the preaching of the Word; and though the media are different and demand explanations appropriate to the three media of pulpit, table, and baptistry, it is the same Lord who is effectively communicating Himself in all three in accordance with the conditions of faith: "This spiritual presence of Christ is to the man who putteth his whole hope and trust of his redemption and salvation in that only sacrifice which Christ made upon the cross."

What is effected by a worthy participation in the Eucharist? It is undoubtedly a remembrance of the ultimate sacrifice on the cross, and the Archbishop insists on this over and over again. There is recollection and gratitude for a finished work by which men may be saved from their sins.

Christ is not only remembered, however, but also spiritually received as the faithful recipient shares in communion; God works in the heart of the recipient in all things necessary to his salvation. This is expressed in the idea of eternal life which is to be regarded both as a future realization of the purpose of God for His people, and also as a present gift which is bestowed in time and will be consummated beyond death. The presence of Christ and His very life are in the believer rather than on a table or altar in material substances.

Thus, Cranmer argues, the Eucharistical communion produces ethical effects in character and conduct. There is, as it were, an offering which the faithful give to God as a response to the offering which God has provided for them. Any thought that a man can accept the Holy Spirit without manifesting the fruits of the Spirit is a grave error. "Wherefore," writes Cranmer, "whose heart soever this holy sacrament, communion and supper of Christ will not kindle with love to his neighbors and cause him to put out of his heart all envy, hatred and malice and to grave in the same all amity, friendship and concord, he deceiveth himself, if he think that he hath the Spirit of Christ dwelling within him." In this way faith and works are united in sustained obedience, and the life of Christ is continued in the life of each believer. Participation in the sacrament is itself an act of obedience which sustains and depends on that which initiates it. The analogy is pressed that just as eating and drinking ordinary food nourishes and strengthens the physical body, so sharing in the Lord's Supper nourishes and strengthens the soul for the fight against evil.

Further, the bonds of union which unite Christians in the Church are strengthened. Cranmer follows St. Paul closely in teaching that participation in this sacrament is not just an individual matter. The unity of the Body of Christ is involved, and the faithful "so be joined unto Christ; and also together among themselves, that they do make but one mystical body of Christ, as St. Paul saith: 'We be one bread and one body, as many as be partakers of one bread and one cup.'" Thus, the love of Christ for His Church becomes the love which ought to be experienced within His Church. By viewing the dramatic action of the communion service, the hearts of all are inspired to sacrificial concern for the benefit of the community.

All this is said at length and enforced with repetition. Yet the polemical context is always so pressing that Cranmer has to meet the counter arguments of the Roman protagonists; consequently, a great deal of space is allotted to negative arguments. The use of negative arguments is characteristic of almost all the ponderous theological treatises of Cranmer's time, and the practice makes many passages very complex and not always free from ambiguity. Weighty scholarship was marshaled by both sides to support the older and the newer causes. Cranmer's contribution to the momentous struggle added greatly to the Reformed cause and was offered at a time when matters were at a critical stage in England. It is not the novelty of his views, but the correlation of them with the main doctrines of the Reformed party at a level of impressive learning that makes his work on the Lord's Supper one of the great treatises in the history of theology in England.

THE MAGDEBURG CENTURIES

Author: Matthias Flacius (1520-1575) [and others]
Type of work: Church history
First published: 1559-1574

PRINCIPAL IDEAS ADVANCED

[A landmark in the history of ecclesiastical historiography, this thirteen-volume work surveys the history of the Christian Church from the first to the end of the

thirteenth century, devoting a volume to each century (hence the name "Centuries") and following the same order of topics in the treatment of each century. A product of the second generation of the Reformation, its purpose was apologetic and polemical: a defense of Protestantism and an attack on Roman Catholicism.]

The Church suffered a gradual deterioration after the Apostolic age, especially in the Middle Ages.

The Protestant Reformation restored the Church to its pristine purity.

A proper estimate of the *Magdeburg Centuries* requires that this work be seen in its historical context. The historians of the Middle Ages were chroniclers who for the most part recorded local history based on hearsay and often embroidered with legends. The humanists of the Renaissance introduced a critical use of sources and challenged the correctness of some prevailing opinions about the past. Following in their footsteps, the Protestant Reformers discovered in history a useful weapon to combat their opponents. Neither humanists nor Reformers, however, attempted anything more than an occasional foray into one or another corner of the past. It remained for the generation following the Reformation to attempt a bold and systematic interpretation of the whole sweep of the Church's history.

The man who was responsible for the first major undertaking of this kind since Eusebius of Caesarea (c.260-c.340) had written his great *Ecclesiastical History* twelve centuries before was Matthias Flacius. A native of Istria, in the present Yugoslavia, Flacius was diverted from the study of Catholic theology by an uncle who directed his attention to the reform proposals of Martin Luther (1483-1546). In 1541 Flacius went to Wittenberg, where under Luther's influence he finally reached settled religious convictions and adhered to them stead-fastly, and even stubbornly, the rest of his life. For several years he taught in the University in Wittenberg, but when he became involved in a bitter controversy with Luther's colleague and successor, Philip Melanchthon (1497-1560), he found it expedient to move to Magdeburg. Later he was made professor of the New Testament in Jena, but there, too, he became embroiled in quarrels and spent his last years wandering about from Frankfurt to Strasbourg and to Basel.

It was during his stay in Magdeburg that Flacius developed his ambitious project of a history of the Church. "I am contemplating a great undertaking," he wrote to a friend in 1553, "an undertaking which is indeed beyond my strength but which, if carried out, could be of extraordinary benefit to the church. . . . I desire that a history of the church be written in which may be described, chronologically and systematically, how the true church and its religion gradually deteriorated from its original purity and simplicity in the time of the apostles. . . . The history should also describe how from time to time the church has also been restored by some truly godly men, how the light of truth now shone more brightly and now was more or less obscured by the growing darkness of godlessness, until finally in our own time, when truth appeared to be almost completely annihilated, through the boundless blessing of God true religion has been restored in its purity once again." In these words we have a good description not only of the early plan but also of the actual execution of the work.

The first thing Flacius did was to gather about himself a number of collaborators. A "society" was organized, headed by five "inspectors." Besides Flacius, these included Ebeling Allemann, a consul; Martin Copus, a physician; and John Wigand and Matthew Judex, clergymen, all living in Magdeburg. Through correspondence and the dispatching of emissaries, source materials were then gathered. "Traces of the church's history should be sought in the oldest documents," Flacius suggested. "The true history should be drawn out of the very depths of the sources and brought to light." The most diligent of the collectors of source materials was Marcus Wagner. He searched the libraries of Denmark, Scotland, Austria, and various parts of Germany. Books and manuscripts were bought, parts of others were laboriously copied, and everything was shipped to Magdeburg. There, under the direction of the inspectors, seven students were hired to copy excerpts from the assembled books and manuscripts. These were then arranged by century and divided according to predetermined topics. In all of this, Wigand reported, Flacius was "the captain and chief pilot."

The materials for each century were arranged in the same order according to sixteen topics, which became chapters in the published work. The first was a brief preview of a century, "that the reader may know what he ought to look for." The second described the extent of the Church, and its geograph-

ical expansion or retraction in a given century. The third recorded the persecutions suffered or the peace enjoyed. Major emphasis was given to the fourth chapter, headed "The Teaching of the Church." Here the findings were arranged according to a recurring pattern: teachings about the Scriptures, God, creation, angels, man and the Fall, original and actual sin, law, Gospel, predestination, justification, faith, good works, prayer, baptism, confession and absolution, the Lord's Supper, church, ministry, miracles, Antichrist, human traditions, marriage, magistracy, death, the end of the world, the Last Judgment, Heaven and Hell, and Purgatory. This long chapter is followed by the fifth, which treats the heresies of a given century. The sixth describes the rites and ceremonies employed by the Church and adds a section on the "customs of Christians." The seventh deals with the organization of the Church, the eighth with schisms, and the ninth with councils convened during a given century. The three succeeding chapters provide some account of the lives of prominent bishops, heretics, and martyrs. The thirteenth chapter describes miracles reported to have occurred. The fourteenth describes the location and condition of the Jews, and this is followed by a chapter given to an account of other religions. The final chapter reports the political changes that have taken place in the Roman Empire.

The first three volumes, which surveyed the first three centuries of the Church's history in the fashion indicated, were published in quarto by John Opirinus in Basel in the year 1559. They bore the title *Ecclesiastica historia . . . secundum singulas centurias . . . congesta per aliquot stu-*

diosos et pios viros in urbe Magde-burgica; that is, "Ecclesiastical History, century by century, compiled by a number of learned and godly men in the city of Magdeburg." The fourth volume appeared from the same press in 1560, the fifth and sixth in 1562, the seventh and eighth in 1564, the ninth in 1565, the tenth and eleventh in 1567, the twelfth in 1569, and the thirteenth in 1574. Three additional volumes, covering the fourteenth to sixteenth centuries, were in preparation but were not completed when, one after another, the leaders of the project died, and accordingly these volumes were never published.

The most obvious weakness of this history is its mechanical plan. The arrangement of the materials by centuries is arbitrary and does not do justice to movements in the life of the Church which were not confined so neatly within the span of a century. Apart from the centurial plan, the treatment of topics within each volume as separate and unrelated units contributes to the impression of artificiality. Persecutions are reported in the third chapter, but martyrs are not dealt with until the twelfth. Heresies are treated in the fifth chapter, but heretics not until the eleventh. Much more serious is the fact that, although the greatest emphasis is placed on the doctrines and the proclamation of the Church, what is said about teachings and beliefs is not related at all to how Christians lived and worshiped. The disjunction of the chapters is such that the reader is confronted with a lifeless mass of data and does not receive an organic impression of the Church as a living organism. Moreover, the rigidity with which the order of topics is pursued in volume after volume made it impossible to organize materials around men and movements that give a particular age its distinctive character.

The diligence in assembling sources at a time when great libraries and bibliographical tools were not yet available has already been mentioned. The compilers also gave evidence of a critical use of these sources. It was relatively easy to demonstrate that certain teachings and practices which were widely believed to have originated with the Apostles were actually of much later origin. It required more acumen to show that some canons and decrees of the early Middle Ages were forgeries. The objectivity of such historical criticism becomes suspect, however, when it is observed how uncritical the centuriators were in accepting as genuine the spurious epistle of Pontius Pilate to Emperor Tiberius. One can hardly avoid the conclusion that the underlying apologetic and polemical purposes of the history influenced its writers to be credulous when they were defending their own positions and critical when they were attacking the positions of their opponents. A case in point is the difference in the treatment of ancient and medieval miracles.

Despite such serious shortcomings in the *Magdeburg Centuries,* this work was a notable achievement. It was distinguished from all preceding works in the field of Church history by the comprehensiveness of its treatment, by the clarity of its organization, and by the extraordinary richness of its detail. It was reprinted and widely used. In the eighteenth century several attempts were made to revise and complete the work, but none of these was carried to a conclusion. Perhaps the best evidence of the greatness of Flacius' achievement was the fact that this "pestilential work," as it was called, was imitated by Roman Catholic opponents. Casare Baronius (1538-1607) undertook to demonstrate that the Church during the Middle Ages represented a continuation and not a deterioration of the Apostolic Church. This he attempted by gathering an equally prodigious amount of information and arranging it in a rigidly chronological fashion, year by year. The fruits of his labors were published in the twelve volumes of his *Annales ecclesiastici* (Rome, 1588-1607), which traced the history of the Church to the end of the twelfth century.

THE LIFE OF ST. TERESA OF ÁVILA

Author: Saint Teresa of Ávila (Teresa de Cepeda y Ahumada, 1515-1582)
Type of work: Spiritual autobiography
First published: 1562

PRINCIPAL IDEAS ADVANCED

True devotion consists in complete resignation of the self to God, who will work the good through those who obey Him.

The pillar of devotion is mental prayer, of which the first degree entails great human effort, although in subsequent degrees supernatural grace is chiefly effective.

The Christian ought to obey the Church even when it is wrong, confident that God will overrule its errors.

When St. Teresa wrote her *Life,* she still had twenty years to live. Her celebrated autobiography, therefore, gives no indication of the busy career as organizer and administrator upon which she was shortly to enter. Hitherto she had been preoccupied with her interior life, with supernatural visitations, and with mental prayer. The *Life,* accordingly, is devoted largely to these matters. Yet it is not a devotional manual or a treatise on mystical theology, but an animated personal narrative. Its bulk attests the vigor which the author brought to everything she did, just as its content betokens her lively sensibility and keen intelligence.

Teresa wrote her *Life* on the instruction of one of her spiritual advisors, and the book was ostensibly for the use of priests and nuns. Her language is racy and idiomatic, and her story unfolds in an easy and informal manner.

If Teresa devotes comparatively little attention to the external events of her life, this is because up to the time when she founded her first monastery, there were not many events to relate. She laments the passing of childhood innocence, and the "wicked" life into which she fell at an early age. She finds little cause to complain of her parents, except that her mother read "tales of chivalry," and allowed these to fall into the hands of her children; but one of her cousins, with whom she liked to play, is severely censored for leading her into vain and frivolous practices. As she tells it, her fear of a bad reputation kept her from mortal sin, and she would have nothing to do with boys. But, because she was an active and self-willed girl, she seemed to herself always to be doing something wrong, especially considering her firm conviction that we must despise the world and strive for the joys of Heaven.

Teresa had her first taste of convent life when, on the death of her mother, she was placed in an Augustinian monastery as a boarder. Though she found life in the convent pleasant, she could not decide to give up the world entirely. This resolution was taken after she had returned to live with relatives, when, through the influence of religious books and the congenial example of a friend, she decided to enter the Carmelite monastery in Ávila. Because her father would not give his consent to her becoming a nun, she prevailed upon one of her brothers to take her to the convent; but, notified by the nuns of his daughter's action, the father came and "offered up his Isaac on Mount Carmel."

A serious illness, which overtook Teresa when she was in her early twenties, brought her to the threshold of death and left her with a paralysis from which she was three years in recovering. Earlier, Teresa had prayed that she might experience sickness in order to learn patience, and at first she bore her affliction with joy; but later, thinking how much better she could serve God in health, she prayed to be made whole. That, she says, was a mistake. We ought "to resign ourselves absolutely to the disposition of our Lord, who knows best what is for our good."

Teresa has little that is specific to tell us concerning her next fifteen years. These years cannot have been uneventful; but, as Teresa looks back over them, they seem to have been a time of lukewarmness and compromise, mainly due to her neglect of prayer: "I could wish I had permission to say how often at this time I failed in my duty to God, because I was not leaning on the strong pillar of prayer. I passed nearly twenty years on this stormy sea, falling and rising, but rising to no good purpose, seeing that I went and fell again."

When she was forty years old, a change took place which she regards as her true conversion. A picture of the wounded Christ and a copy of St. Augustine's *Confessions* were instrumental in bringing her to a new pitch of devotion. Kneeling before the picture, she felt as never before her inability to do anything of herself, and she was finally able to place her complete confidence in God. "It seems to me that I said to Him that I would not rise up till He granted my petition. I do certainly believe that this was of great service to me, because I have grown better ever since." The trouble had been that, from the time that she recovered from her illness, she had been trying to "reconcile God and the world." Now "the grounds of the warfare" were changed; having accepted "the vanity of the world," and having resigned herself to serving God in everything, she found a joy that she had not known since the time of her illness.

As Teresa entered upon her new commitment, she became increasingly dissatisfied with the lax discipline of the Carmelite order. When it came to her attention that the original rule had been much stricter, she determined to set up her own monastery and to govern it according to the original rule. Her efforts met with determined opposition from the city of Ávila and from numerous groups within the Church. The Father Provincial of her order, after first granting her permission, bowed to pressures and told her to abandon her plans. There were those, however, who encouraged her to go ahead, and by proceeding secretly, she was able to present the Provincial with a *fait accompli*. She had some struggles with Satan, who ventured to suggest that she had failed in her obedience; but she fended off the temptation by promising before the Holy Sacrament not to enter the house without the Provincial's permission. This he granted, after rebuking her (mistakenly, as she avers) for being motivated by the desire for fame.

In her struggles to found her monastery, Teresa was partly sustained by visions and voices, which, from her fortieth year, came to her with increasing frequency. Once, when she was having difficulty paying the workmen, St. Joseph, who was her particular saint and for whom her monastery was to be named, appeared to her, assuring her that God would provide the means. Another time, Mary and Joseph appeared together with a garment which they draped about her as a sign that she was cleansed from her sins, after which they promised that her desires to build the monastery would be realized. Another time it was the saintly hermit, Peter of Alcantara, then deceased, who appeared for the purpose of advising Teresa in the matter of an endowment which she had under consideration.

Of her "voices" or "locutions," Teresa says: "[They] are so frequent that I cannot count them; many of them are

reproaches, and He sends them when I fall into imperfections. They are enough to destroy a soul. They correct me, however; for His Majesty gives both counsel and relief." Teresa explains that, although not heard with the bodily ear, these voices are perfectly distinct, and impossible to shut out or ignore; furthermore, she believes, there can be no possibility of confusing the voice of God with that of evil spirits or with suggestions of one's own mind. "The words formed by the understanding effect nothing," she says; "but, when our Lord speaks, it is at once word and work; and though the words may not be meant to stir up our devotion, but are rather words of reproof, they dispose a soul at once, strengthen it, make it tender, give it light, console and calm it."

Teresa's ecstasies, transports, and raptures occasioned much discussion in her own time. Her early advisors inclined to say that her experiences were of Satanic origin, and she suffered great anxiety until she found more understanding confessors. The *Life* abounds in careful descriptions of these mystical experiences, since part of Father Ibañez's purpose in having her write the *Life* was to put these experiences on record.

Of more value, however, to the student of religion is Teresa's lengthy discourse on mental prayer. Speaking without reference to the standard theological works on the subject, and recounting only what she had learned by experience, Teresa distinguishes four degrees of prayer. These, she says, may be compared to four ways of watering a garden. The first degree of prayer requires great effort on man's part and is like drawing water from a well bucket by bucket. Beginners in prayer must practice meditation, self-examination, and humiliation; and, despite the great labor involved, the rewards seem small. At the second degree, which Teresa compares to the introduction of an irrigation pump, supernatural aids are given. Some of man's other faculties begin to co-operate and to assist the will, and the spiritual satisfactions are great. The third state of prayer is like a running brook, in that the inspiration is provided by God's Spirit, and nothing remains to man's faculties save to direct its flow. Finally comes the prayer of union, in which the soul is freely watered as by a gentle shower of rain, at the cost of no human effort. The secret of progress in mental prayer, says Teresa, in words which were given to her by the Lord, is: "[The soul] undoes itself utterly, My daughter, in order that it may give itself more and more to Me: it is not itself that lives, it is I." Teresa was of the opinion that numerous devout persons who practice faithfully the first stage of prayer are permitted to experience the second stage, but that comparatively few attain to the third and fourth stages. The fourth stage, the prayer of unity, is not (we are reminded) the same as ecstasy or rapture.

A faithful daughter of the Counter Reformation, Teresa accepted on principle the absolute authority of the Catholic Church. To many mystics the institutional framework of religion has been an intolerable constraint, and there have been devout Catholics who felt little or no need for the sacraments. Not so, Teresa, for whom devotion to God required that one first do violence to the self. But obedience had a curious twist in the case of Teresa. Fully aware that Churchmen are fallible, she obeyed them as a matter of principle,

but was, meanwhile, confident that God would shortly overrule human folly. Thus, when the Father Provincial called her to account for having secretly built her monastery, she saw herself in the role of Christ before the Sanhedrin: "I prayed and implored our Lord to help me, and my father St. Joseph to bring me back to his house. I offered up to him all I was to suffer, rejoicing greatly that I had the opportunity of suffering for his honour and of doing him service. I went persuaded that I should be put in prison at once; but this would have been a great comfort. . . . When [the Provincial] came, I was summoned to judgment, rejoicing greatly at seeing that I had something to suffer for our Lord. . . . I thought of Christ receiving sentence, and I saw how this of mine would be less than nothing."

As a matter of fact, Teresa was the founder of one of those distinctive orders that find their place in the Roman Catholic Church. With the able assistance of the zealous young monk who came to be known as St. John of the Cross (1542-1591), she established the Reformed or Discalced ("barefoot") order of Carmelites, and she promulgated a new type of mystical devotion which has not always been well-received within the Church. In many respects, the quietism of Miguel Molinos (1640-1697), who was imprisoned by the Inquisition for teaching that God visits men's souls by direct illumination without the aid of Gospel or sacrament, was a development of Teresa's teaching; and the Discalced Carmelites in France were particularly sympathetic to quietist teachings. (See, for example, Brother Lawrence [Nicolas Herman, c.1605-1691], *The Practice of the Presence of God*.)

DE REGNO CHRISTI

Author: Martin Bucer (1491-1551)
Type of work: Church doctrine; systematic theology
First published: 1577

PRINCIPAL IDEAS ADVANCED

The Church is the Kingdom of Christ, in which a covenant relationship with God has been established.

The doctrine of predestination means an election to salvation; salvation is dependent upon the eternal counsel of God, and for that reason man may be absolutely certain about salvation.

Special ministers are appointed by God to be responsible for doctrine and discipline within the Church; the elect allow themselves to be governed and guided by these ministers, who also teach, confining themselves strictly to the Holy Scriptures.

The marks of the true Church are the Scriptural character of its doctrine, the proper administration of the sacraments, its discipline, and its care of the poor.

The Kingdom of Christ is to be established in England by a reorganization of the political, social, and religious institutions within the country, so that the law of God will become the moral ideal for all.

In 1549, Martin Bucer, the Reformer of Strassburg, was invited to come to England by the Archbishop of Canterbury, Thomas Cranmer (1489-1556). It had been determined by Cranmer that Bucer would become Regius Professor of Theology at the University of Cambridge. While in England, Bucer wrote a book entitled *De regno Christi* (*Of the Kingdom of Christ*, written 1550; published in the *Scripta anglicana*, 1577). Bucer presented his book to King Edward VI, the reigning monarch of England at that time.

De regno Christi is Bucer's mature theological work, and it is the closest to a systematic theology of any of his works. In *De regno Christi*, Bucer was concerned to apply the doctrines of the Reformed Protestant Church to the political order. The fundamental ideas of the Reformation—concerning sin, grace, justification, and sanctification—were reproduced basically in harmony with the position of Martin Luther (1483-1546) and Philipp Melanchthon (1497-1560).

Bucer's work is a theologian's attempt to draw out the practical implications of theological ideas. Chapters on education, relief of the poor, marriage and divorce, business and the trades, judges, prisoners and penalties present in detail Christian suggestions for the conduct of practical affairs. The book is more an essay in social reform than it is a standard work of Reformed theology. Bucer concerns himself with the Church and its relationship to the state, and with the problem of how the Christian faith could be best exhibited to and practiced in the secular world.

For Bucer, theology was Biblically-oriented, and he believed that the

Christian faith was relevant to every aspect of man's life. Church organization and Church discipline were, he believed, essential ingredients of the Christian Gospel, and could be employed to make religion more meaningful to man.

In *De regno Christi* Bucer defined the nature of the Kingdom of Christ as "an administration and attainment of the eternal salvation of the elect of God, by which he himself, our Lord and King of heaven, by his doctrine and discipline administered through special ministers appointed for that purpose . . . gathers his elect to himself and incorporates them in himself and his church, and in it so governs them that, purged more fully from their sins, they may live well and blessedly." Bucer emphasized, therefore, the moral character of the Kingdom. The Gospel was to be the source of moral power. Love is the norm for the Kingdom. When love is established among men, then Christ rules. Morality was also conceived to be law. The Old Testament and the New Testament are not to be distinguished as Martin Luther had done in terms of Law and Gospel, said Bucer. Rather, the will of God, which is given in the whole Bible, is to be realized in all of the activities of life and to include the whole social and cultural life of man. The Kingdom comes only when the commandments of God and the truth of the Bible have permeated all life.

The Kingdom, however, consists also of the elect; that is, of those whom God has chosen for participation in the Kingdom. But election is realized only by the incorporation of the Christian into the Church of Christ. The Church is the "Kingdom of Christ" in which a new covenant with God has been established.

Bucer's idea of predestination is related closely to his concept of *Spirit*. Christ, who grants election by His Spirit, has by this act constituted the Church. The elect are those who have received the Spirit and are enabled to believe the Word and to live a virtuous life based upon the Holy Scriptures. The Kingdom of Christ is, therefore, Christ's lordship over those whom He has elected. It is they who make up the Christian Church. The Church is, furthermore, an institution or organization with offices and a polity, which permit the elect to form a community. The elect can gather about the Church; they can hear the Word and be obedient to the Word in their lives. Christ rules the Church through the ministers, which are his instruments for Church order. The elect, Bucer said, allow themselves to be guided and directed by the "ministry," which is "regularly constituted." This community is a community of love, whose membership is dependent upon ethical obedience to the commandments of God and Christ.

Throughout Bucer's discussion of the Kingdom of Christ, there is an emphasis upon its moral character, as well as upon the moral demands upon the individual which make him part of the Kingdom. In addition, Bucer emphasized Church discipline. Christ's "order" is superior to all human institutions, and for that reason, obedience to His word and commandments contribute to the shaping of human life. The word of Christ must be obeyed as a law.

Bucer never set up a sharp contrast between the Kingdom of Christ and the secular order. The political order has a spiritual task, he insisted. The ruler or the magistrate must be responsible to the community to provide the best life for its citizens. He must promote the highest ideals of morality, peace, and concord. But because Bucer asserted that the highest kind of morality is founded upon religion, it is the duty of the magistrate to establish the true religion in his country. The temporal order must be so constructed that the moral power of the Kingdom can influence the lives of every subject within it. Bucer asserted that although the secular government had to contribute to the creation of the Kingdom, the true magistrate is the Christian magistrate—all others are tyrants. The magistrate who is a Christian, and who serves the state, must not use religion for the maintenance of peace (as the tyrants do), but must propagate the Christian Gospel so that the Kingdom might be established. In this way, a Christian magistrate or ruler can serve the Church in a *direct* way. The Christian state is therefore that political structure which attempts to place all life under the law of the Bible.

Bucer called the Christian state the "commonwealth"; that is, that human community in which the welfare of the people is guaranteed by the Christian consciousness of the government. But the Christian state is also that state which has best utilized the political structures available, with the result that peace is a reality within that state.

Bucer did not believe that there should be a distinction between the state and the Kingdom. Legislation is based upon the precepts of Christ and the Decalogue, which Bucer equated with the law of God. Bucer did not believe that the existence of such a state might weaken the traditional forms of the Christian faith. According to Bucer, the sovereign in a kingdom (in England for example) is obliged, by virtue of his divinely appointed office, to promote a reformation of the Church. Bucer thereby provided the first distinctively Protestant theory of the supremacy of the British monarchs in matters involving the Church.

Bucer's plan to reorganize the Church in England presupposed that all of the social, cultural, and political life of England must be reconstituted according to the law of God. It was the responsibility of the state, however, to insure the welfare of its citizens. To do so involved the establishment of universities and schools, the regulation of begging, usury, and class differentiation. Bucer also believed that it was the task of the state to regulate marriage and divorce laws.

The type of Church structure and polity which is designated by the term Reformed ("Calvinistic") is in essence based upon the ideas of Martin Bucer. It was John Calvin, the Reformer of Geneva, who carried out Bucer's ideas and made them normative for the Reformed Church in Europe.

The Reformation had taken place in Strassburg sometime in the early 1520's. A group of highly educated and respected preachers had been converted from Roman Catholicism to the newly-expressed Lutheran Protestant faith. Bucer was the leader of this group within the Strassburg church community. The city council in Strassburg had encouraged the acceptance of evangelical practices in the parishes of the city, and the council permitted preachers to be elected by the separate parishes within the city. A reorganization of the Church took place soon after, which included the concept of Church property, the role of education within the churches, the nature of welfare programs, as well as a moral code ("Sittenmandat") and other policies to revitalize the Reformation church of Strassburg. The city council subsequently ordered the appointment of church wardens to help supervise the care of souls in the parishes. The wardens were elected by the city council and had as their task "the supervision of ministers," and the building of a vigorous Christian congregation in the city. Later the wardens received the right to determine true doctrine and to encourage discipline and regulate morality. In 1539, Bucer, recognizing the ineffectiveness of the office of church warden, insisted that the Church be constructed along the lines of the New Testament. There were to be four classes of officers: preachers, elders, teachers, and deacons. (It is easy to see the similarity between this and Calvin's "Ordonnances ecclesiastiques.") The elders, with the preachers, were to be responsible for the moral and religious discipline of the Church members, and were empowered to admonish and even excommunicate if necessary.

Bucer's order for the administration of the Church was based upon the belief that the government was responsible for the temporal and eternal welfare of its subjects. The government had to regulate religion; it was to be the guardian of a temporal order which supervised and ordered man's duties toward God. The true religion was to be established, and all idolatry destroyed. A moral atmosphere was also to be created which would be compatible with the true religion. The Church and its various functions, however, had to be respected, because it alone could determine the nature of preaching, the administration of the sacraments, and other spiritual acts within the Church.

Bucer's plan for the Church of England was based upon his Strassburg experiences. He wanted to create a "Christian commonwealth," in which Christ would be the King, governing through His Word. Christ's vicars, Bucer wrote, are the preachers who administer the Word and the teachers who interpret the Word. The sociopolitical order must be subject to the Word of God. Since under the Word of God, the civil government maintains order within the society, it may use the power of law and the sword. The Church also exists under the Word of God, and thus the Word of God becomes the authority for the related spheres of Church and state.

Although Bucer was not completely successful in establishing his Church orders in Strassburg, and although he was unable to transform the Church of England in any direct way, his program for the Kingdom of Christ has influenced entire generations of Christians in their considerations of the nature of Church polity and of the relationship of Church and state.

A TREATISE OF REFORMATION WITHOUT TARRYING FOR ANY

Author: Robert Browne (c.1550-1633)
Type of work: Separatist polemics (polemical theology)
First published: 1582

PRINCIPAL IDEAS ADVANCED

The respective spheres of Church and state must be sharply distinguished.

The Church is a voluntarily gathered congregation, united by covenant, and characterized by the personal holiness (righteousness) of its members.

The work of reformation must be carried forward without delay, until the suppression of all wickedness in the Church is accomplished.

The chief means of reformation is the power of preachers to excommunicate Church members that persist in wickedness.

The chief significance of this treatise is that it marks the point at which a strain in the Reformed tradition breaks away from this tradition and assumes an identity of its own. Brownism is the outgrowth of Elizabethan (Calvinistic) Nonconformity, which stands at the opposite extreme within the Reformed tradition from the "Erastianism" that underlay the Anglican establishment, and that was explicitly espoused by John Whitgift, Archbishop of Canterbury from 1583 to his death in 1604. The Archbishop regarded Church and state as simply two aspects of the one body politic, to be governed by the Crown in Parliament. The Puritans or Nonconformists strove for a Church that would be free from state control, while using the state to enforce the "godly discipline" that its exponents drew from the pages of Sacred Writ. Robert Browne virtually asserted the mutual independence of Church and state. While he did not hesitate to ascribe to the state an unlimited sovereignty in civil matters, he wholly denied its competence to interfere with the proper functioning of the Church, which he described as the inward and spiritual rule of Christ over His people by means of the Word, with such outward organization as this spiritual rule will give rise to.

Robert Browne was born of a family that had long been prominent in Rutlandshire. The date of his birth lies between 1550 and 1556. He was educated at Corpus Christi College, Cambridge, then considered a breeding ground of Nonconformity. Obtaining his bachelor's degree in 1572, he taught school for a while, but he was subsequently dismissed for his extreme religious views. After serving as a private tutor and preaching on the side, disdaining episcopal authorization, he settled in Norwich (1580) where he gathered, together with Robert Harrison (died c.1585), an assembly that may be regarded as the first Independent or Congregational church in England. The constitutional basis of this church was the covenant that was signed by all the members in 1581. Persecution that included the arrest of Browne and members of his church induced the two leaders and a group of their followers to take refuge in the Low Counties. In 1581 they settled in Middelburg, Zeeland, then a center of English commerce with the continent.

Here Browne published three treatises (1582) that were often bound together, and that constitute the bulk of his literary output. The longest of these, *A Booke which sheweth the life and manners of all true Christians; Also the pointes and partes of all divinitie, that is of the revealed will and worde of God, are declared by their severall Definitions, and Divisions in order as followeth,* is a systematic exposition of Browne's theology. The title is representative of the content: while "all divinitie" is discussed, Browne's main interest is in Christian life and conduct. Of central importance is his definition of the Church: "The Church planted or gathered, is a companie or number of Christians or beleeuers, which by a willing couenant made with their God, are vnder the gouernment of god and Christ, and kepe his lawes in one holie communion: because Christ hath redeemed them vnto holiness & happiness for euer, from which they were fallen by the sinne of Adam. The Church gouernment, is the Lordshipp of Christ in the communion of his offices: whereby his people obey to his will, and haue mutual vse of their graces and callings, to further their godliness and welfare."

A Treatise upon the 23. of Matthewe . . . is incomplete, and has often been omitted in published editions. Here Browne reprobates the use of (Aristotelian) logic and rhetoric in the exposition of the Bible, and sets forth his conception of proper Bible study, illustrating it by means of the exposition of verse one of Matthew 23. The text breaks off shortly after the point at which he had commenced to do the same thing for verses two and three. His approach is to expound the meaning of the verse and any difficulties that may be contained in it, to show the relation of the verse to the whole body of divinity, and to reveal whatever difficulties that may arise in connection with it; then to make the application, which includes proofs, rebukes, and exhortations. It is in this passage that he denies both that the Church of England is a true Church, and that those who refuse to separate from the fellowship of the former can in fact belong to the latter. He denounces the bishops as Romish beasts, and describes the alleged calling of Anglican clergy as illusory, because of the treatment they accord Christ and those who would restore Him to His rightful place in the Church. Sacraments administered within the Anglican establishment are said to be no more valid than those of the Church of Rome.

A Treatise of reformation without tarrying for anie, and of the wickednesse of those Preachers which will not reforme till the Magistrate commaunde or compell them is the best-known of the three treatises. It might be argued that it represents a more consistent application of the principles advanced by the French reformer John Calvin (1509-1564) in *The Necessity of Reforming the Church,* written some thirty-eight years earlier. Both Calvin and Browne affirm that Jerusalem is to "be built again . . . even in troublous times" (Dan. 9:25); Browne goes further and explains that this is true even though it is the magistrate that is causing the trouble, and that reformation must not tarry "for anie." Both Calvin and Browne were charged with subverting the authority of princes and alienating men from the Church; both reply that their opponents are "the men which trouble Israel," because they are rebelling against the rule of God (I Kings 18:18). Where Calvin had argued that certain great and fatal abuses had required the immediate reformation of religion, Browne argues that Protestantism is guilty of tolerating and practicing wickedness, and that *any* wickedness in the church is inconsistent with the Church's character as "the house of the living God, the pillar and ground of truth" (I Timothy 3:15). Browne was thus advocating the very rigorism that Calvin had disowned. It might be argued, however, that Browne's position was at least approximated by the later practice, if not the earlier theory, of Calvinist Geneva. ". . . there is nothing which the Lorde will not breake," wrote Browne, "if it be against his glorie, neither anie wickednes which the gouernement of his Churche is not able to put downe." As at Geneva, the chief weapon of Church government is to be excommunication. The name of God is said to be polluted by the presence of wicked persons at the communion table. The righteousness of God's people is interpreted to the effect that no open wickedness is to be allowed to continue among them: offenders are to be admonished and reclaimed, or, if this proves impossible, to be separated from the Church. "Therefore doth Paule call that parte of church gouernment, which is to separate the vngodlie, the power of our Lorde Iesus Christ." He adds, "For thereby are the Kings bounde in chaines, and the Nobles with fetters of yron, that they may execute vppon them, the iudgement that is written,

Such honor bee to all his Saintes" (Psalm 149:8,9). While the emphasis seems to lie on personal imperfections, institutional faults are to be remedied as well: the observance of Christmas, Easter, Whitsuntide, and other such "traditions," which Browne says were "receyued from Baal," are to be abolished.

Browne is emphatic in distinguishing between spiritual and civil government, and he counts upon New Testament texts for proof. Where Christ says that His Kingdom is not of this world (John 18:36), the fact is that bishops and magistrates rule over the Anglican establishment, which is therefore a part of the world. According to I Corinthians 12, Christ's spiritual Kingdom has a certain hierarchical structure all its own: ". . . first Apostles, secondlie Prophetes, thirdlie, teachers, &c. Also helpers and spiritual guides." All these are understood as charismatic gifts, to be recognized and utilized by the churches. The present leaders of the Church of England are called blind guides, builders who reject the Kingdom and Spirit of God, to whom Christ is a stumbling-block. Refusing to see the spiritual implications of Christ's parable of the leaven (Matthew 13:33), they want Christ's Kingdom set up "with observation" (Luke 17:20); that is, by order of Parliament or the decrees of the bishops; until then they are unwilling to do anything, and continue to wear the yoke of Antichrist. Despising the true honor that comes from God alone (Job 5:44), they insist on honors bestowed by men, such as "The right Honorable my Lorde. &c. who is my very good Lord and Maister." Christ says that His Kingdom is within men (Luke 17:21), and Browne understands this above all in a moral sense: "Goe to therefore, and the outwarde power and ciuil forcings, let us leaue to the Magistrates . . . but let the Church rule in spirtuall wise, and not in worldlie maner: by a liuelie lawe preached, and not by a ciuill lawe written: by holinesse in inwarde and outwarde obedience, and not in straightnesse of the outwarde onelie."

Adopting the traditional image of the two swords, Browne accuses the clergy of having failed to use the sword that belongs to them, namely excommunication, and having borrowed the sword of the civil magistrate to inflict all sorts of nonspiritual penalties. As a result, the clergy is said to be despised by the people.

The proper task of the civil magistrate is "to rule the common wealth in all outwarde Iustice, to maintaine the right, welfare, and honor thereof, with outward power, bodily punishment, & ciuil forcing of men." Browne relies upon this affirmation of the legitimacy of the magistrate to answer the charge of Anabaptism hurled against him. When it is said that Moses, the kings of Judah, or the leaders of the post-exilic community in Jerusalem had not only a civil but also a spiritual authority, Browne replies that as spiritual guides they prefigured and foreshadowed the Kingdom of Christ, which since His coming in the flesh is no longer exercised in shadow and type, but directly and properly; moreover, there are certain functions with respect to the Church which pertain to English magistrates as much as to Old Testament kings. Both are to protect the rights of the Church, as much as those of any other member of the commonwealth; both are to supply the temporal necessities of the Church; both

may enforce Church laws on Church members; and both may command reformation. The last-named function, which is Browne's main concern, he attributes to the magistrate as a right, rather than a duty. Basically, reformation is the responsibility of the Church, and it is the preachers' shame that they wait for the magistrate to compel them to do their proper duty. Since when, asks Browne, is it the sheep's place to force the shepherd to do his job? Browne's criterion for distinguishing Christian from non-Christian magistrates is whether the magistrate supports or opposes the churches' proper functioning. A government that forcibly removes and imprisons divinely called preachers, whose call has been approved and ratified by the Church, thereby demonstrates its non-Christian character. While the civil government is charged with providing the temporal necessities of the Church, the Church is not ultimately dependent on this support. Browne notes that historically the Church has flourished most when the state was openly hostile. The state as such is exempt from Church control. But the magistrate as an individual is as much subject to pastoral care and discipline as any other Christian. A Christian magistrate will willingly submit to Church discipline; and with non-Christian magistrates the Church has nothing to do.

Browne flatly rejects the common theological distinction between ordinary and extraordinary callings. Lawful pastors and preachers of the present day, he asserts, are no more subject to state control than were the Apostles and Prophets. In fact, all ministers of the New Covenant surpass in dignity John the Baptist, who in turn outranked all that came before him

(Luke 7:28). Yet Scripture attributes to the prophet Jeremiah power over the nations, to pull up and root out, to build and to plant (Jeremiah 1:10). So the government of the Church is included in the pastor's calling. This conception of the role of the pastor marks a further departure from mainline Calvinism, which insisted on placing Church government in the hands of a representative body that included, in addition to ministers, a number of lay elders.

For Browne the covenant is of central importance, but he is not a covenant theologian, either of the Continental or of the English school. The covenant idea functions for him in much the same way it functioned for the continental Anabaptists; namely, as the foundation of Church polity. It implies three principles: the outward autonomy of the individual congregations, the voluntary principle with respect to Church membership, and visible holiness as the specific characteristic of the visible Church. So Browne calls attention to the fact that Israel's covenant with its death penalties did not take effect until it had been voluntarily embraced (Exodus 19:3-8). He denies that covenant blessings can be inherited, thus striking at the heart of covenant theology; each generation, he affirms, must enter into covenant with God by a free choice of its own. Hence a Christian is defined as one who "is redeemed by Christ vnto holines & happines for euer & professeth the same by submitting him self to his lawes and gouernmēt." "The Lordes kingdome is not by force . . . ," Browne writes, "for it is the conscience and not the power of man that will drive vs to seeke the Lordes kingdome. . . ."; for "the Lordes people is of the willing sorte." He uses the verse that "the kingdom of God suffereth violence, and the violent take it by force" (Matthew 11:12) to prove that it requires effort to attain the Kingdom, a persistent pressing on, and that the worthy, who do so persistently press on, must not tarry for the unworthy. The constitutive element of the Church is therefore the holiness of its members, and the toleration of any open wickedness means a denial of the very nature of the Church. Christian morality, however, goes beyond the avoiding of what is unlawful to the doing of that which is most expedient. Browne recognizes a measure of human autonomy in ethics when he assigns the determination of what is most expedient to the individual.

Shortly after the publication of Browne's three treatises trouble arose in his church which led to his removal from the pastorate and the disintegration of his congregation. The majority, led by Robert Harrison, joined the regular English church in Middelburg, which was then pastored by the Puritan Thomas Cartwright (1535-1603). Others accompanied Browne to Scotland, apparently after he had composed *A Trve and Short Declaration, Both of the Gathering and Ioyning together of Certaine Persons: and also of the Lamentable Breach and Division which fell amongst them,* late in 1583, and *An answer to Master Cartwright His Letter for Ioyning with the English Churches,* which seems to have been published in 1584. When he continued to expound his separatist convictions and denied the jurisdiction of the Scottish Kirk over him, he was briefly jailed, early in 1584. Returning to England, he was imprisoned at the instance of the bishop of London for giving expression to his views, and was later excommunicated by the bishop of Peterborough for failing to answer to a charge of unauthorized preaching. This excommunication, which threatened him with perpetual imprisonment under the writ *De excommunicato capiendo,* may have been instrumental in procuring his formal (and humiliating) submission to the Church of England, which took place in 1586. He now procured a teaching position, which he held until 1591, when, through the good offices of his kinsman Lord Burghley (1520-1598; the leading member of Queen Elizabeth's Privy Council), he was made rector of Achurch-with-Thorpe, a small Northamptonshire village. He apparently retained this position until his death in 1633. It was openly said during his lifetime that though outwardly conforming, he retained his convictions concerning the nature and polity of the Church. It also appears that he was afflicted with a form of intermittently violent insanity that led to his final imprisonment (in Northampton Gaol, for assaulting a policeman) that lasted from 1631 until his death.

Though Robert Browne outwardly renounced his views, the term "Brownist" came to be applied to every form and degree of separatism. In 1618, *An Arrow against the Separation of the Brownists* distinguished three groups: the followers of Francis Johnson (1562-1618), who separated from the Church of England because of its alleged corruptions without denying that both it and the Church of Rome are true Churches; the followers of John Robinson (c.1575-1625; pastor of the Pilgrim Fathers), who denied that the Church of England was a true Church but allowed religious fellowship with the godly within it; and the followers of Henry Ainsworth (1571-c.1622), who renounced all religious fellowship with the Church of England and all its members. While the Puritans that settled the Massachusetts Bay and the Connecticut Valley insisted that they were not separatists or Brownists, their views were not far removed from those of Browne, and Browne is commonly regarded as the father of Congregationalism. The Independents, who flourished under Oliver Cromwell (1599-1658, creator of the New Model Army; Lord Protector of England, 1653-1658), substantially reflected in their theory and practice the views of Browne.

Congregationalism has been described by the German theologian and sociologist Ernst Troeltsch (1865-1923) as the unhappy marriage of Calvinism with the sect type. The unhappiness of this marriage apparently prompted many of its children to turn to a purer form of sectarianism. John Smyth (c.1554-1612) was only the most prominent of many separatists who ceased to be Calvinists and became General Baptists. But we should also note a second marriage between Calvinism and sectarianism, from which issued the Particular (Regular) Baptists, who shared with Browne his Calvinistic theology, his congregational polity, his recognition of the civil authority of magistrates, and his denial of the validity of any baptism that is not administered on the authority of a "gathered" Church. Finally, we should see in Browne a pioneer of two principles that have decisively influenced the religious history of (English-speaking) America: the voluntary principle with respect to Church membership, which he championed unequivocally, and the principle of separation of Church and state, which he espoused with remarkably few reservations.

THE DARK NIGHT OF THE SOUL

Author: Saint John of the Cross (1542-1591)
Type of work: Manual for mystical contemplation
First transcribed: c.1587

PRINCIPAL IDEAS ADVANCED

The goal of man's soul is ascent toward union with God, and in order to attain this goal the soul must pass through several dark nights.

The dark night of the senses is first, in which all attachment to the outer world is cut off and the direction of the self is turned completely inward.

The self cut off from sense is not peaceful but must pass through a spiritual dark night, since the soul must be emptied of all content, made completely arid, if it hopes for union with God.

Since its origin in the turmoil of John's stormy life and final imprisonment, *The Dark Night of the Soul* has been a classic and a manual for contemplative mysticism. Born in a fertile but decadent Spain as the result of an attempt at monastic reform, this single work has had extraordinary influence on all who seek to understand and to follow the spiritual and mystical way in the religious life. Furthermore, its highly structured form offers in its own way a complete theology.

The ascent to Mount Carmel is the theme, and in the ascent the soul will experience several dark nights in preparing itself for union with God. Instruction is necessary so that the soul may learn to free itself from all that is temporal. Yet even this is not enough, since the spiritual itself can be a burden. Complete nakedness and freedom is the goal, since only a spirit thus free of both temporal and spiritual impediments can hope for union with God.

Darkness actually provides security and protection for the soul, John writes; consequently, darkness properly entered into is not to be feared but is to be sought as the soul's ally. The suspension of the senses produces bliss, although not before the soul has gone through the preliminary torment that darkness and absence first produce. Not to see is also to remain unseen, so that sensual and spiritual darkness protects as much as it also seems to destroy. Advance in such a spiritual life requires careful instruction and advice.

Such doctrine, of course, seems difficult if not impossible or contradictory to those not used to such devious routes. Without any question, to follow John's advice means to go against the natural order, or at least to reverse it, but the advice is, nevertheless, not without its own logic or its own explanation. The nature of the dark night can be made intelligible, although its grasp requires some subtlety and some progression on its path. Darkness is the means to achieve divine light; what appears its opposite is actually the means thereto. Perfect union with God requires the emptying, the transformation of the self.

Human knowledge itself cannot reveal these mystical trails or lessen the darkness through which the soul must pass, since the darkness is the inevitable result of the very attempt to transcend human reason and to prepare the soul for a higher level. Ordinary experience is not sufficient to give an accurate description of the soul's journey. Only the person himself who travels the dark road can have an inner awareness of it, and even he cannot express it adequately in words. Words describe the approach and the stages of preparation, but they are not adequate to the state itself.

Not everyone will allow himself to be led in this manner; thus, few can hope to come to understand this way. In fact most souls impede God's activity by resistance and imprudent behavior; they refuse to surrender themselves to God. The self must be surrendered first before the way can be understood, and few are willing to do that. Even souls who venture to allow themselves to be led spiritually will at first believe themselves to be completely lost, since God leads them along a lofty path of dark contemplation and spiritual aridity.

Such a soul is filled with darkness, misery, and affliction, so that the difficult task for the spiritual counselor is to develop the sensitivity to distinguish this low state of the normal soul, a state brought on by spiritual advance, from the lost and directionless state of the abnormal soul. Those who begin the development of a spiritual life expecting immediate rewards are in for disappointment, since their first progress will have all the outer appearance of a loss, and to the undiscerning their condition will seem no different from the morbid condition of one abandoned by God. Inexperienced counselors, such as Job's, will jump at the conclusion that such a soul must harbor evil, and they will fail to discern the first stage of spiritual progress.

Spiritual progress has as its first fruits the knowledge of one's own misery, and this is perhaps the greatest affliction a soul can feel. In the first night of contemplation, God gives the soul this light of self-knowledge, but it is a terribly revealing light, the first effect of which is to plunge the soul into a lower condition. Increased sin also causes a similar affliction, so by what signs can a spiritual advance which is genuinely purgative be distinguished from the anguish of increased burden? An apparent loss may precede an actual deepening, but on the other hand some think themselves to be advancing spiritually when actually their spirituality amounts to nothing.

The road is not smooth or even upward in an advance toward God, but instead it is filled with dark night and with apparent immediate losses. Such a night is caused by purgation, by emptying present content, and the first such cleansing involves the sensual part of the soul, leading to the first dark night of sense and desire. The second dark night involves the spiritual part of the soul. These first two nights involve the active part of the soul, but after them comes passive or infused contemplation, when the soul has ceased its activity and is subjected to God.

The purgation of the sensual part of the soul is experienced at the start of contemplation, but the night of the spiritual life comes only to persons more advanced in the spiritual life, when God has begun to raise them toward a state of union with Him. The first dark night is caused by the soul's emptying and purging itself of all sense appetites regarding the external things of the world. Step by step a soul frees itself from all desire for the things of the world which it possesses, and such a denial and loss is like night to all of man's senses.

Such a road must be traveled by faith, since its way is as dark to the understanding as it has now become to the senses. God at this point is also like a dark night to a soul in this state of emptying itself of desire for the sense world. The last part of such a night, however, is like the end of night or the early dawn, close to the light of day or close to the divine light. Absence and purging bring darkness as a necessary testing stage. Faith is required since reason cannot guide here, but the transition to light by means of elimination and darkness is necessary.

Deprived of the pleasure which the desire for things makes possible, the soul enters its own dark night. Because of desire, natural man is nourished and fed by whatever his powers and faculties take pleasure in. Emptying itself of all things, the soul that has denied and cast away and silenced pleasure and desire remains as in the darkness of night. Of course, this denial is especially depressing because it is a denial not only of physical delights but also of internal pleasures.

What possesse and harm the soul are not the things of the world but rather the will and desire for them. What enters into the soul is not the thing but the desire for it, so that the elimination of desire is by far the most important goal. The affections which a soul has for creatures is pure darkness in the eyes of God. He who loves a creature becomes as low or lower than the creature. The soul that loves anything other than God renders itself incapable of transformation and thus incapable of pure divine union.

A man who has desires is a slave to them, and thus freedom cannot dwell in a heart that is subject to desires. The elimination of desires brings temporary darkness and even torment, but it also brings genuine freedom to a soul so detached. The love of God and the affection for creatures are contraries. One will does not have room both for a love of creatures and a love of God; one or the other must be eliminated if spiritual purity is to be achieved. Desires make the soul dark and blind, although advance brings a form of temporary blindness too. Even the least desire tarnishes the soul and makes it impure. If one is to enter into divine union, all desire and attachment living in the soul must die.

These things the soul can actively do for itself, but once having passed through the night of sense and desire, the spiritual night begins, and here the soul's activity begins to cease, for it has made itself passive before God by its sensual purity and spiritual rigor. The four natural passions of joy, hope, fear, and grief must be silenced and tranquilized, and in its silence the spiritual soul finds quietude and rest.

Nothing now wearies the upward flight of the soul, and nothing oppresses it when it is cast down. To achieve this state, the soul must be set on fire by a longing for the things of the spirit.

The dark nights of the spirit, faith, hope, and love, are for the soul nights of great promise. The soul seeks a "secret ladder," the steps of which are hidden both to sense and understanding, so that with respect to the natural light of reason the soul is left in darkness.

The soul goes forth in darkness, passing beyond all the limits of nature and reason, in order to ascend by the divine ladder of faith, which leads to and penetrates the innermost being of God. Faith as a marvelous means to God is comparable to midnight before the dawn. The brilliance of the light of faith finally overwhelms and eclipses the light of the understanding. Supernatural being, communicated by love and grace, overcomes the dark night of the soul.

HISTORY OF THE REFORMATION IN SCOTLAND

Author: John Knox (c.1505-1572)
Type of work: Reformation Church history
First published: 1587 (complete edition: 1644)

PRINCIPAL IDEAS ADVANCED

The reformation of religion in Scotland was a rebellion not against lawful authority, but against the unjust and un-Christian use of authority by Church and state.

The persecution of its critics by fire and sword is evidence that the Roman Catholic Church was an instrument of Satan for the suppression of the true Evangel of Jesus Christ in Scotland, and continuance of the rule of this form of religion should be prohibited.

The preservation of the proceedings and documents of the Scottish Reformers would vindicate the justice of their cause and assist in the establishment of an authentic Apostolic Church.

The History of the Reformation of Religion within the Realm of Scotland by the Scottish Reformer John Knox is a combination of a collection of historic documents, a vindication of a party cause, a nationalist broadside, a virulent Anti-Romanist treatise, and an autobiographical diary. It is certainly one of the most exciting books in all the vast literature of the Reformation. There is a rough, unfinished feeling about it as if a polished literary style would have been unsuited to the stormy events narrated. The author was passionately devoted to the cause he advocated, and he was himself the chief Reformer in the movement whose history he reports. If some books of religious history can be classed as objective, Knox's *History* is not one of them. Every page of it is written with a bias that is unconcealed and uncompromising. His pen is a weapon, his ink is undiluted, and his inspiration is the belief that he was fighting a battle for God and the Gospel.

So far as is known no attempt was made to publish the works in Knox's lifetime, though the Second Book seems to have been prepared for publication should events have taken a turn such that a vindication of the Protestant cause would have been necessary. Much of the narrative was written while the events being recorded were actually happening and, hence, it reflects the mood of the changing fortunes of the Protestant party. The reader feels that he is actually on the scene, feeling the tensions of the moment, and watching the gyrations of the nobles and Reformers as they watched the gyrations of one another.

The personal correspondence of the Scottish Reformer shows that he was capable of great tenderness and concern for domestic matters, but when he was confronting the public affairs of religion in Scotland, he was aflame with holy fire and the indignation of an Elijah facing the priests of Baal. He knew what was at stake in success or failure. On the continent of Europe and in England he had been on familiar terms with many of the leaders of the Reformed cause, and he had seen at first hand the immensity of the struggle to initiate, and then to sustain, freedom from the Roman Church. No one could accuse Knox of illusions about the price that had to be paid.

His own introduction to the gravity of the issues left an indelible mark on his outlook. In the *History* he tells of his first involvement when attending upon George Wishart in Lothian, near Edinburgh. Wishart was apprehended as a preacher of reform in 1546, and he was burned alive at St. Andrews at the instigation of, and in the presence of, Cardinal Beaton. This was John Knox's first lesson in the realities of the Roman version of ecclesiastical power, and one lesson was enough. Thereafter he spoke of "bloody wolves," "bloody butchers," "monsters and hypocrites," "sergeants of Sathan," and "that Roman Antichrist." Knox was an implacable foe of what he regarded as the knavery, lechery, cupidity, and inhumanity of the Roman Catholics. He objected also to the theological errors of the idolatry of the Mass and the commercializing of the Evangel. His fiery language, black and white categorizing, scorn of trimmers, surging invective, outrageous innuendoes, all tumble together in a tempest of eloquence: "I am called, Madam, to ane publict functioun within the Kirk of God, and am appointed by God to rebuk the synnes and vices of all." Thus spoke John Knox about himself to his Queen.

This vivid chronicle of Scottish affairs consists of five books, the first four certainly written by Knox, and the fifth by an unknown person. The Laing manuscript is generally conceded to be that which Knox himself supervised in transcription, and it was published by David Laing in his definitive edition "The Works of John Knox," in 1846-1848. The first edition by Vautrollier, 1586-1587, was suppressed; and the second by David Buchanan, 1644, included the fifth book. The writing is full of vernacular phrases, involving both Scottish and English usage, and it finds parallels for everything in Biblical antecedents, especially in the accounts of the kings and prophets of Israel. An excellent version with modernized spelling, edited by William Croft Dickinson, appeared in 1949.

What is now Book Two was the first part of the *History* to be written, and only as the work proceeded and opportunity permitted was the rest added. About the middle of Book Two, a reference to October, 1559, establishes the date of composition of that part. In September, 1560, Thomas Randolph, Scottish agent for Queen Elizabeth of England, wrote to Sir William Cecil, the English Secretary of State, that he had spoken to John Knox about his *History*, of which at that date one book had been written. In the year immediately following, Book Three was added, and Book One was undertaken in 1566 as an introduction and background. Book Four followed later in the same year. There are clear evidences that revisions were being made right up to the Reformer's death in November, 1572. His secretary, Richard Bannatyne, reported to Parliament that he had "certain scrolls, papers, and minutes" of things done after 1564 which needed to be put in "form and order," and it is possible that some of this material was used for Book Five. Within the work as a whole there is some overlapping of accounts, and subsequent editors have sifted out errors which the author's own revision did not catch.

If the *History* is taken in its final form, the narrative opens with an account of the first martyrs for reform at the beginning of the fifteenth century, "after that horrible and universal defecteuon from the trewth which hes cume by meanes of that Romane Antichrist," and it closes with the arrival of the Reformer in Scotland in May, 1559, to take up again the rapidly advancing cause. The cumulative effect of persecution on those who were disgusted with the rapacity and morals of the clergy is emphasized. Of the burning of Patrick Hamilton, for example, it was said that, "the reik of Maister Patrick Hammyltoun hes infected as many as it blew upoun." The French alliance became critical with the marriage in 1558 of the young Queen Mary (1542-1587) to the Dauphin Francis, for it tied Scotland to the strong Roman Catholic dynasty in France, and the repercussions of this in the relations with England were momentous, especially when Mary became Queen Consort of France. Her mother, Mary of Guise (1515-1560), was Regent in Scotland, and she had to depend increasingly on the resident French forces. The fact that Frenchmen were appointed to offices of state exasperated many of the Scottish nobility. Thus, self-interest stimulated recruitment to the reform cause.

In Scotland the Reformation was not a revolt of priests, but a revolt of sections of the people and the civil leaders. It was both a reformation and a revolution. The Scottish nobility had always been a rough and turbulent lot with longstanding family feuds to settle, a state of affairs that Knox did not fail to describe and evaluate caustically. No one needed to counsel him on the mixed motives of the men around him. The acceptance by the Scottish Parliament of the Confession of Faith (in August 1650) but vacillation concerning the *Book of Discipline* (1560) indicates the obtuseness of party men who condemned the papacy but would not finance adequately the Protestant ministry.

Many of the abuses to which the Scottish reform platform called attention were paralleled in other lands—abuses such as the rapacity of the Church, the centralization of power in the prelates, and the ineffectiveness of self-reform. It was a combination of local factors, however, rather than a single item, that produced the explosion; for example, the brutal repression of criticism, circulation of information about successful reform elsewhere, the French involvement, the duplicity of the Queen and her mother, and the zeal of Knox himself.

The Second Book is as much a repository of documents as it is an apologetic for the Protestant Lords of the Congregation, as the important alliance of anti-French noblemen was called. Clearly religion, politics, economics, and family rivalries all played a part in the Scottish Reformation. Knox highlights the irritation caused by the presence of the French, for he considered that the document might have to be utilized in influencing opinion at the Court of England. Every effort was made to show that amid all the alarms and skirmishes of this period, peaceable and legal means of action were pressed to settle matters. The Lords were not rebels, anti-royalists, or a brawling fringe group, but men with a just cause desirous of stable government and friendship with England.

Sufficient strength was gathered to depose the Queen Regent, but the reinforcement of the French troops reduced the Reform party to despondency. Appeal was made to England for more open assistance, and the Second Book ends with a prayer which catches the mood of that hour: "Look upoun us, O Lorde, in the multitude of thy mercyes for we ar brought evin to the deape of the dongeoun."

The Regent's famous taunt comes at the beginning of Book Three, "Whair is now Johne Knox his God? My God is now stronger than his, yea even in Fyff," Fife being the shire in which the Lords had been strong. Her "blasphemous rayling" was short-lived. An English army entered Scotland to reinforce the faltering Protestant nobility, the Treaty of Leith was negotiated, the French were removed, and the Parliament of Scotland accepted the Confession of Faith in 1560. Even at the moment of triumph, however, there was disappointment. The *First Book of Discipline,* designed to order the Scottish Church and to provide for a Reformed ministry, was subscribed to by representatives of the Great Council of Scotland, and they promised to enforce its provisions. They defaulted. So Knox incorporates the book in full, but says that he does it "to the end that the posteriteis to come may juge. . . ." Having ousted the avaricious prelates, he was faced with the avariciousness of a "corrupt generatioun."

The young and beautiful Queen Mary, a widow two years after her marriage to Francis, arrived from France in August, 1561, on a day that was overcast and unseasonably "dolorous," which many of the godly read as an ominous portent. Mass was celebrated in Holyrood Abbey and the fears of the Protestants multiplied. Knox, in an interview with his Queen, used courteous but plain words, and said that he would be "also weall content to lyve under your Grace as Paull was to lyve under Nero." Princes who murdered the godly should be opposed, he argued; and he wrote,

"Thair blynd zeall is no thing but a verray mad phrenesie; and thair foir, to tack the sweard frome thame, to bynd thair handis, and to cast thame selfis in preasone, till that thei be brought to a more sober mynd, is no disobedience against princes, but just obedience, becaus that it aggreith with the will of God." There was no court flattery in such sentiments.

The Queen had her own type of answer, and the struggle for power intensified. Knox was arraigned for treason, but he defended himself boldly and successfully. The attack came next at the General Assembly itself in a long and powerful offensive on Knox's opinions on the respective rights of the Queen, the people, and the Assembly on political and religious obedience, and again the skill of the Reformer frustrated the Queen's spokesmen.

The style of the Fifth Book lacks the sparkle and pungency of the other four. It covers events from 1564 to the renunciation of the Crown by the Queen in favor of her infant son James, and the appointment of a Regency again. Her second marriage, in 1565, to Henry Stuart, Lord Darnley, was a mistake; and her third, in 1567, to the Earl of Bothwell was disastrous. In the end Knox was still minister at Greyfriars Kirk in Edinburgh; the Queen abdicated in 1567, and she was committed as a prisoner to Lochleven Castle.

There is drama in Knox's story of the Scottish Reformation. Great ideas took possession of the minds of men and forced the pace of history. If God predestines events as Calvinism taught and as John Knox believed, it was a predestination which inspired rather than discouraged those who were influenced by it. Reform of the medieval Church called for tremendous courage, for the idea of toleration on both sides was unthinkable. Entrenched power had to be challenged not only in theory, but also by the willingness to live dangerously. The Old Testament was of greater assistance than the New Testament at least as an armory of precedents for sixteenth century polemics.

The intertwining of the economic and the spiritual, the greed of the worldlings and the patriotism of the nationalists, the unchastity of the religious office holders and the domestic principles of the pious, make assignment of motives a difficult exercise. But the moral force within the reform movement can easily be discerned. The Reformers may have been superstitious, ignorant, and cantankerous, but they knew that the clergy had taken vows which they were supposed to keep. When the clergy were corrupt and rapacious, even the most dull-witted could see a need for change. The Reforming party exploited this loose living in appeals for support and for the denunciation of all the existing ecclesiastical regime. If the morals of the Roman Antichrist were low, the Reformers argued, the value of Roman theology and of the Roman claims to authority could be no better.

No doubt the Reformers were intolerant and fanatic at times, but they were willing to seek open debate that all the world might examine the justness of their cause. The *History* of John Knox was just such an enterprise. It attempts to preserve the documents which would vindicate the conduct of his party against misrepresentation and to record both the acts of the Scottish Reformers and the abuses of political and religious power which provoked their rebellion.

A TREATISE OF EXCOMMUNICATION

Author: Thomas Erastus (1524-1583)
Type of work: Ecclesiology
First published: 1589

Principal Ideas Advanced

The visible Church must be sharply distinguished from the invisible Church.
The visible Church is a community based on a common faith, from which no one professing that faith should be excluded.
Christian princes and magistrates have the right and duty of governing the Church in their dominions, and to deal with violations of the moral code.

Thomas Erastus was born Thomas Lieber or Lüber in Baden, Switzerland, in 1524. He grew up in the Reformed (Zwinglian) faith. His baccalaureate was acquired in Basel, and his doctorate in medicine in Bologna.

In 1557 he began to teach at the University of Heidelberg, and in 1559 (and again in 1573) served as rector of the university. He not only lectured on medicine, but also was widely known and esteemed as a skillful physician, and as an opponent of the anti-traditionalist Theophrastus Paracelsus (1493-1541). In 1560 he assisted the Reformed theologian Peter Boquinus (died 1582) in his debate against the Lutheran theologian Johann Stoessel (1524-1576) and gained the respect of Frederick III, Elector Palatine from 1559 to 1576, who embraced the Reformed faith after this Heidelberg debate. Erastus served on the Church council of the Palatinate until 1564, and in every way exerted himself to advance the Reformed religion. Though

the bulk of the population remained Lutheran, the policy of the Palatinate after 1566 was increasingly oriented towards the various Reformed bodies of Western Europe, which looked largely to Geneva for leadership. As a result, the partisans of Geneva, led by the theologian Caspar Olevianus (1536-1587; co-author of the Heidelberg Catechism of 1563), became increasingly insistent in their demand for a system of presbyteries that would include lay elders and that would exercise Church discipline, including the power of excommunication; that is, depriving Church members of the privilege of participating in the Lord's Supper. When one of the Genevan party, the English exile George Withers, proposed the thesis (in 1568) that a well-ordered Church includes a presbytery that shares with the ministers the exercise of Church discipline and that is able to excommunicate even princes, there were riots, and Erastus felt himself constrained to write in opposition to the excommunicators. He formulated his views in 103 theses, which he sent to a number of divines outside the Palatinate. His views were to some extent endorsed by the theologians of German-speaking Switzerland, notably by Henry Bullinger (1504-1575) of Zurich and Johannes Haller (1523-1575) of Berne. The opposite point of view was most ably presented by Theodore Beza (1519-1605), since 1564 the leading minister in Geneva, and echoed by the three Heidelberg theologians whose views had been solicited by the elector. Before the end of 1569 Erastus had compressed his views into seventy-five theses, to which he appended his *Confirmatio thesium* (a five-book reply to Beza and a one-book reply to the Heidelberg theologians). The whole work was printed in 1589, probably in London and with the encouragement of Archbishop John Whitgift (c.1530-1604).

The Latin title of the seventy-five theses succinctly indicates the author's frame of reference: *Explicatio gravissimae questionis, utrum excommunicatio quatenus religionem intelligentes et amplexantes a sacramentorum usu propter admissum facinus arcet, mandato nitatur divino, an excognita sit ab hominibus.*

Erastus states that from the beginning of the "Excommunicating Frenzy" (about 1566) he looked upon it as a basically wrong approach, even though he himself at that time held excommunication to be Scriptural. With only about one-thirteenth of the population sympathetic to Reformed doctrine, he felt that a positive approach was essential. The "saving truths" should be propagated so as to bring people into the fellowship of the Church, rather than to expel them. His fundamental charge against excommunication, as indicated by the Latin title, is that it is an invention of men, which he dates from the end of the second century. He professes to admire the zeal and good intentions of those who originated the practice, but notes that excommunication greatly augmented the Church's hold upon men and states, and the growth of superstition.

Erastus argues from the sacraments of the Old Testament Church, which, with Calvin, he holds to be "altogether the same" with respect to the things signified as those of the New Testament Church. Christ himself did not bar Judas (who left before the Last Supper of his own accord, if at all) or the other disciples, even though they had just striven amongst themselves as to who should be the greatest. Erastus elaborately examines the opponents' prooftexts in Matthew 18:15-17, I Corinthians 5:3,11, and I Timothy 5:29. In the case of the first of these passages he concludes that Jesus is teaching the Jews to submit minor differences to the tribunal of their own nation; namely, the Sanhedrin. In the second passage, Paul is speaking of "cutting off" an offender, not from participation in the sacraments, but from life itself and from the suspension of private familiarities, such as eating together. In the third, public rebuke, is mentioned but not excommunication.

Actually the sacraments are not to be construed as means of penalizing men for their wrongdoings, but rather as inducements to true conversion: "The end and designes of this Institution of the Lords Supper, are, that we may commemorate in the most solemn manner the Death of our Lord: That we may pay our Homage in a publick Recognition and Thankfulness, for the

Deliverance he hath purchased for us: That we may remind our selves, and by our presence bear testimony to others, that we have no other Food of Life, but a Crucified Saviour; no other Drink, but his Bloud poured out for us; That we may declare our selves as well penitent for our past course of Life, as that we have enter'd upon thoughts and resolutions of a better; and that we embrace the Christian Doctrine, are the members of Christ, belong unto his Church, in which we desire piously and religiously both to live and to die. . . . He that by the aid and impulse of the Holy Spirit hath the thoughts of his heart right at the time of his receiving, the Scripture turns him not away; but God only knows whether and how long he will hold on to his good purposes and resolutions. 'Tis our duty to hope always the best of all men, however we may sometimes be mistaken: nay, we ought to address our hearty prayers to God, that he would vouchsafe to strengthen and confirm both us and them in all true Religion and Virtue. But still the sinner is to be told of his faults, is to be reprehended, admonished, and advised, that he may so try himself that (as the Apostle cautions) he eat and drink not Damnation to himself."

Of fundamental importance for Erastus's conception of the proper relationship of Church and state is the distinction between the invisible and the visible Church. These two bodies are not mutually inclusive; hence, what unites men to one does not necessarily unite them to the other. Erastus says: ". . . we are made Members of Christ . . . by that Faith alone which worketh by Charity: and 'tis by Infidelity onely that we fall from this Consortship. And therefore no body can give us admission into this Society, or shut the doors upon us, but he that can impart to us a lively Faith, and again withdraw it at his pleasure."

Membership in the Church is based on profession of this faith, approbation of the same doctrine, and use of the same sacraments. Since "the whole World are to be invited, and by all the Allurements and Arts of men, won and brought into" participation in the first two of these marks, it is most unreasonable that they should be deprived of the third. Moral failings do not debar men from the fellowship of the Church. The extent of Christ's external kingdom should be no narrower now than the boundaries set unto the Jews, among whom all the circumcised were admitted to the privileges of the Temple, while wrongdoers were punished by civil punishments.

Erastus asserts that the office of the lay (nonteaching) elder is not Scriptural, since in New Testament times the elders and bishops were one and the same. The nearest approach to it is Paul's suggestion that the Church institute a tribunal to determine causes between its members. (I Corinthians 6:1-6). Erastus admits the legitimacy of such an institution as long as the Church is "under a Profane Government (as in the Dominions of Turks and Papists)," and he assigns to it the task of admonishing disorderly ministers and profligate members. But such a function becomes obsolete as soon as the civil magistrate becomes Christian, pious, and orthodox: " 'Tis a most pernicious Error, and big with dangerous consequence, that so many think no better of a Christian Magistracy, than of an Heathen one, whose power is to be allowed of no farther than meer Temporals." The Calvinistic presbyteries are superfluous, since Christian rulers have the right not only to order the religion of their dominions but also to deal with every manner of vice. The position of Christian rulers today is analogous to that of the rulers of the Jewish state under the Old Testament. However, "'twas lawful for the High Priests under the Old Testament, to meddle with the arts of Government and Secular affairs, as they were the Types of Christ our King and High Priest: but under the Gospel 'tis another case, IT SHALL NOT BE SO WITH YOU, says Christ."

Erastus quotes Wolfgang Musculus (1484-1563) to the effect that nature does not allow two absolute and independent governments over the same people without one being subordinate to the other.

Wolfgang Musculus, professor of Greek and Theology in Berne, was the most consistent and thorough exponent of the view that would make the Church a department of the state, the view generally known as Erastianism. The Magisterial Reformation (Lutheran, Reformed, Anglican) depended everywhere on the civil government (the magistrate) for its success; where it triumphed, it was perhaps inevitable that state Churches should develop that were with various degrees of completeness subject to the control of the state.

German-speaking Switzerland apparently had no doubt that the authority of the magistrate extended permanently to the control of the religious life of the community; Ulrich Zwingli (1484-1531), Henry Bullinger, and Rudolf Gualter (1519-1586), who succeeded one another as head minister in Zurich, all shared the basic convictions of Musculus and Erastus, which found their ideal in the Christian state. When John Whitgift (from 1583, Archbishop of Canterbury), sought for a theoretical justification of the Anglican state Church, he found it in this German-Swiss tradition. His Calvinistic opposition, the Puritans, meanwhile contended for the kind of ecclesiastical autonomy and discipline that had been won in Geneva after a long and bitter struggle. The Calvinist and Zwinglian views of Church polity had collided in Lausanne in the 1540's and 1550's, and their contest in the Palatinate was but a renewal of this struggle. Only after the Palatinate had reverted to Lutheranism at the death of Frederick III (1576) and all the Reformed professors had been expelled from the University of Heidelberg (Erastus was professor in Basel the last three years of his life), did the two Reformed factions coalesce.

When Theodore Beza published his *Tractatus pius et moderatus de vera Excommunicatione, et christiano Presbyterio, Erasti manuscriptis thesibus oppositus* in 1590, it was in this more irenic atmosphere. While he upholds the Genevan Church polity as the ideal towards which all churches should strive, he recognizes that polity may legitimately vary with local conditions. He asserts that the whole controversy would have been unnecessary if Erastus had all along maintained his final position that he is not concerned to retain those in the Church who do not profess the pure Christian doctrine. But for Beza such a profession is nullified by blasphemy, immorality, or unbelief; for there can be no salvation without sanctification. Excommunication serves to safeguard the glory of God as well as the safety of the individual, lest he eat and drink to his own condemnation. The visible Church is not only a confessional community (as for Erastus) but also a divinely instituted school of salvation and of the Christian life (analogous to Erastus's Christian state, but on a higher level). It approaches far closer to the invisible Church than Erastus had thought proper. Beza does not question the political (civil) sovereignty of the state in this treatise, but he distinguishes, as Erastus had refused to distinguish, between the person and the office of the magistrate: as a person, even the highest magistrate is subject to the discipline (and excommunication) of the Church.

TREATISE ON THE LAWS OF ECCLESIASTICAL POLITY

Author: Richard Hooker (c.1554-1600)
Type of work: Anglican apology
First published: Books I-IV, 1594; Book V, 1597; Books VI-VIII, 1648-1662

PRINCIPAL IDEAS ADVANCED

Christian society is taught both by the natural light of reason and by the supernatural light of Scripture.

The Presbyterians are mistaken in supposing that Scripture, which contains the whole truth necessary for salvation, also gives detailed instructions for the government of Christian society.

Since the ceremonies and discipline of the Church of England serve the cause of Christianity, they ought not be exchanged for those of Geneva.

Hooker's *Ecclesiastical Polity* is commonly regarded as laying the foundations of Anglican theology, providing, as it does, a well-reasoned case for the existence of a national Church, a Church faithful to the essential principles of the Reformation, subject to the decrees of the Crown, and guided by a decent respect for tradition. The work was composed in response to the criticisms of the Elizabethan settlement which were launched against it by Presbyterians, such as Thomas Cartwright (1535-1603). Hooker divided his subject into eight books, of which only the first five were published during his lifetime. The books beyond the first five are sometimes omitted in modern editions, but they are particularly interesting as sources of Hooker's ideas on the doctrine of the episcopacy and on the relation of Church and state.

Hooker stood in the line of renaissance humanism which drew alike from Christian and pagan sources. His account of the moral and civil law is especially indebted to Aristotle, but he owes his views of the relation between nature and grace, reason and revelation, and civil society and the Church to Thomas Aquinas. On these classic grounds he stood to do battle with the strict partisans of the Protestant Reformation, who, although not without classical learning, strove on principle to purge the Church of its non-Hebraic accretions and maintained that for the Christian the only rule of faith and practice is to be found in the Old and New Testaments.

The Puritans with whom Hooker had to contend (not to be confused with the later Puritans, who were often Independents and Congregationalists) were Presbyterians who took the Churches of Geneva and Scotland as their models. The zeal and singleness of mind with which the Presbyterians pressed their cause was an expression of that severe piety which finds its center in submission to the irresistible decrees of a Sovereign God who leaves nothing to the agency of man. As God justifies His elect by the death and resurrection of His Son and sanctifies them by the power of His Spirit, so He instructs and governs them by the Scriptures, preached and applied by those whom He has called to be His ministers. Since the Scriptures, being perfect, tell us everything that God wills us to do, either expressly or by legitimate inference, anything done without Scriptural warrant is presumptuous and sinful. Chief among the principles which the Scriptures lay down are: government by ministers, lay-elders, and deacons; a simple order of worship consisting of psalms, prayers, offerings, and the preaching of the Word; the observance of weekly Sabbaths but not of holy days; and the authority of the Church, through its ministry, to discipline the ungodly and to command the civil power. Besides these matters of Church polity, however, the Scriptures also give a complete regimen for men in their daily life. Such, at least, was the Presbyterian teaching which challenged the existing order of the Church of England and to which Hooker attempted to reply. His book, which is a polemic from beginning to end, owes its bulk to the detail with which he treats a multitude of particular charges made against the practice of the English Church by a number of Presbyterian writers.

Hooker acknowledged the genius of Calvin and praised his achievements in the city of Geneva, but the Calvinist dogma that Scriptural principles provide an exclusive and sufficient rule of life was, he maintained, as dangerous as the claims which the Anabaptists made for their visions and revelations. For to pretend that the whole rule of life is contained in the Scriptures is to subvert the foundations of governments, families, and corporations, which have never been based on Scriptural injunctions but on universal principles of human nature which manifest themselves in custom and through reason. Even to use the Scriptures wisely, says Hooker, presupposes reason and discretion in man.

Whereas jealousy for the sovereignty of the Creator's will led the Puritans to deprecate any excellence that might be claimed for the creature, reverence for the Creator's wisdom led Hooker to affirm the universal goodness of God's handiwork. He maintains that God's will is simply His affirmation of His own eternal law, and that nothing takes place within the created world except by the law of nature which the Creator has laid down. Like Aristotle, Hooker represents the world in teleological terms by describing each creature as having a natural end toward which it strives. Man's nature, no less than that of other creatures, is governed by wholesome dispositions, which lead him to form societies and to invent useful arts. Moreover, man has been endowed with reason, by means of which he is able to apprehend the laws which govern his estate, as is witnessed by morality, civil justice, and the "law of the nations" (*ius gentium*). According to Hooker, we are just as much bound to acknowledge God's law when it is disclosed in nature as we are bound to acknowledge it when it is revealed in the Scriptures.

The necessity for the Scriptures, says Hooker, arises when the natural must be supplemented by the supernatural. The light of nature would, Hooker believes, have been sufficient for man's spiritual as well as for his physical wants had he remained faithful to the duty taught by reason. The good to which his soul aspires is that union with God which is the natural perfection of the intellect. Because of his disobedience, however, man has lost that good, and nature provides no way of recovering it or of escaping the punishment which follows from violating the law. Thus, in His wisdom, God has seen fit to provide a supernatural way, by the incarnation and death of His Son, and it is this new way, together with the duties it imposes, that the Scriptures declare. Admittedly, the Scriptures also comment on our natural condition and present an excellent summary of the moral law. But the primary purpose for which the Bible was given is to provide that supernatural light which teaches the way of salvation; the Scriptures are perfect only in that they omit nothing necessary for man to reach salvation. Thus, the Romanists are in error when they maintain that the Scriptures must be

supplemented by tradition. But the Puritans are also in error whenever, by their devious exegesis, they undertake to draw from the Scriptures all sorts of instructions which God never intended.

Having thus laid down the respective functions of reason and revelation, Hooker was in a position to formulate his principles of ecclesiastical polity. He makes a distinction which the Presbyterians were unwilling to allow; namely, a distinction between matters of faith and matters of polity. Since the former, says Hooker, have to do with truth, they are the same for all times and places, but the latter have to do with virtue, and hence they vary according to circumstances. It is reasonable, therefore, to believe that the Scriptures contain all that is needful to faith but do not lay down rules for the worship and government of the Churches. The facts are, says Hooker, that at no time has the Church been governed by Scriptural rules (even Calvin's Geneva kept the use of wafer cakes in communion and the custom of godparents at baptism, neither of which is warranted by the Scriptures), nor are the Puritans able to extract that "complete, particular, immutable form of church polity" which they affirm the Scriptures contain. But it is not surprising that immutable laws are not provided by God, for He has given man both reason and discretion, and He requires man to use these natural endowments as far as they avail.

Hooker's position, therefore, with respect to worship and discipline, was that the Church should follow local usage insofar as it serves the goal of salvation. The development of English common law is, he says, an example of the way in which customs grow up and come to have the force of law. When the need arises, particular customs should be changed; but for remedying defects it is not necessary or in the least desirable to pull down the whole social fabric. Similarly, according to Hooker, the visible Church (for matters of polity do not apply to the mystical Body of Christ, which is the invisible Church) is composed of social groups, united in their declaration of the common faith but divided by differences in race, language, custom, location, and civil allegiance. The common end of all churches is to bring men into more perfect fellowship with God through Christ. But how this is to be done may vary from place to place. Feasts and fasts, vestments and ceremonies, tithes and endowments need not be uniform so long as they perform useful functions in the life of the Church.

The Calvinists had arguments besides those based on the Scriptures. As uncompromising champions of pure Christianity against what they considered the anti-Christianity of Rome, they urged that, as a matter of strategy, the Reformed churches in all countries should follow the order of Geneva so as to present a strong and united front against the enemy, and furthermore, that because the danger of apostasy to Rome was an ever-present reality, true Christians should make every effort to avoid any practice which might seem to unite them with Rome. Against these proposals, Hooker defended the English way, which he described as the practice of avoiding sharp breaks with the past and of doing all things in moderation. Writing while the French Catholics and Protestants were engaged in civil war, Hooker was able to maintain that English gradualism is better suited than French radicalism to gain the end which both desired.

In the matter of Church government, Hooker argued for the retention of the episcopacy as against government by presbytery, and he was not inclined to admit that the Genevan and Scottish Churches had any right to their innovation. He denied that the Scriptures give any warrant for the Presbyterian practice of ordaining lay elders, and he maintained that bishops are the successors of the Apostles. An important part of his plea concerned the power of ordination, which he maintained was the prerogative of bishops, although apparently he left room for exceptions.

The most far-reaching difference between the positions advocated by Hooker and by the Presbyterians had to do with the relationship between the Church and the state. Neither party favored the separation of Church and state; the question was simply whether the Church was to be subject to the civil power, or vice versa. The Presbyterians maintained a position similar in some respects to that of Rome. They denied that the magistracy has any say in the government of the Church, but they alleged that the magistracy is under the rule of the Scriptures, which none but the ministry of the Church is authorized to interpret. Hooker, for his part, defended the Elizabethan settlement, according to which Parliament advised the monarch on matters civil, while the hierarchy advised it on matters ecclesiastical, with the government vested in the Crown.

Hooker's calm and moderate plea had little influence in his own day or in the strife-torn years to come. But with the restoration of the episcopacy after the civil wars, his work quickly came into eminence, chiefly as a platform for the Latitudinarian party. In addition, his excellent discussion of natural and civil law, of the role of reason in determining justice, of government by consent of the governed, and of the advantages of gradual change over sudden revolution, was to exercise permanent influence on English political thought.

TRUE CHRISTIANITY

Author: Johann Arndt (1555-1621)
Type of work: Christian ethics
First published: 1606

Principal Ideas Advanced

The purpose of the Holy Scriptures is to restore human nature from the Fall.
To love Christ is to copy Christ's most holy life, to transcribe in one's own life the humility, meekness, and patience of Christ; it is to turn from sin and self-love, in true inward repentance and faith, thereby inheriting the promises of grace and the joy of life eternal.

Johann Arndt, the author of *True Christianity,* was a forerunner of Pietism. Against the orthodoxy of his day Arndt stressed the necessity of an inner experience with God. He had little interest in theological controversy and external formality in religion. Instead, Arndt sought to inspire an inner sense or feeling which corresponds to the performance of external duties. The whole intention and design of his book is to explain how Adam is to die and how Christ is to live in us.

According to Arndt, Christianity consists of a true, lively, and practical faith, which brings forth unfeigned godliness and the proper fruits of righteousness. To be a Christian is not only to believe in Christ, but also to live in Him as He again lives in us.

Conformity to the image of God, according to which man was created, consists in the conformity of man's soul, of his mind and spirit, of his powers and faculties, to the Divine Being and His attributes, virtues, and properties, to the extent that such can be imaged in a creature.

Man ought to understand, Arndt emphasizes, that as the image bearer man is united to God in a union which is the soul's chief tranquillity, its only true rest, from which flow peace, joy, and eternal happiness.

The disobedience of man to God in the Fall of Adam divested man of perfect righteousness and stripped him of the divine image, so that man became spiritually dead, inwardly like the Devil, altogether earthly, and given to self-love and self-will.

Arndt claims that man's fallen nature

is restored in Christ by a new birth, a work of the Holy Spirit, by which a child of damnation and wrath is transformed into a child of salvation and grace. The sinner is made righteous through faith, the Word, and the sacraments. The powers of his soul are enlightened, renewed, and sanctified. Every Christian undergoes a twofold birth; the one is after the flesh, but the other after the spirit; the first is natural, while the second is supernatural, spiritual, holy, and blessed. By the second birth a new being is formed, a new man is begotten and produced, a new creature is born in whom the image of God is again manifest.

True repentance, writes Arndt, is wrought in the soul by the Holy Spirit. Man acknowledges his transgressions and he concedes that God's wrath is justified; he is truly sorry for the evil that he has done, and by faith he now perceives the grace of God in Jesus Christ, and thereby he obtains remission of his sins.

The carnal pleasures are mortified, self-love and pride are crucified, when a man becomes a true Christian. The Christian does not simply cease committing great and outward sins, but he also looks inward and searches the inmost recesses of the mind and heart in order finally to convert himself from self-love to divine love, from worldly lusts to a spiritual life, from a participation in sensual pleasures to an enjoyment of the virtues of Christ, by walking in His steps and believing in His word.

The true Christian tames and mortifies his own will and permits himself to be led by the will of God. The true inward penitent offers a contrite heart as the best and most acceptable sacrifice to God. His heart is heavy with earnest sorrow for having offended a good and gracious God. He is full of fear and trepidation, and yet he is sustained by a lively faith.

True Christian faith, according to Arndt's conception, is a solid trust, a certain and firm persuasion of the grace of God promised to us in Christ. By faith the remission of sins is freely conferred upon us, not for any merits of our own, but for Christ's alone. The forgiveness of our sins is our justification, which is eternal before God, for it is neither of men nor of angels, but it takes place because of the obedience of the Son of God Himself, by His most perfect ransom and precious merits. The good work of Christ is appropriated by us, and applied to us, so that neither the imperfections of our life nor any of our sins now condemn us, for they are covered by the veil of grace.

Where true faith is, there Christ is with all His righteousness and holiness, with all His merits, justification, adoption, and inheritance of life eternal. The habitation of Christ within the heart of the believer is a quickening principle, a vital force, an effectual transformation. Faith transplants the believer into Christ and gives Christ freely to him. The heart is made clean, the soul is sanctified, the seed of God is sown in man, so that the heart is purged of earthly thirsts and easily soars heavenward.

The Kingdom of God now dwells in the heart of the believer and the very law of God is inscribed upon the human heart. No man can lay claim to Christ and His merits without true repentance. Those who cleave to their sins do not profit by Christ.

The formal Christian has the form

of godliness but denies its power. To profess to believe in Christ and then to lead an un-Christian life is not Christian but anti-Christian. Such mockery is blasphemy; such deception is a new crucifixion of Christ. Where the *life* of Christ is not, Arndt insists, Christ is not. Many make a great noise for religion, but their lives are filled with greed and covetousness, with pomp and pride, insincerity, and fraud. To such lives the life of Christ is by its nature opposed. The life of the Christian is nothing else but the most pure and sincere love of God and of men. It issues forth in courtesy, in meekness, patience, mercy, veracity, purity, and simplicity; in contempt of the world and its honors; in refusal of wealth and pleasures; in the denial of ourselves, and in the bearing of the cross continually, with all manner of affliction, for the sake of Christ; and in daily study and thirst after the Kingdom of God, as motivated by a desire to fulfill the divine will in all things.

True Christians are few in number, Arndt declares; God alone knows where and who they are; but whoever they are, Christ both is and will be with them. Anyone who does not imitate the life of Christ has not yet seriously repented and is not to be reputed a true child of God. For the sake of Christ, the Christian must be willing to die to all his sins, to his own self, and to the world.

Man ought to love nothing other than God, and it is impossible to love God unless a person is sincerely displeased with all his sins. Self-love corrupts true judgment, expels virtue, and blinds the understanding.

Contempt of ourselves is the first step to obtaining acceptance with God, Arndt writes. To find grace and mercy, a Christian ought to declare himself unworthy in his own judgment, and he ought to trust only in the heavenly grace of Jesus Christ.

Not the Christian name, but a Christian life is the mark of the true Christian, a life of love and humility, unspotted by sin, and marked by perfect righteousness.

Arndt concludes by insisting that Christ alone is the medicine of the soul, the source of honor, the fount of good works, and a remedy against all calumnies. Christ crucified is ever before us as a book of life, from which we may learn the sacred wisdom of God. The crucified Christ presents us with the deplorable sight of our sins, and He enables us to recover from the Fall by leading us to a sight of the most gracious will, providence, and fatherly care of God.

THE DECLARATION OF SENTIMENTS

Author: Jacobus Arminius (1560-1609)
Type of work: Theology
First published: 1608

PRINCIPAL IDEAS ADVANCED

The view of predestination which holds that God has decreed to save particular persons and to condemn others without any consideration of their own free decisions is not contained in the writings of Scripture, nor is it compatible with the justice, wisdom, and goodness of God, nor with the nature of man, created in the image of God.

God has rather decreed to appoint His Son as the redeemer of mankind so that those who repent and persevere will be saved.

God's decree to save and to damn particular persons has its foundation in His foreknowledge, so that He elects those whom He knows will believe and He condemns those whom He knows will reject the grace offered to them.

Jacobus Arminius was born in the Netherlands in 1560. From 1603 until his death in 1609 he served the University of Leyden as a Professor of Divinity. His theological views are distinctive for a particular theory of predestination which bears his name. Most significant among his collected works, translated from the Latin in three volumes, are his *Apology against Thirty-One Defamatory Articles* (1609) and his *Declaration of Sentiments* (1608). In both these works Arminius attempts to vindicate himself against attacks that had been made by those who opposed his views on predestination and accused him of attempting to introduce innovations into theology.

The system of doctrine defended by Arminius has exerted considerable influence and has been the source of much controversy. It was formally condemned by the Synod of Dort which convened from November of 1618 to May 1619, since the supporters of Arminius presented a Remonstrance against the decisions of the Synod of Dort, they were at first known as Remonstrants, but in subsequent years they were designated as Arminians.

In his *Declaration of Sentiments* Arminius rejects the views of predestination that were held in his day. It

was believed that God had precisely and absolutely decreed to save certain men by His grace or mercy, and to condemn others by His justice. God had, moreover, made such a decree without any consideration of righteousness or sin, obedience or disobedience, on the part of any one class of men.

In order to execute His decree, it was further held, God determined to create Adam, and all men in him, in a state of original righteousness; besides which God then ordained them to commit sin, that they might become guilty of eternal condemnation and be deprived of original righteousness.

God had, moreover, according to the conventional view of predestination, positively willed to save certain persons, and to that end He had decreed them not only to salvation but also to the means of salvation. God had decreed to conduct and to bring such persons to faith in Christ Jesus and to perseverance in that faith. God would lead such persons to these results by a grace that is irresistible, so that it would not be possible for those He has elected to do anything other than believe, persevere in faith, and be saved.

By His absolute will God had foreordained some people to perdition and had decreed to deny to them that grace which is necessary and sufficient for salvation. Since He would not in reality confer grace upon them, they would be placed neither in a condition of possible salvation nor in any capacity for believing or for being saved.

Some theologians of Arminius's day presented a more modified view than the conventional one just described. They refused to lay down the Creation or the Fall as a mediate cause foreordained by God for the execution of the preceding degree of predestination. Others did not allow any part of election and reprobation to begin until after the Fall of man.

No matter how this doctrine of predestination was modified, Arminius found it unacceptable in its currently accepted formulations. Arminius argues that such a doctrine is no part of the foundations of Christianity. Christianity is founded on the decree of God by which Christ is appointed to be the Savior and Head of those who will be made heirs of salvation. The doctrine of predestination does not comprise within it the whole or any part of the Gospel, Arminius insists. The Gospel consists partly of an injunction to repent and believe, and partly of a promise to bestow forgiveness of sins, the grace of the Spirit, and eternal life. The doctrine of predestination does not even tell us what kind of men God has predested; such a doctrine embraces a mystery known only to God, a mystery as to which persons are to be saved and how many. It is a doctrine that is not necessary to salvation, either as an object of knowledge, belief, hope, or performance.

Arminius continues by pointing out that the doctrine of predestination was never admitted, decreed, or approved in any council, either general or particular, for the first six hundred years after Christ. Moreover, none of those doctors of the Church who held orthodox views for the first six hundred years after Christ ever propounded or approved this doctrine. It does not even agree with the harmony of the confession published in the name of the Reformed and Protestant Churches at Geneva, and it is doubtful whether it agrees with the Belgic Confession and the Heidelberg Catechism.

When strictly maintained, Arminius argues, the doctrine of predestination is repugnant to God's wisdom because it represents Him as decreeing something for an end which is not good; namely, eternal perdition. The doctrine is repugnant to the justice of God because it affirms that God has absolutely willed to save certain individuals and has decreed their salvation without having any regard for their righteousness or obedience. It is opposed to His justice because it affirms that God wishes to subject His creatures to misery, although He does not consider the creature to be a sinner. The doctrine is repugnant to the goodness of God, a goodness which is a disposition in God to communicate His own goodness insofar as His justice considers it to be proper. The doctrine of predestination ascribes to God the act of willing the greatest evil to his creatures; and it claims that from all eternity He preordained that evil for them, even before He determined to bestow any good upon them.

Such a doctrine, Arminius writes, is contrary to the nature of man, for man was created after the divine image, which consists of the knowledge of God and holiness; thus, man was qualified, empowered, and placed under obligation to love, worship, and serve

God. The doctrine is inconsistent with the freedom of man's will, in which, and with which, man was created; furthermore, the doctrine is prejudicial to man's inclinations and to his capacity for the eternal fruition of salvation in that the majority of men are thought to be prevented from salvation not in consequence of any preceding sin, but solely because of predestination.

The strict view of predestination is diametrically opposed to the act of creation, Arminius continues. To intend the eternal perdition of a creature is not to communicate a good, but a preparation for the greatest evil. Reprobation is an act of hatred, an act which derives its origin from hatred, whereas creation is the communication of good; creation is a perfect act of God, by which He manifests His wisdom, goodness, and omnipotence, and creation is therefore not subordinate to any other preceding act of God.

The doctrine of predestination is at open hostility with the nature of eternal life and eternal death. The former is described as a crown of righteousness and the latter as the wages of sin, so that neither the one nor the other is determined by decree apart from any consideration of sin and obedience.

The doctrine is also inconsistent with the nature and properties of sin, Arminius argues. If a person is under the unavoidable necessity of sinning because of the divine decree, sin could not be called disobedience and rebellion, nor could it be the cause which moves the divine will to reprobate.

Predestination is likewise repugnant to the nature of divine grace, Arminius claims, for predestination interferes with free will, and makes grace irresistible. The doctrine is injurious to the glory of God for, according to the doctrine, God is the author of sin, so that in fact God moves to sin by an act that is unavoidable. Moreover, the doctrine is highly dishonorable to Jesus Christ, since it excludes Christ from that decree of predestination which predestinates the end, and it does not make Christ the foundation of election.

Such a doctrine is also hurtful to the salvation of men; it discourages solicitude about being converted from sin unto God; it extinguishes zeal for prayer and good works. It takes away the fear and trembling with which we are commanded to work out our own salvation, and it produces a despair. It inverts the order of the Gospel and is in open hostility to its ministry, and it very easily renders pastors negligent. It subverts the very foundation of religion by undermining a love for justice and hatred of sin.

In contradistinction to the generally accepted opinion, Arminius held that with respect to the salvation of sinful man, the first absolute decree of God was to appoint His son, Jesus Christ, as Mediator and Savior, who by His own death might destroy sin, and by His obedience might obtain the lost salvation and communicate it by His own virtue.

The first decree was followed by a second decree in which God decreed to receive into favor those who repent and believe, and, in Christ, for His sake and through Him, to effect the salvation of such penitents and believers as persevered to the end, but to damn as aliens from Christ and to leave in sin, and under wrath, all unbelievers and impenitent persons.

In a third divine decree God decreed to administer in an efficacious and in a sufficient manner the means which are necessary for faith and repentance; and He decreed to have such administration instituted according to divine wisdom and justice.

In a fourth decree God decreed to save and to damn certain particular persons. This decree had its foundation, however, in the foreknowledge of God. From all eternity God knows those individuals who will, through His prevenient grace, believe, and who through his subsequent grace will persevere, and He also knows those who will not believe and will not persevere.

Such a view of predestination is the sum and substance of the Gospel, Arminius writes. This doctrine is not subject to any of the preceding criticisms. For in His providence, God both wills and performs good acts, whereas He only freely permits those which are evil. In his primitive condition, after creation, man was enabled to perform the truly good, with the assistance of divine grace. In his fallen state, man, of and by himself, is in-

capable of thinking, willing, or doing what is really good. He must first be regenerated and renewed by the Holy Spirit, and even then he is in constant need of divine grace. To the latter is to be ascribed the commencement, the continuance, and the consummation of all good. For grace is a gratuitous affection by which God looks kindly towards a sinner and gives His Son so that whoever believes in Him inherits eternal life and is justified in the eyes of God. Grace is an infusion, into the human understanding, will, and affections, of the gifts of the Holy Spirit, of faith, hope, and charity, without which man is unable to do anything good. Grace is the perpetual assistance which enables the regenerate man actually to will what is good; it enables God and man to will and to work together, so that man may do the good that He wills. The grace imparted by the Holy Spirit is sufficient to enable men to repent, and to believe and keep the commandments of God.

INTRODUCTION TO THE DEVOUT LIFE

Author: Saint Francis of Sales (1567-1622)
Type of work: Spiritual counsel
First published: 1609

Principal Ideas Advanced

The religious life is not a special vocation for a few Christians, but a possibility and so a duty for all.

It is not achieved without ordered discipline, which makes possible a steady progression away from sin and towards virtue.

Each stage of the devout life has its own basic requirements, and we are shown how we can practice the disciplines of meditation and prayer.

The *Introduction to the Devout Life* was the outcome of prolonged experi-

ence as a director of souls. As Provost of Geneva, Francis of Sales had offered counsel to men and women in search of spiritual guidance, and he had written a large number of letters dealing with specific problems or perplexities. He had accumulated a good deal of material, and the incentive to set it in due order came from his association with Mme. de Charmoisy, an earnest and able woman married to a relative of his, who placed herself under St. Francis's direction. For her, St. Francis composed a series of letters of instruction, and he then rearranged and rewrote the material and published it as the *Introduction to the Devout Life*. St. Francis was perfectly aware that his work represented a breach with tradition. He was a bishop (though, since Geneva was his see, he was nonresident), and it had always been assumed that bishops would be concerned with practical affairs. But it seemed to him eminently appropriate that a chief shepherd should guide and direct men's souls. Moreover, it had previously been taken for granted that a spiritual director would chiefly be preoccupied with the needs of those who, having isolated themselves, could give their whole attention to such matters. "Those who have treated of devotion," he wrote, "have almost all had in mind the instruction of persons very much withdrawn from the society of the world, or at all events they have taught a kind of devotion which leads to this complete withdrawal. My intention is to instruct those who live in towns, in households, at the court, and who, by reason of their circumstances, are obliged to lead an ordinary life in outward show." It had been generally assumed that such people, involved as they were in secular activities, could not be expected to give any serious thought to devotion. But St. Francis would not concede this point; he writes that "a vigorous and constant soul can live in the world without receiving any worldly taint." He concedes that it will not be an easy task; those who undertake it will need help, and St. Francis proposes to provide it. He states that he has no illusions about the difficulties which are involved in living a disciplined religious life in secular surroundings, and he expresses his hope that his little book will encourage those who have hitherto assumed that the undertaking is impractical.

The *Introduction to the Devout Life* was planned with great care, and St. Francis himself points out to the reader the general pattern which this guide book of the spiritual life will follow. He assumes that anyone who embarks upon a course of devotion must have responded to holy impulses, but at first these may represent no more than an intermittent desire to be better than in the past. These vague promptings must therefore be confirmed and consolidated, and to this end St. Francis lays down a course of simple meditations. Initially, of course, he defines devotion (which "is no other thing than a true love of God"), he describes its nature and its excellence, and he demonstrates its relevance to all kinds of life. There is no single pattern of holiness, he claims. The monk pursues one path, the bishop another; in spite of their different activities both strive after the same end. In the same way the married person, the soldier, the courtier, the lawyer may exercise a genuine religious vocation in a diversity of ways, but all aim at true devotion. And here St. Francis observes that most of the patriarchs and holy men of scripture were engaged in callings which took them into the world and kept them there. But good will requires guidance, and a spiritual director is consequently necessary.

St. Francis was aware that discipline is an inseparable part of devotion and that discipline springs from the simple fact that our lives stand in need of cleansing and reform. We must admit our involvement in mortal sin and turn from it. We must learn not only to restrain the evil act but also to rebuke the evil impulse. But this can be achieved only if we train ourselves to control our appetites and desires. At this point the shrewd and practical wisdom which marks the *Introduction* begins to emerge. In order to help us to root "sin and the principal affections to sin" from our hearts, St. Francis sets out a series of meditations, one for each day, to be used in a prescribed order.

The subject of the first meditation is creation; we then turn to the end for which we were created, the benefits which God bestows upon us, the nature of sin, the significance of death, the inevitability of judgment, the pains of Hell, and the joys of Heaven. The last two meditations deal with the decisive choices which the believer makes: the way he "elects" Heaven and selects the devout life.

The series of meditations follows a clear sequence, and each one is developed according to a simple pattern. The believer first prepares himself for meditation; he consciously places himself in the presence of God and asks for guidance and inspiration. Next he ponders, one by one, the chief "considerations," by which St. Francis means the essential facts which determine our posture and position with regard to the subject under study. This

kind of serious reflection naturally awakens emotional responses ("affections") and prompts some kind of moral decision ("resolution"). In this section, St. Francis sets forth as many as half a dozen points which ought to be embraced by our widening reflection. As the meditation draws to a conclusion, the neophyte is instructed to include at least three steps: thanksgiving for God's mercies as these are suggested by the subject under consideration; oblation, in which he offers himself to God; petition, which invokes God's aid in bringing to good effect the affections and resolutions awakened by the meditation. Finally, the believer pauses to consider in retrospect what has engaged his mind and soul, and to "gather a little nosegay of devotion from the considerations which he has made, in order to inhale its perfume throughout the day."

At this point, St. Francis's method appears with special clarity. His system is devised to meet the needs of ordinary people. It does not make unrealistic demands upon time, but sets forth step by step a means by which any earnest seeker can discipline his life. The wisdom of St. Francis's approach is based on a profound understanding of the human mind. He is aware of the difficulties involved; he asks enough to be demanding, but not so much as to be discouraging. Renouncing the old life means that we forsake not evil in general, but those forms of it to which we happen to be inclined. So he offers directions for turning away from venial sins, from "affection to useless and dangerous things," and from evil inclinations.

The purpose of the *Introduction* is primarily positive, and St. Francis therefore turns to the constructive disciplines which lift the soul to God. Prayer, of course, is of supreme importance, but many people fail in this discipline because they are uninstructed. "Above all," says St. Francis, "I recommend to you prayer of the mind and heart, and especially that which has for its subject the life and passion of our Lord; for by beholding him often in meditation, your whole soul will be filled with him; you will learn his disposition, and you will form your actions after the model of his." But St. Francis is too wise to believe that people will learn how to pray by being exhorted to do so. Therefore he sets forth a system of meditation. The first step is to master the art of placing oneself in the presence of God, and here St. Francis enumerates four ways by which one can learn to do so. One should begin with "a lively and attentive apprehension of the omnipresence of God"; then one realizes that the God who is everywhere is, in a special way, in the heart of the worshiper; the third stage is to realize the particular concern which the Savior feels for all His people; the fourth is to use the imagination to visualize Christ in His concrete acts of mercy and love, so that by dwelling in His presence one can dwell in the presence of God. But this is by no means the whole essence of preparation for prayer. One should also specifically invoke God's aid and ponder the mystery of His grace. Finally, one turns to "affections" and "consideration" and recapitulation.

The devout life is one in which the virtues of Christian discipleship are increasingly manifested, writes Francis. But even the devout man needs counsel. Consequently St. Francis considers one by one the various virtues which ought to appear more consistently in the devout lives. He begins with patience, and then he proceeds to humility, both as an outward aspect and as inward disposition. He shows how humility helps us to come to terms with our own nature, and with what wisdom it must be exercised, lest we gain a reputation for hypocrisy. He points out the need of gentleness in our dealings with others and the inescapable demand that we learn to control our anger. By the same token, we should treat ourselves with similar restraint, "never fretting at ourselves or at our imperfections." It is one thing to have a firm and dispassionate dislike of our faults; it is another to nag ourselves about them. In discharging our daily tasks we must always be diligent and careful, never anxious or worried. Chastity must be preserved but need not be equated with celibacy: St. Francis holds virginity in high esteem but has wise counsel for married people, and he insists on the honorableness of the marriage bed. He dwells on the importance of poverty of spirit—which need not be incompatible with the possession of wealth. He is concerned that the true nature of friendship be appreciated. There are vain friendships and evil ones, but when properly understood friendship is one of God's good gifts, and it should be cherished in the spirit of gratitude. St. Francis has wise words on company; he explains how to use it and when to withdraw from it. He examines clothes and the standards by which we judge them; speech, and the standards to which it should conform; games and recreations, and the ways of determining their moral value. Some forms of recreation are permissible but dangerous, and here we need to exercise great care. In addition we must learn to be faithful both on great occasions and on small ones, and in all things we must manifest a just and reasonable spirit.

It is never a simple matter to live a life marked by such virtues. The Christian will always encounter temptations; he must be prepared to meet them. St. Francis advises everyone to learn a proper measure of indifference to the comments of the children of this world. We shall find that we are constantly in need of courage. St. Francis was not concerned merely to emphasize the fact of temptation; he wanted to help the Christian to understand its nature and overcome its power. He distinguishes between small temptations and great ones, and he shows how each type is to be mastered.

What St. Francis envisages is a regular course of discipline, renewed year by year, by means of which the Christian can steadily grow in grace. To achieve spiritual growth involves careful examination of ourselves and of our progress: How do we stand toward God? Have we advanced in understanding and mastery of ourselves? Do our relationships with others adequately reflect our spiritual concerns?

Then, with the care which characterizes all his work, St. Francis turns to the enumeration of "considerations" which will promote our advance. We must dwell on the serious importance of the soul and the high excellence of the virtues. We must dwell on the example of the saints, and we must meditate deeply on the love which Christ bears us. We must lose ourselves in the contemplation of the eternal love of God for us. Then we must make sure that all these thoughts and emotions issue regularly in such conduct as both reflect and confirm them.

Anyone who reads the *Introduction to the Devout Life* will have no difficulty in understanding its great and continuing influence. It provides the foundation for one of the recognized systems of spiritual direction in the Roman Church. In all Christian bodies, thousands have found, and still find, that this book of religious counsel is sane, wise, deeply perceptive, and unfailingly helpful.

THE TRUTH OF THE CHRISTIAN RELIGION

Author: Hugo Grotius (1583-1645)
Type of work: Apologetics
First published: 1622

PRINCIPAL IDEAS ADVANCED

That the Christian religion is more reasonable and more worthy of acceptance than any other religion is evident from the authority and trustworthiness of its sacred books, from the superiority of its precepts and doctrines, and from the inferior teachings of paganism, Judaism, and Islam.

The truth of the Christian religion is as certain as the truth of reason, as the evidence of the senses, and as other truths based upon the testimony of trustworthy witnesses.

The Truth of the Christian Religion, written by Hugo Grotius in 1622, seeks to demonstrate that Christianity is true by examining the evidence in its support, and by comparing Christianity with pagan religion, Judaism, and Mohammedanism.

The work is divided into six books. Book One seeks to demonstrate that there is but one all-perfect God who is the cause of all things and the Governor of the universe. Book Two offers arguments in support of the thesis that Christianity is true and that it excels all other religions. Book Three deals with the authority of the Old and New Testaments, and Books Four, Five, and Six, respectively, compare Christianity with paganism, Judaism, and Mohammedanism to demonstrate that Christianity alone is the true religion, the religion which man must embrace if he is to attain happiness after this life.

Religion is not foolish or empty, Grotius writes, since the existence of God is proven by the rational necessity of a first cause and by the universal assent of every nation. By our senses we observe that some things have a beginning and cannot be the cause of their own existence, for if they were self-caused, they would have been before they were, which is impossible. Such contingent things must then have derived their existence from something else; namely, from God, a cause which never had a beginning but exists necessarily. What exists necessarily cannot be a species of beings and must therefore be a single being, to which all perfection belongs in an infinite degree; therefore, God is a living infinite God, eternal, omnipotent, omniscient, and completely good.

When it is said that God is the cause of all things that have a real existence, writes Grotius, we do not mean that God is the cause of evil actions, for man and some other intelligences superior to man were created by God with a liberty of acting, and liberty is not itself evil although it may be the cause of what is evil.

That the world is governed by the providence of God is evident from the fact that men and animals provide for their young, which perfection, as it is a part of goodness, ought not to be excluded from God. An all-wise, omnipotent being cannot but know, direct, and govern everything which is done, for He seeks always to promote the good of the whole.

God is concerned with the deeds of men, Grotius assures the reader. Since in this life the wicked often go unpunished while the righteous suffer, we can expect judgment after this life, an expectation confirmed by the traditions of almost all civilized people, which is in no way repugnant to reason, but is rather supported by a natural desire of immortality and by a sense of impending judgment.

That the Christian religion is most true and certain is evident from certain matters of fact and from the nature of its doctrine. That there was such a person as Jesus, that He died an ignominious death and yet was worshiped after His death by wise men, is generally acknowledged, not only by Christians, but also by Jewish and pagan sources.

That Jesus was worshiped after His death by wise men is explicable solely on the assumption that they found that the reports concerning His miracles and resurrection were true and founded upon the sufficient testimony of credible witnesses.

There is no reason, Grotius insists, to assume that the belief in the Resurrection of Jesus is false, for the belief does not involve the contradiction of affirming that the same person was alive and dead at the same time; it asserts, rather, that a dead man was restored to life by the power of the One who first gave life to man. By raising Christ from the dead, God the Father put his seal of approval upon the work of his Son and confirmed the truth of His doctrine.

Not only is the Christian religion based upon historical facts, Grotius argues, but its very doctrines are inherently superior to all others. The worship that it prescribes, the rewards that it offers, the precepts it enjoins, and the method by which it is to be propagated are in keeping with man's moral nature and with a conception of an all-wise, all-good, and all-powerful God; Christianity is therefore more excellent, more perfect, and more worthy of devotion than any other religion.

The reward promised by Christ to His disciples goes beyond earthly pleasures, writes Grotius. The end of man is another life after this, in which there is no death, pain, or sorrow, but only the highest joy, not only in the soul, but in the resurrected body. Man will behold God; all things will be glorified.

The Christian religion excels all other religions in the exceeding purity and holiness of its precepts, both in the worship of God, and in other particulars. Christian worship is free of cruelty, of human sacrifice and lewdness. It teaches men to worship God with a pure mind and through the performance of right acts. The chief part of religion consists in a steadfast faith, sincere obedience, trust in God's promises, and in a true love both of God and of one's neighbor, not in a servile obedience prompted by fear of punishment. Christian service is a joyful service, which is enjoined upon the believer, who prays not for riches and honor, but only for such things as are for the glory of God, for whatever leads to eternity, for the pardon of past sins, and for the inspiration of the Holy Spirit.

The Christian religion further excels all others in the manner in which it was delivered and propagated. The divine nature of its teacher is apparent from the testimony of Jesus' disciples, who described Him as being without sin. What He commanded others to do, He did himself; He was faithful to God throughout his life; He was a lover of mankind, even of His persecutors. He was seen after His return to life, and He was taken up into Heaven, where He obtained the highest power; He was himself possessed with the glory that He promised. His doctrines spread with remarkable success, in spite of persecution and without the use of force, so that their very success ought to be regarded as greater than any miracle.

To understand fully the Christian religion, Grotius avers, it is necessary to go to the books that contain it. The books of the New Testament were written by those whose names they bear. The authors knew about the matters of which they wrote, and since they had no desire to lie, what they said must be true, since falsity proceeds either from hypocrisy or ignorance. God has in fact given remarkable testimony to the sincerity of the authors of the New Testament by working miracles through them.

The writings of the New Testament

contain nothing that is impossible nor disagreeable to reason. The books are free of inconsistencies, and what they declare is further confirmed by the books of the Old Testament and by the records of the Jewish religion.

Present-day Judaism, while superior to paganism, has only a part and the beginning of the truth, writes Grotius. The Jews are the offspring of holy men; they were often visited by the prophets of God. The Messiah was born of them, and they were the first teachers of Christianity.

The Jews ought not to look upon Christians as their enemies, Grotius declares; rather they ought to accept the miracles of Christ as sufficiently attested and as based upon the same kind of evidence which persuades the Jews of the miracles done by Moses and Elisha.

The authority of a doctrine cannot be more effectually recommended to man by God than by the working of miracles. The miracles of Christ ought, therefore, to be taken as signs of the truth of what Jesus taught. He urged the worship of the true God and taught men to reverence the writings of Moses. Jesus himself observed the Law of Moses when on earth; no part of the ancient Law was subsequently abolished, except whatever precepts had no intrinsic goodness in them.

Jesus ought to be accepted by the Jews as their own Messiah, says Grotius; He fulfills the extraordinary promise of the Messiah which is found in the books of the Old Testament itself. That He was of the seed of David, that He was born of a virgin, healed the sick, was the instructor of all nations, and suffered and died—all these truths were foretold by the prophets.

The further superiority of Christianity to paganism and Mohammedanism is readily seen, Grotius contends. Reason alone is sufficient to show that there is but one God, the cause of all things. It is foolish to pay homage to many deities and spirits, some of which are evil. To worship departed men, stars, gross matter, brute creatures, and things lacking real existence is most disagreeable to right reason.

The wisest heathens shared many of the principal beliefs of the Christian religion; for instance, that religion does not consist of ceremonies but is in the heart, that the soul is immortal, and that the divine nature can be joined to the human. What is found as disorganized belief among the pagans is unified by the Christian religion, and what is difficult to believe in Christianity is matched in paganism by things far more incredible.

A confrontation of Christianity and Mohammedanism shows that the latter is directly opposed to Christianity, writes Grotius. Mohammedanism is calculated for bloodshed; it delights much in ceremonies, and it encourages belief while refusing critical examination.

Mohammed and his followers admit that Jesus, Moses, and the disciples were sent by God, and yet many things in the Koran contradict their teachings. For example, the Apostles teach that Jesus died on the cross, rose again from the dead, and was seen by many persons; Mohammed says that Jesus was secretly taken into Heaven before the Crucifixion, and that what was fixed to the cross was only an effigy of Him.

To assert that the Koran is uncorrupted and that the writings of Moses and of the disciples of Jesus are corrupted overlooks the fact that copies of the Gospels in many languages were disseminated throughout the world and have been preserved by many sects.

A further comparison of Christianity and Islam discloses the superiority of the former, continues Grotius. Mohammed says that Jesus was the promised Messiah, born without a human father; that He healed the sick and restored the dead to life; and that He was taken up into Heaven. Mohammed says that he himself was sent with arms, not miracles; and the body of Mohammed rests in the grave. Christianity was propagated by miracles and by the blood of the martyrs; the teachers of Islam did not endure any grievous troubles, nor do they undergo death for their faith. Mohammedanism spread by the sword; its precepts are also inferior in that divorce is permitted, revenge is enjoined, and needless rituals and prohibitions are reintroduced.

Grotius concludes his apology by arguing that Christians can safely put their trust in the God, who made all things, and they may be fully persuaded that He takes care of man; and furthermore, Christians can have faith in Jesus, since there is no other Savior. The holy doctrine of Christ is to be preserved as a valuable treasure, and the Scriptures are to be read by Christians prepared to obey God; through being faithful, they will inherit a future happiness.

THE WAY TO CHRIST

Author: Jakob Boehme (1575-1624)
Type of work: Mystical theology
First published: 1623-1682

PRINCIPAL IDEAS ADVANCED

Deity exhibits a threefold nature as Father, Son, and Holy Spirit; the first being Abyss, or Ungrund, *which is beyond all the determinate realities of nature and creation, and which also exhibits opposing aspects of love and wrath; the second, or Son, being the wisdom and love which redeems man as well as the rest of creation; the third being the vitality in nature and creation.*

Man, who is a creation or objectivation of God, has a twofold nature, one which aspires to communion with God, and the other which persists in the arrogant self-centeredness which is the source of evil.

Nature, or creation, also shows a twofold aspect, being in itself alienation from God and hence a lower and evil realm, yet being in relation to Deity the sacramental realm in which God is manifested.

The writings and life of Jakob Boehme may both be regarded as the expression of the mystical exaltation which was literally the defining characteristic of this remarkable man. The claim he made for one of his writings, that "not Art but the Holy Spirit wrote this," might well be extended to include all his numerous writings, and as far as the facts can now be made out, his life as well. The great illumination in which, as Boehme put it, "the Gate was opened to me" occurred in 1600 at the age of twenty-four, and the impact of this experience may be seen in the whole subsequent course of his life. Yet it is also important to note that from childhood onward a kind of direct religious perception of great clarity and intensity was a quality of all Boehme's life and experience.

He lived his entire life, except for a few months of enforced exile, in his native town of Goerlitz in Germany. His parents were farmers, but apparently because of delicate health he was apprenticed to the cobbler's trade. In 1599 he married a butcher's daughter. Of this happy union were born four sons and probably two daughters.

Following the illumination of 1600, Boehme began to write down his experiences. However, his first book *Aurora* did not appear until 1612. It aroused the violent opposition of the Lutheran pastor, Gregorius Richter, who secured from the local government a prohibition of any further writing by the inspired shoemaker. Boehme respected this ban until 1618, when he began again to write and publish his mystical reflections, which seemed to Richter dangerous heresies.

The Three Principles appeared in 1619, *The Three-fold Life of Man, Answers to the Forty Questions of the Soul, The Six Great Points,* and other books in 1620, and *Signatura rerum* in 1621. Yet the bulk of Boehme's writing was published posthumously. The present volumes, *The Way to Christ,* was actually not originally written as a single book, but as a series of tracts on the common theme of redemption in Christ. They were written between 1622 and 1624, and at least two of them were unfinished at the author's death in 1624. In that year a friend published three of them, *Of True Repentance, Of True Resignation,* and the *Supersensual Life* under the title *The Way to Christ.* A second edition, which followed four years later, added two more tracts, and by the 1682 edition of Boehme's works the number had grown to eight. The first English translation was made in 1644. The most recent English translation by John Stoudt in 1947 includes seven tracts, omitting *On The Four Complexions* because of its antiquated psychology.

Pastor Richter continued to attack Boehme, who responded with a dignified defense of *The Way to Christ.* Opposition led to a few months of exile in Dresden and other cities in 1624, where the greatness of his thought was acknowledged and acclaimed. He returned home to Goerlitz later the same year, where he died on November 20.

Boehme's influence on subsequent religious and philosophic thought has been strong and varied. The year of his death was also the year of George Fox's birth, symbolizing Boehme's influence on Fox and the Quakers. An equally great impact may be seen on the Anglican, William Law. Romantic philosophers and literary men in Germany, England, and America show an influence of which Hegel, Schelling, and Emerson are only three illustrations.

Boehme's viewpoint has been characterized as Christian Gnosticism and theosophy. Yet these terms are accurately descriptive only if they are taken in a strictly etymological sense, designating a kind of knowledge which occurs as a direct aspect of religious experience and which illuminates the mysteries of God and the world. Boehme's writings everywhere assume that there is such a knowledge and that he is in possession of at least some aspects of it.

Other identifiable influences on Boehme's mind range from the Bible, which he knew thoroughly and quoted perceptively, through the tradition of western mysticism to the alchemy of Paracelsus. This last influence affected his vocabulary more than it did the content of his message.

Boehme's writing is remarkably objective in character. It is about God and the world, rather than himself. Yet, between the lines there is a clear and persistent symbolic reference to the human self and its relation to ultimate reality. Also, Boehme's writing is a product of the tragic time of war and upheaval in which he lived. The fascination shown in his writings for evil, conflict, and tragedy must be regarded as a response to his age.

One must not neglect to add that Boehme is a powerful religious genius expressing through his writings his own unique vision. In this respect, he has been characterized as the last great Western mystic.

His system of thought is obscure, complex, and not everywhere consistent. Also, the importance of the system in relation to specific individual insights varies widely from document to document. The most basic category of the system is the threefold nature of Deity as Father, Son, and Holy Spirit, with the Father generally characterized as the *Ungrund* or Abyss. The Abyss is literally no-thing, for it is beyond the realm of nature and creatureliness where things exist. He (or It) is conceived voluntaristically, and exhibits two wills, respectively good and evil, love and wrath, light and darkness. The concept of Deity or Godhead as Abyss may be regarded as the result of Boehme's attempt to find onto-logical foundation for his radical view of human freedom. It is a freedom pregnant with all the possibilities of evil, conflict, and tragedy.

In contrast to the Father, the Son is all light and wisdom, and to Him the enlightened soul clings in faith and salvation. The Son is the redeemer from all the world's tragic evil. Boehme's conception of the Virgin Sophia is in effect a mystical feminine rendering of the Logos. The third person of the Trinity is an expression of the indwelling vitalities which guide the course of the world upward to God. The world of nature and creature is an objectification, or as Boehme put it, an exhalation or emanation of deity.

Boehme's interpretation of mysticism emphasizes voluntarism and freedom in both God and man. Like God, man has two wills, one an aspiration toward God, and the other an arrogant self-centeredness, which is the fruitful and characteristic source of evil in human life. The radical and irreducible freedom of man is, according to Boehme, to be redeemed or saved in Christ. Hence, the importance of *The Way to Christ* in the author's whole work and system of thought.

Of the seven treatises which comprise *The Way to Christ,* all but one are essentially religious in nature, and that one, entitled *Of Divine Contemplation,* while basically philosophical, is by no means irrelevant to religion.

The other six can be characterized as working documents emerging from the author's full and rich religious life. Taken as a group, these essays constitute a kind of last testament from the author.

The first of the tracts, entitled *Of True Repentance*, was written in 1622 and 1623, and its purpose is accurately characterized in the title. The essay alternates between exposition of the theme and prayers and confessions which exemplify the process of repentance. There is also dialogue with the reader, who is assumed to be a fellow traveler on the road to repentance. There are also instructions for resistance of temptation. The quality of religious life here expressed is intense, clear, and profoundly Christian.

The treatise contains an extended dialogue between the soul and the Virgin Sophia. The latter has been likened to the world-soul of Hegel or Goethe, yet, as previously indicated, a kind of mystical feminine interpretation of the Logos seems a more appropriate and adequate characterization. Boehme uses a wealth of erotic imagery, already current in the tradition of mysticism, to characterize the religious life and its unique quality of immediate knowledge. "The Gates of the Paradisiacal Rose-garden are only understood by those children of Christ who have experienced it," he writes, or again he asserts of repentance, "The Person who wants to reach divine contemplation and speak with God within himself must follow this Process and then he will reach it."

The second tract, *Of True Resignation*, deals with the resignation of the creaturely and natural self to God. Resignation means not impersonal or stoical acquiescence, or Oriental oblitera-

tion of selfhood, but rather a conforming of the human will to God. It is the want of this conformity which is the source of evil in all its manifold aspects. In this respect, the treatise might be characterized as an inquiry into the origin and conquest of evil.

The discussion begins with a distinction between the arrogant vanity of the creature taken in himself and the achievement of a will in harmony with God. This leads to a distinction between the God-centered reason, which is Eternal Light, and the man-centered reason, which boasts its egocentric viewpoint.

The process of resignation by which the latter is changed into the former is no mere acquiescence or negation of selfhood, but a dynamic transformation of the human will. "There is no other way to God than through a new mind which turns away from evil and enters into repentance for past sins, departing from iniquity, willing it no more but enveloping its will in Christ's Death. . . ."

Both man's faith and God's grace are paradoxically related in the process of repentance. The whole process, moreover, is essentially inward. Externalities of religion are in themselves completely futile. Boehme never tires of saying that the realities of religion achieve authenticity only in proportion to their inwardness.

Of Regeneration, or, Of the New Birth, written in 1622, continues many of the lines of thought of the first two tracts. Regeneration is held to consist of replacing the old and evil will of Adam with the new will of Christ in a man's life. The old and evil will is characterized as it emerges in Adam and is reproduced in his descendants. Its taproot is a self-centered and evil imagination, and its outcome is a replacement of the divine light and vitality by fleshly vanity, darkness, and evil imagination.

Boehme speculates concerning the nature of the Fall of Adam, concluding that it took place not with the eating of the fatal apple, but in Adam's sleep, during which it is asserted that "he died to the angelical world . . . and . . . departed from the eternal image which was of God's generation." During this same sleep Eve was taken from Adam's rib. Upon awakening, both man and woman began their fallen life of evil and external imagination.

The fourth treatise, *Of the Supersensual Life, A Dialogue Between a Scholar and His Master,* was also written in 1622. The Disciple opens the conversation by asking how he may come to the "supersensual life" in which he sees God and hears him speak. The Master replies that to do this he must "leap" into the realm beyond natural and creaturely reality. Asked if it is far, the Master replies, "It is within you."

The conversation then concerns the ways in which this change is to be effected. The Master says first that one must be silent as God was before creation. The Disciple asks how he can achieve this state without "destroying Nature." The Master's answer is that a detachment of the self from the world of things is a first step.

The conversation turns to the radical paradox involved in loving and hating the self. The Master argues for a hatred for the creaturely self of arrogance and self-will, and yet he affirms the self with which man seeks God. Asked where love dwells in man, the Master replies in a similar spirit, that love dwells "in that place in man where he is not." Such love burns out the "I-ness"; that is, the egotism in natural and creaturely man.

The Disciple shifts the conversation again by asking where the soul goes after death. The Master's successive responses add up to the conclusion that Heaven and Hell are not to be regarded as locations, but as actualization of the relations of God's love and wrath to man. The Master continues to reflect upon the theme of Judgment Day, arguing that in that day the strife, tension, and tragedy of history will be surmounted by God's love.

The fifth tract, dated 1624, is entitled *A Dialogue between an Enlightened and Unenlightened Soul.* The conversation begins between the troubled and unenlightened soul and the Devil, and continues between the unenlightened or troubled soul and an enlightened soul. To the modern reader it is reminiscent of the allegorical conversations of John Bunyan of a generation after Boehme.

To the Devil, the soul asserts her inherent nobility, and the Devil replies with an elaboration of the Biblical temptation "to be a real Lord of heaven and earth." Once she has succumbed to temptation, evil proliferates in the troubled soul in the forms of arrogance, avarice, envy, and wrath.

In this sorry condition, the troubled soul meets Jesus Christ, who counsels repentance. However, the Devil is on hand to prevent this course and to counsel worldliness. At this point, an enlightened soul becomes the troubled soul's advisor and guide. She suggests surrender, and explains the upward path to salvation. As a consequence "the Distressed Soul now began her walk under Christ's patient guidance.

. . . Thus did she come again to true rest and become a child of God."

The sixth tract, *Of Divine Contemplation*, was written in 1622 and was unfinished at the author's death. It is essentially a philosophic meditation on the basic themes of Boehme's thought, on God, good, and evil, man's mind and will, and the realm of nature. We begin with human reason which acknowledges its limits, yet knows that it has originated from the supernatural ground of God's essence. Indeed, the suffering, conflicting wills of nature and creation likewise presuppose a divine will. Conversely, out of the strife and anguish of creation come the faith and peace of God.

Human life and, indeed, all of creation are regarded as objectivations of the divine will. Yet beyond all will and willing is that which is without will and is eternally one; namely, the Abyss or *Ungrund*. The beginning of all substance is the Logos; and the world is to be regarded as emanated Logos, "disposed into individualities." The unique designation of each thing is known as its signature. Such, in brief and summary statement, is Boehme's vision of God and God's creation.

The final tract of the volume, *Of Divine Prayer*, was written in the last year of its author's life; the essay is unfinished. The philosophical reflections of the previous treatise are here turned to religious practice in a discussion of the nature and art of prayer. As in the first treatise, the method alternates between exposition of the theme and practical illustrations of it.

Real prayer, the author assures us at the outset, is inward in nature. It is a disposition of the human heart, rather than a form of words. This disposition is a distinctive attitude of dependence on God; it is the essential function of prayer to realize or fulfill this dependence.

Prayer is not similar to an address to any worldly king, for the good reason that before God man has no rights whatsoever, yet from God man receives in abundance, as did the prodigal son from his father.

The greater part of this treatise is not argument or exposition, but confessions, acts of repentance, and prayers for varied occasions of human life. Of such prayers related to the other themes of the book man's way to Christ consists. In summary, *The Way to Christ* may be said to consist of expositions of some of the many aspects of this path, together with Boehme's own travel diary along the way.

DEVOTIONS UPON EMERGENT OCCASIONS

Author: John Donne (c.1573-1631)
Type of work: Devotional essays
First published: 1624

PRINCIPAL IDEAS ADVANCED

Sudden illness reminds man of his frailty and by removing customary distractions may bring man closer to life's essentials.

Physical illness affords man an insight into the sickness of the soul which is sin.

Each man is a world possessing both temporal (physical) and eternal (spiritual) qualities.

Each man's origin is the same: God.

No man is able to escape involvement in the life of all men.

Few who say "No man is an island" are aware of their indebtedness to Dean John Donne and his *Devotions upon Emergent Occasions*. Few who have read Ernest Hemingway's *For Whom the Bell Tolls* connect the title with the musings of a bed-ridden Anglican prelate of the sixteenth century. So profound and eloquent are Donne's meditations on life, illness, and death that it is not surprising to find them receiving the tribute of passing into the common speech and being mined as a source of titles for contemporary literary works.

The form of the *Devotions* is unusual in that each of the twenty-three portions into which the book is divided represents a stage of the author's illness and recovery. In clinical detail every sympton of both physical and mental condition is described. Though the occasion of the *Devotions* was an actual serious illness, the presence of Donne's characteristic stylistic devices suggests that the completed work is the result of careful composition after his recovery.

The work abounds with wit, extended similes and allusions, erudition in widely varying fields, and paradox, all infused with a passionate sincerity.

The work begins with a description of the first stages of Donne's illness. "Variable, and therefore miserable condition of man; this minute I was well, and am ill, this minute. I am surpriz'd with a sodaine change, and alteration to worse, and can impute it to no

cause, nor call it by any name." There is no doubt as to the reality of his attack, for by Section Three he is bed-ridden and by Section Four the doctor is summoned. Section Five is entitled "The Physitian Comes" and Six, "The Physitian Is Afraid." In Sections Eight through Twelve the doctor consults with others and takes various measures to test the disease. However, the treatment is not successful as the title of Section Thirteen reveals: "The sickness declares the infection and malignity thereof by spots." The crisis comes and in Sections Sixteen through Eighteen are found the patient's famous meditations on death, passages written as the bells in an adjoining church toll. By Section Nineteen Donne has passed the crisis, for "At last, the Physitians, after a long and stormie voyage, see land; they have so good signes of the concoction of the disease, as that they may safely proceed to purge." The remaining sections deal with the treatment offered by the doctors, and the work ends with a warning against "the fearefull danger of relapsing."

A curious framework for devotional meditations is this with its discourses on the relative importance of the heart, brain, and liver, and reference to such quaint medical practice as the applying of pigeons to Donne's feet in order to draw the "vapors" from his head. How is it that such a volume of quaint and curious lore should prove so enduring? The answer lies in the fact that Donne used this most private and yet most universal of experiences, illness, as the point of departure for his far-ranging contemplative excursions. The pigeon-purging may be cited as an illustration of his method.

On the theory that "vapors" caused the illness, Donne's doctors applied pigeons at his feet to draw the vapors from his head. Donne takes the occasion of this purging to muse upon his responsibility for the vapors: "What have I done, either to breed or to breath these vapors?" Though he is told it is his melancholy, Donne holds that it is rather his study and his calling which has caused him this suffering: "I have done nothing wilfully, perversely toward it, yet must suffer in it, die by it."

Not long content to remain at the factual level Donne employs this personal problem as an analogy for the ills of the state: "These vapors in us, which wee consider here pestilent, and infectious fumes, are in a State infectious rumors, detracting and dishonourable Calumnies, Libels. The Heart in that body is the King; and the Braine, his Councell; and the whole Magistracie, that ties all together, is the Sinewes, which proceed from thence; and the life of all is Honour, and just respect, and due reverence; and therefore, when these vapors, these venimous rumors, are directed against these Noble parts, the whole body suffers."

Donne finds religious significance in this pigeon-purging. God has provided this remedy in nature as a "type" or symbol to man that by the visitation of the Holy Spirit the vapors of sin shall descend and be trod under foot. One is reminded of the descent of the dove at the baptism of Jesus. Donne exhorts his readers to join him in drawing down the vapors of pride, wit, and self-will to the simplicity of the sacraments and obedience to the word of God.

Though there is much to admire in the *Devotions,* most readers find it too introspective, too erudite and esoteric, too metaphysical. Other manuals of devotion such as *The Imitation of Christ* by Thomas à Kempis (c.1380-1471), *The Scale of Perfection* by Walter Hilton (d.1396), *Private Devotions* by Lancelot Andrewes (1555-1626), or the essays *Holy Living* and *Holy Dying* by Jeremy Taylor (1613-1667), are less difficult in content and more direct in style. For one unfamiliar with Donne's work it is difficult to believe that the *Devotions* is a natural reflection of the author's religious sentiments. Yet when the *Devotions* is put next to Donne's other works, it is apparent that it is a characteristic expression. Displays of wit and learning abound throughout the whole of Donne's work from his early love poetry through his sermons and prayers.

Whatever the obstacles of Donne's style it is certain that the three sections (Sixteen to Eighteen) dealing with the tolling bell have earned for this work a secure niche in the history of English letters and the literature of Christian devotion. The passages are best appreciated when read aloud, for then the force of the argument and the felicity of the speech are most apparent. Donne hears the bells of the church adjoining his house toll for the funeral of a neighbor: "Here the Bells can scarse solemnise the funerall of any person, but that I knew him, or knew that he was my neighbor; we dwelt in houses neere to one another before, but now hee is gone into that house, into which I must follow him."

Donne reflects that this may well have been himself whose death is being noted. "Why might not I have been that man, that is carried to his grave now?" The balm of death as an end of suffering causes Donne to remark: "God hath kept the power of death in his owne hands, lest any man should bribe death. If man knew the game of death, the ease of death, he would solicite, he would provoke death to assist him, by any hand, which he might use."

With the further tolling of the bell Donne is moved to think of the Church universal and of the brotherhood of humanity: "All mankinde is of one Author, and is one volume; when one Man dies, one Chapter is not torne out of the booke, but translated into a better language; and every Chapter must be so translated; God emploies several translators; some peeces are translated by age, some by sicknesses, some by warre, some by justice; but God's hand is in every translation; and his hand shall binde up all our scattered leaves againe, for that Librarie where every booke shall lie open to one another. . . ."

There is perhaps no finer section in the *Devotions* for observing Donne's most characteristic style and content. Having used the metaphor of the Author and His book to speak of the universal Church and of man's eternal destiny, Donne develops his metaphor of the bell: "No man is an Iland, intire of it selfe; every man is a peece of the Continent, a part of the maine; if a Clod bee washed away by the Sea, Europe is the lesse, as well as if a Promontories were, as well as if a Mannor of thy friends or of thine owne were; any mans death diminishes me, because I am involved in Mankinde; And

therefore never send to know for whom the bell tolls: It tolls for thee."

In these passages are found the reasons for the *Devotions'* becoming a classic of literature and devotion. Here are themes of perennial and universal interest treated with consummate artistry. For the reader not sharing Donne's religious faith the *Devotions* has the appeal of dealing with situations no human being avoids: illness, mortality, and musings over the meanings and mysteries of life. Any reader is able to appreciate these themes and to be moved by the manner of their presentation, a manner which, with unforgettable literary effectiveness, portrays passionate human concern.

From the beginning, however, the *Devotions* has held an audience which sees in it strong Christian teaching. Though the validity of the *Devotions* is as much dependent on Donne the man as on Donne the Dean, the two were one, and the work deserves a reading on the theological level. To read it solely as introspective literature is to misread it, for the literary devices were used to add power and vividness to basic theological positions.

In these passages cited above, for example, the rhetoric should not be allowed to obscure the central theological affirmation: "I am involved in mankinde." No wavering here, no romantic isolation, no psychic narcissism, but instead a coherent statement supported by logical reasons which have the compelling power of an exact science. Through the medium of enforced isolation and suffering Donne learned the paradoxical truths of the Gospel: one finds by losing, one is never less alone than when alone. The nearly mortal illness becomes a symbol of the human condition not only in its frailty and sinful inperfection but in its need to realize the meaning of suffering in the providence of God. By losing all the customary securities and by being withdrawn from the usual distractions, Donne could concentrate upon the fundamental matter of his relationship to God. As his illness may be taken for the sinful state of man, so the recovery may be seen as the redemption, and the relapse as the falling back into sin. The tenth expostulation, for example, made against the serpent in Eden, follows a discussion of the body's sickness as symbolizing the sickness of the soul.

The reader who is familiar with Donne's other works is best able to appreciate the place of death in the *Devotions*. Donne was a child of his age in his preoccupation with death, but in the *Devotions* he views it in a less bizarre manner than he does elsewhere. He is neither hysterical nor unconcerned, nor does he long excessively for it. He sees it as part of God's providential plan to bring an end to man's sinning. He prays: "Let this prayer therefore, O my God, be as my last gasp, my expiring, my dying in thee; That if this bee the hour of my transmigration I may die the death of a sinner, drowned in my sins, in the blood of thy sonne. And if I live longer, yet I may now die the death of the righteous, die to sinne, which death is a resurrection to a new life. Thou killest and thou givest life."

As he had recovered from his illness, so would his soul recover to rise at the last to return to its source in God. Aware though he was of the sickness of sin, Donne never so identified human finitude with sin as to forget his Christian affirmation of his divine origin and of his being a joint heir with Christ. Even if he were merely dust and ashes, Donne observes, he could still speak unto the Lord since the Lord is Creator even of dust and ashes. But Donne insisted that he was nothing less than the breath of God, and thus it was right that he should breathe the pious expostulations of the *Devotions*. No contemporary reader can fail to benefit from the testimonies of this man whose physical and spiritual suffering forged his art and his humanity into one matchless instrument for the service of God.

OF CONSCIENCE, ITS POWER AND CASES

Author: William Ames (1576-1633)
Type of work: Puritan ethics and casuistry
First published: 1630

Principal Ideas Advanced

Conscience is the judgment of the practical intellect, by which a conclusion is drawn from the moral law as to one's state before God or to the moral character of one's actions.

Casuistry, or the study of cases of conscience, is a necessary discipline because of the liability of conscience to error and doubts.

The virtues as formulated in classical philosophical ethics can properly be evaluated only by reference to the divinely revealed moral law and the evangelical doctrine of redemption and grace.

The moral law summarized in the Decalogue is substantially the same as the natural law which provides the synteresis or major premise of the syllogism of conscience.

William Ames, a son of Puritan parents, studied at Christ's College, Cambridge, under William Perkins (1558-1602). In 1610, he left England and became a preacher in the Hague. In Holland, he defended Calvinism against the Remonstrants and served as a secretary at the Synod of Dort in 1618. From 1622 to 1632 he was Professor at Franeker. His most influential writings were his *Medulla theologiae* or *Marrow of Theology* (1627), in which, under the influence of Petrus Ramus (1515-1572), he develops theology as a practical science, and his *De conscientia eius iure et casibus,* in which he follows his teacher Perkins in developing a doctrine of conscience with detailed investigation of difficult cases.

Ames defines conscience as man's judgment of himself, according to his subjection to God's judgment. Conscience as a judgment belongs not to the will or emotions, but to the intellect. Although the will may incite the understanding to moral judgment and although emotional states are its consequence, conscience itself, according to the etymology of the word and its usage in Scripture, is a practical judgment of the understanding. Ames differs from his teacher, William Perkins, who represented conscience as a faculty of the soul. Conscience is the very act of moral judgment, by the power of the understanding, and it flows from

a certain habit of the soul. In this view, Ames is in agreement with Thomas Aquinas, as opposed to Scotus, Bonaventura, and Durandus, who defined conscience as a habit of the soul.

The judgment of conscience in such acts as accusing, excusing, or comforting is discursive and may be formulated in a practical syllogism. "The Major of that Syllogisme, wherein the whole judgement of conscience is laid open, treateth alwaies of the Law, the Minor of the fact and state; and the conclusion of the relation that ariseth from our fact or state, by reason of that Law; which is either guilt or spirituall Joy." Conscience is thus a "Law," a "Witness," and a "Judge" in relation to the major premise, minor premise, and conclusion respectively (Romans 2:14,15; Revelation 20:12; I John 5:10).

The major premise is given by the synteresis or repository of law; the minor is called syneidesis, and the conclusion, the *krísis* or judgment itself. "Synteresis is properly an intellectuall habit, whereby we give our consent to the principles of morall action. It differeth not therefore from the Law of nature which is naturally written in the hearts of all men: but in respect onely."

Synteresis can never be completely extinguished or lost in its principle. No man is so depraved as to be completely without a conscience. In its widest sense synteresis includes all consequences following from the principles of natural law and all practical truths accepted by faith in divine revelation. An enlightened conscience receives the precepts of Scripture in addition to the natural law and its consequences. The adequate and full rule of conscience is thus the revealed will of God. Although men are bound in conscience to observe properly instituted human laws, human laws qua human are not binding.

In discussing problems relating to erroneous, doubtful, and scrupulous consciences, Ames proceeds from a division of human actions into good, bad, and indifferent. Conscience can make an indifferent action to be either good or bad and a good action to be evil, but not an evil action to be good. The erroneous conscience binds, in that to act against its judgment is sinful, even when it judges something unlawful to be lawful. The necessity of sinning that arises in this case is due to the error of conscience, not to the nature of the law. Nothing may be done of which the conscience is in doubt. In doubtful cases the safest alternative should be chosen. Action against irrational scruples of conscience, however, is recommended.

In considering the minor premise of the syllogism of conscience, Ames raises the question of how it is possible for a man to do anything against a dictate of conscience which precedes or accompanies his action. Ames replies by denying the intellectualist doctrine that the will is determined by the last practical judgment of the understanding. Although a man cannot will what he does not know, a simple apprehension of an object, without any practical judgment, may suffice to elicit an act of will. The understanding propounds what is good to the will "with a kind of indifferency of judgement, as not having any necessary connexion with the universal good." Though the will is determined by the understanding as to the specification or kind of thing to be willed, yet it enjoys a liberty of exercise in which it moves itself, the understanding, and the other faculties. This doctrine of the primacy of the will distinguishes Ames's account of man's moral nature from the view of the primacy of the intellect commonly adopted by Reformed theologians.

From the conclusion of the practical syllogism follows either an excusing and approval or accusation and condemnation, together with suitable affections of joy or sorrow. Men do not always draw the logical conclusion even when the premises are admitted. A conscience that judges rightly is said to be honestly good; one which excuses and comforts to be peaceably good. Ever since man's Fall, the conscience can be both honestly and peaceably good only by the sprinkling of the blood of Christ and by the sanctification of the Spirit. Among the corollaries derived by Ames from the thirty-eight positions summarizing Book I of the treatise are the following: "The greatest violation of conscience is the greatest sin. The greatest anguish of conscience is the greatest punishment. . . . The interpretation of the Scriptures, or a judgement to discerne Gods will for a man's selfe, in his own conscience, belongs to every man."

Book II opens with a definition of a case of conscience as "a practical question, concerning which, the conscience may make a doubt." Cases are matters of doubt to be resolved by argument and include all questions in which, the general doctrine of faith and obedience being supposed, inquiry is made into a man's duty on particular occasions. Cases of conscience are divided into two classes, those concerning a man's state before God and those concerning actions performed in that state. Puritan casuistry characteristically treats inquiry into the state of the soul as the fundamental occupation of conscience. Assurance of salvation is held to be attainable, though with difficulty, in this life. Consequently, a man must examine himself as to his being in a state of sin or of grace. This question can be resolved by examination of one's behavior, outward and inward, by the attitude of the heart toward God's law, by a reflex act of the mind, and by a certain spiritual feeling. The remainder of Book II discusses cases relating to the state of man, under such headings as the state of sin, postponement of conversion, preparation for conversion, effectual calling, temptations against faith, adoption, sanctification, the conflict between flesh and spirit, progress in sanctification, the first-fruits of glorification in the feeling of God's love, temptations, and conscience of sin. The book closes with a series of selected propositions from *De tentationibus*, a work by William of Auvergne (c.1180-1249), Bishop of Paris.

The last three books of the *De conscientia* concern cases relating to moral duties. In these books Ames achieves an impressive synthesis of Biblical moral teaching and Aristotelian ethical theory. The Aristotelian framework provides a skeleton which is clothed with the living body of Scriptual precepts. Book III discusses basic ethical principles, including the cardinal virtues, while the two remaining books examine cases arising from the implications of the Decalogue.

Ames begins with a consideration of obedience in general, since the duty which God requires of man consists in obedience to His revealed will. Obedience requires knowledge, with which is associated the fear of God. Humility, uprightness, and zeal are dealt with in relation to obedience; peace of conscience is considered as a consequence of obedience. A discussion of virtue follows, in which the Aristotelian analysis of virtue as a habit is illustrated and supported by an abundance of Biblical texts. Virtue is not set in antithesis to pleasure, but pleasure and joy flowing from the exercises of virtue are observed to be signs that a virtue has been acquired. The particular virtues are then analyzed, first prudence or spiritual wisdom, with which watchfulness is associated, then fortitude, in connection with which assurance, perserverance, and patience are examined, and finally temperance; a chapter on drunkenness follows. For each virtue, Ames inquires as to its nature and the motives and means for acquiring it.

After the virtues, good works are discussed as well as the adiaphora (indifferent things), voluntary action, and sins of heart, speech, and behavior. Good works must not only be in conformity with the law of God as to their matter, but also be performed from the right motives and directed to the glory of God. The conscience of sinful men is not a sufficient or infallible rule, but only a rule subordinated to the Word of God. Ames adopts the probabilioristic position in casuistry and advises the choice of the safer side in doubtful cases; that is, the side in which there is no danger of sinning. On the question of choosing between two sins, Ames holds that, in the case of apparent conflict of duties, the greater duty absolves a person from the performance of the lesser. Choosing the lesser of two evils refers to physical rather than moral evil. But if a person supposes he must commit one of two sins, conscience can pass no judgment in favor of either, although the person who commits the lesser sin, sins less.

Voluntary action is analyzed in Scholastic Aristotelian fashion. Actions are rendered involuntary by violence, chance, and such ignorance as is the cause of the action. Ignorance of the law does not excuse, and willful ignorance is itself sin and increases the guilt of sins that result from it.

Book V, Chapter I, contains an important discussion of the nature and types of law. After considering four paradigm cases of the use of "jus," Ames distinguishes natural and positive law. Natural law consists of practical principles known by nature and of the consequences derived from those principles. Positive divine law is added to natural law by special revelations. Natural law is the same as the eternal law, but positive law is not thus designated. The case of Abraham's being commanded to slay his son is no suspension of the natural law, but only a change of the matter with which the law is conversant. Only man as a rational being is properly subject to natural law. Yet all things have a natural inclination to their end. Man possesses some such inclinations in common with animals. A striking appeal is made to texts (Isaiah I:3, Jeremiah 8:7, 2 Timothy 3:3, Jude 10) accentuating the unnaturalness of sin by reference to the behavior of brute beasts. The *jus gentium* embraces both natural and positive law and something intermediate, so far as it derives from common agreement and custom. The commands of the natural law are inadequately formulated as "to live honestly, not to injure anyone, and to give every one his own." This is in part tautological and in part ambiguous. The Golden Rule is both natural and divine law, but it may not be applied indiscriminately. Civil law must be based on the natural law, either as a conclusion from general principles or as the determination and application of a general rule. Civil law makes not good men, but good citizens. The moral law of the Decalogue is identical with the natural law, except for the determination of the seventh day in the Fourth Commandment. The necessity for republication of the natural law in the Ten Commandments stems from the depravity of nature which entails blindness of reason, perversity of will, and disturbance of emotions. The human heart retains but a remnant of the law, which, like an old painting, must be restored with a new brush. Right practical reason is found pure and entire nowhere except in God's written Law.

RELIGIO MEDICI

Author: Sir Thomas Browne (1605-1682)
Type of work: Personal religious commentary
First published: 1642 (pirated); 1643 (authorized)

Principal Ideas Advanced

The world of faith and the world of science are marvelously intertwined, and the one should never be divorced from the other.

Reason and belief are complementary, but the pervasive atmosphere of man's religious quest should be one of mystery and wonder.

The manifold marvels of the world delight those who see in them God's handiwork, and they deliver men from arbitrary dogmatism.

Religio medici, a justly celebrated work of private musings on religious truths, was written by Sir Thomas Browne, probably in 1635. It circulated in manuscript for some years, and after surreptitious editions had appeared in 1642, Browne himself published it in 1643. The author was thus a comparatively young man, but he writes with a whimsical detachment that would seem appropriate in a person twice his age. He writes as a doctor, and he admits that medical men have a poor reputation for religious zeal; but he also writes as a Christian, and his faith is no conventional pattern of belief. Others may owe their religion to baptism and education; Browne is a Christian because, having studied the matter with care and reflected on it at length, he finds himself "obliged by the principles of grace and the laws of mine own reason, to embrace no other name but this."

At the very outset Browne insists that zeal is compatible with charity. He considers that he stands in the tradition of the Reformation, but he dislikes divisive labels. He accepts discipline in his personal life, but sees no reason why it should issue in a surly temper. "My common conversation I do acknowledge austere," he writes, "my behavior full of rigor, sometimes not without morosity; yet at my devotion I love to use the civility of my knee, my hat, and hand, with all those outward sensible motions which may express or promote my invisible devotion."

Browne expresses a regard for forms of religious observance when such forms are helpful and not superstitious, and he is able to respond to the devotional forms of those from whom he differs: "I could never hear the Ave-Mary Bell without an elevation, or think it a sufficient warrant, because they erred in one circumstance, for me to err in all, that is, in silence and dumb contempt." So he describes an attitude at once strict with himself and charitable towards others, combining exacting standards of moral behavior with a tolerance of ceremonial forms. This freedom from the fury of contemporary religious invective is one of the most striking features of Browne's work. He does not accept a position because some authority has propounded it, nor reject it because some one reputed to be an opponent has supported it. When Scripture does not answer his questions, he does not borrow the rules of his religion either from Geneva or from Rome.

The strong appeal of *Religio medici* lies partly in the spirit which pervades it, partly in the material with which it deals. Browne takes a subject of fundamental importance. He deals with man's relation to his God and to the world about him, and he deals with both aspects of his subject with candor, originality, and great imaginative power. Throughout his work he maintains a delicate balance between two kinds of reality and two types of knowledge. He is concerned with faith and science, with God and the world of phenomena, with the knowledge that comes only because God reveals it and with the truth which we grasp only because we search for it. His approach is at times akin to that of Sir Francis Bacon (1561-1626), but he presses forward with the examination of God and his works with greater zeal than his famous predecessor ever did. It is an open question as to the extent to which *Religio medici* can be regarded as an expression of the scientific ferment of the age. It is Browne's aim to keep his sources in just equipoise. He will neither ignore the distinctive sources of truth which God's Word provides nor will he shut his eyes to the evidence of nature: "Thus there are two books from which I collect my divinity; besides that written one of God, another of his servant Nature, that universal and public manuscript, that lies expans'd unto the eyes of all. . . ." He is troubled that Christians so often "disdain to suck divinity from the flowers of Nature." But Browne does not intend to make the opposite mistake, and become so engrossed in the examination of Nature that he forgets God. He will so study all phenomena that he will be able to detect the wise purpose that has fashioned them, and he will recognize in all things created the functional beauty of means perfectly adapted to ends. "And thus," he says, "I call the effects of Nature the works of God, whose hand and instrument she only is." Or, as he more succinctly expresses it, "Nature is the art of God."

Browne therefore refuses to subscribe to the sharp distinction between natural and revealed religion. His delight in the "general beauty in the works of God" delivers him from the narrowness which characterizes many of his contemporaries, but his respect for Scripture saves him from the perils of a vague natural pantheism. And above all, he is constantly overawed by the majesty of the central theme of all religious speculation. In one of his most telling phrases he urges his readers to "think magnificently about God," and no words could more accurately convey the distinctive quality of his book.

It would be a mistake to regard *Religio medici* as a serious contribution to the study of either science or religion, or even of the relations of the one to the other. There is the evidence of much delight in the world which science studies, but few explicit references either to the tasks or achievements of science. There is constant consideration of religious subjects, but little attempt to work out anything approaching a system of divinity. Browne allows great scope to revelation. He also insists on the place of reason and the role which it should play in the religious life. "The world," he says, "was made to be inhabited by beasts, but studied and contemplated by man: 'tis the debt of our reason we owe unto God, and the homage we pay for not being beasts."

Browne's emphasis on man's rationality is carefully balanced by an awareness of the limits of the utmost that man can know. He admits that there are truths which "serve as luminaries in the abyss of knowledge," but he is also aware that everything runs out into mystery. There is an obscurity too deep for our reason, and thus, he says, "I teach my haggard and unreclaimed reason to stoop unto the lure of faith." Browne affirms the proper role of reason and yet insists on its due subordination. It is this attitude which explains the contemplative quality of his book. He observes the visible phenomena of the world about him, but he also ponders unseen and unfathomable truths. He reflects on the wisdom and eternity of God and finds that the one renews and the other confounds his understanding. He knows that God is wise in all things, "wonderful in what we conceive, but far more wonderful in what we comprehend not."

Nor is a due and proper balance merely the formal pattern of Browne's thought. Man's life is composed of many parts. Reason often clashes with faith, and emotion often disturbs reason. We are exposed to the perils of something that approximates to an inner civil war, "for there is in our soul a kind of triumvirate, or triple government of three competitors, which distracts the peace of this our commonwealth." "Sturdy doubts and boisterous objections" attack the serenity of man's spirit, and are artfully employed by our ancient enemy, the tempter, to work us ill. So Browne introduces his vivid picture of playing at chess with the Devil, who yields a pawn in order to gain a queen, "and whilst I labored to raise the structure of my reason, he strived to undermine the edifice of my faith."

Browne does not minimize the problems of belief. He is well aware of the difficulties in the sacred narratives and of the incongruities in the Biblical text. He can construct a comprehensive catalogue of doubts and can cite all the problems latent in the miracles. He is a believer, but without the arrogance of dogmatism, and he is constantly reminded that the citadel of faith is built on the edge of the abyss of doubt. He will believe, but he will "never betray the liberty of my reason"; he is willing to question, but he refuses to become obsessed with doubts. Browne is thus concerned with both faith and reason, and their relation constituted the central problem of his age. But it can hardly be claimed that Browne made a serious contribution to its philosophical solution. It may be questioned whether he even recognized the central issue in the problem. His mind makes sorties into this complicated jungle and lights up its obscurities, but it never demarcates the boundaries of the problem. To change the figure of speech, his subtle intelligence plays like summer lightning over the landscape of man's terrestrial life, but it never strikes with electrifying power to the center of man's problems.

There is a mystical bent to Browne's writings, but he can hardly be regarded as a genuine mystic. He is aware of the mysterious dimensions of life, but he does not intend to lose himself in them. The true mystic can hardly retain the slightly quizzical quality which marks Browne's outlook. Nor can the mystic survey life with the somewhat detached objectivity which Browne maintains. But perhaps the fundamental reason why he never loses himself in a cloud is that his religious faith coalesces with a strong ethical seriousness. Here, again, we can observe an unusual combination of qualities. Browne is mystical, yet concerned with the problems of daily life; he is metaphysical, but intensely moral; he contemplates eternity, but he has no intention of escaping from the responsibilities of time. He delights in beauty but he does not "feed on rainbows." He dwells in a rarefied atmosphere, but it is not "too thin for breathing."

A book like *Religio medici* draws on many sources, but depends on none of them. It reflects Stoic influence and shows traces of Scholasticism. Browne's mind has been shaped by science and by contacts with men of varying backgrounds. His greatest obligation is to Platonism, which inculcated the charitable outlook, the broad and generous tolerance which pervades his book. The wide variety of his intellectual interests is clear to even the most casual reader; one is aware that a keen and well-instructed mind has ranged widely over the field of human thought and knowledge; it has brought home much curious lore, although the author communicates it in almost random fashion.

This explains the immediate appeal of *Religio medici* to its contemporaries. The seventeenth century was an age of shifting cross currents, and Browne touched its interests at many points. He made only an amateur's contribution to the central problems of authority and faith, but he placed these great issues in a new perspective. He proved that it is possible to be earnest about these important matters without descending to foul-mouthed and bad-tempered dogmatism. He gave his age what it badly needed: a fresh expression of an individual man's belief. He showed that man is a true microcosm and that the visible world is a reflection of the invisible world. He showed that a subject of fundamental importance could be treated with entire candor by an author of imaginative power, originality, and good will. But the book would not have retained its unique place as a literary and religious classic unless it possessed qualities which appeal perennially to men. The engaging character of its author inevitably attracts all save the most doctrinaire minds. His curiosity, his charity towards others, his humility about himself, and his sense of the mystery and wonder of life make him a rare and delightful companion. His wit flickers over the most solemn subjects, yet his basic seriousness and sincerity are never in doubt. And he clothes his thought in a form peculiarly appealing and appropriate. He has an inexhaustible gift for epigram. His turns of expression are as arresting as they are quaint. He can be colloquial and magniloquent by turns. He can awaken the emotions and give poetic form to universal human feelings. He can bring the beauty and power of the spiritual world within the reach of the ordinary person. The somber magnificence, lit by flashes of quaint wit, give to *Religio medici* a quality which it shares with few other books. It lives because it speaks to something undying in the heart of man.

THE BLOODY TENENT OF PERSECUTION

Author: Roger Williams (c.1603-1683)
Type of work: Christian social philosophy
First published: 1644

PRINCIPAL IDEAS ADVANCED

It is the prerogative of God alone to punish those who reject Christianity.

In the realm of civil affairs Christians are to associate on a basis of equality with all men, whatever their religious convictions.

Old Testament references to instances in which the rulers of Israel punished idolaters provide no warrant for the later civil rulers to suppress false religious beliefs, for the teachings of Christ regarding the treatment of non-Christians have superseded the teachings of the Old Testament.

Roger Williams, author of *The Bloody Tenent of Persecution,* was born into a shopkeeper's family in London, probably in 1603. His education at Charterhouse and at Pembroke Hall, Cambridge University, was made possible by the generous support of Sir Edward Coke.

While still in England, Williams became aligned with the Puritans, a religio-political party which regarded the Church of England as inadequately purified of Roman Catholic features of belief and ceremony. He adopted the views of the radical or "Separatist" Puritans, who advocated separation from the Church of England rather than internal reform efforts.

Williams sailed for New England in December of 1630 and arrived in Boston on February 5, 1631. He rejected the ministerial call of the church in Boston because of that church's refusal to separate from the Church of England. An offer from the church at Salem was withdrawn after Governor John Winthrop expressed disapproval. Williams then left for the colony at Plymouth, which was avowedly separatist. Here he lived for two years, making his living by farming, but also occasionally preaching in the Plymouth church. He became increasingly unhappy because of the non-separatist implication of the behavior of Plymouth church members who attended Church of England services during visits in England. Finally, in 1633, he left Plymouth and returned to Salem, where he was fondly remembered. There he became an unofficial assistant to the pastor.

At Salem, Williams enlisted enthusiastic support for his separatist views, but his religious and political teachings alarmed the rulers of the colony. He insisted that the rightful owners of the land inhabited by the colonists were the Indians, and that the royal charter provided no valid claim. He declared that an oath constituted a religious affirmation and that, therefore, magistrates had no right to require oaths of unregenerate persons. He claimed, further, that the civil authorities had no right to enforce the first four commandments, which define religious duties, and that the magistrates' responsibility was limited to enforcing those commandments the violation of which resulted in social disorder.

The civil and ecclesiastical leaders of Massachusetts were spurred to a determined effort to silence Williams when, in the spring of 1635, the church at Salem chose Williams to succeed their deceased minister, Samuel Skelton. At the July meeting of the General Court of Massachusetts Bay, Williams was asked to appear and explain his views. Fellow ministers who appeared as witnesses testified that Williams should be removed because of his heretical views, but they were powerless to interfere with the affairs of an independent Congregational church. The General Court, however, was in a position of greater power. Salem was petitioning the General Court for land in Marblehead Neck, and the General Court refused to act on the petition unless the Salem church dismissed Williams. Williams himself broke the deadlock when he insisted that his church break with all other Congregational churches in Massachusetts because of their violation of the principle of local congregational autonomy in calling for government aid in suppressing his unpopular views. In effect he was asking his parishioners to declare that their church alone was the true church, and this the majority of them were unwilling to do.

In October of 1635 the General Court again required Williams to appear, and he was charged with denying the authority of the magistrates in religious matters and with spreading seditious ideas through letters. Williams adamantly defended his acts, and he was sentenced to banishment. Initially he was allowed six weeks in which to leave the colony, but he was later granted permission to remain until the next spring.

Forbidden to preach publicly, he continued to present his views in meetings at his home. Williams received word in January, 1636, that the exasperated colonial authorities planned to deport him immediately to England. He fled to the wilderness south of Massachusetts, where he was helped through the winter by Indians. In the summer of 1636 he founded the village of Providence, which grew rapidly because of the influx of refugees from Massachusetts. In 1644 he secured from Parliament a charter which designated Providence and several other settlements as the colony of Rhode Island.

It was during his stay in London in 1643-44 that Williams wrote and had published his *The Bloody Tenent of Persecution*. His stay in England was a feverishly busy one which saw the publication of several works, including his brilliant anthropological study of New England Indians entitled *A Key into the Language of America*, a book which immediately established his reputation and fame.

Although written in great and obvious haste, *The Bloody Tenent of Persecution* contained thoughts which Williams had been formulating for eight years. The book was designed to refute the philosophy of Church-state relations which the civil and religious authorities of Massachusetts had decided upon, as well as to state Williams's own views. The special target of the book was the Reverend John Cotton (1584-1652), acknowledged dean of the Massachusetts clergy and one of the chief figures in the prosecution of Williams. The first half of *The Bloody Tenent of Persecution* replies directly to Cotton's criticisms of a tract written in Newgate prison by an Anabaptist. The second half attempts to rebut a document entitled *A Model of Church and Civil Power* which the associated ministers of Massachusetts Bay had sent to the people of Salem in the autumn of 1635 in an attempt to show them the errors of Williams's teachings. Williams mistakenly attributed the document largely to the hand of Cotton, who had nothing to do with its writing. Still, Williams correctly interpreted Cotton's thinking on the question of Church-state relations, and Cotton felt compelled to defend his views. In 1647 he published a book bearing a typical seventeenth century polemical title, *The Bloody Tenent Washed, and Made White in the Blood of the Lambe.* In 1652 Williams issued a rejoinder entitled *The Bloody Tenent Yet More Bloody by Mr. Cotton's Endeavour to Wash it White in the Blood of the Lambe.*

The confusing and disorganized quality of *The Bloody Tenent of Persecution* is remedied to a certain extent by twelve lucid one-sentence statements by which Williams opens the book. Most of the statements are basic propositions which are developed and defended in the book, while others are simple descriptions of the contents of the book. Following the list of twelve statements is an address to Parliament in which he urges that body—at that time largely Presbyterian—not to use its powers to enforce or proscribe religious belief. After the appeal to Parliament comes a statement addressed "to every courteous reader." In some of the most eloquent prose of the book, Williams points out the inconsistency of a political policy which permits citizens to read the Bible but which

does not allow them to interpret the Bible in any fashion other than that approved by the state.

Williams next moves into the first of the two main parts of his book, the first part being directed against Cotton's answer to the tract mentioned above. Cotton—arguing in the fashion of a scholastic logician—acknowledges the wrongness of persecuting any conscience that is "rightly informed," and he also maintains that it is wrong to punish an erroneous conscience until after one or two admonitions. If, however, the sinner continues in his error, then he may be punished, for once he has been instructed he no longer sins out of obedience to conscience, but against his conscience. In the case of minor matters, those in error may be tolerated if they exhibit a spirit of Christian meekness and love. If, however, one professes even minor error in an arrogant and boisterous spirit so that he disturbs the civil peace, then he is to be punished according to the seriousness of the disturbance.

The question which is most natural to a modern mind is, How could Cotton so confidently set himself up as the judge of right and wrong conscience? Williams, on the other hand, saw the issue—as did Cotton—as a matter of correct interpretation of the Scriptures. He agreed with Cotton that the passages concerning the wheat and the tares (Matthew 13:24-30, 37-43) are crucial for understanding how heretics and non-Christians should be treated by ecclesiastical and civil authorities. In the parable of the wheat and the tares the master instructs his servants to leave the tares alone in order not to damage the wheat. In response to his disciples' request for an explanation of the parable, Jesus states that the tares will be destroyed by fire at the Final Judgment.

Cotton interpreted the tares as Church members, outwardly holy, who at heart were not Christians. Because churches and ministers cannot be certain who the real Christians are, they must not presume to rid the Church of hypocrites. Both the civil and Church authorities, however, are able to recognize those who openly deny or pervert the faith of the Church and lead others into heresy or schism, and both the state and the Church have the right to admonish and suppress such persons.

Williams's reply to Cotton takes the form of a dialogue between "Peace" and "Truth," both of whom serve as the author's protagonists. The dialogue develops a lengthy and involved exegesis of the Biblical passages concerning the wheat and the tares. Williams declares that the tares refer neither to hypocrites within the Church nor to disturbers of the civil peace. Jesus clearly had in mind "anti-Christian idolaters," those who reject Christianity. Jews, Moslems, and persons of other non-Christian persuasions and of no religious persuasion at all will eventually be judged and punished of God. It is not, however, the function of the Christian Church or of civil governments to suppress non-Christians. Indeed, in the realm of civil affairs, it is proper for Christians and non-Christians to deal with one another freely and to enjoy the same rights. The virtues which make for civil order and harmony have no special relationship to Christianity or any other religion. Just and stable civil societies may exist quite independ-

ently of Christian influence. The skills which are necessary for governing men are to be compared with the specialized skills of a physician, a musician, or a ship's pilot. None of these skills has any necessary relationship to the religious faith of the practitioner, and religious profession should not be a test of office for the magistrate any more than for a ship's pilot.

Within the setting of civil society, Williams's argument goes on, a church has the same nature and status as a medical society or a business corporation. A religious society has its own functions, which are distinctly separate and different from those of a civil society. Civil harmony and order are the responsibility of the state and not of the Church. Christians have a duty as Christians to protect the purity and integrity of their churches, but they have no warrant whatsoever for ridding civil society of Jews, Moslems, pagans, and others who do not properly belong in the Church. Such persons are clearly qualified for full membership in civil society.

John Cotton and other New England ministers were able to cite in favor of the Church-state arrangement in Massachusetts numerous Old Testament accounts of cases in which religious and civil leaders co-operated in violently suppressing idolaters. Williams acknowledges that ancient Israel did engage in such practices. He argues, however, that ancient Jewish society existed by a special covenantal arrangement with God, an arrangement which has existed with no other people, which has been superseded by Christ, and which, therefore, has no authority as a model for Christians.

By its very nature, Williams affirms, Christianity tolerates opposition and rejection, and it seeks to persuade only through peaceful means. By its very nature it cannot be communicated through coercive means. Furthermore, attempts to suppress religious error usually result in more fanatical devotion to the erroneous views.

Williams makes it clear that he is no religious indifferentist. Toleration of religious error is to be distinguished from approval. Evil is to be tolerated for the sake of greater good, both the greater good of civil harmony and that of the promotion of Christianity through appropriate means. Because Christianity is the true religion, the civil magistrate owes it his approbation and the submission of his own will. To non-Christian religions the magistrate owes permission but not approbation. In his official capacity, however, he owes equal protection both to the worshipers of Christ and to those who reject Christ.

The civil and ecclesiastical rulers of Massachusetts, Williams charges, have confused the "garden" which is the Church with the "wilderness" which is the world. By compelling outward conformity with the ways of Christ, they have produced a confused mixture of the Church and the world, so that the Church contains the unregenerate as well as the regenerate. Such a national church conforms to the Old Testament, but it has no warrant in the teachings or example of Christ. Christ appointed no civil authorities to promote and defend His Church.

The fame of Williams and of his greatest book rests largely upon the support which they provide for the doctrine of separation of Church and state. *The Bloody Tenent of Persecution* articulates a clear theory of both Church and state, but it is important to note that Williams's insistence upon separation was motivated chiefly by his concern for the purity and integrity of the Church as a community of regenerate men. He was not motivated —as have been many thinkers since the eighteenth century—by the belief that the state, if left free to act on the basis of reason instead of religious dogmas, can continually improve the quality of human existence.

THE KEYS OF THE KINGDOM OF HEAVEN

Author: John Cotton (1584-1652)
Type of work: Church polity
First published: 1644

PRINCIPAL IDEAS ADVANCED

The Keys of the Kingdom are the key of knowledge and the key of order; the latter may be considered to be two keys representing the powers of Church order: liberty, which belongs to the brethren; and authority, which belongs to the elders.

The recipients of the Keys are individual churches and not presbyteries or bishops.

Although independent of each other, churches ought to be associated for their mutual benefits into synods.

The Church's power does not extend to temporal affairs.

John Cotton, who for twenty years was vicar of St. Botolph's Church, Boston, Lincolnshire, fled England to avoid being arrested for his refusal to kneel at the sacrament and was involved, shortly after coming to Massachusetts, in Anne Hutchinson's (c.1591-1643) revolt against the New England clergy. He and John Winthrop (1588-1649) opposed the antinomian beliefs of Anne Hutchinson. When Mrs. Hutchinson was condemned in 1637 by the General Court, Cotton devoted his full effort to the preservation of peace and order in the New England churches. In the *Keys of the Kingdom,* and in other works of like character, Cotton set forth what was, in effect, the official teaching of the New England churches on the subject of Church polity. Two English divines, Thomas Goodwin (1600-1680) and Philip Nye (1596-1672), both members of the Westminster Assembly, contributed a joint introduction and saw the work through the press. Testifying to the virtual identity between "the Congregational way" in New England and in the mother country, they praise the author for having described a middle-way between Brownism (see Robert Browne, c.1550-1633) and Presbyterianism. The error of the former, they say, lies in drowning the votes of the elders in the popular majority, and that of the latter in swallowing up the interests of the people in the jurisdiction of the presbytery; whereas, the wisdom of Cotton's plan lies in the balancing of powers and privileges so that, while action is not impeded, the danger of tyranny is removed.

Cotton derived the title of his book from the words of Christ to Peter, in Matthew 16:19: "To thee will I give the keys of the Kingdom of Heaven; and whatsoever thou shalt bind on earth, shall be bound in Heaven; and whatsoever thou shalt loose on earth, shall be loosed in Heaven." Cotton distinguishes two sorts of keys. The first is the key of *knowledge,* which, he says, belongs to all Christians alike, because every man is responsible for knowing the Scriptures and believing on Christ for his justification. To exercise the key, Cotton says, it is not necessary for a person to be a member of a church, although normally it is expected that he will. In the present work, Cotton is not primarily concerned with this first key, but with the second, that of *order.* This key is "the power whereby every member of the Church walketh orderly himself, according to his place in the Church, and helpeth his brethren, to walk orderly also."

Properly speaking, there are, according to Cotton, two keys of order. The first is that of power, or interest, or, as it is called in the Scriptures, *liberty.* This power belongs to the people. It includes the right to choose their own officers, to send out missionaries, to refuse membership to undesirable persons, to join with their officers in excommunicating offenders from the sacraments, and to enter into communion with other churches. When the congregation has serious cause to complain against its officers, it may appeal to a synod representing the several churches; and, if they get no satisfaction, they can withdraw their support.

The second key of order is that of *authority*. It is vested in officers (elders and deacons) chosen by the people. These have the right to preach, to teach and to exhort, to call the church together, to examine candidates for membership, to ordain officers upon their being selected by the congregation, to inform the people of the law in cases of disciplinary action, to pronounce sentence after the people have determined the matter of guilt, and to withdraw the ordinances from the people in cases where the whole congregation is stubbornly at fault.

Cotton was careful to base his teaching upon the Scriptures, and he appeals frequently to the practice of the churches in the Acts of the Apostles. Another passage often referred to is Matthew 18:18, in which it is reported that, concerning the brother taken in a fault, Christ commanded that, if he proved obdurate, he should be brought before the Church. It was to the Church that Christ said, "Whatsoever ye shall bind on earth shall be bound in Heaven; and whatsoever ye shall loose on earth shall be loosed in Heaven." Cotton regards this passage as giving the true sense of Christ's words to Peter when he gave him the Keys of the Kingdom. Following Augustine, Cotton says, "Peter received the keys in the name of the Church."

Besides Scripture, however, Cotton had before him the example of English civil law. In a well-ordered Commonwealth, he says, there is a "right and due establishment and balancing of the *liberties* or *privileges* of the people (which in a true sense, may be called a *power*) and the *authority* of the Magistrate." In like manner, he continues, the safety of the Church lies in "the right and due settling and ordering of the holy *power* of the *privileges* and *liberties* of the Brethren, and the ministerial *authority* of the Elders." The English practice of trial by jury affords a close parallel to the way in which Cotton conceives people and officers conjointly exercising discipline. The verdict of a jury is, Cotton says, an exercise of popular liberty, whereas the judge's sentence is an act of authority. Each has a power of judgment, but the powers are different, and neither is effective without the other.

After having distinguished the different keys, Cotton raises the question as to who is the "first subject of the power of the keys." Cotton's answer, fundamental to the whole principle of independency, is that the "particular Church or Congregation" is the "first subject of all Church offices, with all their spiritual gifts and power." He finds no suggestion in the New Testament of a national church, or any hierarchy or church court, such as there was among the Jews. The Apostles, he says, were ministers plenipotentary, empowered to establish churches, and, where no church was, to exercise the power otherwise vested in a church. But the New Testament gives no indication that this exceptional office was intended to be permanent. On the contrary, as churches were established in various parts of the world, they became the residual seat of power, and the keeper of the two keys of Church order. Thus, "the Brethren of a particular Church or a Congregation, are the first subjects of Church Liberty . . . ; the Elders of a particular Church, are the first subjects of

Church Authority"; and "both the Elders and Brethren, walking and joining together in truth and peace, are the first subjects of all Church Power, needful to be exercised in their own body."

In the course of proving these propositions, mainly through interpreting Scriptural texts, Cotton establishes the chief points of Congregational, as distinguished from Episcopal and Presbyterian, Church polity. Each congregation is equal in authority to every other; their elders or overseers likewise have equal power; and it rests with the individual congregation, not with a bishop or presbytery, to certify the calling of a minister and, with the local elders, to ordain him.

Cotton holds back, however, from the most extreme form of independency. While he sees the dangers of any kind of union to the independency of particular churches, he is also aware of the constant tendency of churches to degenerate and to fall into apostasy. He finds it one of the duties, therefore, of particular churches to consult and consent together on weighty matters, and to assume mutual care for one another; and the Scriptures are his authority (for example, the Conference at Jerusalem, Acts 15) for holding that "a Synod of Churches, or of their messengers" has immediate power from Christ, the head of the Church, to undertake disciplinary measures where particular churches fall into grievous error. The need for such a higher authority is imperative in cases where a congregation is rent by factions. Christ, says Cotton, gives authority to a church only when it is "agreeing together in the name of Christ" (Matt. 18:19). Where there is disagreement, the Church loses its power, rendering it necessary for the synod to take action. Scripture indicates, however, that synods should exercise their power with great restraint, so as not to diminish the liberty and authority of the particular congregation; thus, the Jerusalem Conference resolved not to lay upon the churches "other *burthen,* but those necessary things."

One further question was of major importance to the New England churches, as it was also to the churches of England. This was the question of the relation between the Church and the Commonwealth. It seemed clear to Cotton that, since the Kingdom of Heaven does not include the "world," but only the Church, and, in the world to come, Eternal Life, there is no warrant for inferring, with the Papists and with some Presbyterians, that Christ gives the Church power to bind and loose in temporal affairs. Inasmuch as it derives its power from Christ, the Church must insist that, within its own province, it is independent of the secular power; at the same time, it must recognize that Christ has given to the magistrate the power of the sword, and that, in matters which concern civil peace, the Church must obey its earthly rulers.

Many, if not most, Churchmen in our day would agree with the following of Cotton's opinions in the matter of Church and state: namely, that the Church should submit to hold property under the laws of the state; that it should support the state with public prayers in times of national calamity; and that, when persecuted, it should refrain from resorting to force in its own defense.

But one opinion which John Cotton shared with his brethren and with most Churchmen of his day, both in

Europe and in America, was the one to which Roger Williams (c.1604-1683) took exception; namely, that the establishment of pure religion is a concern of civil peace. To support this view, Cotton has to turn to the Old Testament, where it is often pointed out that Israel's misfortunes were due to the nation's having forsaken the worship of Jehovah. A Christian Commonwealth, Cotton concludes, must take whatever action is necessary, "partly by commanding, and stirring up the Churches, and Ministers thereof to go about it in their spiritual way; partly also by civil punishments upon the wilful opposers, and disturbers of the same," in order to see that religion is kept true to the word of God. Cotton draws the line, however, at forcing men to enter into full religious communion. Here, he insists, the prerogatives of the Church to receive and exclude people from membership are at stake. To employ civil power at this point would be "not a *Reformation*, but a *Deformation* of the Church."

Cotton's influence on both ecclesiastical and civil affairs was equal to that of any New England minister of his time. His contemporary, William Hubbard, wrote: "Whatever he delivered in the pulpit was soon put into an order of court, if of a civil, or set up as a practice in the church, if of an ecclesiastical concernment." Cotton has sometimes been called an opponent of democracy, because, when treating of the classical alternatives of democracy, aristocracy, and monarchy, he stated that democracy is not countenanced by Scripture. But if we understand by democracy a workable arrangement in which the powers of the people are balanced against the powers of government, Cotton was a democrat, and he may be considered to have been one of the architects of the American system.

LEX REX

Author: Samuel Rutherford (c.1600-1661)
Type of work: Theology; political philosophy
First published: 1644

PRINCIPAL IDEAS ADVANCED

Nature has endowed every man, and hence every community of men, with the right of self preservation, and this right can never be surrendered to any civil power.

All power of government is from God mediated through the people or their representatives, and the purpose of the will of God in this regard is the good of men.

The relationship between a ruler and his subjects is based on their consent so that in the event of a ruler becoming a tyrant and acting to the destruction of the people or their liberties, they may resist lawfully, as a community, by reverting to the law of nature which was given by God for their protection.

By an extension of the natural law of self preservation, nations may lawfully assist other nations that are subject to tyranny.

When *Lex rex, a Dispute for the Just Prerogative of King and People* appeared in 1644 it was an immediate sensation. Members of the Westminster Assembly of Divines were said to be excited about its devastating attack on the absolute power of kings, and Samuel Rutherford, one of the Scottish Commissioners to the Assembly, was the object of high praise for his grasp of one of the most thorny issues of the times. Seventeen years later, in 1661, the Restoration of Charles II to the throne of the Three Kingdoms reversed the political climate and *Lex rex* was solemnly burned at Edinburgh and St. Andrews by order of the Scottish Parliament. Its author would most surely have been executed had not his death intervened.

Lex rex (*The Law and the Prince*) is a treatise on constitutional law as it related to the royal authority. The Stuart Kings James I and Charles I had asserted absolutism as a divine right of kings; they claimed to be above positive law and to be responsible directly to God for their discharge of the royal function. The claim was supported in an extreme form by John Maxwell, sometime Bishop of Ross, in a book entitled *Sacro-sancta regum majestas or The Sacred Prerogative of Christian Kings,* and *Lex rex* was written by Samuel Rutherford, Professor of Divinity at St. Andrews, as a rejoinder.

The book was written as a series of questions and answers, the questions being about such debated issues as whether government is warranted by the law of nature, and whether a kingdom may lawfully be purchased by the sole title of conquest.

The answer to the question as to whether government is warranted by a divine law makes a distinction which pervades the whole discussion. Government in general is from God; hence, support of it is an act of piety. On the other hand, a particular form of government, such as a monarchy, aristocracy, or democracy, is a human institution for the good of man; that is, there is a clear distinction warranted by the light of nature as well as by the Scriptures between the principle of government and the person designated to govern.

Again, another basic opinion is offered on the question as to whether government rests on a state of nature. Certainly it is natural for man to live in societies, but the mode of society he prefers is quite a different matter. There is nothing in the nature of things that determines one man to be a king and another to be a subject. "All men be born equally free," Rutherford writes. Magistrates are appointed in accordance with a natural desire for orderly social life as a secondary stage in the idea of what is natural, having its most obvious expression in family life where a father governs his household.

If government is in the form of a monarchy, it is not because monarchy is the immediate appointment of God, for other forms could also have divine approbation. Mediately, however, a monarchy may be from God as He guides His people to choose a form of magistracy. Actually the power of government is in the people, for every man has the right to preserve himself from violence; and consequently the people appoint as many officers for government as their safety and peace warrant. "No man cometh out of the womb with a diadem on his head, or a sceptre in his hand," Rutherford writes; but the people may put these symbols there as they delegate this or that person by divine guidance to be their prince, as Saul was chosen by the free suffrages of the people and anointed by Samuel, the prophet. The arguments of John Maxwell in support of God's immediate choice of a king independent of the people are so much rubbish, Rutherford claims; and in the course of his book he pursues his adversary relentlessly down a labyrinth of polemical alleys, flays him with Scripture and pagan tome, scorns his argumentative powers with virulent counterattack, and demonstrates that, "this Plagiarus hath not one line in his book which is not stolen." This "unchurched Prelate," Rutherford argues, referring to Maxwell, either proves too little, or too much, or nothing at all, and does not even do justice to the authors from whom he steals his material.

The king and lower magistrates hold their offices under God, it is contended in *Lex rex*, not only in the sense that they are chosen by God through the parliament of the people, but also because God endows them with gifts of government. Physically the king is "but a mortal man" with the same passive capacity as all other men. As Solomon asked for divine assistance for his royal task, so do all other rulers require grace for the discharge of their function. The authority of government in a prince is superior to that enjoyed by other men, but

it is a matter of degree. Parents, employers, and magistrates all have authority by God in some measure. If "the necessity and temper of a commonwealth" require a monarchical government, then the king is the supreme civil authority, but he is only one among many other ranks of authority all of whom are responsible to God for the governmental gifts with which they have been endowed by divine favor. They are not appointees of the king so much as appointees of the people acting in concert, and they may discharge their functions independently of the royal power. Samuel Rutherford is emphatic on this point that all civil authorities are not delegates of the king but expressions of the natural and divine power resident in the citizens; that if there is a divine right of kings, there is also a divine right attached to all ranks of magistracy and a divine right of the people as a whole. He says, "The constitution is so voluntary, as it hath below it the law of nature for its general foundation, and above it, the supervenient institution of God, ordaining that there should be such magistrates, both kings and other judges, because without such, all human societies should be dissolved."

In Question IX a critical turn in the exposition is raised by the query, "Whether or no sovereignty is so from the people, that it remaineth in them in some part, so as they may, in case of necessity, resume it." It is certainly not true that any individual can take upon himself the right to remove a tyrant, for the power of government originates in the citizens as a whole, or their representatives. "The subject of royal power, we affirm, the first and ultimate, and native subject of all power, is the community," Rutherford insists. Should tyranny develop, this same community can act to redress the wrong. God never gave any magistrate the power to perpetrate wickedness, but only to promote the good. The tyrant is a servant of Satan, and it is the obligation of godly men to resist the works of the Devil. Not all the power of the people is vested in a parliament, and not all the power of a parliament is vested in the king. No arbitrary power is given to either parliament or king, "nor is there any arbitrary power in the people, or in any mortal man." Clearly the community retains the right to reform in cases of flagrant abuse of power, though they "are to suffer much before they resume their power."

It matters not whether a king inherits his throne by birth or achieves it by war, all government is conditional, as is abundantly illustrated in the Old Testament which Samuel Rutherford accepts as a final criterion for every phase of human activity. When Rutherford appeals to the law of nature he never doubts that it concurs with Scripture, for God who speaks through both cannot be thought to contradict Himself. In Question XVIII, "What is the law of the king, and his power?" Rutherford dips into Biblical exegesis in a tremendous display of learning to demonstrate from an awesome array of authorities in divinity that the prophet Samuel did not sanctify tyranny or teach that the only resort of a people was to pray and suffer patiently. A similar exhaustive treatment is given in a crucial passage in the New Testament in Question XXXIII, "Whether or no the place, Rom. XIII, I, proves that in no case is it lawful to resist the king." Because the passage speaks of "the powers that are ordained of God" and not of kings only, Rutherford claims that it tells more against "the cavaliers' unlawful wars against the parliament and estates of two kingdoms."

The practical question of the justification of a defensive war against Charles I was uppermost in the mind of the author, and especially the Scottish involvement with the English parliamentary forces. Not only had the general questions of Church and state been raised acutely for the whole Protestant cause by the Counter-Reformation, but the fact of civil war in Britain was in urgent need of theological and constitutional defense. Samuel Rutherford had been deeply involved in the struggle in Scotland to re-establish Presbyterian church government after the imposition of episcopacy under Archbishop William Laud (1573-1645). The tremendous effort which was necessary was successfully concluded in 1638, and *Lex rex* echoed many of the arguments which had been used for the Scottish "Second Reformation." This local concern appears in Question XXXVII, "Whether or no it be lawful that the Estates of Scotland help their oppressed brethren, the Parliament and Protestants of England, against Papists and Prelates now in arms against them, and killing them, and endeavouring the establishment of Popery, though the King of Scotland should inhibit them." Examples of assistance to the distressed are educed from Scripture; Scottish help for European Protestants is cited, and the help that England gave to the Reformation in Scotland is recalled. God is not pleased with "lip-love" to one's neighbor. We are our brother's keeper; we must bear one another's burdens, and the law of gratitude demands action. Not least, a victory of the Papists and Prelates in England would expose Scotland to the same fate: "We should but sleep to be killed in our nest, if we did not arise and fight for King, church, country, and brethren." Rutherford is careful to show that he is not fighting the King as such, but defending him against his true enemies who have turned him against his own good.

A discussion of the merits of monarchy follows, a question which the author faces unwillingly. "It is a dark way," he says. Unlimited monarchy is clearly bad. There must be restraints against the possible subversion of all laws, liberties, and religion at the hands of a wicked prince. No doubt there are good points in all forms of civil order, and as good a case as any can be made out for a monarchy. Samuel Rutherford declares himself undecided, for he recognizes that all human structures are open to sin, and a monarch is no nearer wisdom than other magistrates. Perhaps the convenience of a monarchy is its best support. If the king fails in his duty and covenant with the people, and if he will not suffer correction, then he may be dethroned by God, through the instrument of the people. The right of self preservation is natural and cannot ever be surrendered; and when a king becomes a tyrant and destroys his subjects, they are released from their fiduciary bond, and they may oppose and depose him. *Salus populi, suprema lex*: the safety of the people is the supreme law.

Lex rex in its title preserves the priority which ought to prevail. The king is not above the law, for he is obliged to administer the laws enacted by parliament. In Question XLIII Samuel Rutherford asserts the state of the matter in the history and laws of Scotland, and in the confessions of faith of the Protestant churches. By the coronation oath King Charles I swore that he would maintain the true religion and rule according to the will of God and the laws of the land, and in this way he accepted limitations on his royal power, and the primacy of law as the foundation of responsible government.

This great work of Rutherford had been preceded in Scotland by the celebrated treatise *De jure regni apud Scotos* of George Buchanan (1506-1582), a scholar and humanist of international fame and tutor to James VI of Scotland, to whom Buchanan dedicated his book in 1579. James VI became James I of the united kingdoms of Scotland and England, and his son, Charles I, was the monarch about whom Rutherford was concerned. John Knox (c.1505-1572) in his *History of the Reformation in Scotland* had faced the same issue with Mary, Queen of Scots, the grandmother of Charles I. The core of the solution to the constitutional question is the same in these three works by Scotsmen; namely, that monarchs are responsible to God and the people and cannot place themselves above the public good. The authority of a king is relative to his use of it. "I desire," wrote Buchanan, "that the people from whom he derived his power, should have the liberty of prescribing its bounds; and I require that he should exercise over the people only those rights which he has received from their hands." In the light of these senti-

ments it is not surprising that Buchanan's book met with the same fate as

that of Rutherford's and was banned
in Scotland.

DE RELIGIONE LAICI

Author: Edward Herbert, First Lord of Cherbury (1583-1648)
Type of work: Theology
First published: 1645

PRINCIPAL IDEAS ADVANCED

All religions rest their claims partly on reason and partly on faith.

*What they rest on reason is common to all religions and consists in five catho-
lic truths.*

*The beliefs which rest on faith are of two kinds: those concerning the past,
and those concerning the future.*

*Faith concerning things past has partly to do with historical beliefs, which are
profitable insofar as they support the catholic truths, and partly with mystifica-
tions, which are useful only to enhance the authority of priests.*

*Faith concerning things future is more directly authenticated in the human
breast, and such faith gives hope for a blessed immortality.*

Part of Lord Herbert's interest in religion undoubtedly arose from the desire to find a practical foundation for
toleration and peace. As English am-
bassador to France under James I, he
was well acquainted with the extent of
religious dissension in his time: Europe was embroiled in the Thirty
Years' War; Holland was torn with the
Arminian controversy; France was
restless under the Edict of Nantes, and
England was on the verge of revolution. Religion, Herbert said, ought to
lay upon men an obligation to peace;
hence, when one beheld the clergy almost everywhere inciting to animosity
and strife, there was reason to inquire
whether they had not mixed vain and
pernicious matters with the truth. In
De religione laici, Herbert provides
the layman with an apparatus for dis-

criminating true from false belief, and
for bringing the clergy to book.

But Herbert's interests in religion
went deeper. Living at a time when
the New Learning was regarded by
many as a means of extending man's
domination over nature, Herbert was
more impressed with the prospects
which it opened for the development
of man's inner life. In this respect, his
essay on lay religion is no mere political tract, but a sermon designed to
point men on the way to their perfection.

Herbert's underlying philosophy is
set forth in *De veritate* (1624),
where, as the title suggests, his purpose was to examine truth, and to distinguish knowledge from "revelation,
probability, possibility, and error." The
essay describes man as a microcosm,

endowed with inner forms of apprehension which naturally conform with all objects of the universe. Native instincts give man true images of the natural world, and provide him with "common notions" by means of which to understand them. By an inner sense, he has infallible knowledge of fundamental truths of metaphysics and morals. Error comes in on the discursive level, so that man has need of a method which will enable him to ask the right questions in the right circumstances. A major purpose of *De veritate* was to provide that method. In distinction from knowledge, which has its foundation in man's natural faculties, "revelation" depends on the authority of him who proclaims it. Insofar as revelation makes claims respecting the past, it must be judged, like all history and tradition, in terms of probability; insofar as it makes claims respecting the future, it appeals to a special faculty of the soul which yearns for the eternal and infinite.

In *De religione laici*, Herbert does little more than apply these principles to the problems of religious knowledge. All religions, he says, have at their foundation certain "common notions," which answer to natural instincts in man, and therefore are true: "namely, 1. That there is some supreme divinity. 2. That this divinity ought to be worshiped. 3. That virtue joined with piety is the best method of divine worship. 4. That we should return to our right selves from sins. 5. That reward or punishment is bestowed after this life is finished." These articles, which Herbert calls "our catholic truths," do not depend at all on a particular faith or religious tradition, having been "acknowledged as true throughout the world, by every

age." They are, in his opinion, not merely the foundation of positive religion, but are by themselves sufficient for piety and virtue. Thus, every religion has its basis in reason.

Every teaching beyond these catholic truths pertains to faith; and, as we have seen, faith must be distinguished, according as it is directed toward the past or toward the future. Faith in the future, says Herbert, "proceeds from the highest faculty of the soul," being the root of all piety and devotion. "For by the light of this Faith we gaze upon God, with its tongue we speak to Him, with its hand we lay hold upon Him; in no other way are we inspired, exalted, preserved." Presumably there would be little quarrel between faith and reason, or between different religious traditions, if people were more zealous in this branch of faith. Unfortunately, religious teachers lay most of their stress upon the other kind of faith, directed toward the past. This kind of faith, which corresponds to no natural faculty, depends upon the reports and testimonies of men, and is more or less probable according to circumstances. "Mankind is given complete liberty regarding Faith about the past, and regarding doctrines proceeding from such Faith," Herbert writes.

For Herbert, the Christian religion possesses no special prerogatives over the other religions of mankind; God is not tied to any time or place. Yet, because Herbert was writing for Europeans, he applied his criteria particularly to the Jewish Scriptures, and asks, "What in the Sacred Scriptures may be called the pure and undisputed word of God?" It is certain, he says, that not everything in the Bible has equal authority, because included in it are the words of "villains, women, beasts, nay of the devil himself." First, we find there "our catholic truths, which as the undoubted pronouncements of God, transcribed in the conscience, are to be set apart and preserved," while the rest is brought under investigation. Second, we find a great deal of Hebrew history, and "no small heap of miracles published among them." These stories were told, according to Herbert, with the obvious purpose of applying and enforcing the catholic truths. How many of the stories a man believes, after considering the likelihood of each one's claim to be true, and whether a particular story does indeed promote piety and morality as it was intended to do, is for each man to decide. Third, there is a mass of esoteric material, "special covenants, secret and allegorical allusions, nay even some expressions too concise, or incoherent, and difficult to understand." Here, in the special covenants, Herbert finds the origins of most of the special claims which divide the churches. On grounds cited later by Rousseau's Savoyard priest, that a man must be impossibly erudite to determine the merits of alternate interpretations, and that God does not make exact scholarship a requirement for salvation, Herbert argues that this part of Scripture can be ignored by the layman; it is, he claims, the special preserve of priestly orders and serves as a means of mystifying the people and enhancing the authority of the priests.

Herbert admits that, in urging men to stick to the catholic truths, he is taking something away from religion, but, he says, he is taking nothing away from virtue and piety. As an instance, he takes the teachings of the Church respecting the remission of sin. Our reason tells us that God will forgive a man if he repent of his sin, but only on the condition that he mend his ways. The priests, however, drawing from the third class of Scriptural matter, hedge forgiveness about with all sorts of provisions and special dispensations, and so make repentance either too light or too heavy, in either case defeating the purpose of Universal Providence. Granted that by these means "the herd may sometimes be impelled to a juster pattern of life," they are rendered no more virtuous at heart, nor are they spared the implacable judgment to come.

Herbert does not deny the value of a priestly group. Unlike the later freethinkers, who, as Steele said, without the word "priestcraft" would be struck dumb, he grants the need of men set apart as teachers of the young, as preachers of virtue, as public intercessors, and as ministers of charity and mercy. We are reminded that Herbert had a celebrated example of the virtuous priest in his own brother, the poet, George Herbert (1593-1633).

Priests of virtuous and exemplary life, Edward Herbert says, ought to be revered because they "check the headlong license of the common people, they call attention to the means of eternal salvation engraved on the conscience, they introduce penitence, they make known God the Rewarder, they improve all things, finally, in the direction of moral excellence." In this way, faith and tradition fortify reason, without taking anything away from it.

The lay believer, whom the author has in view, is designated throughout the treatise as "the Wayfarer," a term which means something more than "pilgrim," in view of Herbert's cabalistic and Neoplatonic affinities. Herbert describes each man as passing through four "lives": in the parental seed, in the womb, in this world, and in the world to come. He points out that, as each of these lives changes into its successor, something gross and rudimentary is left behind, and that the new life is by contrast more full and satisfying. This process, says Herbert, establishes a probability in favor of a blessed immortality. But in these matters, dealing with the higher kind of faith, we are not left with mere probable inference. Among the faculties of our mind, we are told in *De veritate*, is one which longs for "eternal and infinite objects"; not to be confused with the ordinary faculties by which we calculate the future, it is "a divine intellectual faculty" and "a supernatural sense which proceeds directly from God." By means of it man comprehends the infinity of worlds, both large and small, the transcendence of God, who "fills, informs, and encompasses the infinite itself in the vastness of His unity"; by it he further knows the sublimity of his own being, and that it can attain to all these things. For, "since the faculty of sight reaches to the sun and even to the stars, while the understanding and the will refer to the infinite and eternal, is it to be supposed that in spite of our aspirations we do not reach and grasp them?" Once we have cast off the limitations of the flesh, we shall find "that the secrets of all things are revealed, and that nothing exists in the infinite which we may not hope to attain."

Lord Herbert is sometimes called "the father of Deism" because his five catholic truths became a sort of *credo* in anti-clerical circles. But popular Deism owes more to Newton and Locke than to Herbert, whom Locke was at special pains to refute. It is more correct to think of him as a link in the long history of English Platonism and as having as his successors Lord Shaftesbury, Coleridge, and the Cambridge Platonists.

THE FOUNDATIONS OF FREEDOM

Author: John Lilburne (c.1614-1657) and associates
Type of work: Puritan political philosophy
First published: 1648

PRINCIPAL IDEAS ADVANCED

The people of a nation should decide who should receive the power of government.

Government must serve the interests of the people and its power is limited by the natural liberties of man.

Of all freedoms, that of conscience in matters of religion is first in importance.

All men are to be equal before the law with no special privileges or exemptions by reason of birth or function.

The importance of documents is not measured by their length. *The Foundations of Freedom: or An Agreement of the People* is a mere pamphlet in size, but it is a concentrated precipitation of ideas that had been germinating in England ever since Magna Carta (June 15, 1215), the eminent curb on the arbitrary power of government. The Second Agreement, as the 1648 pamphlet is usually called, was the product of a committee of sixteen appointed by the groups most involved in planning political strategy; namely, the Parliament, the Army, the Independents, and the Levellers. It had been preceded by tremendous activity by the Levellers, as the associates of Lilburne were nicknamed, who were determined to oppose the tyrannical use of power by any party in England. The position of the country at the time when the Second Agreement was drawn up was unsettled to the point of being dangerously explosive. The council of Army officers had decided to be rid of King Charles, and Parliament had just been purged of its Presbyterian strength. The Independents were in power, especially in the Army. The time had come, the Levellers believed, when decisive action should be taken to reform the constitutional basis of government by an assembly elected by the "well affected" of the people on a broadly distributed franchise.

Briefly, the proposal was to dissolve the existing Parliament speedily and elect a Commons of three hundred to be called the Representative. All citizens twenty-one years of age and over, except those of the servant class or who had declared themselves to be disaffected by support of the King, or who were opposed to the Agreement, were to be included in the electorate. The Representative would hold office for periods of seven years. Careful arrangements were laid down for the electoral process to insure the absence of corruption.

In anticipation of the successful completion of the election, the Levellers specified the powers of the new national assembly in a document of nine articles; namely, *The Foundations of Freedom*. The document deals with such matters as conscription, recrimination, equal privileges, interference with lawful process, preservation of common rights, emergency measures, corruption, and the subordination of the Army to the decisions of the Representative. Above all, and placed first, freedom of conscience in religious matters is to be firmly upheld. The Representative is not "to compel by penalties or otherwise, any person to any thing in or about matters of Faith, Religion, or God's Worship, or to restrain any person from the professing of his Faith, or exercise of Religion according to his conscience, in any house or place (except such as are or shall be set apart for the publick Worship)." The actual arrangements for the general settlement of religion is left to the discretion of the Representative so long as it does not involve compulsion or the promotion of Popery.

Thereafter the most clamant grievances calling for redress are listed, all of them being flagrant abuses which the Levellers had been speaking about for some time. No one should be compelled to witness against himself or be left in custody without trial for longer than three months, and at the trial all communications were to be in English. Business is not to be restrained, public levies are to be equitable, debtors are not to be imprisoned, life and limb are to be respected, tithes for the support of the clergy are to be abolished, interest on loans is not to exceed six per cent per annum, and in general flagrant injustices are to be rectified.

The whole document is an extraordinary example of the flowering of democratic ideas, and it anticipated much that was later enacted in the modern British Commonwealth, the United States, and in other areas where representative democracy has been established.

Lilburne recorded in *Legal Fundamental Liberties* that the points of greatest sensitivity were the items on freedom of conscience and the right of the Representative to punish where no law covered the case. Army men were in favor of some restriction on liberty of conscience, and in this they were not alone in the land. For years the Presbyterian party had spoken of this liberty as a hydraheaded monster. It was argued that since religion covered a large territory, to permit man to define the limits of liberty would be inviting anarchy. On the other side there were many who were just as strongly convinced that coercion in religious affairs was indefensible. The pulpit and the members of the congregation should both be free to speak their minds as they believed God was leading them. Such a doctrine was advocated in the Baptist meetings which Lilburne and some of his associates attended. These men had suffered scorn and privation at the hands of state religion, and they were in no mood to permit power of persecution to have legal status in their blueprint for a better world. Freedom to dissent and to be protected in their sustentation of it was a fundamental freedom. As dili-

gent students of the Bible, they had come to know their status in the Kingdom of God as the priesthood of all believers, and they were not prepared to settle for a second-class citizen status in the Kingdom of England. The rank and file of the Army were also now a vocal group, and they supported religious liberty as the key to all other liberties.

Lilburne and his friends had expected that the Agreement of the People would be submitted to the people forthwith, first to the regiments and then to the districts. Their chagrin was bitter when the document was submitted instead to a council of officers, who proceeded to open up the Agreement for revision and then to produce their own version. Lilburne's opinion on these proceedings was caustic. The officers were "a pack of dissembling juggling knaves," full of deceit and looking to their own interests. He published his copy of the Agreement, agreed to by a majority of the committee of sixteen, under the title *Foundations of Freedom,* with a prefatory epistle commending it. Thus this notable expression of democratic ideas was made available to great numbers who were eager for a constitutional settlement and demanded it along these lines.

Despite the frustration of seeing a revised form of the Agreement submitted by the council of officers to the Purged Parliament but allowed to lie there without action, it was a high moment in Leveller religious and political aspirations. John Lilburne had succeeded as a result of his stormy career in and out of prison in identifying some of the major ills of England and in obtaining agreement on some remedies by a composite committee of responsible persons. Since the electorate was not to be confined to property owners, the governing assembly would be genuinely a people's Representative. The law's vexatious delays, under which he had long suffered, would be mitigated, and the clergy whom he despised would be shorn of their legalized plunder, called "tithes."

It might have been expected that some reference would be made to Kingship and the House of Lords. There matters apparently were left open, the principal point being that whoever governed was to exercise power in the interests of the people. This was in accordance both with the ancient maxim that the safety of the people is the supreme law, and also with the main thrust of Biblical example. Saul was made King of Israel by the popular acclamation of the people, as the pamphleteers stated again and again. In the Independent Churches the common man demanded a voice in the church meeting as a saint of God, able to read the Word of God as well as any parson, major general, or noble. Here in the church meeting democratic ideas were nurtured and freedom was translated from theory to actuality, and ideas fostered here were applied to larger issues.

Lilburne was in many ways vain and inclined to quarrelsomeness, but he knew the minds of the common people, and he had an immense following, as was obvious when he was suffering imprisonment from time to time. The Levellers knew how to organize petitions and could obtain many thousands of signatures in a few days. Their main leader never lost a chance to exploit his misfortunes by telling all (with running commentary) in a pamphlet. He was so well versed in the law and in expressing himself that, although *The Foundations of Freedom* is said to have been drawn up by "several well-affected Persons," it can be safely assumed that John Lilburne had a considerable part in framing it, and, in any case, was so identified with its ideology and publication that it may well be ascribed to him.

The "Principle which we profess," he wrote in the preface, is "To do unto you, as we would all men should do unto us," and this Gospel precept he believed was the rule of equity. In signing it "Thy truehearted Countryman," he was expressing his sense of identity with all the "well affected," as well as his belief that authority in government rests finally with the people at large, and that its aim is to promote and preserve their liberties.

PRECES PRIVATAE

Author: Lancelot Andrewes (1555-1626)
Type of work: Devotional manual
First published: 1648

Principal Ideas Advanced

God is revealed both in nature and in history.

Each day of the week offers distinctive reasons for the prayerful worship of God.

Although penitence involves confession, it also expresses the hope of reconciliation with God.

Thanks should be given to God for the wonders of His creation and for the particular blessings which men enjoy.

Master of Pembroke College, Bishop of Chichester, of Ely, and of Winchester, chaplain to Elizabeth I, to James I, and to Charles I, Lancelot Andrewes was one of the great public figures in the history of the English Church. He was, at the same time, a profoundly contemplative person who spent hours each day in meditation and prayer, drawing upon a wide range of devotional materials, which he gradually composed into a personal prayer book.

Andrewes's manuscript copy of his book seems to have been lost, but copies had been made, for one of them was presented by Andrewes to William Laud (1573-1645), later Archbishop of Canterbury. The original was a polyglot work, mostly in Latin, but with portions in Greek and in Hebrew. As early as 1630 printed versions in English began to appear. The task of correcting, translating, and editing the work has engaged scholars through the years, culminating in an excellent critical edition by F.E. Brightman in 1903.

Preces privatae, sometimes anglicized to *Private Devotions,* is remarkable in that, although nearly every sentence in it is drawn from some other author—either from the Scriptures or from some earlier devotional work—Andrewes has built the materials into an edifice of his own, like a chapel constructed of stones brought together from many places. What sets it apart from numerous other devotional works which affect the language of tradition is that Andrewes has mined not so much felicitous expressions as determinate thoughts. Moreover, he rarely takes from any one passage more than the two or three lines which are needed in terms of the architecture of the whole. Hence, if one is interested in a collection of the well-known prayers of the Church, he must look elsewhere.

We have spoken in terms of a chapel, for, although Andrewes was a bishop, the *Preces* was composed to meet the needs not of the Church but of the individual believer. But, even as in chapels there are differences of style, so there is diversity in works of devotion. Some are boldly irregular, with obscure crypts and lofty vaults, pierced by shafts of colored light; others are orderly, well-lighted, and carefully appointed. Andrewes's work is of the latter sort. Patiently detailed and logically divided, it offers an interesting parallel to the scientific works of Francis Bacon, who likewise combined zeal for classification with a feeling for the importance of real things. Not in flights of ecstasy but in steady, controlled awareness of all that is taking place both within the soul and outside in the world, Andrewes finds man's highest fulfillment. The devotional life, as Andrewes describes it, is a systematic endeavor to lift the mind out of infantile slumber into the full waking consciousness of responsible manhood. Like others of his time, Andrewes was aware of man's inner conflicts, and he devoted many pages to acts of penitence; but he never lost sight of the great procession of creation, of God's revelation in nature and in secular history, as well as in Scripture, so that he regarded confession and penitence as but parts of a complete regimen, which take their place alongside acts of praise, thanksgiving, and intercession.

In the struggles which were threatening to rend the Established Church at that time, Andrewes followed Richard Hooker (c.1554-1600), who tried to preserve the Church's Catholic heritage against the attacks of the Presbyterians. Andrewes's disagreement with the Low Church party in England hinged on the celebrated Puritan principle, according to which Scripture is held to be the sole rule of faith and practice. The Puritans did, indeed, develop a rich and profound devotional life based exclusively upon Biblical passages, but by their rule they were prevented from offering to God prayers which originated outside the sacred canon. Andrewes follows the principle elaborated by Hooker; namely, that God's revelation is as wide as the creation, and that the guidance of the Holy Spirit is present in the teaching and liturgy of the Church, no less than in the pages of Holy Writ. Puritans would, therefore, object to many passages in the Preces, which are drawn from the Apocrypha, from the Church Fathers, from medieval Horae and Breviaries, and even from the prayerbooks of Jewish syna-

gogues. Still, they could hardly quarrel with the main conception of the work, which is guided entirely by Biblical conceptions, notably God's revelation of Himself in the works of creation, in the divine names, and in redemptive history. These themes interweave and reinforce one another in ways which reveal profound feeling for Biblical typology.

Andrewes's prayers fall into two broad categories: those appointed to special times, and those framed according to special subjects. The first third of the book is devoted to prayers for the morning and the evening. The series of seven morning prayers, one for each day of the week, is especially noteworthy because of the sensitive use made of Biblical symbols and types. Thus, on Sunday, Andrewes commemorates the creation of light, the resurrection of Christ, and the sending of the Holy Spirit; on Monday, the creation of the firmament, the giving of the Law, and the prayers of Job and of the Canaanitish women; so, on through until Saturday, when he commemorates the Sabbath, the burial of Christ, the cessation of sins, and the souls of the departed.

Of the remaining portion of the Preces the largest section is devoted to prayers of penitence. Several complete penitential prayers are given, expressing contrition, confessing sins, pleading for mercy, purposing amendment, petitioning for help, and drawing assurance. The language, drawn chiefly from Scripture, is explicit and firm. The emotional power is largely latent, lying not in the expressions themselves but in the associations which they call forth from a mind thoroughly acquainted with the Scriptures. A reference to "Magdalene at the feast, Peter in the hall, the robber on the rood," is characteristic. On the same page, we read of those who forsook "angel's food" for "leeks and garlick," and "the Father's table" for "swine's husks." This is followed by an allusion to the Galatian Christians: "Woe is me, woe is me insensate! Who did bewitch me in this sort to play the fool?" Then comes a further reflection on the parable of the Prodigal Son: "O if Thou but vouchsafe to receive me, my mind is wholly to return: for then it was better with me than now it is." Such is the texture of nearly the whole book. The feelings it calls forth are of the kind which the believer consciously shares with the whole of Christ's Church.

But, with Andrewes, penitence is not so much an affair of feeling as it is one of reason. His confession is a full indictment of himself by the Law, by God's mercy, by comparison with other creatures and less fortunate men, and it is as detailed and specific as the Devil himself could have drawn up. But his plea for mercy is no less carefully argued. The divine nature, the divine names, a multitude of promises, redemptive acts, and parables are used to overthrow any fear or scruple which might prevent the soul from approaching God. Here is a faith that knows its kinship to reason, yet manages to avoid the excesses of legalism and dogmatism.

Andrewes's prayers of thanksgiving are chiefly notable for their comprehensive attention to detail. A typical prayer begins with a meditation on the seven days of creation, surveys the general station of man, then enlarges upon the atoning work of Christ, to praise Him "for all the good things He did, the evil things He suffered, from the cratch to the cross," for His triumph over death, and for the gift of the Holy Spirit. There is hardly an event in the Gospel narrative that is not worked into this lengthy meditation, as the mind is led from the nativity through the stages of Christ's earthly ministry, to His rejection, condemnation, torture, and crucifixion. To the story of Christ's passion, beginning with the hour of His arrest and ending with the release of His spirit upon the cross, Andrewes devotes more than one hundred items. The cumulative power of this long narrative is then effectively discharged by means of a prayer from the Sarum *Horae* (Paris, 1514), based on the ritual for anointing the various members of the body in Extreme Unction, which mentions the sacred head, hands, side, and feet of the Savior and concludes, "And I, Lord, am wounded in soul: behold the multitude, the length, the breadth, the depth of my wounds, from the crown of the head to the sole of the feet, and by thine heal mine."

A different kind of thanksgiving, of which Andrewes includes several examples, tells the particular blessings which God has bestowed upon the worshiper, including the nation, the city, the church into which he was baptized, the schools which he has attended, the parishes and dioceses which he has served, his family, friends, and neighbors. Sometimes he mentions these in general expressions, drawn from tradition; but at other times he anatomizes his life in circumstantial language, as in the following: "Glory be to Thee, o Lord, for that I am, I am alive, I am rational; for nurture, preservation, governance; for education, citizenship, devotion, religion; . . . for my parents honest and good, teachers, benefactors ever to be remembered, colleagues likeminded, hearers attentive, friends sincere, retainers faithful. . . ; for all these and all things else which we wot of, which we wot not of, open and privy, . . . I confess to Thee and will confess, I bless Thee and will bless, I give thanks to Thee and will give thanks, all the days of my life."

The work also contains prayers of intercession both general and special, and prayers for special occasions, such as before attending Holy Mysteries, and before going on a journey. Because the work was never intended for publication, but only for Andrewes's own use, it is freighted with allusions to the stirring times in which the author lived. The prayers are formally interesting in that they reflect, in both phraseology and thought, the influence of the liturgies of the ancient Greek Church; they are personally moving in that they express a constant humility. But if the reader is always conscious of the author, he is more vividly aware of the continuing consciousness of Christendom. The work will always be cherished by Christians who value their connection with the Church invisible as well as visible, triumphant as well as militant.

THE RULE AND EXERCISE OF HOLY LIVING AND HOLY DYING

Author: Jeremy Taylor (1613-1667)
Type of work: Spiritual direction
First published: 1650, 1651

PRINCIPAL IDEAS ADVANCED

The benefits of Heaven are reserved for those who have lived and died in a holy manner.

Holy living consists in remembering our heavenly calling while practicing our calling on earth, and in living sober, just, and godly lives.

Holy dying is an art to which each man must accustom himself before he loses his strength; there is no salvation for the deathbed penitent.

In order to prepare himself for his heavenly destiny, man must overcome the attractions of the present life; sickness, as a kind of penance and mortification of the flesh, is to be accounted a blessing.

A clergyman who sided with the royalist cause, Jeremy Taylor spent the years of the Puritan ascendancy in Wales, as chaplain to Richard, Earl of Carbery, to whom the present work is dedicated. In the preface to *The Rule and Exercise of Holy Living,* Taylor refers to the scattered condition of the Church during those Puritan years; many Christians were deprived of the Church's ministrations and, thus, individual Christians were left to find their own salvation.

Taylor's book is designed to trace

the "narrow way to heaven" in a straightforward way, without controversy and speculation. "I have told what men ought to do, and by what means they may be assisted; and in most cases I have also told them why; and yet with as much quickness as I could think necessary to establish a rule, and not to engage in homily or discourse."

The Rule and Exercise of Holy Dying was originally published as a separate work. It was begun during the last illness of Lady Carbery and was composed especially to help her. She died, however, before the work was completed. "She knew how to live rarely well," writes Taylor, "and she desired to know how to die; and God taught her by an experiment." Together, the two books constitute a detailed handbook for Christian living, together with suitable prayers for every occasion.

Taylor stood in the High Church tradition, for he was a protégé of Archbishop Laud. In opposition to the Puritan principle, that the Scriptures alone provide the rules of faith and practice, Taylor took the broad view of Christian origins, and he depended on instruction from extra-Biblical as well as Biblical sources. Although he was as ready as the Puritans to use Scriptural examples of his rules, he was just as likely to draw illustrations from one of the Fathers or from some Greek historian. For example, charity is enjoined on the recommendation of St. Jerome, who wrote, "I do not remember to have read that ever any charitable person died an evil death," and of Cyrus the Persian, who said on his deathbed, "I have been a lover of mankind, and a friend, and merciful; and now I expect to communicate in that great kindness which he shows that is the great God and Father of man and mercies."

Taylor also repudiated the Protestant teaching of justification by faith alone, and he argued that the covenant of grace, no less than the covenant of nature, lays a strict obligation on man. "Either you must renounce your religion," he says, "or submit to the impositions of God and thy portion of sufferings." He explains that, whereas in the Old Testament, pardon of sins consisted in no more than the removing of the punishment, in the Gospel it includes turning a man from his iniquities. Pardon of sins, he says, is sanctification; a man is not forgiven unless he forgives; he is not saved unless he live a holy life. Stories of deathbed repentance were particularly odious to Taylor. "Our religion," he says, "hath made a covenant of sufferings, and the great business of our lives is sufferings." Thus, it is incredible that God will "take a deathbed sigh or groan, and a few unprofitable tears and promises, in exchange for all our duty." The main complaint Taylor makes against the Roman Church is concerning its teaching that Extreme Unction will save a soul from Hell.

Following in the way that Richard Hooker (c.1554-1600) marked out for the Church of England, Taylor seeks to identify Christianity, at least in its moral aspects, with "the law of nature and great reason." Christianity has regard for all the fundamental necessities of life, underwrites all its natural relations, and leads to the consummation which God intended when he created man. Taylor finds the divisions of man's duty in the words of Paul, that we should live "soberly, righteously, and godly in this present world." The first of these, says Taylor, comprises our duties to ourselves, including temperance, chastity, modesty, and contentment; the second, our duty to our fellows, including obedience to superiors, responsibility to inferiors, fulfillment of contracts, and restitution of wrongs committed; the third, our duty to God, including both internal and external actions of religion.

Of special interest, in view of the political upheavals of the times, is Taylor's account of obedience to superiors. As his own loyalty to the royal family would suggest, he upholds the absolute right of kings over subjects. Other obligations, he says, rest on contract, but obedience to superiors, whether parents or the king, derives from the command of God. Obedience, he explains, is a complex virtue, including nearly all others—humility, self-denial, charity to God and to others, and victory over unruly passion. For this reason, rebellion is "the most unnatural and damned impiety," worse even than idolatry. That men should count it otherwise betokens, in Taylor's view, a fundamental perversion of the order of creation, the same kind of unreasonableness which led Satan and his hosts to revolt against their King. But even the devils preserve their appointed ranks and obey their superiors in rebellion. Heedless of all order, and deluded by the vain promises of ambition and greed, men hope to better their worldly estate by a crime which will damn them for eternity.

The contrast between this world and eternity is fundamental to Taylor's piety. Although he recognizes that a man's trade or profession is a calling, and that in some sense we serve God in performing honestly the work of this world, he nevertheless maintains that our proper service to God lies in acts of devotion which prepare the soul for Heaven. He urges us to take the utmost care of our time, to employ every possible moment in prayers, reading, meditating, and performing works of charity, "ever remembering so to work in our calling, as not to neglect the work of our high calling." He says that what we sow in minutes and spare parts of our time will bring us eternal rewards, for "God rewards our minutes with long and eternal happiness; and the greater portion of our time we give to God, the more we treasure up for ourselves."

Reasoning in this way, Taylor is led to take an extreme stand against all those things which tend to bind our affections to this world. He warns against "balls and revellings," "garish and wanton dresses," "banquets and perfumes," "feasts and liberty," and "the company of women that are singers." To humble the flesh he recommends exercises similar to those developed by Buddhists and Jains. We are to reflect on the uncleannesses which the body sends out from "its several sinks," one of the foulest of which is situated in the middle of the face. If this is not enough to wean us from the flesh, we may visit hospitals and charnel houses in order to acquaint ourselves with the body in its various stages of decay. He relates the story of a young hermit who, having failed by prayer and fasting to overcome his passion for a young lady, and hearing that she had died, secretly visited her vault and wiped the moisture from her decaying carcass with his mantle. Henceforth, when temptation returned, all he had to do to overcome it was to wrap his face in the mantle.

From these precepts, it will be seen how exactly Taylor agrees with the claim that "to live is Christ, and to die is gain." Holy living is, in his opinion, but a preparation for holy dying; since the latter is the gate of Heaven, sickness and old age are not to be considered as enemies but as friends. The sick man, in Taylor's view, is nearer to Heaven than the healthy man, because Heaven consists in the absence of sinful affections; in sickness the soul begins to untie "the strings of vanity that made her upper garment cleave to the world and sit uneasy." While the flesh sits uneasy, the spirit "feels itself at ease, freed from the petulant solicitations of those passions which in health" never abate. Even the groans of the sick man are so many penances by which the soul is prepared for Heaven.

Taylor was writing during troubled times, and he may on that account have been inclined to exaggerate the suffering of human life. "As our life is very short," he writes, "so it is very miserable. . . . God, in pity to mankind, lest his burden should be insupportable, and his nature an intolerable load, hath reduced our state of misery to an abbreviature." These words were written during the time that Hobbes, from a different philosophical perspective, was commenting on the shortness and incommodiousness of life. Unlike Hobbes, Taylor found a redeeming feature in man's suffering, arguing with the Stoics that there is no evil except in relation to men's desires, and that desires can be controlled. It is part of the discipline that God has set before us, says Taylor, that we should bear pain joyfully. Few

outside the Roman communion have written with greater enthusiasm for the suffering of martyrs. "God could not choose but be pleased with the delicate accents of martyrs," he writes, "when in their tortures they cried out nothing but 'Holy Jesus,' and 'Blessed be God.'" Moreover, he ventures, "if we had seen St. Polycarp burning to death, or St. Lawrence roasted upon his gridiron, or St. Ignatius exposed to lions, or St. Sebastian pierced with arrows . . . we should have been in love with flames, and have thought the gridiron fairer than the ribs of a marital bed; and we should have chosen to converse with those beasts, rather than those men that brought those beasts forth. . . ."

Perhaps Taylor's enthusiasm for the martyrs is excessive, yet there is no question that, from the literary point of view, Taylor is one of the great artists of seventeenth century prose, with scarcely an equal in his love for a beautiful expression and a recondite reference. Nevertheless, if all worldly things are vanity, why should Lucan and Petronius be spared? One can use them to moralize with, but Taylor goes beyond this, as when, in a peroration on our duty toward departed loved ones, he tells Petronius's story of the young widow of Ephesus who, after vowing to die in her husband's sepulchre, was wooed by a guard there, and afterward, when her new husband needed an extra corpse, contributed the body of her first. All of this Taylor recounts in full detail, merely to emphasize the impropriety of immoderate grief.

Tolstoy, when the distaste for life drove him to condemn the world, did not spare his art. Was Taylor less perspicacious? Or, profoundly touched with the sadness of man's condition, was he employing his muse to help make men's grief more tolerable? More likely, he reasoned that in cultivating the art of rhetoric he was doing no more than exercise the calling which was laid upon him, and, as it were, sweetening the medicine that it was his duty as a physician of souls to minister. Among the prayers of intercession which he frames is one for the clergy: "Remember them that minister about holy things; let them be clothed with righteousness, and sing with joyfulness. Amen."

THE SAINTS' EVERLASTING REST

Author: Richard Baxter (1615-1691)
Type of work: Devotional meditations
First published: 1650

PRINCIPAL IDEAS ADVANCED

In God's loving purpose a final rest is designed for His children, and their highest felicity consists in attaining this rest.

The achievement of this goal requires on our part serious examination of our present position and earnest consideration of the character of that rest which awaits us.

The goal also presupposes constant discipline of various kinds and at different levels, in order that our present lives may qualify us for our future state and prepare us to enjoy it.

The *Saints' Everlasting Rest* was one of Richard Baxter's earliest works; it has always been his most famous one. When he wrote it, Baxter had already laid down the lines along which his lifework would proceed. He had demonstrated his remarkable gifts as a preacher and pastor, and the first phase of his notable ministry at Kidderminster was behind him. He had refused the chaplaincy of Oliver Cromwell's regiment of horse, but had served in a similar capacity with Colonel Whalley, and had been deeply shocked at the ferment of heretical ideas at work in the parliamentary army. Then serious illness overtook him. He found a refuge in the home of Lady Rouse, but he was convinced that his days were numbered and that his end was near. It was in this mood that he conceived his book, and it is the background of this anticipation of death which gives his work its distinctive quality. Baxter always wrote with the urgency of a man persuaded that his life was trembling on the brink of eternity, with little time in which to fulfill his mission.

His point of departure is a text of Scripture: "There remaineth therefore a rest to the people of God" (Heb. 4:9). Even in the natural life of man there is nothing so welcome to us as rest; "it is not our comfort only, but our stability." For the Christian, rest has a more intense significance; "it is the perfect, endless enjoyment of God by the perfected saints." This is the believer's final destiny, but it is a state open only to those who choose God "for their end and happiness." The goal must be clearly envisioned and resolutely pursued. We must also realize our present need, and acknowledge our basic dependence upon God. "When once we begin to trust our stock of habitual grace and to depend upon our own understanding or resolution, for duty and holy walking, we are then in a dangerous, declining state." The next step, Baxter writes, is to have "an inward principle of spiritual life." God does not treat us as inanimate objects; there must be that within us which can respond to His promptings. We can make no progress, however, unless we propose to enter by the proper gate, and "Christ is the door, the only way to this rest."

So far Baxter has been preoccupied with prolegomena. Can we define this rest more closely? It means, in the first place, that we no longer need to rely upon the means of grace which sustain us in our present state. The heavenly rest also means a perfect freedom from all evils. It involves, Baxter writes, "the highest degree of the saints' personal perfection, both of body and soul." But the core "and principal part of this rest is our nearest enjoyment of God, the chief good." This in turn presupposes the complete and wholly satisfying exercise of all our powers in the enjoyment of God. We progressively discover the true significance of that much-neglected duty, praise, and through the praise of God we unify our whole being. Knowledge

finds its proper content and takes its rightful place. Love proves to be a profoundly personal yet a completely mutual relationship, and we see how remote is our true rest until we realize that God always loves us with a constancy to which our love of Him responds with ever-increasing completeness. We discover that mutual joy is the outcome of mutual love, and Baxter seems fully launched on his exploration of the inner meaning of the heavenly rest when he checks himself; such confident penetration of ultimate mysteries must be the result of man's spiritual pride, and Baxter returns to matters where Scriptural evidence promises a more assured knowledge.

It is clear that certain climactic experiences will be the prelude to the everlasting rest. Christ will appear; the general resurrection will take place; the Last Judgment will separate the saints from the sinners, and the saints will be crowned. Then all will discover the excellencies of the rest laid up for those who will receive it. They will see that it is a purchased possession, yet a free gift; it belongs to saints and angels, yet it derives its joys immediately from God himself. From this we may confidently assume that it will also be seasonable, because it will come to those wearied with the trials and burdens of an evil world. It will be suitable, in that it will be perfectly adapted to the new nature of the glorified saints. It will be perfect, since sin and suffering will have no place in the experience of the saints. And it will be everlasting.

So great a privilege is reserved for those for whom it is specifically designed. It will belong to the people of God, to those who have been chosen in God's good providence before time began. They are elect. They have been given to Christ. They have been born again. They know their own unworthiness, and they try to disguise neither the helplessness of the creature nor the all-sufficiency of Christ. Their will is consequently changed; they consciously enter into a new covenant with Christ, and they persevere in the spiritual duties which they have undertaken. The privileges of the saints are set in sharper contrast by comparing them with those who will forfeit this rest. The unregenerate will lose the personal perfections of the saints. They will have "no comfortable relation to God, nor communion with him." They can expect no part in the profound joys which belong to those who respond to God, know His nature, see His face, and experience His love. They will also forfeit the blessed society of angels and glorified saints. But all their losses will be heightened because the dimness of their understanding will be cleared away, and with fuller knowledge and clearer consciences they will know the measure of their failure. This means that those who lose the saints' rest forfeit all the enjoyments of time (their delusory interest in God and Christ, their hopes, their false peace of conscience, their secular joys, their sensual delights), but they also suffer all the torments of Hell.

Such serious considerations should surely compel the believer to give the most earnest heed to the rest of the saints. It is not surprising that the worldly and the profane neglect the matter; it is beyond measure strange that the godly do so. Magistrates, ministers, and ordinary persons are equally remiss in this regard, and to disturb those who are so foolishly secure, Baxter addresses a series of "awakening questions" alike to the upright and to the sinners. Perhaps this kind of discipline will break through the security of the complacent, and acquaint them with the terrors to which they will be subject while their title to the saints' rest remains in question. Self-examination can lead to certainty on this matter. That is why unregenerate natures, worldly companions, and Satan himself combine to discourage us. And since assurance does not come quickly, it is easy to grow discouraged and forbear the effort. Since it is dangerous to be wrong on this matter, it is necessary to make the effort, and Baxter lays down simple rules to govern our self-examination. Lest we be deluded, we must ask ourselves two simple but vital questions: (1) Do we make God our chief good? (2) Do we heartily accept Christ as our Lord and Savior?

The people of God ought to excite others to seek this rest. It is obvious and unfortunate that they fail to do so. This necessary task would begin in pitying the misery of men's souls. It would proceed through an appropriate course of education to the provision of suitable "public ordinances." Men properly qualified by learning and eloquence have a particular duty to urge others to seek this rest; so have those acquainted with sinners, those who have wealth or influence, and physicians who attend the dying.

No reasonable man will expect that the saints' everlasting rest will be available on earth. Our present afflictions are too great, even though they may stimulate us to hasten toward our true goal. We are too likely to rely on our comforts and cling to them. To do so is to court disaster, because those who seek the creature rather than the Creator inevitably invite trouble. But if we cannot enjoy heavenly rest on earth, at least we can plan for it. We can train ourselves to contemplate the joys of Heaven, and this will both encourage a proper disposition and evidence a Christian frame of mind. Thus, we shall avoid the obstacles to the kind of life which entitles us to enjoy the saints' rest. We shall not live in any known sin. We shall not let our outlook be circumscribed by worldly horizons. We shall not be lured into sharing the company of the ungodly. Specious theories will not beguile us in religion, and we shall avoid a proud and slothful spirit. In addition we shall practise the duties which promote this kind of life. We shall keep our minds on Heaven, because we realize that where our treasure is our hearts will rightly be at home, and we shall make every possible effort to know our true interest in this kind of disciplined yet otherworldly attitude. We must train ourselves to talk often and seriously about the abundant life. In every task we undertake we should strive to raise our hearts to the plane on which such life becomes possible. This will require an alert vigilance to detect and improve all possibilities and events. We should develop the neglected habit of praise. We should dwell often on the thoughts of God's infinite love. We should be sensitive to the promptings of the Holy Spirit. And this exalted conception of the devotional life rests ultimately on a simple and elementary duty: we must not neglect our bodily health. Baxter writes, "Thy body is a useful servant if thou give it its due, and no more than its due."

A disciplined religious life does not unfold automatically, and Baxter devotes much space to detailed instructions regarding the time and place suitable for "heavenly contemplation," as well as the temper most appropriate to it. Meditation and prayer should not be at the mercy of impulse or desire. There should be stated, suitable, and frequent times set aside for it each day. The Lord's Day offers exceptional opportunities, and we should not neglect the incitements of affliction, or disappointment, or bereavement. The place where we engage in this discipline of prayer should be suitably private and quiet, lest interruptions distract or noise disturb us. There is a frame of mind which conduces to meditation. Our minds must be free from secular preoccupation. Godly thoughts have little chance when they are constantly being jostled by worldly interests. This means that we must embark on this discipline "with the greatest solemnity of heart and mind. There is no trifling in holy things." So we should begin with a proper sense of the greatness of this undertaking, and of the profound seriousness of the issues at stake.

"Heavenly contemplation" is supported by what Baxter calls "consideration," which he defines as "the great instrument by which this heavenly work is carried on." It "opens the door between the head and the heart." It provides the standards which guide the affections, and it maintains a due sense of proportion in every phase of our life. It gives reason its due place and maintains it in proper vitality. But in keeping the proper balance between the various elements of our personal life, we must allow the emotions to play their appropriate role. The emotions cannot be left to chance excitement; they must be trained and exercised. Baxter therefore examines the contribution to the full life made by love, desire, hope, courage or boldness, and joy. These emotions must be given due and deliberate exercise. The order in which they should be practiced does not have to be always the same. All of them need not be "exercised" on all occasions, and the interrelations between them may vary from time to time. But they can be gathered up and given full scope in two important disciplines: soliloquy and prayer.

It is difficult, as Baxter admits, to maintain the spiritual glow at full intensity. He knew the limitation of abstract reasoning, so he allows a place to "sensible objects," provided they are cautiously used. Since the heart is always treacherous, we shall do well to ponder its reluctance to take its duty seriously, its disposition to waste its opportunities through trifling, its habit of wandering from the point, and its eagerness to cut short its spiritual exercises. We need to be continually on our guard.

And so, in conclusion, Baxter gives an example of what he means by "heavenly contemplation." In a mood of sustained exultation he passes from meditation on the saints' rest to a long prayer that we may all so consider our final destiny that we shall not forfeit the rest "which remaineth to the people of God." But it is possible for the preacher to be cast away, and his final word is a plea for the author himself: "O suffer not the soul of thy most unworthy servant to be a stranger to those joys which he describes to others . . . that so these lines may not witness against me; but proceeding from the heart of the writer, may be effectual, through thy grace, upon the heart of the reader, and so be the savior of life to both! Amen."

A PRIEST TO THE TEMPLE

Author: George Herbert (1593-1633)
Type of work: Pastoral theology
First published: 1652

PRINCIPAL IDEAS ADVANCED

The pastor is Christ's deputy in the task of bringing men back to obedience toward God.

With the teaching of Scripture and of the Church the pastor mingles knowledge of the human heart and of worldly circumstances.

His preaching is characterized by holiness rather than by eloquence.

Visiting among the people, he is "in God's stead," admonishing, rewarding, and blessing the flock.

He must know law and medicine in order to be all things to his people.

George Herbert left a promising career as a scholar, poet, and courtier to take holy orders. His book of religious verse, *The Temple* (1633), shows the attraction which wealth, beauty, honor, and conviviality held for him, and with what effort he persuaded himself of their vanity. *A Priest to the Temple,* alternately entitled *The Country Parson, his Character, and Rule of Holy Life,* is a prose work, composed while he was rector of the rural parish of Bemerton. Because Herbert lived only three years longer after his ordination, the book is not so much the wisdom of a seasoned clergyman as it is the ideal with which an exceptionally perceptive and devout man entered the vocation. But coming at a time in history when the Church of England was engaged in defining its position, Herbert's model priest proved a helpful guide for others besides the author, and played an important role in molding the Anglican priesthood.

The book comprises thirty-seven short chapters, bearing such titles as "The Parson's Knowledge," "The Parson in His House," and "The Parson in Circuit." The parson whom we meet in these chapters considers himself to be Christ's deputy in the task of "reducing Man to Obedience to God," and he shares both the dignity and authority, and the patience and mortification of his Lord. Appointed to labor among poor and hard-working people, the pastor lives a simple, abstemious life, avoiding any luxury which will add to the burden of those he serves, and endeavoring by his example to inculcate in them the virtues of sobriety, cleanliness, and honesty. Wherever he goes, he is Christ's minister, admonishing, catechizing, and blessing the people. He is ordinarily sad, from thinking on the Cross of Christ and on the sins of the world, and from observing daily the spectacle of ungodliness and misery; yet, be-cause he knows that perpetual severity is hard to bear and that a good disposition is a help to virtuous living, he occasionally condescends to human frailty, and mingles some mirth in his conversation. He is distinguishable from his Puritan counterpart by his peaceableness, his willingness to bear with his people in their love for old customs, his freedom from the extremes of scrupulosity, and his pride in God's house and the quality of its appointments.

Without making his parson a bookish man, Herbert gives primary importance to the parson's knowledge of Scripture, of Christian doctrine, and of practical affairs. It is presupposed that he has received a good schooling, has read the Fathers and the Schoolmen, and is capable of understanding commentaries on the Scriptures. But study needs to be supplemented by prayer and self-discipline, and Herbert says that the parson's library is his holy life. Herbert suggests that each parson should, in his early years, compose his own book of Divinity, using the Church Catechism as a basis; for, he says, although the world is full of such books, "every mans own is fittest, readyest, and most savory to him." Such a book will become a storehouse of material for sermons, when "diversly clothed, illustrated, and inlarged," and will help make the pastor a good catechist, which is part of his responsibility.

Herbert exalts the office of preaching. His parson regards the pulpit as "his joy and his throne." He chooses texts that are devotional rather than controversial, "moving and ravishing texts, whereof the Scriptures are full"; and he interprets these in their whole and obvious meaning, instead of crumbling them into parts as many expositors are wont to do. He will use every art to bring the Scripture's meaning home to his hearers, including specific allusions to local affairs with which the people are familiar, and he will illustrate his meaning in terms of ordinary experience gleaned from "tillage and pastorage." But his sermon never will become an exhibition of wit, learning, and eloquence, or lose the character of holiness.

Herbert never speaks of Sunday as the Sabbath, but, as the day set apart for public worship, Sunday is considered to be the most important day of the week for the rural pastor. As soon as the pastor awakes on that morning, he falls to work, like a market-man on market day, beginning with prayers for himself and for the people, that nothing will take place which is unworthy of the majesty of those offices which he is about to perform. When the hour comes, he goes, with his family attending him, to the Church, where he reads the divine service twice, preaches in the morning, and catechizes in the afternoon. He spends the rest of the day visiting the sick, reconciling neighbors that are at variance, and personally admonishing those whom his sermons do not reach. In the evening, he entertains some of his neighbors, taking occasion to discourse on things both profitable and pleasant, both as concerns the Church and the state. Having performed these things, he permits himself the thought that he has "in some measure, according to poor and fraile man, discharged the publick duties of the Congregation"; and he closes the day, as he began it, with prayer that the Almighty may accept his imperfect service and improve upon it.

On weekday afternoons, the country parson is found "in circuit" among his people. "When he comes to any house, first he blesseth it, and then as hee finds the persons of the house imployed, so he formes his discourse." Always he "is in Gods stead to his Parish," commending and censuring what he finds. If anything is well spoken, he enlarges it; if ill said, he corrects it. "This is called keeping Gods watch." The parson does not lack boldness to speak the word of admonition to the rich when he finds them idle, ill-employed, or over-indulgent, it being in his mind how many things want doing in the land, and how important it is that every man find his vocation. But the parson by preference visits the humbler of his flock, finding no person or care beneath his attention. "Wherfore neither disdaineth he to enter into the poorest Cottage, though he even creep into it, and though it smell never so lothsomly. For both God is there also, and those for whom God dyed: and so much the rather doth he so, as his accesse to the poor is more comfortable, then to the rich; and in regard of himselfe, it is more humiliation."

Charity to the poor is one of the parson's chief obligations. "The Countrey Parson," Herbert says, "is full of Charity; it is his predominant element." He is openhanded with his own small competence, even where it is a question of not "providing a stock for his children," for he assures himself that he better provides for them by lending his money to God than by putting it in the bank. But his concern extends beyond the satisfaction of men's material wants. He tries to teach men that every creature has his good things only from God, that God rewards men's labors, and that He especially remembers the compassionate. Herbert distinguishes between the charity of the pastor and that of lay people. Christians are to give to the poor as unto Christ, but when the priest gives, this is more on the order of God ministering his gifts to men. Therefore, the priest properly requires of those who receive of him that they say their prayers, the creed, and the commandments, and if they are perfect in these he rewards them, even as in all his charities he gives most to those who live best. "So is his charity in effect a Sermon."

Even though the country parson takes his spiritual duties seriously, he is not one to suppose that his responsibility ends with the cure of souls. On the contrary, he "desires to be all to his Parish, and not onely a Pastour, but a Lawyer also, and a Phisician." When controversies arise, he will try them, as judge, in the presence of three or four able members of the parish, and, after consulting with them, will hand down judgment. As judge, he will always hew to exact justice, down to the value of a pin, but afterwards, as pastor, he may admonish for charity. Sometimes, if the case be difficult, he will recommend that it be carried to the courts, in which case he will try to prevail on the contesting parties to go to law as brethren and not as enemies. Similarly, when sickness arises, he or his wife, or if neither has any skill, "a young practicioner" whom the parson keeps in his house for the benefit of his parish, will ever be at hand to help. The study of anatomy and medicine, particularly of herbs, will be throughout his life a pleasant diversion from his theological studies, and a great service to the people.

Living close to the people, it is im-

portant that the country parson be married. Herbert considers virginity a higher state than that of matrimony, but circumstances being what they are, the unmarried priest must exercise excessive precautions against scandal; hence, it is ordinarily better to be married, but to a woman who completely shares the parson's aims, and who, by her skill and sympathy, will make his a model household, and will be able to assist in the ministry to the sick and the poor. Both his children and the household servants will be brought up in an exemplary fashion, so that when they go forth, each will carry the ministry into his ranks. For, "as in the house of those that are skill'd in Musick, all are Musicians; so in the house of a Preacher, all are preachers."

Herbert's Christianity has three main articles: that man fell from God by disobedience, that Christ is the means of calling men back to God, and that the priesthood has the task of carrying on Christ's work of reconciliation. Repentance and new obedience are the aims which he has always in view, but he is not disposed, with his brother Edward (see *De religione laici*, 1645), to minimize the efficacy of such institutions as the sacraments and the priestly benediction. In the presence of the mystery of holy communion, says George Herbert, the priest himself is thrown into confusion, and prays, "Lord, thou knowest what thou didst, when thou appointedst it to be done thus; therefore doe thou fulfill what thou didst appoint; for thou art not only the feast, but the way to it." With the reformers, he wishes to remove from religion all that is superstitious, and all that is tawdry and degrading, but without taking anything away from the holiness and reverence with which these things are performed. But some reformers, in their efforts to avoid idolatry, have, he complains, gone to the opposite extreme of "coldness and Atheism." Herbert's picture of the rural church, decently appointed, but in nothing extravagant, is a pleasant alternative to the starkness of the Puritan chapels, as well as to the luxury of the Catholic cathedrals, and has become the model for Anglican church builders, much as his parson has become a model for the Anglican clergy.

DIDACTICA MAGNA

Author: Johannes Amos Comenius (1592-1670)
Type of work: Philosophy of Christian education
First published: 1657

PRINCIPAL IDEAS ADVANCED

Man's life on earth is merely a preparation for his life in Heaven.
Education is essential if man is to live profitably on earth.
The child should be educated in knowledge, virtue, and piety, for these virtues correspond to the three parts of the soul.
Didactic is the art of education, and, like other arts, its successful practice consists in imitating the order of nature.
All children should receive the same education until the age of twelve, and this teaching, which should be conducted in the vernacular, should comprehend the principles of science, art, and humane learning, as well as morality and religion.

Johannes Amos Comenius (Komensky) was a bishop of the Church of the Bohemian Brethren, who, partly because of the Thirty Years' War, lived much of his life as an exile in Poland, England, Sweden, Germany, Hungary, and Holland. His success as a teacher, and his industry in preparing graded materials for young pupils, led both the English and the Swedish governments to consult him in connection with their programs of educational reform. The *Didactica magna* was written in Bohemian between 1628 and 1632, but was first published in a Latin version at Amsterdam in 1657.

Comenius believed that he was merely implementing two suggestions made by Martin Luther in 1525, who asked, first, that there be schools founded in every town and village for the instruction of all children "in useful knowledge, in morality, and in religion," and, second, that some better method of instruction be evolved so that, instead of resisting learning, children might be drawn to it. Comenius brought to his task the enthusiasm of an age which is remembered for the work of Francis Bacon (1561-1626), and René Descartes (1596-1650).

In spite of the wars that had left

him homeless, Comenius believed that a new day was dawning in Europe. Scientific advances and mechanical inventions suggested to him that great benefits would accrue to morality and religion if men were to bring to the cultivation of human nature the same diligence and acumen which they had applied to understanding and mastering the physical environment.

Comenius is a reminder, however, that the harbingers of the New Learning did not completely break their ties with the Platonized Christianity which underlies so much of Western culture. He believed that the visible world was created to be a nursery for man, and that it would endure no longer than was necessary for the number of the elect to be filled up. He writes that man's life occurs in "the mother's womb, the earth, and the heaven." As the first place of life is preparatory to the second, so the second is preparatory to the third, and the third will abide forever.

Education, as Comenius describes it, is but the preparatory part of man's life on earth. Unlike other infants, the human child must be taught if it is to realize its full potentialities. There is one, and only one, way to do this efficiently: specialists must take the children in hand and fashion them into men and women, or, more specifically, into Christian men and women. Because of the limited number of years which God has allotted to man on earth, it is of utmost importance that the education be completed by the time the person reaches physical maturity.

The scope of man's education, says Comenius, corresponds to the tripartite nature of the soul. Man's intellect is given him for the purpose of knowl-edge; his will for the purpose of choosing between what is advantageous and what is harmful; his memory for the retention of all things hitherto learned and for reminding him of his dependence upon and his duty toward God. "From this it follows," Comenius writes, "that man is naturally required to be: (1) acquainted with all things; (2) endowed with power over all things and over himself; (3) to refer himself and all things to God, the source of all." Man's chief end, says Comenius, is to serve God, His creatures and ourselves, and to enjoy the happiness that comes from knowing, using, and loving these three rightly. Both as respects serving and enjoying, "Learning, Virtue, and Piety" are essential prerequisites. All else (health, strength, beauty, riches, honor, friendship, good-fortune, long life) are "but extrinsic ornaments of life," like the case of a watch or the trappings of a horse. "It follows, therefore, that we advance toward our ultimate end in proportion as we pursue Learning, Virtue, and Piety in this world."

Comenius recognizes no limits to the scope of human knowledge. He accepts the view that man is a microcosm, in which the whole universe is inwardly comprehended. All knowledge is present to man, just as a plant or tree is present in the seed. He cites Pythagoras as saying that, because man naturally possesses all knowledge, a boy of seven, if properly questioned, should be able to answer correctly all questions of philosophy; and, except that he believes that the mind ripens more slowly than Pythagoras suggests, Comenius agrees. In another place, however, he cites Aristotle's teaching that the mind is "a blank tablet on which nothing was written, but on which all things may be engraved." That there may be a conflict between thinking of the mind as a seed and as a blank tablet does not seem to have occurred to him.

Comenius admits that "exact or deep knowledge" of all the arts and sciences is more than any man can acquire in a whole lifetime, much less during his formative years; nevertheless, since the child of God is destined to know all things, his education should be universal in scope. 'That is to say, he should learn the principles, causes, and uses of all the important things in the world; for he must never, in his journey through life, encounter anything so strange to him that he cannot form a true judgment concerning it and turn it to its proper use.

To this end, a systematic organization of education is necessary. Everywhere, in nature as well as in art, says Comenius, order is "the soul of affairs." He cites as examples the solar system, insect societies, the human body, military organizations, and machines. Seemingly impossible undertakings are brought to completion by "the all-ruling force of order; that is to say, the force derived from arranging all the parts concerned according to their number, size, and importance, and in such a manner that each one shall perform its own proper function as well as work harmoniously with and assist the other parts whose action is necessary to produce the desired result." If the goal of educating all children in all knowledge seems a formidable one, says Comenius, that is because we have not hitherto acquired the educational art.

"Didactic," says Comenius, "signifies the art of teaching." He calls his work the "Great Didactic" because it comprises "the whole art of teaching all things to all men, and indeed of teaching them with certainty, so that the result cannot fail to follow." The business of any art is to eliminate chance by means of circumspection. By studying nature and learning its way, the artist or craftsman is able to bring things to pass with the same infallible certainty which characterizes the course of nature itself. Hitherto teachers have possessed no art, comparable to that of the engineer or the horticulturalist, which would enable them to say, "In so many years I will bring this youth to such and such a point; I will educate him in such and such a way." But Comenius expresses confidence that his method will supply the lack.

Comenius's universal claims for his method rest upon his avowedly *a priori* method. Unlike educationists who depend merely upon experience, he sought out the principles upon which education must be based. His method consists in finding suitable analogies in nature and in the crafts. For example, a bird chooses the springtime to multiply its species; similarly, a gardener, to set out his plants; so, "the education of men should be commenced in the springtime of life." Again, before the bird lays an egg, it prepares a nest; a gardener, before he begins to set plants, has the soil, the tools, and the tender slips all in readiness; so, the teacher must first prepare maps, phrase books, diagrams, and models, and must observe the right order in presenting subject matter.

Although Comenius sometimes writes as if the mind develops organically, all that he means to suggest is that the texture of the brain is at some times better suited to receive impressions than at others. For the most part, he uses purely mechanical models. The mechanism of a clock interests him, and it suggests a model for understanding everything in creation. Not merely man's bodily movements, but those of his soul also, may be understood in terms of "the weights" of desire which incline it this way and that, with reason serving as an "escapement" which makes is possible to blend the active and passive elements. More pertinent to the educational art is the parallel with printing. Comenius invents the term "didachography" after the analogy of "typography," and he develops at length the concept of impressing knowledge on the mind by uniform symbols ("class-books"), ink ("the voice of the teacher"), and pressure ("the school-discipline, which keep the pupils up to their work and compels them to learn"). "Our discovery of didachography," says Comenius, "facilitates the multiplication of learned men in precisely the same way that the discovery of printing facilitated the multiplication of books," enabling us for the first time to expect the fulfillment of the divine prediction, "The earth shall be full of the knowledge of God, as the waters cover the sea."

Comenius's *a priori* principles led him to numerous practical innovations, which cause twentieth century educationists to place his name along with those of Johann Pestalozzi (1746-1827) and Friedrich Froebel (1782-1852) as one of the founders of modern pedagogy. One of his contributions is the insistence on the use of visual aids. The mind, he says, is like a mirror: ". . . in order that the mirror may duly receive the images of the objects, it is necessary that these latter be solid and visible, and be also placed before the eyes." Mere verbal presentations are like clouds, and make an unsatisfactory impression. For example, a skeleton and models of the nerves and viscera should be used in teaching anatomy; and pictures should be used in teaching the vocabulary of foreign languages. Another application of his principles was the rule that no materials should be permitted to enter the mind of a learner which would prevent his receiving images without confusion. Scholars should have books, written specifically for them, which contain nothing except the matter that the educator wishes to impress upon their minds. Further, instruction should be carefully graded, so that the child will have time to master simple materials before more complicated ones are introduced. This, in turn, demands lesson plans and schedules. The school year should contain the same number of days each year, so that each class may complete its allotted task, and all the students will enter the next grade together. "This," he adds, "is an exact analogy of the method used in printing when all the copies of the first page are printed first, then those of the second page, and so on."

Comenius's principles also suggested to him numerous reforms in connection with school curricula. For one thing, his insistence on universal knowledge led him to place natural science and the crafts alongside the seven liberal arts. Further, his theory of child development led him to argue for what he calls a "vernacular school," for all children ages six to twelve. A "Latin school" for students thirteen to nineteen would, according to his plan, prepare pre-professional students for the university.

One of Comenius's objections to the schools of his time was the result of their neglect of morals and piety. In his *Didactica* he seeks to remedy this. He urges that sciences, arts, and languages be taught as "purely subordinate subjects," so that the child will understand that "all that does not relate to God and the future life is nothing but vanity." Thus, the Holy Scriptures must "rank before all other books." Children, he reminds us, are "plants of Paradise." The schools have the responsibility for seeing that the students develop into "steadfast and noble-minded" men and women. Or, to change the figure somewhat, children are soft and malleable substances which can take any shape, and the schools are "forging places of humanity," in which virtuous and godly men are fashioned.

The reforms suggested by Comenius follow *a priori* from his principles. However, in spite of urging that "this art of instilling true virtue and piety may be elaborated on a definite system and introduced into schools," Comenius has almost nothing to say about how this can be done. His chief recommendation is that the teaching of pagan authors should be eliminated. There is nothing of value in them, he says, that cannot be found in Hebrew and Christian writers, and there is much that is vicious and false, which could only corrupt the image which Christian education is trying to impress on the young.

OLIVER CROMWELL'S LETTERS AND SPEECHES

Author: Oliver Cromwell (1599-1658)
Type of work: Letters and speeches
First published: 1845

PRINCIPAL IDEAS ADVANCED

God is at work in the affairs of nations and individuals, and it behooves all men of serious outlook to walk in humble obedience to God's will.

It is easier to recognize God's guidance in dramatic events or in personal experiences than in the more complicated developments of political life.

The complexities of public life lay upon the righteous the duty to work together in fulfilling God's purposes.

Oliver Cromwell's letters and speeches are documents which give personal quality to the narrative of a remarkable career. Cromwell was a writer only in the most incidental sense. Primarily he was a man of action, and he bestrode the middle years of the seventeenth century as the supreme example of the Puritan soldier and statesman. To an extent seldom true of great men, fame was thrust upon him by circumstances. Until the outbreak of the first civil war of the Puritan Revolution, he was a relatively obscure figure: a country gentleman of modest means and a silent back-bencher in the House of Commons. He had had no training in the arts of war; he became a remarkably successful soldier, and the German Imperial General Staff used to cite him as one of the most notable examples of a great cavalry leader. When the Long Parliament assembled, no one would have guessed that among all its members Cromwell was the one destined to attain supreme political power.

In Cromwell's *Letters and Speeches* we catch glimpses, fleeting and none too frequent, of this amazing development. The earliest letters show us an active member of parliament organizing the military concerns of his party in the area which he represented. The need was urgent; the requisite steps were obvious, and Cromwell writes with directness and vigor concerning issues both complex and confused. His commands are clear and explicit, and we can see the resources of the eastern counties being mobilized to serve the parliamentary cause. What is even more important, we can already detect the distinctive attitudes which made Cromwell a great military leader. He realized that the quality of an army depends on the character of its men. He approved the zeal shown by the leaders at Huntingdon in raising a company of foot, but he wanted to see it changed into a troop of horse, "which indeed will by God's blessing, far more advantage the cause than two or three companies of foot; especially if your men be honest, godly men, which by all means I desire." "I beseech you," he writes on another occasion, "be careful what captains of horse you choose, what men be mounted: a few honest men are better than numbers. . . . If you choose godly honest men to be captains of horse, honest men will follow them. . . . I had rather have a plain russet-coated captain that knows what he fights for, and loves what he knows, than that which you call 'a gentleman' and is nothing else. I honor a *gentleman* that is so indeed!" His sense of the importance of the cause, together with his sympathy with the men who supported it, explains the invincible morale of the force which Cromwell raised and led. This made the Ironsides one of the most famous regiments in history.

Many of his letters directly concern military developments. Immediately after the battle of Marston Moor (1644), he sent a beautiful message of sympathy to Colonel Valentine, whose son had been killed. The letter begins with a vivid account of the encounter, of how his wing had charged and scattered Prince Rupert's horse troops and then the enemy foot soldiers: "God made them as stubble to our swords. . . . Give glory, all the glory, to God." He refers movingly to his friend's loss, but adds, "let this public mercy to the Church of God make you to forget your private sorrow." After the battle of Naseby (1645) the same note recurs. "Sir," writes Cromwell to the Speaker of the House, "this is none other but the hand of God; and to him alone belongs the glory, wherein none are to share with him." But he realized that divine mercies are mediated through human agents, in this case the honest men who had served parliament faithfully, and who must not be discouraged. "He that ventures his life for the liberty of his country, I wish he trust God for the liberty of his conscience and you for the liberty he fights for."

It is at this point that one of Cromwell's great concerns begins to emerge clearly from the *Letters*. Distinctions of religious affiliation are often magnified; among soldiers fighting for a great cause, they become irrelevant. In a long dispatch after the storming of Bristol, he concluded with a strong plea for toleration: "Presbyterians, Independents, all have here the same spirit of faith and prayer; the same presence and answer; they agree here, have no names of difference: pity it is it should be otherwise anywhere! All that believe have the real unity, which is most glorious; because inward and spiritual, in the Body and the Head. . . . And for brethren in things of the mind we look for no compulsion, but that of light and reason."

Though there is no doubt of the graphic quality of Cromwell's military dispatches (after all there is no source for the first and second civil wars to compare with his letters), the center of interest gradually shifts to other matters. There was the uneasy and increasingly disturbing political maneuvers which culminated in the second civil war and which slowly brought Cromwell to the reluctant conclusion that the duplicity of King Charles I ("that man of blood") made it impossible to trust him any further. There was the turmoil in the army, culminating in the Putney debates. There was trouble with the Presbyterian faction in Parliament; there were the earliest attempts to fashion a new constitution by which the country could be governed. By sheer necessity, Cromwell was pushed by events and by the vacuum at the head of affairs into the position of supreme power as Lord Protector (1653). His aims were clear, but it was far from obvious how they

could be achieved. Here, too, the *Letters and Speeches* reveal the increasingly acute dilemmas which Cromwell faced. The problems of the Church were in themselves difficult to deal with. How could the ministry be maintained? Were tithes an intolerable affront to the freedom of religious worship (as some of the sects claimed) or were they, under existing circumstances, the only possible way of supporting the Church? Was toleration synonymous with confusion?—or was it a sincere and promising attempt to translate man's religious freedom into feasible social forms? It is true that certain groups, like the Anglicans and Roman Catholics, suffered a measure of persecution, but Cromwell claimed that such repression was prompted by political, not by religious, motives; these people suffered, not for their convictions but because they engaged in subversive activities. In his attitude to the Jews, Cromwell was more openminded than most of his contemporaries. But the task of giving effect to a policy of toleration was always difficult, and Cromwell found himself beset with problems. As time passed, the extremer elements among the Puritan sects were increasingly hostile; they were more vocal in their abuse, more ready to engage in plots.

The urgent, indeed the insoluble, problem of the Protectorate was that of devising a system of government which could preserve order and maintain public confidence. This is the difficulty with which Cromwell's speeches are increasingly preoccupied. His dilemma was that he believed in ruling with the people's consent, but he was unable to secure it. The disconcerting but inescapable fact was that his rule rested on force. He was the head of the state because he was the commander of the army. Military rule is expensive and unpopular, and the experiment of maintaining order by the major-generals did nothing to commend the Protectorate to the people. Cromwell tried more than once, and by more than one method, to secure a parliament that would prove co-operative. But even when its members were chosen by a method designed to guarantee similarity of outlook and aim, the result was the same. In his first speech to the first parliament of the Protectorate, he could refer to a dayspring of divine prophecy and hope, and urge the members to struggle toward it. He could even speak of resigning his authority into their hands, but before long he was sternly reminding them that he was responsible for order and could not allow them to tamper with the foundations of government. The problems created by parties form a constant refrain in his addresses, and he complained bitterly on the spirit of faction which jeopardized the achievements of the Protectorate. That these achievements were both genuine and considerable, he left them in no doubt. The reform of the law, the settling of the Church, the maintenance of peace at home, the establishment of respect abroad—these formed a notable record, yet all the time those who should have co-operated with him were intent on fomenting trouble. Cromwell was well aware that France and Spain held his power in wholesome awe, and he wrote to Cardinal Mazarin with an authority which English rulers had not recently been able to assume. He could intervene with effect on behalf of Continental Protestants, but he could not get English Puritans to agree among themselves or to unite in his support.

This problem of unity became increasingly urgent, and among other things it explains the episode which occupies so much space in the latter part of the *Letters and Speeches:* the offer of the crown to Cromwell (1656). This might have re-established a pattern of authority with which Englishmen were familiar, and the majority of the nation might have settled down under a new dynasty. But in the army the suggestion caused deep concern, and Cromwell finally rejected it because it further jeopardized the precarious unity upon which his regime rested.

The *Letters and Speeches* are a source of primary importance for the history of the English civil wars, the Commonwealth, and the Protectorate. Here we see events through the eyes of one of the chief participants in them, a man, moreover, who had an amazing gift for direct and vivid narrative. We can share in the turmoil of battle and we can appreciate the mounting perplexities which made government so difficult. As we close the work we can appreciate how fortunate Cromwell was in the hour of his death. We realize how insoluble were the difficulties besetting "the rule of the saints" and how inevitable therefore was the restoration of Charles II. But the great value of the work does not relate to political developments. This is a Christian classic because it is a clear and moving revelation of the character of one of the greatest of the Puritans. We do not see, of course, the whole of Cromwell's very complex nature. From other sources we know that when faced with a difficult problem he often suffered agonies of indecision, but when he acted, he did so with swift and irresistible force. We can sense a little of the former quality in some of the political letters and speeches from the later years of his life. We can see the decisive vigor clearly enough in the early letters describing his activities during the initial stages of the first civil war. When he felt that he was fighting the Lord's battles his characteristic qualities appear most clearly. Then his sense of God's presence and his submission to God's will find humble expression. Events become the stage on which the divine purpose is being accomplished, and it is his high privilege to be a fellow laborer in this great task. This is what makes his battle dispatches among the great documents of militant Puritanism.

But there is a less public side to Cromwell's religious life. He can write to friends and relatives with a directness which makes his Christian convictions both clear and contagious. He can write, too, with a simplicity largely free from the dogmatism which sometimes defaces the expressions of Puritan beliefs. And he can deal wisely with the spiritual perplexities of others. His letter on the spirit of fear and the spirit of love is still one of the most perceptive statements on an important theme. Fear, he says, is the natural result "of a bondage spirit," and is the antithesis of love: "The voice of fear is: If I had done this; if I had avoided that, how well it had been with me! . . . Love argueth in this wise: What a Christ have I; what a Father in and through him! What a name hath my Father: merciful, gracious, long-suffering, abundant in goodness and truth; forgiving iniquity, transgression and sin. What a nature hath my Father: he is LOVE;—free in it, unchangeable, infinite! . . . This commends the love of God: it's Christ's dying for men without strength, for men whilst sinners, whilst enemies. And shall we seek for the root of our comforts within us,—what God hath done, what he is to us in Christ is the root of our comfort: in this is stability, in us is weakness. Acts of obedience are not perfect, and therefore yield not perfect grace. Faith, as an act, yields it not; but 'only' as it carries us into him, who is our perfect rest and peace; in whom we are accounted of, and received by the Father,—even as Christ himself. This is our high calling. Rest we here, and here only."

DUCTOR DUBITANTIUM

Author: Jeremy Taylor (1613-1667)
Type of work: Moral theology
First published: 1660

PRINCIPAL IDEAS ADVANCED

Conscience is man's rational capacity for knowing the laws by which God governs him for his own perfection.

All law is of divine origin; the teachings of Christ perfect the law which is present to man's natural understanding.

Human law derives its authority from God, and thus it is to be obeyed as a matter of conscience.

Jeremy Taylor completed his *Ductor dubitantium* in time to dedicate it to the new king, Charles II, upon the restoration of the Stuart dynasty to the throne of England. The dedication was appropriate to the occasion. Better than Thomas Hobbes (1588-1679), who had been Charles's tutor, Taylor expresses the principles to which the Stuarts gave their allegiance. In Taylor's view, the king, like Moses, descends from God to the people with the two tables of the law (religious and civil) in his hand. Under no law himself except that of God, the king is governed solely by "the arguments . . . of conscience." A book on conscience, therefore, seemed particularly apt to both king and people.

The artificiality of the title (for the work was written in English and bears the subtitle, *The Rule of Conscience in all her General Measures*) prepares the reader for a work of erudition. Taylor does not draw his examples from his own time, nor does he venture to set forth rules based on his own pastoral experience. Rules and cases alike are taken from classic literature, from the Church Fathers, from civil and canon law, and from Spanish and Italian books of casuistry. Even his method of subordinating cases to rules he borrows from antiquity. "I took my pattern," he says, "from Tribonianus the lawyer, who out of the laws of the old Romans collected some choice rules which give answer to very many cases that happen."

Ductor dubitantium, which comprises the last two volumes of Taylor's collected works, is divided into four books of unequal length. The first book is a discussion of conscience in its various modes (true and false, confident and doubtful, probable and certain). The second is an exposition of divine law, drawn chiefly from the New Testament. The third book, by far the longest, is an exposition of human law, with special reference to civil law, ecclesiastical law, and the law of fathers of families. The fourth book, which is comparatively brief, is a discussion of the questions of free agency and of human happiness. It is characteristic of Taylor that he finds Aristotle's doctrine of the four causes underlying his divisions. Conscience, he says, is the formal cause of good and evil; the laws of God and man are their material cause; and man's freedom and his happiness, respectively, are their efficient and final causes. Taylor describes his book as "a general instrument of moral theology," and, while he hopes that it will be useful to laymen who are learned and wise enough to "guide themselves in all their proportions of conscience," he warns that in difficult cases men ought to consult a priest. It is mainly for such pastors of souls that the work is intended.

Taylor maintains that conscience belongs to the rational part of man. He is careful to distinguish conscience from both the natural tendencies which man shares with the lower animals, and the kind of practical intelligence which we call prudence. Conscience is the part of man's reason by which he judges according to law. Taylor explains that God governs nature by providence and rational beings by commands. Strictly speaking, there is no law in nature; law is superadded. Similarly, conscience is not a natural faculty, but a gift. But law and conscience are needed to perfect man's nature, and one of the indications of the rightness of conscience is whether it accords with our natural tendencies.

There are two kinds of judgment included under the name of "conscience." The first (designated in Greek by the word *synteresis*) is the knowledge which men have of moral axioms; the second (designated by the word *syneidesis*) is the capacity which they have for recognizing the moral character of particular acts. For example, in the affair of Bathsheba, David might reason: "Whatsoever is injurious ought not to be done; but to commit adultery is injurious; therefore it ought not to be done." This, says Taylor, is the first act of conscience, by means of which the mind is supplied with principles of action. The second act of conscience applies the conclusion of this syllogism to the particular case. Thus: "Adultery ought not to be done; this action I am about to do is adultery; therefore it ought not to be done."

Because conscience is the part of man's reason which informs him of God's commands, he is always bound to obey it. But numerous questions about the fallibility and certainty of conscience now arise. In general, Taylor's confidence in man's reason, both moral and speculative, is strong and constant. There are, of course, matters that are beyond our ken, in which case ignorance is unavoidable, but a great deal of ignorance can be overcome and is therefore inexcusable.

Taylor holds that a man ought to obey his conscience even when it is in error, for though he sins in obeying an erroneous conscience, he sins even more in defying it.

A conscience is not erroneous unless it carries the conviction of being right. More frequent is the doubtful conscience, which needs to be instructed, usually not in principles but in their application. Here the art of casuistry comes into play, and Taylor accommodates the reader with rules for balancing various types of probability and for tempering justice with charity. Taylor avoids the excesses to which some casuists have gone, but he does not take the easy course of omitting knotty problems. Thus, in discussing whether it is lawful to bribe a corrupt judge to make him do justice, Taylor argues that, although bribery is an ill-sounding word, to give money is itself an indifferent thing; and that, if a judge is ready to receive money on any terms, giving him money to do a good act is not necessarily to commit a fault.

While the formal correctness of an act depends upon whether one follows his conscience, its material correctness depends upon its conformity to law. Therefore, the most profitable way of leading the doubtful conscience is to instruct it concerning the various kinds of law.

All law, according to Taylor, has divine origin; because God is pre-eminently a rational being, all law is naturally intelligible to man. From the first commands that a child can learn to the highest rules of ascetic religion, God's law is one continuous whole. Christianity is neither more nor less than the moral law of nature in its final perfection. It "binds no more upon us than God did by the very reason of our nature." In the Old Testament, God modified these laws according to man's weakness, as when, by Moses, He permitted polygamy, although monogamy is the rule of nature; similarly, He instituted religious ceremonies, such as circumcision, which go beyond the requirements of natural piety. But when Christ came, these pedagogical devices were swept aside, and God's law was exhibited in its simplicity and perfection. Even the worship demanded by Christ is, according to Taylor, purely spiritual: "The whole design of the laws of Jesus Christ is to be perfective of the spirit, and His religion is a spiritual service; that is, permanent and unalterable, virtuous and useful, natural and holy, not relative to time and place, or any material circumstances, nor integrated by corporal services."

Taylor distinguishes, however, just as the Roman Church has always done, between precepts and counsels; that is to say, between those words of Christ (chiefly prohibitions) which bind the Christian absolutely, and those which, though they point the way to perfection, must be understood as being relative to the individual's strength and stature, and which, therefore, bind in varying degrees. Speaking of the Sermon on the Mount, Taylor writes that it is a great mistake to suppose that everything spoken there is a law; many parts of it are "progressions and degrees of Christian duty." On the other hand, Taylor is careful to note that these counsels of perfection are not optional. God, he says, follows the course of our natures, and although in the early stages of our walk He accepts our minimal duties, he expects us to pass on towards perfection.

Turning to laws which have their origin in human commands, Taylor reiterates the principle that all law derives its authority from God. The authority of the parent over his child, like that of the prince over his people, and of the bishop over his flock, derives from the divine institution, and is enforced and authenticated to man's reason by the teaching of Scripture. Numerous questions of conscience arise from the conflict between human laws and divine, and Taylor freely admits that there are cases in which a man is bound to follow his conscience in disobedience of the commands of men. In their legitimate spheres, however, authorities ought to be revered. Thus, children ought never to marry contrary to their parents' command; parishioners ought never to hold conventicles against their bishop's order; and citizens ought never to assemble or organize themselves in defiance of the king's command.

These principles, of course, particularly those which bear upon the authority of the bishop and of the prince, were all being tested in Taylor's time, as well as the further question concerning the prince's authority over the Church. Taylor takes his stand on the side of the prince wherever possible. He holds that Parliament acted treasonably in raising arms against the Crown, and thus Parliament deserved to be punished accordingly; that Presbyterians and Independents were guilty of disobeying the Apostolic order of bishops; and that Papists and Presbyterians alike subverted the divine institution in maintaining that the Church has any political authority over the prince. The prince, according to Taylor, is under the law of God, so that when he does wrong it is possible to reason with him, but it is never permissible to censure him in public. Moreover, a mere citizen may find it difficult to understand the justice of the king's cause, because public morality stands on a different footing from that of private morality.

Taylor is an interesting example of the new rationalistic tendencies at work within seventeenth century English theology. He holds uncompromisingly to the Scriptures and to the creeds, but at the same time he argues that revelation is perfectly intelligible to human reason. Traditional theology has often distinguished between human reason and divine, and it has maintained that while there is a proportionality between the two, divine reason is often incompatible with human reason. Taylor denies that this is true. To allege that God tells us something and means something different from what we can understand Him to mean would be, he says, to charge God with hypocrisy.

In addition to maintaining that Christianity is inherently reasonable, Taylor also maintains that, by accumulating probable arguments, one can demonstrate the truth of all its teachings. "Since," he says, "there is . . . nothing to be said for any other religion, and so very much for Christianity, every one of whose pretences can be proved as well as the things themselves do require, and as all the world expects such things should be proved; it follows that the holy Jesus is the Son of God, that His religion is commanded by God, and is that way by which He will be worshipped and honored. . . . He that puts his soul upon this cannot perish; neither can he be reproved who hath so much reason and argument for his religion." Perhaps it is not overventuresome to find here the seeds of those lay developments in religious thought later exemplified in John Locke's *The Reasonableness of Christianity* (1695), and in John Toland's *Christianity not Mysterious* (1696).

A CHRISTIAN DIRECTORY

Author: Richard Baxter (1615-1691)
Type of work: Pastoral theology
First published: 1665

PRINCIPAL IDEAS ADVANCED

Because the only good in this life is that which tends to man's eternal happiness, man ought to employ his time and energies with a view always to God's glory and his soul's salvation.

Nothing which is contrary to God's law is ultimately good; hence, it is never permissible to disobey God's comandments in order to advance what we believe is good.

God has set some men in authority over others; civil magistrates and religious authorities have their power from God and not from those over whom they rule.

It is the duty of all men in this troubled world to forbear one another and to seek peace.

Richard Baxter wrote *A Christian Directory* when, because of his nonconformism, he was no longer permitted to preach. The work, which fills five large volumes, is devoted mainly to "practical cases of conscience, and the reducing of theoretical knowledge into serious Christian practice." It was, he maintained, a necessary labor because the Romanists were still far ahead of Protestants in this department of theology, even after the good beginning made by Jeremy Taylor in his *Ductor dubitantium* (1660).

The contents of *A Christian Directory* are propounded as rules or directions rather than as questions and answers, so as to enable the reader to resolve his own particular cases. Beginning with directions for the conversion of sinners and the strengthening of weak Christians, Baxter sets forth seventeen "Grand Directions," in which the essential obligations of the baptismal covenant are explained under the heads of the believer's duties to the three Persons of the Trinity. The particular directions which make up the rest of the work are distributed under four heads: Christian ethics (or private duties); Christian economics (or family duties); Christian ecclesiastics (or Church duties); and Christian politics (or duties to our rulers and neighbors).

A theological moderate in his day, Baxter was too much of a rationalist to please the Calvinists, and too much of a Biblicist to please the Arminians. Baxter took it for granted that the Scriptures are the Word of God, and he agreed with the Puritans generally that the Bible contains "whatever it is necessary that man believe, think, or do, in all ages and places of the world." But he maintained that, in order to be effective, the Scriptures must be addressed to men's reason. The Devil, he said, keeps his hold on men by silencing reason and causing it to slumber; but the Scriptures in their very nature excite reason, and effective preaching consists in showing men that sin is unreasonable. Baxter's constant plea for tolerance in matters of religion was based upon his confidence in the power of reason to overcome enmity and sloth.

When Baxter speaks of reason, he seems ordinarily to have had in mind the prudential judgment which distinguishes man from animals and by means of which man conducts his worldly business. All that man needs to do is to extend the scope of his understanding until it includes his immortal destiny, and he will quickly see the need for reconciliation to God and the truth of those matters revealed in Holy Scripture.

In Baxter's view, the things of this world are little more than "dreams and shadows, and valuable only as they serve us in the way of heaven." Our present life and circumstances are given us on trial, in order that we may prepare ourselves for the life that is to come after. An eternity, either of happiness or misery, awaits every man. Whence it follows that the only good in this life is that which tends toward our eternal happiness;

whatever distracts us from that goal is evil.

The sobriety with which Baxter and most Puritans faced life is implicit in their acceptance of the rational scheme of things. Man dare not stop until he has rationalized every move that he makes. Here, for instance, is the basis for the Puritan's characteristic attitude toward sports and toward sensuous pleasure. Recreation in itself is lawful and even, for some men, a duty; it serves to exhilarate the spirits and to exercise the natural parts so as to fit the body and mind for better serving God. Similarly, the satisfaction of our fleshly appetites is in itself good; God desires to give man greater pleasure, not less, and he approves the delights of the senses as long as they are kept subordinate to heavenly delights. But all our activities must be kept under the government of reason: "Take nothing and do nothing merely because the sense or appetite would have it; but because you have reason so to do."

The most characteristic manifestation of Baxter's attempt to rationalize the whole of human life is his attitude toward the use of time: "Time being man's opportunity for all those works for which he liveth, and which his Creator doth expect from him, and on which his endless life dependeth: the redeeming or well improving of it, must needs be of most high importance to him." Not merely are we accountable for not wasting a minute; we are held for putting every minute to the best possible use. Here the good is enemy of the best. Sleep beyond what is necessary for health, inefficient work habits, and leisurely habits of dressing and dining are all "thieves of time" and hence to be avoided. One can waste time in the performance of devotional exercises; busy persons are advised to have a child or a servant read to them a chapter from the Bible while they are dressing or at table. Everyone must, of course, have some time during the day for private prayer and meditation, but those fitted for an active life cannot lawfully take as much time for these matters as the aged and the weak. Indeed, the contemplative life, so much lauded by the Romanists, is reserved by Baxter for those who are disqualified from active labor.

So far, it has been possible to set forth Baxter's thought in terms of consequential ethics. The Christian religion appears as a higher kind of prudence: "That only is good in this life, which tendeth to the happiness of our endless life; and that is evil indeed in this life, that tendeth to our endless hurt." But man cannot know in detail the conditions of true happiness; hence, for direction in life one must obey the laws which God has revealed to man in nature and in the Scriptures. Baxter's thought here assumes the characteristics of formalistic ethics.

The clearest examples of Baxter's ethical method are cases connected with telling the truth. Baxter discusses typical moral dilemmas in which a person is given the alternative of either permitting obvious evil to take place or telling a lie: "Is it not contrary to the light of nature, to suffer . . . a parent, a king, myself, my country, rather to be destroyed, than to save them by a harmless lie?" "No," answers Baxter. In the first place, we can never be certain that our falsehood will accomplish the end we hope for. In the second place, there are lawful means enough to save lives when saving lives is what is best. The rule, therefore, is "Obey God, and trust him with your lives, and he can save them without a lie, if it is best: and if it be not, it should not be desired." Baxter gives a comparable answer to the question whether it is lawful to steal bread in order to save one's life. He admits that the common good takes precedence over private good, and that property rights may be violated if the public interest is at stake; but to take another man's property for one's private benefit, even though it be to preserve one's life, is forbidden.

The basis for Baxter's social philosophy is provided by strong determination always to obey the law of God, and not by any attempt on his part to estimate the consequences of man's actions. To oppress one's fellow man is wrong, according to Baxter, because he who keeps men so destitute that they die of sickness is a murderer; and murder is always wrong. Slavery is not wrong in every circumstance, there being different kinds of slavery; but catching Negroes by piracy in order to sell them is thievery of the worst sort; moreover, it is a heinous sin to buy such a slave, except for the purpose of setting him free. All killing in war is murder if the war be unjustly waged. The professional soldier is worse than a thief, because thieves kill only an occasional individual, but soldiers murder thousands at one time. Whether a man ought ever to bear arms is a more difficult question. Baxter, who served as a chaplain with the Parliamentary armies during the Civil War, finds it almost impossible to determine whether particular wars are just or unjust. A wise man, he avers, may prefer to be "abused as a neuter" than to risk being guilty of the blood of an unjust war.

The reader must not infer from the abridged form in which we have cited Baxter's directions that he had a few simple rules by means of which every moral problem may be resolved. On the contrary, as the length of his *Directory* attests, Baxter was fully aware that circumstances alter cases, and that each case must finally be decided on its individual merits. Thus, while he held that outright lying is never permitted, he was willing to grant that there are times when intentional deception is a duty, for instance in the case of a physician or a statesman, "for," says Baxter, "all dissimulation is not evil, though lying be." In order to deal with the wide variety of instances which present themselves, the author frequently turns aside from the practice of setting out directions, and poses typical questions. For example, in connection with his directions concerning the relations of husbands and wives, he takes up eighteen questions dealing with the problem of separation and divorce. To the question, "Who be they that may or may not marry again when they are parted?" Baxter's reply is that a person released on the grounds of the other's adultery may remarry, but not any person released on any other ground. Still, he says, one must consider the possibility of reconciliation; and how necessary it is to the well-being of the innocent party to marry again. In the last analysis, the best he can say is that there is no absolute prohibition against the innocent party's remarrying.

The difficulty which we often face in discovering our duty must not mislead us into supposing that one opinion concerning it is as good as another; "The 'esse' is before the 'scire,' " Baxter writes; "the thing is first true or false before I judge it to be so." Whenever we are in doubt we must keep distinct "the being of a duty," and "the knowledge of a duty."

Baxter declares that one of the most dangerous errors of his time is the view that a man is bound to do everything that his conscience tells him is the will of God. No man, says Baxter, has the duty to obey his conscience when it is in error. One must avoid sin by avoiding error. "God hath appointed means for the cure of blindness and error as well as other sins; else the world were in a miserable case."

Baxter introduces a third major principle of obligation, besides those of prudence and obedience to law; namely, that of authority. According to Baxter, God, who is Lord of all the world, has delegated power to men in their various social relations. Thus, He has given the husband authority over the wife, and parents authority over children. In like manner, He has ordained that rulers shall have power over nations, and that the ministry shall lead the Church. Some part, therefore, of every man's duty consists in obedience to those over him.

In discussing the issue of political sovereignty, Baxter takes a position somewhere between those who argue for the divine right of kings and those who argue for the sovereignty of the people. In Baxter's opinion, the people determine, by their explicit or implicit consent, whether they shall be governed by a king, or by an aristocracy, or by elected representatives; but in choosing who shall govern them, they do not bestow power on the government, any more than a woman bestows

authority on the husband she chooses, or the soldier on the commander under whom he enlists: "Rulers therefore are God's officers, placed under him in his kingdom, as he is the universal, absolute sovereign of the world; and they receive their power from God, who is the only original of power." The power which individuals have over their own lives is of a different kind from civil or political power; the latter is brought into being by God's act and not by resignation of His natural power to an artificial head.

Baxter's theory of Church government is similar to his theory of politics, except for his contention that in the Scriptures God specifies how churches are to be governed in spiritual matters; namely, by elders or presbyters set apart and ordained for this purpose. Baxter argues that the word "church" ought to be applied only to particular assemblies of believers, just as the word "school" is applied to particular assemblies of scholars. There are many schools in England, as there are many churches; but it would be absurd to speak of the School of England. So, there can be no national church. But, says Baxter, the temporal affairs of the churches must fall under the civil power; the magistrate or king, and not the presbytery, has authority over "the temple, the pulpit, the tithes, &c."

It must be remembered that Baxter wrote on these matters during one of the great formative periods of Western political and ecclesiastical history, and that he personally had much at stake. At the time of the Restoration, he was offered a bishopric by Charles II, but he refused; and when the Act of Uniformity was imposed shortly thereafter, he chose to cast his lot with the persecuted ministers. Meanwhile, Quakers, Anabaptists, Independents, Presbyterians, Jesuits, Erastians, Arminians, high and low Anglicans, and numerous other parties were bitterly contending for positions of power. In Baxter's writings, on the other hand, there is almost complete absence of a spirit of contention. From time to time he raises his voice against the exclusivist claims of a religious party, notably the Romanists; but mainly he was interested in restoring unity. He declares that he accepts the Puritan principle, according to which the Scriptures are the only rule of worship and government, but he points out that the Scriptures are silent on a great many matters, and insists that what is not forbidden is lawful. He says, paraphrasing the Cambridge philosopher, Henry More (1614-1687), "It would do much more good in the world, if all parties were forwarder to find out and commend what is good in the doctrine and worship of all that differ from them. This would win them to hearken to reforming advice, and would keep up the credit of the common truths and duties of religion in the world, when the envious snarling at all that others do, both tend to bring the world to atheism, and banish all reverence of religion, together with Christian charity from the earth."

Although Baxter's voice of reason and moderation was little heeded in his time, his writings exercised great influence on the development of nonconformist thought in subsequent generations. Unfortunately, his intellectualism and legalism are easier for men to emulate than the high religious spirit with which his own thinking was always imbued.

GRACE ABOUNDING TO THE CHIEF OF SINNERS

Author: John Bunyan (1628-1688)
Type of work: Spiritual autobiography
First published: 1666

PRINCIPAL IDEAS ADVANCED

The memory of past mercies helps support the Christian in his time of trial.
There is no salvation in mere adherence to Church ritual nor in attempting to fulfill the works of the law.
Only those are saved who receive the "new birth," and whose sins are removed by the blood of Christ.
Trials and temptations alternate with joy and peace while the Christian is in this world, compelling him to rely absolutely on Christ for his full deliverance.

Grace Abounding to the Chief of Sinners records John Bunyan's inner struggles from his childhood through the first term of his imprisonment. It is the closest thing to an autobiography of any of his numerous books, but those who turn to it in hopes of finding a circumstantial account of the author's life are disappointed. The book is a spiritual exercise, in many ways comparable to the *Confessions* of St. Augustine. Bunyan set down the record of his own fears and deliverances in order to assist the members of his congregation during the time he was prevented from ministering among them. He hoped that when they read it they would realize what God had done for each of them; for, says Bunyan, the remembrance of God's help in time past is a great support to the Christian in his temptation.

Bunyan tells but little of his boyhood. His parents, although of low social standing, made the effort necessary to have him taught reading and writing, but we infer that they were not especially devout. As a child, however, John Bunyan was tormented with thoughts of his soul's damnation. He writes, at the age of nine or ten, "in the midst of my many sports and childish vanities, amidst my vain companions, I was often much cast down and afflicted in my mind therewith, yet could I not let go my sins." These fears abated with the passing years, and Bunyan became "the very ringleader of all the youth that kept [him] company, into all manner of vice and ungodliness." But, though he avoided religion, and took pleasure in reviling it, his heart trembled whenever he saw a religious man doing anything wicked.

It was only after he had served his term in the Parliamentary army and was married to a young woman of Christian upbringing, that Bunyan began to read Christian books and to attend church services. The outward forms of religion took great hold upon him. He admired the liturgy, the vestments, and the choir, and he was quite carried away with "a spirit of superstition," as he later came to view it. He attended church two times a day and recited and sang with the others; but he did not alter his way of life. Once, after the parson had preached against Sabbath sports, he was playing a game of cat when he seemed to hear a voice from Heaven saying, "Wilt thou leave thy sins and go to heaven, or have thy sins and go to hell?" He paused in the midst of his play long enough to reckon that he was damned already for former sins; then, in a kind of despair, he returned to his game.

During this time, however, he overcame his habit of swearing. He had been reproached for his profane language by a shopkeeper who was herself no model of virtue. A secret shame made him wish that he might be a child again and that his father might teach him to speak more decently, for the habit of swearing was too strong, he thought, for him ever to give it up. Yet, from that day on, to his great astonishment, he did not swear any more, and he found that he spoke better and more pleasantly than before.

An acquaintance grew up between Bunyan and a man who talked much about the Bible; and, liking the talk, Bunyan began reading the Scriptures for himself, especially the historical parts, for he could make nothing out of the epistles of Paul. The result was a complete conversion in his outward manner of life. He gave up dancing, Sabbath games, and even his great passion, bell-ringing, to undertake a life of rigid self-denial. The Bible seemed to him a book of rules which he had to follow if he were to gain Heaven, but, as he then understood it, if now and then he should break one of the rules, all he had to do was to repent and to promise that he would do better next time. He went on in this way for a year or more. Giving up his pleasures cost him many a struggle, but he was wonderfully satisfied in his own eyes, and he thought that he "pleased God as well as any man in England."

Working one day at his trade in Bedford, he heard three or four women sitting at a door in the sun, talking in the manner of nonconformists about things that had not hitherto entered his hearing. Bunyan, who "was now a brisk talker also in matters of religion," readily entered the discussion, but he could not understand at first what the women meant by "a new birth," and "their miserable state by nature," and how it was that "God had visited their souls with his love in the Lord Jesus." Much affected, he went not long after to consult Mr. Gifford, their pastor. "In a dream or vision," he says, "I saw [these people at Bedford] as if they were set on the sunny side of some high mountain, there refreshing themselves with the pleasant beams of the sun, while I was shivering and shrinking in the cold, afflicted with frost, snow, and dark clouds." A wall surrounded the mountain, and Bunyan saw himself testing it, trying to find a gap through which he might pass, and finally succeeding in squeezing through and sitting down with them in the sun. The mountain, Bunyan explains, signifies the Church; the sun, God's merciful face; the wall, the Word which separates the Christian and the world; and the gap in the wall, Jesus Christ.

Henceforth Bunyan read the Scriptures more zealously than before, but, having passed through formalism and legalism, he found experimental religion to contain new and greater vexations. In the first place, everything now seemed to hang on the validity of God's Word, particularly on His promises. How could one be sure that the Scriptures were not fables? How could one know that Christ is God's Son? "Everyone," he writes, "doth think his own religion rightest, both Jews and Moors and Pagans! and how if all our faith, and Christ, and Scriptures, should be but a think-so too?" But there was always the further question whether, supposing the Scriptures are true, he in particular were one of God's elect. Mostly it was the latter doubt that troubled Bunyan. His sense of God's presence and of Christ's mediation was too vivid for him long to be troubled by atheism. But, knowing the contradictions of his own heart, he was unable to go for any length of time without uncovering some evidence which, in the light of God's Word, seemed to number him among the reprobate. So persistent and so encompassing was this fear, that Bunyan devotes approximately a third of *Grace Abounding* to narrating the struggles to which it gave rise.

Bunyan had been permitted to experience many of the joys and consolations to which his evangelical friends testified. For instance, there was the time he was traveling into the country, thinking about the wickedness of his heart, when the Scriptural passage came to his mind which declares that God has "made peace through the blood of his cross." "I was made to see," he says, "that God and my soul were friends by this blood; yea, I saw that the justice of God and my sinful soul could embrace and kiss each other through this blood. This was a good day to me; I hope I shall not forget it."

Reading the Bible, he found ever deeper meanings disclosing themselves: "Oh! now, how was my soul led from truth to truth by God! even from the birth and cradle of the Son of God to his ascension and second coming from heaven to judge the world." It seemed to him that Christ spoke to him through the pages of the Gospel and made them talk with him and comfort him. He was sure that his soul cleaved to Christ, and that his love for Christ was "as hot as fire."

At this moment of pride, Satan disclosed to him a secret resentment against Christ, and a temptation to sell Him in exchange for the good things of this life: "Sometimes it would run through my thoughts, not so little as a hundred times together, Sell him, sell him, sell him!" The temptation stayed with Bunyan for days and weeks. Moreover, a fear constantly haunted him that would sometime weaken and yield to the temptation. Then, one morning, while he was lying on his bed and answering the tempter, "No, no, not for thousands, thousands, thousands," he was aware that there passed through his heart the thought, "Let him go, if he will!" With this, the struggle ended. "Down fell I, as a bird that is shot from the top of a tree, into great guilt, and fearful despair." The Scriptural verses which speak of Esau selling his birthright and finding no place of repentance stood in judgment over him. He was sure he had committed the unpardonable sin and that he would be numbered with those who, having been enlightened and then having fallen away, find it impossible to renew their repentance. Now all those passages which speak of the fullness of Christ's grace were so many coals of fire heaped on his head. For, this one who so loved sinners as to wash them from their sins in His own blood was the very one of whom Bunyan had said, "Let him go if he will." God could forgive David and Peter, and even the wicked Manasseh, great as their sins were; but, Bunyan believed, their sins were not the same as his: "This one consideration would always kill my heart, my sin was point-blank against my Saviour."

After months of gloom, brightened with only occasional streaks of hope as one or another Scriptural passage gave brief encouragement of forgiveness, Bunyan at last found assurance in the account of those "cities of refuge" which Joshua ordained as sanctuaries for persons found guilty of manslaughter. Bunyan noted that willful murderers were not given refuge, but only those who had not lain in wait to shed blood and had not hated the slain man; and this seemed to fit his case: "I hated him not aforetime; no, I prayed unto him, was tender of sinning against him; yea, and against this wicked temptation I had strove for a twelvemonth before; yea, and also when it did pass through my heart, it did in spite of my teeth; wherefore I thought I had a right to enter this city, and the elders, which are the apostles, were not to deliver me up." Bunyan was encouraged to reread the various Scriptures which had previously condemned him. Considering them carefully, and weighing "their scope and tendency," he was able to discriminate between his sin and that for which God casts men away.

Bunyan now enjoyed sufficient consolation to seek admission into the fellowship of Mr. Gifford's congregation, and after two or three years he was marked by some of its leading members as one suited to be a preacher. It appeared, upon trial, that he had unusual gifts for proclaiming the Gospel; and within a short time hundreds were coming to hear him preach. Then, after about five years, he was arrested by the Crown in its drive for religious uniformity. Presumably he could have remained at liberty if he had given bond to stop preaching; but, unable to do this, he chose to go to prison.

Bunyan goes on to show that, despite his preaching, during the whole time he was never without temptations. After the first few times he took communion with Mr. Gifford's congregation, he experienced a temptation to blaspheme the ordinance, and he was forced to pray to God to keep him from cursing those who received the cup. Another time, when overcome with sickness, his sense of guilt made him afraid of death, until he remembered the Scriptural passage which says, we are "justified by his grace, through the redemption that is in Christ Jesus." Another time, when "a great cloud of darkness" hid from him the face of Christ, he was seized by the expression, "I must go to Jesus." "At this," he says, "my former darkness and atheism fled away, and the blessed things of heaven were set within my view." He asked his wife if there were a Scriptural passage which says, "I must go to Jesus," but she could not tell. Then, like a bolt, it came to him: "Ye are come unto mount Sion, . . . and to Jesus the mediator of the new covenant, and to the blood of sprinkling, that speaketh better things than of Abel."

Bunyan notes, in the conclusion of his book, that his fears and consolations seemed to alternate in a remarkable way. "I have wondered much at this one thing," he writes, "that though God doth visit my soul with never so blessed a discovery of himself, yet I have found again, that such hours have attended me afterwards, that I have been in my spirit so filled with darkness, that I could not so much as once conceive what that God and that comfort was with which I have been refreshed." In short, there is no end to the Christian warfare. The abominations of the human heart are with us always, compelling us daily to trust in Jesus to help us and carry us "through this world."

Grace Abounding is written in the simple and unadorned language of one who is making a confession to God. Bunyan lays a kind of restraint on himself, noting, in his Preface, "I could have enlarged much in this my discourse. . . . I could also have stepped into a style much higher than this in which I have here discoursed, and could have adorned all things more than here I have seemed to do, but I dare not. God did not play in convincing of me, the devil did not play in tempting of me . . . ; wherefore I may not play in my relating of them, but be plain and simple, and lay down the thing as it was." The result is, nonetheless, a great work of art, quite as affecting in its way as *The Pilgrim's Progress,* in which Bunyan did permit himself the enlargement which seemed out of place here.

PARADISE LOST

Author: John Milton (1608-1674)
Type of work: Religious epic poem
First published: 1667

Principal Ideas Advanced

Satan conspired with other fallen angels to corrupt Adam and Eve through temptation.

God realized that man would fall, but He granted man His grace, for man's fall was to be through temptation by evil; and He decided to send His Son to answer death with sacrificial death and thus to achieve man's salvation.

In the guise of a serpent Satan led Eve to eat the fruit of the Tree of Knowledge, and Adam shared her disobedience; hence, Adam and Eve were banished from Eden, but not before hearing how the Son of God would become a man and would give His life for all men.

Paradise Lost is generally conceded to be one of the greatest poems in the English language; and there is no religious epic in English which measures up to Milton's masterpiece. Dante's *Divine Comedy* rivals it as poetry, and in the opinion of many critics Dante's poem exceeds Milton's in poetic virtue; but the *Comedy* is an Italian work, and hence comparison is to some extent not possible.

To say that *Paradise Lost* is a great poem means that persons who know poetry and who judge it, and who have been accepted by most educated men as qualified to judge, have been more strongly drawn to Milton's poem than to most other poems in the language. There is no question but that the principal appeal of the poem resides in its poetic quality: the quality of the imagery, and the quality of the work as a composition in which sound and rhythm contribute sentiment and color to meaning. But it is interesting to consider to what extent the Christian idea accounts for much of the poem's power; a new dimension of understanding is achieved once one considers Milton's work as a serious response to the problem of evil, as something other than a sentimental attempt to "justify the ways of God to men."

Poetry does religion a service in that it contributes drama and feeling to events, mythical or historical, on which the injunctions of religion rest. But religion does poetry a service in that it provides literature with a subject matter that appeals to man's deepest feelings. When a religion which has moved men for centuries inspires a poet whose use of poetic form is masterful enough to justify his taking that religion as his subject, the result can be a creative phenomenon which is itself capable of surviving the centuries. So it is with Dante's *Divine Comedy* and Milton's *Paradise Lost*.

If Milton had by temperament and the ordinary adventures of life been drawn into the sectarian task of apologizing for some particular version of the Christian faith, his work would surely have been affected; *Paradise*

Lost, as an attempt to cast the struggle between good and evil into imagery of universal significance, could not have been written. But Milton disliked the emphasis on ritual in the English Church, and he resisted his father's efforts to lead him to the ministry. His interest in reforming the corrupt clergy led him to ally himself with the Presbyterians, with whom he later became dissatisfied; and his love of freedom led him to be critical of Parliamentary censorship of the press (*Areopagitica,* 1644). He supported those who regarded Charles I as a threat to the freedom of the English people, and his *Tenure of Kings and Magistrates* (1649) presented an argument in favor of executing tyrants. He was appointed, in 1649, Latin Secretary to Oliver Cromwell, and his active defense of the Commonwealth government, as in his *First Defense of the English People,* led to his blindness two years later. The Restoration (1660) forced him into hiding, but he soon found that the new government was willing to allow him to continue his poetic labors.

Thus, it was as a champion of religious integrity and of human freedom that Milton came to the task of putting into poetic form the great story of man's Fall. In considering how Adam and Eve were led to taste the forbidden fruit, Milton was able to draw upon his experience of corruption in both Church and state. The resultant poetic myth has a frightening relevance to the life of any man, and the tragedy of man's Fall is relieved only by the creative intervention of Christ (whose regenerative effect is portrayed and praised in Milton's minor poem, *Paradise Regained,* which was completed in 1667).

The story of *Paradise Lost* is the familiar Genesis drama, together with embellishments suggested by Milton's imagination at work on other Biblical material and (probably) on such other literary works as Phineas Fletcher's *Locustoe* (1627) (or its English version, *The Apollyonists*); Giambattista Andreini's sacred drama, *L'Adamo* (1614); and Joost van den Vondel's *Lucifer* (1654).

Milton begins his poem by stating its subject:

> Of Man's first disobedience, and
>   the fruit
> Of that forbidden tree whose mortal taste
> Brought death into the World,
>   and all our woe,
> With loss of Eden, till one
>   greater Man
> Restore us, and regain the blissful Seat,
> Sing, Heavenly Muse. . . .

He asks the Muse to illumine "what in me is dark . . . / That, to the highth of this great argument,/ I may assert Eternal Providence,/ And justify the ways of God to men."

The usual problem for a religious man is the problem of justifying his ways to God. But philosophers and theologians, and other persons who find themselves challenging the grounds of their religious convictions, are faced with a unique and disturbing problem: the problem of justifying the ways of God to man. The problem arises because of the presence of evil in the world. If God is the creator of all being, then He is the author of death and suffering; and how is this consequence to be made compatible with the idea of God as an omniscient, omnipotent, benevolent Father?

It is clear from the outset of *Paradise Lost* that Milton has no quarrel with God. He asks, not for a divine explanation, but for insight concerning the cause of the fall of man: "Say first . . . what cause/ Moved our grand Parents, in that happy state,/ Favoured of Heaven so highly, to fall off/ From their Creator, and transgress his will. . . ." Man was created as an innocent being; there was nothing in his nature which of its own account could lead to transgression. So Milton must have reasoned, for he asks his question about the cause of the Fall so as to suggest that the cause could not have been *in* man, but from the outside. Thus, he asks, "Who first seduced them to that foul revolt?" The answer is immediately forthcoming: "The infernal Serpent . . . ," Satan, the "Arch-Enemy," who because of pride rebelled against God and then, in league with the fallen angels, conspired to attack God through corrupting His creation, man.

The religious use of Satan as the image of evil is ineffective if Satan is conceived to be the entire cause of moral evil. If Satan is the author of evil, God is powerless to hold Satan in check; and if anyone is to blame for the Fall of man, it must be Satan, not man. Milton's problem, then, is the problem which an initial consideration of the problem of evil provokes: the problem of using the image of evil, Satan, in such a manner as not to diminish the glory of God or to minimize the responsibility of man.

It is unlikely that any resolution of the latter problem can be entirely satisfactory to the mind of man. If Adam and Eve were innocent; if prior to the seductive blandishments of the Serpent, they had known only the good; if no experience provided them with evidence by which to recognize evil at work, how then can they be held accountable for succumbing to temptation? The answer must be that God created man with the freedom to choose, and He demanded obedience; man was expected to obey not because he had reasons, but because there was a sufficient cause of moral obedience; namely, the injunction from God Himself. But to accept God as the sufficient ground of obedience must be an act of faith; it could not, at least with Adam and Eve, have been a commitment justified by experience of good and evil. And although faith in God is superior to any other faith, it could not have been known to be superior (and, in any case, once the dependence on God is known to be a superior kind of dependence, it is no longer faith; such knowledge rests on experience).

Perhaps, then, there is no way of intellectually solving the problem in regards to Adam and Eve. But if Adam and Eve are taken, not as first parents, but as images of human beings faced with the choice between good and evil; if the story of their Fall is taken not as a case in support of moral recrimination, but as an argument for obedience to God; and if the hope of Paradise regained is shown to be justified through faith in Christ, the "greater Man" who can "restore us," then the tale of Paradise lost becomes an effective expression of that Christian commitment by which the problem of evil is not so much solved as settled. The answer, then, is like Christ's answer to the Grand Inquisitor (in Dostoevski's *The Brothers Karama-*

zov); His kiss was not an argument or a proof; it was an act of wholehearted acceptance of the other.

Milton's poem tells how Satan, after debating the matter with the fallen angels, decides to fly to the world, there to attempt the perversion of man (Books I and II). God observes Satan's journey to earth, and He tells His Son that Satan will succeed in the effort to corrupt Adam and Eve (Book III). Milton then describes God as asking the question which Satan's temptation of man suggests: If man falls, whose fault is it? God's answer—and it is an answer to which the poet must give priority—is that the Fall will be no one's fault but man's. Speaking of man, God says wrathfully, "Whose fault?/ Whose but his own? Ingrate, he had of me/ All he could have; I made him just and right,/ Sufficient to have stood, though free to fall." God justifies His gift of freedom to man by declaring that obedience through necessity would be morally worthless; such obedience would give no pleasure to God. "They themselves decreed/ Their own revolt, not I," God declares, and thus He frees Himself from the possible accusation that He is to blame for man's Fall. However, man is to find grace, God decides, because man's Fall is to be brought about by temptation wrought by the angels whose fall, unlike man's, was "Self-tempted, self-depraved. . . ." The Son of God welcomes His Father's words; it would be inconsistent with the divine nature if man were to be denied grace after a fall brought about by Satan's fraud as well as by man's folly. Christ then offers to become mortal and to pay "death for death," in order that neither man nor Justice will die eternally.

Milton's resolution of the problem of evil, then, is the central Christian resolution. Man was created a free moral agent; if he errs, he, not the evil to which he succumbs, is to blame. But evil is whatever tempts man, and if man were in no way tempted, it is unlikely that he would fall. Thus, God's grace is not inappropriately granted, although it is freely given. Christ's sacrifice will be genuine, for He will suffer and die as a man; but His sacrifice will be regenerative, for the Resurrection will show that the divine is more powerful than evil: ". . . I shall rise victorious . . . Death his death's wound shall then receive, and stoop/ Inglorious, of his mortal sting disarmed. . . ."

In sending Raphael to tell Adam of Satan's rebellion and of Satan's plot against their innocent state, God provides Adam and Eve with the knowledge they need to choose good in preference to evil (Books V-VIII). Thus, Milton universalized the Adam myth; Adam becomes as every man in that he knows of evil and of the seductive power of temptation. The Biblical Adam enjoyed no such advance warning. Eve, also, has ample warning, for she overhears the angel's advice to Adam; furthermore, on the morning of the temptation, Adam pleads with her not to leave his side. But she declares herself strong enough to resist evil (Book IX).

When Satan in the guise of the Serpent succeeds in persuading Eve to taste the fruit of the Tree of Knowledge, he wins because of Eve's pride and over-confidence (Book IX). As Milton portrays her, Eve is no ignorant child of nature; she is woman warned; consequently, she is everywoman, just as Adam is everyman.

Christ is sent to judge the sinners (Book X). In sending the divine Son, "Man's Friend, his Mediator," God shows the mercy which, prior to man's Fall, He had decided upon. The God of Genesis is a wrathful God, intemperate in His judgment; but the God of *Paradise Lost* judges man in His person as Christ. Thus, man has no recourse; he cannot blame God for man's disobedience, nor can he accuse God of intolerance. Man's only hope of salvation, then, is through Christ. Michael is portrayed both as the angel who is to lead Adam and Eve from Paradise and as the bearer of the news that man is to have Christ as Savior (Books XI and XII).

What Milton accomplished in *Paradise Lost* is the transformation of the Biblical account of man's Fall into a Christian myth, a promise of salvation through Christ. In casting this new story into some of the clearest and most moving poetry in the English language Milton performed an artist's service to his God.

PENSÉES

Author: Blaise Pascal (1623-1662)
Type of work: Reflections on the Christian religion
First published: 1670

PRINCIPAL IDEAS ADVANCED

Man must learn to reflect upon himself and seek to understand himself in relation to the rest of nature; the Socratic dictum, "Know thyself," becomes the guiding principle of philosophical and religious inquiry.

The human condition is characterized by a peculiar ambivalence of misery and grandeur; on the one hand, man experiences a disproportion within himself and in his relation to nature; on the other hand, he is the highest of all creatures and sovereign over the world of nature.

Man's rational knowledge suffers significant and far-reaching limitations; the heart plays a more important role than does reason in disclosing both the human condition and the reality of God.

The existence of God is not settled by metaphysical demonstrations of the rational intellect; the issue is settled through a concrete existential decision in which man must wager either for the existence of God or against it.

The fundamentals of the Christian religion are its belief in the corruption of human nature and its doctrine of redemption through Jesus Christ.

Pascal's *Pensées* (*Thoughts*) consists of fragmentary notes and aphorisms which he had intended to use in the writing of an "Apology for the Christian Religion." Ill health and an untimely death precluded the realization of this project. In the effort to preserve Pascal's acute insights into human life and his suggestive observations about God and religion, the Port-Royalists compiled and edited the fragmentary notes of the projected "Apology" eight years after Pascal's death. It is in the form of this revision that the notes have come down to us today.

Like the Athenian Socrates, Pascal teaches that the task of the existing individual is to know or understand himself. "One must know oneself. If this does not serve to discover truth, it at least serves as a rule of life, and there is nothing better." Pascal does not disparage man's efforts to gain knowledge of the vast expanses of the universe, but he suggests that before entering upon such a quest man would do well to reflect seriously upon himself and to see what proportion or disproportion there exists between himself and nature. In pursuing this basic question of self-knowledge Pascal formulates some penetrating insights into the life of man. His *Pensées* is to be understood not as an attempt at a formulation of a systematic philosophy or theology but rather as an attempt at an elucidation of the human condition in its manifold concreteness.

When man once reflects upon himself, he finds that his condition is characterized by a pervading ambivalence and ambiguity. In comparison with the Infinite, he is nothing; in comparison with the nothing out of which he has been made, he is the crown of creation. On the one hand, he is incurably limited in power and wisdom; on the other hand, he is but a little lower than the angels. He is capable of the lowest, but also capable of the highest. He bears the stamp of finitude, but he also carries with him the image of the Infinite. This is the essential ambiguity or paradox which characterizes the human condition. "What a chimera then is man! What a novelty! What a monster, what a chaos, what a contradiction, what a prodigy! Judge of all things, imbecile worm of the earth; depositary of truth, a sink of uncertainty and error; the pride and refuse of the universe!" Man stands at the crossroads between the finite and the Infinite; in him flesh and spirit meet. There is both a misery and a grandeur which qualifies the existence of man.

Man's ineradicable finitude imposes some clearly defined limits on the reach and range of human reason. Man as a "thinking reed" exhibits the power of reason, but he does so only under the conditions of a limited and fractured existence. Man remains incapable of certain knowledge; his highest rational principles are never immune to doubt. "Our reason is always deceived by fickle shadows; nothing can fix the finite between the two Infinites, which both enclose and fly from it." There is an inescapable uncertainty or existential doubt which is part of the human condition.

It is necessary to distinguish this existential doubt of which Pascal speaks from the calculated, methodological doubt of Descartes. The doubt of Descartes was a provisional doubt, to be used as a technique for arriving at indubitable propositions and to be suspended the moment that such propositions are made known. Pascalian doubt is neither calculated nor provisional. It is part of the finitude of man, indicating an element of insecurity and risk in every existential truth. Such a doubt can never be overcome or even assessed through the exercise of man's rational faculty. This does not mean that reason must thus be displaced. It does mean, however, that knowledge involves more than simply the response of the mind and that in dealing with those truths which concern man most deeply "the heart has its reasons, which reason does not know."

The threat of emptiness and meaninglessness is another determinant of the human condition. Man seeks to find satisfaction and meaning for his life in the pursuit of various finite and temporal goods, but his endeavors fail to provide an ultimate satisfaction or a final meaning. In the section entitled, "The Misery of Man Without God," Pascal examines the threat of emptiness in connection with the phenomenon of diversion. Man seeks various diversions and distractions so as to fill the emptiness or void of his existence; this is why men love bustle, noise, and amusements. But this frantic pursuit of various activities and amusements fails to provide satisfaction. It only diverts man's thoughts from himself. Indeed, the pursuit is undertaken for the purpose of escaping from himself, for man lacks the courage to face the weariness, emptiness, and despair which threaten his existence. Men will spend entire days chasing hares which they would not have accepted prior to the chase. They are not interested in the object of the chase, but only in the chase itself, which diverts their thoughts from themselves and screens them from the existential negativities of their condition. It is for this reason that solitary confinement is the most horrible of all punishments. All avenues for diversion are cut off and the self must contend with itself in its solitude. Man lives and moves in emptiness, engaged in an abortive search for satisfaction through diverting activities, refusing to accept his finitude and the conditions of his estranged existence.

It is this description of the human condition as it is characterized by its various negativities that drives Pascal to his wager for the existence of God. The wager thus becomes a matter of existential concern. In no sense is the wager for Pascal an objective, disinterested, calculated undertaking, the outcome of which remains a matter of indifference. It has to do with a possible answer, or lack of such, to the ultimate issues of life. If God does not exist, the human condition is threatened with final despair. The wager thus confronts man with an existential choice qualified by ultimate concern. The wager is formulated in terms of a forced option which presents an inescapable decision. Either God exists or He does not. Shall one decide for His existence or against it? There is no rule of certainty to govern one's decision. It remains a matter of risk. Man is thus confronted with an inescapable decision in the presence of an inescapable uncertainty. In the face of this inescapable uncertainty he wagers. If he believes in God, and if God does exist, he gains everything; if he believes, and God does not exist, he suffers only a finite loss. On the other hand, if he disbelieves, and God exists, he loses everything; and if he disbelieves, and God does not exist, he reaps only a finite gain. The odds thus favor belief in God's existence. If one believes, there is an infinity to gain and only a finite truth to lose; if one disbelieves, there is an infinity to lose and only a finite truth to gain.

It is evident that the truth of God's existence cannot be determined through the use of pure reason. Pascal breaks with the whole tradition of natural or philosophical theology. "The metaphysical proofs of God are so remote from the reasoning of men, and so complicated, that they make little impression; and if they should be of service to some, it would be only during the moment that they see such demonstration; but an hour afterwards they fear they have been mistaken." The philosophical proofs, in the last analysis, are rejected by Pascal on two counts: they lack certainty and they remain irrelevant to religious experience.

Thus, the God of the philosophers is displaced by the God of Abraham, Isaac, and Jacob, and by the God who revealed Himself decisively in Jesus Christ. Pascal had written the fragmentary notes compiled in the *Pensées* in preparation for an apology for the Christian religion. This intention is evident throughout. Only the Christian religion has provided man with an adequate picture of the distortions and corruptions present in man's nature, and with a teaching of deliverance from this condition through redemption by Jesus Christ. As a committed adherent to this religion, Pascal in his theological reflections remains consistently and emphatically Christocentric. "Not only do we know God by Jesus Christ alone, but we know ourselves only by Jesus Christ. We know life and death only through Jesus Christ. Apart from Jesus Christ we do not know what is our life, nor our death, nor God, nor ourselves."

DISCOURSE CONCERNING THE HOLY SPIRIT

Author: John Owen (1616-1683)
Type of work: Puritan theology
First published: 1674

PRINCIPAL IDEAS ADVANCED

The doctrine of the Holy Spirit is clearly grounded in Scripture.

The Spirit was active at the first creation, has been revealed in power in the old and new dispensations, and is responsible for the new creation.

The work of the Spirit is seen in raising the believer to new life and in maintaining him in progressive holiness.

What a former generation knew as "Owen on the Holy Spirit," but which is the *Discourse Concerning the Holy Spirit,* is a massive and composite work in five sections, representing one of the major theological contributions of one of the greatest of the later English Puritan writers. Owen was chiefly, but by no means exclusively, a theologian. The first stage of his Oxford career was cut short by William Laud (1573-1645), who objected to Owen's Puritan views, but these views were responsible for Owen's rapid rise under the protection of Oliver Cromwell (1599-1658). As dean of Christ

Church and vice-chancellor of Oxford, Owen played an important role on a stage far wider than the university. His administrative experience gave him practical wisdom, which was combined with both evangelical fervor and Christian charity. When the restoration of Charles II drove him into nonconformity he was already a learned scholar, a famous theologian, and a prominent public figure. During the remaining two decades of his life he poured out a stream of major works, most of which arose out of the controversies of the period.

Many of Owen's books dealt with the central doctrines of Christianity. His works on the Spirit are neither abler nor more extensive than his works on the atonement and the Trinity, but they deal with a subject which had been consistently neglected. The doctrine of the Holy Spirit had never received the dogmatic development accorded to the other central affirmations of the faith, and Owen's work is important not only because of the quality of his thought, but also because it examines with great thoroughness a topic which has usually been accorded the most perfunctory treatment.

The first of Owen's five works on the Holy Spirit is A Discourse Concerning the Holy Spirit, itself a book of 650 quarto pages. It was followed by The Reason of Faith (1677), The Causes, Ways and Means of Understanding the Mind of God (1678), The Work of the Holy Spirit in Prayer (1682) and On the Work of the Holy Spirit as a Comforter (1693, posthumously). These, it is obvious, cumulatively represent a sustained preoccupation with the doctrine of the Holy Spirit to which there are few (if any) parallels in the history of theology.

Owen treats his subject with the expansiveness, even prolixity, which a seventeenth century theologian felt free to claim and in which his contemporaries were willing to indulge him, but even a modern reader senses at once that we have here the work of a great man exploring a great subject.

In the first book of the Pneumatologia (the foundation work among the five) Owen deals with the preliminary topics which a thorough examination of the subject presupposes. The Scriptures speak of spiritual gifts and promise them. This in itself, Owen writes, would make the Spirit an important subject of study—particularly when one considers the central place which the Spirit occupies in the Bible. But when misguided enthusiasts invest their fantasies with the Spirit's authority, and when men glorying in their own intelligence presume to slight its significance, the task of examining Scriptural teaching on the subject assumes more than passing importance. Men can be guided by false spirits as well as by the divine Spirit, but we have been given a rule by which to test them (I John 4: 1-3).

The next step is to consider the names and titles by which the Bible speaks of the Spirit, for if there is confusion at the beginning we can hardly hope for clarity as we proceed. We must also be aware of the nature of the reality with which we are dealing, and Owen is concerned at the outset to establish the personal character of the Spirit. He argues that the nature of God is the foundation of all religion, and what this nature is we know because of divine revelation. God has revealed Himself as Three in One, and from this we can see that the Spirit is not an impersonal cosmic energy, but a manifestation, an activity of the Godhead itself. The very language of Scripture is conclusive proof that the Spirit is personal; the properties assigned to it (to *Him*) presuppose a personal subsistence. This divine personal Spirit is active now and has been active from the very beginning. Creation was accomplished through His instrumentality, and Owen carefully examines the distinctive role of the Spirit therein. The whole Godhead, of course, was involved in creation, and the Spirit's special task was to perfect what the Father created. So Owen examines what the Spirit did in spreading out the heavens and marshaling their hosts, in fashioning the earth and making the creatures who inhabit it, and, most significantly of all, in creating man. The same Spirit who creates preserves all things, both natural and moral. But there are mysteries here which cannot be easily probed nor lightly disregarded. In relation to God's will, the Spirit is described as given or sent in relation to His own will. He is spoken of as proceeding or coming.

The strongly Biblical foundation of Owen's theology is seen in the way he deals with the activity of the Spirit as this is described in both the Old and New Testaments. Under the old dispensation he finds that the way was prepared for the new, and he examines the significance of prophecy, inspiration, miracles, and the special gifts which can be directly attributed to the Spirit. In every area, the natural faculties of men's minds were heightened, whether the area involved was political, moral, intellectual, or physical. The importance of the Spirit in the new dispensation which was inaugurated in the New Testament can be seen in the fact that the full outpouring of the Spirit is the great promise concerning the new creation. The ministry of the Gospel rests on this promise, a promise which extends to all believers. Each person is commanded to pray for the Spirit. On the eve of His departure Christ solemnly promised to send His Spirit. He even specified the ends which the gift of the Spirit would serve, and He made clear that the new creation (to be completed by the Spirit) would be the principal means by which God's glory would be made known. The Head of this new creation is Christ, and we can see the significance of the Spirit if we observe the way in which the presence and power of the Spirit are made manifest in Christ.

At this point Owen embarks on a careful discussion, worked out in considerable detail and in strict loyalty to trinitarian presuppositions, of the part played by the Spirit in the Incarnation of the Word. It is clear that the Holy Spirit is the immediate efficient cause of all divine operations. It is of the Spirit that Scripture speaks in connection with the conception of Jesus. It is the Spirit which accomplishes the sanctification of His human nature. He anoints the Savior with power and gifts; the Spirit guides, conducts, and supports Christ throughout His ministry. The Spirit is responsible for miraculous works, but He also endows Christ with the spiritual graces of love, zeal, submission, faith, and truth. The Spirit sustains Christ in the final ordeal of His crucifixion and death, and in the triumph of His resurrection. And since the ascension of Christ the Spirit bears witness to Christ and brings to mind the truth as it is in Him. In all this, the implications for a doctrine of the Godhead are carefully noted, The faith proclaims one God, not three, and in every activity of the Godhead all three persons are involved.

Owen deals with great sophistication with the most complex and subtle theological truths. But he does not forget that the New Creation concerns men and women. In particular, it concerns them as they are members of the Church, for the Church is built upon the foundation of the promise of the Spirit, and the erection of the Church is likewise committed to the Spirit. The Spirit performs the work of Christ in those who are the members of Christ's Body, and thus the Spirit is the author of all grace.

Owen, it is clear, is a careful and Biblical theologian, but he is competent to proceed further and construct an elaborate superstructure on the Spiritual foundations. A great deal of the interest and value of his principal book on the Spirit lies in his exposition of the stages of the New Creation. The focal points of an elaborate discussion of the new life in the believer are regeneration and sanctification. The presuppositions of the new life are provided in the Gospel, especially in the Incarnation and the atonement. But man is dead in trespasses and sins. Regeneration declares that what has been dead can be made alive. The Good News has been proclaimed; it must be appropriated, and the distinguishing mark of Owen's work is the close connection he establishes between the Holy Spirit and the reawakening of the soul that is sunk in sin. A new creature is formed, with a new nature and capable of a new life. This is not a magical transformation. It has the most profound moral significance, and it requires, on man's part, a specific response. Man must be converted; he must turn from his sin. His mind, his affections, his conscience must be touched. But a man cannot simply decide to abandon his sins by his own wisdom and in his own strength. Hence, Owen carefully studies the state of corruption into which man has been plunged by his sin. The mind has been deprived of saving light, and it is overwhelmed by a darkness which is both objective and subjective. So the natural man lives in a state which is described as spiritual death.

Owen's careful study of nature and sin is the necessary prelude to a consideration of the work of the Spirit in regeneration. There is no possibility of new life for people living and dying in a state of sin. The vicious circle must be broken; deliverance is by God's grace alone, and the agent of God in this new act of creation is the Holy Spirit. This is all much less remote from modern experience than the twentieth century reader might suppose. The analysis of man's plight is conducted with great psychological insight, and it is significant that the argument is enforced by an appeal to the experience of that profound psychologist, St. Augustine.

The new life will be a holy life, and it will be progressively so. Owen therefore studies with equal care the power of the Spirit in sanctifying the believer. This subject also presupposes a study of sin, not now as a past state of bondage and death but as a present and dangerous alternative to holiness.

The filth of sin must be purged away; it can be purged away by the blood of Christ. Then the task of strengthening the believer begins.

Sanctification is a progressive advance that is open only to the believer whose life is filled and transformed by the Spirit. Here the positive work of sanctification comes under careful scrutiny.

The value and importance of Owen's work on the Spirit is considerable. Historically this is one of the most faithful and complete reflections of the Puritan mind. The main lines of Calvinist thought are clearly present. God, His presence, His power, His continuing activity are the presuppositions of the work. The great doctrines of Reformed theology appear one by one. In particular, Owen shows with some care how election is the cause of and a motive for holiness. It is clear, also, that the best type of Puritan theology was never abstract or theoretical. The argument is constantly related to practical issues, and the great theological doctrines are applied to the immediate necessities of man's situation. Even more important is the fact that Owen provides perhaps the only Protestant study, on a major scale, of one of the neglected doctrines of Christian theology. In recent years there have been numerous signs of a revival of interest in the theological implications of the Spirit. So far most of the books which reflect this renascence have been small in scale and many of them have been slight in significance. Owen may sometimes be diffuse, but he is always massively learned and soundly Biblical. His argument is developed in great detail, and both in aim and in effect his work is impressively constructive.

TREATISE CONCERNING THE SEARCH AFTER TRUTH

Author: Nicholas Malebranche (1638-1715)
Type of work: Philosophical theology
First published: 1674

PRINCIPAL IDEAS ADVANCED

God is the sole cause of events in nature and of corresponding perceptions in the human mind.

The laws which God has prescribed are so disposed that events and perceptions exist in perfect parallel, activity in nature being the occasion, but not the cause, of activity in the mind.

By the senses we learn to preserve the body, but the senses often deceive us; the highest truth is to be found in the immediate awareness of God and in the apprehension of the ideas in the divine mind.

The *Treatise Concerning the Search After Truth* is the principal work of Nicholas Malebranche, a French priest trained at the Sorbonne and a member of the Oratory. Malebranche was profoundly influenced by the philosophy of René Descartes (1596-1650) and of Descartes' disciple, Arnold Geulincx (1624-1699); the philosophy which emerged is known as occasionalism.

Malebranche posits a parallelism between events in nature and events in the mind, a parallelism due to the activity of God. Malebranche inherited Descartes's dualism between extension and thought. Extension and thought were considered by Malebranche to be too dissimilar to interact; each, then, must act according to its own law, without affecting the other. God has so regulated matters that when the will acts there is movement in the body and when there is an injury to the body pain occurs. The physical event is the "occasion" of the mental event, without being its cause.

The human mind, says Malebranche, is situated between God, its Creator, and material beings; it is intimately related to God and is thus exalted above all things, while because of its connection with the body, it is prone to misery and error. The relation of our minds to our bodies is not one of absolute necessity, but our mind's relation to God is absolutely indispensable, natural, and necessary.

The nature of all things is regulated by the will of God, Malebranche claims; the human soul is so united to God that it receives from the eternal truth, which presides over the understanding, a knowledge of its duty. To the degree that the mind increases its union with God, it grows more luminous, and when unaffected by its union with the body, and solely attentive to the pure ideas of the mind, while listening to God, the mind cannot possibly fall into error, for God does not deceive those who interrogate Him.

Knowledge is acquired through the attention of the mind, not by sensations and passions, writes Malebranche. The opposition that the body makes to the mind should be withstood; sensible things are not to be made the object of our attention, and the reports of the senses are to be subjected to disbelief.

Malebranche claims that the truth of all things must be pronounced by the mind, according to its internal light, without listening to the confused and false verdict of the senses and imagination. Our senses, he writes, are given to us solely for the preservation of our body, and it is because of them that we fall into error. The senses are most exact in telling us of the relations which our body has to bodies around us, but they are incapable of instructing us concerning the nature of bodies. The senses are never to be raised above the understanding. We ought never to give our entire consent to anything that is not entirely evident. To doubt the senses out of prudence and caution, because of wisdom and penetration of mind, is the mark of the true philosopher. The moving force of bodies is nothing but the action of God, for bodies have no force to move themselves; their moving force is the will of God, which is always efficacious.

God by His efficacious will performs whatever is performed by the motion of bodies and the wills of minds. Creatures have no efficacious action themselves; God's power is communicated to them by means of natural laws which God established on their account.

Man wills and determines himself, says Malebranche, only to the extent that God causes him to will; man alone sins, but sin, error, and concupiscence are nothing; in themselves man's volitions are impotent; God works all notwithstanding them, for man's volitions produce nothing.

God is to be seen in all things, writes Malebranche; we ought to be sensible of His power and force in all natural effects. No power, force, or efficacy is to be attributed to secondary or natural causes. In everything it is God that works all; nothing resists Him, because He can do whatever He wills.

According to Malebranche, "God by the first of Natural Laws positively Wills and consequently causes the Collision of Bodies; and afterwards employs this Collision as an Occasion of establishing the Second Natural Law; which regulates the communication of motions; . . . thus the actual Collision is the Natural, or Occasional, Cause of the Actual Communication of Motions; . . . these two Natural Laws . . . are sufficient to produce such a world as we see. . . ."

To attain truth, says Malebranche, the philosopher must realize that the thoughts of the soul which depend upon the body concern only the body and thus are either obscure or false. In any case, such thoughts can serve only to unite us to sensible goods and to what procures them. It is not only necessary to rid ourselves of the delusions of sense, Malebranche warns, but also we must guard against the deception caused by the vision of our imagination and the impressions that other men's imagination exercise upon our mind. Truth is obtained by the admission of the clear ideas which the mind, or pure understanding, receives through its necessary union with the divine Logos.

The limitation of the mind is a source of error, Malebranche points out, for the mind cannot grasp anything of an infinite nature. Human reason cannot comprehend such mysteries as the Trinity. Since the principles of the Christian faith are not known to reason, reason must submit to faith in the Scriptures.

Our minds are dependent upon God for all their thoughts, writes Malebranche. God has in Himself the ideas of all the beings He has created, and since God is united by His presence with our souls, in that He is the place of spirits, as space is the place of bodies, the mind can see the ideas in God which represent created beings. The mind can see all the works of God in God. We can see only what God desires us to see. Our sufficiency is of God, not of ourselves. God is the light that enlightens every man. Men are entirely impotent without God. Unless we know God in some way, we know nothing at all. When we see material and sensible things, we do not have sensations of them in God, but they proceed from God, who acts upon us. When we perceive something sensible two factors appear: pure idea and sensation. Sensations are modifications in our soul caused within us by God. Pure ideas, which are joined to sensations, are in God, and we know them only because God discloses them to us. The idea in God is joined to the sensation in us by God; thus, when objects are present, we believe them to be so, and we have the proper sentiments and passions with relation to them.

The senses and imagination are confined to sensible things, Malebranche writes, but the pure intellect, our understanding or reason, enables us to have pure ideas and to see truths in God and to learn eternal laws.

The dependence of our minds upon the will of God enables us to perceive all things through the presence of God, who comprehends everything in the simplicity of His essence. God makes our souls to feel pain and pleasure and all other sensations by the union He has instituted between our souls and bodies. By means of the union between the will of man and the representation of the ideas included in the divine essence, God enables our souls to know whatever they know; this union is caused by the will of God; He alone can enlighten us.

According to Malebranche, "God is the intelligible world, or the place of Spirits, as the material world is the place of bodies. That is, from His Power they receive all their modifications; that 'tis in His Wisdom they discover all their Idea's; and 'tis by His love they are influenced with all their regulated motions: And because His Power and His Love are nothing but Himself; let us believe with St. Paul, that He is not far from every one of us, and that in Him we live and move, and have our Being."

There are four ways by which the mind knows things, writes Malebranche. The first is the manner by which the mind knows God. God alone penetrates the mind and discloses Himself to it, by enlightening the mind from His own substance. We see God with an immediate and direct vision. Although the knowledge that we have of God in this life is imperfect and confused, God is intelligible by Himself immediately.

The second way of knowing things is the way by which we know bodies; that is, by their ideas, by reference to

something different from themselves. Bodies together with their properties are seen in that divine being which contains them in an intelligible manner; they are seen in God, and thus they are seen in the most perfect manner. Whatever is lacking in our knowledge of extension, its figures and motions, is attributable to the defectiveness of our minds, not to the defectiveness of the divine ideas.

The third way that the mind knows is the way by which it knows the soul; that is, by means of internal sensation, or conscience. The soul is known not by reference to the idea of the soul, nor is it seen in God; the soul is known, although imperfectly, by conscience, by reference to what one feels within. The *existence* of the soul is more clearly apprehended than is the existence of the body, but the *nature* of the soul is less well known than is the nature of the body.

The fourth way by which the mind knows is the way by which it knows the souls of other men and of pure intelligences; that is, by conjecture. By conjecture we know that the souls of other men are of the same species as our own. We presume that what we feel in ourselves is felt by others, and that God influences other spirits just as He influences our own.

The mind of man is limited, Malebranche claims; it is by nature subject to error. Even the least things have infinite relations which are beyond the scope of a finite mind.

Just as bodies move in the material world, so spirits move toward God in the spiritual world. By faith, writes Malebranche, we know that the order of nature has been inverted by sin, and we realize that our inclinations are disordered, so that instead of seeking

God, we seek our ultimate end in our-selves. But we are properly inclined only when we are inclined to the good in general, only when we love our neighbors as well as ourselves.

The cause of our adhesion to sensible things is sin, says Malebranche, for sin has estranged us from God, and thus we are now made dependent on our bodies. Since the Fall of Adam God is withdrawn from us, and we know Him as our good only by the grace of Jesus Christ. God alone is our true good, and whatever is real in the motions of the mind is the work of God, although He is not the author of our sin, or of our concupiscence. Actual grace is necessary before we can act rightly. The mind of man is preserved by God so that it can know and love Him. Whatever God wills is proper solely because He wills it, and He is just.

One of the most deplorable consequences of original sin, writes Malebranche, is that we no longer see God in all things and love Him in His works. The mind wanders and forgets God, who enlightens the mind. In a sense, the mind wills and determines itself, insofar as God causes it to will, for otherwise there would be no future reward and punishment; but inasmuch as God is the cause, man is inclined to will the good.

God acts in the simplest way and always with order, Malebranche concludes. God is an infinitely perfect being, whose knowledge and wisdom are without limits, so that every means by which He wishes to execute His designs are known to Him. The salvation of man is accomplished by repentance, self-denial and obedience, through Christ Jesus and His grace.

AN APOLOGY FOR THE TRUE CHRISTIAN DIVINITY

Author: Robert Barclay (1648-1690)
Type of work: Apologetics
First published: 1676 (Latin); 1678 (English)

PRINCIPAL IDEAS ADVANCED

The Christian faith is a living and vital experience, not a formal pattern of scholastic ideas, yet it can be presented as an ordered system without sacrificing its reality.

Man's true felicity is to know God, and this knowledge can be appropriated only by those who are enlightened by the Spirit; but this Spirit is clearly related to Scripture and to the work accomplished by Jesus Christ, who brings us into a new and living relationship with God.

Christian witness must be translated into appropriate forms of life if it is to affect those about us.

In his *An Apology for the True Christian Divinity* Robert Barclay pro-vides, as the subtitle of his work announces, "an explanation and vindication of the Principles and Doctrines of the People Called Quakers." It was one of the earliest formal statements of the position of the Society of Friends, and in many ways it remains the most important and impressive of Quaker manifestoes. It stands in its own right, however, as one of the major theological works of an age much given to theological writing. Barclay's Scottish background may explain a degree of formal theological structure not common in Quaker works, and it also accounts for occasional traces of Calvinism not wholly congenial to his coreligionists.

Barclay opens his work with a characteristically Quaker address to King Charles II: "As it is inconsistant with the truth I bear, so it is far from me to use this epistle as an engine to flatter thee . . . ," but he takes occasion to repeat the story of Quaker sufferings and to reaffirm their innocence. He reminds the king of the degree to which his own career reflects the marvels of divine providence, and he submits that this should surely teach the king not only a humble awareness of the precariousness of human dignities but also a keen awareness of "how hateful the oppressor is both to God and man." At the forefront of his work, Barclay places a noble plea for liberty of conscience.

To explain his method, Barclay adds a greeting "unto the friendly reader" and a letter "to the clergy . . . unto whose hands these [theological theses] may come." He has no intention, he says, of relying on scholastic subtleties; the "simple, naked truth" which God has given men for their guidance has been overlaid by "school-divinity" which "brings [us] not a whit nearer to God, neither makes any man less

wicked or more righteous than he was."

The main body of the *Apology* consists of fifteen propositions. Barclay gives them initially in condensed form and then expounds each of them in detail. He begins with the true foundation of knowledge. The height of all happiness is to know God, and therefore "the true and right understanding of this foundation and ground of knowledge is that which is most necessary to be known and believed in the first place." This knowledge can come only in an appropriate and appointed way, and Barclay's second proposition defines immediate revelation. The testimony of the Spirit "is that alone by which the true knowledge of God hath been, is, and can be only revealed," and it is by the agency of the Spirit that He has disclosed himself. Because there is an inner and essential consistency in the truth, the witness of the Spirit can never contradict the outward testimony either of the Scriptures or of right and sound reason, but this does not imply that the testimony of the Spirit can in any way be subjected to any external standard. The inward illumination of divine revelation "is that which is evident and clear of itself, forcing, by its own evidence and clearness, the well-disposed understanding to assent, irresistibly moving the same thereunto."

Barclay's next step is to consider Scripture and to examine its relation to direct revelation. The Bible contains the record of the revelations of the Spirit of God to the saints, and these are preserved for us in the form of history, prophecy, and "a full and ample account of the chief principles of the doctrine of Christ." Yet the Scriptures are a secondary, not a primary source, "because they are only a declaration of the fountain and not the fountain itself, therefore they are not to be esteemed the principal ground of all truth and knowledge, nor yet the adequate primary rule of faith and manners." The Scriptures are always subordinate to the Spirit. By the Spirit we know that the Scriptures testify to the truth; by the Spirit we, like the inspired authors, are led into all truth. "Therefore according to the Scriptures, the Spirit is the first and principal leader." The necessity of the truth so revealed is emphasized by the natural state of the men to whom it is disclosed. We are the posterity of Adam, which "is fallen, degenerated and dead, deprived of the sensation or feeling of this inward testimony or seed of God, and is subject unto the power, nature and seed of the serpent." The subtle influence of our fallen condition pervades our whole being; we can know nothing aright, and all our thoughts about God and about spiritual things are unprofitable. Here the Socinians and Pelagians, who exalt a natural light, are clearly wrong, but so are those who believe that the seed of iniquity is imputed to infants before they actually join themselves to it by transgression.

The fifth and sixth propositions concern the universal redemption which has been wrought on behalf of man by Jesus Christ. Barclay introduces the subject with a catena of Scriptural texts, all of which emphasize God's mercy toward the sinner and the all-embracing scope of the salvation which He has wrought in Christ. "The saving and spiritual light" thus shed abroad is no less universal than "the seed of sin" which it counteracts. What is necessary is that men improve "the first and common grace," and

where this happens it is easy to believe that those who stand outside the pale of formal grace may be saved. Some of the old philosophers and all who happen to live where the Gospel has not been preached are not beyond hope, provided they do not resist that grace which in a measure is granted to all. "This certain doctrine then being received (to wit) that there is an evangelical and saving light and grace in all, the universality of the love and mercy of God towards mankind (both in the death of his beloved Son, the Lord Jesus Christ, and in the manifestation of the light in the heart) is established and confirmed against all the objections of such as deny it." So the benefits of Christ's death are not restricted to those who have "the distinct outward knowledge of his death and sufferings"; those who are excluded from this knowledge "by some inevitable accident" may also be made partakers in the mystery of His death. If they allow "his seed and light" to work in their hearts they are brought into fellowship with the Father and the Son; by the indwelling power of the Spirit they are turned from the evil to the good; they learn to do to others as they would be done by, and by thus obeying the inclusive injunction of Christ they manifest their obedience to His will. The error of those who have taught universal redemption has usually lain, says Barclay, in making salvation dependent on outward knowledge of the truth as it is in Christ, but salvation actually comes through "that divine and evangelical principle of light and life, wherewith Christ hath enlightened every man that comes into the world."

The results of universal redemption now demand attention, and in the seventh proposition Barclay considers justification. The result of receiving the light is "an holy, pure, spiritual birth" within us, and it is manifested in holiness, righteousness, purity "and all these other blessed fruits which are acceptable to God." What Barclay means by a holy birth is clear: it is Jesus Christ formed within us and working His works in us. As we are sanctified, so we are justified in the sight of God. But the new relationship with God is in no way due to our initiative nor is it the result of anything we do; it is the work of Christ, "who is both the gift and the giver, and the cause producing the effects in us." When this new relationship becomes a reality, the "body of death and sin" is crucified and removed. Our hearts are united and subjected to the truth; they no longer respond to the suggestions of evil but are free from actual sinning and transgressing of the law of God. In this sense we can be described as perfect, but perfection allows for growth, and if we cease to attend on the Lord we shall discover to our cost that we are never beyond the reach of sin.

Perserverance is the subject of the ninth proposition. Barclay claims that the gift of the inward grace of God is sufficient to enable us to work out our salvation, but if we resist God's gift, we become subject to condemnation. When grace has been at work in a life to cleanse and renew that life and to lead it toward fuller perfection, it is still possible to fall from grace and to make a shipwreck of faith. Nevertheless, it is also possible to attain such an increase and stability in the truth that we need no longer fear total apostasy.

Barclay now turns to questions which touch the distinctive Quaker witness concerning the life of the Christian community. His tenth proposition deals with the ministry. Every true minister is ordained, prepared, and supplied by the gift or light of God. By the leading and moving of the Spirit a minister should be guided to work where, when, how, and among whom it is right to work. The person who is inwardly illuminated by God ought to preach, whether or not he has received human training or authorization, while those who lack the Heaven-imparted gift, even when admirably qualified, may be no better than deceivers. Those who have been taught and inspired by God will share freely what they have received, and they will not look for reward or treat their vocation as a source of profit. Related to the ministry is worship (the subject-matter of the eleventh proposition). "All true and acceptable worship of God is offered in the inward and immediate moving and drawing of his own Spirit, which is neither limited to places, times, or persons." Worship as devised by men and prescribed as to form is "abominable idolatry in the sight of God," and men of sensitive spirit will separate from all such travesties.

In the twelfth and thirteenth propositions Barclay sets forth the Quaker position on sacraments. The New Testament speaks of "one baptism," but it points to "a pure and spiritual thing, to wit, the baptism of the spirit and fire, by which we are buried with him, that being washed and purged from our sins, we may 'walk in newness of life.' " He dismisses the baptism of infants as "mere human tradition," lacking Scriptural warrant. In the same way, the communion of the body and blood of Christ is inward and spiritual. It is a participation in His life by which our inward nature is daily nourished by His indwelling presence. Barclay concedes that Christ's disciples for a time kept up the outward observance of the rite, but this was a temporary concession to the weakness of new believers. As in the case of other signs, like washing one another's feet, it was but the shadow of better things, and it ceased among those who had obtained the substance of spiritual understanding.

In the fourteenth proposition Barclay limits the power civil magistrates can claim in matters which are purely religious. The Quakers never denied the authority of civil power in the government of this world, but they hotly denied the right of the magistrate to interfere in questions beyond his competence. God had reserved to Himself power and dominion over conscience, and He alone can rightly govern and instruct it. It is therefore a transgression of God's prerogatives to force the conscience of any man; to do so by killing, fining, banishing, or imprisoning, especially on the ground of mere differences in worship or belief, is the sure evidence of "the spirit of Cain the murderer." No man, of course, can invoke conscience in order to prejudice his neighbor in life or estate, or to veil conduct prejudicial to society. An appeal to conscience cannot be the refuge of hypocrites or scoundrels.

In his final proposition Barclay comes to outward forms of social behavior. The pattern of man's life will be governed by his true purposes, and since the chief end of all religion is to redeem man from the spirit and vain conversation of this world and to lead him to inward communion with God, it follows that all the vain customs and habits of the world will be rejected by those who come to the true fear of God. "Hat honour" and all other forms of social obsequiousness, together with "all the foolish and superstitious formalities" involved, must be repudiated. So must "unprofitable plays, frivolous recreations, sportings and gamings," which waste precious time and divert man's attention from its proper objects. The man of sensitive spirit will forsake these things "as knowing they are contrary to the will of him who redeems his children from the love of this world and its lusts and leads them in the ways of truth and holiness, in which they take delight to walk."

So Barclay reaches his conclusion. The system he has outlined is described by him as being clear, consistent, and Scriptural. He states that the Quakers may be few in numbers and humble in social status, but they can justly claim to enjoy God's blessing and to know His presence. And in characteristic seventeenth century fashion, the book ends with an ejaculation of praise and an outpouring of prayer.

THE PILGRIM'S PROGRESS

Author: John Bunyan (1628-1688)
Type of work: Religious allegory
First published: Part I, 1678; Part II, 1684

Principal Ideas Advanced

Christian, a lonely pilgrim, makes his way from the City of Destruction to the Celestial City.

He encounters various obstacles—including the Slough of Despond, the Hill of Difficulty, the giant Despair, and a treacherous river—but he is aided by Evangelist, three Shining Ones, Discretion, Prudence, Piety, Charity, Hopeful, and others.

Christian's wife, Christiana, also makes the journey to the Celestial City; she and her sons are assisted by Mercy, Mr. Greatheart, Mr. Honest, Mr. Valiant-for-truth, Mr. Steadfast, and others.

Christian's adventures are an image of the lonely experience of conversion; Christiana's pilgrimage shows that the courageous journey of the exceptional person (her husband) makes the way easier for others.

In a versified "Apology for his Book," John Bunyan, the English preacher and author, tells how his celebrated allegory, *The Pilgrim's Progress*, came into being. While he was engaged in writing a more conventional work on Christian living, Bunyan found that the analogy of the pilgrim kept creeping into his work, and the references to the pilgrim grew to such proportions that, as a workmanly writer, Bunyan was obliged to excise them. For his own satisfaction, however, he set down the allegory on separate pages, where he could give reign to his imagination without fearing men's reproaches for the novelty of it. When, after many doubts, he decided to publish the first part, the work won immediate popularity. Its influence was so great that another writer ventured (as happened with Cervantes' *Don Quixote*) to publish a second part. Bunyan himself, therefore, returned to the theme and issued his own sequel, thus completing the work as we know it. In the closing paragraph of Part II, Bunyan tentatively promises a third installment, which, however, he never wrote.

Part I recounts the pilgrimage of Christian, a lonely soul, who made his way, not without encouragement and instruction, but mainly by his own sincerity and valor, to the Celestial City. Misunderstood by his family, scorned and persecuted by his neighbors, he fled from his native place, The City of Destruction, with a burden on his back and a book in his hand. He had no directions to follow except the word of Evangelist, who told him to make for the Wicket Gate, but even this he could not see. For illumination he had only an uncertain light. Before he reached the Gate, Christian fell into the Slough of Despond, and afterwards was waylaid by Mr. Worldly-Wiseman, who would have him turn aside to the comfortable village of Morality. But Evangelist found the pilgrim and again showed him the Wicket Gate, through which Christian entered, and came up a hill to the Cross, where his burden fell off his back. Three Shining Ones then clothed him with new raiment, set a mark on his forehead, and gave him a roll with a seal upon it—his safe-conduct to the Celestial City. After climbing the Hill of Difficulty, Christian fell asleep and dropped his roll, which he must later come back for. He found fellowship and encouragement at the Palace Beautiful in the presence of the damsels Discretion, Prudence, Piety, and Charity. But he still had to fight Apollyon in the Valley of Humiliation, and he barely escaped martyrdom (which befell his companion Faithful) at Vanity Fair. Once, when the way was rough, he climbed a stile in order to walk in By-path Meadow, only to lose his way and find himself at Doubting Castle, where he fell prey to the giant Despair. After languishing in a dungeon, Christian remembered the key of Promise and made his escape. He was now nearing the Delectable Mountains, from which he could see his journey's goal. But there remained the river which all must cross; in passing through it Christian was nearly drowned by the remembrance of his sins, but he was sustained by the hand of his companion Hopeful, with whom at last he entered the Celestial City.

Part II relates how Christian's wife and sons, moved by his death, undertook the journey upon which they had refused to accompany him. They were accompanied by a young woman named Mercy, and from time to time as they progressed along the route, others joined them: Mr. Greatheart, who was commissioned to be their conductor, Mr. Honest, Mr. Valiant-for-truth, Mr. Steadfast, as well as Mr. Feeble-mind, Mr. Ready-to-halt (who traveled on crutches), Mr. Despondency, and the latter's daughter, Mrs. Much-afraid. They covered the same ground as did Christian, yet their experiences were not the same. It is notable that Christiana and her companions bore no burdens: at the place of the Cross, where Christian was delivered of his burden, they only paused to reflect on the meaning of Christ's death. The enemies which Christian had fought, and others besides, were ably subdued by Greatheart. The town of Vanity still kept its Fair, but a Christian community also flourished in its midst, and there were other signs that the witness of Christian and Faithful had not been without effect. There, as elsewhere on the journey, they stayed awhile to refresh themself in Christian homes. The sons grew to manhood, married, and took their places of responsibility alongside Greatheart, who, thus reinforced, drew up plans to assault Doubting Castle and liberate any who were imprisoned there (notably, Mr. Despondency and Mrs. Much-afraid). Thus, they all came to Beulah Land, in the Delectable Mountains, and settled with other pilgrims to await their particular calls to cross the river. When the call came to Christiana, she had time to bless her children, to encourage her companions, and to bequeath her few belongings to the poor. She entered the river calmly with the words, "I come, Lord, to be with thee, and bless thee," and, though her children wept, Mr. Greatheart and Mr. Valiant played upon the cymbal and harp for joy.

The lonely adventure of Christian in Part I reflects Bunyan's personal experience of conversion, his long imprisonment under Charles II (which was voluntary, in the sense that by abjuring his calling he could probably have been set free), and the mingled passions engendered by a Calvinistic conviction, which knows that things are not what they seem and which is nevertheless unable to penetrate to what they are. The journey is, however, that of an exceptional person. As a pastor and spiritual counselor, Bunyan came to understand that salvation is not restricted to those who serve God directly. As path-breakers and heroes, the pastors make it possible for others less doughty to follow after. These lives, being less exposed, may even realize a kind of perfection denied to the former, as Solomon in some ways surpassed his father David. Even those of little faith (Mr. Feeble-mind, Mr. Ready-to-halt, and the others) complete the journey when they are fortunate enough to fall in with the company of more resolute believers. Not so, however, for those of bad faith (Mr. Worldly Wiseman, Mr. Formalist, Mr. Talkative, Mr. By-ends) who, presumably, have all experienced convictions of sin and have feared for their state, but "understand not that such convictions tend to their good; and therefore they do desperately seek to stifle them, and presumptuously continue to flatter themselves in the way of their own hearts."

The conception of life as a pilgrimage had been exploited by other writers prior to the time of Bunyan. So had the method which dramatizes spiritual struggles in terms of the hazards of nature and the malice of men. Bunyan's originality appears in the power and conviction which the allegory takes in his hands. Fanciful pictures from medieval tales of chivalry and poetical symbols from the Holy Scriptures combine with realistic descriptions and characterizations from Eng-

lish village and country life to form a story which not merely demands credence for itself but tends to give the lie to our everyday way of viewing things.

The Pilgrim's Progress is a mirror of the spiritual awakening known as Puritanism. John Bunyan was not one of the originators of that movement, for he was active late in the seventeenth century; rather, his work was a faithful expression of the transformation which the Reformed teaching worked in the lives of ordinary people. Countless details in the work reflect the warmth and sincerity of the spirit of these men and women, which was grave and serious, but not in the least wanting in vigor or cheer. Bunyan's love of good food, his enthusiasm for music, his appreciation of feminine grace and masculine courage, and above all his delight in the company of family and friends help the reader to form a true picture of what Puritanism was in its prime. But the value of the work does not lie in these details. While he was a thorough Puritan, the author's genius enabled him, like every great artist, to transcend the time and the locale in which he wrote, and to present the character of the Puritan Englishman in its universal aspects. In contemporary terms, *The Pilgrim's Progress* tells how a man, with a circle of his fellows, is lifted out of the mass where nobody really exists, and, by way of hard decisions and fast commitments, wins the dignity of a name—*Christian*.

THE TRUE INTELLECTUAL SYSTEM OF THE UNIVERSE

Author: Ralph Cudworth (1617-1688)
Type of work: Apologetics
First published: 1678

PRINCIPAL IDEAS ADVANCED

The physical system of the world, made intelligible by the science of mechanics, needs to be integrated into a more comprehensive intellectual system, which includes life and mind.

There is universal and public truth, directly discernible to human reason.

The existence of God, demonstrable by pure reason, is also necessary to the understanding of movement and order in nature.

Besides the mechanical causes in nature, a plastic or purposive cause is at work in nature.

The soul, being the effective agent in the life of the body, is also, in man, a compendium of the Divine Mind.

Religious and moral knowledge, as well as scientific, are based on natural truth, inherent in reasonable beings; Christian revelation was necessary to retrieve men from error and re-establish them in the right way.

Ralph Cudworth was a fellow and master at Cambridge University and, with his friend Henry More (1614-1687), a leader in the philosophical group known as the Cambridge Platonists. *The True Intellectual System of the Universe* is a massive fragment. Its three volumes comprise only Book One of the original project, which was to have consisted of three books: the first directed against atheism; the second, against the teaching that God's will is sovereign over truth and justice; the third, against fatalism and predestination. It is clear that Cudworth's first concern lay in vindicating the eternity of moral principles, and man's freedom and responsibility, but he went into such detail in his argument against atheism that he failed to achieve his initial goal. From the point of view of the modern reader, this is unfortunate. We would readily have seen Book One shortened by two-thirds, in order to have the rest of the argument, for Cudworth is worth reading when he is expounding his own philosophy, but he is wearisome and unprofitable when he turns to the history of philosophy to buttress his position.

In entitling his work *The True Intellectual System of the Universe,* Cudworth intended to show that what he was doing in the sphere of man's moral and religious concerns was analogous to what his contemporaries among the natural philosophers were doing when they sought to describe the true *physical system* of the universe. A thorough-going rationalist, Cudworth was not satisfied with a philosophy which, though it makes the corporeal world intelligible, leaves morality and religion in a state of confusion. He was alarmed by atheistic philosophers, like Thomas Hobbes, who too hastily affirmed that the physical system is all there is, but he was hardly less disturbed by theistic philosophers of nominalist turn, often abetted by religious authoritarians, who, although they continued to affirm belief in God and moral principles, contended that these exceed the powers of understanding. *The True Intellectual System* seeks to avoid both these conclusions, and, without taking anything away from the science of mechanics, to integrate the physical system into a more universal system in which the noncorporeal parts of the universe are also included.

Cudworth's confidence in the possibility of such a system depends upon the old distinction between knowledge and opinion, a distinction which had been effectively revived in the seventeenth century by Galileo and Descartes. The truth or falsity of all universal and abstract propositions, he maintains, is directly evident to man's mind. "In these intelligible ideas of the mind, whatsoever is clearly perceived to be, is; or which is all one, is true. Every clear and distinct perception is an entity or truth, as that, which is repugnant to conception is a non-entity or falsehood." Sense experience, by contrast, is a private thing, relative to the one who possesses it. It was one of the great achievements of the new physics, says Cudworth, to show that colors, tastes, and odors, which we naturally and habitually attribute to the physical world, are actually fancies and passions in us, and that the only qualities which really belong to matter are extension, magnitude, figure, position, motion, and rest. These latter qualities, being abstract and universal, are clearly and directly perceived by every rational being, and constitute "a public, catholic, and universal truth." In Cudworth's opinion, Descartes had forsaken solid ground in maintaining that our certainty with respect to self-evident truth rests on the veracity of our Maker, rather than on the necessity which the mind discovers in its ideas. He particularly complains against the thought, allowed by Descartes, that the sum of four and four might have been other than eight, if God had willed it so. These irrationalist elements were to reappear in the Christian apologetics of the Common Sense school, but Cudworth rigorously opposed them, insisting that the real is inherently rational, and that it is the prerogative of spiritual beings to apprehend the real.

It is part of Cudworth's polemic against the atheists to argue that all men naturally have the idea of one omnipotent and omniscient God, upon whose Providence the world depends. This part of his demonstration is, as he says, philological, rather than philosophical, being a kind of natural history of religion, based on Greek and Latin sources. The pagans were polytheistic, but, Cudworth maintains, this did not prevent them from having knowledge of the Supreme Numen, or universal God. The ancients believed in both minor deities and in a supreme god, and they distinguished between them; their fault consisted in making offerings to natural deities of worship which should have been reserved as offerings for the true God. In spite of numerous errors, Cudworth maintains, pagan theologians arrived at a remarkably clear apprehension of God, even approximating the idea of three eternal substances within the unity of the Divine Being. Atheism, on the other hand, nowhere represents the natural belief of men, and philosophers such as Democritus, who deny the existence of God, show thereby that they possess the idea of that which they deny.

Cudworth's favorite proof for the existence of God is the celebrated ontological argument, which holds that the idea of a perfect being includes the idea of His existence. While Cudworth rejects the argument in the form in which Descartes stated it, he accepts that modification of it best known through the writings of Leibniz. As Cudworth frames it, the proof requires two steps. Because the idea of a being whose essence includes, among all other perfections, necessary existence, is not inconceivable, it follows that such a being is at least possible. But of a necessary being, it further follows that if it is possible for it to be then it *must* be, because "if it might have been, though it be not, then would it not be a necessary existent Being." Hence, Cudworth concludes: "God is either impossible to have been, or else he is. For if God were possible, and yet be not, then is he not a necessary but a contingent Being, which is contrary to the hypothesis."

The ontological proof, says Cudworth, is as valid as any proof in geometry; nevertheless, he concedes, it may not convince the generality of men, because the capacity of the recipient must be taken into account. He therefore offers, as a further proof, the kind of argument found in Locke's *Essay on Human Understanding* (1690), which rests on the assumption that there must be as great power in a cause as there is in its effect. It is agreed, says Cudworth, between theists and atheists that "something or other did exist from all eternity, without beginning." The only question between them is whether this being is to be thought of as "a perfect Being and God, or the most imperfect of all things whatsoever, inanimate and senseless matter." To the unprejudiced mind it is perfectly evident "that lesser perfections may naturally descend from greater," but "utterly impossible, that greater perfections, and higher degrees of being, should rise and ascend out of lesser and lower." He concludes: "Wherefore it is certain, that in the universe things did not thus ascend and mount, or climb up from lower perfection to higher; but, on the contrary descend and slide down from higher to lower: so that the first original of all things was not the most imperfect, but the most perfect Being."

It is this principle, that the less perfect can only be understood in the light of the more perfect, which provides the basis for Cudworth's "intellectual system of the universe." As we have seen, he welcomed the mechanist, or, as he called it (disregarding the differences between Empedocles and Democritus, and between Descartes and Gassendi), the "atomist" theory of the corporeal world. Much better than the Aristotelian doctrine of occult qualities, the atomist theory "renders the corporeal world intelligible to us; since mechanism is a thing that we can clearly understand, and we cannot clearly and distinctly conceive any thing in bodies else." But, by making a clear distinction between mental and physical qualities, the atomists not merely enable us to form a clear idea of the material world, but also demonstrate that the material world is not intelligible in material terms alone. Since matter is nothing but "extended bulk," there must be, in addition to matter, some incorporeal substance to account for order and movement in the world, as well as for life and thought. The atomist theory, therefore, far from requiring atheism, is properly a help toward establishing theism, and this, Cudworth maintains, following the line of argument of the French Catholic Epicurean, Pierre Gassendi (1592-1655), was evident to the discoverers of the theory; namely, the Eleatic and Pythagorean philosophers. They were led to atomism, as a means of understanding the corporeal world, by the principle *ex nihilo nihil,* but they were consistent enough to see that, by the same principle, there must be something besides atoms to account for their motion and arrangement. The atheistic atomists, Democritus in ancient and Hobbes in modern times, were motivated by moral rather than by intellectual considerations. Without God, their systems are unintelligible, but their desire to escape from moral responsibility is so strong that they are content with an imperfect system.

Just as the atomist theory is compatible with belief in God, so is it compatible with human freedom; but for this to be so, says Cudworth, some amendment must be made in the Cartesian world-view. A difficulty arises from the fact that when Descartes rejected the Aristotelian doctrine of essential causes, he also rejected "all final and intending causality." It follows that, in order to account for law and order in the world, Descartes had either to leave the whole natural order of things to mechanical causation, or to fall back on the constant and immediate intervention of God Himself. But when he took the alternative of assuming a natural order, he acknowledged, in effect, that there is no purpose in nature, and that what seems purposive is merely the result of chance. This is contrary to reason, as well as destructive of freedom and morality. Hence, Descartes sometimes leaned to the other alternative, by explaining the order of the world in terms of God's immediate activity. But this alternative is no less deleterious to morality than the former, besides the fact that an assumption of God's intervention cannot explain the slow, sometimes bungling manner in which nature achieves its purpose. It is reasonable, therefore, says Cudworth, to infer that between the Divinity and the mechanical and fortuitous nature, there is an artisan nature, "subservient to deity, as the manuary opificer, and drudging executioner thereof." This world-fashioning "plastic nature," as More and Cudworth call it, is recognizably the World-Soul of Neoplatonic philosophy. It is an incorporeal substance, because endowed with life and mind, but it acts in a somnambulant fashion, without choice and discretion, and has a Higher Providence presiding over it.

The souls of men and animals, says Cudworth, are immaterial, but their life is bound up closely with matter. Descartes was wrong in identifying the soul with consciousness or thought, and, in consequence, he failed to understand the soul's role in presiding over the life of the body, not only in men but also in animals. Souls, says Cudworth, are formed by plastic nature, but they are independent agents. Although their activity does not require local motion, it is not without any spatial connection, "having not only such an essential inside, bathos, or profundity in it, wherein it acteth and thinketh within itself, but also a certain amplitude of active power ad extra, or a sphere of activity upon body." Like Lord Herbert of Cherbury (1583-1648), Cudworth describes minds as microcosms, each one recapitulating within itself the essential structure of the world. As God continually comprehends in his archetypal intellect the sum total of all that ever is or could be, so the mind of man, being a kind of "ectypal model or derivative compendium," virtually and potentially contains within itself the totality of all forms, which are unfolded and displayed "as occasion serves and outward objects invite."

In a separate essay, entitled *Concerning Eternal and Immutable Morality*, intended as part of the *magnum opus*, but first published in 1731, Cudworth develops his thesis that moral good and evil are discerned by the mind in the same way as are other essential truths. The argument is directed mainly against those who, like Hobbes, maintain that justice is based merely on convention. Cudworth seeks to show that moral qualities exist "by the necessity of their own nature," and are knowable by us through our intellectual powers. But the essay is directed also against certain philosophers and theologians who, while acknowledging that morality transcends the will of man, base it on the arbitrary will of God. Concerned always to assert the rationality and intelligibility of things, Cudworth insists that the will and power of God, although they command the existence of all created things, cannot cause things to be anything other than whatever the necessity of their natures demands. It is not by command that an act is just or unjust; all that laws do is to stipulate that an act must be performed, on pain of punishment. Cudworth's inquiry takes him to the highest reaches of metaphysics. "There is," he says, "in the scale of being a nature of goodness superior to wisdom, which therefore measures and determines the wisdom of God, as his wisdom measures and determines his will." Some innovators, he complains, have limited the idea of God, making it consist of nothing but will and power. They had better follow the wisdom of Plotinus and of the Jewish cabalists, who expressed the divine nature in the mystical representation of an infinite circle, whose inmost center is simple goodness, whose inner area is wisdom, and whose circumference is will or activity.

While Cudworth writes as a Christian, his attitude toward Biblical and ecclesiastical authority is latitudinarian. In *The True Intellectual System* there is very little reference to revealed religion, the most explicit statement being a sketch, never developed, in the outline to Chapter Four. Somewhat in the manner used by Locke in *The Reasonableness of Christianity* (1695), Cudworth suggests that because men failed to make proper use of their natural reason, and fell into superstition and idolatry, God, out of compassion, "designed himself to reform the religion of the pagan world, by introducing another religion of his own framing instead of it." There is nothing absurd, he says, in the supposition of the Divine Glory indwelling the pure soul and body of the Messiah; indeed, Christ's death and resurrection have vindicated the divine plan, since paganism has, through their means, been effectively destroyed. Moreover, Cudworth finds the Christian doctrine of the Trinity, although a mystery, better in accord with the demands of reason than the Platonist doctrine, for, whereas the latter tried to maintain that the three hypostases or persons are numerically one (*monoousios*), the Nicene Fathers maintained no more than that the three persons are essentially the same (*homoousios*). This claim left Cudworth vulnerable to the charge by orthodox churchmen that he was a Tritheist.

The *True Intellectual System* en-joyed considerable popularity well into the eighteenth century, mainly outside theological circles. It was translated into Latin and subjected to a learned commentary by the German scholar J. L. Mosheim, in 1733. That it is no longer extensively studied is due largely to its excessive and uncritical use of historical materials. We can still appreciate seventeenth century Christian philosophy, but not the historiography of that time.

DISCOURSES UPON THE EXISTENCE AND ATTRIBUTES OF GOD

Author: Stephen Charnock (1628-1680)
Type of work: Puritan theology
First published: 1682

PRINCIPAL IDEAS ADVANCED

The existence of God is known by all men and can be demonstrated by rational argument.

Eternity, immutability, omnipresence, omniscience, infinite wisdom, and omnipotence are incommunicable attributes of God.

These attributes, together with such moral attributes as holiness, goodness, and patience, and the prerogative of sovereign dominion over all creatures, are manifested in God's works of creation, providence, and redemption.

After ministering in Southwark for a time, Stephen Charnock became a fellow of New College, and later Senior Proctor at Oxford (1649-1656). He went to Dublin as chaplain to the Governor, and in 1675 he accepted a call to Crosby Square, where he remained as one of the ministers ejected under the Restoration.

The *Discourses upon the Existence and Attributes of God,* published posthumously, is a classic of Reformed nat-ural theology. Charnock draws heavily on the work of Thomas Aquinas and other Scholastics, while he works within the framework of Biblical revelation. His interest is practical as well as speculative. A discourse on practical atheism follows that on the existence of God, and the discourse of God as a spirit leads to a discussion of spiritual worship. Each of the discourses (including those on the attributes of eternity, immutability, omnipresence, knowledge, wisdom, power, holiness, goodness, dominion, and patience) begins with the exposition of a text of Scripture and ends with "uses" or applications to Christian experience and practice.

After expounding the words of Psalm 14, "The fool hath said in his heart, There is no God," Charnock argues that the folly of atheism is revealed by the light of reason, as stated in Romans 1:19-20 and other passages of Scripture. The first rational argument he advances for the existence of God is that of the *consensus gentium:* There has been a universal, constant and uninterrupted, natural and innate agreement in the notion of a God and practice of religion. This consent could not be by mere tradition, nor by political contrivance, nor the effect of fear.

The second reason Charnock gives for believing in God is the cosmological proof, which Charnock considers to be not merely a probable, but a demonstrative truth. The objects and persons of the world declare the existence of a God in their production, harmony, preservation, and purposes. No creature can make itself, nor can any creature make the world. It follows that there is a first cause of things, which we call God. The harmony of the world's parts, contrary qualities linked together and one thing subservient to another, declare the being and wisdom of God.

The third reason is from the nature and constitution of man the microcosm. The whole model of the body is grounded upon reason, each member having its exact proportion, distinct office, and regular motion, while the soul is the greatest glory of this lower world, in the vastness of its capacity,

the quickness of its motions, its union with the body and, above all, in the witness of conscience to the moral law and the judgment of God, together with the vastness of the desires in man and his real dissatisfaction in everything below himself.

The fourth and last reason is drawn from extraordinary occurrences in the world, including extraordinary judgments, miracles, and fulfilled prophecies.

Among the "uses" may be mentioned the pernicious consequences of atheism for nations and for individuals, including the atheist himself, the wisdom of being firmly settled in the truth of God's existence, and the folly, once the existence of God is admitted, of not worshiping Him and thinking often of Him.

The eternity of God is discussed by Charnock on the basis of Psalm 90:2. Eternity is a negative attribute, excluding beginning, end, and succession. There is no succession in the knowledge of God or in His decrees. God is His own eternity, and all His perfections are eternal. Scripture accommodates itself to human weakness in using the language of time to describe the divine eternity. God's eternity is evident in the name "I AM" (Exodus 3:14). God has life in Himself. Eternity is implied by God's immutability, infinite perfection, omnipotence, and original causality. Eternity is an incommunicable attribute, proper to God alone. Even if a creature existed from all eternity by the will of God, its eternal existence would in the nature of things be merely contingent, not necessary.

The immutability of God, expressed in Psalm 102:26-27, concerns His being and perfections. God is unchangeable in His essence. Otherwise He would not truly be, or be perfectly blessed. God's knowledge is immutable. Otherwise He would not be omniscient or a fit object of trust to any rational creature. God knows not by species, but by His own nature and by one intuitive act. Since His knowledge and will are the cause of all things, the distinction between past and future does not affect the knowledge which God has. The manner of God's knowledge is incomprehensible to a finite creature, even to one in Heaven. God is also unchangeable in will and purpose. The will of God is God willing. God's will and understanding concur in everything. There can be no reason for change in the will of God, neither lack of foresight, nor natural instability, nor want of strength. Things willed by God are not immutable as is the divine will itself.

Charnock argues also that the immutability of God's will is consistent with its liberty. God is also unchangeable as to place, because he has ubiquity. Immutability is implied by God's perfection, simplicity, eternity, infinity, and omnipotence, as well as by the order and government of the world. Furthermore, immutability is an incommunicable attribute; no creature can be unchangeable in its nature. There was no change in God when He created the world, Charnock writes, for there was no new will or power in Him, nor a new relation acquired by Him. Nor was there any change in the divine nature of Christ when He assumed human nature: "The glory of his divinity was not extinguished nor diminished, though it was obscured and darkened under the veil of our infirmities." Repentance and other affections are ascribed to God anthropomorphically, but they cannot involve any change in God. Nor does a change of laws by God imply any change in God.

God is omnipresent; that is, He is essentially everywhere present in Heaven and earth. Bodies are circumscribed in their places; angels and spirits are present at one point only at one time, while God alone fills all places, yet so as not to be contained in them. Our knowledge of God, Charnock argues, is by way of negation; omnipresence is a denial of limitation of place. There is also an influential omnipresence of God, universal with all creatures. God is essentially present in all places, with all creatures, without any mixture, without any division or multiplication of Himself, not by extension or diffusion, but totally in every part of the world as well as beyond the world. Omnipresence is also an incommunicable attribute; the human nature even of the exalted Christ is not omnipresent.

Psalm 147:5 is the text for Charnock's discourse on God's knowledge. God has an infinite knowledge and understanding. All nations acknowledge the knowledge as well as the existence of God. God has a knowledge of vision, by which he knows Himself and all real things, past, present, and future, as well as a knowledge of simple understanding, the object of which is all things possible though not willed by Him. The knowledge of things possible is only speculative in God, while the knowledge of things decreed is practical as terminating in the act of creation. There is a knowledge of approbation as well as apprehension in God. God alone knows Himself comprehensively and by His own essence. Thus, God transcends all creatures, and His understanding is truly infinite.

God knows all creatures, Charnock argues, all their actions and thoughts, as well as all their evils and sins. He knows all future things. What is now past was once future. God has predicted future events; God knows His own will and therefore must know all the future. If He did not know all future things, He would be mutable in His knowledge. God foreknows all creatures, certainly and eternally, incommunicably and incomprehensibly. God knows all future contingencies, all chance events and free choices. What is accidental with respect to the creature is not so for God. If God did not foreknow the free choices of men, he could not govern the world. He foreknows free acts, whether good, indifferent, or sinful. But God's foreknowledge does not deprive the human will of freedom. No man is compelled in any of his voluntary actions. God's foreknowledge does not add to the sequence of human actions, but only beholds them as present, as arising from their proper causes. God foreknows events because they will come to pass; but events are not made to be future by God's knowledge of them. God foreknows not only our actions, but also the manner of those actions as free. God's foreknowledge and human freedom are alike certain, even though the human understanding cannot fully reconcile them.

The mode of God's knowledge is incomprehensible to us. He knows by His own essence, by one act of intuition, not discursively or successively as we do. He knows all things independently, distinctly, infallibly, immutably, and perpetually; that is, in act.

The wisdom of God is distinct from knowledge. Wisdom consists in acting for a right end, in observing all circumstances for action, in willing and acting according to a right judgment of things. Knowledge has its seat in the speculative understanding, wisdom in the practical.

Charnock describes the Son of God as the essential and personal wisdom of God. The wisdom of God is identical with the divine essence. Wisdom is the property of God alone, as Pythagoras admitted in preferring to be called a lover of wisdom rather than wise. God alone is wise necessarily, originally, perfectly, universally, perpetually, incomprehensibly, and infallibly. The wisdom of God is taught by Scripture and is abundantly evident in the government of the world. As the fountain of all wisdom in the creatures, God is Himself infinitely wise.

Charnock's discourse on the power of God follows an exposition of the twenty-sixth chapter of Job. The power of God is not to be understood in terms of His authority and dominion, but by reference to His strength to act. Absolute power is that by which God is able to do all things possible; ordinate power is that by which He does what He has ordained to do. Absolute power does not respect things repugnant to the nature of God. God's ordinate power is free and belongs to His will. "The power of God," Charnock writes, "is that ability or strength whereby he can bring to pass whatsoever he please, whatsoever his infinite wisdom can direct, and whatsoever the infinite purity of his will can resolve."

With Aquinas, Charnock would rather say that some things are impossible than say that God cannot do them. Some things are impossible by their own nature; for example, contradictions. Some are impossible because of the nature of God or His glorious perfections. Thus, it is impossible for God to be ignorant or lie. Other things are impossible as a consequence of the determined will of God. Reasons advanced by Charnock for accepting the doctrine of divine omnipotence are: (1) the power that is in creatures, (2) the infinite perfection of God, (3) the simplicity of God, and (4) the miracles that have been in the world. The power of God appears in creation, government and, most admirably, in redemption.

The moral character of God is examined in Charnock's remaining discourses on the attributes of holiness, goodness, dominion, and patience. The same method of exposition exemplified in the preceding discourses on the incommunicable attributes is followed. The discourse on the dominion of God stresses the prerogative of sovereignty. Sovereignty or dominion is not bare power, Charnock asserts, but the "right of making what he pleases, of possessing what he made, of disposing of what he doth possess." The notion of sovereignty is inseparable from the notion of a God. This dominion is independent and absolute, yet not tyrannical, and managed by the rules of wisdom, righteousness, and goodness. Divine sovereignty extends over all creatures and is eternal in its foundation and duration, though exercised only from the creation. The first act of sovereignty is making laws, which is essential to God. As proprietor and lord of His creatures, God manifests His dominion in choosing some persons for eternal life and in bestowing grace where He pleases, disposing the means of grace to some, not to all. The dominion of God is manifested further in His government of men and nations and, finally, in the work of redemption in Christ.

Charnock concludes the discourse on God's dominion with an exhortation to humility, praise and thankfulness, promotion of the honor of this sovereign, fear and reverence, prayer and trust, obedience and patience. The discourses on the attributes are appropriately followed by one on the divine providence. Consideration of these sublime and profound themes may elicit the expression of admiration and adoration in the words of Romans 11:33, "O the depth of the riches both of the wisdom and knowledge of God! How unsearchable are his judgments, and his ways past finding out!"

THE PRACTICE OF THE PRESENCE OF GOD

Author: Brother Lawrence (Nicholas Herman, c.1605-1691)
Type of work: Devotional manual
First published: 1692, 1694 (Present collection, 1703)

PRINCIPAL IDEAS ADVANCED

Instead of approaching God in the way prescribed in books, it is sufficient to place oneself directly in God's presence and surrender all one's acts to His direction.

God can be served as well in the kitchen or on the battlefield as in the Church while receiving the Sacrament.

The service of God is primarily an affair of the will and not of the understanding.

God is to be served for His own sake only, and not for the benefits which His service brings.

The Practice of the Presence of God is a memoir on the life and thought of a lay monk known as Brother Lawrence (Nicolas Herman). The book has lately enjoyed great popularity with Protestants. Brother Lawrence wrote but little and destroyed most of what he wrote because it seemed inadequate. But Abbé Joseph de Beaufort, the superior of the Parisian monastery where Lawrence lived, gathered up a few letters and some fragments of meditations, and he supplemented these with notes from conversations and with his own recollections, to present the picture of a truly unforgettable character.

In his youth, Brother Lawrence had been a soldier; then, after being wounded in battle, he became a gentleman's valet. In the monastery he served for fifteen years in the kitchen until, because of his lameness, he was put to work as a cobbler. What makes his manual one of the most highly esteemed devotional works is the true simplicity of its authority.

When he was asked in his old age by what method he had arrived at his constant sense of God's nearness to him, Lawrence usually said that his method was to throw away all methods. "Having found in several books different methods for going to God and various practices of the spiritual life, I thought that this would serve rather to trouble my soul than to make easy for me what I aspired to and sought after, which was nothing else

than a means of belonging wholly to God. This made me resolve to give all for all." Chiefly, Lawrence emphasized the necessity of simply believing that God is present in all His creatures, that He is wise, merciful, and all-sufficient. When he first began his practice, he used to arrange his work so that he had time to pray between duties. Then he accustomed himself to speak to God while he was working. In the end, he ceased to observe separate times of prayer, except those enforced on him by the discipline of the community. "It was a great mistake," he said, "to believe that the time of prayer should be different from the other, for we are as much obligated to be united to God by action, at the time of action, as by prayer in its time."

Lawrence admits that, at first, he had difficulty in setting aside distracting thoughts and fixing his mind on God. But in time, the practice of talking with God became habitual, and the sense of God's presence rarely left him. "I possess God as tranquilly in the bustle of my kitchen—where sometimes several people are asking me different things at one time—as if I were on my knees before the Blessed Sacrament. My faith sometimes even becomes so enlightened that I think I have lost it; it seems to me that the curtain of obscurity is drawn, that the endless, cloudless day of the other life is beginning to dawn."

One of the most popular passages in the book is that in which Lawrence tells how he relies on God to help him when he has a particularly difficult or unpleasant chore to perform. One must, he says, speak to God very frankly, saying, "My God, I would not be able to do that, if Thou didst not help me." Then God gives him strength. Trips outside the monastery to purchase supplies were a chore; he felt he had no head for business; furthermore, he was lame. But "he simply told God that it was his affair, after which he found that everything turned out nicely." Although he had an aversion for kitchen work, he gained considerable skill during the fifteen years that he was occupied there. He said, "I turn my little omelette in the pan for the love of God; when it is finished, if I have nothing to do, I prostrate myself on the ground and adore my God, Who gave me the grace to make it, after which I arise, more content than a king. When I cannot do anything else, it is enough for me to have lifted a straw from the earth for the love of God."

Brother Lawrence's first sense of God's goodness and love came to him when he was eighteen. One winter day, while he was looking at a tree stripped of its leaves and thinking that in the spring it would have flowers and foliage, "he received a profound impression of the providence and power of God, which was never effaced from his soul." For many years however, he did suffer from a sense of his sinfulness and from fear lest he should be rejected by God. All of a sudden, a change took place: "My soul, which until then was always troubled, felt a profound interior peace, as if it were in its center and place of repose." After that time, his fears never returned. He merely placed

his sins before God and trusted for mercy. Sometimes it seemed to him that God took him by the hand and paraded with him before the heavenly court, "to show off the miserable one whom it pleased Him to honor."

Lawrence drew a sharp distinction between the understanding and the will, discounting the former. "In the way of God," he said, "thoughts count for little, love does everything." He disparaged the practice of meditating on great subjects, such as sin and death, Heaven and Hell, and he recommended instead that men concentrate on "doing little things for the love of God." Thoughts, he said, spoil everything; that is where evil begins. His advice was to reject every thought that enters the mind insofar as it is not relevant to the task one has in hand. Even so, one ought not let his mind run ahead of what he is doing. When the time comes for action, one sees in God "as in a clear mirror" all that is necessary to do for the present.

In the ordinary round of duty, Lawrence paid no attention to what his hands were doing, nor could he afterwards remember what he had done, his mind being entirely fixed on God, thanking Him and "making an infinity of other acts." On those occasions when his occupation diverted him from thinking of God, "there came to him some remembrance which took possession of his soul, giving him some most engrossing idea of God." At such times, he was frequently so exalted that he was moved to dance and sing for joy. Losing himself in God, he achieved a remarkable indifference to things affecting his own welfare. His superior says that no jealousies, fears, or disappointments seemed to touch him; yet it was not as if he were withdrawn from what transpired around him. He took an interest in the welfare of all in the monastery and was charitable toward the unfortunate who came to the gate seeking alms. He possessed "great common sense," and, although he was not fond of declaring his thoughts, when obliged by his superiors to declare his thoughts on some question, "his answers were so clear and to the point that they needed no comment." Eventually, his reputation extended outside the monastery, and people turned to him as a spiritual director.

It is important to recall that Brother Lawrence lived at the time during which quietism was making its appearance among French Catholics, and that the monastery in which he lived belongs to the "discalced" (barefoot) branch of the Carmelite order, which owed its foundation to the sixteenth century Spanish mystics, St. Teresa (1515-1582) and St. John of the Cross (1542-1591), who gave quietism its initial impulse. How far Brother Lawrence himself was influenced by the movement is uncertain; but the Abbé, in holding him up as an exemplar, was clearly supporting the cause that sent Mme. Guyon (1648-1717) to the Bastille. Like the quietists, Brother Lawrence sought to love God without any consideration of his own advantage. Says Abbé de Beaufort, "Far from loving God in return for His benefits, he had so disinterested a charity that he would have loved God even though there had been no punishment to avoid nor any reward to attain, and desiring only the good and glory of God and forming his Heaven of the accomplishment of his holy Will." The surges of joy which Lawrence experienced were not ungratefully received; still, he warned against the danger of cherishing the gift for its own sake and neglecting to raise one's thoughts to the Giver. In his opinion, raptures and ecstasies are found only in devotees who fall into that error.

Students of world-religions may find in the way of Brother Lawrence an analogy to the "yoga of selfless action" represented in the *Bhagavad Gita.* Like Krishna in that work, Lawrence is able to advise a soldier that, far from destroying the courage of men at arms, the presence of God fortifies them even on the most dangerous occasions: "A brief remembrance of God, an interior act of adoration, even while one may be running with sword in hand, are prayers which, however short they are, are nevertheless pleasing to God."

THE JOURNAL OF GEORGE FOX

Author: George Fox (1624-1691)
Type of work: Spiritual autobiography
First published: 1694

PRINCIPAL IDEAS ADVANCED

The power of the Lord is over all His works, and manifests itself in the affairs of men.

In the experience of one of His servants, therefore, we see how this power operates: how it leads him in his quest, satisfies him with a growing understanding of the truth, and sustains him in all trials and adversities.

The Lord, who "had a great people to be gathered," drew them together into the Society of Friends.

The Journal of George Fox is one of the most remarkable religious works in the English language. For its directness, simplicity, vividness, and spiritual power it has few equals. And yet it is a book which it is not easy to classify. Strictly speaking it is not a journal at all, since it does not profess to be a day-by-day account of a man's experience. It is a fragment of autobiography, composed in mid-career, and never completed. Fox was a prolific author, but he preferred to use an amanuensis rather than to write himself. About 1675 he dictated to his son-in-law, Thomas Lower, an account of his life till that date. What approximates most closely to a journal is the section describing his travels in the West Indies and on the American continent. After Fox's death, the task of editing his autobiographical remains was committed to Thomas Ellwood, and it was in Ellwood's edition that the world knew this work until early in the twentieth century. Ellwood took his task seriously, perhaps too seriously. He tamed somewhat the vigor of Fox's unconventional style. At appropriate points he inserted letters or manifestoes which Fox had written, and he provided a narrative to carry the story beyond the point at which Fox's own account ceased. He also secured from William Penn a prefatory tribute to Fox, and this remains one of our most illuminating pictures of this remarkable man.

Fox briefly indicates his relatively humble origin, and he describes his earnest attitude as a child. His relatives thought such seriousness must be the mark of a future minister, but his father apprenticed him to a shoe maker. When he was about nineteen, he passed through an intense and prolonged spiritual crisis. The suggestion that he join his companions at the public house in drinking healths aroused scruples in his mind, and he withdrew—immediately from the company of his associates, gradually from that of his friends and relations. For some time he traveled "up and down as a stranger in the earth, which way the Lord inclined my heart," and he attributes his wanderings to the fact that he was "afraid both of professor and profane, lest, being a tender young man," he should be injured by associating with either.

Gradually the pattern of Fox's mature convictions began to take shape. He says that the true believers were those who had been born of God and had passed from death unto life; he realized that to go to Oxford or Cambridge was in itself no sufficient preparation for the ministry. He discovered that in Christ there was an answer to his doubts and temptations, and that the secret of spiritual victory lay in Christ's presence and power. "Christ, who had enlightened me, gave me his light to believe in," Fox writes; "he gave me hope, which he himself revealed in me; and he gave me his spirit and grace, which I found sufficient in the deeps and in weakness."

Fox's new insight made him impatient of the old ways, and his convictions combined with his nature to make him uncompromising in denouncing them. So began the long series of interruptions of public worship, rebukes to blind preachers, challenges to existing patterns both in church order and social convention. His methods awakened resentment; this often showed itself in violent forms. The upshot of disturbing one church service was a rush of angry parishioners, who swept him into the church yard and severely beat him. In describing such episodes Fox is amazingly detailed and circumstantial. As the blows rained about his head, he noted the expressions on the faces of his assailants and the precise inflections of the words they used.

The vividness with which many of these incidents are recounted carries us back into the midst of seventeenth century life. Nowhere else do we get so photographic, yet so living a picture of the words and actions of those who make up that elusive body, the populace of a bygone age. In the midst of this vibrant setting we have this strangely vital man. It is easy to sympathize with his antagonists. Often Fox seems deliberately, even wantonly, provocative. He seems to assert a doctrinaire witness in a particularly offensive manner. He seems to provoke the violence in submitting to which he finds his superior virtue vindicated. To concede this is merely to admit that not all readers find Fox a consistently attractive figure. The rebukes which he administered to others might indicate unyielding honesty, but they give the impression of self-consciously superior virtue. The letters which he wrote from prison were not calculated to conciliate the officers of the law,

and when face to face with his critics Fox was no less blunt in denouncing the shortcomings of others and insisting on his own rectitude.

But even those who disliked him were compelled to admire his courage and his integrity. He feared the face of no man. When driven from a town by brutal mobs he often returned at once, ready to face again the worst that they could do. A threatening group hemming him round or a man with a drawn sword caused him no dismay. This courage was unquestionably one element in the strange ascendency which he established over others. Violent crowds became quiet, hostile men "became loving," and Fox could pass on to continue among others this revolutionary work which he was everywhere initiating.

Related to Fox's courage was his integrity. People recognized his sincerity and responded to it. After his imprisonment in Scarborough Castle, the soldiers bore generous tribute to his quality. "He is as stiff as a tree and as pure as a bell, for we could never stir him." It was sincerity, reinforced by unfailing courage, which compelled others to give heed to his witness. But it was not simply the testimony of a brave and honest man which gained their reluctant admiration. The story of Fox's life bears constant witness to his ability to win the loyalty and adhesion of men and women of education and social prominence. Margaret Fell (later his wife), Thomas Ellwood, Isaac Penington, and William Penn all testify to his capacity to touch people of the upper as well as the lower strata of society. The explanation lies in the amazing spiritual vitality to which *The Journal* bears witness. "The power of the Lord" is a phrase constantly on

Fox's lips. To this he always attributed the hold he established over groups and individuals. "And the truth of the Lord came over him so that he grew loving." The vigor of a rugged personality might explain the way he sometimes overbore opposition; it cannot account for the degree to which he won over those whom he silenced.

Though Fox frequently conciliated his antagonists, the victory was often slow in coming, and in the meantime he had abundant experience of the suffering which religious nonconformity could cause. The narrative is punctuated with accounts of trials and imprisonments. We see how hard it was, in the face of strong prejudice, to secure even the rights which the law guaranteed to a prisoner. Fox always insisted on what he regarded as his due rights; he did not hesitate to argue with his judges, to call them to task, or to denounce them. Such conduct increased the likelihood that he would be committed to prison, and so we have detailed descriptions of the interiors of a large number of seventeenth century jails. We see the ordinary discomforts to which prisoners were usually condemned: cold in winter, heat in summer, insanitary conditions, vexations from the jailer and from fellow inmates, as well as the problems of securing food and drink in the casually organized prisons of the day. Sometimes Fox found himself consigned to a dungeon; in Doomsdale in Launceston he stood in excrement over his boot tops and was almost always stifled by the stench. Accounts of such hardships are an inseparable part of almost all early Quaker journals; the comments explain why mortality was so high among prisoners and why the Friends made such persistent efforts to secure the release of their companions. As a picture of judicial methods and penal conditions in the seventeenth century, the *Journal* is both a historical source of great importance and a human document of intensely moving interest.

As the *Journal* progresses we witness the emergence of the Society of Friends. Fox was an organizer of some capacity, and he provided the Quakers with a structure which saved them from the fate which most of the small sects of the seventeenth century suffered. This, in its full development, lies beyond the period with which the *Journal* deals. But we can also observe something of greater interest than the fashioning of an institutional structure; we can trace the development of the distinctive witness of the Society of Friends. Perhaps most important of all is the insistence on the inwardness and vitality of religion. This explains the protest against forms, ceremonies, observances, and sacred buildings. But this was the negative aspect of an important positive truth. It is not enough to quote Christ and His Apostles; the decisive question is, "What canst thou say?" Men must learn to listen to the Spirit of Christ speaking in their hearts. If we would only pause to hear Christ's voice, we could live in the power of His endless life, we are told. The "inner light" is another way of expressing the same truth. It is important to notice that this inward and personal illumination of the believer was, for Fox, related in the most intimate way with the figure of Jesus of Nazareth. This association gave concreteness and character to his interpretation of the Spirit.

Less vital but more immediately observable were certain other aspects of

Quaker belief. The pattern of silent worship begins to emerge, though Fox was on occasion a vehement preacher and was much given to forceful and vocal prayer. The *Journal* abounds in incidents which illustrate Fox's refusal to remove his hat when customary social usage demanded this gesture; indeed, the problem of "hat honor" figures prominently in the accounts of the legal proceedings in which Fox was so frequently involved. So, too, does his refusal to swear. Since taking an oath had an important preliminary role in a prisoner's testimony, it was always possible, if other methods failed, to sentence Fox to prison for contempt of court. "Plain speech" also had legal as well as social implications. Fox believed that the distinction between "thou" and "you" in personal address rested on hypocritical obsequiousness, and that evangelical simplicity required us to address all alike as "thou." But when applied to magistrates and judges, this had disconcerting results.

In Fox's *Journal* the repudiation of violence is clearly present. When a fellow prisoner at Scarborough threatened to fight him, Fox walked up to him with his hands in his pockets, and pointed out "what a shame it was for him to challenge a man whose principle he knew was not to strike." In London, when a rough soldier threatened to kill all Quakers, Fox went to him and offered to submit to his violence, "and the truth came so over him that he grew loving."

What principally emerges from the *Journal* is a vivid picture of a remarkable man. The book is noteworthy for its originality, sincerity, and power because these are precisely the qualities which mark the man himself. The graphic directness of the work shows us the age and its people, but above all the *Journal* makes us aware of Fox. He was, as William Penn said, "an original, being no man's copy." Penn's preface forms an excellent epitome, since it is the tribute of one great religious leader to another. Fox, Penn tells us, "was a man that God endued with a clear and wonderful depth, a discerner of others' spirits, and very much a master of his own." So he was able to open the truth to others, and bring them under its constraint. His "exemplary sobriety, humility, gravity, punctuality, charity and circumspect care in the government of church affairs" made those whom he gathered about him a society able to maintain itself in the world and to bear an increasingly effective witness. "Never heed," said Fox on the eve of his death; "the Lord's power is over all weakness and death; the Seed reigns, blessed be the Lord." This admirably epitomized the testimony of his life. It explains the abiding influence of his most remarkable book, the *Journal*. And it justifies the "short epitaph" with which Penn closes his tribute: "Many sons have done virtuously in this day, but dear George Fox thou excellest them all."